WITHDRAWN
USJ Library

THE SPIRITUALITY
OF THE
AMERICAN
TRANSCENDENTALISTS

THE SPIRITUALITY OF THE AMERICAN TRANSCENDENTALISTS

SELECTED WRITINGS
OF RALPH WALDO EMERSON,
AMOS BRONSON ALCOTT,
THEODORE PARKER,
AND HENRY DAVID THOREAU

Edited with Introductions and Notes
by
Catherine L. Albanese

ISBN 0-86554-258-9

The Spirituality of the American Transcendentalists
Copyright © 1988
Mercer University Press, Macon, Georgia 31207
All rights reserved
Printed in the United States of America

The paper used in this publication meets the minimum requirements
of American National Standard for Information Sciences—
Permanence of Paper for Printed Library Materials, ANSI Z39.48-1984.

Library of Congress Cataloging-in-Publication Data
The Spirituality of the American transcendentalists :
    selected writings of Ralph Waldo Emerson, Amos Bronson
    Alcott, Theodore Parker, and Henry David Thoreau / edited
    with introduction and notes by Catherine L. Albanese.

x + 360 pp. 7" x 10"
Bibliography : p. 345
Includes index.
ISBN 0-86554-258-9
    1. Transcendentalism (New England). 2. Spirituality.
I. Albanese, Catherine L.
B905.S65 1988   87-34730
810'.8'0382—dc19   CIP

Contents

Preface vii
Acknowledgments ix
Introduction 1

Part I
RALPH WALDO EMERSON 29

THE LORD'S SUPPER 34
NATURE 45
THE DIVINITY SCHOOL ADDRESS 76
THE OVER-SOUL 91
SELF-RELIANCE 106
POEMS (Selections) 127
FATE (Selection) 141

Part II
AMOS BRONSON ALCOTT 145

THE DOCTRINE AND DISCIPLINE OF HUMAN CULTURE 151
ORPHIC SAYINGS (Selections) 164

Part III
THEODORE PARKER 179

A DISCOURSE OF THE TRANSIENT AND PERMANENT IN CHRISTIANITY
  (Selection) 185
A DISCOURSE OF MATTERS PERTAINING TO RELIGION (Selections) 201
A SERMON OF THE DELIGHTS OF PIETY 217

Part IV
HENRY DAVID THOREAU 233

A WEEK ON THE CONCORD AND MERRIMACK RIVERS (Selections) 239
THE MAINE WOODS (Selection) 266
CIVIL DISOBEDIENCE (Selection) 275
WALDEN (Selections) 289

Bibliography 345
Index 353

To the memory of my grandmother
Lucia Macaluso Albanese
(1888-1981),
in her own way
a Transcendentalist

Preface

Ralph Waldo Emerson, Amos Bronson Alcott, Theodore Parker, Henry David Thoreau—the names of these four New Englanders have come down to us in the annals of American literary and cultural history because of their manifest embodiment, each in his own way, of American Transcendentalism. What is often forgotten, however, is that the concerns that spawned the Transcendental movement were essentially religious: the American Transcendentalists thought, wrote, spoke, and lived a distinctive spirituality.

Fashioned from a mingling of past and present, of orthodox and heterodox, of West and sometimes East, this spirituality, or its record, occupies the pages that follow. Transcendentalism has been called rationalist and intuitive, Puritan and Gnostic, coldly ethereal and warm with energies not unlike those expressed in the revivals. Its spirituality was at least an affirmation of the intuitive faculty in every individual and a call to listen to inner and natural voices. It celebrated conscience and private integrity and, in one way or another, impelled each Transcendentalist toward public action in defense of principle. It proclaimed "self-culture" (a concept derived from the Unitarians) but could also, without contradiction, at times envision and enact experiments in community. Transcendental spirituality often repudiated the churches but sought the revelation of the divine in nature. It turned resolutely from gospel miracles yet found a source of law and direction in the correspondences perceived between the different elements of creation.

In this volume Emerson's writings move from his renunciation of the theological and ritual basis of his regular ministry in "The Lord's Supper" to his Transcendental manifestos in *Nature* and *The Divinity School Address,* and then to other essays and poems that have become classic in the canon of the American Renaissance. Alcott is represented in his statement of educational idealism in his early *Doctrine and Discipline of Human Culture* and in samplings from his often-derided "Orphic Sayings." Excerpts from Parker's *Discourse of the Transient and Permanent in Christianity* are followed by reflections on inspiration and popular American religion from his lengthy *Discourse of Matters Pertaining to Religion* and then the spiritual program of his frequently overlooked *Sermon of the Delights of Piety.* Finally, Thoreau speaks in these pages through excerpts from his *Week on the Concord and Merrimack Rivers* and *The Maine Woods,* through selections from his essay "Civil Disobedience," and through an extended series of passages—in fact, a condensation—from his classic *Walden.*

Compelled by their vision and the need to live it in New England's rapidly changing nineteenth-century landscape, these Transcendentalists were responding to the upheavals of the early industrial era. Their religious and moral convictions emerged as works of synthesis in the context of the demands of their spirits and their times. Their legacy—created in the midst of a society experiencing acute growing pains—reflects their world and has something still to say to our own.

Acknowledgments

Pursuing the sources of allusions and quotations in Transcendental writing has been a bit like tracking the hound, bay horse, and turtledove of Henry David Thoreau's *Walden*. "Many are the travellers I have spoken concerning them, describing their tracks and what calls they answered to." Acknowledgments in numerous individual notes attest the extent of my debts, for I have found it necessary, in light of the near-encyclopedic knowledge reflected in these texts, to consult not only students of English and American literature but also classical and medieval scholars, specialists in Judaica and French literature, and, among others, even a biologist. Here I should mention especially the assistance of David L. Barr (New Testament) and of Willis M. Stoesz (Eastern religions) in identifying references. Both are former colleagues in the Religion Department at Wright State University.

Stephen Haas, Emily Lehrman, and Diane T. Marketti, all of the Wright State University Library, helped me in the task of locating references. Mr. Haas, now of the University of Massachuetts Library in Boston, assisted in locating modern editions in the bibliography and also prepared the index. Joy L. Iddlings, through Wright State Interlibrary Loan, furnished numerous hard-to-find editions of nineteenth-century and earlier works. Librarians at Antioch College in Yellow Springs, Ohio, likewise offered gracious help and cheer, and particular thanks are due, among them, to Steven Duffy and Bruce W. Thomas. Throughout the project my Wright State student Lisa Hauck rendered invaluable assistance in various tasks.

A grant from the Research Council of Wright State University offered early encouragement for the work, and the office of Dean Eugene B. Cantelupe in the College of Liberal Arts there provided faithful support along the way. Dean Cantelupe's successor, Perry D. Moore, assisted the publication of the completed work generously. Later an award from the Committee on Research at the University of California, Santa Barbara, supported production of the index. Marvin Bergman, former acquisitions editor at Mercer, offered insightful commentary and suggestions regarding annotations. Meanwhile, for typing a lengthy and demanding manuscript, Jane Reese, Connie Lockwood, and Veda D. Horton deserve extensive praise and gratitude. My parents, Louis and Theresa Albanese, as always, wholeheartedly encouraged my endeavor.

Introduction

In the 1830s a group of young people in New England began a revolution. Unlike many another revolution that had been and that would be, this one involved no physical weapons. Instead, as the leading revolutionary, Ralph Waldo Emerson noted years later: "The young men were born with knives in their brain, a tendency to introversion, self-dissection, anatomizing of motives."[1] The young men—and women—mostly in their twenties and thirties, took fire with a shared vision of the elements in the old order that needed overturning and the aspects of the new that they embraced. Yet they refused to organize in any conventional sense and institutionalize their revolution. Emerson, in *The Dial,* explained that those who shared in the revolution had "no external organization, no badge, no creed, no name. They do not vote, or print, or even meet together. They do not know each other's faces or names. They are united only in a common love of truth, and love of its work."[2] The statement summarized their view of radical transformations in New England society, and it was perhaps exaggerated. For at least the nucleus of the revolution did have a label and a creed. The participants did know each other's names and faces; they met together; and their works made their way into print. But it was the elusive quality of the group and what they said and did that the statement in *The Dial* reflected.

The movement of these New Englanders has been called Transcendentalism, and they have been called Transcendentalists. The name came first in derision because, critics mocked, in their enthusiasm for German and Kantian philosophic idealism the revolutionaries walked with their heads in the clouds while their feet scarcely touched the ground. The young people who bore the brunt of the criticism were mostly Unitarian in background, mostly middle class, and mostly educated at Harvard. Their movement was based in or near Boston, and at its center it included a group of some thirty or so. Among them were Ralph Waldo Emerson (1803-1882), Amos Bronson Alcott (1799-1888), Theodore

---

*A note to the notes: I have deliberately adopted the practice of capitalizing the terms *Gods* and *Goddesses* in the annotations that follow. For a historian of religions, either all Gods and Goddesses are real or none of them is. I prefer all.

[1] Ralph Waldo Emerson, *Historic Notes of Life and Letters in New England,* in Ralph Waldo Emerson, *The Complete Works of Ralph Waldo Emerson,* ed. Edward Waldo Emerson, centenary ed. (Boston: Houghton, Mifflin, 1903-1904) 10:329.

[2] Ralph Waldo Emerson, "The Editors to the Reader," *The Dial* 1:1 (July 1840): 2.

Parker (1810-1860), Henry David Thoreau (1817-1862), Margaret Fuller (1810-1850), George Ripley (1802-1880), James Freeman Clarke (1810-1888), Frederic Henry Hedge (1805-1890), Convers Francis (1795-1863), William H. Furness (1802-1896), Orestes Brownson (1803-1876), Elizabeth Palmer Peabody (1804-1894), William Henry Channing (1810-1884), Jones Very (1813-1880), and (William) Ellery Channing (1818-1901).[3]

Always nebulous, the group and the movement acquired some definition with the meetings of the Transcendental Club. Beginning on 19 September 1836 with six or seven present, like-minded friends met from time to time for an evening's conversation on topics of mutual concern. Often prompted by the arrival of Frederic Henry Hedge from Bangor, Maine, where he ministered to a church, these meetings attracted many of Boston's liberal elite, and their discussions ranged over such themes as the problems of "American genius," the "education of humanity," Harvard College, law, truth, Emerson's journals, property, and worship. By 1839 club members were actively planning a periodical to give expression to their views, and by July 1840 the first number of *The Dial* was sounding a new era in American literature. Club members, however, understood their revolution as, first and foremost, spiritual. The works that they produced, both in *The Dial* and independently, need to be seen primarily not as belles lettres or philosophy but as records of a religious quest. A glance at the forces that helped to shape Transcendentalism will aid us in understanding its spirituality.

THE BACKGROUND

The Transcendentalists created a religion of newness, and like all revolutionaries, they stressed their independence from the past. But like all revolutionaries, they were in many ways its product, just as they were also the product of the collision of that past with the present.

First, the Transcendentalists were children of the Puritan settlers of New England, who had early exhibited a mystical strain and an ability to find God in nature. Perry Miller has spoken of this mystical strain among the Puritans and of the persistence of their attempt "to confront, face to face, the image of a blinding divinity in the physical universe."[4] Even from a rationalistic perspective, Cotton Mather (1663-1728) in his *Christian Philosopher* (1721) had extolled the revelation of God in nature with its abiding order and harmony. Later, Jonathan Edwards (1703-1758), the great Puritan theologian, found nature an occasion for meeting God more intuitively. He recalled in an autobiographical narrative how he had gone walking alone in his father's pasture.

> And as I was walking there, and looking up on the sky and clouds, there came into my mind so sweet a sense of the glorious *majesty* and *grace* of God, that I know not how to express. . . . After this my sense of divine things gradually increased, and became more and more

---

[3]Except for James Freeman Clarke, the names in this list are drawn from Alexander Kern's well-known inventory. See Alexander Kern, "The Rise of Transcendentalism," in Harry Hayden Clark, ed., *Transitions in American Literary History* (1954; rpt., New York: Octagon Books, 1967) 249. It is curious that Kern omits Clarke from his list since he cites the Transcendentalist later in the extensive essay.

[4]Perry Miller, "From Edwards to Emerson," in *Errand into the Wilderness* (New York: Harper & Row, Harper Torchbooks, 1967) 185.

lively, and had more of that inward sweetness. . . . God's excellency, his wisdom, his purity and love, seemed to appear in every thing; in the sun, moon, and stars; in the clouds, and blue sky; in the grass, flowers, trees; in the water, and all nature; which used greatly to fix my mind.[5]

The mystical strain was also expressed in such Puritan "heresies" as the Quaker doctrine of the inner light and the antinomian teaching of Mistress Anne Hutchinson (1591-1643), who defied religious authorities to speak, certain of the more authoritative presence of the Holy Spirit within herself. Likewise, the Puritan penchant for keeping intimate journals and diaries revealed an introspective concern for the condition of the soul and the presence or absence of grace. Thus, whether outwardly in nature or inwardly in the self, the Puritans possessed a sensitivity to the God who was immanent as well as transcendent. They gave to their Transcendental heirs a religious culture in which nature and the interior life were respected in the light of divinity, and they encouraged a seriousness and intensity of purpose in the pursuit of spiritual things. As Octavius B. Frothingham wrote in his classic study: "Transcendentalism simply claimed for all men what Protestant Christianity claimed for its own elect."[6]

Beyond that, Puritan philosophic thinking had favored the Platonic tradition with its idealism and its system of analogy between the material world and the spiritual realm. At the same time, Puritan inwardness and idealism were woven into the fabric of a culture that, with its austerity and asceticism, also emphasized the world. Imbued with a sense of high morality and calling by God in every profession, the Puritans moved with confidence and ability. They were pragmatic, efficient, and industrious people who succeeded at what they tried and who tried very much.

Even as they rebelled against their past, the Transcendentalists continued to embody these Puritan tendencies and qualities. Indeed, as Harold Goddard argued in 1908, "On the whole the most conspicuous similarity of these transcendentalists was simply their *Puritan character.*"[7] Like their ancestors, the Transcendentalists wrote their own footnotes to Plato as they fashioned a spirituality that moved them to speak to the condition of their times. Like their ancestors, too, they were haunted by their sense of morality and the moral law, and they thought of the task of spreading their new gospel as a vocation, a calling by God. The Transcendentalists preached with a confidence and an optimism that matched their ancestors' sense of intimacy with God.

Meanwhile, that sense of intimacy was reflected in a predilection for the interior life and a cultivation of mystical themes. The intimacy was also reflected in a celebration of nature as the abode of spirit, when Transcendentalists, in a form of spiritual pragmatism, pointed to nature's religious usefulness. While these qualities in many cases went further

---

[5]Jonathan Edwards, "Personal Narrative," in Clarence H. Faust and Thomas H. Johnson, eds., *Jonathan Edwards: Representative Selections,* American Century Series, rev. ed. (New York: Hill and Wang, 1962) 60-61.

[6]Octavius B. Frothingham, *Transcendentalism in New England: A History* (1876; rpt., Gloucester MA: Peter Smith, 1965) 108.

[7]Harold C. Goddard, *Studies in New England Transcendentalism* (1908; rpt., New York: Hillary House, 1960) 183. (Emphasis Goddard's.)

than earlier Puritan expressions, the seeds of Transcendental religious culture could still be found in Puritanism.

Second, the Transcendentalists were children of the Unitarians who emerged from the liberal wing of Puritanism. In a gradual process during the second half of the eighteenth century and the early part of the nineteenth, the Unitarians had achieved a separate identity. In Boston and its neighborhood, the preaching from Puritan pulpits increasingly emphasized morality and upright character. Less and less, this preaching spoke of human depravity and the old Calvinist teaching of election by God. When in the 1730s and 1740s the Great Awakening brought enthusiastic religion and revivalism to New England as elsewhere, liberal Christians warned of its dangers and preached a rational religion of sobriety and restraint. There were straws in the wind, as when, in 1785, King's Chapel in Boston revised its liturgy to avoid reference to the Trinity and when, in 1805, Harvard College appointed the Reverend Henry Ware, then a liberal Christian, as Hollis Professor of Divinity. Eventually, in 1825, the tensions and institutional crises that had occurred throughout eastern Massachusetts came to a head in the formation of the American Unitarian Association.

The Unitarians emphasized the rationalism that had already been part of Puritanism, and they allied it with the Enlightenment philosophy of John Locke (1632-1704). This Englishman, in his famous *Essay Concerning Human Understanding* (1690), had taught a doctrine of epistemological materialism. Rejecting the traditional theory that human beings possessed knowledge through innate ideas, Locke argued that the mind was a tabula rasa, a clean slate on which knowledge was recorded through the impression of the senses and then subject to reflection to create ideas. In a mechanical way, the world affected the sense organs, forming the ideas that were faithful representations of reality. Hence, scientific work was possible, and rationalism—the agenda of the Enlightenment—was sustained and fortified.

For the Unitarians, the sensationalist philosophy of John Locke had religious consequences. In the theological quest for certainty, they found evidence for the truth of Christianity in the miracles to which the gospels witnessed. Here was proof through the senses for the authenticity of the character of Jesus and the message that he preached. Here, in short, was a rational argument for the faith of a liberal nineteenth-century person. So, as Perry Miller wrote, "In Boston and Salem, the centers of shipping and banking, ministers preached rationality rather than dogma, the Newtonian universe and the sensational psychology rather than providence and innate depravity."[8] In so doing, the Unitarians created an intellectual and spiritual freedom that the Transcendentalists would harvest, much to the chagrin of their fellow religionists.

Freedom from dogma was related to the further emphasis among the Unitarians on individual responsibility. With its cultivation of morality as the essence of the Christian message, Unitarianism, perforce, turned to the individual who struggled for righteousness. Vernon L. Parrington has called this emphasis on individual responsibility a rediscovery of the "original principle" of Protestantism, which had been "tacitly denied by

---

[8]Miller, "From Edwards to Emerson," 193.

Calvinistic orthodoxy."⁹ Moreover, if individuals were responsible, Unitarians saw them as intrinsically *capable* of acting responsibly; and original sin gave way in Unitarian thought before human goodness. Perhaps it was more than coincidence, therefore, that the Unitarians—as part of their teaching—had turned from the Trinity to the unity of God. For the individual who lived out the moral life as a solitary self, the unity of God and the earnest and exemplary character of Jesus seemed compelling symbols. The divine community of a Trinity appeared not nearly so meaningful.

Rationalist and Lockean, championing freedom, individual responsibility, and human goodness, the Unitarians refined their moral theology through their appropriation of Scottish common-sense philosophy. As expounded by Thomas Reid (1710-1796) and his followers, among them Dugald Stewart (1753-1828) and Thomas Brown (1778-1820), Scottish common sense adhered to much of Locke's empiricism but argued for the self-evidence of fundamental principles of reason ("common sense") as the ground for knowledge of the objective world. It argued, too, for a moral sense—a basic intuitive sense by means of which people distinguished between good and evil and understood the principles on which moral action was built.

The Transcendentalists came to regard Lockean sensationalism as the enemy to be destroyed in the service of the spirit. Indeed, the case can be made that without the goad of John Locke their revolution might not have been fought. However, it was John Locke as mediated through the rationalism of Unitarian preaching that disturbed them most. Their revolt again and again witnessed to the barrenness and coldness they found in the rational message of their church. Emerson once told Divinity School students at Harvard that a minister of the time was "plainest prose, the prose of prose. He is a Warming-pan, a Nightchair at sick beds & rheumatic souls." He called Unitarianism an "icehouse" with "coldness continually increasing," and he castigated the preaching of one minister as "the most ominous shaking of Unitarian husks & pods out of which all corn & peas had long fallen."¹⁰ His friend Alcott, although not formally a Unitarian, shared many of these sentiments regarding their clergy when he wrote:

> The intellect of preachers seems still wandering among the mysteries of a dark and antiquated theology. . . . They lead us through a bewildering labyrinth of theory, of book-work, far away from the ever-present and all-pervading Deity. They lead us to what man has said and thought and recorded in books, rather than to what He who made man has recorded in living character.¹¹

---

⁹Vernon L. Parrington, *Main Currents in American Thought,* vol. 2 of *The Romantic Revolution in America, 1800–1860* (1927; New York: Harcourt, Brace & World, Harvest Books, 1954) 373.

¹⁰Ralph Waldo Emerson, *The Journals and Miscellaneous Notebooks of Ralph Waldo Emerson,* ed. William H. Gilman et al. (Cambridge: Harvard University Press, Belknap Press, 1960–) 5 (1 April 1838): 471; 8 (26 June 1842): 182; (March 1843): 355. Ralph Waldo Emerson to Margaret Fuller, 6 September 1839, in Ralph Waldo Emerson, *The Letters of Ralph Waldo Emerson,* ed. Ralph L. Rusk (New York: Columbia University Press, 1939) 2:222.

¹¹Amos Bronson Alcott, *Journals* (1828), quoted by Odell Shepard, *Pedlar's Progress: The Life of Bronson Alcott* (1937; rpt., New York: Greenwood Press, 1968) 126. Unfortunately, the published journals of Alcott contain only a small portion of the total material that he left.

But if, as Perry Miller has said, Transcendentalism was the "natural reaction of some descendants of Puritans and Quakers to Unitarian and commercial times,"[12] there was much of Unitarianism that the Transcendentalists continued to uphold. Unitarian overthrow of traditional Christian doctrine, in general, freed the Transcendentalists to pursue their own, more radical speculations. More specifically, Unitarian rejection of the orthodox Trinity cleared the ground for the mystical unitarianism of Transcendentalists who spoke of divine Mind and Reason and the Oversoul. Unitarian-bequeathed Scottish common-sense philosophy, with its teaching of the moral sense, blended with new sources of Transcendental thinking to support the spirituality based on the primacy of intuition. Thus, Unitarian stress on individual responsibility and optimism regarding human goodness became also the Transcendental gospel. Unitarian self-culture, the active flowering of its individualism, was appropriated by the Transcendentalists and, as we shall see, developed even further.

Children of the Puritans and the Unitarians, the Transcendentalists also found many of the new sources for their thought and spirituality in Europe. For the Transcendentalists were, third, the children of the Europeans, especially in their Romantic phase. Members of the "new school" grew enthusiastic about the transcendental philosophy of the German scholar Immanuel Kant (1724-1804), which challenged the tabula rasa doctrine of John Locke and the British empiricists. For Kant, knowledge was mediated through a series of mental categories that shaped the raw data of experience. Thus, knowledge was partly ideal (the product of the mind) and partly empirical (the product of the senses).[13] The Transcendentalists turned eagerly as well to Friedrich H. Jacobi (1743-1819), another German thinker, who countered the Kantian philosophy to argue for the direct and immediate knowledge of intuition in an idealism that was more complete and more mystical. A third German hero for the Transcendentalists was Johann G. Fichte (1762-1812), who exalted the human mind as the ultimate reality, going beyond Kantian idealism by denying the existence of an objective, external world. Other Germans, too, drew Transcendental approval and enthusiasm, among them Friedrich Schleiermacher (1768-1834), the theologian of pietism who identified religion with feeling.

German influences reached the Transcendentalists in various ways. In 1819 the return of two New Englanders—Edward Everett and George Ticknor—from studies in Göttingen, Germany, and then in 1822 the return of a third—George Bancroft—excited interest in German literature. Later, from 1825, Charles T. C. Follen (1796-1840) taught German at Harvard, and among the founding members of the Transcendental Club, Frederic Henry Hedge spent four years studying in Germany. However, the Transcendentalists got much of their German at second hand; and in the final analysis it was the work of Samuel Taylor Coleridge (1772-1834) and, in some measure, of other English Romanticists like Thomas Carlyle (1795-1881) and William Wordsworth (1770-1850) that influenced them more.

Coleridge had been introduced to an American audience in 1829, when James Marsh (1794-1842), a Calvinist cleric and professor at the University of Vermont, produced an

---

[12]Miller, "From Edwards to Emerson," 189.

[13]My discussion here and in much of what follows relies on Paul Boller. See his chapter "Intuitional Philosophy" in Paul F. Boller, Jr., *American Transcendentalism, 1830-1860: An Intellectual Inquiry* (New York: G. P. Putnam's Sons, 1974) 34-63.

American edition of the Englishman's *Aids to Reflection.* In a preliminary essay and notes to the book, Marsh stressed Coleridge's distinction between the Reason and the Understanding, which was based on Kantian terms but also a simplification and a transformation of them. For Coleridge—as interpreted by Marsh—Reason was the high faculty of intuition that could have direct and positive knowledge of spiritual things, while Understanding was the lesser faculty that dealt with the material world. The American Transcendentalists made this distinction basic to their understanding of spirituality. A number of them never came to terms with the original philosophy of Immanuel Kant, although they thought that, through Coleridge and Marsh, they had.

If German and English Romantics made their mark on the Transcendentalists, so, to some extent, did the French. Eclecticism, especially in the work of Victor Cousin (1792-1867), found a congenial audience among Transcendentalists such as George Ripley and Orestes Brownson. Cousin, along with Théodore Jouffroy (1796-1842) combined Scottish common sense with German idealism and other sources, arguing that each possessed truths that could be understood intuitively. Meanwhile, the Neoplatonic and metaphysical tradition of Europe—with its long history preceding the rise of Romanticism—had been discovered by many of the Transcendentalists; and new spiritual heroes were found in men such as Emanuel Swedenborg (1688-1772) and Jacob Boehme (1575-1624).

The Transcendentalists absorbed Neoplatonism with their Platonism, for they read Plato with the aid of the introductions and translations of Thomas Taylor, a British scholar who gave his readings a Neoplatonic and mystical cast. Emerson was also greatly affected by his discovery of Sampson Reed (1800-1880), a young Swedenborgian whose speaking and writing introduced the Transcendental leader to the prolific Swedish mystic. When, in 1826, Reed published his *Observations on the Growth of the Mind,* Emerson could not praise it enough in his journal: "a book of such a character as I am conscious betrays some pretension even to praise. It has to my mind the aspect of a revelation, such is the wealth & such is the novelty of the truth unfolded in it."[14] Still more, Emerson studied Swedenborg's own works, in which the doctrine of correspondences between the earth and various spiritual spheres was developed. Swedenborg spoke in his writings with the authority of one who had had direct experience, for he was a visionary who claimed the revelations of angelic and spirit visitors. Although in later life Emerson would qualify some of his earlier enthusiasm for Swedenborg himself, the effect of his teachings proved to be profound and lasting.

Even more than Emerson, his close friend Alcott was drawn to the Neoplatonic view of things. Alcott's teaching regarding Genesis, or Lapse, was drawn from the ancient Neoplatonic doctrine of the emanation of the Many from the One. For Alcott, human beings were emanations from the divine Mind, although it was only in rare and brief moments of heightened consciousness that men and women became aware of their true origins. Human beings, thought Alcott, had "lapsed" from Mind, while nature itself was a lapse from humanity, "Man in ruins."[15] So much was Alcott drawn to the metaphysical worldview that, as Alexander Kern has remarked, "much of Alcott's obscurity lay in the fact that he was by temperament as well as by reading an heir of the hermetic mystical tradition."[16]

---

[14]Emerson, *Journals and Miscellaneous Notebooks,* 3 (10 September 1826): 45.
[15]Shepard, *Pedlar's Progress,* 454.
[16]Kern, "Rise of Transcendentalism," 271.

Later, *The Harbinger,* a periodical begun by the Transcendentalist commune at Brook Farm in 1845, strongly reflected Swedenborgian thinking. Various other Transcendentalists spoke with approval and admiration of Swedenborg and Boehme and of general Neoplatonic teaching. But the ecumenism of the Transcendental spirit extended beyond the esoteric tradition of Europe to embrace, in time, the spirituality of the East.

Here, with the movement already in its heyday, the Orient acted not as a first teacher but, instead, as a corroborator of what the Transcendentalists already knew. The excitement of discovering spiritual insights and experiences similar to their own among strange and distant people was strong, and both Emerson and Thoreau have left literary records of their encounters with the East.[17] From India, the *Bhagavad Gita,* certain texts of the *Vedas,* the *Laws of Manu,* and, from China, even the sayings of Confucius whetted Transcendental appetites. Read in inaccurate translations and mingled eclectically with other sources, the Eastern works proved malleable to Transcendental reconstruction. The union of Brahman with Atman, the forms of yoga, the harmonial disciplines of spiritual paths, all found reincarnations in the "new-school" synthesis. Thus, from one perspective, because the reconstructed Orient told the Transcendentalists what they already believed, they read the Eastern classics simply for support and confirmation. But from another perspective, their gesture of openness toward a spirituality totally other was a testimony to the Romantic spirit of expansiveness and inclusion. In the end, that Romantic spirit had been kindled by the gift of Europe.

Whatever the largesse of the European gift, however, the Transcendentalists were, fourth and finally, the children of their contemporary America. Outside the Puritan-turned-Unitarian enclaves of Boston, a new America was living through an era of material and mental ferment.[18] The industrial revolution was bringing the factory system of collective manufacturing and, with it, the dislocation of many farm people who settled in company towns. A transportation revolution was introducing canals and steamboats and, most important, railroads. Meanwhile, cities grew, swelled by the arrival of rural migrants and foreign immigrants; and the frontier was being pushed further and further west by others still. In 1828 Andrew Jackson (1767-1845) assumed the presidency, and the triumph of the hero from Tennessee—to the horror of conservative Whigs—became the symbol of the popular democracy of the age. The economy alternately boomed on a tide of speculation and crashed with its own weight.

Like their economy, Americans were strained by the pressures of the times. A subculture of ultraism, or extremism, attracted many, while some immersed themselves in numerous reform movements for causes like temperance, antislavery, peace, and women's rights. Revivals and new religious movements flared in the "burnt-over" district of New York state, without a doubt the California of the nineteenth century. Experiments in life-style brought communal living to some and nontraditional sexual arrangements to

---

[17]For what is still the best discussion of the relationship of leading Transcendentalists to Eastern thought, see Arthur E. Christy, *The Orient in American Transcendentalism: A Study of Emerson, Thoreau, and Alcott* (1932; rpt., New York: Octagon Books, 1978).

[18]For a more extensive discussion, on which the present one is based, see Catherine L. Albanese, *Corresponding Motion: Transcendental Religion and the New America* (Philadelphia: Temple University Press, 1977) 122-50.

others. Alternative forms of healing such as herbal medicine, homeopathy, and, after 1840, hydropathy flourished, and vegetarianism attracted notice.

In the midst of this world of rapid change and continuing social upheaval, the Transcendentalists responded in complex and ambiguous fashion. Conceptually, they were often ambivalent about an America so mindlessly on the move, fearing for the materialism of the era and the absence of more lasting values. "Things are in the saddle," Emerson wrote, "and ride mankind."[19] Nonetheless, their ambivalence did not prevent the Transcendentalists from throwing themselves into various reform movements—as in the case of Theodore Parker's work for antislavery—or experimenting with different life-styles—as at Brook Farm and Fruitlands, as we shall see. In truth, at a deeper level, the Transcendentalists shared the excitement of their times in a vision in which flux was at the heart of things. Emerson thought that Boston, when seen from a stage coach, offered a "ludicrous pathetic tragical picture," but, he said, "get into the railroad car & the Ideal Philosophy takes place at once."[20]

> One has . . . a practical confirmation of the ideal philosophy that Matter is phenomenal whilst men & trees & barns whiz by you as fast as the leaves of a dictionary. As our teakettle hissed along through a field of mayflowers, we could judge of the sensations of a swallow who skims by trees & bushes with about the same speed. The very permanence of matter seems compromised & oaks, fields, hills, hitherto esteemed symbols of stability do absolutely dance by you.[21]

"Machinery & Transcendentalism agree well," Emerson decided.[22]

That agreement was revealed chiefly in the language with which the Transcendentalists expressed their vision of religious truth, a language in which motion was everywhere, and revolution and the "newness" were celebrated. While this language was often the language of nature, it was more often the language of movement and change. In other words, whatever the content of the Transcendental message in substantive terms, it tended to be written in the kinetic mode. True, more conservative Transcendentalists, who remained Unitarians, spoke the message of Jesus Christ and Christianity, while their radical friends contemplated ultimate things in terms more pantheistic and universal. All, however, saw the spiritual world as a world in flux. The gospel became an energizing word; water was transformed into a river or a current; light into a flame or fire. Wind and breath, circles and circulation, birth and growth were all preferred metaphors for spiritual truth. In short, the Transcendentalists, in tune with their times, were inaugurating a language and a religion of process.

THE TRANSCENDENTAL REVOLUTION

The inheritors of a complex past and present, the Transcendentalists went about their revolution with conscious intent. In so doing, they thought, wrote, and acted in new ways that went beyond their legacy, putting forward a distinctive spirituality as the expression of their vision. In exploring the background for their movement, we have already seen

---

[19]Ralph Waldo Emerson, "Ode Inscribed to W. H. Channing," in Emerson, *Complete Works*, 9:78.

[20]Emerson, *Journals and Miscellaneous Notebooks*, 4 (15 April 1834): 277.

[21]Ibid., 4 (10 June 1834): 296.

[22]Ibid., 8 (May 1843): 397.

parts of the concrete achievement of the Transcendentalists, but it is important here to discuss that achievement systematically, however briefly.

Alexander Kern has summarized the main features of Transcendental thought in examining the mental shifts that gave rise to the movement. Philosophically, the Transcendentalists were intuitive idealists who rejected Lockean sensationalism, moving from the moral sense of the Scottish school to a belief in the direct and immediate knowledge of reality. At the same time, Kern tells us, the Transcendentalists rejected the mechanistic universe of the Enlightenment for a vitalistic, organic view of nature in which it became symbolic of spiritual things. In organized religious terms, they moved from the conservative and rationalistic Unitarian posture in which most of them were reared to a clear articulation of the divinity of human beings. In literature, they turned from neoclassical theories to Romantic ideas of symbol as the revelation of artistic vision. And in social thought, they tended to ignore collective and communal understandings to emphasize individual integrity and human freedom in the context of personal development.[23]

Distinctive thought meant distinctive writing, and the full list of Transcendental publications would require a volume in itself to discuss. Still, it is worth noting at least a few of these contributions. Indeed, the year in which the Transcendental Club first met—1836—has been called the annus mirabilis of the movement, because in that remarkable year so many Transcendental writings made their way into print. In 1836 Emerson's *Nature* authoritatively proclaimed the revolution and the gospel of the new school. Eighteen hundred thirty-six was also the year in which Alcott published the first volume of his *Record of Conversations on the Gospels,* an account of his experiment in education in the Temple School.

In that year, too, George Ripley reviewed James Martineau's *Rationale of Religious Inquiry* in the pages of the official Unitarian *Christian Examiner,* creating a controversy because he disparaged the usefulness of miracles as Christian evidence. Likewise, William H. Furness published *Remarks on the Four Gospels,* in which he challenged the miraculousness of the resurrection of Jesus, arguing that the supernatural was contained in the natural world. Orestes Brownson published *New Views of Christianity, Society, and the Church,* locating Unitarian history in the context of two warring social systems, the material and the spiritual, with Unitarianism being a victory for materialism. Meanwhile, a tract written by Convers Francis, *Christianity as a Purely Internal Principle,* offered a Transcendental testament to the Christian aim: "to purify and sweeten the fountains in the deep places of the soul, that refreshing influences may thence go forth."[24]

The collective character of the Transcendental enterprise was evident in a series of periodicals published by members of the group. The earliest of these, *The Western Messenger,* appeared in Cincinnati in 1835, ostensibly devoted to Unitarian Christianity. With James Freeman Clarke and, later, William Henry Channing among its editors, however, the *Messenger* occupied a central place in the evolution of the Transcendental movement until the periodical's demise in 1841. Its subscription list, which included nearly one hundred readers from New England in 1836, reflected a continual dialogue with New En-

---

[23]Kern, "Rise of Transcendentalism," 251.

[24]Convers Francis, *Christianity as a Purely Internal Principle,* in *Tracts of the American Unitarian Association,* 1st ser., 9:105 (Boston: Leonard C. Bowles, 1836) 8.

glanders.[25] The steady interest of the editors of the Unitarian *Christian Register and Boston Observer* in its appearance and content provided still another sign of the *Messenger*'s influence in the East. In fact, the *Register* pursued a regular policy of printing extracts and even complete articles culled from its pages. During the years of its publication, the *Messenger* offered a capsule summary of the development of American liberalism from Calvinism to eventual Transcendentalism, and especially in 1838 and 1839, its shift toward Transcendental beliefs and values became most noticeable. Articles treated the new views; Emerson was defended against his critics; his poems and Jones Very's sonnets made almost their first public appearances. The *Messenger* also featured excerpts from Emerson's addresses, and brief extracts from his writings began to be used as fillers.[26]

Yet the *Messenger* was eclipsed in its role as vehicle for the new views by the well-remembered *Dial,* which appeared for a brief four-year span beginning just nine months before the *Messenger* ended. At an organizational meeting held in 1839, Margaret Fuller was designated editor (followed later by Emerson, with George Ripley assuming business responsibility and an editorial advisory role). Alcott suggested the journal's title, offering the name he had used for parts of his diary. The "Dial" meant a sundial, and for the Transcendentalists so humble a commodity as a sundial could assume symbolic and spiritual proportions. As early as 1836, Convers Francis had compared the relationship between an individual's spiritual life and the divine nature to that between a sundial and the sun.[27] And James Freeman Clarke thought the title "excellent" and "significant of those who believe in the progress of time and who watch it, not in the bustle of a city, but amid the flowers and leafiness of a garden walk." "The name," he said, "speaks of faith in Nature and in Progress."[28] So *The Dial* tied its sense of time to organic perceptions and to a motion that followed the periodicity of the planetary system. Ideas of nature, progress, and correspondence were joined in its title—a hermetic sign for the initiated and a clue to the spiritual revolution it hoped to perpetrate.

Publishing poetry, articles on religious, literary, and social issues, excerpts from spiritual classics, and book reviews as well as other critical commentaries, *The Dial* announced its editorial creed with each issue: "The pages of this Journal will be filled by contributors . . . whose hearts are more in the future than in the past; and who trust the

---

[25]*The Western Messenger* 2:5 (December 1836): 352; also cited by Clarence L. F. Gohdes, *The Periodicals of American Transcendentalism* (1931; rpt., New York: AMS Press, 1970) 37.

[26]For a fuller discussion, from which this one is derived, see Catherine L. Albanese, "Charon and the River: The Changing Religious Symbols of Six American Transcendentalists" (Ph.D. diss., University of Chicago, 1972) 207-12.

[27]Convers Francis, "Discourse 3," *Three Discourses Preached before the Congregational Society in Watertown* (Cambridge MA: Folsom, Wells & Thurston, 1836) 52. Even earlier, as Emerson recorded in his journal *(Journals and Miscellaneous Notebooks* 4 [15 July 1832?]: 33), *The New Jerusalem Magazine* had observed that Emanuel Swedenborg saw "the visible world & the relation of its parts as the dial plate of the invisible one." Emerson later used the quotation in *Nature* (1836). See Samuel Sandels, "Emanuel Swedenborg," *The New Jerusalem Magazine* 5 (July 1832): 437.

[28]James Freeman Clarke to Margaret Fuller, 24 May 1840, *The Letters of James Freeman Clarke to Margaret Fuller,* ed. John Wesley Thomas (Hamburg: Cram, de Gruyter, 1957) 138.

living soul rather than the dead letter. It will endeavor to promote the constant evolution of truth, not the petrifaction of opinion."[29]

Some of Emerson's best poems and lectures were printed in these pages. So, too, was Fuller's article, "The Great Lawsuit; Man versus Men—Woman versus Women," which she later developed into *Woman in the Nineteenth Century* (1845), the first significant treatise on feminism in the United States. Alcott contributed many of his "Orphic Sayings," while Parker and Thoreau, along with Ripley, Clarke, and both Channings, also offered material for the journal. But despite its high aim to "occupy a station on which the light may fall; which is open to the rising sun; and from which it may correctly report the progress of the hour and the day," among its contemporaries *The Dial* was often either condemned or ridiculed. "The editors and reviewers of its day could make nothing of it," wrote Octavius B. Frothingham, himself once a Transcendentalist.[30]

A third Transcendental periodical, edited by Orestes Brownson, overlapped *The Dial* during part of its short history. Published from 1838 to 1842, *The Boston Quarterly Review* left most of its articles unsigned, although a few were initialed. In the first issue, Parker—who wrote marginal notes on his own copy—contributed an article, as did William Henry Channing, John Sullivan Dwight, and, among others, Brownson himself. In fact, throughout the periodical's existence, Brownson was the overwhelming contributor, and his logical, expository style so influenced the tone of the journal that Clarence Gohdes has called it "the most philosophical of all the periodicals connected with the [Transcendental] movement."[31] Yet *The Boston Quarterly Review* mixed religion and literature with its philosophy, printing some of Alcott's "Orphic Sayings" and at one time proposing a union with the projected *Dial* (a suggestion rejected by Fuller and Emerson). Moreover, Brownson actively identified with the Democratic party in his review and generally lived up to his reputation as a "reform man."

A fourth, short-lived Transcendental periodical also devoted itself to issues of social reform. Established in New York City in 1843 by William Henry Channing, *The Present*, like *The Boston Quarterly Review*, was mostly an outlet for the writing of its editor. Channing concentrated on religious and social philosophy—a plan for "Christian Union"—heavily influenced by the thought of the French socialist and communitarian Charles Fourier (1772-1837). Still, again like *The Boston Quarterly Review*, *The Present* found space for a series of Alcott's sayings that, in fact, stretched to two installments. But after only a year and twelve issues, *The Present* ceased to publish.

Other Transcendental periodicals came and went, invariably rather quickly. There was, for example, Elizabeth Palmer Peabody's *Aesthetic Papers*, which published only one number (1849), and *The Massachusetts Quarterly Review* edited by Parker, which appeared in three volumes (1847-1850). There was a second *Dial*, which endured for a year (1860) in Cincinnati. And in New England a late journal, *The Radical*, kept afloat for

---

[29]*The Dial*, editorial message appearing on the cover of each volume.

[30]Frothingham, *Transcendentalism in New England*, 137.

[31]Gohdes, *Periodicals of American Transcendentalism*, 80. Gohdes's book is the definitive study of *The Boston Quarterly Review, The Present,* and other periodicals of American Transcendentalism. See also, Albanese, "Charon and the River," 239-42, for a brief discussion of *The Boston Quarterly Review* and *The Present*.

nearly seven years (1865-1872), an outgrowth of views fostered by the earlier Transcendental movement.

Outside the pages of these periodicals, the Transcendentalists proved to be prolific authors, contributing to other journals and publishing independently as well. Emerson, after the publication of *Nature,* wrote voluminously, mostly essays and lectures. Alcott, too, continued to publish into his old age, offering collections of aphorisms and conversations. Parker's writings later extended some fifteen volumes in the American Unitarian Association edition (1907-1911), best known among them his ringing declaration of faith in the sermon "The Transient and Permanent in Christianity" (1841). More slowly and quietly, Thoreau produced expressions of his inner and outer life; his *Walden* (1854), "Civil Disobedience" ("Resistance to Civil Government," 1849), and *Week on the Concord and Merrimack Rivers* (1849) justly numbered among the classics of American literature. The ambitious Ripley enlisted the aid of his friends for the fourteen-volume *Specimens of Foreign Standard Literature* (1838-1842), a series of translations of French and German works. Fuller, Ellery Channing, Furness, and Very (with Emerson's help), as already noted, published their works; and other Transcendentalists likewise found their way into print.

While the Transcendentalists thought and wrote in distinctive ways, they revealed the extent of their commitment by *acting* distinctively. First, they experimented with new life-styles and their symbolic encodement in ceremonial forms; and second (and here the record is mixed), they devoted themselves to contemporary efforts for social reform. Of the two new life-styles that the Transcendentalists explored, self-culture—with its name and fundamental concept already articulated by the Unitarians—was the more basic. Communal living, according to a Utopian model, attracted some of the Transcendentalists, like Alcott and Ripley; but it raised serious questions for others, including Emerson and Thoreau. Self-culture, however, remained the requirement for all.

Emerson, the leader, articulated the notion of self-culture for the others who, as in the case of Thoreau, added their footnotes to the Emersonian scheme. "I cannot find language of sufficient energy to convey my sense of the sacredness of private integrity," Emerson wrote flatly in one essay.[32] It is this sense of private integrity that made self-culture a distinctive ideal, related to traditional Western mysticism but also somewhat separate from it. Much of the mysticism of the West worked to diminish what we, in a post-Freudian era, would call the ego, the sense of personal and autobiographical power, prestige, and self-confidence that each of us possesses. While Christian mysticism resisted the Eastern formulation in which the self is extinguished and absorbed into the divine, it also taught the value of humility and self-abasement in seeking an experience of close communion with God.

The Transcendental understanding of self-culture was predicated on a different view of things. It would be too simple—and, in fact, a distortion—to say, as many critics have,

---

[32]Ralph Waldo Emerson, "Lectures on the Times," *The Dial* 3:1 (July 1842): 12. For a related and more extensive discussion of self-culture, see Albanese, *Corresponding Motion,* 151-73; and for Emerson's debt to Unitarianism for the concept of self-culture, see David Robinson, *Apostle of Culture: Emerson as Preacher and Lecturer* (Philadelphia: University of Pennsylvania Press, 1982) esp. 7-35.

that the Transcendentalists merely and selfishly exalted the ego. What they did was far more complex and far more interesting. Sharing the insights of many Western mystics, they desired to seek within themselves the divine fountain of life, and they understood such intimacy as a radical force that would mean the revision of their former lives. But the revision was based on an overwhelming sense that the God who dwelled within was the God who empowered the ego, enabling it to fulfill all of its capacities and goals. In other words, there was a way in which, in Transcendental self-culture, the energy that pulsed at the mystical Center was channeled into autobiographical and, in a corrected sense, egoistic concerns. It was this that made the "private integrity" of the self so sacrosanct and made Transcendental individualism a doctrine akin to mysticism. The genius of the new life-style was that it captured the power unleashed by moments of mystical intensity, used them in the service of the ego, and at the same time, even as it maintained and expanded the ego, transfigured it. Thus the ego began to resemble something beyond its ordinary condition, something—in a word—divine.

Self-culture was therefore the chief activity for those who participated in the movement. The experiments with communal living that engaged some of the Transcendentalists need to be seen as one way to implement the basic task. They hoped that Utopian communities might foster the social conditions in which each self, each reconstituted ego, would flourish and grow in an atmosphere of freedom, support, and trust. So it was that Ripley and those who joined him from 1841 created Brook Farm, while Alcott and others, on a smaller scale, in 1843 initiated Fruitlands. In so doing, the Transcendentalists joined a small army of experimenters in the nineteenth century—Shakers, Rappites, Owenites, Fourierists, Oneidans among them—who sought the answer to religious or social ills in the establishment of planned communities.

Brook Farm—"a French Revolution in small, an Age of Reason in a patty-pan," as Emerson later called it[33]—began in the imagination of George Ripley. By 1840 Ripley had grown restive in his (Unitarian) ministry to a church on Purchase Street in Boston. The parish was surrounded by a deteriorating neighborhood, and Ripley's concern for the people who lived there blended with the Transcendental ideal of self-culture to suggest an experiment in economic and social democracy. The community he proposed would support the efforts of its members to engage in reform projects. No poorer folk joined the Brook Farm community, however, than the Transcendental middle class. The community was organized as a joint stock company in which members held the shares and so some proprietary interest. Ripley, who resigned from his ministry, for the most part led Brook Farm, and to the community flocked a series of Transcendental notables, most of them as frequent visitors rather than members. On a farm of some 160 acres in West Roxbury, Massachusetts, the cooperative community at first numbered about twenty but later averaged close to seventy. Every effort was made, according to the Brook Farm Constitution, to fit work to the "capacities, habits, and tastes" of the different members; and indeed each member was exhorted to "select and perform such operations of labor, whether corporal or mental, as shall be deemed best suited to his own endowments and the benefit of the Association."[34]

---

[33]Emerson, *Historic Notes*, 364.

[34]Brook-Farm Association for Industry and Education, "Constitution," in Frothingham, *Transcendentalism in New England*, 161.

It was clear that freedom was a cardinal principle at Brook Farm. "No member of the Association shall ever be subjected to any religious test," declared the constitution. "Nor shall any authority be assumed over individual freedom of opinion by the Association, nor by one member over another; nor shall any one be held accountable to the Association, except for such overt acts, or omissions of duty, as violate the principles of justice, purity, and love, on which it is founded."[35]

In this ideological climate, members of Brook Farm worked at agriculture, crafts, and light industries and established a highly regarded school. Although some, like Nathaniel Hawthorne, grew less enthusiastic for manual labor as the months passed, for the most part morale was high, with theater and concerts, games and dances, and long Transcendental "conversations." The list of social reforms that members of Brook Farm later endorsed sounds, as Ripley's biographer Charles Crowe has observed, "like a reform catalogue of the age replete with anti-currency men, labor reformers, Grahamites, hydropaths, Swedenborgians, and representatives of dozens of reform and religious sects."[36] Ripley invited speakers on all issues, and perplexed women's rights advocates found themselves greeted with alternate boredom and hostility by Brook Farm women who voted, held office, and performed equal duties beside men. Meanwhile, the Brook Farm school combined theoretical learning with laboratory and field work and cultivated the industrial arts. The school's approach to learning reflected the larger community, where it was hoped that abolition of a division of labor would lead each member to freedom.

Ultimately, the web of reform activities at Brook Farm led the community to become Fourierist. Ripley had been convinced by the socialist ideas of Charles Fourier through the teaching of Fourier's American disciple Albert Brisbane (1809-1890). By 1844 Brook Farm had become a phalanx, a self-sufficient Fourierist community in theory representing all the different possibilities of human personality and talent. But two years later a fire destroyed the nearly completed central "phalanstery," and in a matter of months the community ended.

Despite Ripley's efforts, Emerson had refused to become involved in the community, thinking that the demands of solitary self-culture were too compelling to admit of communal endeavor. "Shall I raise the siege of this hencoop & march baffled away to a pretended siege of Babylon?" Emerson had written to Ripley on the subject.[37] Thoreau, likewise, preferred the solitude of Walden Pond (1845-1847) to a community venture. But Parker was, as his biographer Henry Steele Commager declares, "practically a member," visiting several times a week and being visited by a group of Brook Farmers at his regular Sunday services.[38] So was Fuller, who liked to hold conversations there; and Al-

---

[35]Ibid., 160.

[36]Charles Crowe, *George Ripley: Transcendentalist and Utopian Socialist* (Athens: University of Georgia Press, 1967) 161. For a brief and useful discussion of Brook Farm, see Boller, *American Transcendentalism,* 122-28. The classic study is Lindsay Swift, *Brook Farm: Its Members, Scholars, and Visitors* (1900; rpt., Gloucester MA: Peter Smith, n.d.).

[37]Emerson, *Journals and Miscellaneous Notebooks,* 7 (17 October 1840): 408.

[38]Henry Steele Commager, *Theodore Parker,* 2d ed. (1960; rpt., Gloucester MA: Peter Smith, 1978) 51.

cott visited and spoke but, instead of staying, founded his own community at Fruitlands, near the town of Harvard, Massachusetts.

Like Brook Farm, Fruitlands grew first in imagination. During a trip to England in 1842, Alcott wrote to his wife, Abigail, about his desire to plant in New England "the new state of things."[39] In England, Alcott had met a fellow traveler in Charles Lane, who came to America, paid Alcott's outstanding debts, and purchased a ninety-acre farm where his and Alcott's Transcendental ideas of community might be tested. Lane and his young son joined the five members of the Alcott family and a few others for the experiment. As at Brook Farm, individualism was valued, but Alcott, in his zeal, enacted a series of prohibitions that in practice were totalitarian. The use of meat, alcohol, tea and coffee, and milk was forbidden, as was the use of potatoes, which did not grow toward the sun. So, too, was the wearing of cotton and woolen garments, both the products of slavery and exploitation—cotton the slavery of black people and wool the slavery of sheep. Cold-water bathing was the rule for the community, which arose and retired with the sun. Meanwhile, Lane tried to introduce celibacy (thus separating Bronson and Abigail Alcott), and this—combined with the poor farming record of the community—brought Fruitlands to a swift conclusion.

The experiment had lasted seven months. For that short time Fruitlands was a testimony to the absoluteness with which Transcendental ideals could be upheld as well as their sometime impracticality. Still, if Alcott and some of the other Transcendentalists were driven by an impossible dream of purity and paradise on earth, the spiritual intensity that motivated Fruitlands also issued in Transcendental efforts for social reform. Beyond the arrangements of individual life-style, a number of Transcendentalists ventured to improve not only their own "hencoop" but the "Babylon" of America as well.

Already, in their revolt against Unitarianism, the Transcendentalists were taking a stand regarding an established order that, for them, required correction. It is no surprise, therefore, that the need to reform the church yielded a series of experimental ministries at the margin of the Unitarian establishment and outside it. In 1836 Brownson had formed the experimental Society for Christian Union and Progress, abolishing pew ownership to further his ministry to the working class and preaching social reform and progress. Clarke founded the Church of the Disciples in 1841 with a broad doctrinal statement, flexible ritual arrangements, and, again, a system of free pews. Parker, surviving a formal "tea" that verged on a heresy trial and then ostracism by other Unitarians, became the leader of the Twenty-Eighth Congregational Society in 1845. Abolishing the proprietary pew system as well as the regular collection, he eventually presided over the largest congregation in Boston.

William Henry Channing, after a youthful experiment in 1837 as minister of New York City's poor, returned to Brooklyn in 1842 and then, in 1843, to the Christian Union he established in New York City on principles of "Humanity, Wisdom, and Holiness." Later in Boston in 1846, Channing again worked to apply his principles in the Religious Union

---

[39] Amos Bronson Alcott to Mrs. A. B. Alcott, 16 July 1842, in Amos Bronson Alcott, *The Letters of A. Bronson Alcott,* ed. Richard L. Herrnstadt (Ames: Iowa State University Press, 1969) 85. For a short discussion, see Boller, *American Transcendentalism,* 120-22. The classic study is Clara Endicott Sears, *Bronson Alcott's Fruitlands* (1915; rpt., Philadelphia: Porcupine Press, 1975).

of Associationists, a Fourierist "church" including members from various denominations who all subscribed to the associationist gospel of Universal Unity.

Channing's linkage of Christianity with Fourierist social reform, as at Brook Farm, pointed toward the larger focus of Transcendental moral effort. Government, economy, education, and the dynamics of the social process all were objects of concern, as different events brought various problems to the attention of the Transcendentalists. Their overriding concerns were for equality and justice for all, and even the less socially involved among them, like Emerson, were quick to notice when justice had been violated and equality ignored. Emerson, it was true, provided the rationale for the more hesitant who did not plunge headlong into reform activity, arguing that each person must accomplish self-reform before the general conditions of life in society could be changed. "I wish to break all prisons. I have not yet conquered my own home."[40] Yet Emerson thought, too, that he and others must earn their bread "by the hearty contribution of our energies to the common benefit," that they "must not cease to *tend* to the correction of flagrant wrongs, by laying one stone aright every day." "What is a man born for but to be a Reformer, a Remaker of what man has made?" he asked rhetorically, moving beyond daily life to the wider realm of social structures.[41]

The concerns of his age forced Emerson, however reluctantly, into the public arena. Indeed, Moncure Conway, an early biographer, called Emerson "the first American scholar to cast a dart at slavery," noting that in 1831 Emerson "admitted an abolitionist to lecture on the subject in his church, and in the following year another was invited to his pulpit." This, noted Conway, was at a time when William Lloyd Garrison was "regarded as a vulgar street-preacher of notions too wild to excite more than a smile."[42] Still more, Emerson opened his church to the Society for the Abolition of Slavery, which held annual meetings there. He befriended abolitionists and hosted them at his home. He publicly protested the assassination of Elijah P. Lovejoy, an outspoken abolitionist who died at Alton, Illinois, in 1837, defending his press. And the same year Emerson delivered an address at the Second Church in Boston on the subject of slavery. "I regret to hear that all the churches but one, and almost all the public halls in Boston, are closed against the discussion of the question," James Cabot reported him saying.[43]

Indian Removal also brought Emerson's protest, when the Cherokees were forced from Georgia and surrounding states in accordance with a treaty to which they had not assented. Emerson's private journal revealed how much the problem disturbed him; and although he felt helpless and ineffectual, he addressed a citizens' meeting in Concord and the next day sent an open letter to President Martin Van Buren. Temperance and the cause of peace enlisted Emerson's support and so, theoretically, did the issue of women's rights. If by temperament and inclination Emerson turned inward, self-culture had not led him

---

[40] Emerson, *Journals and Miscellaneous Notebooks*, 7 (17 October 1840): 408.

[41] Ralph Waldo Emerson, *Man the Reformer*, in Emerson, *Complete Works*, 1:247-48.

[42] Moncure Daniel Conway, *Emerson at Home and Abroad* (Boston: James R. Osgood, 1882) 299.

[43] James E. Cabot, *A Memoir of Ralph Waldo Emerson* (Boston: Houghton, Mifflin, 1887) 2:425. The lecture, "Slavery" (1837), is missing. For further discussion of Emerson and reform, see Albanese, *Corresponding Motion*, 145-48, and Boller, *American Transcendentalism*, 101-107.

to ignore the world. Along with Thoreau, he was perhaps the most reluctant Transcendentalist of the four in this volume when it came to real involvement in reform efforts, but still he did not spurn the problems of his time as he pursued his more personal goals.

Thoreau, as we shall see, militantly defended the individual against the encroachments of society. His exposition (1848 and 1849) of what came to be called civil disobedience was preceded by his abstention, for a number of years, from paying his poll tax to the state of Massachusetts. Its government, Thoreau thought, implicitly supported slavery. When, in 1846, the Mexican War augured more territory for slaveholders and, at the same time, Massachusetts grew less lenient in its tax-collecting policies, Thoreau spent one memorable night in jail. Perhaps less known, he also worked to help slaves escape to freedom in Canada. And in his "Plea for Captain John Brown," Thoreau early and publicly defended the abolitionist who had raided Harpers Ferry.[44]

Even more active than Thoreau in the antislavery effort was Parker, who burned himself out in this and other causes to die in his fiftieth year. Henry Steele Commager has called him the "universal reformer,"[45] and it seemed that wherever injustice existed Parker was sure to notice—and act. The Peace Society of Massachusetts, the work of Dorothea Dix for the insane, penal reform, the abolition of capital punishment, the common-school movement of Horace Mann, all received Parker's active endorsement. But his greatest cause was antislavery, and after the passage of the Fugitive Slave Act in 1850 he was an ardent abolitionist, joining William Lloyd Garrison and Wendell Phillips in their work. Because one sermon against slavery was so impassioned, he was addressed by Samuel Gridley Howe as "The Reverend Thunder and Lightning." Like Thoreau, Parker worked with fugitive slaves, concealing them and helping them to reach freedom in Canada. A member of the Vigilance Committee to safeguard the fugitives from arrest and return to the South, he participated in an abortive effort in 1854 to free Anthony Burns, a Virginia slave, from the courthouse where he was being held.[46]

Among the group who mobbed the courthouse with Parker was Alcott. His wife, the former Abigail May, was the sister of the noted abolitionist minister Samuel J. May, and Alcott himself became a dedicated antislavery crusader. He heard Garrison speak in 1830, thought his lecture "full of truth and power," and dispatched a communication on Garrison's behalf to *The Boston Daily Advertiser*.[47] A few weeks later he was among the group who formed the Preliminary Anti-Slavery Society from which came, two years afterward, the New England Anti-Slavery Society. And supplying an example for Thoreau, Alcott was arrested (although never jailed) for refusing to pay his town tax to a slave-sanctioning government.[48]

---

[44]For a good, brief discussion of Thoreau and civil disobedience, see Boller, *American Transcendentalism*, 107-12.

[45]Commager, *Theodore Parker*, 151-67. "The Universal Reformer" is the title of the chapter.

[46]See Boller, *American Transcendentalism*, 132-33, and Commager, *Theodore Parker*, 151-247.

[47]Amos Bronson Alcott, *The Journals of Bronson Alcott*, sel. and ed. Odell Shepard (Boston: Little, Brown, 1938) (15 October 1830) 25.

[48]Ibid., "Mrs. Alcott's Journal" (17 January 1843) 150-51. The tax was paid, almost surely, by Ebenezer Rockwood Hoar, a leading Concord citizen. Thoreau's tax was paid by (most probably) an aunt, after he had spent the night in jail.

Like Parker, who was for universal reform, Alcott attended meetings of the Convention of Non-resistants, the Convention of the Friends of Universal Reform, the Come-outer Convention, the Groton Convention, and the Chardon Street Convention. In Europe, he was present at anti-Corn-Law conferences, met with Chartists and persons committed to Promoting Health and Chastity, and at Alcott House, an experimental school and community named in his honor, mingled with the zealots of reform.[49]

As this last suggests, most significant of all Alcott's reform efforts were those in education. Early associated with experimental schools based on new theories of education, in Boston Alcott challenged the educational establishment with his program. He opposed the time-honored practice of recitation by students, introduced the inductive method, and taught that a school ought to be enjoyed. Influenced by the theories of the Swiss educator Johann Heinrich Pestalozzi (1746-1827), Alcott thought of education as a religious and moral enterprise that should draw from the child the knowledge he or she already possessed. In his most celebrated educational venture, the Temple School in Boston, he endeavored to put these ideas into practice until the publication, in 1836, of his *Record of Conversations on the Gospels* (to be discussed later) ruined both the school and Alcott's career.

We have already seen Ripley's concern for the poorer class in Boston and his socialism in both its pre-Fourierist and Fourierist phases. Even after the failure of Brook Farm, Ripley—who assumed responsibilities with Horace Greeley's *New-York Tribune*—continued to affirm the values of association on Fourierist principles. Likewise William Henry Channing, who worked to reform the church, embedded his efforts in his larger concern for the Fourierist reform of society.

Meanwhile Brownson linked himself with Jacksonian democracy, embracing the Democratic party and its fight for equality. He read the work of Fourier and other European advocates of socialism and saw the main theme of history as class struggle. In a two-part article published in *The Boston Quarterly Review* in 1840, Brownson outlined his radical social theory in a form that gained him notoriety, if not fame. "The Laboring Classes" proved a thoroughgoing critique of the social system based on wages and a call for economic and social equality. Fuller, too, made lasting contributions to reform, mostly in the field of women's rights. Her already-noted *Woman in the Nineteenth Century* taught that freedom for women would enable the divine energy to fill nature as never before. Later, Fuller traveled to Italy, apparently married the Marchése Angelo Ossoli, and participated with him in the Italian revolution of 1848-1849 as a follower of Giuseppe Mazzini.[50]

Hence, these Transcendentalists and others who counted themselves among them moved with the reformers of their times. If human beings possessed divinity within themselves, the Transcendentalists thought that divinity ought to grow unimpeded by external forces. Both the more mystical, like Alcott, and the less mystical, like Parker, could find a connection between Transcendental ideals and earnest social action. With their sense of

---

[49] Odell Shepard calls Alcott House a "lay monastery" in Shepard, *Pedlar's Progress*, 320. Regarding Alcott and his various reform activities, see Albanese, *Corresponding Motion*, 41-43.

[50] For a further discussion of Fuller and Brownson and social reform, see Boller, *American Transcendentalism*, 112-16, 128-32.

the worth of each human being, the Transcendentalists preached a liberation in which, as Frothingham wrote, "the method of reform followed from the principle." "It was the method of individual awakening and regeneration," he continued, and the Transcendentalist was "less a reformer of human circumstance than a regenerator of the human spirit, and . . . never a destroyer except as destruction accompanied the process of regeneration."[51] In the Transcendental scheme of things, social reform emerged from spiritual issues and concerns and led inevitably back to them.

The Transcendental revolution, in other words, meant the introduction of a new spirituality. There was an experiential religious impulse at the heart of Transcendental thinking, writing, and acting. Translated into a moral passion for rebirth, renewal, and reform of self and world, this religious impulse ran deep and was the ultimate explanation for the vitality of the movement. It is necessary, therefore, to examine Transcendental spirituality in greater detail.

TRANSCENDENTAL SPIRITUALITY

Use of the term *spirituality* has become widespread only in recent times, and most contemporary writers tend to employ the word in an experiential way. Moreover, understandings of spirituality have moved away from concrete to more abstract formulations—not so much to how people live their religious tradition but more to how they link their lives to ultimate meanings and values. In so doing, understandings of spirituality have become less particularized and more general.[52] Jon Alexander has cited, as an example of these tendencies, the representative definition of spirituality by a well-known Roman Catholic theologian. For Hans Urs von Balthazar, spirituality means "that basic practical or existential attitude of man which is the consequence and expression of the way in which he understands his religious—or more generally, his ethically committed—existence." It is "the way in which he acts and reacts habitually throughout his life according to his objective and ultimate insights and decisions."[53]

Something of this perspective on spirituality is necessary in order to fathom the Transcendentalists. If we are to glimpse the fundamental sources of their enthusiasm and action, we must locate them with reference to a broad understanding. We must see their spirituality as a system for making sense of the world and meeting its power, a system built on a worldview and its expression in experience and action. In other words, we must see that Transcendental spirituality told members of the movement how, in the most basic sense, the world was constructed and, as important, provided ritual means—in a sacred setting—and moral means—in the setting of everyday life—for the expression of these insights. In so doing, Transcendental spirituality mediated to members of the movement a qualitative, experiential dimension to living.

---

[51]Frothingham, *Transcendentalism in New England*, 155.

[52]See the discussion in Jon Alexander, "What Do Recent Writers Mean by Spirituality?" *Spirituality Today* 32:2 (September 1980): 247, 250, 253-54.

[53]Hans Urs von Balthazar, "The Gospel as Norm and Test of All Spirituality in the Church," quoted ibid., 251.

The worldview on which Transcendental spirituality was based was the ancient idea of correspondence.[54] In numerous cultures throughout the world, explanatory theories arose concerning the relationship of the human community to the cosmos. For many, that relationship was best expressed by describing the human community as a microcosm—literally, a "small world"—that reflected the macrocosm, the "great world" that was its source. The macrocosm could be understood as the realm of the divine and the spirit or the domain of nature, both views conveying the sense of transcendence and ultimacy contained in notions of the great cosmos. Arising from these formulations, too, was the sense of a law implicit in the scheme of things, a controlling providence, a natural or moral law that unfolded in the very order that the cosmos represented.

While the results of this kind of thinking are too extensive to be analyzed adequately here, we can point to four practical consequences that impinge on spirituality. First, the worldview of correspondence between microcosm and macrocosm led people to think of the nature of the universe and the spiritual realm as prior and thus fostered a reverence for the natural or divine order. Second, correspondence implied that the way to learn the truth about human life was to look at the cosmos, taking note of what it was and said and what time or rhythm it kept. Third, if human life was illuminated by viewing it from a cosmic perspective, then, in the correspondential scheme of things, it also acquired greater "reality" because it was grounded on the prior and greater pattern of the cosmos. And fourth, since correspondence taught that the microcosm was simply a small-scale replica of the macrocosm, it followed that there was no radical break between the sacred and the profane and that, therefore, all of human life was religious.

These insights took shape both as directives for the particular community and for the distinct individual. For both community and individual, they issued in the requirement of harmony with cosmic law; for the individual, they meant mysticism. Since the universe was prior and, with its larger dimensions, offered an object lesson in how the law should unfold in ordered and rhythmic sequence, the central task for the community became attuning itself to the cosmic or the divine and spiritual, living in harmony with natural law. A community that did so realized intrinsically its own value, and it understood that all things were holy so long as its openness to the cosmic wholeness prevailed. Measured against this pattern, the Transcendentalists were seekers after communal harmony. Their writings in this volume and elsewhere offer ample testimony to their regard for nature and, beyond it, the divine and spiritual source of life. The Transcendentalists' scrutiny of nature and reflection on the moral law witness to their status as pupils of the macrocosm; their attempts to emulate it by bringing the American community into harmony are also everywhere apparent. Finally, with their rebellion against their contemporary Christianity, their vision reflected a landscape in which the sacred could not be cordoned off. Harmony with the cosmos led ultimately, for them, to the "secular" world in which commodity and profit held sway. There was a cosmic pattern for the proper existence even of all this.

---

[54]For a fuller discussion of the worldview of correspondence, see Albanese, *Corresponding Motion*, 3-21. Frederick Streng's concepts of harmony with cosmic law and mystical insight through spiritual discipline have assisted me in this formulation. See Frederick J. Streng, *Understanding Religious Life*, 2d ed. (Belmont CA: Dickenson Publishing, 1976) 99-125.

Seen in more individualistic terms, from the Transcendental perspective one did not need to attend a church in order to be religious. Indeed, it seemed more correct to wander in nature and catch there a glimpse of spirit. It also seemed pointless to struggle to rid oneself of faults and to work at "charitable" relationships according to memorable Puritan canons. Rather, one should seek the moral expression that arose from a rightly ordered life, without artificial thought or effort. Disorder would always be evident in the lack of mental peace, in the failure of health, in the frenetic quest after fortune, in stepping out of "place." On the other hand, real religion meant life that quietly affirmed spiritual truth through one's duty in the midst of the ordinary. It meant living in tune with the divinity within oneself, listening intently for the answering divinity in nature and spirit. In short, living in harmony with cosmic law meant cultivating the ground for mysticism.

The possibility for mystical experience was contained in the idea of correspondence, since correspondence made it possible to collapse the dimensions of space and time. If the correspondential worldview taught that the universe *answered* and that nothing was isolated from the process, then it followed that inner equaled outer, that space was coterminous with time, and that both could be made to disappear or, alternately, be used to full advantage. On the purely pragmatic and material level, this was a rationale for magic and the office of the magician, since a magician was simply an adept who had learned to take advantage of the basic unity of the world. On the spiritual level, however, correspondence supplied the rationale for a direct apprehension of divine reality in which space, time, the self, and the world fell away. At least theoretically, it suggested the unitive consciousness that has accompanied so much of mysticism, even in the West. Since a harmony existed between microcosm and macrocosm, there could be optimism about the basic possibilities of human beings. Each piece of the world—each human being—was in essence like the power behind the whole, and so it was possible for each human being to realize that identity and celebrate it. In terms closer to Transcendental language, human beings were divine; and, empowered by their divinity, they should live expansively, learning to control and order the world.

However, if the worldview at the basis of Transcendental harmony and mysticism was correspondence, the kind of correspondence admits of an important qualification. Unlike a more traditional cosmos, the universe to which the Transcendentalists sought attunement was a world set in motion to a degree and with an intensity that offered a marked contrast to quiet and contemplative rhythms. On a theoretical level, the Transcendentalists pondered the meaning of correspondence by using the language of process, life, force, energy, and emanation. On a poetic, or more intuitive, level, they found spiritual meaning in natural, or sometimes Christian, realities caught on the wing. We have already noticed this quality in the vision of the Transcendentalists and have linked it to their experience with an America in a state of flux and ferment. Here it is important to extend the discussion by pointing to its relationship to spirituality.

"When man rests he stinks," Emerson had once observed.[55] Indeed, the spirituality of kinetic correspondence pervaded his public and private writings. Thus, contemplating the river of his thoughts he could say:

---

[55]Emerson, *Journals and Miscellaneous Notebooks,* 7 (14 April 1839): 190. Emerson subsequently deleted this entry from his journal.

> When I watch that flowing river, which, out of regions I see not, pours for a season its streams into me, I see that I am a pensioner; not a cause but a surprised spectator of this ethereal water; that I desire and look up and put myself in the attitude of reception, but from some alien energy the visions come.[56]

As he and others received the energy, their mandate was to flow with the stream:

> Nature ever flows, stands never still. Motion or change is her mode of existence. The poetic eye sees in Man the Brother of the River, & in Woman the sister of the River. Their life is always transition. Hard blockheads only drive nails all the time; forever remember; which is fixing. Heroes do not fix but flow, bend forward ever & invent a resource for every moment.[57]

Finally, ego was fused with the suprapersonal, as Emerson confessed:

> Above his life, above all creatures I flow down forever a sea of benefit into races of individuals. Nor can the stream ever roll backward or the sin or death of a man taint the immutable energy which distributes itself into men as the sun into rays or the sea into drops.[58]

The kinetic vision of correspondence was articulated individually by the other Transcendentalists who shared Emerson's worldview. Alcott, for example, sometimes defined his kinetic spirituality by reflecting on sexual themes. "Fluids form solids," he told his journal. "Mettle [sperm] is the Godhead proceeding into the matrix of nature to organize Man. Behold the creative jet! And hear the morning stars sing for joy at the sacred generation of the Gods!"[59] By contrast, in the more ascetic (and perhaps more static) spirituality of Thoreau, movement still came, here through the metaphor of travel. John Aldrich Christie has studied Thoreau as "world traveler"[60]; and as Christie has shown, although most of Thoreau's travels were adventures of the mind, many of his most compelling spiritual utterances were born of physical travel. One thinks of his meditations in *A Week on the Concord and Merrimack Rivers* and of his stark encounter with sacred power climbing the mountain of Ktaadn in *The Maine Woods*.[61]

For both Alcott and Thoreau, as for Emerson, there was an overriding resemblance between different spheres, between different levels of the world. What happened in nature provided a moral lesson for human life; and if nature was kinetic, the parallel with human life, as these Transcendentalists experienced it in nineteenth-century America, was suggestive. The parallel hinted that, in keeping with the worldview of correspondence, which collapsed sacred and profane reality into unity, the contemporary world of America provided its own macrocosm. It acted as a source from which the Transcendentalists were drawing moral lessons and projecting the quality of motion onto nature. Because Tran-

---

[56] Ralph Waldo Emerson, "The Over-Soul," 92 in this volume.

[57] Emerson, *Journals and Miscellaneous Notebooks,* 7 (6 December 1840): 539-40.

[58] Ibid. (23 April 1841): 435.

[59] Alcott, *Journals* (31 March 1839):121.

[60] John Aldrich Christie, *Thoreau as World Traveler* (New York: Columbia University Press, 1965).

[61] See Henry David Thoreau, *A Week on the Concord and Merrimack Rivers* and *The Maine Woods,* in this volume.

scendental spirituality was kinetic, it was related to the everyday world in which the Transcendentalists lived.

Of course, when we take up the cases of Transcendentalists like Parker and Brownson, kinetic correspondence leaves the world of reflection to be embodied in vigorous activity. But the intensity of their style should not obscure the fact that, for *all* the Transcendentalists, a worldview unfolded in experience, action, and way of life.

There were, first, moments of heightened spiritual awareness and experience. Fuller spoke of a unitive experience in which she was absorbed into God.[62] Parker possessed, as Goddard said, a "highly emotional nature, and confidence in the validity of spiritual intuitions; and his belief in the possibility of the soul's immediate communion with God yields to that of few mystics in sincerity and fervor."[63] Thoreau had had his Ktaadn and his morning ablutions at Walden Pond. Emerson had spoken of becoming a "transparent eyeball" and being "part or parcel of God."[64] Alcott and Very had acquired reputations among their contemporaries for their mysticism. For all of them, a keen awareness of the present, of moral meaning, of the relationship of nature's life and law to the human condition, and of their capacity for deep reflection had witnessed to the power of immediate experience in their lives.

But the Transcendentalists could not always count on the unprompted revelation of the sacred. Like other human beings, they, too, came down from the mountain. Like other human beings, they needed to recapture their sense of the sacred through formal acts of ritual and to live out that sense in an ethic that encompassed their everyday behavior.

Ritual among the Transcendentalists took a variety of forms: the keeping of private journals (often to be shared), stylized modes of communing with nature, equally stylized "conversations." As inheritors of the Puritan tradition of spiritual autobiography and self-examination, the Transcendentalists frequently kept journals or commonplace books. Emerson, Alcott, Parker, Thoreau, and Fuller all followed the custom; and Lawrence Buell has shown how, like their ancestors, they considered the keeping of a journal to be a "solemn task." However, unlike their Puritan forebears, they distrusted the "very idea of a structured spiritual development" and instead kept their diaries to facilitate the spiritual process that was self-culture.[65] Meanwhile, communing with nature came through the morning walks in which Emerson, Alcott, and other Transcendentalists delighted. It came through bathing in Walden Pond, as Thoreau did, with studied spiritual discipline. Or it came, in the case of Parker, through the bouquet of flowers placed in his pulpit by friends when he preached.[66]

---

[62]The incident is cited by Paul Boller in *American Transcendentalism*, 82.

[63]Goddard, *Studies in New England Transcendentalism*, 125-26.

[64]Ralph Waldo Emerson, *Nature*, ch. 1, in this volume.

[65]Lawrence Buell, *Literary Transcendentalism: Style and Vision in the American Renaissance* (Ithaca NY: Cornell University Press, 1973) 275, 277.

[66]For Thoreau, see, in this volume, Henry David Thoreau, *Walden*, ch. 2, "Where I Lived, and What I Lived For." Octavius B. Frothingham, in his biography of Parker, cited the flowers that were placed in Parker's pulpit, adding that "his love for wild flowers was almost a passion: he watched for their annual return, and knew where, for miles around, he should find their first blooming." See Octavius B. Frothingham, *Theodore Parker: A Biography* (Boston: J. R. Osgood,

Conversation, however, provided the communal act that, with its public and collective character, most clearly fulfilled the conditions for ritual. And for the Transcendentalists, such conversation meant ritual as vehicle for strong experience. Thus, in his journal Emerson confided an ideal of conversation that seemed almost an account of Quakers at meeting, of people being filled with the spirit:

> In conversation, we pluck up the eternal Termini which bound the common of Silence on every side. The parties are not to be judged by the spirit they partake & even express under this pentecost. Tomorrow they will have receded from this highwater mark. Tomorrow you shall find them stooping under the old packsaddles. Yet let us enjoy the cloven flame whilst it glows on our walls. When each new speaker strikes a new light, emancipates us from the oppression of the last speaker to oppress us with the greatness & exclusiveness of his own thought, then yields us to another redeemer, then we seem to recover our rights, to become men.[67]

Emerson continued to describe the process:

> In common hours society sits cold & statuesque. We all stand waiting, empty, knowing possibly that we can be full. . . . Then cometh the god & converts the statues into fiery men, & by a flash of his eye burns up the veil which shrouded all things & the meaning of the very furniture, of cup & saucer, of chair & clock & tester is manifest. The facts which loomed so large in the fogs of yesterday . . . have strangely changed their proportions all that we reckoned settled shakes now & rattles and literatures, cities, climates, religions leave their foundations & dance before our eyes.[68]

Conversation flourished among the Transcendentalists especially in the meetings of the Transcendental Club from 1836 to 1840. "As an organized movement," Lawrence Buell tells us, "Transcendentalism can almost be said to have begun and ended as a discussion group."[69] Hence, Emerson, in exalting conversation, was indirectly pointing to the spiritual significance of the club. Besides the club, however, there were also formal conversations conducted by individual Transcendentalists. In 1833 Elizabeth Palmer Peabody offered a series for the public, repeating the gesture several times in later years, while Fuller, too, initiated conversations in Boston from 1839 to 1844. Alcott made conversation the basis of his career as an educator and, as he grew older, led discourses in New England and throughout the Midwest. And although what the Transcendentalists liked most about their conversations was their openness to spontaneity (as Emerson's meditations showed), in truth, the *act* of coming together to await the spirit was a studied ritual performance. By means of the rite, Transcendentalists could attune themselves to one another and to what lay beyond. They could find their own corresponding motion and through that motion return empowered to the ordinary world.

1874) 242-43. John White Chadwick also remembered that "my earliest recollection of his name is in connection with the flowers upon his pulpit, instanced as one proof of his awful wickedness; flat paganism, and no less." See John White Chadwick, *Theodore Parker: Preacher and Reformer* (1900; rpt., St. Clair Shores MI: Scholarly Press, 1971) 213.

[67]Emerson, *Journals and Miscellaneous Notebooks*, 7 (28 May 1840): 360.
[68]Ibid.
[69]Buell, *Literary Transcendentalism*, 77.

Hence, accomplished ritual led out of the sacred setting and into the everyday. Here Transcendental morality was an authentic expression of the system of Transcendental spirituality. We have already seen this morality at work in the reform activity of many in the group. And the experiments with self-culture and with communalism were programmatic schemes based on a Transcendental spirituality of correspondence. Above all ways of living was the great commandment of harmony—with self and with others through a free disclosure of the self. So self-culture and communalism became moral paths, and reform the overplus of people who sought to liberate others. Coupled with the Transcendental sense of the divinity immanent in every person was a powerful ethic of spiritual democracy. It made a difference in the thinking of members of the group, but the protected, middle-class background of many prevented democracy of thought from becoming the radical democracy of practice. To a considerable extent, the Transcendentalists lived their lives as spiritual elitists.

Theoretical democrats but practical elitists, still, they had very much to say to America about how to live, and they did try to embody these prescriptions in their behavior. They felt the excitement of the new America of the nineteenth century, and they shaped their correspondence to correspond with it. Yet they wanted to temper the frenetic activity around them with a sense of inwardness and the authoritative voice of the self. And they wanted to introduce others to the givenness of a nature with its highest use not, as Emerson said, for commodity, but for discipline and morality.[70] Their ethic, begun in regard for nature and the divine, in the end returned to the need for reverence. Respect the divinity of your self, the Transcendentalists said; respect the divinity in nature. Their legacy, their spiritual revolution, has sought the roots of our being both in self and in nature.

DIRECTIONS IN TRANSCENDENTAL SPIRITUALITY

This volume contains some of the writings of four leading Transcendentalists, gathered because they are key expressions of their spirituality. It is worth noting the different directions taken by these authors and worth pursuing the question of how and in what sense these works are particularly significant as expressions of Transcendental spirituality.

Ralph Waldo Emerson's inclusion needs little, if any, explanation. He was clearly the leader of the movement and its most gifted writer. The presence of some of his major statements in a work devoted to spirituality should highlight their importance as religious documents, since all too often they have been seen mostly as literary or philosophical writings. Amos Bronson Alcott, Emerson's closest friend, was the person who most continuously gave voice to the mystical tendencies in Transcendentalism. He also clearly exemplified its departures from traditional Christianity and its appropriation of a revived Neoplatonism in the metaphysical tradition of the West. And he demonstrated more thoroughly than the others the implications of self-culture for education.

The third writer in the volume, Theodore Parker, struggled throughout his career as a Unitarian minister to reconcile his Transcendentalism with organized Christianity and to use his Transcendentalism as the spur for public efforts at moral and social reform. He is a compelling representative of the Christian side of Transcendentalism and an equally compelling representative of Transcendental activism.

---

[70]See Emerson, *Nature,* ch. 5.

Finally, Henry David Thoreau, a "second-generation" Transcendentalist, was a younger man than Emerson and many of the others, and he pursued Emerson's strictures regarding the religious experience of nature with a new attention to the precise details of the natural world. More than even Emerson himself, he lived by the creed of self-reliance, a witness to the inner resources of the solitary self in its spiritual growth. He especially demonstrated the fascination of members of the movement with Eastern, and notably Hindu, religious thought.

While it is tempting to argue for the incorporation of other materials and other figures, various considerations have led to this selection. The works here chosen represent major directions in Transcendental spirituality from major figures in the movement. Yet, as we have seen, spirituality for the Transcendentalists permeated all of life. Hence, the Transcendentalists expressed their spirituality often not in condensed writings on traditional religious topics but, rather, much more diffusively, in ways intertwined with general observations about their life and times. The diffusive nature of their statements represents something of an editorial challenge, and problems have been resolved in three ways.

First, the selections are substantive and extensive, thus preserving as much as possible the integrity of original documents. Second, the work of fewer rather than more Transcendentalists has been included. Space—at least in a book—is not endless, and there cannot be an indefinite number of selections. (Indeed, the four who are included are represented by only a fraction of their published work: there is an embarrassment of Transcendental riches and the need—often exercised arbitrarily—to deny space to some materials.) Third, frequently an anthologized approach has been employed, sometimes interpolating short explanations to fill in narrative gaps.

Although some of the works selected for this volume rank high in the canons of American literature (notably those of Emerson and Thoreau), these documents are not uniformly great literature. Some of them have never appeared in anthologies devoted to Transcendentalism, and at least one of them, Alcott's "Orphic Sayings," has been the butt of ridicule from his day to our own. Hence, these works are here not because they necessarily contain the best writing in the movement (although some of them do) but, instead, because they are clear and definitive expressions of different directions in Transcendental spirituality. In short, these writings are representative: they are well-articulated statements even when, as in Alcott's case, they are deficient in some other respects.

These works are here, too, because they are authoritative. They are the written wisdom of persons who might be said to "know" because they have experienced—who, in their different ways, have put their lives on the line as embodiments of spiritual concerns. The authors of these writings are persons for whom spirituality is, in the words of Paul Tillich about religion, the "ultimate concern."[71] Moreover, these works are here because they speak to their particular situations with a language that contains a universal quality. This is not to say that they record experience that corroborates with that of all people for all time. In fact, the Transcendentalists saw themselves embroiled in a struggle against quite specific problems in their contemporary Christianity and in American social, political, and economic life. Rather, in the Transcendentalists' efforts to articulate the issues,

---

[71]See Paul Tillich, *Systematic Theology* (Chicago: University of Chicago Press, 1967) 1:12-14, 110-11, 214-16.

in their appropriation of so many spiritual and intellectual traditions to do so, and in their posing and resolving—to an extent—certain key spiritual questions, they were speaking to the human condition, at least as the Western tradition had come to recognize it. Fascinated by problems of the transient and the permanent, they intently followed their own transitive era, and in so doing they were able to enunciate a spirituality that touches on the abiding concerns of the West.

Finally, these Transcendental works are here because they speak with inspiration. The word *inspiration* is much maligned in our usage, accompanied, as it is, by superficial and sentimental overtones. Yet in its etymological meaning it speaks to the staying quality, the endurance, of these writings: because they are inspired, a life has been breathed into them that is breathed out again onto succeeding generations of readers. The Transcendentalists tapped more than their rational selves in composing these works. They touched their creative depths in which, in their language, the part of human beings that is divine lives and grows. The words of the Transcendentalists, although often dressed in the ponderous prose of the Victorian era, still possess flesh and fire. Their words still offer entry into a place of inner contemplation, an invitation to harmony. Perhaps the observation of Paul Boller, though offered in another context, best summarizes why these writings have been chosen:

> The perennial appeal of the Transcendentalists has rested largely on their impassioned quest for noble ways of using the great gifts of life. The Transcendental revolt began in religion, and though it soon moved into other realms of life it remained essentially religious in its quest for meaning and purpose. It was at heart an effort to eliminate the false, artificial, meretricious, and stylized and to clear the way for an honest, direct, natural, and deeply felt response to the miracle of creation.[72]

---

[72]Boller, *American Transcendentalism*, 205.

Part I

RALPH WALDO EMERSON

INTRODUCTION

In 1847 Ralph Waldo Emerson penned a letter to an Englishwoman who wanted to write a short memoir of him, thanking her but declining to send materials. "I am concerned to say I have no history no anecdotes no connexions no fortunes that would make the smallest figure in a narrative," he told her. "My course of life has been so routinary, that the keenest eye for point or picture would be at fault before such remediless commonplace."[1] Although Emerson was protesting too much (no doubt trying to maintain distance and protect his privacy), there was some truth in what he had said. A national seer and saint in his own lifetime, there was still and always an unmistakable bourgeois quality about him, an air of middle-class respectability and routine that coexisted with the mystical doctrine he preached.

If Emerson combined a mystical spirituality with distinct bourgeois instincts, he stood in the Puritan tradition of his New England ancestors who, paradoxically, blended these qualities in their everyday lives. Counting both sides of his family, he had come from eight generations of clergy, with his father, William, a liberal Boston minister and his grandfather, also William, an army chaplain who died during the Revolutionary War. Meanwhile, Emerson's mother, Ruth Haskins, was the daughter of a prosperous distiller, and with this parental background Emerson was born into Boston's stolid and respectable inner circle. In due course he attended the eminent Boston Latin School and then matriculated at Harvard, where seven Emersons in five generations had preceded him. Like his peers and colleagues, politically he became a Federalist (later a Whig), and religiously as a young man he was a Unitarian.

The details of his biography—"commonplace," as he called them—may be quickly summarized. While at Harvard he began teaching during the summers and continued to do so to support himself, although he disliked the job. Then, after studying divinity, he was ordained to preach in 1826 and later became junior pastor of the Second (Hanover Street) Church in Boston. In 1829 he married the fragile, still-teenage Ellen Tucker, but two years later she died from tuberculosis. It was not the first time that Emerson would experience so nearly this scourge of the nineteenth century, for in 1834 it killed his brother Edward and in 1836 took his (youngest) brother Charles Chauncy. Meanwhile, in 1832 Emerson struggled with a general discomfort in his ministry and, particularly, with religious scruples concerning his administration of the Lord's Supper to his congregation. Coming to a decision, he regretfully resigned his pastorate and by the end of the year was sailing for Europe. There, after landing in Malta, he traveled in Italy, Switzerland, France, England, and Scotland, meeting various persons of distinction and, especially, literary

---

[1]Ralph Waldo Emerson to Mary Botham Howitt, 30 September 1847, in Ralph Waldo Emerson, *The Letters of Ralph Waldo Emerson,* ed. Ralph L. Rusk (New York: Columbia University Press, 1939) 3:418.

figures such as William Wordsworth, Samuel Taylor Coleridge, and—what was the beginning of a lifetime friendship and correspondence—Thomas Carlyle.

The trip to Europe proved a season of excitement and sifting for the troubled New Englander. There would be two later trips abroad, one in 1847–1848 and another, in his old age, in 1872–1873, but neither of the later trips would make so deep an impression as this one did. After Emerson returned home in the fall of 1833, he eventually (1834) took up residence in Concord and began an independent career of writing and public lecturing, at first in New England but gradually extending the range of his travels until he was lecturing in the Mid-Atlantic states, the Middle West, and—by his later years—even as far away as San Francisco. Nineteenth-century towns before the Civil War frequently possessed a lyceum in which public lectures or courses of lectures were held—a middle-class attraction that perhaps occupied the place that the cinema would in the twentieth century. It was in these lyceums that Emerson as traveling lecturer addressed his audiences. He was, from all reports, immensely popular and extremely good at it; and, supplemented by other sources of income, the lecturing made him a prosperous man.

If Emerson's public life assumed a routinized character as he became a traveling salesman of the spirit, so did his private existence. In 1835 he married Lydia Jackson, whom he delighted in calling Lidian, and she became a companion throughout his life (despite later difficulties and doubts about his Transcendentalism), surviving him when he died in 1882. The couple rejoiced in the birth of their firstborn son, Waldo, in 1836—just after the formation of the Transcendental Club and the publication of *Nature*—and in subsequent years two daughters, Ellen (1839) and Edith (1841), were born to them. Emerson was successful and the little family comfortable until misfortune struck in early 1842 when the young Waldo died very suddenly from scarlet fever. Emerson's sorrow and pain ran deep, and reportedly, years later when he himself was dying, he remembered and spoke of Waldo: "Oh that beautiful boy."[2] Still, the birth of a second son, Edward Waldo, in 1844 must have helped ease the sense of loss. Moreover, Edward Waldo would later prove of great assistance to his father's literary estate, collecting much of the senior Emerson's work and editing it in a uniform edition, the well-known centenary edition of 1903–1904.[3]

The Emerson home in Concord saw frequent visitors, among them various social reformers to whom Emerson played the cordial host; and, as noted in the introduction, he early supported such movements as antislavery and the peace cause. His closest friends, though, were those who shared his Transcendental convictions—Bronson Alcott, Henry David Thoreau, Margaret Fuller, (William) Ellery Channing, and others in the Transcendental Club. By 1840 he was joining with club members to produce *The Dial*, and two years later he became its editor until its demise in 1844. Beyond that, collections of his

---

[2] Ralph L. Rusk, *The Life of Ralph Waldo Emerson* (1949; rpt., New York: Columbia University Press, 1967) 508.

[3] Ralph Waldo Emerson, *The Complete Works of Ralph Waldo Emerson,* ed. Edward Waldo Emerson, centenary ed. (Boston: Houghton, Mifflin, 1903–1904). Edward Waldo Emerson also, with Waldo Emerson Forbes, edited Emerson's collected journals (Boston: Houghton Mifflin, 1909–1914). During Emerson's lifetime, besides his own edition of six volumes of prose published in 1870, there had been a Little Classics edition in 1875. After his death, his daughter Ellen and James Elliot Cabot arranged the Riverside edition of 1883–1893, published by Houghton, Mifflin, in twelve volumes.

essays and poems began to appear. In the 1840s there were *Essays* (1841), *Essays, Second Series* (1844), *Poems* (1846), and *Nature, Addresses, and Lectures* (1849), while the 1850s brought *Representative Men* (1850) and *English Traits* (1856), and the 1860s, *The Conduct of Life* (1860) and a new collection of poetry, *May-Day and Other Pieces* (1867). By 1870, Emerson had revised the first six volumes of his prose, which were published as *The Prose Works,* and he brought forward an additional collection of essays titled *Society and Solitude*. Five years later his elder daughter, Ellen, and James Elliot Cabot used his lectures as the basis for *Lectures and Social Aims,* and the following year he collaborated with them to produce *Selected Poems.*

It was an impressive publishing record, truly—the collected reflections of a man, part poet, part philosopher, and altogether religious seeker, concerned for his age but concerned most of all for the self of each individual in time and eternity. The outer life could be middle class and routine because—partially conditioned by his bourgeois matrix and partially transcending it—it was in the record of his mind and spirit that Emerson lived adventurously. Moreover, in keeping with his vocation as religious seeker, the published work was grounded in the continuing private journals that Emerson kept—a collection of notebooks that spanned the years from 1820 until near the end of his days. Within them he recorded thoughts from his reading and musing, copied passages from other authors that particularly moved him, and sometimes confided material of a more personal nature, such as occasional dreams. As he composed his lectures and essays, he would dip into the passages of his journals, lifting out material and weaving it into the new composition. In this way, the old supported the new and the private supported the public Emerson.

The selections from Emerson's voluminous writings that appear below are only a fraction of his total output. It is fair to say, too, that his religious quest governed, either explicitly or implicitly, nearly all of his work. Hence, a complete introduction to the Transcendentalist's spirituality would mean working one's way through all of his writing—journals, lectures, essays, addresses, and poetry. In the present collection, therefore, only a few representative items are included—with an eye to their classical quality and their ability to portray the various facets of Emerson's spirituality. The selections begin with the sermon Emerson preached to his congregation in 1832 to explain his decision to resign his pastorate. There follows the complete text of *Nature,* the little book of 1836 that announced the Transcendental good news to the world. The Divinity School *Address* of 1838 is included next, marking the lines, in Emerson's view, between the old and the new spirituality, and then—to expand and explore the meaning of that new spirituality—two essays from his first collection of 1841. "The Over-Soul" proclaims the message from the side of the divine source, while "Self-Reliance" looks to the sacredness of each individual. Finally, in a selection from Emerson's poetry and the conclusion of his essay "Fate," his experience is summarized in a biography of the spirit. We gain, as we read, a new sense of the significance of the commonplaces that Emerson, in his letter to the English writer, owned. "Commonplace," we discover, is another way of saying common to human perception and experience—representative, in some way, of the whole.

THE LORD'S SUPPER

Edward Waldo Emerson tells, in his notes to this sermon, of his father's wish not to have any of his preaching preserved, a wish in this case overruled by the family.[1] The reason is clear. The sermon defends Emerson's decision to leave the pulpit of the Second Church in Boston, a decision that was to have momentous consequences for his later life and for American religion and literature. It is a statement of the youthful minister's abhorrence of traditional religious forms and, already in 1832, a call to inwardness and the life of the spirit without the mediation of these externals. During the time Emerson struggled with his decision to leave his pastorate, his journal records his interest in the life of George Fox (1624–1691), the founder of the Quakers, and in Emanuel Swedenborg—both examples, for him, of persons who were genuine.[2] Both were also persons who claimed to be the recipients of direct religious experience unmediated by the rituals of the church.

The sermon is divided by content into two parts. The first—and by far the longer—section offers a scriptural argument against the perpetuity of the rite of the Lord's Supper. It is an argument that, according to Edward Waldo Emerson, Emerson essentially took from his older brother, William, who earlier had objected to the Lord's Supper celebration.[3] The second, and more impassioned, section is Emerson's plea arising from his sense of inner conviction and his growing revulsion for external forms. Rituals, for Emerson, were dead rituals; and so he found it necessary to reject the Unitarian "ordinance"—the Lord's Supper understood by liberal Christians as a sign, or memorial, but also as a means of grace and spiritual improvement. The next few years would make it clear that Emerson turned away from the church's ritual to find what he thought a better means of improvement in nature and the inner voice.[4]

---

[1] See Ralph Waldo Emerson, *The Complete Works of Ralph Waldo Emerson,* ed. Edward Waldo Emerson, centenary ed. (Boston: Houghton, Mifflin, 1903–1904) 11:547.

[2] See Ralph Waldo Emerson, *The Journals and Miscellaneous Notebooks of Ralph Waldo Emerson,* ed. William H. Gilman et al. (Cambridge: Harvard University Press, Belknap Press, 1960–) 4 (15 July 1832?): 31, 33; (18 August 1832): 37.

[3] See Emerson, *Complete Works,* 11:550-51.

[4] The text is that in the centenary edition of Emerson, *Complete Works,* 11:1-25.

THE LORD'S SUPPER

SERMON DELIVERED BEFORE THE SECOND CHURCH
IN BOSTON, SEPTEMBER 9, 1832

> I LIKE a church; I like a cowl,
> I love a prophet of the soul;
> And on my heart monastic aisles
> Fall like sweet strains, or pensive smiles:
> Yet not for all his faith can see
> Would I that cowlèd churchman be.
> Why should the vest on him allure,
> Which I could not on me endure?[1]
>
> THE word unto the prophet spoken
> Was writ on tables yet unbroken;
> The word by seers or sibyls told,
> In groves of oak, or fanes of gold,
> Still floats upon the morning wind,
> Still whispers to the willing mind.[2]

The Kingdom of God is not meat and drink; but righteousness, and peace, and joy in the Holy Ghost.—ROMANS xiv. 17.

IN the history of the Church no subject has been more fruitful of controversy than the Lord's Supper. There never has been any unanimity in the understanding of its nature, nor any uniformity in the mode of celebrating it. Without considering the frivolous questions which have been lately debated as to the posture in which men should partake of it; whether mixed or unmixed wine should be served; whether leavened or unleavened bread should be broken;—the questions have been settled differently in every church, who should be admitted to the feast, and how often it should be prepared. In the Catholic Church, infants were at one time permitted and then forbidden to partake; and since the ninth century the laity receive the bread only, the cup being reserved to the priesthood. So, as to the time of the solemnity. In the Fourth Lateran Council, it was decreed that any believer should communicate at least once in a year,—at Easter.[3] Afterwards it

---

[1] Edward Waldo Emerson has prefixed to the body of the sermon these lines, which form the introduction to his father's poem "The Problem" (1839). See the complete poem in Ralph Waldo Emerson, *Poems,* in this volume.

[2] These lines are also taken from "The Problem."

[3] Held in 1215 under Pope Innocent III, the

was determined that this Sacrament should be received three times in the year,—at Easter, Whitsuntide and Christmas. But more important controversies have arisen respecting its nature. The famous question of the Real Presence was the main controversy between the Church of England and the Church of Rome. The doctrine of the Consubstantiation taught by Luther was denied by Calvin.[4] In the Church of England, Archbishops Laud and Wake[5] maintained that the elements were an Eucharist, or sacrifice of Thanksgiving to God; Cudworth and Warburton,[6] that this was not a sacrifice, but a sacrificial feast; and Bishop Hoadley,[7] that it was neither a sacrifice nor a feast after sacrifice, but a simple commemoration. And finally, it is now near two hundred years since the Society of Quakers denied the authority of the rite altogether, and gave good reasons for disusing it.

I allude to these facts only to show that, so far from the Supper being a tradition in which men are fully agreed, there has always been the widest room for difference of opinion upon this particular. Having re-

---

Fourth Lateran Council established the requirement of an annual confession of sins and communion during the Easter season. Joseph Jungmann cites a growing discontinuance of chalice communion from the twelfth, not the ninth, century. See Joseph A. Jungmann, *The Mass of the Roman Rite: Its Origins and Development,* trans. Francis A. Brunner and rev. Charles K. Riepe (New York: Benziger Brothers, 1959) 512. The "frivolous questions" (above in the text) were controversies in New England churches regarding the sacrament.

[4]The Roman Catholic doctrine of transubstantiation held to the real (i.e., physical) presence of Christ with the consecration of bread and wine at the Mass. The substance had been changed; only the appearances of bread and wine remained. The Lutheran doctrine of consubstantiation taught the real, physical presence of Jesus Christ along with the continuing elements of bread and wine in the Lord's Supper. In other words, the substance of the bread and wine did not disappear when Christ became physically present. John Calvin's teaching, on the other hand, held that the real presence was spiritual. For Church of England views, see nn. 5 through 7 below. The doctrine of the real presence was, in fact, *not* the main controversy with the Roman church.

[5]William Laud (1573–1645), archbishop of Canterbury from 1633, was noted for his High Church position and his opposition to Puritanism in matters of ritual and church discipline. Among his most controversial actions, he designated the communion table the center of the church instead of the pulpit. Because he so an-tagonized the powerful Puritan faction that gained control of the government in 1642, he was finally executed. William Wake (1657–1737), archbishop of Canterbury from 1716, was more willing than Laud to tolerate Nonconformists. His *Real Presence and Adoration of the Host,* a polemic against Roman Catholic views, was published as part of *Preservative against Popery,* edited by Edmund Gibson in 1738.

[6]Ralph Cudworth (1617–1688), important among the group of English scholars known as the Cambridge Platonists, revealed his interest in the Lord's Supper in his *Discourse concerning the True Notion of the Lord's Supper* (1642). Here he considered the ritual as not itself a sacrifice but a "feast upon a sacrifice," like feasts that came after Jewish legal sacrifices. William Warburton (1698–1779) was bishop of Gloucester, England, from 1760 and the author of various ecclesiastical works. Possessing something of a literary reputation as an editor, with Alexander Pope, of the works of William Shakespeare and of Pope's works after his death, he shared Cudworth's view of the Lord's Supper as a sacrificial feast.

[7]Benjamin Hoadley (or Hoadly; 1676–1761) was an English prelate of Low Church inclinations, with a view of the Lord's Supper as a simple commemoration.

cently given particular attention to this subject, I was led to the conclusion that Jesus did not intend to establish an institution for perpetual observance when he ate the Passover with his disciples; and further, to the opinion that it is not expedient to celebrate it as we do. I shall now endeavor to state distinctly my reasons for these two opinions.

I. The authority of the rite.

An account of the Last Supper of Christ with his disciples is given by the four Evangelists, Matthew, Mark, Luke and John.

In St. Matthew's Gospel (Matt. xxvi. 26-30) are recorded the words of Jesus in giving bread and wine on that occasion to his disciples, but no expression occurs intimating that this feast was hereafter to be commemorated. In St. Mark (Mark xiv. 22-25) the same words are recorded, and still with no intimation that the occasion was to be remembered. St. Luke (Luke xxii. 19), after relating the breaking of the bread, has these words: "This do in remembrance of me." In St. John, although other occurrences of the same evening are related, this whole transaction is passed over without notice.

Now observe the facts. Two of the Evangelists, namely, Matthew and John, were of the twelve disciples, and were present on that occasion. Neither of them drops the slightest intimation of any intention on the part of Jesus to set up anything permanent. John especially, the beloved disciple, who has recorded with minuteness the conversation and the transactions of that memorable evening, has quite omitted such a notice. Neither does it appear to have come to the knowledge of Mark, who, though not an eye-witness, relates the other facts. This material fact, that the occasion was to be remembered, is found in Luke alone, who was not present. There is no reason, however, that we know, for rejecting the account of Luke. I doubt not, the expression was used by Jesus. I shall presently consider its meaning. I have only brought these accounts together, that you may judge whether it is likely that a solemn institution, to be continued to the end of time by all mankind, as they should come, nation after nation, within the influence of the Christian religion, would have been established in this slight manner—in a manner so slight, that the intention of commemorating it should not appear, from their narrative, to have caught the ear or dwelt in the mind of the only two among the twelve who wrote down what happened.

Still we must suppose that the expression, "This do in remembrance of me," had come to the ear of Luke from some disciple who was present. What did it really signify? It is a prophetic and an affectionate expression. Jesus is a Jew, sitting with his countrymen, celebrating their national feast. He thinks of his own impending death, and wishes the minds of his disciples to be prepared for it. "When hereafter," he says to them, "you shall keep the Passover, it will have an altered aspect to your eyes. It is now a historical covenant of God with the Jewish nation. Hereafter it will remind you of a new covenant sealed with my blood. In years to come, as long as your people shall come up to Jerusalem to keep this feast, the connection which has subsisted between us will give a new meaning in your eyes to the national festival, as the anniversary of my death." I see natural feeling and beauty in the use of such language from Jesus, a friend to his friends; I can readily imagine that he was willing and desirous, when his disciples met, his memory should hallow their intercourse; but I cannot bring myself to believe that in the use of such an expression he looked beyond the living generation, beyond the abolition of the festival he was celebrating, and the scattering of the nation, and meant to impose a memorial feast upon the whole world.

Without presuming to fix precisely the purpose in the mind of Jesus, you will see that many opinions may be entertained of his intention, all consistent with the opinion that he did not design a perpetual ordinance. He may have foreseen that his disciples would meet to remember him, and that with good effect. It may have crossed his mind that this would be easily continued a hundred or a thousand years,—as men more easily transmit a form than a virtue,—and yet have been altogether out of his purpose to fasten it upon men in all times and all countries.

But though the words, "Do this in remembrance of me," do not occur in Matthew, Mark or John, and although it should be granted us that, taken alone, they do not necessarily import so much as is usually thought, yet many persons are apt to imagine that the very striking and personal manner in which the eating and drinking is described, indicates a striking and formal purpose to found a festival. And I admit that this impression might probably be left upon the mind of one who read only the passages under consideration in the New Testament. But this impression is removed by reading any narrative of the mode in which the ancient or the modern Jews have kept the Passover. It is then perceived that the leading circumstances in the Gospels are only a faithful account of that ceremony. Jesus did not celebrate the Passover, and afterwards the Supper, but the Supper was the Passover. He did with his disciples exactly what every master of a family in Jerusalem was doing at the same hour with his household. It appears that the Jews ate the lamb and the unleavened bread and drank wine after a prescribed manner. It was the custom for the master of the feast to break the bread and to bless it, using this formula, which the Talmudists have preserved to us, "Blessed be Thou, O Lord, our God, who givest us the fruit of the vine,"—and then to give the cup to all.[8] Among the modern Jews, who in their dispersion retain the Passover, a hymn is also sung after this ceremony, specifying the twelve great works done by God for the deliverance of their fathers out of Egypt.[9]

But still it may be asked, Why did Jesus make expressions so extraordinary and emphatic as these—"This is my body which is broken for you. Take; eat. This is my blood which is shed for you. Drink it"?—I reply they are not extraordinary expressions from him. They were familiar in his mouth. He always taught by parables and symbols. It was the national way of teaching, and was largely used by him. Remember the readiness which he always showed to spiritualize every occurrence. He stopped and wrote on the sand. He admonished his disciples respecting the leaven of the Pharisees. He instructed the woman of Samaria respecting living water. He permitted himself to be anointed, declaring that it was for his interment. He washed the feet of his disciples.[10] These are admitted to be symbolical actions and expressions. Here, in like manner, he calls

---

[8] The formula is the Kiddush, the sanctification or blessing of the traditional Jewish Sabbath and holy days given over a cup of wine by the head of the household.

[9] See Exod. 7:8-14:31. But the Passover Haggadah to which Emerson is referring nowhere mentions twelve wonders. He may, however, mean the *Dayyenu* litany, which numbers fifteen verses, each accompanied by the refrain *Dayyenu* ("it would have been enough for us"). The litany is not too far separated from the Kiddush in the ritual. I am indebted to Eric L. Friedland of Wright State University for this observation.

[10] Cf. John 8:3-9; Matt. 16:6, 11; John 4:6-15; Mark 14:3-9; John 13:3-15.

the bread his body, and bids the disciples eat. He had used the same expression repeatedly before. The reason why St. John does not repeat his words on this occasion seems to be that he had reported a similar discourse of Jesus to the people of Capernaum more at length already (John vi. 27-60). He there tells the Jews, "Except ye eat the flesh of the Son of Man and drink his blood, ye have no life in you." And when the Jews on that occasion complained that they did not comprehend what he meant, he added for their better understanding, and as if for our understanding, that we might not think his body was to be actually eaten, that he only meant we should live by his commandment. He closed his discourse with these explanatory expressions: "The flesh profiteth nothing; the words that I speak to you, they are spirit and they are life."[11]

Whilst I am upon this topic, I cannot help remarking that it is not a little singular that we should have preserved this rite and insisted upon perpetuating one symbolical act of Christ whilst we have totally neglected all others,—particularly one other which had at least an equal claim to our observance. Jesus washed the feet of his disciples and told them that, as he had washed their feet, they ought to wash one another's feet; for he had given them an example, that they should do as he had done to them. I ask any person who believes the Supper to have been designed by Jesus to be commemorated forever, to go and read the account of it in the other Gospels, and then compare with it the account of this transaction in St. John, and tell me if this be not much more explicitly authorized than the Supper. It only differs in this, that we have found the Supper used in New England and the washing of the feet not. But if we had found it an established rite in our churches, on grounds of mere authority, it would have been impossible to have argued against it. That rite is used by the Church of Rome, and by the Sandemanians.[12] It has been very properly dropped by other Christians. Why? For two reasons: (1) because it was a local custom, and unsuitable in western countries; and (2) because it was typical,[13] and all understood that humility is the thing signified. But the Passover was local too, and does not concern us, and its bread and wine were typical, and do not help us to understand the redemption which they signified. These views of the original account of the Lord's Supper lead me to esteem it an occasion full of solemn and prophetic interest, but never intended by Jesus to be the foundation of a perpetual institution.

It appears, however, in Christian history that the disciples had very early taken advantage of these impressive words of

---

[11] John 6:63. For the discussion above in the text, see John 6:44-46, which Emerson interprets rather freely. See also John 15:10, which Emerson may have conflated with John 6:56.

[12] Foot washing is performed by the priest-celebrant for a symbolic group of preselected men as part of the ritual for Maundy, or Holy, Thursday. The Sandemanians, also known as Glassites, were a religious sect founded by John Glas (1695–1773), a Scottish Presbyterian who advocated a restoration of the practices of the early church. His son-in-law, Robert Sandeman (1718–1771), became the leader in bringing the movement to both England and America. Foot washing was also practiced by seventeenth- and eighteenth-century German Pietists, by various German Dunker or Brethren groups, and in America by Primitive, or Regular, Baptist congregations. Despite Emerson's next sentence, the rite is still continued to this day among some Brethren and Baptist bodies.

[13] Here Emerson means that the custom was symbolic—a type, or sign, of a spiritual reality.

Christ to hold religious meetings, where they broke bread and drank wine as symbols. I look upon this fact as very natural in the circumstances of the Church. The disciples lived together; they threw all their property into a common stock; they were bound together by the memory of Christ, and nothing could be more natural than that this eventful evening should be affectionately remembered by them; that they, Jews like Jesus, should adopt his expressions and his types, and furthermore, that what was done with peculiar propriety by them, his personal friends, with less propriety should come to be extended to their companions also. In this way religious feasts grew up among the early Christians. They were readily adopted by the Jewish converts, who were familiar with religious feasts, and also by the Pagan converts, whose idolatrous worship had been made up of sacred festivals, and who very readily abused these to gross riot, as appears from the censures of St. Paul.[14] Many persons consider this fact, the observance of such a memorial feast by the early disciples, decisive of the question whether it ought to be observed by us. There was good reason for his personal friends to remember their friend and repeat his words. It was only too probable that among the half-converted Pagans and Jews, any rite, any form, would find favor, whilst yet unable to comprehend the spiritual character of Christianity.

The circumstance, however, that St. Paul adopts these views, has seemed to many persons conclusive in favor of the institution. I am of opinion that it is wholly upon the Epistle to the Corinthians, and not upon the Gospels, that the ordinance stands. Upon this matter of St. Paul's view of the Supper, a few important considerations must be stated.

The end which he has in view, in the eleventh chapter of the first Epistle, is not to enjoin upon his friends to observe the Supper, but to censure their abuse of it. We quote the passage nowadays as if it enjoined attendance upon the Supper; but he wrote it merely to chide them for drunkenness. To make their enormity plainer, he goes back to the origin of this religious feast to show what sort of feast that was, out of which this riot of theirs came, and so relates the transactions of the Last Supper. "I have received of the Lord," he says, "that which I delivered to you." By this expression it is often thought that a miraculous communication is implied; but certainly without good reason, if it is remembered that St. Paul was living in the lifetime of all the apostles who could give him an account of the transaction; and it is contrary to all reason to suppose that God should work a miracle to convey information that could so easily be got by natural means. So that the import of the expression is that he had received the story of an eye-witness such as we also possess.

But there is a material circumstance which diminishes our confidence in the correctness of the Apostle's view; and that is, the observation that his mind had not escaped the prevalent error of the primitive Church, the belief, namely, that the second coming of Christ would shortly occur, until which time, he tells them, this feast was to be kept. Elsewhere he tells them that at that time the world would be burnt up with fire, and a new government established, in which the Saints would sit on thrones;[15] so slow were the disciples, dur-

---

[14] 1 Cor. 11:17-34. Emerson's account of the early Christian community seems also to be drawn from Acts. See Acts 2:44-47; 4:32-35.

[15] See 2 Thess. 1:7-10, which may be what Emerson has in mind. But his memory is faulty since neither here nor elsewhere does Paul of-

ing the life and after the ascension of Christ, to receive the idea which we receive, that his second coming was a spiritual kingdom, the dominion of his religion in the hearts of men, to be extended gradually over the whole world. In this manner we may see clearly enough how this ancient ordinance got its footing among the early Christians, and this single expectation of a speedy reappearance of a temporal Messiah, which kept its influence even over so spiritual a man as St. Paul, would naturally tend to preserve the use of the rite when once established.

We arrive, then, at this conclusion: first, that it does not appear, from a careful examination of the account of the Last Supper in the Evangelists, that it was designed by Jesus to be perpetual; secondly, that it does not appear that the opinion of St. Paul, all things considered, ought to alter our opinion derived from the Evangelists.

One general remark before quitting this branch of this subject. We ought to be cautious in taking even the best ascertained opinions and practices of the primitive Church for our own. If it could be satisfactorily shown that they esteemed it authorized and to be transmitted forever, that does not settle the question for us. We know how inveterately they were attached to their Jewish prejudices, and how often even the influence of Christ failed to enlarge their views. On every other subject succeeding times have learned to form a judgment more in accordance with the spirit of Christianity than was the practice of the early ages.

II. But it is said: "Admit that the rite was not designed to be perpetual. What harm doth it? Here it stands, generally accepted, under some form, by the Christian world, the undoubted occasion of much good; is it not better it should remain?" This is the question of expediency.

I proceed to state a few objections that in my judgment lie against its use in its present form.

1. If the view which I have taken of the history of the institution be correct, then the claim of authority should be dropped in administering it. You say, every time you celebrate the rite, that Jesus enjoined it; and the whole language you use conveys that impression. But if you read the New Testament as I do, you do not believe he did.

2. It has seemed to me that the use of this ordinance tends to produce confusion in our views of the relation of the soul to God. It is the old objection to the doctrine of the Trinity,—that the true worship was transferred from God to Christ, or that such confusion was introduced into the soul that an undivided worship was given nowhere.[16] Is not that the effect of the Lord's

---

fer a sequence in which, after the fire of the Last Judgment, the saints sit upon "thrones." Perhaps Emerson has conflated Rev. 20:4 with Paul.

[16] Although anti-Trinitarianism had played its part in previous church history, the objections Emerson raises were voiced in the late seventeenth century with the rise of English Unitarianism. Still more, Emerson's objections reflect the liberal Christianity of the later eighteenth and early nineteenth century, as it moved toward official Unitarianism. While it is true that the main argument of New England Unitarianism against the doctrine of the Trinity was that it was unscriptural, in his classic and definitive sermon *Unitarian Christianity* (1819) William Ellery Channing explained the practical difficulties of Trinitarianism in language very close to Emerson's: the doctrine of the Trinity was "unfavorable to devotion, by dividing and distracting the mind in its communion with God"; it also harmed devotion "by taking from the Father the supreme affection which is his due, and transferring it to the Son." See William Ellery Channing, *Unitarian Christianity* (Discourse at the Ordination of the

Supper? I appeal now to the convictions of communicants, and ask such persons whether they have not been occasionally conscious of a painful confusion of thought between the worship due to God and the commemoration due to Christ. For the service does not stand upon the basis of a voluntary act, but is imposed by authority. It is an expression of gratitude to Christ, enjoined by Christ. There is an endeavor to keep Jesus in mind, whilst yet the prayers are addressed to God. I fear it is the effect of this ordinance to clothe Jesus with an authority which he never claimed and which distracts the mind of the worshipper. I know our opinions differ much respecting the nature and offices of Christ, and the degree of veneration to which he is entitled. I am so much a Unitarian as this: that I believe the human mind can admit but one God, and that every effort to pay religious homage to more than one being goes to take away all right ideas. I appeal, brethren, to your individual experience. In the moment when you make the least petition to God, though it be but a silent wish that he may approve you, or add one moment to your life,—do you not, in the very act, necessarily exclude all other beings from your thought? In that act, the soul stands alone with God, and Jesus is no more present to your mind than your brother or your child.

But is not Jesus called in Scripture the Mediator? He is the mediator in that only sense in which possibly any being can mediate between God and man,—that is, an instructor of man. He teaches us how to become like God. And a true disciple of Jesus will receive the light he gives most thankfully; but the thanks he offers, and which an exalted being will accept, are not compliments, commemorations, but the use of that instruction.

3. Passing other objections, I come to this, that the use of the elements, however suitable to the people and the modes of thought in the East, where it originated, is foreign and unsuited to affect us. Whatever long usage and strong association may have done in some individuals to deaden this repulsion, I apprehend that their use is rather tolerated than loved by any of us. We are not accustomed to express our thoughts or emotions by symbolical actions. Most men find the bread and wine no aid to devotion, and to some it is a painful impediment. To eat bread is one thing; to love the precepts of Christ and resolve to obey them is quite another.

The statement of this objection leads me to say that I think this difficulty, wherever it is felt, to be entitled to the greatest weight. It is alone a sufficient objection to the ordinance. It is my own objection. This mode of commemorating Christ is not suitable to me. That is reason enough why I should abandon it. If I believed it was enjoined by Jesus on his disciples, and that he even contemplated making permanent this mode of commemoration, every way agreeable to an Eastern mind, and yet on trial it was disagreeable to my own feelings, I should not adopt it. I should choose other ways which, as more effectual upon me, he would approve more. For I choose

---

Rev. Jared Sparks, Baltimore, 1819), in *The Works of William E. Channing, D.D.* (Boston: American Unitarian Association, 1877) 372-73. See also Channing's sermon *Unitarian Christianity Most Favorable to Piety* (Discourse at the Dedication of the Second Congregational Unitarian Church, New York, 1826), ibid., 387, 389. For a historical discussion of modern Unitarianism, see Earl Morse Wilburn, *A History of Unitarianism: In Transylvania, England, and America* (Cambridge: Harvard University Press, 1952). I am indebted to Conrad Wright of the Harvard Divinity School for suggesting the likelihood of Channing's sermon *Unitarian Christianity* as a source for Emerson's ideas.

that my remembrances of him should be pleasing, affecting, religious. I will love him as a glorified friend, after the free way of friendship, and not pay him a stiff sign of respect, as men do those whom they fear. A passage read from his discourses, a moving provocation to works like his, any act or meeting which tends to awaken a pure thought, a flow of love, an original design of virtue, I call a worthy, a true commemoration.

4. The importance ascribed to this particular ordinance is not consistent with the spirit of Christianity. The general object and effect of the ordinance is unexceptionable. It has been, and is, I doubt not, the occasion of indefinite good; but an importance is given by Christians to it which never can belong to any form. My friends, the Apostle well assures us that "the kingdom of God is not meat and drink, but righteousness, and peace, and joy in the Holy Ghost." I am not so foolish as to declaim against forms. Forms are as essential as bodies; but to exalt particular forms, to adhere to one form a moment after it is outgrown, is unreasonable, and it is alien to the spirit of Christ. If I understand the distinction of Christianity, the reason why it is to be preferred over all other systems and is divine is this, that it is a moral system; that it presents men with truths which are their own reason, and enjoins practices that are their own justification; that if miracles may be said to have been its evidence to the first Christians, they are not its evidence to us, but the doctrines themselves;[17] that every practice is Christian which praises itself, and every practice unchristian which condemns itself. I am not engaged to Christianity by decent forms, or saving ordinances; it is not usage, it is not what I do not understand, that binds me to it,—let these be the sandy foundations of falsehoods. What I revere and obey in it is its reality, its boundless charity, its deep interior life, the rest it gives to mind, the echo it returns to my thoughts, the perfect accord it makes with my reason through all its representation of God and His Providence; and the persuasion and courage that come out thence to lead me upward and onward. Freedom is the essence of this faith. It has for its object simply to make men good and wise. Its institutions then should be as flexible as the wants of men. That form out of which the life and suitableness have departed should be as worthless in its eyes as the dead leaves that are falling around us.

And therefore, although for the satisfaction of others I have labored to show by the history that this rite was not intended to be perpetual; although I have gone back to weigh the expressions of Paul, I feel that here is the true point of view. In the midst of considerations as to what Paul thought, and why he so thought, I cannot help feeling that it is time misspent to argue to or from his convictions, or those of Luke and John, respecting any form. I seem to lose the substance in seeking the shadow. That for which Paul lived and died so gloriously; that for which Jesus gave himself to be crucified; the end that animated the thousand martyrs and heroes who have followed his steps, was to redeem us from a formal religion, and teach us to seek our well-being in the formation of the soul. The whole world was full of idols and ordinances. The Jewish was a religion of forms; it was all body, it had no life, and the Almighty God was pleased to qualify and send forth a man to teach men that they must serve him with the heart; that only that life was religious which was thoroughly

---

[17] Here Emerson briefly alludes to the Unitarian view of miracles as Christian evidence, a position that he and other Transcendentalists would later dispute more vigorously.

good; that sacrifice was smoke, and forms were shadows. This man lived and died true to this purpose; and now, with his blessed word and life before us, Christians must contend that it is a matter of vital importance,—really a duty, to commemorate him by a certain form, whether that form be agreeable to their understandings or not. Is not this to make vain the gift of God? Is not this to turn back the hand on the dial? Is not this to make men,—to make ourselves,—forget that not forms, but duties; not names, but righteousness and love are enjoined; and that in the eye of God there is no other measure of the value of any one form than the measure of its use?

There remain some practical objections to the ordinance, into which I shall not now enter. There is one on which I had intended to say a few words; I mean the unfavorable relation in which it places that numerous class of persons who abstain from it merely from disinclination to the rite.

Influenced by these considerations, I have proposed to the brethren of the Church to drop the use of the elements and the claim of authority in the administration of this ordinance, and have suggested a mode in which a meeting for the same purpose might be held, free of objection.

My brethren have considered my views with patience and candor, and have recommended, unanimously, an adherence to the present form. I have therefore been compelled to consider whether it becomes me to administer it. I am clearly of opinion I ought not. This discourse has already been so far extended that I can only say that the reason of my determination is shortly this: It is my desire, in the office of a Christian minister, to do nothing which I cannot do with my whole heart. Having said this, I have said all. I have no hostility to this institution; I am only stating my want of sympathy with it. Neither should I ever have obtruded this opinion upon other people, had I not been called by my office to administer it. That is the end of my opposition, that I am not interested in it. I am content that it stand to the end of the world, if it please men and please Heaven, and I shall rejoice in all the good it produces.

As it is the prevailing opinion and feeling in our religious community that it is an indispensable part of the pastoral office to administer this ordinance, I am about to resign into your hands that office which you have confided to me. It has many duties for which I am feebly qualified. It has some which it will always be my delight to discharge according to my ability, wherever I exist. And whilst the recollection of its claims oppresses me with a sense of my unworthiness, I am consoled by the hope that no time and no change can deprive me of the satisfaction of pursuing and exercising its highest functions.

NATURE

When Emerson published his slim volume *Nature* in 1836, he had produced a manifesto for the emerging Transcendental movement. Seen in juxtaposition to his farewell sermon at the Second Church, *Nature* offers Emerson's spiritual alternative to the inherited forms of the church. Throughout the work he stands in the Platonic lineage and, especially, that lineage as read through a revived metaphysical tradition in the West. Hence, in *Nature* the world of the "not-me" that Emerson celebrates is seen ultimately as a reflection of the one Mind or Spirit present in the human soul and in the realm of the Ideas. Refracted through the Neoplatonic teaching of the One (the Soul) and the Many (Nature), Emerson articulates a Swedenborgian doctrine of correspondence, expresses enthusiasm for magic and miracle, and speaks prophetically of human powers that seem, indeed, godlike. The while he employs the Kantian-Coleridgean distinction between the Reason and the Understanding (as he understands it) to contrast true and deceptive visions of the world. He sees in a hieroglyphic of symbols the means for the Reason to discern the secret message of Spirit encoded in matter.

The metaphysical tradition that Emerson embraces in *Nature* would enjoy a considerable following in the nineteenth century. Even as Emerson owed a debt to Emanuel Swedenborg and the Swedenborgian Church of the New Jerusalem, others—like the followers of Mary Baker Eddy (1821–1910) in Christian Science and followers of forms of mind cure in New Thought—would owe a debt to Emerson. In the twentieth century the "positive thinking" of Norman Vincent Peale (b. 1898) and others also had its roots in Emerson's teaching.

Beyond that, in *Nature* Emerson gives voice to a characteristic American millennialism, a sense that a new age with new powers and energies has dawned or is about to dawn. Despite his idealism, he exalts a landscape that will form the earthly paradise for a later wilderness preservation movement. He speaks with a largeness of vision and a confidence in human capacity that, in a host of different ways, finds expression in the culture of the era. Situated in a new space, Emerson and other Americans concluded that they were also living in a new time and that, as Gods, they should stretch their spirits to the demands of the age.[1]

---

[1] The text is that of Ralph Waldo Emerson, *The Complete Works of Ralph Waldo Emerson,* ed. Edward Waldo Emerson, centenary ed. (Boston: Houghton, Mifflin, 1903–1904) 1:1-77.

NATURE

> A SUBTLE chain of countless rings
> The next unto the farthest brings;
> The eye reads omens where it goes,
> And speaks all languages the rose;
> And, striving to be man, the worm
> Mounts through all the spires of form.[1]

INTRODUCTION

OUR age is retrospective. It builds the sepulchres of the fathers. It writes biographies, histories, and criticism. The foregoing generations beheld God and nature face to face; we, through their eyes. Why should not we also enjoy an original relation to the universe? Why should not we have a poetry and philosophy of insight and not of tradition, and a religion by revelation to us, and not the history of theirs? Embosomed for a season in nature, whose floods of life stream around and through us, and invite us, by the powers they supply, to action proportioned to nature, why should we grope among the dry bones of the past, or put the living generation into masquerade out of its faded wardrobe? The sun shines to-day also. There is more wool and flax in the fields. There are new lands, new men, new thoughts. Let us demand our own works and laws and worship.

Undoubtedly we have no questions to ask which are unanswerable. We must trust the perfection of the creation so far as to believe that whatever curiosity the order of things has awakened in our minds, the order of things can satisfy. Every man's condition is a solution in hieroglyphic to those inquiries he would put.[2] He acts it as life,

---

[1] Emerson prefixed this poem of his, with its evolutionary motif, to the second edition of *Nature* published in 1849. The first edition of 1836, at a time when Emerson was probably influenced strongly by the Neoplatonism of Bronson Alcott, was prefaced by the words of Plotinus: "Nature is but an image or imitation of wisdom, the last thing of the soul; nature being a thing which doth only do, but not know." In the new critical edition of Emerson's writings, Robert E. Spiller suggests that the quotation may have come from Ralph Cudworth's *True Intellectual System of the Universe*, edited by Thomas Birch (1820). See Ralph Waldo Emerson, *The Collected Works of Ralph Waldo Emerson*, ed. Alfred R. Ferguson et al. (Cambridge: Harvard University Press, Belknap Press, 1971–) 1:247. I have relied considerably on Spiller's scholarship in the informational notes that follow, especially in citations of Emerson's sources. My reliance on Spiller continues, too, in the notes to the Divinity School *Address*.

[2] The symbol of Egyptian hieroglyphics was particularly cogent for Emerson. Beginning in the 1820s there had been an Egyptian revival in the United States. In academic circles it took the form of keen interest in Jean-François Champollion's decipherment of Egyptian hieroglyphics with the assistance of the inscriptions on the Rosetta stone (1821). Influenced

before he apprehends it as truth. In like manner, nature is already, in its forms and tendencies, describing its own design. Let us interrogate the great apparition that shines so peacefully around us. Let us inquire, to what end is nature?

All science has one aim, namely, to find a theory of nature. We have theories of races and of functions, but scarcely yet a remote approach to an idea of creation. We are now so far from the road to truth, that religious teachers dispute and hate each other, and speculative men are esteemed unsound and frivolous. But to a sound judgment, the most abstract truth is the most practical. Whenever a true theory appears, it will be its own evidence. Its test is, that it will explain all phenomena. Now many are thought not only unexplained but inexplicable; as language, sleep, madness, dreams, beasts, sex.

Philosophically considered, the universe is composed of Nature and the Soul.[3] Strictly speaking, therefore, all that is separate from us, all which Philosophy distinguishes as the NOT ME, that is, both nature and art, all other men and my own body, must be ranked under this name, NATURE. In enumerating the values of nature and casting up their sum, I shall use the word in both senses;—in its common and in its philosophical import. In inquiries so general as our present one, the inaccuracy is not material; no confusion of thought will occur. *Nature,* in the common sense, refers to essences unchanged by man; space, the air, the river, the leaf. *Art* is applied to the mixture of his will with the same things, as in a house, a canal, a statue, a picture. But his operations taken together are so insignificant, a little chipping, baking, patching, and washing, that in an impression so grand as that of the world on the human mind, they do not vary the result.

NATURE

I

To go into solitude, a man needs to retire as much from his chamber as from society. I am not solitary whilst I read and write, though nobody is with me. But if a man would be alone, let him look at the stars. The rays that come from those heavenly worlds will separate between him and what he touches. One might think the atmosphere was made transparent with this design, to give man, in the heavenly bodies, the perpetual presence of the sublime. Seen in the streets of cities, how great they are! If the stars should appear one night in a thousand years, how would men believe and adore; and preserve for many generations the remembrance of the city of God which had been shown! But every night come out these envoys of beauty, and light the universe with their admonishing smile.

The stars awaken a certain reverence, because though always present, they are inaccessible; but all natural objects make a kindred impression, when the mind is open to their influence. Nature never wears a mean appearance. Neither does the wisest man extort her secret, and lose his curiosity by finding out all her perfection. Nature never became a toy to a wise spirit. The

---

by an older tradition of metaphysical interpretation of hieroglyphics that had come to him from Neoplatonism and Swedenborgianism, Emerson—as did the Swedenborgians—combined the occult and mystical understanding with his awareness of Champollion's work. Hence, throughout *Nature* he is impressed by the "emblematic." For further discussion, see John T. Irwin, *American Hieroglyphics: The Symbol of the Egyptian Hieroglyphics in the American Renaissance* (New Haven: Yale University Press, 1980) 3-14.

[3]Here Emerson's philosophical understanding is based on the Neoplatonic description of the world of the Many in which exist human souls and matter.

flowers, the animals, the mountains, reflected the wisdom of his best hour, as much as they had delighted the simplicity of his childhood.

When we speak of nature in this manner, we have a distinct but most poetical sense in the mind. We mean the integrity of impression made by manifold natural objects. It is this which distinguishes the stick of timber of the wood-cutter from the tree of the poet. The charming landscape which I saw this morning is indubitably made up of some twenty or thirty farms. Miller owns this field, Locke that, and Manning the woodland beyond. But none of them owns the landscape. There is a property in the horizon which no man has but he whose eye can integrate all the parts, that is, the poet. This is the best part of these men's farms, yet to this their warranty-deeds give no title.

To speak truly, few adult persons can see nature. Most persons do not see the sun. At least they have a very superficial seeing. The sun illuminates only the eye of the man, but shines into the eye and the heart of the child. The lover of nature is he whose inward and outward senses are still truly adjusted to each other; who has retained the spirit of infancy even into the era of manhood. His intercourse with heaven and earth becomes part of his daily food. In the presence of nature a wild delight runs through the man, in spite of real sorrows. Nature says,—he is my creature, and maugre all his impertinent griefs, he shall be glad with me. Not the sun or the summer alone, but every hour and season yields its tribute of delight; for every hour and change corresponds to and authorizes a different state of the mind, from breathless noon to grimmest midnight. Nature is a setting that fits equally well a comic or a mourning piece. In good health, the air is a cordial of incredible virtue. Crossing a bare common, in snow puddles, at twilight, under a clouded sky, without having in my thoughts any occurrence of special good fortune, I have enjoyed a perfect exhilaration. I am glad to the brink of fear. In the woods, too, a man casts off his years, as the snake his slough, and at what period soever of life is always a child. In the woods is perpetual youth. Within these plantations of God, a decorum and sanctity reign, a perennial festival is dressed, and the guest sees not how he should tire of them in a thousand years. In the woods, we return to reason and faith. There I feel that nothing can befall me in life,—no disgrace, no calamity (leaving me my eyes), which nature cannot repair. Standing on the bare ground,—my head bathed by the blithe air and uplifted into infinite space,—all mean egotism vanishes. I become a transparent eyeball; I am nothing; I see all; the currents of the Universal Being circulate through me; I am part or parcel of God.[4] The name of the nearest friend sounds then foreign and accidental: to be brothers, to be acquaintances, master or servant, is then a trifle and a disturbance. I am the lover of uncontained and immortal beauty. In the wilderness, I find something more dear and connate than in streets or villages. In the tranquil landscape, and especially in the distant line of the horizon, man beholds somewhat as beautiful as his own nature.

The greatest delight which the fields and woods minister is the suggestion of an occult relation between man and the vegetable. I am not alone and unacknowledged. They nod to me, and I to them. The waving of the boughs in the storm is new to me and old. It takes me by surprise, and yet is not unknown. Its effect is like that of

---

[4]In this record of nature mysticism, Emerson's Neoplatonic doctrine of the Oversoul is in evidence.

a higher thought or a better emotion coming over me, when I deemed I was thinking justly or doing right.

Yet it is certain that the power to produce this delight does not reside in nature, but in man, or in a harmony of both. It is necessary to use these pleasures with great temperance. For nature is not always tricked in holiday attire, but the same scene which yesterday breathed perfume and glittered as for the frolic of the nymphs is overspread with melancholy to-day. Nature always wears the colors of the spirit. To a man laboring under calamity, the heat of his own fire hath sadness in it. Then there is a kind of contempt of the landscape felt by him who has just lost by death a dear friend. The sky is less grand as it shuts down over less worth in the population.

II
COMMODITY

WHOEVER considers the final cause of the world will discern a multitude of uses that enter as parts into that result. They all admit of being thrown into one of the following classes: Commodity; Beauty; Language; and Discipline.

Under the general name of commodity, I rank all those advantages which our senses owe to nature. This, of course, is a benefit which is temporary and mediate, not ultimate, like its service to the soul. Yet although low, it is perfect in its kind, and is the only use of nature which all men apprehend. The misery of man appears like childish petulance, when we explore the steady and prodigal provision that has been made for his support and delight on this green ball which floats him through the heavens. What angels invented these splendid ornaments, these rich conveniences, this ocean of air above, this ocean of water beneath, this firmament of earth between? this zodiac of lights, this tent of dropping clouds, this striped coat of climates, this fourfold year? Beasts, fire, water, stones, and corn serve him. The field is at once his floor, his work-yard, his play-ground, his garden, and his bed.

"More servants wait on man
Than he'll take notice of."[5]

Nature, in its ministry to man, is not only the material, but is also the process and the result. All the parts incessantly work into each other's hands for the profit of man. The wind sows the seed; the sun evaporates the sea; the wind blows the vapor to the field; the ice, on the other side of the planet, condenses rain on this; the rain feeds the plant; the plant feeds the animal; and thus the endless circulations of the divine charity nourish man.

The useful arts are reproductions or new combinations by the wit of man, of the same natural benefactors. He no longer waits for favoring gales, but by means of steam, he realizes the fable of Æolus's bag, and carries the two and thirty winds in the boiler of his boat.[6] To diminish friction, he paves the road with iron bars, and, mounting a coach with a ship-load of men, animals, and merchandise behind him, he darts through the country, from town to town, like an eagle or a swallow through the air. By the aggregate of these aids, how is the face of the world changed, from the era of Noah to that of Napoleon! The pri-

---

[5]These lines are taken from "Man" by the English metaphysical poet George Herbert (1593–1633). In "Prospects," later in the text, five additional verses from the poem are quoted.

[6]Aeolus was keeper of the winds in ancient Greek mythology. During his travels, Odysseus visited Aeolus's island and received as a farewell gift a bag holding all of the winds. While Odysseus lay asleep his men opened the bag; and, blown furiously by the winds, the ship was pushed back to the island of Aeolus (Homer *Odyssey* 10.1-55).

vate poor man hath cities, ships, canals, bridges, built for him. He goes to the post-office, and the human race run on his errands; to the book-shop, and the human race read and write of all that happens, for him; to the court-house, and nations repair his wrongs. He sets his house upon the road, and the human race go forth every morning, and shovel out the snow, and cut a path for him.

But there is no need of specifying particulars in this class of uses. The catalogue is endless, and the examples so obvious, that I shall leave them to the reader's reflection, with the general remark, that this mercenary benefit is one which has respect to a farther good. A man is fed, not that he may be fed, but that he may work.

III
BEAUTY

A NOBLER want of man is served by nature, namely, the love of Beauty.

The ancient Greeks called the world κόσμος, beauty.[7] Such is the constitution of all things, or such the plastic power of the human eye, that the primary forms, as the sky, the mountain, the tree, the animal, give us a delight *in and for themselves;* a pleasure arising from outline, color, motion, and grouping. This seems partly owing to the eye itself. The eye is the best of artists. By the mutual action of its structure and of the laws of light, perspective is produced, which integrates every mass of objects, of what character soever, into a well colored and shaded globe, so that where the particular objects are mean and unaffecting, the landscape which they compose is round and symmetrical. And as the eye is the best composer, so light is the first of painters. There is no object so foul that intense light will not make beautiful. And the stimulus it affords to the sense, and a sort of infinitude which it hath, like space and time, make all matter gay. Even the corpse has its own beauty. But besides this general grace diffused over nature, almost all the individual forms are agreeable to the eye, as is proved by our endless imitations of some of them, as the acorn, the grape, the pine-cone, the wheat-ear, the egg, the wings and forms of most birds, the lion's claw, the serpent, the butterfly, sea-shells, flames, clouds, buds, leaves, and the forms of many trees, as the palm.

For better consideration, we may distribute the aspects of Beauty in a threefold manner.

1. First, the simple perception of natural forms is a delight. The influence of the forms and actions in nature is so needful to man, that, in its lowest functions, it seems to lie on the confines of commodity and beauty. To the body and mind which have been cramped by noxious work or company, nature is medicinal and restores their tone. The tradesman, the attorney comes out of the din and craft of the street and sees the sky and the woods, and is a man again. In their eternal calm, he finds himself. The health of the eye seems to demand a horizon. We are never tired, so long as we can see far enough.

But in other hours, Nature satisfies by its loveliness, and without any mixture of corporeal benefit. I see the spectacle of morning from the hilltop over against my house, from daybreak to sunrise, with emotions which an angel might share. The long slender bars of cloud float like fishes in the sea of crimson light. From the earth, as a shore, I look out into that silent sea. I seem to partake its rapid transformations; the active enchantment reaches my dust,

---

[7]Transliterated, cosmos. The primary meaning of cosmos is order. Only secondarily is the term used to refer to an ornament or decoration—hence, Emerson's "beauty." The third meaning of the word is world or universe.

and I dilate and conspire with the morning wind. How does Nature deify us with a few and cheap elements! Give me health and a day, and I will make the pomp of emperors ridiculous. The dawn is my Assyria; the sunset and moonrise my Paphos, and unimaginable realms of faerie;[8] broad noon shall be my England of the senses and the understanding; the night shall be my Germany of mystic philosophy and dreams.

Not less excellent, except for our less susceptibility in the afternoon, was the charm, last evening, of a January sunset. The western clouds divided and subdivided themselves into pink flakes modulated with tints of unspeakable softness, and the air had so much life and sweetness that it was a pain to come within doors. What was it that nature would say? Was there no meaning in the live repose of the valley behind the mill, and which Homer or Shakspeare could not re-form for me in words? The leafless trees become spires of flame in the sunset, with the blue east for their background, and the stars of the dead calices of flowers, and every withered stem and stubble rimed with frost, contribute something to the mute music.

The inhabitants of cities suppose that the country landscape is pleasant only half the year. I please myself with the graces of the winter scenery, and believe that we are as much touched by it as by the genial influences of summer. To the attentive eye, each moment of the year has its own beauty, and in the same field, it beholds, every hour, a picture which was never seen before, and which shall never be seen again. The heavens change every moment, and reflect their glory or gloom on the plains beneath. The state of the crop in the surrounding farms alters the expression of the earth from week to week. The succession of native plants in the pastures and roadsides, which makes the silent clock by which time tells the summer hours, will make even the divisions of the day sensible to a keen observer. The tribes of birds and insects, like the plants punctual to their time, follow each other, and the year has room for all. By water-courses, the variety is greater. In July, the blue pontederia or pickerel-weed blooms in large beds in the shallow parts of our pleasant river, and swarms with yellow butterflies in continual motion. Art cannot rival this pomp of purple and gold. Indeed the river is a perpetual gala, and boasts each month a new ornament.

But this beauty of Nature which is seen and felt as beauty, is the least part. The shows of day, the dewy morning, the rainbow, mountains, orchards in blossom, stars, moonlight, shadows in still water, and the like, if too eagerly hunted, become shows merely, and mock us with their unreality. Go out of the house to see the moon, and 't is mere tinsel; it will not please as when its light shines upon your necessary journey. The beauty that shimmers in the yellow afternoons of October, who ever could clutch it? Go forth to find it, and it is gone; 't is only a mirage as you look from the windows of diligence.

2. The presence of a higher, namely, of the spiritual element is essential to its perfection. The high and divine beauty which can be loved without effeminacy, is that which is found in combination with the human will. Beauty is the mark God sets upon virtue. Every natural action is graceful. Every heroic act is also decent, and causes the place and the bystanders to shine. We are taught by great actions that the universe is the property of every indi-

---

[8]According to Spiller, Assyria is used here to represent power, while Paphos, the city on Cyprus dedicated to Aphrodite and her worship, is used to represent myth (Emerson, *Collected Works,* 1:248).

vidual in it. Every rational creature has all nature for his dowry and estate. It is his, if he will. He may divest himself of it; he may creep into a corner, and abdicate his kingdom, as most men do, but he is entitled to the world by his constitution. In proportion to the energy of his thought and will, he takes up the world into himself. "All those things for which men plough, build, or sail, obey virtue;" said Sallust.[9] "The winds and waves," said Gibbon, "are always on the side of the ablest navigators."[10] So are the sun and moon and all the stars of heaven. When a noble act is done,—perchance in a scene of great natural beauty; when Leonidas and his three hundred martyrs consume one day in dying, and the sun and moon come each and look at them once in the steep defile of Thermopylæ;[11] when Arnold Winkelried, in the high Alps, under the shadow of the avalanche, gathers in his side a sheaf of Austrian spears to break the line for his comrades;[12] are not these heroes entitled to add the beauty of the scene to the beauty of the deed? When the bark of Columbus nears the shore of America;—before it the beach lined with savages, fleeing out of all their huts of cane; the sea behind; and the purple mountains of the Indian Archipelago around, can we separate the man from the living picture? Does not the New World clothe his form with her palm-groves and savannahs as fit drapery? Ever does natural beauty steal in like air, and envelope great actions. When Sir Harry Vane was dragged up the Tower-hill, sitting on a sled, to suffer death as the champion of the English laws, one of the multitude cried out to him, "You never sate on so glorious a seat!"[13] Charles II., to intimidate the citizens of London, caused the patriot Lord Russell to be drawn in an open coach through the principal streets of the city on his way to the scaffold. "But," his biographer says, "the multitude imagined they saw liberty and virtue sitting by his side."[14] In private places, among sordid objects, an

---

[9]The original edition attributed this quotation to "an ancient historian." Although the 1849 edition cited Sallust, Emerson may have paraphrased the quotation as he remembered it. But Spiller remarks (Emerson, *Collected Works,* 1:248) that these words appear exactly in John Milton's *Apology for Smectymnuus* (John Milton, *The Prose of John Milton,* ed. Charles Symmons [London: J. Johnson, 1806] 1:234).

[10]Edward Gibbon, *History of the Decline and Fall of the Roman Empire* (London: W. Strahan and T. Cadell in the Strand, 1776–1788) 6:489.

[11]In 480 B.C., the Spartan king Leonidas defended the Greeks from the Persians at the mountain pass of Thermopylae where he died, fighting to the last, with his men.

[12]Tradition has it that Arnold von Winkelried in the battle of Sempach (9 July 1386) led the Swiss to victory over the Austrians under Duke Leopold by throwing himself at the enemy and gathering into his body all the Austrian spears he was able to reach. Although he died in the process, he breached the Austrian ranks.

[13]Sir Henry Vane (1613–1662), English Puritan statesman and governor of Massachusetts Bay in 1636, the following year returned to England to continue his political career. In 1662 the Restoration government convicted him of treason, and he was executed.

[14]William Russell (1639–1683) was supposedly implicated in the Rye House Plot, a plan to murder Charles II of England and his brother James (later James II) as they passed Rumbold's Rye House (Hertfordshire) on their way to London. A Whig leader, Lord Russell was executed on weak evidence. Emerson's source for the episode may have been *The General Biographical Dictionary* edited by Alexander Chalmers (new ed. [London: J. Nichols, 1812–1817] 26:493).

act of truth or heroism seems at once to draw to itself the sky as its temple, the sun as its candle. Nature stretches out her arms to embrace man, only let his thoughts be of equal greatness. Willingly does she follow his steps with the rose and the violet, and bend her lines of grandeur and grace to the decoration of her darling child. Only let his thoughts be of equal scope, and the frame will suit the picture. A virtuous man is in unison with her works, and makes the central figure of the visible sphere. Homer, Pindar,[15] Socrates, Phocion,[16] associate themselves fitly in our memory with the geography and climate of Greece. The visible heavens and earth sympathize with Jesus. And in common life whosoever has seen a person of powerful character and happy genius, will have remarked how easily he took all things along with him,— the persons, the opinions, and the day, and nature became ancillary to a man.

3. There is still another aspect under which the beauty of the world may be viewed, namely, as it becomes an object of the intellect. Beside the relation of things to virtue, they have a relation to thought. The intellect searches out the absolute order of things as they stand in the mind of God, and without the colors of affection. The intellectual and the active powers seem to succeed each other, and the exclusive activity of the one generates the exclusive activity of the other. There is something unfriendly in each to the other, but they are like the alternate periods of feeding and working in animals; each prepares and will be followed by the other. Therefore does beauty, which, in relation to actions, as we have seen, comes unsought, and comes because it is unsought, remain for the apprehension and pursuit of the intellect; and then again, in its turn, of the active power. Nothing divine dies. All good is eternally reproductive. The beauty of nature reforms itself in the mind, and not for barren contemplation, but for new creation.

All men are in some degree impressed by the face of the world; some men even to delight. This love of beauty is Taste. Others have the same love in such excess, that, not content with admiring, they seek to embody it in new forms. The creation of beauty is Art.

The production of a work of art throws a light upon the mystery of humanity. A work of art is an abstract or epitome of the world. It is the result or expression of nature, in miniature. For although the works of nature are innumerable and all different, the result or the expression of them all is similar and single. Nature is a sea of forms radically alike and even unique. A leaf, a sunbeam, a landscape, the ocean, make an analogous impression on the mind. What is common to them all,—that perfectness and harmony, is beauty. The standard of beauty is the entire circuit of natural forms,—the totality of nature; which the Italians expressed by defining beauty "il più nell' uno."[17] Nothing is quite beautiful alone; nothing but is beautiful in the whole. A single object is only so far beautiful as it

---

[15]Pindar (518?–438? B.C.) is considered by many the greatest lyric poet of ancient Greece.

[16]Phocion (402?–318 B.C.) was an Athenian general who fought successfully against Philip of Macedon and later urged peace. When the surrender of his Athenian opponent Demosthenes was demanded by Alexander the Great, Phocion—with his embassy—made a successful plea for a resolution of the problem without the surrender that the Athenians refused.

[17]Literally, the more (or many) in one, or in Samuel Taylor Coleridge's translation, the "multitude in unity." Emerson's source for this phrase, which he often used, was Henry Nelson Coleridge, ed., *Specimens of the Table Talk of the Late Samuel Taylor Coleridge* (New York: Harper, 1835) 2:11.

suggests this universal grace. The poet, the painter, the sculptor, the musician, the architect, seek each to concentrate this radiance of the world on one point, and each in his several work to satisfy the love of beauty which stimulates him to produce. Thus is Art a nature passed through the alembic of man. Thus in art does Nature work through the will of a man filled with the beauty of her first works.

The world thus exists to the soul to satisfy the desire of beauty. This element I call an ultimate end. No reason can be asked or given why the soul seeks beauty. Beauty, in its largest and profoundest sense, is one expression for the universe. God is the all-fair. Truth, and goodness, and beauty, are but different faces of the same All.[18] But beauty in nature is not ultimate. It is the herald of inward and eternal beauty, and is not alone a solid and satisfactory good. It must stand as a part, and not as yet the last or highest expression of the final cause of Nature.

IV
LANGUAGE

LANGUAGE is a third use which Nature subserves to man. Nature is the vehicle of thought, and in a simple, double, and threefold degree.

1. Words are signs of natural facts.
2. Particular natural facts are symbols of particular spiritual facts.
3. Nature is the symbol of spirit.[19]

---

[18]The Ideas of the Good, the True, and the Beautiful form a kind of Platonic trinity. For Plato, the Idea of the Good was supreme (*Republic*), but he also viewed the path to the Ideal world as an ascent to Beauty (*Symposium*) and a pilgrimage to Truth (*Phaedo*).

[19]Here and throughout this chapter Emerson employs the hieroglyphic interpretation of language and world. At the basis of the understanding was his appropriation of the ancient

1. Words are signs of natural facts. The use of natural history is to give us aid in supernatural history; the use of the outer creation, to give us language for the beings and changes of the inward creation. Every word which is used to express a moral or intellectual fact, if traced to its root, is found to be borrowed from some material appearance. *Right* means *straight; wrong* means *twisted. Spirit* primarily means *wind; transgression,* the crossing of a *line; supercilious,* the *raising of the eyebrow*. We say the *heart* to express emotion, the *head* to denote thought; and *thought* and *emotion* are words borrowed from sensible things, and now appropriated to spiritual nature. Most of the process by which this transformation is made, is hidden from us in the remote time when language was framed; but the same tendency may be daily observed in children. Children and savages use only nouns or names of things, which they convert into verbs, and apply to analogous mental acts.

2. But this origin of all words that convey a spiritual import,—so conspicuous a fact in the history of language,—is our least debt to nature. It is not words only that are emblematic; it is things which are emblematic. Every natural fact is a symbol of some spiritual fact. Every appearance in nature corresponds to some state of the mind, and that state of the mind can only be described by presenting that natural appearance as its picture. An enraged man is a lion, a cunning man is a fox, a firm man is a rock, a learned man is a torch. A lamb is innocence; a snake is subtle spite; flowers express to us the delicate affections.

---

doctrine of correspondence, especially as articulated at this time by the Swedenborgians. In the long passage that follows, Emerson's reference to the language of ''savages'' reveals nineteenth-century understandings of nonliterate cultures and their speech patterns.

Light and darkness are our familiar expression for knowledge and ignorance; and heat for love. Visible distance behind and before us, is respectively our image of memory and hope.

Who looks upon a river in a meditative hour and is not reminded of the flux of all things? Throw a stone into the stream, and the circles that propagate themselves are the beautiful type of all influence. Man is conscious of a universal soul within or behind his individual life, wherein, as in a firmament, the natures of Justice, Truth, Love, Freedom, arise and shine. This universal soul he calls Reason: it is not mine, or thine, or his, but we are its; we are its property and men. And the blue sky in which the private earth is buried, the sky with its eternal calm, and full of everlasting orbs, is the type of Reason. That which intellectually considered we call Reason, considered in relation to nature, we call Spirit. Spirit is the Creator. Spirit hath life in itself. And man in all ages and countries embodies it in his language as the FATHER.

It is easily seen that there is nothing lucky or capricious in these analogies, but that they are constant, and pervade nature. These are not the dreams of a few poets, here and there, but man is an analogist, and studies relations in all objects. He is placed in the centre of beings, and a ray of relation passes from every other being to him. And neither can man be understood without these objects, nor these objects without man. All the facts in natural history taken by themselves, have no value, but are barren, like a single sex. But marry it to human history, and it is full of life. Whole floras, all Linnæus' and Buffon's volumes, are dry catalogues of facts;[20] but the most trivial of these facts, the habit of a plant, the organs, or work, or noise of an insect, applied to the illustration of a fact in intellectual philosophy, or in any way associated to human nature, affects us in the most lively and agreeable manner. The seed of a plant,—to what affecting analogies in the nature of man is that little fruit made use of, in all discourse, up to the voice of Paul, who calls the human corpse a seed,—"It is sown a natural body; it is raised a spiritual body."[21] The motion of the earth round its axis and round the sun, makes the day and the year. These are certain amounts of brute light and heat. But is there no intent of an analogy between man's life and the seasons? And do the seasons gain no grandeur or pathos from that analogy? The instincts of the ant are very unimportant considered as the ant's; but the moment a ray of relation is seen to extend from it to man, and the little drudge is seen to be a monitor, a little body with a mighty heart, then all its habits, even that said to be recently observed, that it never sleeps, become sublime.

Because of this radical correspondence between visible things and human thoughts, savages, who have only what is necessary, converse in figures. As we go back in history, language becomes more picturesque, until its infancy, when it is all poetry; or all spiritual facts are represented by natural symbols. The same symbols are found to make the original elements of all languages. It has moreover been observed, that the idioms of all languages approach each other in passages of the greatest elo-

---

[20]Carolus (Carl) Linnaeus (1707–1778), author of the *Systema naturae* (1735), was the Swedish botanist and taxonomist who originated the modern scientific system of classification for animals and plants. Georges-Louis Leclerc, comte de Buffon (1707–1788), was a French naturalist and author (with others) of the popular *Histoire naturelle* (1749–1804), in forty-four volumes.

[21]1 Cor. 15:44.

quence and power. And as this is the first language, so is it the last. This immediate dependence of language upon nature, this conversion of an outward phenomenon into a type of somewhat in human life, never loses its power to affect us. It is this which gives that piquancy to the conversation of a strong-natured farmer or backwoodsman, which all men relish.

A man's power to connect his thought with its proper symbol, and so to utter it, depends on the simplicity of his character, that is, upon his love of truth and his desire to communicate it without loss. The corruption of man is followed by the corruption of language. When simplicity of character and the sovereignty of ideas is broken up by the prevalence of secondary desires,—the desire of riches, of pleasure, of power, and of praise,—and duplicity and falsehood take place of simplicity and truth, the power over nature as an interpreter of the will is in a degree lost; new imagery ceases to be created, and old words are perverted to stand for things which are not; a paper currency is employed, when there is no bullion in the vaults. In due time the fraud is manifest, and words lose all power to stimulate the understanding or the affections. Hundreds of writers may be found in every long-civilized nation who for a short time believe and make others believe that they see and utter truths, who do not of themselves clothe one thought in its natural garment, but who feed unconsciously on the language created by the primary writers of the country, those, namely, who hold primarily on nature.

But wise men pierce this rotten diction and fasten words again to visible things; so that picturesque language is at once a commanding certificate that he who employs it is a man in alliance with truth and God. The moment our discourse rises above the ground line of familiar facts and is inflamed with passion or exalted by thought, it clothes itself in images. A man conversing in earnest, if he watch his intellectual processes, will find that a material image more or less luminous arises in his mind, contemporaneous with every thought, which furnishes the vestment of the thought. Hence, good writing and brilliant discourse are perpetual allegories. This imagery is spontaneous. It is the blending of experience with the present action of the mind. It is proper creation. It is the working of the Original Cause through the instruments he has already made.

These facts may suggest the advantage which the country-life possesses, for a powerful mind, over the artificial and curtailed life of cities. We know more from nature than we can at will communicate. Its light flows into the mind evermore, and we forget its presence. The poet, the orator, bred in the woods, whose senses have been nourished by their fair and appeasing changes, year after year, without design and without heed,—shall not lose their lesson altogether, in the roar of cities or the broil of politics. Long hereafter, amidst agitation and terror in national councils,—in the hour of revolution,—these solemn images shall reappear in their morning lustre, as fit symbols and words of the thoughts which the passing events shall awaken. At the call of a noble sentiment, again the woods wave, the pines murmur, the river rolls and shines, and the cattle low upon the mountains, as he saw and heard them in his infancy. And with these forms, the spells of persuasion, the keys of power are put into his hands.

3. We are thus assisted by natural objects in the expression of particular meanings. But how great a language to convey such pepper-corn informations! Did it need such noble races of creatures, this profusion of forms, this host of orbs in heaven, to furnish man with the dictionary and grammar of his municipal speech? Whilst

we use this grand cipher to expedite the affairs of our pot and kettle, we feel that we have not yet put it to its use, neither are able. We are like travellers using the cinders of a volcano to roast their eggs. Whilst we see that it always stands ready to clothe what we would say, we cannot avoid the question whether the characters are not significant of themselves. Have mountains, and waves, and skies, no significance but what we consciously give them when we employ them as emblems of our thoughts? The world is emblematic. Parts of speech are metaphors, because the whole of nature is a metaphor of the human mind. The laws of moral nature answer to those of matter as face to face in a glass. "The visible world and the relation of its parts, is the dial plate of the invisible."[22] The axioms of physics translate the laws of ethics. Thus, "the whole is greater than its part;" "reaction is equal to action;" "the smallest weight may be made to lift the greatest, the difference of weight being compensated by time;" and many the like propositions, which have an ethical as well as physical sense. These propositions have a much more extensive and universal sense when applied to human life, than when confined to technical use.

In like manner, the memorable words of history and the proverbs of nations consist usually of a natural fact, selected as a picture or parable of a moral truth. Thus; A rolling stone gathers no moss; A bird in the hand is worth two in the bush; A cripple in the right way will beat a racer in the wrong; Make hay while the sun shines; 'T is hard to carry a full cup even; Vinegar is the son of wine; The last ounce broke the camel's back; Long-lived trees make roots first;— and the like. In their primary sense these are trivial facts, but we repeat them for the value of their analogical import. What is true of proverbs, is true of all fables, parables, and allegories.

This relation between the mind and matter is not fancied by some poet, but stands in the will of God, and so is free to be known by all men. It appears to men, or it does not appear.[23] When in fortunate hours we ponder this miracle, the wise man doubts if at all other times he is not blind and deaf;

> "Can such things be,
> And overcome us like a summer's cloud,
> Without our special wonder?"[24]

for the universe becomes transparent, and the light of higher laws than its own shines through it. It is the standing problem which has exercised the wonder and the study of every fine genius since the world began; from the era of the Egyptians and the Brahmins[25] to that of Pythagoras,[26] of

---

[22]This quotation from Emanuel Swedenborg was used by Samuel Sandels in "Emanuel Swedenborg," *The New Jerusalem Magazine* 5 (July 1832): 437. It suggests, of course, the future title of the Transcendentalist journal *The Dial*.

[23]This line is from Plotinus *Enneads* 5.5, as quoted in Samuel Taylor Coleridge, *Biographia Literaria* (New York: Leavitt, Lord, 1834) 144-45.

[24]William Shakespeare, *Macbeth,* act 3, sc. 4, ll. 110-12.

[25]The Brahmins (alternatively Brahmans) are the highest and priestly caste in India, who could interpret the sacred books of the Vedas and offer the Vedic fire sacrifice of Hinduism. With the Vedas compiled roughly from 1400 B.C. to 500 B.C., Emerson is here referring to an ancient period.

[26]Pythagoras (582?–507? B.C.) was a pre-Socratic Greek philosopher who founded a secret society known for its doctrine of the transmigration of souls and for its mystical understanding of numbers as the real essence of things.

Plato, of Bacon,[27] of Leibnitz,[28] of Swedenborg. There sits the Sphinx at the roadside, and from age to age, as each prophet comes by, he tries his fortune at reading her riddle.[29] There seems to be a necessity in spirit to manifest itself in material forms; and day and night, river and storm, beast and bird, acid and alkali, preëxist in necessary Ideas in the mind of God, and are what they are by virtue of preceding affections in the world of spirit. A Fact is the end or last issue of spirit. The visible creation is the terminus or the circumference of the invisible world. "Material objects," said a French philosopher, "are necessarily kinds of *scoriæ* of the substantial thoughts of the Creator, which must always preserve an exact relation to their first origin; in other words, visible nature must have a spiritual and moral side."[30]

This doctrine is abstruse, and though the images of "garment," "scoriæ," "mirror," etc., may stimulate the fancy, we must summon the aid of subtler and more vital expositors to make it plain. "Every scripture is to be interpreted by the same spirit which gave it forth,"—is the fundamental law of criticism.[31] A life in harmony with Nature, the love of truth and of virtue, will purge the eyes to understand her text. By degrees we may come to know the primitive sense of the permanent objects of nature, so that the world shall be to us an open book, and every form significant of its hidden life and final cause.

A new interest surprises us, whilst, under the view now suggested, we contemplate the fearful extent and multitude of objects; since "every object rightly seen, unlocks a new faculty of the soul."[32] That

---

[27]Here Emerson may mean Roger Bacon (1214?–1294?), the English Franciscan scientist and scholastic philosopher who was greatly interested in alchemy and reputed for his learning in magic. Or, more likely, Emerson may mean Francis Bacon (1561–1626), the English essayist, philosopher, and statesman whose *Novum Organum* (1620) is the classical argument for the inductive method of science.

[28]Gottfried Wilhelm, Baron von Leibniz (1646–1716), was a German philosopher and mathematician who taught that the ultimate elements in the universe were immaterial monads acted upon according to a principle of preestablished harmony.

[29]The Greeks appropriated the Sphinx from Egypt and made of the representation a winged creature with the upper torso of a woman and the body of a lion. In the Oedipus legend she killed those who could not solve her baffling riddle until, when Oedipus resolved it, she committed suicide.

[30]The French philosopher is Guillaume Oegger (fl. 1800?–1855?), a professor of philosophy and vicar of Notre Dame in Paris who eventually left the church. Oegger, a Swedenborgian with a number of religiophilosophical publications, explored a mystical and metaphysical Christianity that emphasized symbolic themes. The material Emerson uses here may be found in G. Oegger, *The True Messiah; or, The Old and New Testaments, Examined according to the Principles of the Language of Nature,* trans. E. P. Peabody (Boston: E. P. Peabody, 1842) 5, a translation of the introductory section of Oegger's muchlonger work, *Le Vrai Messie,* published in Paris in 1829. Emerson had probably read Oegger in Elizabeth Palmer Peabody's manuscript translation. I am indebted to Pierre Horn of the Modern Languages Department at Wright State University for his assistance in identifying Oegger.

[31]The line is from George Fox (1624–1691), the founder of the Quakers, as quoted in William Sewel, *The History of the Rise, Increase, and Progress of the Christian People Called Quakers* (Philadelphia: Benjamin & Thomas Kite, 1823) 1:115.

[32]Emerson is quoting Samuel Taylor Coleridge, *Aids to Reflection,* ed. James Marsh (Burlington VT: C. Goodrich, 1829) 150-51.

which was unconscious truth, becomes, when interpreted and defined in an object, a part of the domain of knowledge,—a new weapon in the magazine of power.

V
DISCIPLINE

IN view of the significance of nature, we arrive at once at a new fact, that nature is a discipline. This use of the world includes the preceding uses, as parts of itself.

Space, time, society, labor, climate, food, locomotion, the animals, the mechanical forces, give us sincerest lessons, day by day, whose meaning is unlimited. They educate both the Understanding and the Reason.[33] Every property of matter is a school for the understanding,—its solidity or resistance, its inertia, its extension, its figure, its divisibility. The understanding adds, divides, combines, measures, and finds nutriment and room for its activity in this worthy scene. Meantime, Reason transfers all these lessons into its own world of thought, by perceiving the analogy that marries Matter and Mind.

1. Nature is a discipline of the understanding in intellectual truths. Our dealing with sensible objects is a constant exercise in the necessary lessons of difference, of likeness, of order, of being and seeming, of progressive arrangement; of ascent from particular to general; of combination to one end of manifold forces. Proportioned to the importance of the organ to be formed, is the extreme care with which its tuition is provided,—a care pretermitted in no single case. What tedious training, day after day, year after year, never ending, to form the common sense; what continual reproduction of annoyances, inconveniences, dilemmas; what rejoicing over us of little men; what disputing of prices, what reckonings of interest,—and all to form the Hand of the mind;—to instruct us that "good thoughts are no better than good dreams, unless they be executed!"[34]

The same good office is performed by Property and its filial systems of debt and credit. Debt, grinding debt, whose iron face the widow, the orphan, and the sons of genius fear and hate;—debt, which consumes so much time, which so cripples and disheartens a great spirit with cares that seem so base, is a preceptor whose lessons cannot be foregone, and is needed most by those who suffer from it most. Moreover, property, which has been well compared to snow,—"if it fall level to-day, it will be blown into drifts to-morrow,"—is the surface action of internal machinery, like the index on the face of a clock. Whilst now it is the gymnastics of the understanding, it is hiving, in the foresight of the spirit, experience in profounder laws.

The whole character and fortune of the individual are affected by the least inequalities in the culture of the understanding; for example, in the perception of differences. Therefore is Space, and therefore Time, that man may know that things are not huddled and lumped, but sundered and individual. A bell and a plough have each their use, and neither can do the office of the other. Water is good to drink, coal to burn, wool to wear; but wool cannot be drunk, nor water spun, nor coal eaten. The wise man shows his wisdom in

---

[33]Emerson here follows Coleridge's *Aids to Reflection,* as glossed by Marsh, in a distinction between the Understanding and the Reason. (See the introduction to this volume.)

[34]This is a close paraphrase of a line from Francis Bacon's essay "Of Great Place," in his *Essays* (1597). See Francis Bacon, *The Works of Francis Bacon, with a Life of the Author by Basil Montagu* (Philadelphia: M. Murphy, 1876) 1:19. For "pretermitted" (above in the text), read "neglected."

separation, in gradation, and his scale of creatures and of merits is as wide as nature. The foolish have no range in their scale, but suppose every man is as every other man. What is not good they call the worst, and what is not hateful, they call the best.

In like manner, what good heed Nature forms in us! She pardons no mistakes. Her yea is yea, and her nay, nay.

The first steps in Agriculture, Astronomy, Zoölogy (those first steps which the farmer, the hunter, and the sailor take), teach that Nature's dice are always loaded; that in her heaps and rubbish are concealed sure and useful results.

How calmly and genially the mind apprehends one after another the laws of physics! What noble emotions dilate the mortal as he enters into the councils of the creation, and feels by knowledge the privilege to BE! His insight refines him. The beauty of nature shines in his own breast. Man is greater that he can see this, and the universe less, because Time and Space relations vanish as laws are known.

Here again we are impressed and even daunted by the immense Universe to be explored. "What we know is a point to what we do not know."[35] Open any recent journal of science, and weigh the problems suggested concerning Light, Heat, Electricity, Magnetism, Physiology, Geology, and judge whether the interest of natural science is likely to be soon exhausted.

Passing by many particulars of the discipline of nature, we must not omit to specify two.

The exercise of the Will, or the lesson of power, is taught in every event. From the child's successive possession of his several senses up to the hour when he saith, "Thy will be done!"[36] he is learning the secret that he can reduce under his will not only particular events but great classes, nay, the whole series of events, and so conform all facts to his character. Nature is thoroughly mediate. It is made to serve. It receives the dominion of man as meekly as the ass on which the Saviour rode. It offers all its kingdoms to man as the raw material which he may mould into what is useful. Man is never weary of working it up. He forges the subtile and delicate air into wise and melodious words, and gives them wing as angels of persuasion and command. One after another his victorious thought comes up with and reduces all things, until the world becomes at last only a realized will,—the double of the man.

2. Sensible objects conform to the premonitions of Reason and reflect the conscience. All things are moral; and in their boundless changes have an unceasing reference to spiritual nature. Therefore is nature glorious with form, color, and motion; that every globe in the remotest heaven, every chemical change from the rudest crystal up to the laws of life, every change of vegetation from the first principle of growth in the eye of a leaf, to the tropical forest and antediluvian coal-mine, every animal function from the sponge up to Hercules, shall hint or thunder to man the laws of right and wrong, and echo the Ten Commandments. Therefore is Nature ever the ally of Religion: lends all her pomp and riches to the religious sentiment. Prophet and priest, David, Isaiah, Jesus, have drawn deeply from this source. This ethical character so penetrates the bone and

---

[35]This is a paraphrase of a quotation from Bishop Joseph Butler (1692–1752), author of *The Analogy of Religion* (1736). Emerson took the quotation from Robert Plumer Ward's novel *Tremaine; or, The Man of Refinement* (Philadelphia: E. Littell, 1825) 3:125-26.

[36]See Matt. 6:10 and, especially, 26:42.

marrow of nature, as to seem the end for which it was made. Whatever private purpose is answered by any member or part, this is its public and universal function, and is never omitted. Nothing in nature is exhausted in its first use. When a thing has served an end to the uttermost, it is wholly new for an ulterior service. In God, every end is converted into a new means. Thus the use of commodity, regarded by itself, is mean and squalid. But it is to the mind an education in the doctrine of Use, namely, that a thing is good only so far as it serves; that a conspiring of parts and efforts to the production of an end is essential to any being. The first and gross manifestation of this truth is our inevitable and hated training in values and wants, in corn and meat.[37]

It has already been illustrated, that every natural process is a version of a moral sentence. The moral law lies at the centre of nature and radiates to the circumference. It is the pith and marrow of every substance, every relation, and every process. All things with which we deal, preach to us. What is a farm but a mute gospel? The chaff and the wheat, weeds and plants, blight, rain, insects, sun,—it is a sacred emblem from the first furrow of spring to the last stack which the snow of winter overtakes in the fields. But the sailor, the shepherd, the miner, the merchant, in their several resorts, have each an experience precisely parallel, and leading to the same conclusion: because all organizations are radically alike. Nor can it be doubted that this moral sentiment which thus scents the air, grows in the grain, and impregnates the waters of the world, is caught by man and sinks into his soul. The moral influence of nature upon every individual is that amount of truth which it illustrates to him. Who can estimate this? Who can guess how much firmness the sea-beaten rock has taught the fisherman? how much tranquillity has been reflected to man from the azure sky, over whose unspotted deeps the winds forevermore drive flocks of stormy clouds, and leave no wrinkle or stain? how much industry and providence and affection we have caught from the pantomime of brutes? What a searching preacher of self-command is the varying phenomenon of Health!

Herein is especially apprehended the unity of Nature,—the unity in variety,—which meets us everywhere. All the endless variety of things make an identical impression. Xenophanes complained in his old age, that, look where he would, all things hastened back to Unity.[38] He was weary of seeing the same entity in the tedious variety of forms. The fable of Proteus has a cordial truth.[39] A leaf, a drop, a crystal, a moment of time, is related to the whole, and partakes of the perfection of the whole. Each particle is a microcosm, and faithfully renders the likeness of the world.

---

[37]This is a version of the Platonic doctrine of the ascent of the soul from the gross to the Ideal, as in the *Symposium,* in which Socrates argues from the love of beautiful bodies to the love of Beauty.

[38]Xenophanes (570?–480? B.C.), a pre-Socratic Greek philosopher, taught that there was only one God, an eternal and unchanging being who was also closely connected with this world. These ideas probably constituted a doctrine of pantheism. According to Edward Waldo Emerson, his father's notions of the One and the All ("Each and All") were derived from Xenophanes. See Ralph Waldo Emerson, *The Complete Works of Ralph Waldo Emerson,* ed. Edward Waldo Emerson, centenary ed. (Boston: Houghton, Mifflin, 1903–1904) 1:409-10.

[39]An account of Proteus, the immortal Egyptian man of the sea who could assume different shapes, is given in Homer *Odyssey* 4.384-570. When compelled to be truthful, Proteus returned to his proper shape.

Not only resemblances exist in things whose analogy is obvious, as when we detect the type of the human hand in the flipper of the fossil saurus, but also in objects wherein there is great superficial unlikeness. Thus architecture is called "frozen music," by DeStaël and Goethe. Vitruvius thought an architect should be a musician.[40] "A Gothic church," said Coleridge, "is a petrified religion."[41] Michael Angelo maintained, that, to an architect, a knowledge of anatomy is essential. In Haydn's oratorios, the notes present to the imagination not only motions, as of the snake, the stag, and the elephant, but colors also; as the green grass. The law of harmonic sounds reappears in the harmonic colors. The granite is differenced in its laws only by the more or less of heat from the river that wears it away. The river, as it flows, resembles the air that flows over it; the air resembles the light which traverses it with more subtle currents; the light resembles the heat which rides with it through Space. Each creature is only a modification of the other; the likeness in them is more than the difference, and their radical law is one and the same. A rule of one art, or a law of one organization, holds true throughout nature. So intimate is this Unity, that, it is easily seen, it lies under the undermost garment of Nature, and betrays its source in Universal Spirit. For it pervades Thought also. Every universal truth which we express in words, implies or supposes every other truth. *Omne verum vero consonat.*[42] It is like a great circle on a sphere, comprising all possible circles; which, however, may be drawn and comprise it in like manner. Every such truth is the absolute Ens[43] seen from one side. But it has innumerable sides.

The central Unity is still more conspicuous in actions. Words are finite organs of the infinite mind. They cannot cover the dimensions of what is in truth. They break, chop, and impoverish it. An action is the perfection and publication of thought. A right action seems to fill the eye, and to be related to all nature. "The wise man, in doing one thing, does all; or, in the one thing he does rightly, he sees the likeness of all which is done rightly."[44]

Words and actions are not the attri-

---

[40]Madame Germaine de Staël (1766–1817) was a French-Swiss writer whose Paris salon became a center of French political and intellectual life; Johann Wolfgang von Goethe (1749–1832) was, of course, the German poet, novelist, and dramatist who became a leader in the Romantic movement; Marcus Vitruvius Pollio, who lived in the late first century B.C. and the early first century A.D., was a Roman writer on architecture who also worked as an engineer and architect for the emperor Augustus. In his journals, Emerson traced the quotation from Madame de Staël (*Corinne, ou l'Italie,* bk. 4, ch. 3) to, in a variant form, Goethe (*Gespräche mit Eckermann,* 23 March 1829), and ultimately, in much different language, to Vitruvius (*Of Architecture,* bk. 1, ch. 1). See Ralph Waldo Emerson, *The Journals and Miscellaneous Notebooks of Ralph Waldo Emerson,* ed. William H. Gilman et al. (Cambridge: Harvard University Press, Belknap Press, 1960–) 4 (16 November 1834): 337; 6 (1834?): 226, and note.

[41]Robert Spiller offers no information on the source of the quotation from Samuel Taylor Coleridge, and I have been unable to locate it independently.

[42]Literally, every truth accords to truth.

[43]Latin philosophical term for "being."

[44]This is a close paraphrase of material from Thomas Carlyle's translation of Goethe's *Wilhelm Meister's Travels,* ch. 6. For the source, see Thomas Carlyle, *The Works of Thomas Carlyle,* ed. H. D. Traill, centenary ed. (London: Chapman and Hall, 1896–1899) 24:228.

butes of brute nature. They introduce us to the human form, of which all other organizations appear to be degradations. When this appears among so many that surround it, the spirit prefers it to all others. It says, "From such as this have I drawn joy and knowledge; in such as this have I found and beheld myself; I will speak to it; it can speak again; it can yield me thought already formed and alive." In fact, the eye,—the mind,—is always accompanied by these forms, male and female; and these are incomparably the richest informations of the power and order that lie at the heart of things. Unfortunately every one of them bears the marks as of some injury; is marred and superficially defective. Nevertheless, far different from the deaf and dumb nature around them, these all rest like fountain-pipes on the unfathomed sea of thought and virtue whereto they alone, of all organizations, are the entrances.

It were a pleasant inquiry to follow into detail their ministry to our education, but where would it stop? We are associated in adolescent and adult life with some friends, who, like skies and waters, are coextensive with our idea; who, answering each to a certain affection of the soul, satisfy our desire on that side; whom we lack power to put at such focal distance from us, that we can mend or even analyze them. We cannot choose but love them. When much intercourse with a friend has supplied us with a standard of excellence, and has increased our respect for the resources of God who thus sends a real person to outgo our ideal; when he has, moreover, become an object of thought, and, whilst his character retains all its unconscious effect, is converted in the mind into solid and sweet wisdom,—it is a sign to us that his office is closing, and he is commonly withdrawn from our sight in a short time.[45]

VI
IDEALISM

THUS is the unspeakable but intelligible and practicable meaning of the world conveyed to man, the immortal pupil, in every object of sense. To this one end of Discipline, all parts of nature conspire.

A noble doubt perpetually suggests itself,—whether this end be not the Final Cause of the Universe; and whether nature outwardly exists. It is a sufficient account of that Appearance we call the World, that God will teach a human mind, and so makes it the receiver of a certain number of congruent sensations, which we call sun and moon, man and woman, house and trade. In my utter impotence to test the authenticity of the report of my senses, to know whether the impressions they make on me correspond with outlying objects, what difference does it make, whether Orion is up there in heaven,[46] or some god paints the image in the firmament of the soul? The relations of parts and the end of the whole remaining the same, what is the difference, whether land and sea interact, and worlds revolve and intermingle without number or end,—deep yawning under deep, and galaxy balancing galaxy, throughout absolute space,—or whether, without relations of time and space, the same appearances are inscribed in the constant faith of man? Whether nature enjoy a substantial existence without, or is only in the apocalypse of the mind, it is alike useful and alike venerable to me. Be it what it may, it is ideal to me so long as I cannot try the accuracy of my senses.

The frivolous make themselves merry

---

[45]Edward Waldo Emerson here recalls the deaths of Emerson's brothers, Edward Bliss Emerson and Charles Chauncy Emerson, both within two years previous to *Nature's* publication. See Emerson, *Complete Works,* 1:410.

[46]The constellation on the celestial equator.

with the Ideal theory, as if its consequences were burlesque; as if it affected the stability of nature. It surely does not. God never jests with us, and will not compromise the end of nature by permitting any inconsequence in its procession. Any distrust of the permanence of laws would paralyze the faculties of man. Their permanence is sacredly respected, and his faith therein is perfect. The wheels and springs of man are all set to the hypothesis of the permanence of nature. We are not built like a ship to be tossed, but like a house to stand. It is a natural consequence of this structure, that so long as the active powers predominate over the reflective, we resist with indignation any hint that nature is more short-lived or mutable than spirit. The broker, the wheelwright, the carpenter, the tollman, are much displeased at the intimation.

But whilst we acquiesce entirely in the permanence of natural laws, the question of the absolute existence of nature still remains open. It is the uniform effect of culture on the human mind, not to shake our faith in the stability of particular phenomena, as of heat, water, azote;[47] but to lead us to regard nature as phenomenon, not a substance; to attribute necessary existence to spirit; to esteem nature as an accident and an effect.

To the senses and the unrenewed understanding, belongs a sort of instinctive belief in the absolute existence of nature. In their view man and nature are indissolubly joined. Things are ultimates, and they never look beyond their sphere. The presence of Reason mars this faith. The first effort of thought tends to relax this despotism of the senses which binds us to nature as if we were a part of it, and shows us nature aloof, and, as it were, afloat. Until this higher agency intervened, the animal eye sees, with wonderful accuracy, sharp outlines and colored surfaces. When the eye of Reason opens, to outline and surface are at once added grace and expression. These proceed from imagination and affection, and abate somewhat of the angular distinctness of objects. If the Reason be stimulated to more earnest vision, outlines and surfaces become transparent, and are no longer seen; causes and spirits are seen through them. The best moments of life are these delicious awakenings of the higher powers, and the reverential withdrawing of nature before its God.

Let us proceed to indicate the effects of culture.

1. Our first institution in the Ideal philosophy is a hint from Nature herself.

Nature is made to conspire with spirit to emancipate us. Certain mechanical changes, a small alteration in our local position, apprizes us of a dualism. We are strangely affected by seeing the shore from a moving ship, from a balloon, or through the tints of an unusual sky. The least change in our point of view gives the whole world a pictorial air. A man who seldom rides, needs only to get into a coach and traverse his own town, to turn the street into a puppet-show. The men, the women,—talking, running, bartering, fighting,—the earnest mechanic, the lounger, the beggar, the boys, the dogs, are unrealized at once, or, at least, wholly detached from all relation to the observer, and seen as apparent, not substantial beings. What new thoughts are suggested by seeing a face of country quite familiar, in the rapid movement of the railroad car! Nay, the most wonted objects, (make a very slight change in the point of vision,) please us most. In a camera obscura, the butcher's cart, and the figure of one of our own family amuse us. So a portrait of a well-known face gratifies us. Turn the eyes upside down, by looking

---

[47]Former term for nitrogen.

at the landscape through your legs, and how agreeable is the picture, though you have seen it any time these twenty years!

In these cases, by mechanical means, is suggested the difference between the observer and the spectacle—between man and nature. Hence arises a pleasure mixed with awe; I may say, a low degree of the sublime is felt, from the fact, probably, that man is hereby apprized that whilst the world is a spectacle, something in himself is stable.

2. In a higher manner the poet communicates the same pleasure. By a few strokes he delineates, as on air, the sun, the mountain, the camp, the city, the hero, the maiden, not different from what we know them, but only lifted from the ground and afloat before the eye. He unfixes the land and the sea, makes them revolve around the axis of his primary thought, and disposes them anew. Possessed himself by a heroic passion, he uses matter as symbols of it. The sensual man conforms thoughts to things; the poet conforms things to his thoughts. The one esteems nature as rooted and fast; the other, as fluid, and impresses his being thereon. To him, the refractory world is ductile and flexible; he invests dusts and stones with humanity, and makes them the words of the Reason. The Imagination may be defined to be the use which the Reason makes of the material world.[48]

Shakspeare possesses the power of subordinating nature for the purposes of expression, beyond all poets. His imperial muse tosses the creation like a bauble from hand to hand, and uses it to embody any caprice of thought that is uppermost in his mind. The remotest spaces of nature are visited, and the farthest sundered things are brought together, by a subtle spiritual connection. We are made aware that magnitude of material things is relative, and all objects shrink and expand to serve the passion of the poet. Thus in his sonnets, the lays of birds, the scents and dyes of flowers he finds to be the *shadow* of his beloved; time, which keeps her from him, is his *chest;* the suspicion she has awakened, is her *ornament*;

> The ornament of beauty is Suspect,
> A crow which flies in heaven's sweetest
>   air.[49]

His passion is not the fruit of chance; it swells, as he speaks, to a city, or a state.

> No, it was builded far from accident;
> It suffers not in smiling pomp, nor falls
> Under the brow of thralling discontent;
> It fears not policy, that heretic,
> That works on leases of short numbered
>   hours,
> But all alone stands hugely politic.[50]

In the strength of his constancy, the Pyramids seem to him recent and transitory. The freshness of youth and love dazzles him with its resemblance to morning;

> Take those lips away
> Which so sweetly were forsworn;

---

[48]Emerson here follows Coleridge in a distinction between the Imagination and the Fancy parallel to that between the Reason and the Understanding. Imagination is the high faculty of the creative mind as it deals with the material world, seeing the whole in the parts and parts in the whole. Fancy is a lower faculty that builds patterns out of materials already made and juxtaposes, rather than unifies, images of the material world. For a discussion of the distinction and its development in Coleridge's thought, see Basil Willey, *Nineteenth-Century Studies: Coleridge to Matthew Arnold* (New York: Columbia University Press, 1949) 10-26.

[49]William Shakespeare, Sonnet 70, ll. 3-4. Emerson does not quote exactly but is very close.

[50]William Shakespeare, Sonnet 124, ll. 5-7, 9-11. Again, Emerson does not quote exactly.

And those eyes,—the break of day,
Lights that do mislead the morn.[51]

The wild beauty of this hyperbole, I may say in passing, it would not be easy to match in literature.

This transfiguration which all material objects undergo through the passion of the poet,—this power which he exerts to dwarf the great, to magnify the small,—might be illustrated by a thousand examples from his Plays. I have before me the Tempest, and will cite only these few lines.

> ARIEL. The strong based promontory
> Have I made shake, and by the spurs
>   plucked up
> The pine and cedar.[52]

Prospero calls for music to soothe the frantic Alonzo, and his companions;

> A solemn air, and the best comforter
> To an unsettled fancy, cure thy brains
> Now useless, boiled within thy skull.[53]

Again;

> The charm dissolves apace,
> And, as the morning steals upon the night,
> Melting the darkness, so their rising senses
> Begin to chase the ignorant fumes that
>   mantle
> Their clearer reason.
>   Their understanding
> Begins to swell: and the approaching tide
> Will shortly fill the reasonable shores
> That now lie foul and muddy.[54]

The perception of real affinities between events (that is to say, of *ideal* affinities, for those only are real), enables the poet thus to make free with the most imposing forms and phenomena of the world, and to assert the predominance of the soul.

3. Whilst thus the poet animates nature with his own thoughts, he differs from the philosopher only herein, that the one proposes Beauty as his main end; the other Truth. But the philosopher, not less than the poet, postpones the apparent order and relations of things to the empire of thought. "The problem of philosophy," according to Plato, "is, for all that exists conditionally, to find a ground unconditioned and absolute."[55] It proceeds on the faith that a law determines all phenomena, which being known, the phenomena can be predicted. That law, when in the mind, is an idea. Its beauty is infinite. The true philosopher and the true poet are one, and a beauty, which is truth, and a truth, which is beauty, is the aim of both. Is not the charm of one of Plato's or Aristotle's definitions strictly like that of the Antigone of Sophocles?[56] It is, in both cases, that a spiritual life has been imparted to nature; that the solid seeming block of matter has been pervaded and dissolved by a thought; that this feeble human being has pene-

---

[51] William Shakespeare, *Measure for Measure*, act 4, sc. 1, ll. 1-4. Still again, Emerson has come very close but has not quoted exactly.

[52] William Shakespeare, *The Tempest*, act 5, sc. 1, ll. 46-48. Emerson is in error in ascribing these lines to Ariel; they belong to the character Prospero. In his initial lecture on "Shakespear," Emerson made the correct attribution to Prospero. See Ralph Waldo Emerson, *The Early Lectures of Ralph Waldo Emerson*, ed. Stephen E. Whicher et al. (Cambridge: Harvard University Press, Belknap Press, 1966–1972) 1:292.

[53] William Shakespeare, *The Tempest*, act 5, sc. 1, ll. 58-60.

[54] See ibid., ll. 64-68, 79-82.

[55] This is an abbreviated and slightly altered version of a statement Emerson found in Samuel Taylor Coleridge, *The Friend*, 2d ed. (London: Rest Fenner, 1818) 3:158.

[56] Sophocles (496?–406 B.C.), the Greek tragic poet, composed the play *Antigone* around 441 B.C.

trated the vast masses of nature with an informing soul, and recognized itself in their harmony, that is, seized their law. In physics, when this is attained, the memory disburthens itself of its cumbrous catalogues of particulars, and carries centuries of observation in a single formula.

Thus even in physics, the material is degraded before the spiritual. The astronomer, the geometer, rely on their irrefragable analysis, and disdain the results of observation. The sublime remark of Euler on his law of arches, "This will be found contrary to all experience, yet is true;" had already transferred nature into the mind, and left matter like an outcast corpse.[57]

4. Intellectual science has been observed to beget invariably a doubt of the existence of matter. Turgot said, "He that has never doubted the existence of matter, may be assured he has no aptitude for metaphysical inquiries."[58] It fastens the attention upon immortal necessary uncreated natures, that is, upon Ideas; and in their presence we feel that the outward circumstance is a dream and a shade. Whilst we wait in this Olympus of gods, we think of nature as an appendix to the soul. We ascend into their region, and know that these are the thoughts of the Supreme Being. "These are they who were set up from everlasting, from the beginning, or ever the earth was. When he prepared the heavens, they were there; when he established the clouds above, when he strengthened the fountains of the deep. Then they were by him, as one brought up with him. Of them took he counsel."[59]

Their influence is proportionate. As objects of science they are accessible to few men. Yet all men are capable of being raised by piety or by passion, into their region. And no man touches these divine natures, without becoming, in some degree, himself divine. Like a new soul, they renew the body. We become physically nimble and lightsome; we tread on air; life is no longer irksome, and we think it will never be so. No man fears age or misfortune or death in their serene company, for he is transported out of the district of change. Whilst we behold unveiled the nature of Justice and Truth, we learn the difference between the absolute and the conditional or relative. We apprehend the absolute. As it were, for the first time, *we exist*. We become immortal, for we learn that time and space are relations of matter; that with a perception of truth or a virtuous will they have no affinity.

5. Finally, religion and ethics, which may be fitly called the practice of ideas, or the introduction of ideas into life, have an analogous effect with all lower culture, in degrading nature and suggesting its dependence on spirit. Ethics and religion differ herein; that the one is the system of human duties commencing from man; the other, from God. Religion includes the personality of God; Ethics does not. They are one

---

[57]Leonhard Euler (1707–1783) was a prolific Swiss mathematician who was one of the earliest broad developers of calculus. Emerson took Euler's remark from Coleridge, *Aids to Reflection*, 274, 295 (there were two variants).

[58]Anne Robert Jacques Turgot (1727–1781) was a French economist and statesman, comptroller general of finances in France from 1774 to 1776. Emerson probably took the quotation from a book review of Dugald Stewart's *Account of the Life and Writings of Thomas Reid* (1803) in the *Edinburgh Review* 3 (1803–1804): 273.

[59]The lines are a free transcription of Prov. 8:23, 27, 28, 30, with some omissions, and probably from memory. Emerson's most serious change is that he has altered the singular, which in the text refers to wisdom ("I was set up from everlasting," etc.), to the plural—to agree with the Ideas.

to our present design. They both put nature under foot. The first and last lesson of religion is, "The things that are seen, are temporal; the things that are unseen, are eternal."⁶⁰ It puts an affront upon nature. It does that for the unschooled, which philosophy does for Berkeley and Viasa.⁶¹ The uniform language that may be heard in the churches of the most ignorant sects is,— "Contemn the unsubstantial shows of the world; they are vanities, dreams, shadows, unrealities; seek the realities of religion." The devotee flouts nature. Some theosophists have arrived at a certain hostility and indignation towards matter, as the Manichean and Plotinus.⁶² They distrusted in themselves any looking back to these flesh-pots of Egypt.⁶³ Plotinus was ashamed of his body.⁶⁴ In short, they might all say of matter, what Michael Angelo said of external beauty, "It is the frail and weary weed, in which God dresses the soul which he has called into time."⁶⁵

It appears that motion, poetry, physical and intellectual science, and religion, all tend to affect our convictions of the reality of the external world. But I own there is something ungrateful in expanding too curiously the particulars of the general proposition, that all culture tends to imbue us with idealism. I have no hostility to nature, but a child's love to it. I expand and live in the warm day like corn and melons. Let us speak her fair. I do not wish to fling stones at my beautiful mother, nor soil my gentle nest. I only wish to indicate the true position of nature in regard to man, wherein to establish man all right education tends; as the ground which to attain is the object of human life, that is, of man's connection with nature. Culture inverts the vulgar views of nature, and brings the mind to call that apparent which it uses to call real, and

---

⁶⁰See 2 Cor. 4:18.

⁶¹George Berkeley (1685–1753), the Irish idealist philosopher and cleric, taught that matter did not exist independent of perception and that the mind of God observing all was the source of the apparent existence of the material world. The term *Vyasa* (Emerson's "Viasa") means, literally, "arranger" and was used to designate various authors and compilers of ancient Indian writings. Tradition has it that Vyasa was the person who arranged the Vedas (see n. 25 above) and who compiled the great Indian epic, the *Mahabharata*. No historical evidence supports these identifications, and the writings were no doubt the work of many hands. However, Emerson would not have possessed this knowledge; and with a traditional Indian teaching of the illusoriness of matter and the reality of ultimate monism, it is not hard to see why he links Berkeley with "Viasa" in ecumenical fashion.

⁶²Etymologically, theosophists are those learned in divine wisdom, but the term is used more specifically to refer to the occult and metaphysical tradition of the West. After 1875 (much later than this essay), theosophy became linked with the Theosophical Society of Helena P. Blavatsky (1831–1891) and Henry S. Olcott (1832–1907). As part of an earlier theosophical tradition, Manichaeans followed Mani (216?–276?), a Babylonian ascetic who taught a late version of Gnosticism emphasizing a sharp dualism between the divine world of light and spirit and the Satanic realm of darkness and matter. Plotinus (205?–270), the reputed founder of Neoplatonism, taught a theosophical doctrine of the mystical ascent of the soul from the world of the Many to the One.

⁶³For the biblical allusion, see Exod. 16:2-3.

⁶⁴This is a free reading of the opening sentence of the biography of Plotinus (*Vita Plotinus*) written by his disciple Porphyry (232?–304?). Emerson read the book in Latin.

⁶⁵Emerson took the quotation from Michelangelo's Sonnet 51 in Michelagnolo Buonarroti, *Rime di Michelagnolo Buonarroti, il Vecchio,* ed. G. Biagioli (Paris: Presso L'Editore, 1821) 118.

that real which it uses to call visionary. Children, it is true, believe in the external world. The belief that it appears only, is an afterthought, but with culture this faith will as surely arise on the mind as did the first.

The advantage of the ideal theory over the popular faith is this, that it presents the world in precisely that view which is most desirable to the mind. It is, in fact, the view which Reason, both speculative and practical, that is, philosophy and virtue, take. For seen in the light of thought, the world always is phenomenal; and virtue subordinates it to the mind. Idealism sees the world in God. It beholds the whole circle of persons and things, of actions and events, of country and religion, not as painfully accumulated, atom after atom, act after act, in an aged creeping Past, but as one vast picture which God paints on the instant eternity for the contemplation of the soul. Therefore the soul holds itself off from a too trivial and microscopic study of the universal tablet.[66] It respects the end too much to immerse itself in the means. It sees something more important in Christianity than the scandals of ecclesiastical history or the niceties of criticism; and, very incurious concerning persons or miracles, and not at all disturbed by chasms of historical evidence, it accepts from God the phenomenon, as it finds it, as the pure and awful form of religion in the world. It is not hot and passionate at the appearance of what it calls its own good or bad fortune, at the union or opposition of other persons. No man is its enemy. It accepts whatsoever befalls, as part of its lesson. It is a watcher more than a doer, and it is a doer, only that it may the better watch.

---

[66]This is a point on which Emerson and Henry David Thoreau grew to differ. Thoreau was the consummate natural philosopher who delighted in noticing the particularities of specimens he encountered.

VII
SPIRIT

It is essential to a true theory of nature and of man, that it should contain somewhat progressive. Uses that are exhausted or that may be, and facts that end in the statement, cannot be all that is true of this brave lodging wherein man is harbored, and wherein all his faculties find appropriate and endless exercise. And all the uses of nature admit of being summed in one, which yields the activity of man an infinite scope. Through all its kingdoms, to the suburbs and outskirts of things, it is faithful to the cause whence it had its origin. It always speaks of Spirit. It suggests the absolute. It is a perpetual effect. It is a great shadow pointing always to the sun behind us.

The aspect of Nature is devout. Like the figure of Jesus, she stands with bended head, and hands folded upon the breast. The happiest man is he who learns from nature the lesson of worship.

Of that ineffable essence which we call Spirit, he that thinks most, will say least. We can foresee God in the coarse, and, as it were, distant phenomena of matter; but when we try to define and describe himself, both language and thought desert us, and we are as helpless as fools and savages. That essence refuses to be recorded in propositions, but when man has worshipped him intellectually, the noblest ministry of nature is to stand as the apparition of God. It is the organ through which the universal spirit speaks to the individual, and strives to lead back the individual to it.

When we consider Spirit, we see that the views already presented do not include the whole circumference of man. We must add some related thoughts.

Three problems are put by nature to the mind: What is matter? Whence is it? and

Whereto? The first of these questions only, the ideal theory answers. Idealism saith: matter is a phenomenon, not a substance. Idealism acquaints us with the total disparity between the evidence of our own being and the evidence of the world's being. The one is perfect; the other, incapable of any assurance; the mind is a part of the nature of things; the world is a divine dream, from which we may presently awake to the glories and certainties of day. Idealism is a hypothesis to account for nature by other principles than those of carpentry and chemistry. Yet, if it only deny the existence of matter, it does not satisfy the demands of the spirit. It leaves God out of me. It leaves me in the splendid labyrinth of my perceptions, to wander without end. Then the heart resists it, because it balks the affections in denying substantive being to men and women. Nature is so pervaded with human life that there is something of humanity in all and in every particular. But this theory makes nature foreign to me, and does not account for that consanguinity which we acknowledge to it.

Let it stand then, in the present state of our knowledge, merely as a useful introductory hypothesis, serving to apprize us of the eternal distinction between the soul and the world.

But when, following the invisible steps of thought, we come to inquire, Whence is matter? and Whereto? many truths arise to us out of the recesses of consciousness. We learn that the highest is present to the soul of man; that the dread universal essence, which is not wisdom, or love, or beauty, or power, but all in one, and each entirely, is that for which all things exist, and that by which they are; that spirit creates; that behind nature, throughout nature, spirit is present; one and not compound it does not act upon us from without, that is, in space and time, but spiritually, or through ourselves: therefore, that spirit, that is, the Supreme Being, does not build up nature around us, but puts it forth through us, as the life of the tree puts forth new branches and leaves through the pores of the old. As a plant upon the earth, so a man rests upon the bosom of God; he is nourished by unfailing fountains, and draws at his need inexhaustible power. Who can set bounds to the possibilities of man? Once inhale the upper air, being admitted to behold the absolute natures of justice and truth, and we learn that man has access to the entire mind of the Creator, is himself the creator in the finite. This view, which admonishes me where the sources of wisdom and power lie, and points to virtue as to

"The golden key
Which opes the palace of eternity,"[67]

carries upon its face the highest certificate of truth, because it animates me to create my own world through the purification of my soul.

The world proceeds from the same spirit as the body of man. It is a remoter and inferior incarnation of God, a projection of God in the unconscious. But it differs from the body in one important respect. It is not, like that, now subjected to the human will. Its serene order is inviolable by us. It is, therefore, to us, the present expositor of the divine mind. It is a fixed point whereby we may measure our departure. As we degenerate, the contrast between us and our house is more evident. We are as much strangers in nature as we are aliens from God. We do not understand the notes of birds. The fox and the deer run away from us; the bear and tiger rend us. We do not know the uses of more than a few plants, as corn and the apple, the potato and the vine. Is not the landscape, every glimpse of which hath a grandeur, a face of him?

---

[67]John Milton, *Comus,* ll. 13-14, with a few minor alterations in the transcription.

Yet this may show us what discord is between man and nature, for you cannot freely admire a noble landscape if laborers are digging in the field hard by. The poet finds something ridiculous in his delight until he is out of the sight of men.

VIII
PROSPECTS

IN inquiries respecting the laws of the world and the frame of things, the highest reason is always the truest. That which seems faintly possible, it is so refined, is often faint and dim because it is deepest seated in the mind among the eternal verities. Empirical science is apt to cloud the sight, and by the very knowledge of functions and processes to bereave the student of the manly contemplation of the whole. The savant becomes unpoetic. But the best read naturalist who lends an entire and devout attention to truth, will see that there remains much to learn of his relation to the world, and that it is not to be learned by any addition or subtraction or other comparison of known quantities, but is arrived at by untaught sallies of the spirit, by a continual self-recovery, and by entire humility. He will perceive that there are far more excellent qualities in the student than preciseness and infallibility; that a guess is often more fruitful than an indisputable affirmation, and that a dream may let us deeper into the secret of nature than a hundred concerted experiments.

For the problems to be solved are precisely those which the physiologist and the naturalist omit to state. It is not so pertinent to man to know all the individuals of the animal kingdom, as it is to know whence and whereto is this tyrannizing unity in his constitution, which evermore separates and classifies things, endeavoring to reduce the most diverse to one form. When I behold a rich landscape, it is less to my purpose to recite correctly the order and superposition of the strata, than to know why all thought of multitude is lost in a tranquil sense of unity. I cannot greatly honor minuteness in details, so long as there is no hint to explain the relation between things and thoughts; no ray upon the *metaphysics* of conchology, of botany, of the arts, to show the relation of the forms of flowers, shells, animals, architecture, to the mind, and build science upon ideas. In a cabinet of natural history, we become sensible of a certain occult recognition and sympathy in regard to the most unwieldy and eccentric forms of beast, fish, and insect. The American who has been confined, in his own country, to the sight of buildings designed after foreign models, is surprised on entering York Minster or St. Peter's at Rome, by the feeling that these structures are imitations also,—faint copies of an invisible archetype. Nor has science sufficient humanity, so long as the naturalist overlooks that wonderful congruity which subsists between man and the world; of which he is lord, not because he is the most subtile inhabitant, but because he is its head and heart, and finds something of himself in every great and small thing, in every mountain stratum, in every new law of color, fact of astronomy, or atmospheric influence which observation or analysis lays open. A perception of this mystery inspires the muse of George Herbert, the beautiful psalmist of the seventeenth century. The following lines are part of his little poem on Man.

> Man is all symmetry,
> Full of proportions, one limb to another,
> And all to all the world besides.
> Each part may call the farthest, brother;
> For head with foot hath private amity,
> And both with moons and tides.
>
> Nothing hath got so far
> But man hath caught and kept it as his prey;
> His eyes dismount the highest star:
> He is in little all the sphere.
> Herbs gladly cure our flesh, because
>   that they
> Find their acquaintance there.

> For us, the winds do blow,
> The earth doth rest, heaven move, and
> fountains flow;
> Nothing we see, but means our good,
> As our delight, or as our treasure;
> The whole is either our cupboard of food,
> Or cabinet of pleasure.
>
> The stars have us to bed:
> Night draws the curtain; which the sun
> withdraws.
> Music and light attend our head.
> All things unto our flesh are kind,
> In their descent and being; to our mind,
> In their ascent and cause.
>
> More servants wait on man
> Than he'll take notice of. In every path,
> He treads down that which doth
> befriend him
> When sickness makes him pale and wan.
> Oh mighty love! Man is one world, and hath
> Another to attend him.[68]

The perception of this class of truths makes the attraction which draws men to science, but the end is lost sight of in attention to the means. In view of this half-sight of science, we accept the sentence of Plato, that "poetry comes nearer to vital truth than history."[69] Every surmise and vaticination of the mind is entitled to a certain respect, and we learn to prefer imperfect theories, and sentences which contain glimpses of truth, to digested systems which have no one valuable suggestion. A wise writer will feel that the ends of study and composition are best answered by announcing undiscovered regions of thought, and so communicating, through hope, new activity to the torpid spirit.

I shall therefore conclude this essay with some traditions of man and nature, which a certain poet sang to me;[70] and which, as they have always been in the world, and perhaps reappear to every bard, may be both history and prophecy.

'The foundations of man are not in matter, but in spirit. But the element of spirit is eternity. To it, therefore, the longest series of events, the oldest chronologies are young and recent. In the cycle of the universal man, from whom the known individuals proceed, centuries are points, and all history is but the epoch of one degradation.

'We distrust and deny inwardly our sympathy with nature. We own and disown our relation to it, by turns. We are like Nebuchadnezzar, dethroned, bereft of reason, and eating grass like an ox.[71] But who can set limits to the remedial force of spirit?

'A man is a god in ruins. When men are

---

[68]This extensive quotation from George Herbert's poem "Man," also quoted earlier (see n. 5), omits stanzas 1, 2, 7, and 9. The transcription is fairly accurate although spelling is modernized.

[69]Emerson has here conflated two quotations, one from Plato's *Republic,* bk. 5, and one from Aristotle's *Poetics,* ch. 10, as he found them in a review of John Knox's *Remarks on the Supposed Dionysius Longinus* (1827) in the *Edinburgh Review* 54 (1831): 48.

[70]The "certain poet" is probably Bronson Alcott, Emerson's close friend whose Neoplatonic and mystical leanings Emerson at this time strongly approved. Alcott's doctrine of Genesis, or Lapse (man, the "god in ruins"), is paraphrased in the passages that follow, and his celebration of infancy is also suggested. For a discussion of Alcott's thought that is related, see Odell Shepard, *Pedlar's Progress: The Life of Bronson Alcott* (1937; rpt., New York: Greenwood Press, 1968) 453-63. See also, in this volume, Amos Bronson Alcott, "Orphic Sayings," saying 52 and nn. 4 and 27 to the text.

[71]Nebuchadnezzar was king of Babylon from about 605 to 562 B.C. In the Book of Daniel, he is portrayed as a vain and overbearing king who eventually goes mad and is reduced to eating grass. See Dan. 4:25-30.

innocent, life shall be longer, and shall pass into the immortal as gently as we awake from dreams. Now, the world would be insane and rabid, if these disorganizations should last for hundreds of years. It is kept in check by death and infancy. Infancy is the perpetual Messiah, which comes into the arms of fallen men, and pleads with them to return to paradise.

'Man is the dwarf of himself. Once he was permeated and dissolved by spirit. He filled nature with his overflowing currents. Out from him sprang the sun and moon; from man the sun, from woman the moon. The laws of his mind, the periods of his actions externized themselves into day and night, into the year and the seasons. But, having made for himself this huge shell, his waters retired; he no longer fills the veins and veinlets; he is shrunk to a drop. He sees that the structure still fits him, but fits him colossally. Say, rather, once it fitted him, now it corresponds to him from far and on high. He adores timidly his own work. Now is man the follower of the sun, and woman the follower of the moon. Yet sometimes he starts in his slumber, and wonders at himself and his house, and muses strangely at the resemblance betwixt him and it. He perceives that if his law is still paramount, if still he have elemental power, if his word is sterling yet in nature, it is not conscious power, it is not inferior but superior to his will. It is instinct.' Thus my Orphic poet sang.[72]

At present, man applies to nature but half his force. He works on the world with his understanding alone. He lives in it and masters it by a penny-wisdom; and he that works most in it is but a half-man, and whilst his arms are strong and his digestion good, his mind is imbruted, and he is a selfish savage. His relation to nature, his power over it, is through the understanding, as by manure; the economic use of fire, wind, water, and the mariner's needle; steam, coal, chemical agriculture; the repairs of the human body by the dentist and the surgeon. This is such a resumption of power as if a banished king should buy his territories inch by inch, instead of vaulting at once into his throne. Meantime, in the thick darkness, there are not wanting gleams of a better light,—occasional examples of the action of man upon nature with his entire force,—with reason as well as understanding. Such examples are, the traditions of miracles in the earliest antiquity of all nations; the history of Jesus Christ; the achievements of a principle, as in religious and political revolutions, and in the abolition of the slave-trade; the miracles of enthusiasm, as those reported of Swedenborg, Hohenlohe, and the Shakers; many obscure and yet contested facts, now arranged under the name of Animal Magnetism; prayer; eloquence; self-healing; and the wisdom of children.[73] These are ex-

---

[72]Alcott, whose "Orphic Sayings" appear excerpted in this volume, is again suggested, although Robert E. Spiller argues against the identification on the grounds of Emerson's penchant for crafting an alter ego when he wanted to speak as a poet-seer. See Emerson, *Collected Works,* 1:253. The Orphic mysteries were celebrated in ancient Greece, especially in the sixth century B.C. Orphism taught that the human soul was divine but that it was embed-

ded in evil in the world. Through initiation into the Orphic mysteries and through transmigration, the soul could be liberated to reach eternal blessedness. For a fuller account, see the introduction to Alcott's "Orphic Sayings" and n. 6 to the same introduction. Finally, "instinct" in the last words of the "Orphic poet" should be understood as intuition-in-action, the outward expression of immediate inner truth.

[73]Alexander Leopold of Hohenlohe-Waldenberg-Schillingfürst (1794-1849), of noble birth and a prince, became a writer and a Ro-

amples of Reason's momentary grasp of the sceptre; the exertions of a power which exists not in time or space, but an instantaneous in-streaming causing power. The difference between the actual and the ideal force of man is happily figured by the schoolmen, in saying, that the knowledge of man is an evening knowledge, *vespertina cognitio,* but that of God is a morning knowledge, *matutina cognitio.*[74]

The problem of restoring to the world original and eternal beauty is solved by the redemption of the soul. The ruin or the blank that we see when we look at nature, is in our own eye. The axis of vision is not coincident with the axis of things, and so they appear not transparent but opaque. The reason why the world lacks unity, and lies broken and in heaps, is because man is disunited with himself. He cannot be a naturalist until he satisfies all the demands of the spirit. Love is as much its demand as perception. Indeed, neither can be perfect without the other. In the uttermost meaning of the words, thought is devout, and devotion is thought. Deep calls unto deep.[75] But in actual life, the marriage is not celebrated. There are innocent men who worship God after the tradition of their fathers, but their sense of duty has not yet extended to the use of all their faculties. And there are patient naturalists, but they freeze their subject under the wintry light of the understanding. Is not prayer also a study of truth,—a sally of the soul into the unfound infinite? No man ever prayed heartily without learning something. But when a faithful thinker, resolute to detach every object from personal relations and see it in the light of thought, shall, at the same time, kindle science with the fire of the holiest affections, then will God go forth anew into the creation.

It will not need, when the mind is prepared for study, to search for objects. The invariable mark of wisdom is to see the miraculous in the common. What is a day? What is a year? What is summer? What is woman? What is a child? What is sleep? To our blindness, these things seem unaffecting. We make fables to hide the baldness of the fact and conform it, as we say, to the higher law of the mind. But when the fact is seen under the light of an idea, the gaudy fable fades and shrivels. We behold the real higher law. To the wise, therefore, a fact is true poetry, and the most beautiful of fables. These wonders are brought to our own door. You also are a man. Man and woman and their social life, poverty, labor, sleep, fear, fortune, are known to you. Learn that none of these things is superficial, but that each phenomenon has its roots in the faculties and affections of the mind. Whilst the abstract question occupies your intellect, nature brings it in the concrete to be solved by your hands. It were a wise inquiry for

---

man Catholic bishop. He gained renown because of the miraculous cures that were linked to his prayers. The Shakers, or officially the United Society of Believers in Christ's Second Appearing, were a communal, mystical, and millennial sect that flourished in the nineteenth century. Their worship attracted notice because of the ecstatic dancing it involved. Originating from the theories of Franz Anton Mesmer (1734–1815), animal magnetism, or mesmerism, was a healing method based on the belief that a universal energy or fluid was at work in the world, a fluid that the magnetic doctor could, at least in part, control.

[74]The "schoolmen" were the scholastic philosophers of the Middle Ages, men like Anselm of Bec (1033?–1109) and Thomas Aquinas (1225–1274). In making the distinction, Emerson relies on John Norris, *An Essay towards the Theory of the Ideal or Intelligible World* (London: S. Manship and W. Hawes, 1701–1704) 1:159-61.

[75]See Ps. 42:7.

the closet, to compare, point by point, especially at remarkable crises in life, our daily history with the rise and progress of ideas in the mind.

So shall we come to look at the world with new eyes. It shall answer the endless inquiry of the intellect,—What is truth? and of the affections,—What is good? by yielding itself passive to the educated Will. Then shall come to pass what my poet said: 'Nature is not fixed but fluid. Spirit alters, moulds, makes it. The immobility or bruteness of nature is the absence of spirit; to pure spirit it is fluid, it is volatile, it is obedient. Every spirit builds itself a house, and beyond its house a world, and beyond its world a heaven. Know then that the world exists for you. For you is the phenomenon perfect. What we are, that only can we see. All that Adam had, all that Cæsar could, you have and can do. Adam called his house, heaven and earth; Cæsar called his house, Rome; you perhaps call yours, a cobbler's trade; a hundred acres of ploughed land; or a scholar's garret. Yet line for line and point for point your dominion is as great as theirs, though without fine names. Build therefore your own world. As fast as you conform your life to the pure idea in your mind, that will unfold its great proportions. A correspondent revolution in things will attend the influx of the spirit. So fast will disagreeable appearances, swine, spiders, snakes, pests, madhouses, prisons, enemies, vanish; they are temporary and shall be no more seen. The sordor and filths of nature, the sun shall dry up and the wind exhale. As when the summer comes from the south the snow-banks melt and the face of the earth becomes green before it, so shall the advancing spirit create its ornaments along its path, and carry with it the beauty it visits and the song which enchants it; it shall draw beautiful faces, warm hearts, wise discourse, and heroic acts, around its way, until evil is no more seen. The kingdom of man over nature, which cometh not with observation,—a dominion such as now is beyond his dream of God,—he shall enter without more wonder than the blind man feels who is gradually restored to perfect sight.'

THE DIVINITY SCHOOL ADDRESS

Invited by a committee of the graduating class at Harvard's Divinity School to deliver an address to them, Emerson used the occasion (15 July 1838) to instruct them in the task of preaching. Edward Waldo Emerson notes that, four months earlier, his father had observed in his journal that he ought to write to the clergy, exposing "the ugliness and unprofitableness of theology and churches at this day, and the glory and sweetness of the moral nature out of whose pale they are almost shut."[1] We know, too, that from May 1837 Emerson had begun to express his growing displeasure with the preaching of Barzillai Frost, the new minister at the church in Concord where Emerson lived. Thus, Emerson brought a prior agenda to the request of the senior class, and he memorialized the occasion by mounting—sometimes in the words of journal entries that he had made regarding Barzillai Frost—an indictment of the ministry.[2]

The speech that resulted is a resounding affirmation of Emerson's Transcendental doctrine of the moral sentiment. Residing within each individual, this intuitive faculty breathes life into religion because it provides insight into the relationship of the human spirit to the one Mind indwelling all things. Jesus of Nazareth, argues Emerson, was great because of the infusion of the moral sentiment in him, and the God that he was we all can become. As noted in the introduction, Emerson and other Transcendentalists had developed their idea of the moral sentiment at least partially through their contact with the "moral sense" of Scottish philosophy. But here Emerson construes the teaching in a new way, linking it to ideas that resonate with Neoplatonic mysticism. In so doing, he adumbrates a vision of the unity of Soul to which he gives classic utterance in his essay "The Over-Soul." And likewise, he articulates the notions of the integrity and sanctity of the self that form the basis for "Self-Reliance."

Whether or not Emerson intended subsequent events, his address created shock and consternation among more conservative Unitarian ministers of his day, and a bitter controversy raged, spilling over into print. But a number of people had been deeply inspired, among them Theodore Parker. Returning home after hearing the speech, he recorded in his journal:

> I shall give no abstract, so beautiful, so just and terribly sublime was his picture of the church in its present condition. My soul is roused, and this week I shall write the long-meditated sermons on the state of the church and the duties of these times.[3]

---

[1] See Ralph Waldo Emerson, *The Complete Works of Ralph Waldo Emerson*, ed. Edward Waldo Emerson, centenary ed. (Boston: Houghton, Mifflin, 1903–1904) 1:421. The passage is quoted from Emerson's journal for 14 March 1838.

[2] For the classic discussion of Barzillai Frost and the Divinity School *Address,* see Conrad Wright, "Emerson, Barzillai Frost, and the Divinity School Address," in *The Liberal Christians: Essays on American Unitarian History* (Boston: Beacon Press, 1970) 41-61.

[3] Theodore Parker, *Journal;* quoted by Edward Waldo Emerson in Emerson, *Complete Works,* 1:423. The text that follows is that in the centenary edition of Emerson, *Complete Works,* 1:117-51.

AN ADDRESS

DELIVERED BEFORE THE SENIOR CLASS IN DIVINITY COLLEGE, CAMBRIDGE, SUNDAY EVENING, JULY 15, 1838.

In this refulgent summer, it has been a luxury to draw the breath of life. The grass grows, the buds burst, the meadow is spotted with fire and gold in the tint of flowers. The air is full of birds, and sweet with the breath of the pine, the balm-of-Gilead,[1] and the new hay. Night brings no gloom to the heart with its welcome shade. Through the transparent darkness the stars pour their almost spiritual rays. Man under them seems a young child, and his huge globe a toy. The cool night bathes the world as with a river, and prepares his eyes again for the crimson dawn. The mystery of nature was never displayed more happily. The corn and the wine have been freely dealt to all creatures, and the never-broken silence with which the old bounty goes forward has not yielded yet one word of explanation. One is constrained to respect the perfection of this world in which our senses converse. How wide; how rich; what invitation from every property it gives to every faculty of man! In its fruitful soils; in its navigable sea; in its mountains of metal and stone; in its forests of all woods; in its animals; in its chemical ingredients; in the powers and path of light, heat, attraction and life, it is well worth the pith and heart of great men to subdue and enjoy it. The planters, the mechanics, the inventors, the astronomers, the builders of cities, and the captains, history delights to honor.

But when the mind opens and reveals the laws which traverse the universe and make things what they are, then shrinks the great world at once into a mere illustration and fable of this mind.[2] What am I? and What is? asks the human spirit with a curiosity new-kindled, but never to be quenched. Behold these outrunning laws, which our imperfect apprehension can see tend this way and that, but not come full circle. Behold these infinite relations, so like, so unlike; many, yet one. I would study, I would know, I would admire forever. These works of thought have been the entertainments of the human spirit in all ages.

A more secret, sweet, and overpowering beauty appears to man when his heart and mind open to the sentiment of virtue.[3] Then he is instructed in what is above him. He learns that his being is without bound; that to the good, to the perfect, he is born, low as he now lies in evil and weakness.

---

[1] This is the balm-of-Gilead poplar (*Populus candicans*).

[2] Here Emerson is articulating his idealism with its roots in Neoplatonism. He sees the world as an image of Mind and the work of Mind.

[3] Emerson begins his discussion of the moral sentiment, the central theme of his address.

That which he venerates is still his own, though he has not realized it yet. *He ought.* He knows the sense of that grand word, though his analysis fails to render account of it. When in innocency or when by intellectual perception he attains to say,—"I love the Right; Truth is beautiful within and without for evermore. Virtue, I am thine; save me; use me; thee will I serve, day and night, in great, in small, that I may be not virtuous, but virtue;"—then is the end of the creation answered, and God is well pleased.

The sentiment of virtue is a reverence and delight in the presence of certain divine laws. It perceives that this homely game of life we play, covers, under what seem foolish details, principles that astonish. The child amidst his baubles is learning the action of light, motion, gravity, muscular force; and in the game of human life, love, fear, justice, appetite, man, and God, interact. These laws refuse to be adequately stated. They will not be written out on paper, or spoken by the tongue. They elude our persevering thought; yet we read them hourly in each other's faces, in each other's actions, in our own remorse. The moral traits which are all globed into every virtuous act and thought,—in speech we must sever, and describe or suggest by painful enumeration of many particulars. Yet, as this sentiment is the essence of all religion, let me guide your eye to the precise objects of the sentiment, by an enumeration of some of those classes of facts in which this element is conspicuous.

The intuition of the moral sentiment is an insight of the perfection of the laws of the soul. These laws execute themselves. They are out of time, out of space, and not subject to circumstance. Thus in the soul of man there is a justice whose retributions are instant and entire. He who does a good deed is instantly ennobled. He who does a mean deed is by the action itself contracted. He who puts off impurity, thereby puts on purity. If a man is at heart just, then in so far is he God; the safety of God, the immortality of God, the majesty of God do enter into that man with justice. If a man dissemble, deceive, he deceives himself, and goes out of acquaintance with his own being. A man in the view of absolute goodness, adores, with total humility. Every step so downward, is a step upward. The man who renounces himself, comes to himself.

See how this rapid intrinsic energy worketh everywhere, righting wrongs, correcting appearances, and bringing up facts to a harmony with thoughts. Its operation in life, though slow to the senses, is at last as sure as in the soul. By it a man is made the Providence to himself, dispensing good to his goodness, and evil to his sin. Character is always known. Thefts never enrich; alms never impoverish; murder will speak out of stone walls. The least admixture of a lie,—for example, the taint of vanity, any attempt to make a good impression, a favorable appearance,—will instantly vitiate the effect. But speak the truth, and all nature and all spirits help you with unexpected furtherance. Speak the truth, and all things alive or brute are vouchers, and the very roots of the grass underground there do seem to stir and move to bear you witness. See again the perfection of the Law as it applies itself to the affections, and becomes the law of society. As we are, so we associate. The good, by affinity, seek the good; the vile, by affinity, the vile. Thus of their own volition, souls proceed into heaven, into hell.

These facts have always suggested to man the sublime creed that the world is not the product of manifold power, but of one will, of one mind; and that one mind is everywhere active, in each ray of the star, in each wavelet of the pool; and whatever opposes that will is everywhere balked and baffled, because things are made so, and not otherwise. Good is positive. Evil is merely privative, not absolute: it is like cold, which is the privation of heat.[4] All evil is so much death or nonentity. Benevolence is absolute and real. So much benevolence as a man hath, so much life hath he. For all things proceed out of this same spirit, which is differently named love, justice, temperance, in its different applications, just as the ocean receives different names on the several shores which it washes. All things proceed out of the same spirit, and all things conspire with it. Whilst a man seeks good ends, he is strong by the whole strength of nature. In so far as he roves from these ends, he bereaves himself of power, or auxiliaries; his being shrinks out of all remote channels, he becomes less and less, a mote, a point, until absolute badness is absolute death.

The perception of this law of laws awakens in the mind a sentiment which we call the religious sentiment, and which makes our highest happiness. Wonderful is its power to charm and to command. It is a mountain air. It is the embalmer of the world. It is myrrh and storax, and chlorine and rosemary. It makes the sky and the hills sublime, and the silent song of the stars is it. By it is the universe made safe and habitable, not by science or power. Thought may work cold and intransitive in things, and find no end or unity; but the dawn of the sentiment of virtue on the heart, gives and is the assurance that Law is sovereign over all natures; and the worlds, time, space, eternity, do seem to break out into joy.

This sentiment is divine and deifying. It is the beatitude of man. It makes him illimitable. Through it, the soul first knows itself. It corrects the capital mistake of the infant man, who seeks to be great by following the great, and hopes to derive advantages *from another,*—by showing the fountain of all good to be in himself, and that he, equally with every man, is an inlet into the deeps of Reason. When he says, "I ought;" when love warms him; when he chooses, warned from on high, the good and great deed; then, deep melodies wander through his soul from Supreme Wisdom.—Then he can worship, and be enlarged by his worship; for he can never go behind this sentiment. In the sublimest flights of the soul, rectitude is never surmounted, love is never outgrown.

This sentiment lies at the foundation of society, and successively creates all forms of worship. The principle of veneration never dies out. Man fallen into superstition, into sensuality, is never quite without the visions of the moral sentiment. In like manner, all the expressions of this sentiment are sacred and permanent in proportion to their purity. The expressions of this sentiment affect us more than all other compositions. The sentences of the oldest time, which ejaculate this piety, are still fresh and fragrant. This thought dwelled always deepest in the minds of men in the devout and contemplative East; not alone in Palestine, where it reached its purest expression, but in Egypt, in Persia, in India, in China. Europe has always owed to oriental genius its divine impulses. What these holy bards said, all sane men found agreeable and true. And the unique impression of Jesus upon mankind, whose name is not so much written as ploughed into the history of this world, is proof of the subtle virtue of this infusion.[5]

---

[4]The privative doctrine of evil—that it is the absence of order or good—is Neoplatonic. See Plotinus *Enneads* 2.4.16; 3.6.2; 3.6.6-11.

[5]Here Emerson asserts the characteristic Transcendental doctrine, identifying the significance of Jesus with his possession of the moral sentiment.

Meantime, whilst the doors of the temple stand open, night and day, before every man, and the oracles of this truth cease never, it is guarded by one stern condition; this, namely; it is an intuition. It cannot be received at second hand. Truly speaking, it is not instruction, but provocation, that I can receive from another soul. What he announces, I must find true in me, or reject; and on his word, or as his second, be he who he may, I can accept nothing. On the contrary, the absence of this primary faith is the presence of degradation. As is the flood, so is the ebb. Let this faith depart, and the very words it spake and the things it made become false and hurtful. Then falls the church, the state, art, letters, life. The doctrine of the divine nature being forgotten, a sickness infects and dwarfs the constitution. Once man was all; now he is an appendage, a nuisance. And because the indwelling Supreme Spirit cannot wholly be got rid of, the doctrine of it suffers this perversion, that the divine nature is attributed to one or two persons, and denied to all the rest, and denied with fury.[6] The doctrine of inspiration is lost; the base doctrine of the majority of voices usurps the place of the doctrine of the soul. Miracles, prophecy, poetry, the ideal life, the holy life, exist as ancient history merely; they are not in the belief, nor in the aspiration of society; but, when suggested, seem ridiculous. Life is comic or pitiful as soon as the high ends of being fade out of sight, and man becomes near-sighted, and can only attend to what addresses the senses.

These general views, which, whilst they are general, none will contest, find abundant illustration in the history of religion, and especially in the history of the Christian church. In that, all of us have had our birth and nurture. The truth contained in that, you, my young friends, are now setting forth to teach. As the Cultus, or established worship of the civilized world,[7] it has great historical interest for us. Of its blessed words, which have been the consolation of humanity, you need not that I should speak. I shall endeavor to discharge my duty to you on this occasion, by pointing out two errors in its administration, which daily appear more gross from the point of view we have just now taken.

Jesus Christ belonged to the true race of prophets. He saw with open eye the mystery of the soul. Drawn by its severe harmony, ravished with its beauty, he lived in it, and had his being there. Alone in all history he estimated the greatness of man. One man was true to what is in you and me. He saw that God incarnates himself in man, and evermore goes forth anew to take possession of his World. He said, in this ju-

---

[6] In his notes to the text, Edward Waldo Emerson wrote that the divine nature meant "the over-soul, the divine element shared in measure by every soul." (See Ralph Waldo Emerson, *The Complete Works of Ralph Waldo Emerson,* ed. Edward Waldo Emerson, centenary ed. [Boston: Houghton, Mifflin, 1903–1904] 1:426.) For Emerson, to attribute personality to the divine nature was to limit it. In refusing to do so, in one way he was echoing the classical Neoplatonic mystical tradition of the via negativa, the "negative way," which taught that God could best be comprehended by saying what he was not. See Pseudo-Dionysius Areopagita (fl. A.D. 500?), *The Divine Names and Mystical Theology,* trans. John D. Jones (Milwaukee: Marquette University Press, 1980). Pseudo-Dionysius, however, was always interpreted within the bounds of Christian orthodoxy. Here, however, with his teaching of a divine humanity Emerson is moving significantly beyond these borders, initiating, in fact, what will be an attack on (even liberal) Christianity.

[7] Emerson could be provincial at times, as this judgment about the "civilized world" indicates.

bilee of sublime emotion, 'I am divine. Through me, God acts; through me, speaks. Would you see God, see me; or see thee, when thou also thinkest as I now think.' But what a distortion did his doctrine and memory suffer in the same, in the next, and the following ages! There is no doctrine of the Reason which will bear to be taught by the Understanding.[8] The understanding caught this high chant from the poet's lips, and said, in the next age, 'This was Jehovah come down out of heaven. I will kill you, if you say he was a man.' The idioms of his language and the figures of his rhetoric have usurped the place of his truth; and churches are not built on his principles, but on his tropes. Christianity became a Mythus, as the poetic teaching of Greece and of Egypt, before. He spoke of miracles; for he felt that man's life was a miracle, and all that man doth, and he knew that this daily miracle shines as the character ascends. But the word Miracle, as pronounced by Christian churches, gives a false impression; it is Monster. It is not one with the blowing clover and the falling rain.[9]

He felt respect for Moses and the prophets, but no unfit tenderness at postponing their initial revelations to the hour and the man that now is; to the eternal revelation in the heart. Thus was he a true man. Having seen that the law in us is commanding, he would not suffer it to be commanded. Boldly, with hand, and heart, and life, he declared it was God. Thus is he, as I think, the only soul in history who has appreciated the worth of man.

1. In this point of view we become sensible of the first defect of historical Christianity. Historical Christianity has fallen into the error that corrupts all attempts to communicate religion. As it appears to us, and as it has appeared for ages, it is not the doctrine of the soul, but an exaggeration of the personal, the positive, the ritual. It has dwelt, it dwells, with noxious exaggeration about the *person* of Jesus. The soul knows no persons. It invites every man to expand to the full circle of the universe, and will have no preferences but those of spontaneous love. But by this eastern monarchy of a Christianity, which indolence and fear have built, the friend of man is made the injurer of man.[10] The manner

---

[8]The distinction between the Reason and the Understanding, employed by Emerson in *Nature,* is used again here—the distinction borrowed from Immanuel Kant as interpreted by Samuel Taylor Coleridge, with Coleridge read through the eyes of James Marsh.

[9]Here Emerson has taken a position regarding the miracles question, which had been a source of dispute between the more conservative Unitarians and the Transcendentalists. At the time that Emerson was speaking, George Ripley and William H. Furness had already (1836) adopted a public posture that criticized the reliance on miracles as evidence for gospel truth. But Emerson's address opened a new and more bitter phase in the controversy.

[10]Edward Waldo Emerson notes (in Emerson, *Complete Works,* 1:426-27) James Elliot Cabot's description of Emerson's surprise at being misunderstood in this part of his address. He did not intend to belittle Jesus Christ. "Far from this," Cabot wrote, "he was trying to place the reverence for Jesus upon its true ground, out of reach of the reaction that was sure to set in when the claim to an exclusive revelation should lose its force." See James E. Cabot, *A Memoir of Ralph Waldo Emerson* (Boston: Houghton, Mifflin, 1887) 1:343-44. Edward Waldo Emerson also notes (Emerson, *Complete Works,* 1:427) that according to Elizabeth Peabody the written version of the address contained a passage that stated this intent, but for the lack of time Ralph Waldo Emerson did not read it. Later, he decided not to insert the omitted passage. See Elizabeth Palmer Peabody, *Reminiscences of Rev. Wm. Ellery Channing* (Boston: Roberts Brothers, 1880) 363.

in which his name is surrounded with expressions which were once sallies of admiration and love, but are now petrified into official titles, kills all generous sympathy and liking. All who hear me, feel that the language that describes Christ to Europe and America is not the style of friendship and enthusiasm to a good and noble heart, but is appropriated and formal,—paints a demigod, as the Orientals or the Greeks would describe Osiris[11] or Apollo.[12] Accept the injurious impositions of our early catechetical instruction, and even honesty and self-denial were but splendid sins, if they did not wear the Christian name. One would rather be

"A pagan, suckled in a creed outworn,"[13]

than to be defrauded of his manly right in coming into nature and finding not names and places, not land and professions, but even virtue and truth foreclosed and monopolized. You shall not be a man even. You shall not own the world; you shall not dare and live after the infinite Law that is in you, and in company with the infinite Beauty which heaven and earth reflect to you in all lovely forms;[14] but you must subordinate your nature to Christ's nature; you must accept our interpretations, and take his portrait as the vulgar draw it.

That is always best which gives me to myself. The sublime is excited in me by the great stoical doctrine, Obey thyself.[15] That which shows God in me, fortifies me. That which shows God out of me, makes me a wart and a wen. There is no longer a necessary reason for my being. Already the long shadows of untimely oblivion creep over me, and I shall decease forever.

The divine bards are the friends of my virtue, of my intellect, of my strength. They admonish me that the gleams which flash across my mind are not mine, but God's; that they had the like, and were not disobedient to the heavenly vision.[16] So I love them. Noble provocations go out from them, inviting me to resist evil; to subdue the world; and to Be. And thus, by his holy thoughts, Jesus serves us, and thus only. To aim to convert a man by miracles is a profanation of the soul.[17] A true conversion, a true Christ, is now, as always, to be made by the reception of beautiful sentiments. It is true that a great and rich soul, like his, falling among the simple, does so preponderate, that, as his did, it names the world. The world seems to them to exist for him, and they have not yet drunk so deeply of his sense as to see that only by coming again to themselves, or to God in themselves, can they grow forevermore. It is a low benefit to give me something; it is a high benefit to enable me to do somewhat of myself. The time is coming when all men will see that the gift of God to the soul

---

[11]Osiris was the ancient Egyptian deity who ruled the underworld. Murdered, his body scattered to pieces and then restored to life, he was the object of an imposing cultus throughout the Mediterranean world, especially honoring his identification with the life and fertility of nature.

[12]Apollo was one of the leading Olympian deities in ancient Greek religion. Considered the patron of prophecy, music, and poetry, and noted for his archery, he was perhaps most widely known as Phoebus Apollo, the Sun God.

[13]William Wordsworth, "The world is too much with us," l. 10, in *Miscellaneous Sonnets*.

[14]This is another instance of Emerson's Platonism.

[15]Emerson is sounding a theme that he will develop more fully in his essay "Self-Reliance."

[16]Cf. Acts 26:19.

[17]Once more Emerson argues his case in the miracles controversy.

is not a vaunting, overpowering, excluding sanctity, but a sweet, natural goodness, a goodness like thine and mine, and that so invites thine and mine to be and to grow.

The injustice of the vulgar tone of preaching is not less flagrant to Jesus than to the souls which it profanes. The preachers do not see that they make his gospel not glad, and shear him of the locks of beauty and the attributes of heaven. When I see a majestic Epaminondas,[18] or Washington; when I see among my contemporaries a true orator, an upright judge, a dear friend; when I vibrate to the melody and fancy of a poem; I see beauty that is to be desired. And so lovely, and with yet more entire consent of my human being, sounds in my ear the severe music of the bards that have sung of the true God in all ages. Now do not degrade the life and dialogues of Christ out of the circle of this charm, by insulation and peculiarity. Let them lie as they befell, alive and warm, part of human life and of the landscape and of the cheerful day.

2. The second defect of the traditionary and limited way of using the mind of Christ is a consequence of the first; this, namely; that the Moral Nature, that Law of laws whose revelations introduce greatness—yea, God himself— into the open soul, is not explored as the fountain of the established teaching in society. Men have come to speak of the revelation as somewhat long ago given and done, as if God were dead. The injury to faith throttles the preacher; and the goodliest of institutions becomes an uncertain and inarticulate voice.

It is very certain that it is the effect of conversation with the beauty of the soul, to beget a desire and need to impart to others the same knowledge and love. If utterance is denied, the thought lies like a burden on the man. Always the seer is a sayer. Somehow his dream is told; somehow he publishes it with solemn joy: sometimes with pencil on canvas, sometimes with chisel on stone, sometimes in towers and aisles of granite, his soul's worship is builded; sometimes in anthems of indefinite music; but clearest and most permanent, in words.

The man enamored of this excellency becomes its priest or poet. The office is coeval with the world. But observe the condition, the spiritual limitation of the office. The spirit only can teach. Not any profane man, not any sensual, not any liar, not any slave can teach, but only he can give, who has; he only can create, who is. The man on whom the soul descends, through whom the soul speaks, alone can teach. Courage, piety, love, wisdom, can teach; and every man can open his door to these angels, and they shall bring him the gift of tongues.[19] But the man who aims to speak as books enable, as synods use, as the fashion guides, and as interest commands, babbles. Let him hush.

To this holy office you propose to devote yourselves. I wish you may feel your call in throbs of desire and hope. The office is the first in the world. It is of that reality that it cannot suffer the deduction of any falsehood. And it is my duty to say to you that the need was never greater of new revelation than now. From the views I have already expressed, you will infer the sad conviction, which I share, I believe, with numbers, of the universal decay and now

---

[18]Epaminondas (418?–362 B.C.) was a Greek statesman and general from Thebes. He defeated the Spartans so thoroughly at Leuctra (371 B.C.) that he acquired a lasting reputation for the military tactics that had brought him victory.

[19]See Acts 2:1-11.

almost death of faith in society. The soul is not preached. The Church seems to totter to its fall, almost all life extinct. On this occasion, any complaisance would be criminal which told you, whose hope and commission it is to preach the faith of Christ, that the faith of Christ is preached.

It is time that this ill-suppressed murmur of all thoughtful men against the famine of our churches;—this moaning of the heart because it is bereaved of the consolation, the hope, the grandeur that come alone out of the culture of the moral nature,—should be heard through the sleep of indolence, and over the din of routine. This great and perpetual office of the preacher is not discharged. Preaching is the expression of the moral sentiment in application to the duties of life. In how many churches, by how many prophets, tell me, is man made sensible that he is an infinite Soul; that the earth and heavens are passing into his mind; that he is drinking forever the soul of God? Where now sounds the persuasion, that by its very melody imparadises my heart, and so affirms its own origin in heaven? Where shall I hear words such as in elder ages drew men to leave all and follow,—father and mother, house and land, wife and child?[20] Where shall I hear these august laws of moral being so pronounced as to fill my ear, and I feel ennobled by the offer of my uttermost action and passion? The test of the true faith, certainly, should be its power to charm and command the soul, as the laws of nature control the activity of the hands,—so commanding that we find pleasure and honor in obeying. The faith should blend with the light of rising and of setting suns, with the flying cloud, the singing bird, and the breath of flowers. But now the priest's Sabbath has lost the splendor of nature; it is unlovely; we are glad when it is done; we can make, we do make, even sitting in our pews, a far better, holier, sweeter, for ourselves.

Whenever the pulpit is usurped by a formalist, then is the worshipper defrauded and disconsolate. We shrink as soon as the prayers begin, which do not uplift, but smite and offend us. We are fain to wrap our cloaks about us, and secure, as best we can, a solitude that hears not. I once heard a preacher who sorely tempted me to say I would go to church no more.[21] Men go, thought I, where they are wont to go, else had no soul entered the temple in the afternoon. A snow-storm was falling around us. The snow-storm was real, the preacher merely spectral, and the eye felt the sad contrast in looking at him, and then out of the window behind him into the beautiful meteor of the snow. He had lived in vain. He had no one word intimating that he had laughed or wept, was married or in love, had been commended, or cheated, or chagrined. If he had ever lived and acted, we were none the wiser for it. The capital secret of his profession, namely, to convert life into truth, he had not learned. Not one fact in all his experience had he yet imported into his doctrine. This man had ploughed and planted and talked and bought and sold; he had read books; he had eaten and drunken; his head aches, his heart throbs; he smiles and suffers; yet was there not a surmise, a hint, in all the discourse, that he had ever lived at all. Not a line did he draw out of real history. The true preacher can be known by this, that he deals out to the people his life,—life passed through the fire of thought. But of the bad

---

[20]Cf. Matt. 10:37-38 and 19:29.

[21]The preacher Emerson has in mind is the Reverend Barzillai Frost of Concord. (See the introduction to the text.) For more than a year, Emerson had complained in his journals about the preaching of the new minister.

preacher, it could not be told from his sermon what age of the world he fell in; whether he had a father or a child; whether he was a freeholder or a pauper; whether he was a citizen or a countryman; or any other fact of his biography. It seemed strange that the people should come to church. It seemed as if their houses were very unentertaining, that they should prefer this thoughtless clamor. It shows that there is a commanding attraction in the moral sentiment, that can lend a faint tint of light to dulness and ignorance coming in its name and place. The good hearer is sure he has been touched sometimes; is sure there is somewhat to be reached, and some word that can reach it. When he listens to these vain words, he comforts himself by their relation to his remembrance of better hours, and so they clatter and echo unchallenged.

I am not ignorant that when we preach unworthily, it is not always quite in vain. There is a good ear, in some men, that draws supplies to virtue out of very indifferent nutriment. There is poetic truth concealed in all the common-places of prayer and of sermons, and though foolishly spoken, they may be wisely heard; for each is some select expression that broke out in a moment of piety from some stricken or jubilant soul, and its excellency made it remembered. The prayers and even the dogmas of our church are like the zodiac of Denderah[22] and the astronomical monuments of the Hindoos,[23] wholly insulated from anything now extant in the life and business of the people. They mark the height to which the waters once rose. But this docility is a check upon the mischief from the good and devout. In a large portion of the community, the religious service gives rise to quite other thoughts and emotions. We need not chide the negligent servant. We are struck with pity, rather, at the swift retribution of his sloth. Alas for the unhappy man that is called to stand in the pulpit, and *not* give bread of life. Everything that befalls, accuses him. Would he ask contributions for the missions, foreign or domestic? Instantly his face is suffused with shame, to propose to his parish that they should send money a hundred or a thousand miles, to furnish such poor fare as they have at home and would do well to go the hundred or the thousand miles to escape. Would he urge people to a godly way of living;—and can he ask a fellow-creature to come to Sabbath meetings, when he and they all know what is the poor uttermost they can hope for therein? Will he invite them privately to the Lord's Supper?[24] He dares not. If no heart warm this rite, the hollow, dry, creaking formality is too plain, than that he can face a man of wit and energy and put the invitation without terror. In the street, what has he to say to the bold village blasphemer? The village blasphemer sees fear in the face, form, and gait of the minister.

Let me not taint the sincerity of this plea by any oversight of the claims of good men.

---

[22]The temple of the Cow-Goddess Hathor, in Denderah (on the upper Nile in Egypt) from the first century B.C., contained an impressive zodiacal table.

[23]The monuments to which Emerson refers were probably the seventeenth- and eighteenth-century observatories at Jaipur, Delhi, and other places. But contrary to Emerson's estimate, astronomy in India had for centuries been closely intertwined with astrology and so had much to do with the lives of ordinary people, forming the basis for life readings and prognostications.

[24]Emerson had made his position on this ritual clear almost six years previously with the sermon (printed in this volume) "The Lord's Supper."

I know and honor the purity and strict conscience of numbers of the clergy. What life the public worship retains, it owes to the scattered company of pious men, who minister here and there in the churches, and who, sometimes accepting with too great tenderness the tenet of the elders, have not accepted from others, but from their own heart, the genuine impulses of virtue, and so still command our love and awe, to the sanctity of character. Moreover, the exceptions are not so much to be found in a few eminent preachers, as in the better hours, the truer inspirations of all,—nay, in the sincere moments of every man. But, with whatever exception, it is still true that tradition characterizes the preaching of this country; that it comes out of the memory, and not out of the soul; that it aims at what is usual, and not at what is necessary and eternal; that thus historical Christianity destroys the power of preaching, by withdrawing it from the exploration of the moral nature of man; where the sublime is, where are the resources of astonishment and power. What a cruel injustice it is to that Law, the joy of the whole earth, which alone can make thought dear and rich; that Law whose fatal sureness the astronomical orbits poorly emulate;— that it is travestied and depreciated, that it is behooted and behowled, and not a trait, not a word of it articulated. The pulpit in losing sight of this Law, loses its reason, and gropes after it knows not what. And for want of this culture the soul of the community is sick and faithless. It wants nothing so much as a stern, high, stoical, Christian discipline, to make it know itself and the divinity that speaks through it. Now man is ashamed of himself; he skulks and sneaks through the world, to be tolerated, to be pitied, and scarcely in a thousand years does any man dare to be wise and good, and so draw after him the tears and blessings of his kind.

Certainly there have been periods when, from the inactivity of the intellect on certain truths, a greater faith was possible in names and persons. The Puritans in England and America found in the Christ of the Catholic Church and in the dogmas inherited from Rome, scope for their austere piety and their longings for civil freedom. But their creed is passing away, and none arises in its room. I think no man can go with his thoughts about him into one of our churches, without feeling that what hold the public worship had on men is gone, or going. It has lost its grasp on the affection of the good and the fear of the bad. In the country, neighborhoods, half parishes are *signing off,* to use the local term. It is already beginning to indicate character and religion to withdraw from the religious meetings. I have heard a devout person, who prized the Sabbath, say in bitterness of heart, "On Sundays, it seems wicked to go to church."[25] And the motive that holds the best there is now only a hope and a waiting. What was once a mere circumstance, that the best and worst men in the parish, the poor and the rich, the learned and the ignorant, young and old, should meet one day as fellows in one house, in sign of an equal right in the soul, has come to be a paramount motive for going thither.

My friends, in these two errors, I think, I find the causes of a decaying church and a wasting unbelief. And what greater calamity can fall upon a nation than the loss

---

[25]Robert Spiller identifies the "devout person" as Lidian Emerson, Emerson's second wife. See Ralph Waldo Emerson, *The Collected Works of Ralph Waldo Emerson,* ed. Alfred R. Ferguson et al. (Cambridge: Harvard University Press, Belknap Press, 1971–) 1:257. See also Ralph Waldo Emerson, *The Journals and Miscellaneous Notebooks of Ralph Waldo Emerson,* ed. William H. Gilman et al. (Cambridge: Harvard University Press, Belknap Press, 1960–) 5 (3 December 1837): 442.

of worship? Then all things go to decay. Genius leaves the temple to haunt the senate or the market. Literature becomes frivolous. Science is cold. The eye of youth is not lighted by the hope of other worlds, and age is without honor. Society lives to trifles, and when men die we do not mention them.

And now, my brothers, you will ask, What in these desponding days can be done by us? The remedy is already declared in the ground of our complaint of the Church. We have contrasted the Church with the Soul.[26] In the soul then let the redemption be sought. Wherever a man comes, there comes revolution. The old is for slaves. When a man comes, all books are legible, all things transparent, all religions are forms. He is religious. Man is the wonderworker. He is seen amid miracles. All men bless and curse. He saith yea and nay, only. The stationariness of religion; the assumption that the age of inspiration is past, that the Bible is closed; the fear of degrading the character of Jesus by representing him as a man;—indicate with sufficient clearness the falsehood of our theology. It is the office of a true teacher to show us that God is, not was; that He speaketh, not spake. The true Christianity,— a faith like Christ's in the infinitude of man,—is lost. None believeth in the soul of man, but only in some man or person old and departed. Ah me! no man goeth alone. All men go in flocks to this saint or that poet, avoiding the God who seeth in secret.[27] They cannot see in secret; they love to be blind in public. They think society wiser than their soul, and know not that one soul, and their soul, is wiser than the whole world.[28] See how nations and races flit by on the sea of time and leave no ripple to tell where they floated or sunk, and one good soul shall make the name of Moses, or of Zeno,[29] or of Zoroaster,[30] reverend forever. None assayeth the stern ambition to be the Self of the nation and of nature, but each would be an easy secondary to some Christian scheme, or sectarian connection, or some eminent man. Once leave your own knowledge of God, your own sentiment, and take secondary knowledge, as St. Paul's, or George Fox's,[31] or Swedenborg's, and you get wide from God with every year this secondary form lasts, and if, as now, for centuries,—the chasm yawns to that breadth, that men can scarcely be convinced there is in them anything divine.

Let me admonish you, first of all, to go alone; to refuse the good models, even those which are sacred in the imagination of men, and dare to love God without mediator or veil. Friends enough you shall find who will hold up to your emulation Wesleys[32] and Oberlins,[33] Saints and

---

[26]Emerson's idea of the Soul culminates in his Neoplatonic doctrine of the Oversoul. For the fullest discussion, see his essay "The Over-Soul," in this volume.

[27]Cf. Matt. 6:4 and 6:18. Emerson recasts the action-oriented, moral meaning of the text to a more mystical and intuitive one. Emerson's "seeing" is that of the seer.

[28]Cf. Matt. 16:26.

[29]Zeno of Citium (334?–262? B.C.) was the Greek philosopher who founded Stoicism, the austere ethical system based on a unified vision of the cosmos and its immutable laws. (See n. 35 to Ralph Waldo Emerson, "Self-Reliance.")

[30]Zoroaster (628?–551? B.C.) was the prophet of ancient Persia who founded Zoroastrianism, a dualistic religion that conceived the universe in terms of a monumental war between the forces of good and of evil.

[31]See n. 31 to Ralph Waldo Emerson, *Nature*.

[32]John Wesley (1703–1791) was the Anglican minister who founded Methodism.

[33]Jean Frédéric Oberlin (1740–1826) was an Alsatian Lutheran minister noted for his reform efforts in his French pastoral district. Oberlin College, in Ohio, was named for him.

Prophets. Thank God for these good men, but say, 'I also am a man.' Imitation cannot go above its model. The imitator dooms himself to hopeless mediocrity. The inventor did it because it was natural to him, and so in him it has a charm. In the imitator something else is natural, and he bereaves himself of his own beauty, to come short of another man's.

Yourself a newborn bard of the Holy Ghost, cast behind you all conformity, and acquaint men at first hand with Deity. Look to it first and only, that fashion, custom, authority, pleasure, and money, are nothing to you,—are not bandages over your eyes, that you cannot see,—but live with the privilege of the immeasurable mind. Not too anxious to visit periodically all families and each family in your parish connection, —when you meet one of these men or women, be to them a divine man; be to them thought and virtue; let their timid aspirations find in you a friend; let their trampled instincts be genially tempted out in your atmosphere; let their doubts know that you have doubted, and their wonder feel that you have wondered. By trusting your own heart, you shall gain more confidence in other men. For all our penny-wisdom, for all our soul-destroying slavery to habit, it is not to be doubted that all men have sublime thoughts; that all men value the few real hours of life; they love to be heard; they love to be caught up into the vision of principles. We mark with light in the memory the few interviews we have had, in the dreary years of routine and of sin, with souls that made our souls wiser; that spoke what we thought; that told us what we knew; that gave us leave to be what we inly were. Discharge to men the priestly office, and, present or absent, you shall be followed with their love as by an angel.

And, to this end, let us not aim at common degrees of merit. Can we not leave, to such as love it, the virtue that glitters for the commendation of society, and ourselves pierce the deep solitudes of absolute ability and worth? We easily come up to the standard of goodness in society. Society's praise can be cheaply secured, and almost all men are content with those easy merits; but the instant effect of conversing with God will be to put them away. There are persons who are not actors, not speakers, but influences; persons too great for fame, for display; who disdain eloquence; to whom all we call art and artist, seems too nearly allied to show and by-ends, to the exaggeration of the finite and selfish, and loss of the universal. The orators, the poets, the commanders encroach on us only as fair women do, by our allowance and homage. Slight them by preoccupation of mind, slight them, as you can well afford to do, by high and universal aims, and they instantly feel that you have right, and that it is in lower places that they must shine. They also feel your right; for they with you are open to the influx of the all-knowing Spirit, which annihilates before its broad noon the little shades and gradations of intelligence in the compositions we call wiser and wisest.

In such high communion let us study the grand strokes of rectitude: a bold benevolence, an independence of friends, so that not the unjust wishes of those who love us shall impair our freedom, but we shall resist for truth's sake the freest flow of kindness, and appeal to sympathies far in advance; and,—what is the highest form in which we know this beautiful element,—a certain solidity of merit, that has nothing to do with opinion, and which is so essentially and manifestly virtue, that it is taken for granted that the right, the brave, the generous step will be taken by it, and nobody thinks of commending it. You would compliment a coxcomb doing a good act, but you would not praise an angel. The silence that accepts merit as the most natural thing in the world, is the highest applause. Such souls, when they appear, are the Imperial Guard of Virtue, the perpetual reserve, the dictators of fortune. One needs not praise their courage,—they are the heart and soul of nature. O my friends, there are resources in us on which we have not drawn. There are men who rise refreshed on hearing a threat; men to whom a crisis which intimidates and paralyzes the majority,—demanding not the faculties of prudence and thrift, but comprehension, immovableness, the readiness of sacrifice,—comes graceful and beloved as a bride. Napoleon said of Massena, that he was not himself until the battle began to go against him; then, when the dead began to fall in ranks around him, awoke his powers of combination, and he put on terror and victory as a robe.[34] So it is in rugged crises, in unweariable endurance, and in aims which put sympathy out of question, that the angel is shown. But these are heights that we can scarce remember and look up to without contrition and shame. Let us thank God that such things exist.

And now let us do what we can to rekindle the smouldering, nigh quenched fire on the altar. The evils of the church that now is are manifest. The question returns, What shall we do? I confess, all attempts to project and establish a Cultus with new rites and forms, seem to me vain. Faith makes us, and not we it, and faith makes its own forms. All attempts to contrive a system are as cold as the new worship introduced by the French to the goddess of Reason,—to-day, pasteboard and filigree, and ending to-morrow in madness and murder.[35] Rather let the breath of new life be breathed by you through the forms already existing. For if once you are alive, you shall find they shall become plastic and new. The remedy to their deformity is first, soul, and second, soul, and evermore, soul. A whole popedom of forms one pulsation of virtue can uplift and vivify. Two inestimable advantages Christianity has given us; first the Sabbath, the jubilee of the whole world, whose light dawns welcome alike into the closet of the philosopher, into the garret of toil, and into prison-cells, and everywhere suggests, even to the vile, the dignity of spiritual being. Let it stand forevermore, a temple, which new love, new faith, new sight shall restore to more than its first splendor to mankind. And secondly, the institution of preaching,—the speech of man to men,—essentially the most flexible of all organs, of all forms. What hinders that now, everywhere, in pulpits, in lecture-rooms, in houses, in fields, wherever the invitation of men or your own occasions lead you, you speak the very truth, as your life and conscience teach it, and cheer the waiting, fainting hearts of men with new hope and new revelation?

I look for the hour when that supreme Beauty which ravished the souls of those Eastern men, and chiefly of those Hebrews, and through their lips spoke oracles to all time, shall speak in the West also. The Hebrew and Greek Scriptures contain immortal sentences, that have been bread of

---

[34] André Masséna (1758–1817) earned a distinguished reputation as a marshal in Napoleon's army because of the brilliance and success of his military tactics. Emerson's account here is drawn from Barry Edward O'Meara, *Napoleon in Exile; Or, A Voice from St. Helena*. See 4th ed. (Boston: C. Ewer, 1823) 1:183–84.

[35] In the midst of the French Revolution (1793), the Goddess of Reason was enthroned in the cathedral of Notre Dame in Paris and a cultus instituted to honor her and the values of the Enlightenment. But, ironically, the reign of the Goddess ran roughly parallel to the Reign of Terror (1793–1794).

life to millions. But they have no epical integrity; are fragmentary; are not shown in their order to the intellect. I look for the new Teacher that shall follow so far those shining laws that he shall see them come full circle; shall see their rounding complete grace; shall see the world to be the mirror of the soul; shall see the identity of the law of gravitation with purity of heart; and shall show that the Ought, that Duty, is one thing with Science, with Beauty, and with Joy.[36]

---

[36]Emerson closes his address with a paean to correspondence, the fundamental belief out of which his spirituality arises. Note, too, his almost messianic expectation of a "Teacher" to come.

THE OVER-SOUL

This short work appeared in Emerson's first collection of essays published in 1841. Its main theme was one that had already been expressed in *Nature* and, indeed, had recurred in the pages of Emerson's private journals and also in his public lectures. Yet even though he devotes extended thought here to the term and concept, the meaning of Emerson's Oversoul is still not precise. On the one hand, the Oversoul is God; but on the other, it is the divine part of human nature and the overarching collectivity in which all participate. It is the "I" of each "me," but it is an I that transcends biography even as it celebrates it—an I that, like a tree with endless ground roots, encircles the earth and mingles with all that exists. The Oversoul is involved in matter yet moves beyond it as spirit. It is the culminating concept in Emerson's own version of the ideal theory, and it testifies at once to the reality and illusoriness of the material world.

As it comes to us in the essay, the idea of the Oversoul is vintage Emerson—an eclectic blend of Neoplatonism with a likely debt to Gnosticism inherited from the occult-metaphysical tradition of the West, a continued reliance on Coleridge and Swedenborg, and—perhaps unawares—an understanding related to one side of Scottish common sense. From Neoplatonism comes the ancient notion of a World Soul in which all individual souls participate—a bridge from the One to the Many of the material world. From Gnosticism perhaps comes a conviction (discussed in the notes) of the reality of secret knowledge—Emerson's "revelation" —and a divine identity to be sought and reapprehended. Coleridge's exaltation of Reason flowers again in the Reason of the Oversoul, and Swedenborg's affirmation of interiority and his basic doctrine of correspondence flower there, too. Meanwhile, from Emerson's Harvard past, Scottish common sense provides a moral intuitionism that supports and undergirds the synthesis.

Yet even as Emerson ponders the transcending mysteries of the Oversoul, the exaltation of the individual—the "celebration" of Transcendental biography alluded to above—forms a continuing theme. It is a theme that is more thoroughly explored in "Self-Reliance," but still it is in "The Over-Soul" that we learn of minds "grandly simple" and souls that "walk as gods in the earth." There is, in fact, a pragmatic tinge to Emerson's diffuse mystical doctrine: the Oversoul fosters self-culture, and self-culture—besides increasing the kingdom of the spirit—leads to success and happiness on earth.[1]

---

[1] The text is that in Ralph Waldo Emerson, *The Complete Works of Ralph Waldo Emerson,* ed. Edward Waldo Emerson, centenary ed. (Boston: Houghton, Mifflin, 1903–1904) 2:265-97.

THE OVER-SOUL

"But souls that of his own good life partake,
He loves as his own self; dear as his eye
They are to Him: He'll never them forsake:
When they shall die, then God himself shall die:
They live, they live in blest eternity."
Henry More.[1]

Space is ample, east and west,
But two cannot go abreast,
Cannot travel in it two:
Yonder masterful cuckoo
Crowds every egg out of the nest,
Quick or dead, except its own;
A spell is laid on sod and stone,
Night and Day've been tampered with,
Every quality and pith
Surcharged and sultry with a power
That works its will on age and hour.[2]

There is a difference between one and another hour of life in their authority and subsequent effect. Our faith comes in moments; our vice is habitual. Yet there is a depth in those brief moments which constrains us to ascribe more reality to them than to all other experiences. For this reason the argument which is always forthcoming to silence those who conceive extraordinary hopes of man, namely the appeal to experience, is for ever invalid and vain. We give up the past to the objector, and yet we hope. He must explain this hope. We grant that human life is mean, but how did we find out that it was mean? What is the ground of this uneasiness of ours; of this old discontent? What is the universal sense of want and ignorance, but the fine innuendo by which the soul makes its enormous claim? Why do men feel that the natural history of man has never been written, but he is always leaving behind what you have said of him, and it becomes old, and books of metaphysics worthless? The philosophy of six thousand years has not searched the chambers and magazines of the soul. In its experiments there has al-

---

[1] Henry More, "Psychozoia; or, The Life of the Soul," canto 2, stanza 19, in More, *Philosophical Poems* (Cambridge: R. Daniel, 1647). This was the only motto that preceded the essay in the original edition (1841).

[2] This poem, of Emerson's own composition, was later retitled "Unity." It appears under that title (and with a small grammatical change) in Ralph Waldo Emerson, *The Complete Works of Ralph Waldo Emerson*, ed. Edward Waldo Emerson, centenary ed. (Boston: Houghton, Mifflin, 1903–1904) 9:279.

ways remained, in the last analysis, a residuum it could not resolve. Man is a stream whose source is hidden. Our being is descending into us from we know not whence. The most exact calculator has no prescience that somewhat incalculable may not balk the very next moment. I am constrained every moment to acknowledge a higher origin for events than the will I call mine.

As with events, so is it with thoughts. When I watch that flowing river, which, out of regions I see not, pours for a season its streams into me, I see that I am a pensioner; not a cause but a surprised spectator of this ethereal water; that I desire and look up and put myself in the attitude of reception, but from some alien energy the visions come.

The Supreme Critic on the errors of the past and the present, and the only prophet of that which must be, is that great nature in which we rest as the earth lies in the soft arms of the atmosphere; that Unity, that Over-Soul, within which every man's particular being is contained and made one with all other; that common heart of which all sincere conversation is the worship, to which all right action is submission; that overpowering reality which confutes our tricks and talents, and constrains every one to pass for what he is, and to speak from his character and not from his tongue, and which evermore tends to pass into our thought and hand and become wisdom and virtue and power and beauty. We live in succession, in division, in parts, in particles. Meantime within man is the soul of the whole; the wise silence; the universal beauty, to which every part and particle is equally related; the eternal ONE.[3] And this deep power in which we exist and whose beatitude is all accessible to us, is not only self-sufficing and perfect in every hour, but the act of seeing and the thing seen, the seer and the spectacle, the subject and the object, are one. We see the world piece by piece, as the sun, the moon, the animal, the tree; but the whole, of which these are the shining parts, is the soul. Only by the vision of that Wisdom can the horoscope of the ages be read, and by falling back on our better thoughts, by yielding to the spirit of prophecy which is innate in every man, we can know what it saith. Every man's words who speaks from that life must sound vain to those who do not dwell in the same thought on their own part. I dare not speak for it. My words do not carry its august sense; they fall short and cold. Only itself can inspire whom it will, and behold! their speech shall be lyrical, and sweet, and universal as the rising of the wind. Yet I desire, even by profane words, if I may not use sacred, to indicate the heaven of this deity and to report what hints I have collected of the transcendent simplicity and energy of the Highest Law.[4]

If we consider what happens in conversation, in reveries, in remorse, in times of passion, in surprises, in the instructions of dreams, wherein often we see ourselves in masquerade,—the droll disguises only magnifying and enhancing a real element and forcing it on our distant notice,—we shall catch many hints that will broaden and lighten into knowledge of the secret of nature. All goes to show that the soul in man is not an organ, but animates and exercises all the organs; is not a function, like the power of memory, of calculation, of com-

---

[3] Unity and Oversoul are, for Emerson, alternate names for the One, the eternal Idea, or Form, which was the ultimate principle in the Neoplatonic tradition that shaped his thought.

[4] With his Puritan and Unitarian heritage, Emerson understands the One under the character of Law, transforming the moralism of his background into a form of mystical perception.

parison, but uses these as hands and feet; is not a faculty, but a light; is not the intellect or the will, but the master of the intellect and the will; is the background of our being, in which they lie,—an immensity not possessed and that cannot be possessed. From within or from behind, a light shines through us upon things and makes us aware that we are nothing, but the light is all. A man is the façade of a temple wherein all wisdom and all good abide. What we commonly call man, the eating, drinking, planting, counting man, does not, as we know him, represent himself, but misrepresents himself. Him we do not respect, but the soul, whose organ he is, would he let it appear through his action, would make our knees bend. When it breathes through his intellect, it is genius; when it breathes through his will, it is virtue; when it flows through his affection, it is love. And the blindness of the intellect begins when it would be something of itself. The weakness of the will begins when the individual would be something of himself. All reform aims in some one particular to let the soul have its way through us; in other words, to engage us to obey.

Of this pure nature every man is at some time sensible. Language cannot paint it with his colors. It is too subtile. It is undefinable, unmeasurable; but we know that it pervades and contains us. We know that all spiritual being is in man. A wise old proverb says, "God comes to see us without bell;"[5] that is, as there is no screen or ceiling between our heads and the infinite heavens, so is there no bar or wall in the soul, where man, the effect, ceases, and God, the cause, begins.[6] The walls are taken away. We lie open on one side to the deeps of spiritual nature, to the attributes of God. Justice we see and know, Love, Freedom, Power. These natures no man ever got above, but they tower over us, and most in the moment when our interests tempt us to wound them.

The sovereignty of this nature whereof we speak is made known by its independency of those limitations which circumscribe us on every hand. The soul circumscribes all things. As I have said, it contradicts all experience. In like manner it abolishes time and space. The influence of the senses has in most men overpowered the mind to that degree that the walls of time and space have come to look real and insurmountable; and to speak with levity of these limits is, in the world, the sign of insanity. Yet time and space are but inverse measures of the force of the soul. The spirit sports with time,—

"Can crowd eternity into an hour,
Or stretch an hour to eternity."[7]

We are often made to feel that there is another youth and age than that which is measured from the year of our natural birth. Some thoughts always find us young, and keep us so. Such a thought is the love of

---

[5]Emerson drew this proverb from Vicesimus Knox, "Old Spanish Proverbs," in *Elegant Extracts; or, Useful and Entertaining Passages in Prose,* 7th ed. (London: Printed for B. Law, 1797) 2:1035. For this and many of the other identifications in this essay and "Self-Reliance," I am indebted to Joseph Slater's scholarship in Ralph Waldo Emerson, *The Collected Works of Ralph Waldo Emerson,* ed. Alfred R. Ferguson et al. (Cambridge: Harvard University Press, Belknap Press, 1971–) 2:251-53, 229-33.

[6]This is a notably clear statement of the vision of the world that follows from the doctrine of correspondence. All things are made of the same elements, and so all things are ultimately One.

[7]George Gordon Noël (Lord) Byron, *Cain,* act 1, sc. 1, ll. 536-37. The lines are taken, without substantive change, from a statement by Lucifer.

the universal and eternal beauty. Every man parts from that contemplation with the feeling that it rather belongs to ages than to mortal life. The least activity of the intellectual powers redeems us in a degree from the conditions of time. In sickness, in languor, give us a strain of poetry or a profound sentence, and we are refreshed; or produce a volume of Plato or Shakspeare, or remind us of their names, and instantly we come into a feeling of longevity. See how the deep divine thought reduces centuries and millenniums, and makes itself present through all ages. Is the teaching of Christ less effective now than it was when first his mouth was opened? The emphasis of facts and persons in my thought has nothing to do with time. And so always the soul's scale is one, the scale of the senses and the understanding is another. Before the revelations of the soul, Time, Space and Nature shrink away. In common speech we refer all things to time, as we habitually refer the immensely sundered stars to one concave sphere. And so we say that the Judgment is distant or near, that the Millennium approaches, that a day of certain political, moral, social reforms is at hand, and the like, when we mean that in the nature of things one of the facts we contemplate is external and fugitive, and the other is permanent and connate with the soul. The things we now esteem fixed shall, one by one, detach themselves like ripe fruit from our experience, and fall. The wind shall blow them none knows whither. The landscape, the figures, Boston, London, are facts as fugitive as any institution past, or any whiff of mist or smoke, and so is society, and so is the world. The soul looketh steadily forwards, creating a world before her, leaving worlds behind her. She has no dates, nor rites, nor persons, nor specialties nor men. The soul knows only the soul; the web of events is the flowing robe in which she is clothed.

After its own law and not by arithmetic is the rate of its progress to be computed. The soul's advances are not made by gradation, such as can be represented by motion in a straight line, but rather by ascension of state, such as can be represented by metamorphosis,—from the egg to the worm, from the worm to the fly. The growths of genius are of a certain *total* character, that does not advance the elect individual first over John, then Adam, then Richard, and give to each the pain of discovered inferiority,—but by every throe of growth the man expands there where he works, passing, at each pulsation, classes, populations, of men. With each divine impulse the mind rends the thin rinds of the visible and finite, and comes out into eternity, and inspires and expires its air. It converses with truths that have always been spoken in the world, and becomes conscious of a closer sympathy with Zeno and Arrian than with persons in the house.[8]

This is the law of moral and of mental gain. The simple rise as by specific levity not into a particular virtue, but into the region of all the virtues. They are in the spirit which contains them all. The soul requires purity, but purity is not it; requires justice, but justice is not that; requires beneficence, but is somewhat better; so that there is a kind of descent and accommodation felt

---

[8]For Zeno, see n. 29 to Ralph Waldo Emerson, Divinity School *Address*. Arrian, or Flavius Arrianus (95?-175?), was a Greek philosopher, historian, and general. He is probably linked to Zeno here because he edited and wrote commentaries on the *Discourses* of the Stoic philosopher Epictetus (50?-138?). Stoic doctrine, which to a good degree supported Emerson's conception of the world, taught the essential unity of the cosmos, composed of the refined matter that was the fire of Reason. This Reason was the soul and reason of all living creation.

when we leave speaking of moral nature to urge a virtue which it enjoins. To the wellborn child all the virtues are natural, and not painfully acquired. Speak to his heart, and the man becomes suddenly virtuous.

Within the same sentiment is the germ of intellectual growth, which obeys the same law. Those who are capable of humility, of justice, of love, of aspiration, stand already on a platform that commands the sciences and arts, speech and poetry, action and grace. For whoso dwells in this moral beatitude already anticipates those special powers which men prize so highly. The lover has no talent, no skill, which passes for quite nothing with his enamored maiden, however little she may possess of related faculty; and the heart which abandons itself to the Supreme Mind finds itself related to all its works, and will travel a royal road to particular knowledges and powers. In ascending to this primary and aboriginal sentiment we have come from our remote station on the circumference instantaneously to the centre of the world, where, as in the closet of God, we see causes, and anticipate the universe, which is but a slow effect.

One mode of the divine teaching is the incarnation of the spirit in a form,—in forms, like my own. I live in society; with persons who answer to thoughts in my own mind, or express a certain obedience to the great instincts to which I live. I see its presence to them. I am certified of a common nature; and these other souls, these separated selves, draw me as nothing else can. They stir in me the new emotions we call passion; of love, hatred, fear, admiration, pity; thence come conversation, competition, persuasion, cities and war. Persons are supplementary to the primary teaching of the soul. In youth we are mad for persons. Childhood and youth see all the world in them. But the larger experience of man discovers the identical nature appearing through them all. Persons themselves acquaint us with the impersonal. In all conversation between two persons tacit reference is made, as to a third party, to a common nature. That third party or common nature is not social; it is impersonal; is God. And so in groups where debate is earnest, and especially on high questions, the company become aware that the thought rises to an equal level in all bosoms, that all have a spiritual property in what was said, as well as the sayer. They all become wiser than they were. It arches over them like a temple, this unity of thought in which every heart beats with nobler sense of power and duty, and thinks and acts with unusual solemnity. All are conscious of attaining to a higher self-possession. It shines for all. There is a certain wisdom of humanity which is common to the greatest men with the lowest, and which our ordinary education often labors to silence and obstruct. The mind is one, and the best minds, who love truth for its own sake, think much less of property in truth. They accept it thankfully everywhere, and do not label or stamp it with any man's name, for it is theirs long beforehand, and from eternity. The learned and the studious of thought have no monopoly of wisdom. Their violence of direction in some degree disqualifies them to think truly. We owe many valuable observations to people who are not very acute or profound, and who say the thing without effort which we want and have long been hunting in vain.[9] The action of the soul is oftener in that which is felt and left unsaid than in that which is said in any conversation. It broods

---

[9]Here Emerson displays a suspicion of unbridled intellect akin to the warnings of many in the mystical tradition. See, for example, Thomas à Kempis, *The Imitation of Christ* (1424?—trans. Richard Whitford [1530?]) 1:2; 3:43.

over every society, and they unconsciously seek for it in each other. We know better than we do.[10] We do not yet possess ourselves, and we know at the same time that we are much more. I feel the same truth how often in my trivial conversation with my neighbors, that somewhat higher in each of us overlooks this by-play, and Jove nods to Jove from behind each of us.

Men descend to meet. In their habitual and mean service to the world, for which they forsake their native nobleness, they resemble those Arabian sheiks who dwell in mean houses and affect an external poverty, to escape the rapacity of the Pacha,[11] and reserve all their display of wealth for their interior and guarded retirements.

As it is present in all persons, so it is in every period of life. It is adult already in the infant man. In my dealing with my child, my Latin and Greek, my accomplishments and my money stead me nothing; but as much soul as I have avails. If I am wilful, he sets his will against mine, one for one, and leaves me, if I please, the degradation of beating him by my superiority of strength. But if I renounce my will and act for the soul, setting that up as umpire between us two, out of his young eyes looks the same soul; he reveres and loves with me.

The soul is the perceiver and revealer of truth. We know truth when we see it, let sceptic and scoffer say what they choose. Foolish people ask you, when you have spoken what they do not wish to hear, 'How do you know it is truth, and not an error of your own?' We know truth when we see it, from opinion, as we know when we are awake that we are awake.[12] It was a grand sentence of Emanuel Swedenborg, which would alone indicate the greatness of that man's perception,—"It is no proof of a man's understanding to be able to affirm whatever he pleases; but to be able to discern that what is true is true, and that what is false is false,—this is the mark and character of intelligence."[13] In the book I read, the good thought returns to me, as every truth will, the image of the whole soul. To the bad thought which I find in it, the same soul becomes a discerning, separating sword, and lops it away. We are wiser than we know. If we will not inter-

---

[10]There are Gnostic overtones to Emerson's treatment of knowing in this discussion and throughout the essay. The Gnostic sects, in the Mediterranean world from the second century A.D., taught a doctrine of secret, saving knowledge on the part of certain human beings who were awakened by their divine counterpart to the celestial spark within them. Gnosticism blended with Neoplatonism and other teachings in the occult-metaphysical tradition of the West. Emerson differs from traditional Gnostics in this passage and elsewhere in the democratic universality he ascribes to the spark and the knowledge: all human beings possess both.

[11]*Pacha* is a nineteenth-century variant of *pasha*, a military leader or governor in imperial Turkey or North Africa.

[12]Again, Emerson is teaching an apparently Gnostic conception of knowledge, which flows from his understanding of the one soul in all—the Oversoul. There are links, too, between his idea of knowledge and the moral intuitionism of Scottish common-sense philosophy, as was noted in the introduction to the essay. As Emerson consciously identifies the sources of his thought, however, he acknowledges in the next sentence his debt to Emanuel Swedenborg.

[13]Emerson has used a paraphrase of Swedenborg by Caleb Reed in "The Nature and Character of True Wisdom and Intelligence," *The New Jerusalem Magazine* 3 (January 1830): 151. For Swedenborg's own words, see Emanuel Swedenborg, *The Doctrine of the New Jerusalem concerning the Sacred Scripture* (Boston: John W. Folsom, 1795) sec. 91, p. 147.

fere with our thought, but will act entirely, or see how the thing stands in God, we know the particular thing, and every thing, and every man. For the Maker of all things and all persons stands behind us and casts his dread omniscience through us over things.

But beyond this recognition of its own in particular passages of the individual's experience, it also reveals truth. And here we should seek to reinforce ourselves by its very presence, and to speak with a worthier, loftier strain of that advent. For the soul's communication of truth is the highest event in nature, since it then does not give somewhat from itself, but it gives itself, or passes into and becomes that man whom it enlightens; or in proportion to that truth he receives, it takes him to itself.

We distinguish the announcements of the soul, its manifestations of its own nature, by the term *Revelation*. These are always attended by the emotion of the sublime. For this communication is an influx of the Divine mind into our mind. It is an ebb of the individual rivulet before the flowing surges of the sea of life. Every distinct apprehension of this central commandment agitates men with awe and delight. A thrill passes through all men at the reception of new truth, or at the performance of a great action, which comes out of the heart of nature. In these communications the power to see is not separated from the will to do, but the insight proceeds from obedience, and the obedience proceeds from a joyful perception. Every moment when the individual feels himself invaded by it is memorable. By the necessity of our constitution a certain enthusiasm attends the individual's consciousness of that divine presence. The character and duration of this enthusiasm vary with the state of the individual, from an ectasy and trance and prophetic inspirations,—which is its rarer appearance,— to the faintest glow of virtuous emotion, in which form it warms, like our household fires, all the families and associations of men, and makes society possible. A certain tendency to insanity has always attended the opening of the religious sense in men, as if they had been "blasted with excess of light."[14] The trances of Socrates, the "union" of Plotinus, the vision of Porphyry, the conversion of Paul, the aurora of Behmen,[15] the convulsions of George

---

[14]This phrase was used to refer to the poet John Milton in Thomas Gray, "The Progress of Poesy," 1. 101.

[15]In the *Symposium* of Plato, Apollodorus relates how Socrates, on his way with Aristodemus to a banquet at the house of Agathon, stopped in his tracks and remained wrapped in his thoughts while his friend proceeded to the party. Later in the dialogue, Alcibiades recalls another occasion when Socrates remained standing for a twenty-four-hour period, lost in thought. See Plato, *Symposium,* 174D-175B and 220C-D. Plotinus, the founder of Neoplatonism, was observed by his pupil Porphyry to be in ecstatic union with the One on four different occasions. See Porphyry, *On the Life of Plotinus and the Arrangement of His Work,* in Plotinus, *The Enneads,* trans. Stephen MacKenna and ed. B. S. Page, 3d ed. rev. (London: Faber and Faber, 1962) 17. Porphyry displayed mystical inclinations of his own, as revealed in the passage cited above. In the introduction to his translation of Plotinus, Thomas Taylor quoted Porphyry concerning his own and his master's experiences of vision and union. See Thomas Taylor, trans., *Select Works of Plotinus* (London: Published by the Author, 1817) xv, lvii-lxix. Jacob Boehme (Emerson's "Behmen") produced a mystical work in 1612 entitled *Aurora* with which, in English translation (1656), Emerson was familiar. See Ralph Waldo Emerson, *The Journals and Miscellaneous Notebooks of Ralph Waldo Emerson,* ed. William H. Gilman et al. (Cambridge: Harvard University Press, Belknap Press, 1960–) 5 (1 August 1835): 75.

Fox and his Quakers, the illumination of Swedenborg, are of this kind. What was in the case of these remarkable persons a ravishment, has, in innumerable instances in common life, been exhibited in less striking manner. Everywhere the history of religion betrays a tendency to enthusiasm. The rapture of the Moravian and Quietist;[16] the opening of the eternal sense of the Word, in the language of the New Jerusalem Church;[17] the *revival* of the Calvinistic churches; the *experiences* of the Methodists, are varying forms of that shudder of awe and delight with which the individual soul always mingles with the universal soul.

The nature of these revelations is the same; they are perceptions of the absolute law. They are solutions of the soul's own questions. They do not answer the questions which the understanding asks. The soul answers never by words, but by the thing itself that is inquired after.

Revelation is the disclosure of the soul. The popular notion of a revelation is that it is a telling of fortunes. In past oracles of the soul the understanding seeks to find answers to sensual questions, and undertakes to tell from God how long men shall exist, what their hands shall do and who shall be their company, adding names and dates and places.[18] But we must pick no locks. We must check this low curiosity. An answer in words is delusive; it is really no answer to the questions you ask. Do not require a description of the countries towards which you sail. The description does not describe them to you, and to-morrow you arrive there and know them by inhabiting them. Men ask concerning the immortality of the soul, the employments of heaven, the state of the sinner, and so forth. They even dream that Jesus has left replies to precisely these interrogatories. Never a moment did that sublime spirit speak in their *patois*.[19] To truth, justice, love, the attributes of the soul, the idea of immutableness is essentially associated. Jesus, living in these moral sentiments, heedless of sensual fortunes, heeding only the manifestations of these, never made the separation of the idea of duration from the essence of these attributes, nor uttered a syllable concerning the duration of the soul. It was left to his disciples to sever duration from the moral elements, and to teach the immortality of the soul as a doctrine, and maintain it by evidences. The moment the doctrine of the immortality is separately

---

[16]The Moravians, who arose in Bohemia among the followers of the martyred John Huss (1369?-1415), came in contact with Lutheran Pietism through the association in 1722 of a remnant of the original group with Nikolaus von Zinzendorf (1700-1760). The Moravian Brethren were known for the deep strain of subjective feeling they brought to religious observance. The Quietists were followers of a seventeenth-century mystical movement founded in Spain by the priest Miguel de Molinos (1640-1697) that later spread to France. Considered heretical by the Roman Catholic church, Quietism, or Molinism, taught the centrality of passive contemplation.

[17]The "New Jerusalem Church," or, officially, the Church of the New Jerusalem, was the Swedenborgian church. The new critical edition of Emerson's writings supplies "internal sense of the Word" for "eternal sense of the Word," basing its text on the original 1841 edition of the *Essays*. See Emerson, *Collected Works*, 2:167. This reading agrees with the Swedenborgian insistence on an inner mystical meaning for the Word. See Swedenborg, *Doctrine of the New Jerusalem*, 12.

[18]Here, again, the familiar distinction between the Reason and the Understanding forms the background for Emerson's thought.

[19]French for "regional dialect" or "jargon."

taught, man is already fallen. In the flowing of love, in the adoration of humility, there is no question of continuance. No inspired man ever asks this question or condescends to these evidences. For the soul is true to itself, and the man in whom it is shed abroad cannot wander from the present, which is infinite, to a future which would be finite.[20]

These questions which we lust to ask about the future are a confession of sin. God has no answer for them. No answer in words can reply to a question of things. It is not in an arbitrary "decree of God," but in the nature of man, that a veil shuts down on the facts of to-morrow; for the soul will not have us read any other cipher than that of cause and effect. By this veil which curtains events it instructs the children of men to live in to-day. The only mode of obtaining an answer to these questions of the senses is to forego all low curiosity, and, accepting the tide of being which floats us into the secret of nature, work and live, work and live, and all unawares the advancing soul has built and forged for itself a new condition, and the question and the answer are one.

By the same fire, vital, consecrating, celestial, which burns until it shall dissolve all things into the waves and surges of an ocean of light, we see and know each other, and what spirit each is of. Who can tell the grounds of his knowledge of the character of the several individuals in his circle of friends? No man. Yet their acts and words do not disappoint him. In that man, though he knew no ill of him, he put no trust. In that other, though they had seldom met, authentic signs had yet passed, to signify that he might be trusted as one who had an interest in his own character. We know each other very well,—which of us has been just to himself and whether that which we teach or behold is only an aspiration or is our honest effort also.

We are all discerners of spirits. That diagnosis lies aloft in our life or unconscious power. The intercourse of society, its trade, its religion, its friendships, its quarrels, is one wide judicial investigation of character. In full court, or in small committee, or confronted face to face, accuser and accused, men offer themselves to be judged. Against their will they exhibit those decisive trifles by which character is read. But who judges? and what? Not our understanding. We do not read them by learning or craft. No; the wisdom of the wise man consists herein, that he does not judge them; he lets them judge themselves and merely reads and records their own verdict.

By virtue of this inevitable nature, private will is overpowered, and, maugre our efforts or our imperfections, your genius will speak from you, and mine from me. That which we are, we shall teach, not voluntarily but involuntarily. Thoughts come into our minds by avenues which we never left open, and thoughts go out of our minds through avenues which we never voluntarily opened. Character teaches over our head. The infallible index of true progress is found in the tone the man takes. Neither his age, nor his breeding, nor company, nor books, nor actions, nor talents, nor all together can hinder him from being deferential to a higher spirit than his own. If he have not found his home in God, his manners, his forms of speech, the turn of his sentences, the build, shall I say, of all his opinions will involuntarily confess it, let him brave it out how he will. If he have found his centre, the Deity will shine

---

[20]The present is infinite for the inspired person because he or she dwells in the eternity and immutableness of the Oversoul. By contrast, the future is only a limited human experience. The passages that follow are a clear affirmation by Emerson of the mystical vision.

through him, through all the disguises of ignorance, of ungenial temperament, of unfavorable circumstance. The tone of seeking is one, and the tone of having is another.

The great distinction between teachers sacred or literary,—between poets like Herbert, and poets like Pope,[21]—between philosophers like Spinoza, Kant and Coleridge, and philosophers like Locke, Paley, Mackintosh and Stewart,[22]—between men of the world who are reckoned accomplished talkers, and here and there a fervent mystic, prophesying half insane under the infinitude of his thought,—is that one class speak *from within,* or from experience, as parties and possessors of the fact; and the other class *from without,* as spectators merely, or perhaps as acquainted with the fact on the evidence of third persons. It is of no use to preach to me from without. I can do that too easily myself. Jesus speaks always from within, and in a degree that transcends all others. In that is the miracle.[23] I believe beforehand that it ought so to be. All men stand continually in the expectation of the appearance of such a teacher. But if a man do not speak from within the veil, where the word is one with that it tells of, let him lowly confess it.[24]

The same Omniscience flows into the intellect and makes what we call genius. Much of the wisdom of the world is not wisdom, and the most illuminated class of men are no doubt superior to literary fame, and are not writers. Among the multitude of scholars and authors we feel no hallowing presence; we are sensible of a knack and skill rather than of inspiration; they have a light and know not whence it comes and call it their own; their talent is some exaggerated faculty, some overgrown member, so that their strength is a disease. In these instances the intellectual gifts do not make the impression of virtue, but almost

---

[21]George Herbert was known for his religious themes and the quietness of his poetic tone. Emerson's regard for his work is seen in his quotations from Herbert in *Nature* (see nn. 5 and 68 to the essay). On the other hand, Emerson thinks less of the work of Alexander Pope (1688–1744), the English satiric poet known for the wit, polish, and precision of his lines.

[22]Emerson ranks Baruch Spinoza (1632–1677) with Kant and Coleridge as "teachers sacred." The Dutch Jewish philosopher taught a monistic and pantheistic doctrine in which all things participate as one substance in God, or Nature. Emerson views the philosophy of John Locke with far less enthusiasm, as is also the case for the thought of William Paley (1743–1805), James Mackintosh (1765–1832), and Dugald Stewart (1753–1828). Paley, an English theologian, wrote *A View of the Evidences of Christianity* (1794), which pointed to external, rational evidences for the truth of the Christian message—an enterprise in general applauded by Unitarians and deplored by Emerson. Sir James Mackintosh, highly regarded by Unitarian moralists, was a writer on political and historical themes and, after entering Parliament in 1813, a political reformer. Dugald Stewart was the Scottish common-sense philosopher who largely followed the thought of Thomas Reid (1710–1796) in his own philosophical exposition.

[23]Emerson alludes here to the miracles controversy with the Unitarian establishment. For him and for other Transcendentalists, the real sources of power and authority in Jesus were inner. (See the introduction to this volume and n. 9 to Emerson, Divinity School *Address.*)

[24]See Emerson's discussion under "Language" (ch. 4) in *Nature,* where he argues for the spiritual significance of the correspondence between word and thing. Observe, too, the reference (above in the passage) to expectation of one to come, a theme already noted in the Divinity School *Address* (see n. 36 to the address) and present as well in Emerson's "Song of Nature" in this volume.

of vice; and we feel that a man's talents stand in the way of his advancement in truth. But genius is religious. It is a larger imbibing of the common heart. It is not anomalous, but more like and not less like other men. There is in all great poets a wisdom of humanity which is superior to any talents they exercise. The author, the wit, the partisan, the fine gentleman, does not take place of the man. Humanity shines in Homer, in Chaucer, in Spenser, in Shakspeare, in Milton. They are content with truth. They use the positive degree. They seem frigid and phlegmatic to those who have been spiced with the frantic passion and violent coloring of inferior but popular writers. For they are poets by the free course which they allow to the informing soul, which through their eyes beholds again and blesses the things which it hath made. The soul is superior to its knowledge, wiser than any of its works. The great poet makes us feel our own wealth, and then we think less of his compositions. His best communication to our mind is to teach us to despise all he has done. Shakspeare carries us to such a lofty strain of intelligent activity as to suggest a wealth which beggars his own; and we then feel that the splendid works which he has created, and which in other hours we extol as a sort of self-existent poetry, take no stronger hold of real nature than the shadow of a passing traveller on the rock. The inspiration which uttered itself in Hamlet and Lear could utter things as good from day to day for ever. Why then should I make account of Hamlet and Lear, as if we had not the soul from which they fell as syllables from the tongue?

This energy does not descend into individual life on any other condition than entire possession. It comes to the lowly and simple; it comes to whomsoever will put off what is foreign and proud; it comes as insight; it comes as serenity and grandeur. When we see those whom it inhabits, we are apprised of new degrees of greatness. From that inspiration the man comes back with a changed tone. He does not talk with men with an eye to their opinion. He tries them. It requires of us to be plain and true. The vain traveller attempts to embellish his life by quoting my lord and the prince and the countess, who thus said or did to *him*. The ambitious vulgar show you their spoons and brooches and rings, and preserve their cards and compliments. The more cultivated, in their account of their own experience, cull out the pleasing, poetic circumstance,—the visit to Rome, the man of genius they saw, the brilliant friend they know; still further on perhaps the gorgeous landscape, the mountain lights, the mountain thoughts they enjoyed yesterday,—and so seek to throw a romantic color over their life. But the soul that ascends to worship the great God is plain and true; has no rose-color, no fine friends, no chivalry, no adventures; does not want admiration; dwells in the hour that now is, in the earnest experience of the common day,—by reason of the present moment and the mere trifle having become porous to thought and bibulous of the sea of light.

Converse with a mind that is grandly simple, and literature looks like word-catching. The simplest utterances are worthiest to be written, yet are they so cheap and so things of course, that in the infinite riches of the soul it is like gathering a few pebbles off the ground, or bottling a little air in a phial, when the whole earth and the whole atmosphere are ours. Nothing can pass there, or make you one of the circle, but the casting aside your trappings and dealing man to man in naked truth, plain confession and omniscient affirmation.

Souls such as these treat you as gods would, walk as gods in the earth, accepting without any admiration your wit, your bounty, your virtue even,—say rather your act of duty, for your virtue they own as their proper blood, royal as themselves, and over-royal, and the father of the gods. But what rebuke their plain fraternal bearing casts on the mutual flattery with which authors solace each other and wound themselves! These flatter not. I do not wonder that these men go to see Cromwell and Christina and Charles the Second and James the First and the Grand Turk.[25] For they are, in their own elevation, the fellows of kings, and must feel the servile tone of conversation in the world. They must always be a godsend to princes, for they confront them, a king to a king, without ducking or concession, and give a high nature the refreshment and satisfaction of resistance, of plain humanity, of even companionship and of new ideas. They leave them wiser and superior men. Souls like these make us feel that sincerity is more excellent than flattery. Deal so plainly with man and woman as to constrain the utmost sincerity and destroy all hope of trifling with you. It is the highest compliment you can pay. Their "highest praising," said Milton, "is not flattery, and their plainest advice is a kind of praising."[26]

Ineffable is the union of man and God in every act of the soul. The simplest person who in his integrity worships God, becomes God; yet for ever and ever the influx of this better and universal self is new and unsearchable. It inspires awe and astonishment. How dear, how soothing to man, arises the idea of God, peopling the lonely place, effacing the scars of our mistakes and disappointments! When we have broken our god of tradition and ceased from our god of rhetoric, then may God fire the heart with his presence. It is the doubling of the heart itself, nay, the infinite enlargement of the heart with a power of growth to a new infinity on every side. It inspires in man an infallible trust. He has not the conviction, but the sight, that the best is the true, and may in that thought easily dismiss all particular uncertainties and fears, and adjourn to the sure revelation of time the solution of his private riddles. He is sure that his welfare is dear to the heart of being. In the presence of law to his mind he is overflowed with a reliance so universal that it sweeps away all cherished hopes and the most stable projects of mortal condition in

---

[25] Oliver Cromwell (1599-1658) rose swiftly to a role of political leadership during the first English Civil War and in 1654 became lord protector of England, the dictatorial position he held until his death. Christina (1626–1689), queen of Sweden from 1632 to 1654, defied convention to live her life as she chose. Renowned for her enthusiasm for learning and for her patronage of the arts, she eschewed marriage and then, attracted to Roman Catholicism, left Sweden secretly, disguised as a man, and became a Catholic. After his defeat at Oliver Cromwell's hands, Charles II (1630–1685) lived on the Continent until, in 1660, he was restored to the English throne. Friction with Parliament plagued his reign (Charles had Roman Catholic leanings and favored France), and in 1681 he acted to dissolve Parliament and proceeded to rule as an absolutist. James I (1566–1625) of England (also James VI of Scotland) in 1614 dissolved Parliament and ruled without it until 1621, paving the way for the later English Civil Wars. He also displayed an early interest in theological learning and produced works on politics, literary theory, and poetry. For the "Grand Turk" Emerson was probably thinking of Sulayman the Magnificent (1494–1566), or Sulayman I, under whom the Turkish Empire attained the height of its power. Sulayman was a reformer and an avid patron of literature, art, and architecture; and his court was renowned as a place of splendor.

[26] See John Milton, *Areopagitica*, ed. John W. Hales (London: Oxford University Press, 1961) 3. Emerson has made small changes, notably substituting "their" for the "his" of the original.

its flood. He believes that he cannot escape from his good. The things that are really for thee gravitate to thee. You are running to seek your friend. Let your feet run, but your mind need not. If you do not find him, will you not acquiesce that it is best you should not find him? for there is a power, which, as it is in you, is in him also, and could therefore very well bring you together, if it were for the best. You are preparing with eagerness to go and render a service to which your talent and your taste invite you, the love of men and the hope of fame. Has it not occurred to you that you have no right to go, unless you are equally willing to be prevented from going?[27] O, believe, as thou livest, that every sound that is spoken over the round world, which thou oughtest to hear, will vibrate on thine ear! Every proverb, every book, every byword that belongs to thee for aid or comfort, shall surely come home through open or winding passages. Every friend whom not thy fantastic will but the great and tender heart in thee craveth, shall lock thee in his embrace. And this because the heart in thee is the heart of all; not a valve, not a wall, not an intersection is there anywhere in nature, but one blood rolls uninterruptedly an endless circulation through all men, as the water of the globe is all one sea, and, truly seen, its tide is one.

Let man then learn the revelation of all nature and all thought to his heart; this, namely; that the Highest dwells with him; that the sources of nature are in his own mind, if the sentiment of duty is there. But if he would know what the great God speaketh, he must 'go into his closet and shut the door,' as Jesus said.[28] God will not make himself manifest to cowards. He must greatly listen to himself, withdrawing himself from all the accents of other men's devotion. Even their prayers are hurtful to him, until he have made his own. Our religion vulgarly stands on numbers of believers. Whenever the appeal is made,— no matter how indirectly,—to numbers, proclamation is then and there made that religion is not. He that finds God a sweet enveloping thought to him never counts his company. When I sit in that presence, who shall dare to come in? When I rest in perfect humility, when I burn with pure love, what can Calvin or Swedenborg say?

It makes no difference whether the appeal is to numbers or to one. The faith that stands on authority is not faith. The reliance on authority measures the decline of religion, the withdrawal of the soul. The position men have given to Jesus, now for many centuries of history, is a position of authority. It characterizes themselves. It cannot alter the eternal facts. Great is the soul, and plain. It is no flatterer, it is no follower; it never appeals from itself. It believes in itself. Before the immense possibilities of man all mere experience, all past biography, however spotless and sainted, shrinks away. Before that heaven which our presentiments foreshow us, we cannot easily praise any form of life we have seen or read of. We not only affirm that we have few great men, but, absolutely speaking, that we have none; that we have no history, no record of any character or mode of living that entirely contents us. The saints and demigods whom history worships we are constrained to accept with a grain of allowance. Though in our lonely hours we draw a new strength out of their memory, yet, pressed on our attention, as

---

[27] In his notes to the essay, Edward Waldo Emerson observed that this sentence was originally inscribed by his father in his journal on the eve of delivering the Divinity School *Address*. See Emerson, *Complete Works*, 2:432.

[28] Cf. Matt. 6:6.

they are by the thoughtless and customary, they fatigue and invade. The soul gives itself, alone, original and pure, to the Lonely, Original and Pure, who, on that condition, gladly inhabits, leads and speaks through it.[29] Then is it glad, young and nimble. It is not wise, but it sees through all things. It is not called religious, but it is innocent. It calls the light its own, and feels that the grass grows and the stone falls by a law inferior to, and dependent on, its nature. Behold, it saith, I am born into the great, the universal mind. I, the imperfect, adore my own Perfect. I am somehow receptive of the great soul, and thereby I do overlook the sun and the stars and feel them to be the fair accidents and effects which change and pass. More and more the surges of everlasting nature enter into me, and I become public and human in my regards and actions. So come I to live in thoughts and act with energies which are immortal. Thus revering the soul, and learning, as the ancient said, that "its beauty is immense,"[30] man will come to see that the world is the perennial miracle which the soul worketh, and be less astonished at particular wonders; he will learn that there is no profane history; that all history is sacred; that the universe is represented in an atom, in a moment of time. He will weave no longer a spotted life of shreds and patches,[31] but he will live with a divine unity. He will cease from what is base and frivolous in his life and be content with all places and with any service he can render. He will calmly front the morrow in the negligency of that trust which carries God with it and so hath already the whole future in the bottom of the heart.

---

[29]Cf. Plotinus *Enneads* 6.9.11: "the flight of the Alone to the Alone."

[30]See Plotinus *Enneads* 5.8.3, in which Plotinus is referring to the beauty of the Gods. Emerson may have recalled part of the line from the introduction to Thomas Taylor's translation of the *Enneads* in *Select Works of Plotinus:* "All the Gods are venerable and beautiful, their beauty is immense" (Plotinus, *Select Works,* lxxix).

[31]Cf. *Hamlet,* act 3, sc. 4, l. 102.

SELF-RELIANCE

Like "The Over-Soul," "Self-Reliance" appeared as part of Emerson's first collection of essays, published in 1841. Also like "The Over-Soul," parts of it had been taken from earlier lectures. More important here, "Self-Reliance" forms the other side of the teaching articulated in "The Over-Soul." For Emerson the energy that flows into a person from that divine source does not lead to the extinction of individuality, but to its flowering in self-culture. Conversely, the self that is cultivated is a Self thoroughly attuned to the sacred. While much is sometimes made of Emerson's hypothetical reference to being the Devil's child and his indictment of the "foolish philanthropist," the context of the Emersonian rhetoric is often forgotten. Emerson's argument is, in fact, a tour de force for the primacy of being over doing. Like so many in the mystical tradition, he is suspicious of action that dissipates energy, encourages distraction, and arises from social convention. He seeks genuineness, purity, originality, and spontaneity—a doing that issues integrally from a person's being.

Hence, despite his preference for moral categories, Emerson moves beyond the usual understandings of good and evil in this essay. He is a nineteenth-century gnostic as he testifies to a spiritual estate in which such distinctions yield to another order of being. The doing he can affirm completely is the doing that emerges from this estate—even when he applies his ideas, as in the latter part of the essay, to problems in religion, education, art, and the governance of society. Such doing is neither selfish nor contrary to the divine plan according to Emerson. "Accept the place the divine providence has found for you, the society of your contemporaries, the connection of events," he counsels.

Emerson's son and editor was not unaware of the dangers of misreading "Self-Reliance," and his notes to the essay are worth repeating. "It is well to call to mind," he said, "1st, Mr. Emerson's fear of weakening the effect of his presentation of a subject by qualification; 2d, That the Self he refers to is the higher self, man's share of divinity." "Hence," he added, " 'The Over-Soul' should be read after 'Self-Reliance' "[1]—an order that in this volume has been reversed while still observing the link he noted.[2]

---

[1] See Ralph Waldo Emerson, *The Complete Works of Ralph Waldo Emerson,* ed. Edward Waldo Emerson, centenary ed. (Boston: Houghton, Mifflin, 1903–1904) 2:390.

[2] The text is that of the centenary edition of Emerson, *Complete Works,* 2:43-90.

SELF-RELIANCE

"Ne te quæsiveris extra."[1]

MAN is his own star; and the soul that can
Render an honest and a perfect man,
Commands all light, all influence, all fate;
Nothing to him falls early or too late.
Our acts our angels are, or good or ill,
Our fatal shadows that walk by us still.
   Epilogue to {Francis} Beaumont and {John} Fletcher's
   Honest Man's Fortune {2d ed.; 1679}.

Cast the bantling on the rocks,
Suckle him with the she-wolf's teat,
Wintered with the hawk and fox,
Power and speed be hands and feet.[2]

I READ the other day some verses written by an eminent painter which were original and not conventional.[3] The soul always hears an admonition in such lines, let the subject be what it may. The sentiment they instil is of more value than any thought they may contain. To believe your own thought, to believe that what is true for you in your private heart is true for all men,—that is genius. Speak your latent conviction, and it shall be the universal sense; for the inmost in due time becomes the outmost, and our first thought is rendered back to us by the trumpets of the Last Judgment. Familiar as the voice of the mind is to each, the highest merit we ascribe to Moses, Plato and Milton is that they set at naught books and traditions, and spoke not what men, but what *they* thought. A man should learn to detect and watch that gleam of light which

---

[1] "Do not seek [anyone or anything] outside yourself." The source is Persius *Satires* 1.7, although Emerson has transcribed *ne* for *nec*.

[2] This brief verse was composed by Emerson. In Edward Waldo Emerson's edition of his father's works, it appears under the title "Power" as one of a collection of "Quatrains." See Ralph Waldo Emerson, *The Complete Works of Ralph Waldo Emerson*, ed. Edward Waldo Emerson, centenary ed. (Boston: Houghton, Mifflin, 1903–1904) 9:295.

[3] Through one of Emerson's journal entries, the painter has been identified as Washington Allston (1779–1843)—the American artist, a student of Benjamin West, who was also an author. See Ralph Waldo Emerson, *The Journals and Miscellaneous Notebooks of Ralph Waldo Emerson*, ed. William H. Gilman et al. (Cambridge: Harvard University Press, Belknap Press, 1960–) 5 (20 September 1837): 377.

flashes across his mind from within, more than the lustre of the firmament of bards and sages. Yet he dismisses without notice his thought, because it is his. In every work of genius we recognize our own rejected thoughts; they come back to us with a certain alienated majesty. Great works of art have no more affecting lesson for us than this. They teach us to abide by our spontaneous impression with good-humored inflexibility then most when the whole cry of voices is on the other side. Else tomorrow a stranger will say with masterly good sense precisely what we have thought and felt all the time, and we shall be forced to take with shame our own opinion from another.

There is a time in every man's education when he arrives at the conviction that envy is ignorance; that imitation is suicide; that he must take himself for better for worse as his portion; that though the wide universe is full of good, no kernel of nourishing corn can come to him but through his toil bestowed on that plot of ground which is given to him to till. The power which resides in him is new in nature, and none but he knows what that is which he can do, nor does he know until he has tried. Not for nothing one face, one character, one fact, makes much impression on him, and another none. This sculpture in the memory is not without preëstablished harmony. The eye was placed where one ray should fall, that it might testify of that particular ray. We but half express ourselves, and are ashamed of that divine idea which each of us represents. It may be safely trusted as proportionate and of good issues, so it be faithfully imparted, but God will not have his work made manifest by cowards. A man is relieved and gay when he has put his heart into his work and done his best; but what he has said or done otherwise shall give him no peace. It is a deliverance which does not deliver. In the attempt his genius deserts him; no muse befriends; no invention, no hope.

Trust thyself: every heart vibrates to that iron string.[4] Accept the place the divine providence has found for you, the society of your contemporaries, the connection of events. Great men have always done so, and confided themselves childlike to the genius of their age, betraying their perception that the absolutely trustworthy was seated at their heart, working through their hands, predominating in all their being. And we are now men, and must accept in the highest mind the same transcendent destiny; and not minors and invalids in a protected corner, not cowards fleeing before a revolution, but guides, redeemers and benefactors, obeying the Almighty effort and advancing on Chaos and the Dark.[5]

What pretty oracles nature yields us on this text in the face and behavior of children, babes, and even brutes! That divided and rebel mind, that distrust of a sentiment because our arithmetic has computed the strength and means opposed to our purpose, these have not. Their mind being whole, their eye is as yet unconquered, and when we look in their faces we are disconcerted. Infancy conforms to nobody; all conform to it; so that one babe commonly makes four or five out of the adults who prattle and play to it. So God has armed youth and puberty and manhood no less with its own piquancy and charm, and made it enviable and gracious and its claims not to be put by, if it will stand by itself.

---

[4]At the time that Emerson was writing, wrought iron was still used for major construction work, as in railroads and bridges, and so would symbolize strength.

[5]The metaphor is dualistic, underlining Emerson's eclecticism even as he espouses a Neoplatonic monistic doctrine.

Do not think the youth has no force, because he cannot speak to you and me. Hark! in the next room his voice is sufficiently clear and emphatic. It seems he knows how to speak to his contemporaries. Bashful or bold then, he will know how to make us seniors very unnecessary.

The nonchalance of boys who are sure of a dinner, and would disdain as much as a lord to do or say aught to conciliate one, is the healthy attitude of human nature. A boy is in the parlor what the pit is in the playhouse; independent, irresponsible, looking out from his corner on such people and facts as pass by, he tries and sentences them on their merits, in the swift, summary way of boys, as good, bad, interesting, silly, eloquent, troublesome. He cumbers himself never about consequences, about interests; he gives an independent, genuine verdict. You must court him; he does not court you. But the man is as it were clapped into jail by his consciousness. As soon as he has once acted or spoken with *éclat* he is a committed person, watched by the sympathy or the hatred of hundreds, whose affections must now enter into his account. There is no Lethe for this.[6] Ah, that he could pass again into his neutrality! Who can thus avoid all pledges and, having observed, observe again from the same unaffected, unbiased, unbribable, unaffrighted innocence,—must always be formidable. He would utter opinions on all passing affairs, which being seen to be not private but necessary, would sink like darts into the ear of men and put them in fear.

These are the voices which we hear in solitude, but they grow faint and inaudible as we enter into the world. Society everywhere is in conspiracy against the manhood of every one of its members. Society is a joint-stock company, in which the members agree, for the better securing of his bread to each shareholder, to surrender the liberty and culture of the eater. The virtue in most request is conformity. Self-reliance is its aversion. It loves not realities and creators, but names and customs.

Whoso would be a man, must be a nonconformist. He who would gather immortal palms must not be hindered by the name of goodness, but must explore if it be goodness. Nothing is at last sacred but the integrity of your own mind. Absolve you to yourself, and you shall have the suffrage of the world. I remember an answer which when quite young I was prompted to make to a valued adviser who was wont to importune me with the dear old doctrines of the church. On my saying, "What have I to do with the sacredness of traditions, if I live wholly from within?" my friend suggested,—"But these impulses may be from below, not from above." I replied, "They do not seem to me to be such; but if I am the Devil's child, I will live then from the Devil."[7] No law can be sacred to me but that of my nature. Good and bad are but names very readily transferable to that or this; the only right is what is after my constitution; the only wrong what is against it. A man is to carry himself in the presence of all opposition as if every thing were titular and ephemeral but he. I am ashamed to think how easily we capitulate to badges and names, to large societies and dead institutions. Every decent and well-spoken individual affects and sways me more than is right. I ought to go upright and vital, and

---

[6]In Greek mythology, Lethe was the river of forgetfulness, one of the five rivers marking the boundary to the underworld.

[7]Emerson here skirts the edge of a gnostic awareness of evil as part of the sacred. See Hans Jonas, *The Gnostic Religion,* 2d ed. rev. (Boston: Beacon Press, 1963) 105, 130-31.

speak the rude truth in all ways. If malice and vanity wear the coat of philanthropy, shall that pass? If an angry bigot assumes this bountiful cause of Abolition, and comes to me with his last news from Barbadoes,[8] why should I not say to him, 'Go love thy infant; love thy wood-chopper; be good-natured and modest; have that grace; and never varnish your hard, uncharitable ambition with this incredible tenderness for black folk a thousand miles off. Thy love afar is spite at home.' Rough and graceless would be such greeting, but truth is handsomer than the affectation of love. Your goodness must have some edge to it,—else it is none. The doctrine of hatred must be preached, as the counteraction of the doctrine of love, when that pules and whines. I shun father and mother and wife and brother when my genius calls me. I would write on the lintels of the door-post, *Whim*.[9] I hope it is somewhat better than whim at last, but we cannot spend the day in explanation. Expect me not to show cause why I seek or why I exclude company. Then again, do not tell me, as a good man did today, of my obligation to put all poor men in good situations. Are they *my* poor? I tell thee, thou foolish philanthropist, that I grudge the dollar, the dime, the cent I give to such men as do not belong to me and to whom I do not belong. There is a class of persons to whom by all spiritual affinity I am bought and sold; for them I will go to prison if need be; but your miscellaneous popular charities; the education at college of fools; the building of meeting-houses to the vain end to which many now stand; alms to sots, and the thousand-fold Relief Societies;—though I confess with shame I sometimes succumb and give the dollar, it is a wicked dollar, which by and by I shall have the manhood to withhold.

Virtues are, in the popular estimate, rather the exception than the rule. There is the man *and* his virtues. Men do what is called a good action, as some piece of courage or charity, much as they would pay a fine in expiation of daily non-appearance on parade. Their works are done as an apology or extenuation of their living in the world,—as invalids and the insane pay a high board. Their virtues are penances. I do not wish to expiate, but to live. My life is for itself and not for a spectacle. I much prefer that it should be of a lower strain, so it be genuine and equal, than that it should be glittering and unsteady. I wish it to be sound and sweet, and not to need diet and bleeding. I ask primary evidence that you are a man, and refuse this appeal from the man to his actions. I know that for myself it makes no difference whether I do or forbear those actions which are reckoned excellent. I cannot consent to pay for a privilege where I have intrinsic right. Few and mean as my gifts may be, I actually am, and do not need for my own assurance or the assurance of my fellows any secondary testimony.

What I must do is all that concerns me, not what the people think. This rule, equally arduous in actual and in intellectual life, may serve for the whole distinction between greatness and meanness. It is the harder because you will always find those who think they know what is your duty better than you know it. It is easy in the world to live after the world's opinion; it is easy in solitude to live after our own; but the great man is he who in the midst of the crowd keeps with perfect sweetness the independence of solitude.

The objection to conforming to usages that have become dead to you is that it

---

[8] In 1834 slavery had been abolished in Barbados—a fairly recent event at the time of this writing.

[9] Note the scriptural allusions in these two lines, the first of which evokes Matt. 10:37 and the second, Exod. 12:23.

scatters your force. It loses your time and blurs the impression of your character. If you maintain a dead church, contribute to a dead Bible-society, vote with a great party either for the government or against it, spread your table like base housekeepers,—under all these screens I have difficulty to detect the precise man you are: and of course so much force is withdrawn from your proper life. But do your work, and I shall know you. Do your work, and you shall reinforce yourself. A man must consider what a blindman's-buff is this game of conformity. If I know your sect I anticipate your argument. I hear a preacher announce for his text and topic the expediency of one of the institutions of his church. Do I not know beforehand that not possibly can he say a new and spontaneous word? Do I not know that with all this ostentation of examining the grounds of the institution he will do no such thing? Do I not know that he is pledged to himself not to look but at one side, the permitted side, not as a man, but as a parish minister? He is a retained attorney, and these airs of the bench are the emptiest affectation. Well, most men have bound their eyes with one or another handkerchief, and attached themselves to some one of these communities of opinion. This conformity makes them not false in a few particulars, authors of a few lies, but false in all particulars. Their every truth is not quite true. Their two is not the real two, their four not the real four; so that every word they say chagrins us and we know not where to begin to set them right. Meantime nature is not slow to equip us in the prison-uniform of the party to which we adhere. We come to wear one cut of face and figure, and acquire by degrees the gentlest asinine expression. There is a mortifying experience in particular, which does not fail to wreak itself also in the general history; I mean "the foolish face of praise,"[10] the forced smile which we put on in company where we do not feel at ease, in answer to conversation which does not interest us. The muscles, not spontaneously moved but moved by a low usurping wilfulness, grow tight about the outline of the face, with the most disagreeable sensation.

For nonconformity the world whips you with its displeasure. And therefore a man must know how to estimate a sour face. The by-standers look askance on him in the public street or in the friend's parlor. If this aversion had its origin in contempt and resistance like his own he might well go home with a sad countenance; but the sour faces of the multitude, like their sweet faces, have no deep cause, but are put on and off as the wind blows and a newspaper directs. Yet is the discontent of the multitude more formidable than that of the senate and the college. It is easy enough for a firm man who knows the world to brook the rage of the cultivated classes. Their rage is decorous and prudent, for they are timid, as being very vulnerable themselves. But when to their feminine rage the indignation of the people is added, when the ignorant and the poor are aroused, when the unintelligent brute force that lies at the bottom of society is made to growl and mow, it needs the habit of magnanimity and religion to treat it godlike as a trifle of no concernment.

The other terror that scares us from self-trust is our consistency; a reverence for our past act or word because the eyes of others have no other data for computing our orbit than our past acts, and we are loth to disappoint them.

But why should you keep your head over your shoulder? Why drag about this corpse of your memory, lest you contradict somewhat you have stated in this or that public place? Suppose you should contradict yourself; what then? It seems to be a rule of wisdom never to rely on your memory alone, scarcely even in acts of pure

---

[10]See Alexander Pope, *Epistle to Dr. Arbuthnot*, 1.212.

memory, but to bring the past for judgment into the thousand-eyed present, and live ever in a new day. In your metaphysics you have denied personality to the Deity, yet when the devout motions of the soul come, yield to them heart and life, though they should clothe God with shape and color.[11] Leave your theory, as Joseph his coat in the hand of the harlot,[12] and flee.

A foolish consistency is the hobgoblin of little minds, adored by little statesmen and philosophers and divines. With consistency a great soul has simply nothing to do. He may as well concern himself with his shadow on the wall. Speak what you think now in hard words and to-morrow speak what to-morrow thinks in hard words again, though it contradict every thing you said to-day.—'Ah, so you shall be sure to be misunderstood.'—Is it so bad then to be misunderstood? Pythagoras was misunderstood, and Socrates, and Jesus, and Luther, and Copernicus, and Galileo, and Newton,[13] and every pure and wise spirit that ever took flesh. To be great is to be misunderstood.

I suppose no man can violate his nature. All the sallies of his will are rounded in by the law of his being, as the inequalities of Andes and Himmaleh[14] are insignificant in the curve of the sphere. Nor does it matter how you gauge and try him. A character is like an acrostic or Alexandrian stanza;[15]—read it forward, backward, or

---

[11]In his note to this line, Edward Waldo Emerson quoted his father as saying: "I deny personality to God because it is too little—not too much." See Emerson, *Complete Works*, 2:391. This insight is in the tradition of the classical mystical via negativa and fits congruently with other aspects of the mystical worldview articulated by Emerson in the essay.

[12]Cf. Gen. 39:12. Emerson's "harlot" is the wife of Potiphar, the Egyptian captain of the guard.

[13]Pythagoras's biographer Jamblichus recounted that, after the seer returned to his native Samos, he found a lack of enthusiasm among the Greeks for his doctrine. Later, in a reversal, he was considered one of the Gods by his followers. Thomas Taylor translated the account in [Jamblichus of Chalcis,] *Iamblichus' Life of Pythagoras; or, Pythagoric Life, Accompanied by . . . a Collection of Pythagoric Sentences* (London: Printed by A. J. Valpy, 1818) 13-14. Nicholas Copernicus (1473-1543), the Polish astronomer, became the first modern European to argue that the earth and other planets revolved around the sun. But his *De revolutionibus orbium coelestium* did not see publication until Copernicus was on his deathbed in 1543. The Italian Galileo Galilei (1564–1642) challenged the teachings of Aristotle with his experiments concerning motion and, using the telescope, confirmed the Copernican theory. In 1616, when the church declared the Copernican theory dangerous to the faith, Galileo was ordered not to promulgate it. In 1632, however, his *Dialogue on the Two Chief Systems of the World* violated the order, and the following year he was tried by the Inquisition and under pressure disowned his previous teaching. Sir Isaac Newton (1642–1727), the English mathematician and physicist, formulated the law of universal gravitation and the three laws of motion. His *Philosophiae naturalis principia mathematica* (1687) became a foundational scientific work for the West, but as he grew older Newton viewed studies in alchemy, theology, and history as more important.

[14]The Andes and the Himalayas (Emerson's "Himmaleh") are the two loftiest mountain systems in the world.

[15]During the Alexandrian period in Greek literature (from the third century B.C.), poets were fond of using acrostics. But Emerson's "Alexandrian stanza," which spells the same thing forward, backward, and across, is an exaggeration, and Emerson may have been misinformed.

across, it still spells the same thing. In this pleasing contrite wood-life which God allows me, let me record day by day my honest thought without prospect or retrospect, and, I cannot doubt, it will be found symmetrical, though I mean it not and see it not. My book should smell of pines and resound with the hum of insects. The swallow over my window should interweave that thread or straw he carries in his bill into my web also. We pass for what we are. Character teaches above our wills. Men imagine that they communicate their virtue or vice only by overt actions, and do not see that virtue or vice emit a breath every moment.

There will be an agreement in whatever variety of actions, so they be each honest and natural in their hour. For of one will, the actions will be harmonious, however unlike they seem. These varieties are lost sight of at a little distance, at a little height of thought. One tendency unites them all. The voyage of the best ship is a zigzag line of a hundred tacks. See the line from a sufficient distance, and it straightens itself to the average tendency. Your genuine action will explain itself and will explain your other genuine actions. Your conformity explains nothing. Act singly, and what you have already done singly will justify you now. Greatness appeals to the future. If I can be firm enough to-day to do right and scorn eyes, I must have done so much right before as to defend me now. Be it how it will, do right now. Always scorn appearances and you always may. The force of character is cumulative. All the foregone days of virtue work their health into this. What makes the majesty of the heroes of the senate and the field, which so fills the imagination? The consciousness of a train of great days and victories behind. They shed a united light on the advancing actor. He is attended as by a visible escort of angels. That is it which throws thunder into Chatham's voice,[16] and dignity into Washington's port, and America into Adam's eye. Honor is venerable to us because it is no ephemera. It is always ancient virtue. We worship it to-day because it is not of to-day. We love it and pay it homage because it is not a trap for our love and homage, but is self-dependent, self-derived, and therefore of an old immaculate pedigree, even if shown in a young person.

I hope in these days we have heard the last of conformity and consistency. Let the words be gazetted and ridiculous henceforward. Instead of the gong for dinner, let us hear a whistle from the Spartan fife.[17] Let us never bow and apologize more. A great man is coming to eat at my house. I do not wish to please him; I wish that he should wish to please me. I will stand here for humanity, and though I would make it kind, I would make it true. Let us affront and reprimand the smooth mediocrity and squalid contentment of the times, and hurl in the face of custom and trade and office, the fact which is the upshot of all history, that there is a great responsible Thinker and

---

[16] William Pitt, first earl of Chatham (1708–1778), was a British statesman renowned for his eloquent rhetoric. His denunciation of early British policy regarding the Seven Years' War led to his appointment as secretary of state. Later he protested against the Stamp Act of 1765 levied on the American colonies and continued to urge conciliation.

[17] A male in the Greek city-state of Sparta (sixth century B.C.) did not live at home, but rather ate and slept in army barracks. Hence, instead of a "dinner gong" Emerson thinks of the shrill-toned fife, the small transverse flute that, in his experience, accompanied the drum in military marches. While the "Spartan fife" surely brought conformity of a totalitarian sort, here Emerson seems to be thinking, instead, of the spare simplicity associated with the Spartan life-style—a sharp contrast to the conventionality of middle-class life as he knew it.

Actor working wherever a man works; that a true man belongs to no other time or place, but is the centre of things.[18] Where he is, there is nature. He measures you and all men and all events. Ordinarily, every body in society reminds us of somewhat else, or of some other person. Character, reality, reminds you of nothing else; it takes place of the whole creation. The man must be so much that he must make all circumstances indifferent. Every true man is a cause, a country, and an age; requires infinite spaces and numbers and time fully to accomplish his design;—and posterity seem to follow his steps as a train of clients. A man Cæsar is born, and for ages after we have a Roman Empire.[19] Christ is born, and millions of minds so grow and cleave to his genius that he is confounded with virtue and the possible of man. An institution is the lengthened shadow of one man; as, Monachism, of the Hermit Antony;[20] the Reformation, of Luther; Quakerism, of Fox; Methodism, of Wesley; Abolition, of Clarkson.[21] Scipio, Milton called "the height of Rome;"[22] and all history resolves itself very easily into the biography of a few stout and earnest persons.[23]

Let a man then know his worth, and keep things under his feet. Let him not peep or steal, or skulk up and down with the air of a charity-boy, a bastard, or an interloper in the world which exists for him. But the man in the street, finding no worth in himself which corresponds to the force which built a tower or sculptured a marble god, feels poor when he looks on these. To him a palace, a statue, or a costly book have an alien and forbidding air, much like a gay equipage, and seem to say like that, "Who are you, Sir?" Yet they all are his, suitors for his notice, petitioners to his faculties that they will come out and take possession. The picture waits for my verdict; it is not to command me, but I am to settle its claims to praise. That popular fable of the sot who was picked up dead-drunk in the street, carried to the duke's house, washed and dressed and laid in the duke's bed, and, on his waking, treated with all obsequious ceremony like the duke, and assured that he had been insane, owes its popularity to the fact that it symbolizes so well the state of man, who is in the world a sort of sot, but now and then wakes up, exercises his reason and finds himself a true prince.[24]

---

[18]Emerson expresses again his vision of the Oversoul.

[19]Emerson has his history somewhat muddled. Although Julius Caesar (102?–44 B.C.) ruled Rome as dictator from 49 B.C. until his assassination, it was his grandnephew Octavian (63 B.C.-A.D. 14) who, as Augustus, consolidated the form of government that became known as the Roman Empire.

[20]Antony, or Saint Anthony of Egypt (251?–350?), has been called the father of Christian monasticism.

[21]Thomas Clarkson (1760–1846) is credited, along with William Wilberforce (1759–1833), with chief responsibility for the passage of the act in 1807 to abolish the British slave trade.

[22]The Roman general Scipio Africanus Major (Publius Cornelius Scipio Africanus, 236–183 B.C.) conquered Hannibal during the Punic Wars with Carthage. John Milton hailed him as "the height of Rome" in *Paradise Lost,* bk. 9, l. 510.

[23]Emerson articulates a favorite theme—that all history is biography. For the best expression of this idea, see his essay "History," published as the first piece in his collection of 1841 (Emerson, *Complete Works,* 2:1-41).

[24]Emerson's "fable" forms the theme of the induction to William Shakespeare's *Taming of the Shrew,* with the noble a "lord" but not specifically a duke. Although there the sot is "rescued" as a deliberate jest, the mysterious permeability of dream and waking states has

Our reading is mendicant and sycophantic. In history our imagination plays us false. Kingdom and lordship, power and estate, are a gaudier vocabulary than private John and Edward in a small house and common day's work; but the things of life are the same to both; the sum total of both is the same. Why all this deference to Alfred and Scanderbeg and Gustavus?[25] Suppose they were virtuous; did they wear out virtue? As great a stake depends on your private act to-day as followed their public and renowned steps. When private men shall act with original views, the lustre will be transferred from the actions of kings to those of gentlemen.

The world has been instructed by its kings, who have so magnetized the eyes of nations. It has been taught by this colossal symbol the mutual reverence that is due from man to man. The joyful loyalty with which men have everywhere suffered the king, the noble, or the great proprietor to walk among them by a law of his own, make his own scale of men and things and reverse theirs, pay for benefits not with money but with honor, and represent the law in his person, was the hieroglyphic by which they obscurely signified their consciousness of their own right and comeliness, the right of every man.[26]

The magnetism which all original action exerts is explained when we inquire the reason of self-trust. Who is the Trustee? What is the aboriginal Self, on which a universal reliance may be grounded? What is the nature and power of that science-baffling star, without parallax, without calculable elements, which shoots a ray of beauty even into trivial and impure actions, if the least mark of independence appear? The inquiry leads us to that source, at once the essence of genius, of virtue, and of life, which we call Spontaneity or Instinct. We denote this primary wisdom as Intuition, whilst all later teachings are tuitions.[27] In that deep force, the last fact be-

---

appeared as a theme in mythic and metaphysical discourse. In particular, Emerson's sot who wakes to find himself a "true prince" recalls the Gnostic insistence on spiritual awakening. In the classic "Hymn of the Pearl," for example, the king's son goes to Egypt to obtain the One Pearl and there, drugged and asleep, forgets that he is a king's son until he is providentially awakened to his true nature. See Jonas, *The Gnostic Religion*, 112-29.

[25]Emerson no doubt means Alfred the Great (849-899) who fought back the Danes in England and succeeded in maintaining an independent kingdom. The Albanian Scanderbeg, or George Castriota (1404?-1468), a hostage in the court of the Turkish Sultan Murad II, was educated as a Muslim and received the favors of the sultan, including a title and an army command. But when plans were afoot to attack his homeland, he defected and returned to Albania to lead the defense against the Turks. Gustavus is probably Gustavus Adolphus (1594-1632), or Gustavus II, the king of Sweden who fought strenuously in the Thirty Years' War. A strongly religious man, Gustavus envisioned a Christian army and took strong measures to achieve that goal, banning such conduct as raping, torturing, and pillaging.

[26]Emerson has intuitively grasped the importance of the king as a collective symbol. Indeed, the coronation ritual for the king provided a cultic model for later rituals developed for ordinary folk—as in the case, for example, of the Eastern Orthodox marriage rite with its attendant crowns for bride and groom. See E. O. James, *Christian Myth and Ritual: A Historical Study* (1933; rpt., Gloucester MA: Peter Smith, 1973) 1-41, 163-65, passim. Note, too, Emerson's use of the symbol of the hieroglyphic in this passage. (For a discussion, see n. 2 to Ralph Waldo Emerson, *Nature*.)

[27]Intuition is, literally, the teaching—the voice—within. Emerson once more shows us that self-reliance is an expression of the prior reality of the Oversoul.

hind which analysis cannot go, all things find their common origin. For the sense of being which in calm hours rises, we know not how, in the soul, is not diverse from things, from space, from light, from time, from man, but one with them and proceeds obviously from the same source whence their life and being also proceed. We first share the life by which things exist and afterwards see them as appearances in nature and forget that we have shared their cause. Here is the fountain of action and of thought. Here are the lungs of that inspiration which giveth man wisdom and which cannot be denied without impiety and atheism. We lie in the lap of immense intelligence, which makes us receivers of its truth and organs of its activity. When we discern justice, when we discern truth, we do nothing of ourselves, but allow a passage to its beams. If we ask whence this comes, if we seek to pry into the soul that causes, all philosophy is at fault. Its presence or its absence is all we can affirm. Every man discriminates between the voluntary acts of his mind and his involuntary perceptions, and knows that to his involuntary perceptions a perfect faith is due. He may err in the expression of them, but he knows that these things are so, like day and night, not to be disputed. My wilful actions and acquisitions are but roving;—the idlest reverie, the faintest native emotion, command my curiosity and respect. Thoughtless people contradict as readily the statement of perceptions as of opinions, or rather much more readily; for they do not distinguish between perception and notion. They fancy that I choose to see this or that thing. But perception is not whimsical, but fatal. If I see a trait, my children will see it after me, and in course of time all mankind,—although it may chance that no one has seen it before me. For my perception of it is as much a fact as the sun.

The relations of the soul to the divine spirit are so pure that it is profane to seek to interpose helps. It must be that when God speaketh he should communicate, not one thing, but all things; should fill the world with his voice; should scatter forth light, nature, time, souls, from the centre of the present thought; and new date and new create the whole. Whenever a mind is simple and receives a divine wisdom, old things pass away,—means, teachers, texts, temples fall; it lives now, and absorbs past and future into the present hour. All things are made sacred by relation to it,—one as much as another. All things are dissolved to their centre by their cause, and in the universal miracle petty and particular miracles disappear.[28] If therefore a man claims to know and speak of God and carries you backward to the phraseology of some old mouldered nation in another country, in another world, believe him not. Is the acorn better than the oak which is its fulness and completion? Is the parent better than the child into whom he has cast his ripened being? Whence then this worship of the past? The centuries are conspirators against the sanity and authority of the soul. Time and space are but physiological colors which the eye makes, but the soul is light: where it is, is day; where it was, is night; and history is an impertinence and an injury if it be any thing more than a cheerful apologue or parable of my being and becoming.

Man is timid and apologetic; he is no longer upright; he dares not say 'I think,' 'I am,' but quotes some saint or sage. He is ashamed before the blade of grass or the blowing rose. These roses under my window make no reference to former roses or

---

[28]Implicit in this statement is a rebuke to the materialistic notion of miracles held by the Unitarians. The passage that follows may be read similarly.

to better ones; they are for what they are; they exist with God to-day. There is no time to them. There is simply the rose; it is perfect in every moment of its existence. Before a leaf-bud has burst, its whole life acts; in the full-blown flower there is no more; in the leafless root there is no less. Its nature is satisfied and it satisfies nature in all moments alike. But man postpones or remembers; he does not live in the present, but with reverted eye laments the past, or, heedless of the riches that surround him, stands on tiptoe to foresee the future. He cannot be happy and strong until he too lives with nature in the present, above time.

This should be plain enough. Yet see what strong intellects dare not yet hear God himself unless he speak the phraseology of I know not what David, or Jeremiah, or Paul. We shall not always set so great a price on a few texts, on a few lives. We are like children who repeat by rote the sentences of grandames and tutors, and, as they grow older, of the men of talents and character they chance to see,—painfully recollecting the exact words they spoke; afterwards, when they come into the point of view which those had who uttered these sayings, they understand them and are willing to let the words go; for at any time they can use words as good when occasion comes. If we live truly, we shall see truly. It is as easy for the strong man to be strong, as it is for the weak to be weak. When we have new perception, we shall gladly disburden the memory of its hoarded treasures as old rubbish. When a man lives with God, his voice shall be as sweet as the murmur of the brook and the rustle of the corn.

And now at last the highest truth on this subject remains unsaid; probably cannot be said; for all that we say is the far-off remembering of the intuition. That thought by what I can now nearest approach to say it, is this. When good is near you, when you have life in yourself, it is not by any known or accustomed way; you shall not discern the footprints of any other; you shall not see the face of man; you shall not hear any name;—the way, the thought, the good, shall be wholly strange and new. It shall exclude example and experience. You take the way from man, not to man. All persons that ever existed are its forgotten ministers. Fear and hope are alike beneath it. There is somewhat low even in hope. In the hour of vision there is nothing that can be called gratitude, nor properly joy. The soul raised over passion beholds identity and eternal causation, perceives the self-existence of Truth and Right, and calms itself with knowing that all things go well. Vast spaces of nature, the Atlantic Ocean, the South Sea; long intervals of time, years, centuries, are of no account. This which I think and feel underlay every former state of life and circumstances, as it does underlie my present, and what is called life and what is called death.

Life only avails, not the having lived. Power ceases in the instant of repose; it resides in the moment of transition from a past to a new state, in the shooting of the gulf, in the darting to an aim. This one fact the world hates; that the soul *becomes;* for that forever degrades the past, turns all riches to poverty, all reputation to a shame, confounds the saint with the rogue, shoves Jesus and Judas equally aside. Why then do we prate of self-reliance? Inasmuch as the soul is present there will be power not confident but agent.[29] To talk of reliance is a poor external way of speaking. Speak rather of that which relies because it works and is. Who has more obedience than I masters me, though he should not raise his

---

[29]That is, power not merely passive because it hopes now for future expression, but active in its present doing.

finger. Round him I must revolve by the gravitation of spirits. We fancy it rhetoric when we speak of eminent virtue. We do not yet see that virtue is Height, and that a man or a company of men, plastic and permeable to principles, by the law of nature must overpower and ride all cities, nations, kings, rich men, poets, who are not.

This is the ultimate fact which we so quickly reach on this, as on every topic, the resolution of all into the ever-blessed ONE. Self-existence is the attribute of the Supreme Cause, and it constitutes the measure of good by the degree in which it enters into all lower forms. All things real are so by so much virtue as they contain. Commerce, husbandry, hunting, whaling, war, eloquence, personal weight, are somewhat, and engage my respect as examples of its presence and impure action. I see the same law working in nature for conservation and growth. Power is, in nature, the essential measure of right. Nature suffers nothing to remain in her kingdoms which cannot help itself. The genesis and maturation of a planet, its poise and orbit, the bended tree recovering itself from the strong wind, the vital resources of every animal and vegetable, are demonstrations of the self-sufficing and therefore self-relying soul.

Thus all concentrates: let us not rove; let us sit at home with the cause. Let us stun and astonish the intruding rabble of men and books and institutions by a simple declaration of the divine fact. Bid the invaders take the shoes from off their feet, for God is here within.[30] Let our simplicity judge them, and our docility to our own law demonstrate the poverty of nature and fortune beside our native riches.

But now we are a mob. Man does not stand in awe of man, nor is his genius admonished to stay at home, to put itself in communication with the internal ocean, but it goes abroad to beg a cup of water of the urns of other men. We must go alone. I like the silent church before the service begins, better than any preaching. How far off, how cool, how chaste the persons look, begirt each one with a precinct or sanctuary! So let us always sit. Why should we assume the faults of our friend, or wife, or father, or child, because they sit around our hearth, or are said to have the same blood? All men have my blood and I all men's. Not for that will I adopt their petulance or folly, even to the extent of being ashamed of it.[31] But your isolation must not be mechanical, but spiritual, that is, must be elevation. At times the whole world seems to be in conspiracy to importune you with emphatic trifles. Friend, client, child, sickness, fear, want, charity, all knock at once at thy closet door and say,—'Come out unto us.'[32] But keep thy state; come not into their confusion. The power men possess to annoy me I give them by a weak curiosity. No man can come near me but through my act. "What we love that we have, but by desire we bereave ourselves of the love."[33]

---

[30]A metaphorical allusion to Exod. 3:5.

[31]In a mystical vein, Emerson is teaching a form of detachment or holy indifference.

[32]Cf. Isa. 36:16.

[33]The quotation is an inexact rendering of Friedrich von Schiller's epigram "Liebe und Begierde" ("Love and Desire"). Emerson had written the line in his journal in 1839, identifying it as "the great sentiment . . . which Schiller said, or said the like" (Emerson, *Journals and Miscellaneous Notebooks,* 6 [18 June 1839?]: 214). For one possible source, see *Select Minor Poems, Translated from the German of Goethe and Schiller,* ed. John S. Dwight, vol. 3 (1839) of *Specimens of Foreign Standard Literature,* ed. George Ripley (Boston: Hilliard, Gray, 1838–1842) 352. But Emerson changed the meaning, for the line

If we cannot at once rise to the sanctities of obedience and faith, let us at least resist our temptations; let us enter into the state of war and wake Thor and Woden, courage and constancy, in our Saxon breasts.[34] This is to be done in our smooth times by speaking the truth. Check this lying hospitality and lying affection. Live no longer to the expectation of these deceived and deceiving people with whom we converse. Say to them, 'O father, O mother, O wife, O brother, O friend, I have lived with you after appearances hitherto. Henceforward I am the truth's. Be it known unto you that henceforward I obey no law less than the eternal law. I will have no covenants but proximities. I shall endeavor to nourish my parents, to support my family, to be the chaste husband of one wife,—but these relations I must fill after a new and unprecedented way. I appeal from your customs. I must be myself. I cannot break myself any longer for you, or you. If you can love me for what I am, we shall be the happier. If you cannot, I will still seek to deserve that you should. I will not hide my tastes or aversions. I will so trust that what is deep is holy, that I will do strongly before the sun and moon whatever inly rejoices me and the heart appoints. If you are noble, I will love you; if you are not, I will not hurt you and myself by hypocritical attentions. If you are true, but not in the same truth with me, cleave to your companions; I will seek my own. I do this not selfishly but humbly and truly. It is alike your interest, and mine, and all men's, however long we have dwelt in lies, to live in truth. Does this sound harsh today? You will soon love what is dictated by your nature as well as mine, and if we follow the truth it will bring us out safe at last.'—But so may you give these friends pain. Yes, but I cannot sell my liberty and my power, to save their sensibility. Besides, all persons have their moments of reason, when they look out into the region of absolute truth; then will they justify me and do the same thing.

The populace think that your rejection of popular standards is a rejection of all standard, and mere antinomianism; and the bold sensualist will use the name of philosophy to gild his crimes. But the law of consciousness abides. There are two confessionals, in one or the other of which we must be shriven. You may fulfil your round of duties by clearing yourself in the *direct,* or in the *reflex* way. Consider whether you have satisfied your relations to father, mother, cousin, neighbor, town, cat and dog—whether any of these can upbraid you. But I may also neglect this reflex standard and absolve me to myself. I have my own stern claims and perfect circle. It denies the name of duty to many offices that are called duties. But if I can discharge its debts it enables me to dispense with the popular code. If any one imagines that this law is lax, let him keep its commandment one day.

And truly it demands something godlike in him who has cast off the common motives of humanity and has ventured to trust himself for a taskmaster. High be his heart, faithful his will, clear his sight, that he may in good earnest be doctrine, society, law, to himself, that a simple purpose may be to him as strong as iron necessity is to others!

---

reads: "One *loves* what he has; one *desires* what he has not; Only the rich soul loves; only the poor one desires."

[34] In Norse mythology, Thor was the God of thunder and patron of warriors. One account held him to be the son of Woden (Odin), the supreme God and also a God of war. The cults of Woden and Thor were widely prevalent among the German tribes; and the Saxons, of Germanic origin, had brought their beliefs to Britain.

If any man consider the present aspects of what is called by distinction *society,* he will see the need of these ethics. The sinew and heart of man seem to be drawn out, and we are become timorous, desponding whimperers. We are afraid of truth, afraid of fortune, afraid of death, and afraid of each other. Our age yields no great and perfect persons. We want men and women who shall renovate life and our social state, but we see that most natures are insolvent, cannot satisfy their own wants, have an ambition out of all proportion to their practical force and do lean and beg day and night continually. Our housekeeping is mendicant, our arts, our occupations, our marriages, our religion we have not chosen, but society has chosen for us. We are parlor soldiers. We shun the rugged battle of fate, where strength is born.

If our young men miscarry in their first enterprises they lose all heart. If the young merchant fails, men say he is *ruined.* If the finest genius studies at one of our colleges and is not installed in an office within one year afterwards in the cities or suburbs of Boston or New York, it seems to his friends and to himself that he is right in being disheartened and in complaining the rest of his life. A sturdy lad from New Hampshire or Vermont, who in turn tries all the professions, who *teams it, farms it, peddles,* keeps a school, preaches, edits a newspaper, goes to Congress, buys a township, and so forth, in successive years, and always like a cat falls on his feet, is worth a hundred of these city dolls. He walks abreast with his days and feels no shame in not 'studying a profession,' for he does not postpone his life, but lives already. He has not one chance, but a hundred chances. Let a Stoic open the resources of man and tell men they are not leaning willows, but can and must detach themselves; that with the exercise of self-trust, new powers shall appear; that a man is the word made flesh, born to shed healing to the nations; that he should be ashamed of our compassion, and that the moment he acts from himself, tossing the laws, the books, idolatries and customs out of the window, we pity him no more but thank and revere him;[35]—and that teacher shall restore the life of man to splendor and make his name dear to all history.

It is easy to see that a greater self-reliance must work a revolution in all the offices and relations of men; in their religion; in their education; in their pursuits; their modes of living; their association; in their property; in their speculative views.

1. In what prayers do men allow themselves! That which they call a holy office is not so much as brave and manly. Prayer looks abroad and asks for some foreign addition to come through some foreign virtue, and loses itself in endless mazes of natural and supernatural, and mediatorial and miraculous. Prayer that craves a particular commodity, anything less than all good, is vicious. Prayer is the contemplation of the facts of life from the highest point of view. It is the soliloquy of a beholding and jubilant soul. It is the spirit of God pronouncing his works good. But prayer as a means to effect a private end is meanness and theft. It supposes dualism and not unity in nature and consciousness.

---

[35]Stoicism (see n. 29 to Ralph Waldo Emerson, Divinity School *Address*) taught that the highest good was virtue and that virtue consisted in living according to the law of nature. Stoic philosophy exalted duty and the inner resource of a right disposition, inculcating the ethic of *apatheia,* or apathy—an indifference to passion and desire of any sort. Emerson clearly admires the Stoic ethic, but it would be a curious Stoic indeed who taught that "a man is the word made flesh" (cf. John 1:14) and that such a man was "born to shed healing to the nations" (cf. Rev. 22:2).

As soon as the man is at one with God, he will not beg. He will then see prayer in all action. The prayer of the farmer kneeling in his field to weed it, the prayer of the rower kneeling with the stroke of his oar, are true prayers heard throughout nature, though for cheap ends.[36] Caratach, in Fletcher's "Bonduca," when admonished to inquire the mind of the god Audate, replies,—

"His hidden meaning lies in our
    endeavors;
Our valors are our best gods."[37]

Another sort of false prayers are our regrets. Discontent is the want of self-reliance: it is infirmity of will. Regret calamities if you can thereby help the sufferer; if not, attend your own work and already the evil begins to be repaired. Our sympathy is just as base. We come to them who weep foolishly and sit down and cry for company, instead of imparting to them truth and health in rough electric shocks, putting them once more in communication with their own reason. The secret of fortune is joy in our hands. Welcome evermore to gods and men is the self-helping man. For him all doors are flung wide; him all tongues greet, all honors crown, all eyes follow with desire. Our love goes out to him and embraces him because he did not need it. We solicitously and apologetically caress and celebrate him because he held on his way and scorned our disapprobation. The gods love him because men hated him. "To the persevering mortal," said Zoroaster, "the blessed Immortals are swift."[38]

As men's prayers are a disease of the will, so are their creeds a disease of the intellect. They say with those foolish Israelites, 'Let not God speak to us, lest we die. Speak thou, speak any man with us, and we will obey.'[39] Everywhere I am hindered of meeting God in my brother, because he has shut his own temple doors and recites fables merely of his brother's, or his brother's brother's God. Every new mind is a new classification. If it prove a mind of uncommon activity and power, a Locke, a Lavoisier, a Hutton, a Bentham, a Fourier, it imposes its classification on other men, and lo! a new system.[40] In proportion to the

---

[36]Edward Waldo Emerson, in his notes to this passage, recounted an anecdote concerning his father as a divinity student. The elder Emerson had worked on his uncle's farm beside a Methodist who claimed "that men are always praying, and that all prayers are answered." Emerson's first sermon contained as one of its points a reference to these "acted prayers," and the following day he was told by a stranger, "Young man, you'll never preach a better sermon than that." See Emerson, *Complete Works*, 2:394.

[37]In John Fletcher's *Tragedie of Bonduca* (1647), Audate (later Andate) was God of war for the Britons. Caratach, general of the Britons and a character from the play who had particularly impressed Emerson, was quoted here, probably from memory. See John Fletcher, *The Tragedy of Bonduca*, act 3, sc. 1, ll. 81-82; and, for Emerson's enthusiasm for Caratach, see Emerson, *Journals and Miscellaneous Notebooks*, 7 (13 April 1839): 187-88.

[38]The line is from the so-called "Chaldaean Oracles of Zoroaster." See Isaac Preston Cory, *Ancient Fragments of the Phoenician, Chaldaean, Egyptian, Tyrian, Carthaginian, Indian, Persian, and Other Writers*, 2d ed. (London: W. Pickering, 1832) 271. For more on the "Chaldaean Oracles," see n. 53 to Henry David Thoreau, *A Week on the Concord and Merrimack Rivers*.

[39]Emerson is recalling, though not exactly, Exod. 20:19.

[40]Antoine Lavoisier (1743–1794) is the French chemist and physicist credited with founding modern chemistry. His system of classification provided the basis for later

depth of the thought, and so to the number of the objects it touches and brings within reach of the pupil, is his complacency. But chiefly is this apparent in creeds and churches, which are also classifications of some powerful mind acting on the elemental thought of duty and man's relation to the Highest. Such is Calvinism, Quakerism, Swedenborgism.[41] The pupil takes the same delight in subordinating every thing to the new terminology as a girl who has just learned botany in seeing a new earth and new seasons thereby. It will happen for a time that the pupil will find his intellectual power has grown by the study of his master's mind. But in all unbalanced minds the classification is idolized, passes for the end and not for a speedily exhaustible means, so that the walls of the system blend to their eye in the remote horizon with the walls of the universe; the luminaries of heaven seem to them hung on the arch their master built. They cannot imagine how you aliens have any right to see,—how you can see; 'It must be somehow that you stole the light from us.' They do not yet perceive that light, unsystematic, indomitable, will break into any cabin, even into theirs. Let them chirp awhile and call it their own. If they are honest and do well, presently their neat new pinfold will be too strait and low, will crack, will lean, will rot and vanish, and the immortal light, all young and joyful, million-orbed, million-colored, will beam over the universe as on the first morning.

2. It is for want of self-culture that the superstition of Travelling, whose idols are Italy, England, Egypt, retains its fascination for all educated Americans. They who made England, Italy, or Greece venerable in the imagination, did so by sticking fast where they were, like an axis of the earth. In manly hours we feel that duty is our place. The soul is no traveller; the wise man stays at home, and when his necessities, his duties, on any occasion call him from his house, or into foreign lands, he is at home still and shall make men sensible by the expression of his countenance that he goes, the missionary of wisdom and virtue, and visits cities and men like a sovereign and not like an interloper or a valet.

I have no churlish objection to the circumnavigation of the globe for the purposes of art, of study, and benevolence, so that the man is first domesticated, or does not go abroad with the hope of finding somewhat greater than he knows. He who travels to be amused, or to get somewhat which he does not carry, travels away from himself, and grows old even in youth among old things. In Thebes, in Palmyra,[42] his will and mind have become old

---

chemical nomenclature, and his studies of combustion brought the phlogiston theory into disrepute. The Scotchman James Hutton (1726–1797) led the way toward the modern science of geology. His uniformitarian theory held that by watching contemporary geological forces a scientist could reconstruct the past history of the earth, since forces identical to the present had acted in the past. Jeremy Bentham (1748–1832), the English philosopher and political theorist who founded utilitarianism, argued that the basic principle of all morality is the greatest happiness for the greatest number—the so-called utilitarian principle. Charles Fourier (1772–1837), mentioned in the introduction, was the French social philosopher who worked out an intricate scheme for a socialist utopia based on the belief that the natural passions of individuals could flower into a harmonious society.

[41]Not even the Swedenborgian church is immune, in Emerson's view, from the intellectual disease expressed by all creeds and churches.

[42]Thebes was the principal city of Boeotia in ancient Greece, rich in its connections with

and dilapidated as they. He carries ruins to ruins.

Travelling is a fool's paradise. Our first journeys discover to us the indifference of places. At home I dream that at Naples, at Rome, I can be intoxicated with beauty and lose my sadness. I pack my trunk, embrace my friends, embark on the sea and at last wake up in Naples, and there beside me is the stern fact, the sad self, unrelenting, identical, that I fled from. I seek the Vatican and the palaces. I affect to be intoxicated with sights and suggestions, but I am not intoxicated. My giant goes with me wherever I go.[43]

3. But the rage of travelling is a symptom of a deeper unsoundness affecting the whole intellectual action. The intellect is vagabond, and our system of education fosters restlessness. Our minds travel when our bodies are forced to stay at home. We imitate; and what is imitation but the travelling of the mind? Our houses are built with foreign taste; our shelves are garnished with foreign ornaments; our opinions, our tastes, our faculties, lean, and follow the Past and the Distant. The soul created the arts wherever they have flourished. It was in his own mind that the artist sought his model. It was an application of his own thought to the thing to be done and the conditions to be observed. And why need we copy the Doric or the Gothic model?[44] Beauty, convenience, grandeur of thought and quaint expression are as near to us as to any, and if the American artist will study with hope and love the precise thing to be done by him, considering the climate, the soil, the length of the day, the wants of the people, the habit and form of the government, he will create a house in which all these will find themselves fitted, and taste and sentiment will be satisfied also.

Insist on yourself; never imitate. Your own gift you can present every moment with the cumulative force of a whole life's cultivation; but of the adopted talent of another you have only an extemporaneous half possession. That which each can do best, none but his Maker can teach him. No man yet knows what it is, nor can, till that person has exhibited it. Where is the master who could have taught Shakespeare? Where is the master who could have instructed Franklin, or Washington, or Bacon, or Newton? Every great man is a unique. The Scipionism of Scipio is precisely that part he could not borrow. Shakspeare will never be made by the study of Shakspeare. Do that which is assigned you, and you cannot hope too much or dare too much. There is at this moment for you an utterance brave and grand as that of the colossal chisel of Phidias,[45] or trowel of the

---

Greek history and religion. Palmyra was the ancient Syrian city that tradition said was founded by Solomon. The ruins of both cities provide for Emerson a moral metaphor.

[43] As Edward Waldo Emerson noted, there is an autobiographical immediacy to this passage. Saddened by the death of his young wife, Ellen Tucker (1831), and uprooted by his own resignation from the Unitarian ministry (1832), Emerson spent much of 1833 abroad, traveling to Italy as well as to Switzerland, France, England, and Scotland. For Edward Waldo Emerson's comments, see Emerson, *Complete Works*, 3:394-95.

[44] Known for its simplicity, Doric architecture was the earliest type developed by the ancient Greeks, built from the seventh to the second century B.C. Gothic architecture, renowned for its use of space and light, became the dominant European expression from the twelfth century, lasting a period of some four hundred years.

[45] Phidias (500?–432? B.C.) was considered one of the greatest sculptors of the ancient Greek world.

Egyptians, or the pen of Moses or Dante, but different from all these. Not possibly will the soul, all rich, all eloquent, with thousand-cloven tongue,[46] deign to repeat itself; but if you can hear what these patriarchs say, surely you can reply to them in the same pitch of voice; for the ear and the tongue are two organs of one nature. Abide in the simple and noble regions of thy life, obey thy heart, and thou shalt reproduce the Foreworld again.[47]

4. As our Religion, our Education, our Art look abroad, so does our spirit of society. All men plume themselves on the improvement of society, and no man improves.

Society never advances. It recedes as fast on one side as it gains on the other. It undergoes continual changes; it is barbarous, it is civilized, it is christianized, it is rich, it is scientific; but this change is not amelioration. For every thing that is given something is taken. Society acquires new arts and loses old instincts. What a contrast between the well-clad, reading, writing, thinking American, with a watch, a pencil and a bill of exchange in his pocket, and the naked New Zealander, whose property is a club, a spear, a mat and an undivided twentieth of a shed to sleep under! But compare the health of the two men and you shall see that the white man has lost his aboriginal strength. If the traveller tell us truly, strike the savage with a broad-axe and in a day or two the flesh shall unite and heal as if you struck the blow into soft pitch, and the same blow shall send the white to his grave.[48]

The civilized man has built a coach, but has lost the use of his feet. He is supported on crutches, but lacks so much support of muscle. He has a fine Geneva watch, but he fails of the skill to tell the hour by the sun. A Greenwich nautical almanac he has,[49] and so being sure of the information when he wants it, the man in the street does not know a star in the sky. The solstice he does not observe; the equinox he knows as little; and the whole bright calendar of the year is without a dial in his mind. His notebooks impair his memory; his libraries overload his wit; the insurance-office increases the number of accidents; and it may be a question whether machinery does not encumber; whether we have not lost by refinement some energy, by a Christianity, entrenched in establishments and forms, some vigor of wild virtue. For every Stoic was a Stoic; but in Christendom where is the Christian?

There is no more deviation in the moral standard than in the standard of height or bulk. No greater men are now than ever

---

[46]An allusion to the divine inspiration of Pentecost. Cf. Acts 2:3-4.

[47]In this paradisal imagery, Emerson expresses his own form of mythic consciousness. The time of beginnings is the strong time (cf. the "Orphic poet" in Emerson, *Nature,* ch. 8); and by restoring all things to the beginning, all things are made new. Emerson interiorizes the mythic impulse, finding the "Foreworld" in the inner spirit, the heart of every human being. For a discussion of the significance of myths and especially of myths of origin, see Mircea Eliade, *Myth and Reality,* trans. Willard R. Trask (New York: Harper & Row, Harper Torchbooks, 1968) 1-38.

[48]Emerson's source for this travel account may have been James Cook in *The Three Voyages of Captain James Cook around the World* (London: Printed for Longman, Hurst, Rees, Orme, and Brown, 1821) 2:34-48. If so, Emerson has exaggerated both the seriousness of the New Zealander's wound and the swiftness of its healing.

[49]Greenwich, England. The prime meridian runs through the Royal Observatory there, and the nautical calculations would be made in terms of Greenwich.

were. A singular equality may be observed between the great men of the first and of the last ages; nor can all the science, art, religion, and philosophy of the nineteenth century avail to educate greater men than Plutarch's heroes,[50] three or four and twenty centuries ago. Not in time is the race progressive. Phocion, Socrates, Anaxagoras, Diogenes,[51] are great men, but they leave no class. He who is really of their class will not be called by their name, but will be his own man, and in his turn the founder of a sect. The arts and inventions of each period are only its costume and do not invigorate men. The harm of the improved machinery may compensate its good. Hudson and Behring[52] accomplished so much in their fishing-boats as to astonish Parry and Franklin,[53] whose equipment exhausted the resources of science and art. Galileo, with an opera-glass, discovered a more splendid series of celestial phenomena than any one since. Columbus found the New World in an undecked boat. It is curious to see the periodical disuse and perishing of means and machinery which were introduced with loud laudation a few years or centuries before. The great genius returns to essential man. We reckoned the improvements of the art of war among the triumphs of science, and yet Napoleon conquered Europe by the bivouac, which consisted of falling back on naked valor and disencumbering it of all aids. The Emperor held it impossible to make a perfect army, says Las Casas, "without abolishing our arms, magazines, commissaries and carriages, until, in imitation of the Roman custom, the soldier should receive his supply of corn, grind it in his hand-mill and bake his bread himself."[54]

Society is a wave. The wave moves onward, but the water of which it is composed does not. The same particle does not rise from the valley to the ridge. Its unity is only phenomenal. The persons who

---

[50]Plutarch (46?–120?), a Greek biographer, made a profound impression on English literature through his biographies of great Greeks and Romans as they are collected in *The Parallel Lives*. He excelled in depicting the character and moral stature of his "heroes."

[51]For Phocion, see n. 16 to Emerson, *Nature*. Anaxagoras (500?–428 B.C.), the Greek philosopher who perhaps was the teacher of Socrates, was accused of blasphemy and atheism, and fled into exile to die. He believed that there was an all-pervading mind at work in the universe, a kind of mechanical cause of motion that led to the production of things. Diogenes (412?–323 B.C.), the Greek philosopher of Cynicism, esteemed above all a life of simplicity. Virtue for him consisted in the total rejection of a conventional way of life—of external goods, a good name, and civic responsibility.

[52]Henry Hudson (d. 1611?), the English navigator, attempted to find a northern passage to the East and in his third voyage, for the Dutch East India Company, discovered the great river that bears his name. Emerson's "Behring" is probably Vitus Jonassen Bering (1681–1741), the Danish navigator who, serving under Peter the Great of Russia, explored Siberia and reached Alaska. The strait between Siberia and Alaska as well as the sea and an island in the region now bear his name. "Fishing boats," however, seems a rather romanticized and exaggerated description of the equipment of the two men.

[53]By contrast with the earlier Hudson and "Behring," Sir William Edward Parry (1790–1855) and Sir John Franklin (1786–1847) were well-known explorers contemporary with Emerson. Parry discovered the way to the North Pole, while Franklin concentrated his efforts in Northern Canada and, after Emerson's writing, was lost in an attempt to find the Northwest Passage.

[54]See Emmanuel, Comte de Las Cases *Mémorial de Sainte Hélène* 4.7.97.

make up a nation to-day, next year die, and their experience dies with them.

And so the reliance on Property, including the reliance on governments which protect it, is the want of self-reliance.[55] Men have looked away from themselves and at things so long that they have come to esteem the religious, learned and civil institutions as guards of property, and they deprecate assaults on these, because they feel them to be assaults on property. They measure their esteem of each other by what each has, and not by what each is. But a cultivated man becomes ashamed of his property, out of new respect for his nature. Especially he hates what he has if he see that it is accidental,—came to him by inheritance, or gift, or crime; then he feels that it is not having; it does not belong to him, has no root in him and merely lies there because no revolution or no robber takes it away. But that which a man is, does always by necessity acquire; and what the man acquires, is living property, which does not wait the beck of rulers, or mobs, or revolutions, or fire, or storm, or bankruptcies, but perpetually renews itself wherever the man breathes. "Thy lot or portion of life," said the Caliph Ali, "is seeking after thee; therefore be at rest from seeking after it."[56] Our dependence on these foreign goods leads us to our slavish respect for numbers. The political parties meet in numerous conventions; the greater the concourse and with each new uproar of announcement, The delegation from Essex! The Democrats from New Hampshire! The Whigs of Maine! the young patriot feels himself stronger than before by a new thousand of eyes and arms. In like manner the reformers summon conventions and vote and resolve in multitude. Not so, O friends! will the God deign to enter and inhabit you, but by a method precisely the reverse. It is only as a man puts off all foreign support and stands alone that I see him to be strong and to prevail. He is weaker by every recruit to his banner. Is not a man better than a town? Ask nothing of men, and, in the endless mutation, thou only firm column must presently appear the upholder of all that surrounds thee. He who knows that power is inborn, that he is weak because he has looked for good out of him and elsewhere, and, so perceiving, throws himself unhesitatingly on his thought, instantly rights himself, stands in the erect position, commands his limbs, works miracles; just as a man who stands on his feet is stronger than a man who stands on his head.

So use all that is called Fortune. Most men gamble with her, and gain all, and lose all, as her wheel rolls. But do thou leave as unlawful these winnings, and deal with Cause and Effect, the chancellors of God. In the Will work and acquire, and thou hast chained the wheel of Chance, and shall sit hereafter out of fear from her rotations. A political victory, a rise of rents, the recovery of your sick or the return of your absent friend, or some other favorable event raises your spirits, and you think good days are preparing for you. Do not believe it. Nothing can bring you peace but yourself. Nothing can bring you peace but the triumph of principles.

---

[55]Emerson is radical in theory but not in practice. He owned property and made capital investments; and he refused to participate in even the rather moderate joint-stock experiment in communal living at Brook Farm—here, though, for other philosophical reasons.

[56]From the "Sentences of Ali, Son-in-Law of Mahomet, and His Fourth Successor," in Simon Ockley, *The Conquest of Syria, Persia, and Aegypt by the Saracens* (London: Printed for J. Knaplock, J. Sprint, R. Smith, B. Lintott, and J. Round, 1708-1718) vol. 2: *The History of the Saracens,* appendix, p. 2.

POEMS

If the short essay or lecture was one genre in which Emerson typically expressed himself, poetry was surely the other. One complete volume of the twelve-volume centenary edition of his works is devoted to his poems; and during his lifetime he published, as we have seen, several collections: *Poems* in 1846, *May-Day and Other Pieces* in 1867, and—in collaboration with his daughter Ellen and James Elliot Cabot—*Selected Poems* in 1876. Emerson was fond of prefixing to an essay a poem of his own composition that provided a pithy summary of the theme, and his single poems appeared also in journals such as the Transcendental periodicals *The Dial* and *The Western Messenger*.

Some of Emerson's poetry excelled in literary power and stature, some of it was middling, and some was not very good. But independent of the aesthetic merits of each piece, the poems formed a part of the record of his spirit, an expression—however incomplete—of Emerson's sense of the meaning of God, of nature, and of humanity. It is with this understanding of the significance of his poetry that the following selections have been made. Whether widely anthologized or hardly noticed in recent times, together they form a biography of the spirit. They are arranged, therefore, not so much according to the date of their composition as according to the sense of spiritual passage and transition they express.

The series opens with Emerson pondering the problem of his ambivalence toward the institutionalized ministry ("The Problem") and then moves on to explain his decision for spiritual independence ("Self-Reliance"). From there it considers the riddle of the human condition ("The Sphinx") and provides key statements of his Transcendental understanding of God ("Brahma"), nature ("Each and All," "The Rhodora"), and the relationship between nature and human beings ("The Miracle," "Two Rivers"). In these poems, Emerson reconstitutes his world through the power of his spiritual message, but in them also even his seemingly boundless Transcendentalism must confront its limits. Emerson encounters death in the passing of his firstborn son ("Threnody"); habit and custom ("Grace"); and the failing of his own powers ("Terminus"). A context is set for understanding the brief excerpt from his earlier essay "Fate," which is appended to the selections. The transmutation of Fate into Beautiful Necessity is wrought by an Emerson who has faced and accepted the boundaries of his world.

POEMS

THE PROBLEM[1]

I LIKE a church; I like a cowl;
I love a prophet of the soul;
And on my heart monastic aisles
Fall like sweet strains, or pensive smiles;
Yet not for all his faith can see
Would I that cowled churchman be.

Why should the vest on him allure,
Which I could not on me endure?

Not from a vain or shallow thought
His awful Jove young Phidias brought;[2]
Never from lips of cunning fell
The thrilling Delphic oracle;[3]
Out from the heart of nature rolled
The burdens of the Bible old;
The litanies of nations came,
Like the volcano's tongue of flame,
Up from the burning core below,—
The canticles of love and woe:
The hand that rounded Peter's dome
And groined the aisles of Christian Rome
Wrought in a sad sincerity;
Himself from God he could not free;
He builded better than he knew;—
The conscious stone to beauty grew.

Know'st thou what wove yon woodbird's nest
Of leaves, and feathers from her breast?
Or how the fish outbuilt her shell,
Painting with morn each annual cell?
Or how the sacred pine-tree adds
To her old leaves new myriads?
Such and so grew these holy piles,
Whilst love and terror laid the tiles.
Earth proudly wears the Parthenon,
As the best gem upon her zone,
And Morning opes with haste her lids
To gaze upon the Pyramids;

---

[1] The text is that in Ralph Waldo Emerson, *The Complete Works of Ralph Waldo Emerson,* ed. Edward Waldo Emerson, centenary ed. (Boston: Houghton, Mifflin, 1903-1904) 9:6-9. This poem was dated 10 November 1839 and was published in the first issue of *The Dial* in July 1840. Emerson originally titled it "The Priest," and the poem reflects an earlier passage in his private journal in which he expressed his ambivalence concerning the clerical state. (See Ralph Waldo Emerson, *The Journals and Miscellaneous Notebooks of Ralph Waldo Emerson,* ed. William H. Gilman et al. [Cambridge: Harvard University Press, Belknap Press, 1960–] 7 [28 August 1838]: 60.) The issue was, indeed, existential. Although Emerson had resigned from his ministry at the Second Church in 1832, he had continued as a supply preacher for other pulpits. But in 1838, and especially after the Divinity School address, this activity seriously slackened, and Emerson recorded the date of his last sermon as 20 January 1839. (See Ralph L. Rusk, *The Life of Ralph Waldo Emerson* [New York: Columbia University Press, 1949] 273, and William R. Hutchison, *The Transcendentalist Ministers: Church Reform in the New England Renaissance* [Boston: Beacon Press, 1965] 38-39.) Yet even as Emerson struggled here with the question of a vocation to the ministry, the presence of the Oversoul is everywhere—inspiring Phidias, the Delphic oracle, the art of nature and the religious architecture of humanity, and the Pentecost of Christian divines.

[2] For Phidias, see n. 45 to Ralph Waldo Emerson, "Self-Reliance."

[3] The oracle at Delphi, located near the southern slope of Mount Parnassus in Greece, was the vehicle through which, in the temple of the God Apollo, divine messages were communicated to seekers.

O'er England's abbeys bends the sky,
As on its friends, with kindred eye;
For out of Thought's interior sphere
These wonders rose to upper air;
And Nature gladly gave them place,
Adopted them into her race,
And granted them an equal date
With Andes and with Ararat.[4]

These temples grew as grows the grass;
Art might obey, but not surpass.
The passive Master lent his hand
To the vast soul that o'er him planned;
And the same power that reared the shrine
Bestrode the tribes that knelt within.
Ever the fiery Pentecost
Girds with one flame the countless host,
Trances the heart through chanting choirs,
And through the priest the mind inspires.
The word unto the prophet spoken
Was writ on tables yet unbroken;
The word by seers or sibyls told,
In groves of oak, or fanes of gold,
Still floats upon the morning wind,
Still whispers to the willing mind.
One accent of the Holy Ghost
The heedless world hath never lost.
I know what say the fathers wise,—
The Book itself before me lies,
Old *Chrysostom,* best *Augustine,*[5]

And he who blent both in his line,
The younger *Golden Lips* or mines,
Taylor, the Shakspeare of divines.[6]
His words are music in my ear,
I see his cowlèd portrait dear;
And yet, for all his faith could see,
I would not the good bishop be.

SELF-RELIANCE[7]

HENCEFORTH, please God, forever
    I forego
The yoke of men's opinions. I will be
Light-hearted as a bird, and live with God.
I find him in the bottom of my heart,
I hear continually his voice therein.

. . . . . .

The little needle always knows the
    North,[8]
The little bird remembereth his note,
And this wise Seer within me never errs.
I never taught it what it teaches me;
I only follow, when I act aright.

---

[4]For the Andes mountains, see n. 14 to Emerson, "Self-Reliance." Ararat is properly the name for two mountains in eastern Turkey: the Little Ararat and the Great Ararat. Tradition, based on Gen. 8:4, held that Mount Ararat was the place where Noah's Ark came to rest.

[5]Saint John Chrysostom (347?–407)—literally John the Golden-mouthed—a doctor of the church, was considered the greatest of the Greek fathers. He won a wide reputation as a preacher in Antioch and became patriarch of Constantinople. Emerson's "best Augustine," of course, is the widely renowned Saint Augustine (354–430), bishop of Hippo in northern Africa, like John a doctor of the church, and considered one of the four Latin fathers.

[6]Edward Waldo Emerson has identified the Taylor of this line as Jeremy Taylor (1613–1667), the English bishop who wrote on theological and devotional themes. (See Emerson, *Complete Works,* 9:406-407.) Besides being called the Shakespeare of the pulpit, Taylor has been called its (Edmund) Spenser.

[7]The text is that of the centenary edition of Emerson, *Complete Works,* 9:394. The poem, originally untitled, bears the date 9 October 1832 and was written during the troubled period of Emerson's resignation from his ministry at the Second Church.

[8]The needle of the compass. Edward Waldo Emerson recounted an incident late in his father's life, in 1873, when the elder Emerson was traveling with Charles Eliot Norton. Emerson reportedly displayed the pocket compass he kept with him on trips and said, "I like to hold the god in my hands" (Emerson, *Complete Works,* 9:517). The compass of the poem is, for Emerson, the voice of conscience and the voice of divinity directing from within.

THE SPHINX[9]

THE Sphinx is drowsy,
   Her wings are furled:
Her ear is heavy,
   She broods on the world.
"Who'll tell me my secret,
   The ages have kept?—
I awaited the seer
   While they slumbered and slept:—

"The fate of the man-child,
   The meaning of man;
Known fruit of the unknown;
   Daedalian plan;[10]
Out of sleeping a waking,
   Out of waking a sleep;
Life death overtaking;
   Deep underneath deep?

"Erect as a sunbeam,
   Upspringeth the palm;
The elephant browses.
   Undaunted and calm;
In beautiful motion
   The thrush plies his wings;
Kind leaves of his covert,
   Your silence he sings.

"The waves, unashamèd,
   In difference sweet,
Play glad with the breezes,
   Old playfellows meet;
The journeying atoms,
   Primordial wholes,
Firmly draw, firmly drive,
   By their animate poles.

"Sea, earth, air, sound, silence,
   Plant, quadruped, bird,
By one music enchanted,
   One deity stirred,—
Each the other adorning,
   Accompany still;
Night veileth the morning,
   The vapor the hill.

"The babe by its mother
   Lies bathèd in joy;
Glide its hours uncounted,—
   The sun is its toy;
Shines the peace of all being,
   Without cloud, in its eyes;
And the sum of the world
   In soft miniature lies.

"But man crouches and blushes,
   Absconds and conceals;
He creepeth and peepeth,
   He palters and steals;
Infirm, melancholy,
   Jealous glancing around,
An oaf, an accomplice,
   He poisons the ground.[11]

---

[9] The text is that of the centenary edition of Emerson, *Complete Works,* 9:20-25. The poem first appeared in *The Dial* in January 1841, and there are only a few changes from the original in this version. The image of the Sphinx (see n. 29 to Ralph Waldo Emerson, *Nature*) evidently intrigued Emerson, for he used it in various other instances in his writings. (See, for example, "History" in Emerson, *Complete Works,* 2:4 and 32, and the reference, earlier in this volume, in *Nature,* ch. 4.) Emerson's immediate inspiration in the poem was the riddle of the Sphinx in the Oedipus tale. As a divine agent of death, she posed a seemingly insoluble question to which the answer was man himself in the three ages of life. When Oedipus broke the riddle by answering correctly, the Sphinx killed herself. But Emerson does not reconstruct the Oedipus incident; rather, he envisions a dialogue between the Sphinx and a poet who represents humanity. Throughout their discourse, knowledge assumes gnostic proportions, and we catch a glimpse of the mystical identity between the Sphinx, her riddle, and humankind.

[10] In Greek mythology Daedalus, on the island of Crete, conceived and built the labyrinth that housed the Minotaur, the monster with the body of a man and the head of a bull. When he tired of remaining on Crete with King Minos, however, he devised a plan for his own and his son's escape by fashioning feathered wings bound with wax. Although Daedalus by this means safely reached Sicily, his son, Icarus, flew too close to the sun. Its rays melted the wax on the wings so that Icarus fell, plunging into the sea below.

[11] Unlike nature, unconscious and tranquil,

"Out spoke the great mother,
    Beholding his fear;—
At the sound of her accents
    Cold shuddered the sphere:—
'Who has drugged my boy's cup?
    Who has mixed my boy's bread?
Who, with sadness and madness,
    Has turned my child's head?' "

I heard a poet answer
    Aloud and cheerfully,
"Say on, sweet Sphinx! thy dirges
    Are pleasant songs to me.
Deep love lieth under
    These pictures of time;
They fade in the light of
    Their meaning sublime.

"The fiend that man harries
    Is love of the Best;
Yawns the pit of the Dragon,
    Lit by rays from the Blest.
The Lethe of Nature[12]
    Can't trance him again,
Whose soul sees the perfect,
    Which his eyes seek in vain.

"To vision profounder,
    Man's spirit must dive;
His aye-rolling orb
    At no goal will arrive;
The heavens that now draw him
    With sweetness untold,
Once found,—for new heavens
    He spurneth the old.

"Pride ruined the angels,
    Their shame them restores;
Lurks the joy that is sweetest
    In stings of remorse.
Have I a lover
    Who is noble and free?—
I would he were nobler
    Than to love me.

"Eterne alternation
    Now follows, now flies;
And under pain, pleasure,—
    Under pleasure, pain lies.
Love works at the centre,
    Heart-heaving alway;
Forth speed the strong pulses
    To the borders of day.

"Dull Sphinx, Jove keep thy five wits;
    Thy sight is growing blear;
Rue, myrrh and cummin[13] for the Sphinx,
    Her muddy eyes to clear!"
The old Sphinx bit her thick lip,—
    Said, "Who taught thee me to name?
I am thy spirit, yoke-fellow;
    Of thine eye I am eyebeam.

"Thou art the unanswered question;
    Couldst see thy proper eye,
Alway it asketh, asketh;
    And each answer is a lie.
So take thy quest through nature,
    It through thousand natures ply;
Ask on, thou clothed eternity;
    Time is the false reply."

Uprose the merry Sphinx,
    And crouched no more in stone;
She melted into purple cloud,
    She silvered in the moon;
She spired into a yellow flame;
    She flowered in blossoms red;
She flowed into a foaming wave:
    She stood Monadnoc's head.[14]

Thorough[15] a thousand voices
    Spoke the universal dame;
"Who telleth one of my meanings
    Is master of all I am."

Emerson's "man" is conscious, restless, and troubled. The "fall" for Emerson was, indeed, a fall into consciousness.

[12] See n. 6 to Emerson, "Self-Reliance."

[13] Bitter and aromatic plant substances that would stimulate the tear glands of the Sphinx, causing her to clear her eyes.

[14] "Monadnoc," or Monadnock, is an isolated mountain peak in southwestern New Hampshire.

[15] Through (archaic form).

BRAHMA[16]

If the red slayer think he slays,
   Or if the slain think he is slain,
They know not well the subtle ways
   I keep, and pass, and turn again.[17]

Far or forgot to me is near;
   Shadow and sunlight are the same;
The vanished gods to me appear;
   And one to me are shame and fame.

They reckon ill who leave me out;
   When me they fly, I am the wings;
I am the doubter and the doubt,
   And I the hymn the Brahmin[18] sings

The strong gods[19] pine for my abode,
   And pine in vain the sacred Seven;[20]
But thou, meek lover of the good!
   Find me, and turn thy back on heaven.[21]

---

[16] The text is that in the centenary edition of Emerson, *Complete Works,* 9:195. This short work, contributed by Emerson to *The Atlantic Monthly* in 1857, is one of the most often quoted of his poems and, in the nineteenth century, was one of the most provocative. Brahma, in Hindu tradition, is the deity who is the creator of all things. In neuter form, the masculine name Brahma becomes Brahman, the impersonal power or energy that is pure consciousness and the hidden identity of all. It is Brahman as impersonal manifestation that is actually Emerson's subject in this poem, albeit in first-person address. Thus, the poem celebrates the mystical oneness of all things using a Hindu religious metaphor, and it reflects Emerson's familiarity with the *Vishnu Purana* and the *Bhagavad Gita,* both classics of Indian religious literature. Yet, as Edward Waldo Emerson observed in his notes to the poem, as early as 1830 his father had pondered the words of Parmenides that thought and its object were one (Emerson, *Complete Works,* 9:465). And Emerson himself was aware of the arbitrariness of his choice of Brahma. In an anecdote recorded by his son: "Mr. Emerson, much amused when people found 'Brahma' puzzling, said to his daughter, 'If you tell them to say Jehovah instead of Brahma they will not feel any perplexity' " (ibid., 467).

[17] For Emerson's opening lines, cf. *Katha Upanishad* 2.19 and *Bhagavad Gita* 2.19. (For a brief discussion of the *Bhagavad Gita,* see n. 25 to Henry David Thoreau, *A Week on the Concord and Merrimack Rivers.*) Arthur Christy, following David Lee Maulsby in *The Contribution of Emerson to Literature* (1911), identifies Emerson's source as the *Katha Upanishad,* but the quotations from the *Katha Upanishad* and the *Bhagavad Gita* are substantially the same. See Arthur Christy, *The Orient in American Transcendentalism: A Study of Emerson, Thoreau, and Alcott* (1932; rpt., New York: Octagon Books, 1978) 167, and for a useful guide to the entire poem, 164-70.

[18] A member of the highest—the priestly—caste of India.

[19] Emerson's "strong gods" are listed by Edward Waldo Emerson as Indra, Agni, and Yama. (See Emerson, *Complete Works,* 9:466.) Indra is the God of thunder and of war; Agni, the God of fire; and Yama, the God of death.

[20] Edward Waldo Emerson identified the "sacred Seven" as "Maharshis [maharishis] or highest saints" (Emerson, *Complete Works,* 9:466). But to call a maharishi, even if reputed for holiness, a saint is to speak in christianized, and somewhat inaccurate, terms. The first rishis were individuals who heard the sacred words of the Vedas and wrote them down; and, generally speaking, a rishi is someone who sees sacred truth and communicates it. A maharishi is, literally, a great rishi.

[21] Arthur Christy links this final line to *Bhagavad Gita* 8.15-16. See Christy, *Orient in American Transcendentalism,* 168.

EACH AND ALL[22]

LITTLE thinks, in the field, yon red-
    cloaked clown
Of thee from the hill-top looking down;
The heifer that lows in the upland farm,
Far-heard, lows not thine ear to charm;
The sexton, tolling his bell at noon,
Deems not that great Napoleon
Stops his horse, and lists with delight,
Whilst his files sweep round yon
    Alpine height;[23]
Nor knowest thou what argument
Thy life to thy neighbor's creed has lent.
All are needed by each one;
Nothing is fair or good alone.
I thought the sparrow's note from heaven,
Singing at dawn on the alder bough;
I brought him home, in his nest, at even;
He sings the song, but it cheers not now,
For I did not bring home the river
    and sky;—
He sang to my ear,—they sang to my eye.

The delicate shells lay on the shore;
The bubbles of the latest wave
Fresh pearls to their enamel gave,
And the bellowing of the savage sea
Greeted their safe escape to me.
I wiped away the weeds and foam,
I fetched my sea-born treasures home;
But the poor, unsightly, noisome things
Had left their beauty on the shore
With the sun and the sand and the
    wild uproar.
The lover watched his graceful maid,
As 'mid the virgin train she strayed,
Nor knew her beauty's best attire
Was woven still by the snow-white choir.
At last she came to his hermitage,
Like the bird from the woodlands to the
    cage;—
The gay enchantment was undone,
A gentle wife, but fairy none.
Then I said, 'I covet truth;
Beauty is unripe childhood's cheat;
I leave it behind with the games of youth:'—
As I spoke, beneath my feet
The ground-pine curled its pretty wreath,
Running over the club-moss burrs;
I inhaled the violet's breath;
Around me stood the oaks and firs;
Pine-cones and acorns lay on the ground;
Over me soared the eternal sky,
Full of light and of deity;
Again I saw, again I heard,
The rolling river, the morning bird;—
Beauty through my senses stole;
I yielded myself to the perfect whole.

THE RHODORA:
ON BEING ASKED,
WHENCE IS THE FLOWER?[24]

IN May, when sea-winds pierced our
    solitudes,
I found the fresh Rhodora in the woods,
Spreading its leafless blooms in a damp
    nook,
To please the desert and the sluggish brook.

---

[22]The text is that of the centenary edition of Emerson, *Complete Works*, 9:4-6. This poem was first published in February 1839 in *The Western Messenger* as "Each in All." Emerson, the "individualist" of "Self-Reliance," here perceives the aesthetic limits of individuality. The poem's message is one of relationship: beauty comes not through isolation but through organic participation in the life of the larger whole. Objects, in short, require ground. Even more deeply, aesthetics is not a separate aspect of existence but an avenue into the divine mystery. There are mystical overtones to Emerson's yielding to the "perfect whole." For Emerson's own discussion of beauty, see again *Nature*, ch. 3.

[23]Edward Waldo Emerson, in his notes to the poem, cited his father's journal entry regarding Napoleon's love of music. "Hearing the bell of a parish church, he would pause, and his voice faltered as he said, 'Ah! that reminds me of the first years I spent at Brienne; I was then happy'" (Emerson, *Complete Works*, 9:405). (See Emerson, *Journals and Miscellaneous Notebooks*, 9 [1844, 1845]: 135.)

[24]The text is that of the centenary edition of

The purple petals, fallen in the pool,
Made the black water with their beauty gay;
Here might the red-bird come his plumes
    to cool,
And court the flower that cheapens his
    array.
Rhodora! if the sages ask thee why
This charm is wasted on the earth and sky,
Tell them, dear, that if eyes were made
    for seeing,
Then Beauty is its own excuse for being:[25]
Why thou wert there, O rival of the rose!
I never thought to ask, I never knew:
But, in my simple ignorance, suppose
The self-same Power that brought me
    there brought you.

THE MIRACLE[26]

I HAVE trod this path a hundred times
With idle footsteps, crooning rhymes.
I know each nest and web-worm's tent,
The fox-hole which the woodchucks rent,
Maple and oak, the old Divan
Self-planted twice, like the banian.[27]
I know not why I came again
Unless to learn it ten times ten.
To read the sense the woods impart
You must bring the throbbing heart.
Love is aye the counterforce,—
Terror and Hope and wild Remorse,
Newest knowledge, fiery thought,
Or Duty to grand purpose wrought.
    Wandering yester morn the brake,
I reached this heath beside the lake,
And oh, the wonder of the power,
The deeper secret of the hour!
Nature, the supplement of man,
His hidden sense interpret can;—
What friend to friend cannot convey
Shall the dumb bird instructed say.
Passing yonder oak, I heard
Sharp accents of my woodland bird;
I watched the singer with delight,—
But mark what changed my joy to fright,—
When that bird sang, I gave the theme;
That wood-bird sang my last night's dream,
A brown wren was the Daniel
That pierced my trance its drift to tell,
Knew my quarrel, how and why,
Published it to lake and sky,
Told every word and syllable
In his flippant chirping babble,
All my wrath and all my shames,
Nay, God is witness, gave the names.

Emerson, *Complete Works*, 9:37-38. This is another of Emerson's poems published in *The Western Messenger* in 1839 although, according to Edward Waldo Emerson (Emerson, *Complete Works*, 9:418), it was composed in 1834, when Emerson was visiting his uncle in Newton, Massachusetts. The rhodora, belonging to the rhododendron family, is a shrub found from Newfoundland to Pennsylvania. Its flowers are produced in the spring either before or with its leaves—Emerson's "leafless blooms" (l. 3) and its rose-purple blossoms as well as its location distinguish it from other, more common azaleas. As in "Each and All," Emerson in this poem probes the spiritual significance of beauty.

[25]For Emerson's philosophic discussion of the ultimacy of beauty, see *Nature*, ch. 3.

[26]The text is that of the centenary edition of Emerson, *Complete Works*, 9:368-69. Edward Waldo Emerson dated the poem between 1857 and 1865 (Emerson, *Complete Works*, 9:513). Although at this stage in his life, Emerson's days of sharp and direct conflict with the Unitarians were behind him, the title of the poem recalls the controversy over miracles in the midst of which the Transcendentalists articulated their separate identity. As then, so now: Emerson finds miracles in nature. He has sharpened that sense in this poem, however, so that the bird that sings his secret soul assumes the proportions of a clairvoyant being. Even more, lying solidly beneath the flamboyance of the miracle is the ground of correspondence. The bird can tell Emerson's inner story because of the abiding relationship between nature and the human spirit.

[27]The banian, or banyan, is an East Indian tree with branches that produce numbers of trunks. These trunks grow down into the ground, so that the tree is supported by props.

TWO RIVERS[28]

Thy summer voice, Musketaquit,[29]
Repeats the music of the rain;
But sweeter rivers pulsing flit
    Through thee, as thou through
        Concord Plain.

Thou in thy narrow banks art pent:
The stream I love unbounded goes
Through flood and sea and firmament;
Through light, through life, it forward
    flows.

I see the inundation sweet,
I hear the spending of the stream
Through years, through men, through
    Nature fleet,
Through love and thought, through
    power and dream.

Musketaquit, a goblin strong,
Of shard and flint makes jewels gay;
They lose their grief who hear his song,
And where he winds is the day of day.

So forth and brighter fares my stream,—
Who drink it shall not thirst again;[30]
No darkness stains its equal gleam,
And ages drop in it like rain.

THRENODY[31]

The South-wind brings
Life, sunshine and desire,
And on every mount and meadow
Breathes aromatic fire;
But over the dead he has no power,
The lost, the lost, he cannot restore;
And, looking over the hills, I mourn
The darling who shall not return.

I see my empty house,
I see my trees repair their boughs;

---

[28] The text is that of the centenary edition of Emerson, *Complete Works*, 9:248. Emerson wrote "Two Rivers" in 1856 and after considerable revision contributed it to *The Atlantic Monthly*, where it appeared in January 1858. The poem cogently expresses Emerson's belief that "particular natural facts are symbols of particular spiritual facts" (*Nature*, ch. 4). One river in the poem is a geographical entity; the other, a mystical one. Emerson uses the geographical river as a meditative point to lead him to a deeper contemplation of the spiritual stream—that of the Oversoul (cf. the introductory paragraphs in Ralph Waldo Emerson, "The Over-Soul," in this volume).

[29] Musquetaquid ("Grassground"), Emerson's "Musquetaquit," was the Indian name for Concord, and here, more particularly, the Concord River. Even when Emerson first wrote the poem, the use of the term was a romantic throwback to the past. I am indebted to Marcia Moss, librarian at the Concord Public Library, for assisting me here.

[30] Cf. John 4:14.

[31] The text is that of the centenary edition of Emerson, *Complete Works*, 9:148-58. Waldo, the firstborn son of Emerson and his second wife, Lydia Jackson, died 27 January 1842 after a three-day bout with scarlet fever. He was five years and three months old, a boy born with the Transcendental movement during the days when Emerson was first announcing its gospel in *Nature*. "Threnody" is Emerson's lament and memorial to his son and also a record of his attempt to understand and accept. The death of one so dear put Emerson's Transcendental theories on the line, and he struggled to make them practical instruments for dealing with his loss.

The poem was, according to Edward Waldo Emerson, composed in two parts, the first and longer section (ending with "Born for the future, to the future lost!") composed while the father's grief was fresh, and the second section (beginning with "The deep Heart answered, 'Weepest thou?'") composed after Emerson had come to reluctant terms with his son's death. (See Emerson, *Complete Works*, 9:452.) Thus, the poem blends the human poignancy of Emerson's pain, anger, and disbelief as he first mourns the death with his later resignation as he contemplates the continued existence of his son in God. "Threnody" was originally published in Emerson's first volume of poetry, *Poems* (1846).

And he, the wondrous child,
Whose silver warble wild
Outvalued every pulsing sound
Within the air's cerulean round,—
The hyacinthine boy, for whom
Morn well might break and April bloom,
The gracious boy, who did adorn
The world whereinto he was born,
And by his countenance repay
The favor of the loving Day,—
Has disappeared from the Day's eye;
Far and wide she cannot find him;
My hopes pursue, they cannot bind him.
Returned this day, the South-wind searches,
And finds young pines and budding birches;
But finds not the budding man;
Nature, who lost, cannot remake him;
Fate let him fall, Fate can't retake him;
Nature, Fate, men, him seek in vain.

And whither now, my truant wise and sweet,
O, whither tend thy feet?
I had the right, few days ago,
Thy steps to watch, thy place to know:
How have I forfeited the right?
Hast thou forgot me in a new delight?
I hearken for thy household cheer,
O eloquent child!
Whose voice, an equal messenger,
Conveyed thy meaning mild.
What though the pains and joys
Whereof it spoke were toys
Fitting his age and ken,
Yet fairest dames and bearded men,
Who heard the sweet request,
So gentle, wise and grave,
Bended with joy to his behest
And let the world's affairs go by,
A while to share his cordial game,
Or mend his wicker wagon-frame,
Still plotting how their hungry ear
That winsome voice again might hear;
For his lips could well pronounce
Words that were persuasions.

Gentlest guardians marked serene
His early hope, his liberal mien;
Took counsel from his guiding eyes
To make this wisdom earthly wise.

Ah, vainly do these eyes recall
The school-march, each day's festival,
When every morn my bosom glowed
To watch the convoy on the road;
The babe in willow wagon closed,
With rolling eyes and face composed;
With children forward and behind,
Like Cupids studiously inclined;
And he the chieftain paced beside,
The centre of the troop allied,
With sunny face of sweet repose,
To guard the babe from fancied foes.
The little captain innocent
Took the eye with him as he went;
Each village senior paused to scan
And speak the lovely caravan.
From the window I look out
To mark thy beautiful parade,
Stately marching in cap and coat
To some tune by fairies played;—
A music heard by thee alone
To works as noble led thee on.

Now Love and Pride, alas! in vain,
Up and down their glances strain.
The painted sled stands where it stood;
The kennel by the corded wood;
His gathered sticks to stanch the wall
Of the snow-tower, when snow should fall;
The ominous hole he dug in the sand,
And childhood's castles built or planned;
His daily haunts I well discern,—
The poultry-yard, the shed, the barn,—
And every inch of garden ground
Paced by the blessed feet around,
From the roadside to the brook
Whereinto he loved to look.
Step the meek fowls where erst they ranged;
The wintry garden lies unchanged;
The brook into the stream runs on;
But the deep-eyed boy is gone.

On that shaded day,
Dark with more clouds than tempests are,
When thou didst yield thy innocent breath
In birdlike heavings unto death,
Night came, and Nature had not thee;
I said, 'We are mates in misery.'
The morrow dawned with needless glow;
Each snowbird chirped, each fowl must crow;

Each tramper started; but the feet
Of the most beautiful and sweet
Of human youth had left the hill
And garden,—they were bound and still.
There's not a sparrow or a wren,
There's not a blade of autumn grain,
Which the four seasons do not tend
And tides of life and increase lend;
And every chick of every bird,
And weed and rock-moss is preferred.
O ostrich-like forgetfulness!
O loss of larger in the less!
Was there no star that could be sent,
No watcher in the firmament,
No angel from the countless host
That loiters round the crystal coast,
Could stoop to heal that only child,
Nature's sweet marvel undefiled,
And keep the blossom of the earth,
Which all her harvests were not worth?
Not mine,—I never called thee mine,
But Nature's heir,—if I repine,
And seeing rashly torn and moved
Not what I made, but what I loved,
Grow early old with grief that thou
Must to the wastes of Nature go,—
'T is because a general hope
Was quenched, and all must doubt
    and grope.
For flattering planets seemed to say
This child should ills of ages stay,
By wondrous tongue, and guided pen,
Bring the flown Muses back to men.
Perchance not he but Nature ailed,
The world and not the infant failed.
It was not ripe yet to sustain
A genius of so fine a strain,
Who gazed upon the sun and moon
As if he came unto his own,
And, pregnant with his grander thought,
Brought the old order into doubt.
His beauty once their beauty tried;
They could not feed him, and he died,
And wandered backward as in scorn,
To wait an æon to be born.[32]

Ill day which made this beauty waste,
Plight broken, this high face defaced!
Some went and came about the dead;
And some in books of solace read;
Some to their friends the tidings say;
Some went to write, some went to pray;
One tarried here, there hurried one;
But their heart abode with none.
Covetous death bereaved us all,
To aggrandize one funeral.
The eager fate which carried thee
Took the largest part of me:
For this losing is true dying;
This is lordly man's down-lying,
This his slow but sure reclining,
Star by star his world resigning.

O child of paradise,
Boy who made dear his father's home,
In whose deep eyes
Men read the welfare of the times to come,
I am too much bereft.
The world dishonored thou hast left.
O truth's and nature's costly lie!
O trusted broken prophecy!
O richest fortune sourly crossed!
Born for the future, to the future lost!

The deep Heart answered, 'Weepest thou?[33]
Worthier cause for passion wild
If I had not taken the child.
And deemest thou as those who pore,
With aged eyes, short way before,—
Think'st Beauty vanished from the coast
Of matter, and thy darling lost?
Taught he not thee—the man of eld,
Whose eyes within his eyes beheld
Heaven's numerous hierarchy span
The mystic gulf from God to man?[34]

---

[32]In this and the preceding line, Emerson suggests the doctrine of reincarnation.

[33]Here begins the second section of the poem. The "deep Heart" is the divine depth element within Emerson, the Self that is merged with the Oversoul.

[34]The "man of eld" is probably Jesus, whose eyes shone out from the eyes of little Waldo—a reference here to the divinity hidden within the child.

To be alone wilt thou begin
When worlds of lovers hem thee in?
To-morrow, when the masks shall fall
That dizen Nature's carnival,
The pure shall see by their own will,
Which overflowing Love shall fill,
'T is not within the force of fate
The fate-conjoined to separate.
But thou, my votary, weepest thou?
I gave thee sight—where is it now?
I taught thy heart beyond the reach
Of ritual, bible, or of speech;
Wrote in thy mind's transparent table,
As far as the incommunicable;
Taught thee each private sign to raise
Lit by the supersolar blaze.
Past utterance, and past belief,
And past the blasphemy of grief,
The mysteries of Nature's heart;
And though no Muse can these impart,
Throb thine with Nature's throbbing breast,
And all is clear from east to west.

'I came to thee as to a friend;
  Dearest, to thee I did not send
  Tutors, but a joyful eye,
  Innocence that matched the sky,
  Lovely locks, a form of wonder,
  Laughter rich as woodland thunder,
  That thou might'st entertain apart
  The richest flowering of all art:
  And, as the great all-loving Day
  Through smallest chambers takes its way,
  That thou might'st break thy daily bread
  With prophet, savior and head;
  That thou might'st cherish for thine own
  The riches of sweet Mary's Son,
  Boy-Rabbi, Israel's paragon.[35]
  And thoughtest thou such guest
  Would in thy hall take up his rest?
  Would rushing life forget her laws,
  Fate's glowing revolution pause?
  High omens ask diviner guess;
  Not to be conned to tediousness
  And know my higher gifts unbind
  The zone that girds the incarnate mind.

When the scanty shores are full
With Thought's perilous, whirling pool;
When frail Nature can no more,
Then the Spirit strikes the hour:
My servant Death, with solving rite,
Pours finite into infinite.
Wilt thou freeze love's tidal flow,
Whose streams through Nature circling go?
Nail the wild star to its track
On the half-climbed zodiac?
Light is light which radiates,
Blood is blood which circulates,
Life is life which generates,
And many-seeming life is one,—
Wilt thou transfix and make it none?
Its onward force too starkly pent
In figure, bone and lineament?
Wilt thou, uncalled, interrogate,
Talker! the unreplying Fate?
Nor see the genius of the whole
Ascendant in the private soul,
Beckon it when to go and come,
Self-announced its hour of doom?
Fair the soul's recess and shrine,
Magic-built to last a season;
Masterpiece of love benign,
Fairer that expansive reason
Whose omen 't is, and sign.
Wilt thou not ope thy heart to know
What rainbows teach, and sunsets show?[36]
Verdict which accumulates
From lengthening scroll of human fates,
Voice of earth to earth returned,
Prayers of saints that inly burned,—
Saying, *What is excellent,*
As God lives, is permanent;
Hearts are dust, hearts' loves remain;
Heart's love will meet thee again.
Revere the Maker; fetch thine eye
Up to his style, and manners of the sky.
Not of adamant and gold
Built he heaven stark and cold;

---

[35] Jesus, symbol of the divine element, was present in the child Waldo.

[36] Here Emerson recalls the doctrine of correspondence, learning from the physical facts of nature and the spiritual fact that the temporary points beyond itself to the permanent, to that which endures as God lives.

No, but a nest of bending reeds,
Flowering grass and scented weeds;
Or like a traveller's fleeing tent,
Or bow above the tempest bent;
Built of tears and sacred flames,
And virtue reaching to its aims;
Built of furtherance and pursuing,
Not of spent deeds, but of doing.
Silent rushes the swift Lord
Through ruined systems still restored,
Broadsowing, bleak and void to bless,
Plants with worlds the wilderness;[37]
Waters with tears of ancient sorrow
Apples of Eden ripe to-morrow.
House and tenant go to ground,
Lost in God, in Godhead found.'

GRACE[38]

How much, preventing God, how much
    I owe
To the defences thou hast round me set;
Example, custom, fear, occasion slow,—
These scorned bondmen were my parapet.
I dare not peep over this parapet
To gauge with glance the roaring gulf
    below,
The depths of sin to which I had
    descended,
Had not these me against myself defended.

---

[37]Edward Waldo Emerson, in his notes to the poem, observed that in the first part of Plato's *Timaeus* the idea of God "rushing into distribution" was explicated at length (Emerson, *Complete Works*, 9:454). But in the *Timaeus* there is the complicating factor of the relationship between the Demiurge—who created the world—and the heavenly Gods. Moreover, the idea of God's rush into distribution could also, with qualifications, be described as Neoplatonic, with the One—not actively, but through the process of emanation—the source of the Many. See Plato *Timaeus* 29D-30C, 40A-B, 40D-41D, and Plotinus *Enneads* 4.8.6, 5.1.6, 5.2.1.

[38]The text is that of the centenary edition of Emerson, *Complete Works*, 9:359. This brief poem appeared in *The Dial* in January 1842. By

TERMINUS[39]

IT is time to be old,
To take in sail:—
The god of bounds,
Who sets to seas a shore,
Came to me in his fatal rounds,
And said: 'No more!
No farther shoot

Emersonian standards almost traditional, the poem was once mistakenly attributed by Emerson's friends to George Herbert, the English metaphysical poet whom he admired. (See ibid., 510.) Yet it is important to note that, even here, grace is understood in natural rather than supernatural terms. Just as Jesus of Nazareth was radically humanized by Emerson, so, too, was grace. Placed after "Threnody" and before "Terminus," the poem speaks of limits and also sounds a retrospective note.

[39]The text is that of the centenary edition of Emerson, *Complete Works*, 9:251-52. Terminus was the ancient Roman God who watched over boundaries and, as an object, a boundary marker in Rome. According to his son, Emerson wrote this poem more than fifteen years before his death. Already, though, the Transcendentalist had faced his own limits and accepted them. The anecdote that Edward Waldo Emerson recorded concerning the poem is worth repeating:

> In the last days of the year 1866, when I was returning from a long stay in the Western States, I met my father in New York just starting for his usual winter lecturing trip, in those days extending beyond the Mississippi. We spent the night together at the St. Denis Hotel, and as we sat by the fire he read me two or three of his poems for the new May-Day volume, among them "Terminus." It almost startled me. No thought of his ageing [sic] had ever come to me, and there he sat, with no apparent abatement of bodily vigor, and young in spirit, recognizing with serene acquiescence his failing forces; I think he smiled as he read. He recognized, as none of us did, that his working days were nearly done (Emerson, *Complete Works*, 9:489-90).

Thy broad ambitious branches, and thy
  root.
Fancy departs: no more invent;
Contract thy firmament
To compass of a tent.
There's not enough for this and that,
Make thy option which of two;
Economize the failing river,
Not the less revere the Giver,
Leave the many and hold the few.
Timely wise accept the terms,
Soften the fall with wary foot;
A little while
Still plan and smile,
And,—fault of novel germs,—
Mature the unfallen fruit.
Curse, if thou wilt, thy sires,
Bad husbands of their fires,
Who, when they gave thee breath,
Failed to bequeath
The needful sinew stark as once,
The Baresark marrow to thy bones,[40]
But left a legacy of ebbing veins,
Inconstant heat and nerveless reins,—
Amid the Muses, left thee deaf and dumb,
Amid the gladiators, halt and numb.'

   As the bird trims her to the gale,
I trim myself to the storm of time,
I man the rudder, reef the sail,
   Obey the voice at eve obeyed at prime:
'Lowly faithful, banish fear,
Right onward drive unharmed;
The port, well worth the cruise, is near,
And every wave is charmed.'

---

[40] A Berserker, or Berserk—an ancient Scandinavian warrior thought to be invulnerable and known for the wild passion with which he fought.

FATE

The biography of the spirit ends with the concluding paragraphs of Emerson's essay "Fate." Unlike his earlier works in this volume, "Fate" was the product of Emerson's later years, published in 1860 as the lead essay in the collection titled *The Conduct of Life*. "Fate" itself had first been written mostly during 1852, as a letter from Emerson to Thomas Carlyle makes clear. Emerson had remarked in the same letter: "When we find out what Fate is, I suppose, the Sphinx & we are done for; and Sphinx, Oedipus, & world, ought, by good rights, to roll down the steep into the sea."[1]

A quixotic observation, perhaps, for the Transcendental apostle of freedom and individualism, but it is in keeping with Emerson's insight and affirmation in the essay. The Oversoul of earlier years has yielded here to the Beautiful Necessity of boundary and limitation. Power and Fate are the two poles of a dual world in which freedom is, paradoxically, necessary. Because a person, unlike an animal or a plant, can think and will the good, that individual is free and Fate is annulled or converted—to become Necessity. At once free and bound, each person must acquiesce with heart and spirit to what lies beyond ego identity. Only by surrendering to Necessity, Emerson has concluded, can a person experience authentic power and find the liberation of the spirit that each one seeks. The human question and answer, Oedipus and Sphinx against the backdrop of their world, cannot ever be completely understood: Necessity imposes the bounds that make it impossible to understand Necessity completely.[2]

---

[1] Ralph Waldo Emerson to Thomas Carlyle, 19 April 1853, in Ralph Waldo Emerson and Thomas Carlyle, *The Correspondence of Emerson and Carlyle,* ed. Joseph Slater (New York: Columbia University Press, 1964) 485. See also Ralph Waldo Emerson, *The Complete Works of Ralph Waldo Emerson,* ed. Edward Waldo Emerson, centenary ed. (Boston: Houghton, Mifflin, 1903–1904) 6:337, in which Edward Waldo Emerson quotes relevant passages of the letter.

[2] The text is that of the centenary edition of Emerson, *Complete Works,* 6:47-49.

(From) FATE

One key, one solution to the mysteries of human condition, one solution to the old knots of fate, freedom, and foreknowledge, exists; the propounding, namely, of the double consciousness. A man must ride alternately on the horses of his private and his public nature, as the equestrians in the circus throw themselves nimbly from horse to horse, or plant one foot on the back of one and the other foot on the back of the other. So when a man is the victim of his fate, his sciatica in his loins and cramp in his mind; a club-foot and a club in his wit; a sour face and a selfish temper; a strut in his gait and a conceit in his affection; or is ground to powder by the vice of his race;— he is to rally on his relation to the Universe, which his ruin benefits. Leaving the dæmon who suffers, he is to take sides with the Deity who secures universal benefit by his pain.

To offset the drag of temperament and race, which pulls down, learn this lesson, namely, that by the cunning co-presence of two elements, which is throughout nature, whatever lames or paralyzes you draws in with it the divinity, in some form, to repay. A good intention clothes itself with sudden power. When a god wishes to ride, any chip or pebble will bud and shoot out winged feet and serve him for a horse.

Let us build altars to the Blessed Unity which holds nature and souls in perfect solution, and compels every atom to serve an universal end. I do not wonder at a snowflake, a shell, a summer landscape, or the glory of the stars; but at the necessity of beauty under which the universe lies; that all is and must be pictorial; that the rainbow and the curve of the horizon and the arch of the blue vault are only results from the organism of the eye. There is no need for foolish amateurs to fetch me to admire a garden of flowers, or a sun-gilt cloud, or a waterfall, when I cannot look without seeing splendor and grace. How idle to choose a random sparkle here or there, when the indwelling necessity plants the rose of beauty on the brow of chaos, and discloses the central intention of Nature to be harmony and joy.

Let us build altars to the Beautiful Necessity.[1] If we thought men were free in the sense that in a single exception one fantastical will could prevail over the law of things, it were all one as if a child's hand could pull down the sun. If in the least particular one could derange the order of nature,—who would accept the gift of life?

Let us build altars to the Beautiful Ne-

---

[1] Greek mythology contained various accounts of the three Fates (Moirae) and Necessity (Ananke). Perhaps most pertinent here is Plato's version in *The Republic,* in which Necessity is the divine mother of the Fates—Lachesis, Clotho, and Atropos. But it is on the knees of Necessity that the spindle turns on which depend the revolutions of the planets and the other stars. See Plato *Republic* 616C-617D. Elsewhere, the Fates are the daughters of Zeus and Themis (Law, Justice), and they are often conceived in singular form as Moira, or Fate, and linked to understandings of the roles of Fortune (Tyche) and Necessity (Ananke) in human existence. See Mark P. O. Morford and Robert J. Lenardon, *Classical Mythology* (New York: David McKay, 1971) 57, 228-29.

cessity, which secures that all is made of one piece; that plaintiff and defendant, friend and enemy, animal and planet, food and eater are of one kind. In astronomy is vast space but no foreign system; in geology, vast time but the same laws as to-day. Why should we be afraid of Nature, which is no other than "philosophy and theology embodied"?[2] Why should we fear to be crushed by savage elements, we who are made up of the same elements? Let us build to the Beautiful Necessity, which makes man brave in believing that he cannot shun a danger that is appointed, nor incur one that is not; to the Necessity which rudely or softly educates him to the perception that there are no contingencies; that Law rules throughout existence; a Law which is not intelligent but intelligence;—not personal nor impersonal—it disdains words and passes understanding; it dissolves persons; it vivifies nature; yet solicits the pure in heart to draw on all its omnipotence.

---

[2] It has not been possible to locate the source of the quotation, although it has a Goetheian flavor. In Johann von Goethe's *Faust,* for example, the Homunculus confides: "I'm tracking down a pair / Of sages whom I want to question next; / I listened: Nature! Nature! went the text." See *Faust* (trans. Walter Arndt), pt. 2, act 2, ll. 7835-37.

Part II

AMOS BRONSON ALCOTT

INTRODUCTION

Amos Bronson Alcott was the only one in the Transcendental inner circle not born in Boston or its environs, not educated at Harvard, and not grounded in Unitarianism. The outsider even in a group of religious radicals, he embodied in his life the wandering career of a pilgrim and seeker. Alcott had been born in 1799 on a farm in Wolcott, Connecticut. The oldest of the eight children of Joseph Alcox and Anna Bronson, he was descended from an early pioneer family; and by the time he was in his late teens he was pioneering in his own way, making peddling trips to the Carolinas and Virginia.

He had already been confirmed as an Episcopalian and had immersed himself deeply in the spirituality of John Bunyan's *Pilgrim's Progress*. He had also, during these years, experienced presentiments of a divinity present in nature. Then in the Carolinas in 1822 he encountered a Quaker community and, although he never became a Quaker, was strongly attracted to their doctrine of the "inner light" in every person. So it was that, before he ever met the other Transcendentalists, Alcott's world was congruent with theirs. As in the allegories of *Pilgrim's Progress,* things for him were double and possessed a significance that lay behind their first appearance: divinity was present in the world and in human life.

Shaped by these views, Alcott stopped peddling goods and wares and—in his own version of *Pilgrim's Progress*—began to peddle ideas.[1] Although his exposure to formal education had been irregular, in his mid-twenties he began to teach school, first at Bristol but soon at Cheshire, Connecticut. His "Cheshire Pestalozzian School"—named after the Swiss educational reformer—attracted considerable notice and was described by one educator as "the best common school in the state—probably in the United States."[2] But, in a pattern that was to repeat itself in later years, the parents of the Cheshire students became uneasy and then hostile. They sent their children to other schools, and success evaporated as quickly as it had come.

Alcott continued teaching, though, and by 1828 had arrived in Boston and received an invitation from the Boston Infant School Society. So he began the first of a series of experimental schools that would occupy him in Boston for over a decade, except for a period from 1831 to 1833 when he taught in Germantown, near Philadelphia. During these

---

[1]Alcott described his existence at midlife in these terms: "Mind is not always a merchantable commodity; and here's the Pedlar, July 1850, the pack of metaphysic that he is, set bodily, mystically, down in the best market in the world. Athenian times, yet without customer for his handsome wares" (Amos Bronson Alcott, *The Journals of Bronson Alcott*, sel. and ed. Odell Shepard [Boston: Little, Brown, 1838] 232). The metaphor also formed the basis for Shepard's interpretation in Odell Shepard, *Pedlar's Progress: The Life of Bronson Alcott* (1937; rpt., New York: Greenwood Press, 1968).

[2]*Boston Recorder,* 11 May 1827, quoted in Madelon Bedell, *The Alcotts: Biography of a Family* (New York: Clarkson N. Potter, 1980) 18.

years in Boston, educational theory combined with Transcendental faith and friends to support his optimistic endeavors. In this context, the most memorable of his Boston schools was the one, cited in the introduction, that Alcott conducted beginning in 1834 at the Masonic Temple. Here he used space, time, and teacher-student relationships to help achieve the goals of a carefully pondered religious philosophy of education.

Then, in 1835, Alcott started a series of "conversations" with his youthful charges on the New Testament Gospels. Elizabeth Palmer Peabody, Transcendentalist and assistant to Alcott at the school, acted as amanuensis, and by the end of the following year the first volume of *Record of Conversations on the Gospels* appeared. The book implicitly challenged prevalent pedagogical methods by demonstrating an alternative, and it underscored the successes of a man who, without clerical credentials, was deeply involved in the religious and moral training of the young. Worst of all in the eyes of Boston, it recorded his probing questions and answers that touched on the theme of the beginnings of life. Alcott, however carefully and chastely, was broaching the topic of sexuality—in a mixed classroom of children from less-than-six to twelve years old, in nineteenth-century New England.

The results were not slow in coming. Press and clergy hounded Alcott, and his school began to feel the effects. With difficulties compounded in the wake of the financial Panic of 1837, the institution never recovered, moving ignominiously to the Temple basement and then quietly dying in 1838. A short-lived school conducted in Alcott's home failed the following year, the victim of racial prejudice when Alcott accepted a black child.

It was not the end of Alcott's career as an educator, however. Throughout his life, he never ceased to champion "conversation" and to believe in its ennobling effects. A charter member of the Transcendental Club, he was one of its prime conversationalists. Later, from 1848, he increasingly offered formal conversations in Boston and, from 1853 to 1882, launched ten conversational tours of the Midwest.

Meanwhile, in 1859, Alcott accepted a position as superintendent of schools in Concord, an appointment that continued for six years. Then, in the last decade of his life, with William Torrey Harris, Franklin B. Sanborn, and others, he founded the Concord School of Philosophy. For nine successive summers, until Alcott's death in 1888, the school met— at first in his yard and study and then in a rough building erected on his grounds. To the school came various lecturers such as Emerson, Harris, and Sanborn and, of course, Alcott himself. In the context of the school, the conversations continued. Even after a stroke paralyzed Alcott in 1882, the Concord School flourished and in his declining years provided a final tribute to his commitments as an educator.

Educational reform, though, was only the first of a series of social issues that captured Alcott's imagination and energy. As the introduction to this volume noted, he was an early antislavery activist and also participated in meetings for a plethora of reform organizations. Perhaps the apex of this generalized reform activity came in 1842, when—after Alcott had experienced more than five years of public humiliation and failure—Emerson financed a trip to England to hearten him. Here Alcott found support and appreciation in a many-faceted reform movement that commanded a far-larger following than the parallel movement in America. More important, he visited Transcendental sympathizers who had begun a school and community based on his ideas at Alcott House in Ham, Surrey. Among them Alcott encountered Henry Wright and Charles Lane, both of whom returned to

America with him. It was with Lane's support and backing that Alcott, in 1843, began the brief but well-remembered Fruitlands community.

Fruitlands came apart at least partially because of tension between Alcott and Lane over questions of celibacy, for Alcott—ascetic in so many ways—had evolved a spirituality in which sexuality was central. "Wedlock!" he had once written, "blessed union of spirits! blending of two natures in one! Incarnation of love!"[3] Although this embrace of sexual themes was only one side of a religious dialectic that also included a Neoplatonic suspicion of matter, it was based on a spiritual perception that came out of life and not simply theory. Alcott had married Abigail May in 1830, and until her death in 1877, theirs was a relationship of lifelong intimacy—even if disturbed by the formidable differences between an idealist and a strong and practical mate. Marriage brought them Anna in 1831, Louisa in 1832, Elizabeth in 1835, and Abby in 1840—the four sisters of the March family depicted in Louisa May Alcott's later novel *Little Women*. And, as in the novel, there was grief in the Alcott family at the early death of the teenage Elizabeth in 1858. "A family is the heaven of the Soul," Alcott had declared when she was still a little child.[4]

Supported by family and friends, Alcott published, mostly in later life. His earliest work, in 1830—a pamphlet entitled *Observations on the Principles and Methods of Infant Instruction*—was followed in 1836 by another pamphlet, *The Doctrine and Discipline of Human Culture*, the text of which has been included in this volume. In the same year the first part of the two-volume *Record of Conversations on the Gospels* (also called *Conversations with Children on the Gospels*) appeared. Edited by Elizabeth Palmer Peabody, it was joined by the second volume the following year. (Peabody had earlier edited *Record of a School* [1835], which recorded the process of instruction at the Temple School.) Thereafter there were the "Orphic Sayings" in *The Dial* in 1840 and 1841 (reproduced in part here) and *The Boston Quarterly Review* (1841) and similar epigrammatic compositions published in various journals.

It was only in 1865, however, that Alcott came forward with a book again—his privately printed *Emerson*, which was later published in 1882 as *Ralph Waldo Emerson: An Estimate of His Character and Genius, in Prose and Verse*. Meanwhile, his *Tablets* appeared in 1868 and *Concord Days* in 1872. *Table-Talk* followed (1877); and then, in 1881, came the privately printed *New Connecticut: An Autobiographical Poem*, to be edited by Franklin B. Sanborn and republished in 1887. Finally, *Sonnets and Canzonets* (1882) completed the roster of published works.

These productions of Alcott's later years were generally received with interest and respect, for by this time he was venerated as a sage—the result of speaking successes in the Midwest and also of age itself. Alcott was a living reminder of the Transcendental gospel that had shaken an earlier New England and America, and as such he was accorded attention and a measure of homage.

Many years before, his friend Emerson had written to Margaret Fuller concerning Alcott: "He has more of the godlike than any man I have ever seen and his presence rebukes

---

[3] Amos Bronson Alcott, "Psyche" (unpublished MS), quoted in Bedell, *The Alcotts*, 185.

[4] Amos Bronson Alcott, "Psyche: An Evangele" (unpublished MS), quoted in Bedell, *The Alcotts*, 185.

& threatens & raises. He *is* a teacher."[5] That estimate stands as perhaps the best assessment of the man and his message that can be made here. In the pages that follow, we examine Alcott's articulation of Transcendentalism under the character of education in *The Doctrine and Discipline of Human Culture*, and we ponder its many sides in a selection from his oracular "Orphic Sayings." Even among his closest Transcendental friends, we find an Alcott who was "other"—ever a pilgrim in search of the One, ever a teacher moving toward the Many in the strength of his ideas.

---

[5]Ralph Waldo Emerson to Margaret Fuller, 19 and 21 May 1837, in Ralph Waldo Emerson, *The Letters of Ralph Waldo Emerson,* ed. Ralph L. Rusk (New York: Columbia University Press, 1939) 2:76.

THE DOCTRINE AND DISCIPLINE OF HUMAN CULTURE

This short essay was published as a pamphlet in 1836 by James Munroe and Company of Boston. Later the same year the publisher issued the first volume of Alcott's *Record of Conversations on the Gospels,* and the essay was reprinted in full as its introduction. Yet because of the consternation and uproar with which Boston greeted the central text's account of education at the Temple School, the introduction was almost totally ignored. Indeed, even Alcott's twentieth-century biographer Odell Shepard overlooked it in his discussion of the *Conversations on the Gospels* and did not mention it at all as an independent pamphlet.[1]

This pattern of neglect is unfortunate because perhaps nowhere else in his writings does Alcott give so ordered and carefully developed a testimony to his Transcendental spirituality. His more usual method of writing was in the style of the short aphorism, or saying, and by the nature of that genre he could not explore the nuances of an idea in detail. Even in *Doctrine and Discipline* the subheadings at the left margins and the wide separation of paragraphs hint of the epigrammatic style; but here it is only a suggestion, and expositional elements are stronger. Hence it is to *The Doctrine and Discipline of Human Culture,* rather than to Alcott's more widely known "Orphic Sayings," that we turn for an introduction to his thought.

The term *human culture* no doubt came to Alcott from his friend William Russell (1798-1873), the Scottish editor of the *American Journal of Education* with whom Alcott taught in Boston and in Germantown, Pennsylvania, and who later lived with the Alcott family in Boston. For Russell, human culture meant the progressive unfolding of all human capacities from the physical to the mental and the spiritual. Although he did not emphasize the physical, Alcott's understanding, as he explained it in the essay, was not dissimilar. And while it would be inaccurate to say that Alcott took his views whole from Russell, the influence of his friend ran deep. Russell, in fact, "taught" the teacher and was one of the chief formative individuals in his life.[2]

If Russell provided a concept central to Alcott's essay, the Transcendentalist had earlier grown familiar with the theories of the renowned Swiss educator Johann Heinrich

---

[1]Odell Shepard, *Pedlar's Progress: The Life of Bronson Alcott* (1937; rpt., New York: Greenwood Press, 1968) esp. 164-201. In 1960, in an introduction to Amos Bronson Alcott, *Essays on Education (1830–1862) by Amos Bronson Alcott,* ed. Walter Harding (Gainesville FL: Scholars' Facsimiles & Reprints), Harding recounted the publishing history of *The Doctrine and Discipline of Human Culture* and called it "a direct result of Alcott's work at the Temple School and an exposition of the theories he practiced therein" (xi). Harding also noted the lack of attention paid the essay.

[2]For an account on which this one is based, see Shepard, *Pedlar's Progress,* 145-50.

Pestalozzi, who stressed individual development, organic method, and the importance of moral education.³ Moreover, during the time of his association with Russell—besides discovering Plato, Plotinus, Proclus, Boehme, and others—he was reading Coleridge's *Aids to Reflection* with great excitement. All of these and others, too, hover over Alcott's essay, but tracing direct sources for his thought is difficult. Beyond remarking the general Platonic ambience, spotting a few obvious references, and noting the New Testament as the source of most quotations and recognizable allusions, we are left to realize how thoroughly Alcott has synthesized his material, how much what we are reading has become purely and simply Alcott. Blending his temperament, his reading, and his experience, Alcott brought forward his own Transcendental doctrine, a version that must be read alongside the Emersonian statement of self-culture.

More than that, in keeping with Alcott's vocation as an educator, we see here how much the idea of education formed the core of his spirituality. Yet contemporary professional notions of education do not help us to perceive what Alcott is about. "Education" in this essay is a religious concept, the keystone in Alcott's spirituality. It is not a secular institution or a purely intellectual process. Platonic and Neoplatonic in general cast, Alcott's "education" is built on his affirmation that each individual possesses a divine spark and that, enmeshed in matter, the spirit has the capacity to develop its powers and to ascend to the divine. In this reading the teacher becomes a spiritual guide, a mystical master—Alcott's "Genius" in the essay—who helps each soul to unfold itself, encouraging each on the path of ascent. And Jesus, the divine man of the Gospels, is the Teacher among teachers, the great model of what all may become.

In short, *The Doctrine and Discipline of Human Culture* invites its readers not only to seek the highest and the best in the education of their children, but to seek the divine world by bringing to perfection the Idea within themselves. It underlines the Transcendental connection between the reform of society and the reform of self, illustrating by its commitments and concerns that collective goals and individual aspirations were, for the Transcendentalists, two sides of the same spiritual impulse. In the end, with its orientation toward the future and its atmosphere of intense expectation of reform, Alcott's essay is a millennial document.⁴

---

³For a discussion, see ibid., 84-86.

⁴The text is that of the pamphlet: A. Bronson Alcott, *The Doctrine and Discipline of Human Culture* (Boston: James Munroe, 1836).

THE DOCTRINE AND DISCIPLINE OF HUMAN CULTURE

The wind bloweth where it listeth, and ye hear the sound thereof; but ye cannot tell whence it cometh nor whither it goeth; so is every one that is born of the Spirit.
Jesus in Conversation with Nicodemus.[1]

Idea of Man.   MAN is the noblest of the Creator's works. He is the most richly gifted of all his creatures. His sphere of action is the broadest; his influence the widest; and to him is given Nature and Life for his heritage and his possession. He holds dominion over the Outward. He is the rightful Sovereign of the Earth, fitted to subdue all things to himself, and to know of no superior, save God. And yet he enters upon the scene of his labors, a feeble and wailing Babe, at first unconscious of the place assigned him, and needs years of tutelage and discipline to fit him for the high and austere duties that await him.

Idea of Education.   The Art, which fits such a being to fulfil his high destiny, is the first and noblest of arts. Human Culture is the art of revealing to a man the true Idea of his Being[2]— his endowments—his possessions—and of fitting him to use them for the growth, renewal, and perfection of his Spirit. It is the art of completing a man. It includes all those influences, and disciplines, by which his faculties are unfolded and perfected. It is that agency which takes the helpless and pleading Infant from the hands of its Creator; and, apprehending its entire nature, tempts it forth—now by austere, and now by kindly influences and disciplines—and thus moulds it at last into the Image of a Perfect Man; armed at all points, to use the Body, Nature, and Life, for its growth and renewal, and to hold dominion over the fluctuating things of the Outward. It seeks to realize in the Soul the Image of the Creator.—Its end is a perfect man. Its aim, through every stage of influence and discipline, is self-renewal. The body, nature, and life are its instruments and materials. Jesus is its worthiest Ideal. Christianity its purest Organ. The Gospels its fullest Text-Book. Genius its Inspiration.[3] Holiness its

---

[1] Cf. John 3:8. These lines did not appear when the essay was reprinted in *Record of Conversations on the Gospels*. Instead Alcott fused portions of Matt. 18:3 and John 3:3 and 5 to form a new motto for his title page.

[2] Alcott immediately announces the Platonic theme of Idealism that will dominate the essay. In Alcott's version the Idea of the man is his true self, and the man's task is to bring his present, earthly self into conformity with the Idea. For a classic and often-cited discussion of the theory of Ideas, see Plato *Republic* 509D-511E.

[3] The concept of genius was familiar in Romantic circles. In ancient Roman religion the word *genius* was used to describe the guardian

Law. Temperance its Discipline. Immortality its Reward.

History and Type of this Idea. This divine Art, including all others, or subordinating them to its Idea, was never apprehended, in all its breadth and depth of significance, till the era of Jesus of Nazareth. He it was that first revealed it. Over his Divine Intellect first flitted the Idea of man's endowments and destiny. He set no limits to the growth of our nature. "Be Ye Perfect even as my Father in Heaven is Perfect,"[4] was the high aim which he placed before his disciples; and in this he was true to our nature, for the sentiment lives in every faculty and function of our being. It is the ever-sounding Trump of Duty, urging us to the perpetual work of self-renewal. It is the deep instinct of the spirit. And his Life gives us the promise of its realization. In his attributes and endowments he is a Type of our common nature. His achievements are a glimpse of the Apotheosis of Humanity. They are a glorious unfolding of the Godlike in man. They disclose the Idea of Spirit. And if he was not, in himself, the complete fulfilment of Spirit, he apprehended its law, and set forth its conditions. He bequeathed to us the phenomena of its manifestation; for in the Gospels we have the history of Spirit accomplishing its mission on the earth.[5] We behold the Incarnate One, dealing with flesh and blood—tempted, and suffering—yet baffling and overcoming the ministries of Evil and of Pain.

Idea and Type misapprehended. Still this Idea, so clearly announced, and so fully demonstrated in the being and life of Jesus, has made but little advance in the minds of men. Men have not subdued it to themselves. It has not become the ground and law of human consciousness. They have not married their nature to it by a living Faith. Nearly two millenniums have elapsed since its announcement, and yet, so slow of apprehension have been the successors of this Divine Genius, that even at this day, the deep and universal significance of his Idea has not been fully taken in. It has been restricted to himself alone. He stands in the minds of this generation, as a Phenomenon, which God, in the inscrutable designs of his Providence, saw fit to present, to the gaze and wonder of mankind, yet as a being of unsettled rank in the universe, whom men may venture to imitate, but dare not approach. In him, the Human Nature is feebly apprehended, while the Divine is lifted out of sight, and lost in the ineffable light of the Godhead. Men do not deem him as the harmonious unfolding of Spirit into the Image of a Perfect Man—as a worthy Symbol of the Divinity, wherein Human Nature is revealed in its Fulness. Yet, as if by an inward and irresistible Instinct, all

---

spirit of a person, thought to be a kind of second (divine) self. Great achievements and intellectual prowess were understood as the work of the genius, and thus, gradually, the modern usage resulted. Alcott's meditations share with the Roman view of genius the sense of its divinity (indeed, Jesus for him is a "Divine Genius") and its existence almost as a separate force.

[4]Cf. Matt. 5:48.

[5]For Alcott, the divine Jesus points the way to the divinization of humanity. Although this and other passages in the essay appear Hegelian in flavor, Alcott had no knowledge of Hegel at this time. Even much later, as Odell Shepard wrote in another context, Alcott knew Hegel "hardly at all" (Odell Shepard, *Pedlar's Progress: The Life of Bronson Alcott* [1937; rpt., New York: Greenwood Press, 1968] 475). For the seemingly related Hegelian ideas, see G. W. F. Hegel, *The Philosophy of History*, pt. 2, sec. 3, ch. 2.

men have been drawn to him; and, while diverse in their opinions; explaining his Idea in different types, they have given him the full and unreserved homage of their hearts. They have gathered around the altars, inscribed with his perfections, and, through his name, delighted to address the God and Father of Spirits. Disowning him in their minds, unable to grasp his Idea, they have deified him in their hearts. They have worshipped the Holiness which they could not define.

Era of its Revival. It is the mission of this Age, to revive his Idea, give it currency, and reinstate it in the faith of men. By its quickening agency, it is to fructify our common nature, and reproduce its like. It is to unfold our being into the same divine likeness. It is to reproduce Perfect Men. The faded Image of Humanity is to be restored, and man reappear in his original brightness. It is to mould anew our Institutions, our Manners, our Men. It is to restore Nature to its rightful use; purify Life; hallow the functions of the Human Body, and regenerate Philosophy, Literature, Art, Society. The Divine Idea of a Man is to be formed in the common consciousness of this age, and genius mould all its products in accordance with it.

Means of its Revival. The means for reinstating this Idea in the common mind, in order to conduce to these results, are many. Yet all are simple. And the most direct and effectual are by apprehending the Genius of this Divine Man, from the study of those Records wherein his career is delineated with so much fidelity, simplicity, and truth. Therein have we a manifestation of Spirit, while undergoing the temptations of this corporeal life; yet faithful to the laws of its renovation and its end. The Divine Idea of Humanity gleams forth through every circumstance of his terrestrial career. The fearful agencies of the Spirit assert their power. In him Nature and Life are subordinated to the spiritual force. The Son of God appears on Earth, enrobed in Flesh, and looks forth serenely upon Man. We feel the significance of the Incarnation; the grandeur of our nature. We associate Jesus with our holiest aspirations, our deepest affections; and thus does he become a fit Mediator between the last age and the new era, of which he was the herald and the pledge. He is to us the Prophet of two millenniums. He is the brightest Symbol of a Man that history affords, and points us to yet fuller manifestations of the Godhead.

Ideal of a Teacher. And the Gospels are not only a fit Text-Book for the study of Spirit, in its corporeal relations, but they are a specimen also of the true method of imparting instruction. They give us the practice of Jesus himself. They unfold the means of addressing human nature. Jesus was a Teacher; he sought to renovate Humanity. His method commends itself to us. It is a beautiful exhibition of his Genius, bearing the stamp of naturalness, force, and directness. It is popular. Instead of seeking formal and austere means, he rested his influence chiefly on the living word, rising spontaneously in the soul, and clothing itself at once, in the simplest, yet most commanding forms. He was a finished extemporaneous speaker. His manner and style are models. In these, his Ideas became like the beautiful, yet majestic Nature, whose images he wove so skilfully into his diction. He was an Artist of the highest order. More perfect specimens of address do not elsewhere exist. View him in his conversation with his disciples. Hear him in his simple colloquies with the people. Listen to him when seated at the wellside discoursing with the Samaritan woman, on the IDEA OF WORSHIP; and at night with Nicodemus, on SPIRITUAL RENEWAL.[6] From facts and objects the most familiar, he slid easily and simply into the highest and holiest themes, and, in this unimposing guise, disclosed the great Doctrines, and stated the Divine Ideas, that it was his mission to bequeath to his race. Conversation was the form of utterance that he sought.[7] Of formal discourse but one specimen is given, in his Sermon on the Mount; yet in this the inspiration bursts all forms, and he rises to the highest efforts of genius, at its close.

Organ of Instruction.
This preference of Jesus for Conversation, as the fittest organ of utterance, is a striking proof of his comprehensive Idea of Education. He knew what was in man, and the means of perfecting his being. He saw the superiority of this exercise over others for quickening the Spirit. For, in this all the instincts and faculties of our being are touched. They find full and fair scope. It tempts forth all the powers. Man faces his fellow man. He holds a living intercourse.[8] He feels the quickening life and light. The social affections are addressed; and these bring all the faculties in train.

Speech comes unbidden. Nature lends her images. Imagination sends abroad her winged words. We see thought as it springs from the soul, and in the very process of growth and utterance. Reason plays under the mellow light of fancy. The Genius of the Soul is waked, and eloquence sits on her tuneful lip. Wisdom finds an organ worthy her serene, yet imposing products. Ideas stand in beauty and majesty before the Soul.

Organ of Genius.
And Genius has ever sought this organ of utterance. It has given us full testimony in its favor. Socrates—a name that Christians can see coupled with that of their Divine Sage—descanted thus on the profound themes in which he delighted. The marketplace; the workshop; the public streets were his favorite haunts of instruction. And the divine Plato has added his testimony, also, in those enduring works, wherein he sought to embalm for posterity, both the wisdom of his master and the genius that was his own.[9] Rich text-books these for the study of philosophic genius. They rank next in finish and beauty, to the specimens of Jesus as recorded by his own beloved John.

Genius alone Renews.
It is by such organs that Human Nature is to be unfolded into the Idea of its fulness. Yet to do this, teachers must be men in possession of their Idea. They must be men of their kind; men inspired with great and living Ideas, as was Jesus. Such alone are worthy. They alone can pierce the customs and conventions that hide the Soul from itself. They alone can release it from the slavery of the corporeal life, and give

---

[6] See John 4:7-26 and 3:1-21.

[7] Here begins the theme, which Alcott will develop in the following passage, of conversation as religious act and fittest means to his spiritual ends. Alcott's Transcendental ritual of conversation is thus given a theoretical foundation. Note, too, that through conversation Jesus, the divine Idea, teaches other divine Ideas.

[8] Cf. Ralph Waldo Emerson, *The Journals and Miscellaneous Notebooks of Ralph Waldo Emerson,* ed. William H. Gilman et al. (Cambridge: Harvard University Press, Belknap Press, 1960–) 7 (28 May 1840): 360. (See the quotations from the passage in the introduction to this volume.)

[9] In his *Dialogues* Plato used the figure of Socrates to develop arguments and views of his own, and scholars have had difficulty in ascertaining with complete certainty which teachings were those of Socrates and which those of Plato.

it back to itself. And such are ever sent at the call of Humanity. Some God, instinct with the Idea that is to regenerate his era, is ever vouchsafed. As a flaming Herald he appears in his time, and sends abroad the Idea which it is the mission of the age to organize in institutions, and quicken into manners.[10] Such mould the Genius of the time. They revive in Humanity the lost idea of its destiny, and reveal its fearful endowments. They vindicate the divinity of man's nature, and foreshadow on the coming Time the conquests that await it. An Age preëxists in them; and History is but the manifestation and issue of their Wisdom and Will. They are the Prophets of the Future.

Genius misapprehended.   At this day, men need some revelation of Genius, to arouse them to a sense of their nature; for the Divine Idea of a Man seems to have died out of our consciousness. Encumbered by the gluts of the appetites, sunk in the corporeal senses, men know not the divine life that stirs within them, yet hidden and enchained. They revere not their own nature. And when the phenomenon of Genius appears, they marvel at its advent. They cannot own it. Laden with the gifts of the Divinity it touches their orb. At intervals of a century it appears. Some Nature, struggling with vicissitude, tempts forth the Idea of Spirit from within, and unlooses the Promethean God to roam free over the earth.[11] He possesses his Idea and brings it as a blessed gift to his race. With awe-struck visage, the tribes of semi-unfolded beings survey it from below, deeming it a partial or preternatural gift of the Divinity, into whose life and being they are forbidden, by a decree of the Eternal, from entering; whose law they must obey, yet cannot apprehend. They dream not, that this phenomenon is but the complement of their common nature; and that in this admiration and obedience, which they proffer, is both the promise and the pledge of the same powers in themselves; that this is but their fellow-creature in the flesh.[12] And thus the mystery remains sealed, till at last it is revealed, that this is but the unfolding of human nature in its fulness; working free of every incumbrance, by possessing itself.

Idea of Genius.   For Genius is but the free and harmonious play of all the faculties of a human being. It is a Man possessing his Idea and working with it. It is the Whole Man—the central Will—working worthily, subordinating all else to itself; and reaching its end by the simplest and readiest means. It is human nature rising superior to things and events, and transfiguring these into the image of its own Spiritual Ideal. It is the Spirit working in its own way, through its own organs and instruments, and on its own materials. It is the Inspiration of all the faculties of a Man by a life conformed to his Idea. It is not indebted to others for its manifestation. It draws its life from within. It is self-subsistent. It feeds on Holiness; lives in the open vision of Truth; enrobes itself in the light of Beauty; and bathes its powers in the fount of Temperance. It aspires after the Perfect. It loves Freedom. It dwells in Unity. All men have it, yet it does

---

[10] Note the millennial and messianic theme, which is also present in Emerson's writings. Cf., in this volume, Ralph Waldo Emerson, Divinity School *Address*, "Threnody."

[11] In Greek mythology, Zeus bound Prometheus, sent a shaft through his body, and set an eagle against him that would eat at his liver each day—all because Prometheus had maneuvered Zeus into choosing an inferior sacrificial portion and had stolen fire from the Gods for the benefit of humanity. See Hesiod *Theogony* 521-67.

[12] This and what follows provide a particularly clear expression of Alcott's belief—as Emerson's—that human beings are to be "as Gods."

not appear in all men. It is obscured by ignorance; quenched by evil; discipline does not reach it; nor opportunity cherish it. Yet there it is—an original, indestructible element of every spirit; and sooner or later, in this corporeal, or in the spiritual era—at some period of the Soul's developement—it shall be tempted forth, and assert its claims in the life of the Spirit. It is the province of education to wake it, and discipline it into the perfection which is its end, and for which it ever thirsts. Yet Genius alone can wake it. Genius alone inspire it. It comes not at the incantation of mere talent.[13] It respects itself. It is strange to all save its kind. It shrinks from vulgar gaze, and lives in its own world. None but the eye of Genius can discern it, and it obeys the call of none else.

Wane of Genius.   Yet among us Genius is at its wane. Human Nature appears shorn of her beams. We estimate man too low to hope for bright manifestations. And our views create the imperfection that mocks us. We have neither great men, nor good institutions. Genius visits us but seldom. The results of our culture are slender. Thirsting for life and light, Genius is blessed with neither. It cannot free itself from the incumbrance that it inherits. The Idea of a Man does not shine upon it from any external Image. Such Corporeal Types it seeks in vain. It cries for instruction, and none satisfies its wants. There is little genius in our schoolrooms.

Those who enter yearly upon the stage of life, bearing the impress of our choicest culture, and most watchful discipline, are often unworthy specimens of our nature. Holiness attends not their steps. Genius adorns not their brow. Many a parent among us—having lavished upon his child his best affections, and spared no pains which money and solicitude could supply, to command the best influences within his reach—sees him return, destitute of that high principle, and those simple aims, that alone ennoble human nature, and satisfy the parental heart. Or, should the child return with his young simplicity and truth, yet how unarmed is his intellect with the quiver of genius,[14] to achieve a worthy name, and bless his race. The Soul is spilt out in lust; buried in appetite; or wasted in vulgar toils; and retreats, at last, ignobly from the scene of life's temptations; despoiled of its innocence; bereft of its hopes, and sets in the dark night of disquietude, lost to the race.

Cause of Declension.   Yet not all depravity nor ignorance is to be laid at the door of our Institutions. The evil has two faces. It is deeper in its origin. It springs from our low estimate of human nature, and consequent want of reverence and regard for it.[15] It is to be divided between parents and institutions. The young but too often enter our institutions of learning, despoiled of their virtue, and are of course disabled from running an honorable intellectual career. Our systems of nursery discipline are built on shallow or false principles; the young repeat the vices and reproduce the opinions of parents; and par-

---

[13]Alcott's distinction is similar to the Coleridgean distinction between Imagination and Fancy or Reason and Understanding. See n. 48 to Ralph Waldo Emerson, *Nature;* and see, too, the introduction to this volume. Alcott read Coleridge's *Aids to Reflection* many times, and Coleridge's *Biographia Literaria* was almost as important for him. See Shepard, *Pedlar's Progress*, 151, 155, 159-60.

[14]That is, the child's intellect is weak because unarmed with the arrows of genius.

[15]Here Alcott inverts the orthodox Christian doctrine of original sin. The "deeper" evil is not original depravity, but rather the refusal to comprehend the divine Idea within human nature.

ents have little cause to complain. They cannot expect fruits of institutions, for which they have taken so little pains to sow the seeds. They reap as they sow. Aiming at little they attain but little. They cast their own horoscope, and determine by their aim the fate of the coming generation. They are the organized Opportunity of their era.

Faith of Genius. To work worthily, man must aspire worthily. His theory of human attainment must be lofty. It must ever be lifting him above the low plain of custom and convention, in which the senses confine him, into the high mount of vision, and of renovating ideas. To a divine nature, the sun ever rises over the mountains of hope, and brings promises on its wings; nor does he linger around the dark and depressing valley of distrust and of fear. The magnificent bow of promise[16] ever gilds his purpose, and he pursues his way steadily, and in faith to the end. For Faith is the soul of all improvement. It is the Will of an Idea. It is an Idea seeking to embody and reproduce itself. It is the All-Proceeding Word going forth, as in the beginning of things, to incarnate itself, and become flesh and blood to the senses.[17] Without this faith an Idea works no good. It is this which animates and quickens it into life. And this must come from living men.

Genius alone Inspires. And such Faith is the possession of all who apprehend Ideas. Such faith had Jesus, and this it was that empowered him to do the mighty works of which we read. It was this which inspired his genius. And Genius alone can inspire others. To nurse the young spirit as it puts forth its pinions in the fair and hopeful morning of life, it must be placed under the kindly and sympathising agency of Genius—heaven-inspired and hallowed—or there is no certainty that its aspirations will not die away in the routine of formal tuition, or spend themselves in the animal propensities that coexist with it.[18] Teachers must be men of genius. They must be men inspired. The Divine Idea of a Man must have been unfolded from their being, and be a living presence. Philosophers, and Sages, and Seers,—the only real men—must come as of old, to the holy vocation of unfolding human nature. Socrates, and Plato, and the Diviner Jesus, must be raised up to us, to breathe their wisdom and will into the genius of our era, to recast our institutions, remould our manners, and regenerate our men. Philosophy and Religion, descending from the regions of cloudy speculation, must thus become denizens of our common earth, known among us as friends, and uttering their saving truths through the mouths of our little ones. Thus shall our being be unfolded. Thus the Idea of a man be reinstated in our consciousness. Thus Jesus be honored among us. And thus shall Man grow up, as the tree of the primeval woods, luxuriant, vigorous—armed at all points, to brave the winds and the storms of the finite and the mutable—bearing his Fruit in due season.

Idea of Inspiration. To fulfil its end, Instruction must be an Inspiration. The true Teacher, like Jesus, must inspire in order to unfold. He must

---

[16] An allusion to the rainbow that was the sign of God's covenant with Noah (Gen. 9:13-16).

[17] This is an especially clear example of Alcott's fusion of Platonic and Christian material. The "All-Proceeding Word" (cf. John 1:14) equals the Idea equals Faith.

[18] Alcott's remarks echo the Neoplatonic teaching about the descent of the soul into a corporeal state, its enchainment in a body. See Plotinus *Enneads* 4.8.3-4.

know that instruction is something more than mere impression on the understanding. He must feel it to be a kindling influence; that, in himself alone, is the quickening, informing energy; that the life and growth of his charge preëxist in him. He is to hallow and refine as he tempts forth the soul. He is to inform the understanding, by chastening the appetites, allaying the passions, softening the affections, vivifying the imagination, illuminating the reason, giving pliancy and force to the will; for a true understanding is the issue of these powers, working freely and in harmony with the Genius of the soul, conformed to the law of Duty. He is to put all the springs of Being in motion. And to do this, he must be the personation and exampler of what he would unfold in his charge. Wisdom, Truth, Holiness, must have preëxistence in him, or they will not appear in his pupils. These influence alone in the concrete. They must be made flesh and blood in him, to reappear to the senses, and reproduce their like.—And thus shall his Genius subordinate all to its own force. Thus shall all be constrained to yield to its influence; and this too, without violating any Law, spiritual, intellectual, corporeal—but in obedience to the highest Agency, co-working with God. Under the melting force of his Genius, thus employed, Mind shall become fluid, and he shall mould it into Types of Heavenly Beauty.[19] His agency is that of mind leaping to meet mind; not of force acting on opposing force. The Soul is touched by the live coal of his lips.[20] A kindling influence goes forth to inspire; making the mind think; the heart feel; the pulse throb with his own. He arouses every faculty. He awakens the Godlike. He images the fair and full features of a Man. And thus doth he drive at will the drowsy Brute, that the Eternal hath yoked to the chariot of Life, to urge man across the Finite![21]

Hallowed Genius.
To work worthily in the ministry of Instruction, requires not only the highest Gifts, but that these should be refined by Holiness. This is the condition of spiritual and intellectual clearness. This alone unfolds Genius, and puts Nature and Life to their fit uses. "If any man will know of the Doctrine, let him do the will of my Father," said Jesus;[22] and he, who does not yield this obedience, shall never shine forth in the true and full glory of his nature.

Quenching of Genius.
Yet this truth seems to have been lost sight of in our measures of Human Culture. We incumber the body by the gluts of the appetites; dim the senses by self-indulgence; abuse nature and life in all manner of ways, and yet dream of unfolding Genius amidst all these diverse agencies and influences. We train Children amidst all these evils. We surround them by temptations, which stagger their feeble virtue, and

---

[19]Alcott's metaphor is taken from his knowledge of contemporary printing techniques in which type metal was poured into molds to harden.

[20]A reference to the vision of Isaiah (Isa. 6:1-8) in which one of the seraphim touched Isaiah's lips with a burning coal, inaugurating his career as a prophet.

[21]An allusion, most likely, to the *Phaedrus* of Plato in which the human soul is depicted as a charioteer with two winged horses, one noble and the other not. In the Platonic myth, the ignoble beast tries to drag the chariot down while the heavenly horse seeks to move aloft. Here Alcott mentions only the ignoble beast and, unlike Plato, characterizes him as drowsy rather than vicious. See Plato *Phaedrus* 246A-248B, 253C-254E.

[22]Cf. John 7:17. Alcott, probably recalling the scripture from memory, has substantially paraphrased and reinterpreted.

they fall too easily into the snare which we have spread. Concupiscence defiles their functions; blunts the edge of their faculties; obstructs the passages of the soul to the outward, and blocks it up. The human body, the soul's implement for acting on Nature, in the ministry of life, is thus depraved; and the soul falls an easy prey to the Tempter. Self-Indulgence too soon rings the knell of the spiritual life, as the omen of its interment in the flesh. It wastes the corporeal functions; mars the Divine Image in the human form; estranges the affections; paralyzes the will; clouds the intellect; dims the fire of genius; seals conscience, and corrupts the whole being. Lusts entrench themselves in the Soul; unclean spirits and demons nestle therein. Self-subjection, self-sacrifice, self-renewal are not made its habitual exercises, and it becomes the vassal of the Body. The Idea of Spirit dies out of the Consciousness; and Man is shorn of his glories. Nature grows over him. He mistakes Images for Ideas, and thus becomes an Idolater. He deserts the Sanctuary of the Indwelling Spirit, and worships at the throne of the Outward.[23]

Means of Reform.
Our plans of influence, to be successful, must become more practical. We must be more faithful. We must deal less in abstractions; depend less on precepts and rules. We must fit the soul for duty by the practice of duty.[24] We must watch and enforce. Like unsleeping Providence, we must accompany the young into the scenes of temptation and trial, and aid them in the needful hour. Duty must sally forth an attending Presence into the work-day world, and organize to itself a living body. It must learn the art of uses. It must incorporate itself with Nature. To its sentiments we must give a Heart. Its Ideas we must arm with Hands. For it ever longs to become flesh and blood. The Son of God delights to take the Son of Man as a co-mate, and to bring flesh and blood even to the very gates of the Spiritual Kingdom. It would make the word Flesh, that it shall be seen and handled and felt.

Spiritual Culture.
The Culture, that is alone worthy of Man, and which unfolds his Being into the Image of its fulness, casts its agencies over all things. It uses Nature and Life as means for the Soul's growth and renewal. It never deserts its charge, but follows it into all the relations of Duty; at the table it seats itself, and fills the cup for the Soul; caters for it; decides when it has enough; and heeds not the clamor of appetite and desire. It lifts the body from the drowsy couch; opens the eyes upon the rising sun; tempts it forth to breathe the invigorating air; plunges it into the purifying bath; and thus whets all its functions for the duties of the coming day. And when toil and amusement have brought weariness over it, and the drowsed senses claim rest and renewal, it remands it to the restoring couch again, to feed it on dreams. Nor does it desert the Soul in seasons of labor, of amusement, of study. To

---

[23]The entire passage suggests Alcott's commitment to asceticism, a commitment that he had the opportunity to exercise later in his experiment at Fruitlands (see the introduction to this volume). Alcott's conception of "sin" in the passage is, in general, Platonic and Neoplatonic. See Plato *Phaedo* 81B-82A and Plotinus *Enneads* 1.8.4, 14. See also *Enneads* 2.4.10 for a discussion of the relationship, based on Plato, between matter and "spurious reasoning."

[24]While Alcott's writing has been criticized for its airiness, his reference to "the practice of duty" shows him drawing pragmatic conclusions from his theories.

the place of occupation it attends it, guides the corporeal members with skill and faithfulness; prompts the mind to diligence; the heart to gentleness and love; directs to the virtuous associate; the pure place of recreation; the innocent pastime. It protects the eye from the foul image; the vicious act; the ear from the vulgar or profane word; the hand from theft; the tongue from guile;—urges to cheerfulness and purity; to forbearance and meekness; to self-subjection and self-sacrifice; order and decorum; and points, amid all the relations of duty, to the Law of Temperance, of Genius, of Holiness, which God hath established in the depths of the Spirit, and guarded by the unsleeping sentinel of Conscience, from violation and defilement. It renews the Soul day by day.

Self-Apprehension. Man's mission is to subdue Nature; to hold dominion over his own Body; and use both these, and the ministries of Life, for the growth, renewal, and perfection of his Being. As did Jesus, he must overcome the World, by passing through its temptations, and vanquishing the Tempter. But before he shall attain this mastery he must apprehend himself.[25] In his Nature is wrapt up the problem of all Power reduced to a simple unity. The knowledge of his own being includes, in its endless circuit, the Alphabet of all else. It is a Universe, wherein all else is imaged. God—Nature—are the extremes, of which he is the middle term, and through his Being flow these mighty Forces, if, perchance, he shall stay them as they pass over his Consciousness, apprehend their significance—their use—and then conforming his being to the one; he shall again conform the other to himself.[26]

Childhood a Type of the Godhead. Yet, dimmed as is the Divine Image in Man, it reflects not the full and fair Image of the Godhead. We seek it alone in Jesus in its fulness; yet sigh to behold it with our corporeal senses. And this privilege God ever vouchsafes to the pure and undefiled in heart; for he ever sends it upon the earth in the form of the Child. Herein have we a Type of the Divinity. Herein is our Nature yet despoiled of none of its glory.[27] In flesh and blood he reveals his Presence to our senses, and pleads with us to worship and revere.

Misapprehension of Childhood. Yet few there are who apprehend the significance of the Divine Type. Childhood is yet a problem that we have scarce studied. It has been and still is a mystery to

---

[25]Cf. John 16:33. And for "apprehend himself," cf. Socrates' remark that "the unexamined life is not worth living," in Plato *Apology* 38A.

[26]Alcott's "man" must conform himself to God but must also tame nature, conforming it to himself. Thus, unlike some versions of the theory of correspondence, Alcott's version—as his friend Emerson's (see Emerson, *Nature,* ch. 8)—fosters domination over nature as surely as does the biblical teaching (not based on the doctrine of correspondence) in Genesis (Gen. 1:28).

[27]Cf. William Wordsworth, "Ode: Intimations of Immortality from Recollections of Early Childhood," ll. 64-74, esp. ll. 64-66: "But trailing clouds of glory do we come / From God, who is our home: / Heaven lies about us in our infancy!" Odell Shepard has suggested that Wordsworth's "Ode" worked "like yeast among all his [Alcott's] thoughts" (*Pedlar's Progress,* 81), although Shepard later argued for the independence of Alcott's "conviction that childhood is essentially innocent" (ibid., 82). Here it is important to note that the theory of the preexistence of souls and their recollection of a prior state was basic to Wordsworth's poem and also part of Platonic teaching (see, for example, Plato *Phaedrus* 248E-250C).

us. Its pure and simple nature; its faith and its hope, are all unknown to us. It stands friendless and alone, pleading in vain for sympathy and aid. And, though wronged and slighted, it still retains its trustingness; still does it cling to the Adult for renovation and light.—But thus shall it not be always. It shall be apprehended. It shall not be a mystery and made to offend. "Light is springing up, and the dayspring from on high is again visiting us."[28] And, as in times sacred to our associations, the Star led the Wise Men to the Infant Jesus, to present their reverent gifts, and was, at once, both the herald and the pledge of the advent of the Son of God on the earth; even so is the hour approaching, and it lingers not on its errand, when the Wise and the Gifted, shall again surround the cradles of the New Born Babe, and there proffer, as did the Magi, their gifts of reverence and of love to the Holiness that hath visited the earth, and shines forth with a celestial glory around their heads;—and these, pondering well, as did Mary, the Divine Significance, shall steal from it the Art—so long lost in our Consciousness—of unfolding its powers into the fulness of the God.[29]

Renovation of Nature.
And thus Man, repossessing his Idea, shall conform Nature to himself. Institutions shall bear the fruits of his regenerate being. They shall flourish in vigor and beauty. They shall circulate his Genius through Nature and Life, and repeat the story of his renewal.

Human Renewal.
Say not that this Era is distant. Verily, it is near. Even at this moment, the heralds of the time are announcing its approach. Omens of Good hover over us. A deeper and holier Faith is quickening the Genius of our Time. Humanity awaits the hour of its renewal. The renovating Fiat has gone forth, to revive our Institutions, and remould our Men. Faith is lifting her voice, and, like Jesus near the Tomb of Lazarus, is uttering the living words, "I am the Resurrection and the Life, and he that Believeth, though dead in doubts and sins, shall be reassured of his Immortality, and shall flourish in unfading Youth! I will mould Nature and Man according to my Will. I will transfigure all things into the Image of my Ideal."[30]—And by such Faith, and such Vision, shall Education work its mission on the Earth. Apprehending the Divine Significance of Jesus—yet filled with the assurance of coming Messiahs to meet the growing nature of Man—shall inspired Genius go forth to renovate his Era; casting out the unclean spirits and the demons that yet afflict the Soul. And then shall Humanity, leaving her infirmities, her wrongs, her sufferings, and her sins, in the corrupting grave, reappear in the consciousness of Physical Purity; Inspired Genius; and Spotless Holiness. Men shall be one with God, as was the Man of Nazareth.

---

[28]Cf. Luke 1:78-79. Alcott changes the emphasis of the passage to suit his purposes, but his choice is poetically appropriate since the biblical passage is part of the prophecy, or "song," of Zacharias preceding the birth of John the Baptist.

[29]Cf. Matt. 2:1-11. Alcott reinterprets the passage along mystical lines.

[30]Cf. John 11:25. Alcott's quotation begins with a paraphrase of the scriptural verse, but his references to "unfading Youth" and what follows are his own additions and reinterpretations. His millennialism becomes a climactic affirmation, linking New Testament themes of exorcism and resurrection with the mystical message that all will be as Jesus was—one with God (see below in the text).

ORPHIC SAYINGS

When *The Dial* appeared for the first time in July 1840, a collection of fifty "Orphic Sayings" was offered to the public in its pages. In a departure from the publishing practice of the time, the name of the author, A. Bronson Alcott, was written in full under the title. Emerson had advised then-editor Margaret Fuller to include Alcott's name so that those who had heard Alcott speak would think of the man as they read the words. Emerson's advice reflected his own perplexity with the material his friend had given him. With its fusion of Platonic, Neoplatonic, and Christian themes in a series of pithy, sometimes paradoxical, epigrams, Alcott's contribution revealed a version of the Transcendental gospel not too different from Emerson's own. Moreover, when Emerson had criticized an earlier manuscript for Alcott—the unpublished "Psyche"—he had urged his friend to condense his ideas. Still, Emerson expressed his ambivalence toward the new work in letters to Margaret Fuller articulating varying degrees of endorsement and distance.[1]

If Emerson, Transcendental friend and critic, expressed ambivalence concerning the "Orphic Sayings," the non-Transcendental press greeted them with ridicule and made them a public symbol for the "vagaries" of *The Dial* and Transcendentalism. *The Boston Transcript* parodied one of the epigrams under the title "Gastric Sayings," while other newspapers such as *The Boston Daily Advertiser* were not far behind in their jokes at Alcott's expense. Even so, *The Dial* accepted an additional fifty of his "Orphic Sayings" and published them in its issue of January 1841. After that, however, it refused to take more. Orestes Brownson's *Boston Quarterly Review* published a series of twelve "Orphic Sayings," naming A. Bronson Alcott as their author, and Alcott also managed to slip another twelve unobtrusively into his "Days from a Diary," a selection culled from his journals that was printed in *The Dial*.[2] Later he continued to write in epigrammatic style, and although no further "Orphic Sayings" appeared, there were still "sayings."[3]

The habit of ridiculing Alcott's "Orphic Sayings," unfortunately, has prevented them from receiving the serious attention they deserve. "Much-ridiculed but little-read," as

---

[1] Ralph Waldo Emerson to Margaret Fuller, 8 April 1840, in Ralph Waldo Emerson, *The Letters of Ralph Waldo Emerson,* ed. Ralph L. Rusk (New York: Columbia University Press, 1939) 2:276; Ralph Waldo Emerson to Margaret Fuller, 24 April 1840, ibid., 291-92; Ralph Waldo Emerson to Margaret Fuller, 8 May 1840, ibid., 294. After *The Dial* was published, Emerson came around squarely to an endorsement of Alcott's work. He told Fuller that Alcott's contribution was of "great importance," since outside of it there was "little that might not appear in any other journal" (Ralph Waldo Emerson to Margaret Fuller, 8 July 1840, in Emerson, *Letters*, 2:313).

[2] A. Bronson Alcott, "Orphic Sayings," *The Boston Quarterly Review* 4:4 (October 1841): 492-94; A. Bronson Alcott, "Days from a Diary," *The Dial* 2:4 (April 1842): 423-25.

[3] See A. Bronson Alcott, "Sayings," *The Present* 1:5-6 (15 December 1843): 170-72, and A. Bronson Alcott, "Sayings," ibid., 7-8 (15 January 1844): 261-62.

Odell Shepard said, they contain—as he also said—"better things by far . . . than those who prefer to take their literary opinions at second hand suspect."[4] In fact, in a more recent treatment, Madelon Bedell has called them "a brilliant essay in philosophical dialectics."[5] If they are that, they are also something more. Though the sayings are sometimes cast in labored and antiquated language, Alcott gives a ringing affirmation of his Transcendental faith. Even though self-consciously, he speaks with the voice of the "Orphic poet" whose message Emerson had recorded in *Nature*.[6] Indeed, Alcott's evocation of Orphism in the title of this work is particularly apt. More than a recollection of Emerson's work, his sayings are prose poems—pieces of sacred "conversation"—meant, like those of the first Orpheus, to demonstrate the power of the soul over nature. And like the Orphic Mysteries associated with the name of the poet-musician, Alcott's "Orphic Sayings" teach the divinity of the human spirit and the possibility of its liberation from evil. They speak of the preexistence and transmigration of the soul, and they disdain the eating of animal flesh. Above all, they are mystical teachings that seek to fuse speech and action, life and experience, as the Orphic Mysteries of ancient Greece had done.

Alcott does not organize his sayings to follow a logical sequence, although they do follow a "mytho-logic" in which, often, one saying is associatively or thematically related to the next. It might be said, too, that Alcott writes in concentric circles, so that thematic material is repeated throughout his collection and meaning reinforced by each new affirmation. The collection of "Orphic Sayings" that appears below contains roughly two-thirds of the first 100 that were published in *The Dial*, selected to give a sense of their range.[7] Their continuity with many of Alcott's ideas earlier expressed in *The Doctrine and Discipline of Human Culture* is apparent; and, as in *Human Culture*, the symbol of the child is supreme. At the same time, Alcott's epigrams are the record of a nineteenth-century American who celebrates self-culture with an antinomian fervor and rejects customs, usages, and institutions as "sepulchres" even as he embraces universal divine law. Still more, they are the record of an American steeped in the language of Christian scripture—a man who spoke of asceticism and mysticism, but who also knew the way of the prophet and was deeply concerned about the reform of society.

---

[4]Odell Shepard, "Introduction," in Amos Bronson Alcott, *The Journals of Bronson Alcott*, sel. and ed. Odell Shepard (Boston: Little, Brown, 1938) xviii; Odell Shepard, *Pedlar's Progress: The Life of Bronson Alcott* (1937; rpt., New York: Greenwood Press, 1968) 505.

[5]Madelon Bedell, *The Alcotts: Biography of a Family* (New York: Clarkson N. Potter, 1980) 156.

[6]See Ralph Waldo Emerson, *Nature*, ch. 8, in this volume and nn. 70 and 72 to the text. Ancient Greek legend had it that Orpheus—the Thracian musician who loved and lost the nymph Eurydice in Hades—had founded the Orphic Mysteries. The mysteries celebrated Orpheus and honored him as composer of the sacred poems that provided the source of Orphic teaching. Mystical in tenor, this teaching affirmed the soul's divine origin and the possibility of liberation from evil through the Orphic Mysteries and also through the transmigration of the soul. It fostered a life of ascetic discipline in practices such as abstinence from meat, and it fused myth, ritual, life-style, and religious experience into a coherent whole.

[7]The text is from A. Bronson Alcott, "Orphic Sayings," *The Dial* 1:1 (July 1840): 85-98, and A. Bronson Alcott, "Orphic Sayings," *The Dial* 1:3 (January 1841): 351-61.

(From) ORPHIC SAYINGS

I.

THOU art, my heart, a soul-flower, facing ever and following the motions of thy sun, opening thyself to her vivifying ray, and pleading thy affinity with the celestial orbs. Thou dost
>
> the livelong day
> Dial on time thine own eternity.[1]

II. ENTHUSIASM.

Believe, youth, that your heart is an oracle; trust her instinctive auguries, obey her divine leadings; nor listen too fondly to the uncertain echoes of your head.[2] The heart is the prophet of your soul, and ever fulfils her prophecies; reason is her historian; but for the prophecy the history would not be. Great is the heart: cherish her; she is big with the future, she forebodes renovations. Let the flame of enthusiasm fire alway your bosom. Enthusiasm is the glory and hope of the world. It is the life of sanctity and genius; it has wrought all miracles since the beginning of time.

IV. IMMORTALITY.

The grander my conception of being, the nobler my future. There can be no sublimity of life without faith in the soul's eternity. Let me live superior to sense and custom, vigilant alway, and I shall experience my divinity; my hope will be infinite, nor shall the universe contain, or content me. But if I creep daily from the haunts of an ignoble past, like a beast from his burrow, neither earth nor sky, man nor God shall appear desirable or glorious; my life shall be loathsome to me, my future reflect my fears. He alone, who lives nobly, oversees his own being, believes all things, and partakes of the eternity of God.

V. VOCATION.

Engage in nothing that cripples or degrades you. Your first duty is self-culture, self-exaltation: you may not violate this high trust. Your self is sacred, profane it not. Forge no chains wherewith to shackle your own members. Either subordinate your vocation to your life, or quit it forever: it is not for you; it is condemnation of your own soul. Your influence on others is commensurate with the strength that you have found in yourself. First cast the demons from your own bosom, and then shall your word exorcise them from the hearts of others.[3]

---

[1] Alcott had originally intended this poetic line as an inscription for his journal for the year and, in an earlier moment, had given *The Dial* its title based on that of his planned diary. The origin of the metaphor may have been Swedenborgian, since Emanuel Swedenborg had seen the visible world as a (sun) dial for the invisible one (see n. 27 to the introduction of this volume). Here Alcott seems consciously to be evoking the title of the new Transcendental journal in a piece he has contributed for its first issue.

[2] Alcott's suspicion of intellectuality runs through "Orphic Sayings." Such suspicion, resembling Emerson's (see n. 9 to Ralph Waldo Emerson, "The Over-Soul") and going further, has been a recurring theme in the mystical tradition.

---

[3] Cf. Matt. 7:3-5—although Alcott has con-

X. APOTHEOSIS.

Every soul feels at times her own possibility of becoming a God; she cannot rest in the human, she aspires after the Godlike. This instinctive tendency is an authentic augury of its own fulfilment. Men shall become Gods. Every act of admiration, prayer, praise, worship, desire, hope, implies and predicts the future apotheosis of the soul.

XI. DISCONTENT.

All life is eternal; there is none other; and all unrest is but the struggle of the soul to reassure herself of her inborn immortality; to recover her lost intuition of the same, by reason of her descent amidst the lusts and worship of the idols of flesh and sense. Her discomfort reveals her lapse from innocence; her loss of the divine presence and favor.[4] Fidelity alone shall insaturate the Godhead in her bosom.

XIII. CHOICE.

Choice implies apostacy. The pure, unfallen soul is above choice. Her life is unbroken, synthetic; she is a law to herself, and finds no lust in her members warring against the instincts of conscience. Sinners choose; saints act from instinct and intuition: there is no parley of alien forces in their being.[5]

XIV. INSTINCT AND REASON.

Innocent, the soul is quick with instincts of unerring aim; then she knows by intuition what lapsed reason defines by laborious inference; her appetites and affections are direct and trustworthy. Reason is the left hand of instinct; it is tardy, awkward, but the right is ready and dextrous. By reasoning the soul strives to recover her lost intuitions; groping amidst the obscure darkness of sense, by means of the fingers of logic, for treasures present alway and available to the eye of conscience. Sinners must needs reason; saints behold.[6]

XV. IDENTITY AND DIVERSITY.

It is the perpetual effort of conscience to divorce the soul from the dominion of

---

flated texts to speak not of removing logs and specks from eyes, but of casting demons from hearts. Cf. also the theme of Emerson's "Self-Reliance" and his statement in his journal, "Shall I raise the siege of this hencoop & march baffled away to a pretended siege of Babylon?" (Ralph Waldo Emerson, *The Journals and Miscellaneous Notebooks of Ralph Waldo Emerson,* ed. William H. Gilman et al. [Cambridge: Harvard University Press, Belknap Press, 1960–] 7 [17 October 1840]: 408.)

[4] Alcott's lapsarian doctrine (cf. saying 62) is a recasting of the Neoplatonic teaching of the descent of the soul into matter (see Plotinus *Enneads* 4.8). Human beings, Alcott held, had "lapsed" from their true and divine source in Mind. See the discussion in the introduction to this volume and also in Odell Shepard, *Pedlar's Progress: The Life of Bronson Alcott* (1937; rpt., New York: Greenwood Press, 1968) 453-57. Shepard notes (454) the contrast between the notion of universal descent and the nineteenth-century doctrine of evolution and progress—a doctrine to which Alcott in his own way subscribed, as *The Doctrine and Discipline of Human Culture* illustrates.

[5] Cf. Ralph Waldo Emerson in "Self-Reliance": "That source, at once the essence of genius, of virtue, and of life, which we call Spontaneity or Instinct. We denote this primary wisdom as Intuition, whilst all later teachings are tuitions." (See also n. 27 to the essay.) For a different side of Alcott's thinking, see saying 61.

[6] Note that here and throughout "Orphic Sayings" Alcott employs "reason" in a manner decidedly different from the Coleridgean usage appropriated by Emerson and other Transcendentalists. The difference, however, seems semantic more than substantive. The contrast between the nonmediated (im-mediate) vision/knowledge of God by the saints and the labored understanding by other human beings undergirds the anti-intellectualism associated with the mystical tradition.

sense; to nullify the dualities of the apparent, and restore the intuition of the real. The soul makes a double statement of all her facts; to conscience and sense; reason mediates between the two. Yet though double to sense, she remains single and one in herself; one in conscience, many in understanding; one in life, diverse in function and number. Sense, in its infirmity, breaks this unity to apprehend in part what it cannot grasp at once. Understanding notes diversity; conscience alone divines unity, and integrates all experience in identity of spirit. Number is predicable of body alone; not of spirit.

XVI. CONSCIENCE.

Ever present, potent, vigilant, in the breast of man, there is that which never became a party in his guilt, never consented to a wrong deed, nor performed one, but holds itself above all sin, impeccable, immaculate, immutable, the deity of the heart, the conscience of the soul, the oracle and interpreter, the judge and executor of the divine law.

XVII. THEOCRACY.

In the theocracy of the soul majorities do not rule. God and the saints; against them the rabble of sinners, with clamorous voices and uplifted hand, striving to silence the oracle of the private heart. Beelzebub marshals majorities. Prophets and reformers are always special enemies of his and his minions. Multitudes ever lie. Every age is a Judas, and betrays its Messiahs into the hands of the multitude. The voice of the private, not popular heart, is alone authentic.

XVIII. SPEECH.

There is a magic in free speaking, especially on sacred themes most potent and resistless. It is refreshing, amidst the inane common-places bandied in pulpits and parlors, to hear a hopeful word from an earnest, upright soul. Men rally around it as to the lattice in summer heats, to inhale the breeze that flows cool and refreshing from the mountains, and invigorates their languid frames. Once heard, they feel a buoyant sense of health and hopefulness, and wonder that they should have lain sick, supine so long, when a word has power to raise them from their couch, and restore them to soundness. And once spoken, it shall never be forgotten; it charms, exalts; it visits them in dreams, and haunts them during all their wakeful hours. Great, indeed, is the delight of speech; sweet the sound of one's bosom thought, as it returns laden with the fragrance of a brother's approval.

XX. ACTION.

Action translates death into life; fable into verity; speculation into experience; freeing man from the sorceries of tradition and the torpor of habit. The eternal Scripture is thus expurgated of the falsehoods interpolated into it by the supineness of the ages. Action mediates between conscience and sense: it is the gospel of the understanding.[7]

XXI. ORIGINALITY.

Most men are on the ebb; but now and then a man comes riding down sublimely in high hope from God on the flood tide of the soul, as she sets into the coasts of time,

---

[7]In contrast to his earlier allusion to reason in saying 14, Alcott's usage here conforms, generally, to Coleridge's distinction between the Reason and the Understanding. For Coleridge, the Understanding reflects on information derived from the senses but does so, not on its own authority, but on that of a faculty beyond itself. See Samuel Taylor Coleridge, *Aids to Reflection,* "Aphorisms on That Which Is Indeed Spiritual Religion," aphorism 8; and see also the introduction to this volume.

submerging old landmarks, and laying waste the labors of centuries. A new man wears channels broad and deep into the banks of the ages; he washes away ancient boundaries, and sets afloat institutions, creeds, usages, which clog the ever flowing Present, stranding them on the shores of the Past. Such deluge is the harbinger of a new world, a renovated age. Hope builds an ark; the dove broods over the assuaged waters; the bow of promise gilds the east; the world is again repeopled and replanted.[8] Yet the sons of genius alone venture into the ark: while most pass the rather down the sluggish stream of usage into the turbid pool of oblivion. Thitherward the retreating tide rolls, and wafted by the gales of inglorious ease, or urged by the winds of passion, they glide down the Lethean waters, and are not.[9] Only the noble and heroic outlive in time their exit from it.

XXII. VALOR.

The world, the state, the church, stand in awe of a man of probity and valor. He threatens their order and perpetuity: an unknown might slumbers in him; he is an augury of revolutions. Out of the invisible God, he comes to abide awhile amongst men; yet neither men nor time shall remain as at his advent. He is a creative element, and revises men, times, life itself. A new world preexists in his ideal. He overlives, outlives, eternizes the ages, and reports to all men the will of the divinity whom he serves.

XXIV. BREAD.

The hunger of an age is alike a presentiment and pledge of its own supply. Instinct is not only prophetic but provident. When there is a general craving for bread, that shall assuredly be satisfied; bread is even then growing in the fields. Now, men are lean and famishing; but, behold, the divine Husbandman has driven his share through the age, and sown us bread that we may not perish; yea, the reapers even are going forth, a blithe and hopeful company, while yet the fields weep with the dews of the morning, and the harvests wave in yellow ripeness. Soon shall a table be spread, and the age rejoice in the fulness of plenty.[10]

XXV. PROPHET.

The prophet, by disciplines of meditation and valor, faithful to the spirit of the heart, his eye purified of the motes of tradition, his life of the vestiges of usage, ascends to the heights of immediate intuition: he rends the veil of sense; he bridges the distance between faith and sight, and beholds spiritual verities without scripture or mediator. In the presence of God, he communes with him face to face.[11]

XXIX. REVELATION.

The standing problem of Genius is to divine the essential verity intimated in the life and literature of the Past, divesting it of historical interpolations; separating the foreign from the indigenous, and translating

---

[8] Cf. Gen. 6:13-9:17.

[9] Note, in light of the earlier allusion to Genesis, Alcott's mixing of metaphors. The "Lethean waters" are classical in inspiration, representing the boundary to the underworld of Hades where—succumbing to ease and passion in Alcott's view—souls forget their true origins.

[10] Alcott reconstitutes scriptural motifs to supply his own millennial vision. Cf. Matt. 13:24-30, 36-40; Mark 4:28-29; Ps. 128:1-4; Mic. 4:3-4.

[11] Alcott's prophet is, judging from the description, a mystic. But Alcott makes it clear elsewhere that the prophet is one who communicates the vision (see saying 74).

the letter of the universal scripture into the spirit of contemporaneous life and letters.

XXX. CRITICISM.

To justify criticism unity of mind is essential. The critic must not esteem difference as real as sameness, and as permanent in the facts of nature. This tendency is fatal to all sound and final thinking: it never penetrates to the roots of things. All creative minds have been inspired and guided by the law of unity: their problem is ever to pierce the coarse and superficial rind of diversity, and discover the unity in whose core is the heart and seed of all things.

XXXI. CALCULUS.

We need, what Genius is unconsciously seeking, and, by some daring generalization of the universe, shall assuredly discover, a spiritual calculus, a novum organon,[12] whereby nature shall be divined in the soul, the soul in God, matter in spirit, polarity resolved into unity; and that power which pulsates in all life, animates and builds all organizations, shall manifest itself as one universal deific energy, present alike at the outskirts and center of the universe, whose center and circumference are one; omniscient, omnipotent, self-subsisting, uncontained, yet containing all things in the unbroken synthesis of its being.

XXXIII. EACH AND ALL.[13]

Life eludes all scientific analysis. Each organ and function is modified in substance and varied in effect, by the subtile energy which pulsates throughout the whole economy of things, spiritual and corporeal. The each is instinct with the all; the all unfolds and reappears in each. Spirit is all in all. God, man, nature, are a divine synthesis, whose parts it is impiety to sunder. Genius must preside devoutly over all investigations, or analysis, with her murderous knife, will seek impiously to probe the vitals of being.

XXXIV. GOD.

God organizes never his attributes fully in single structures. He is instant, but never extant wholly, in his works.[14] Nature does not contain, but is contained in him; she is the memoir of his life; man is a nobler scripture, yet fails to outwrite the godhead. The universe does not reveal, eternities do not publish the mysteries of his being. He subjects his noblest works to minute and constant revision; his idea ever transcends its form; he moulds anew his own idols; both nature and man are ever making, never made.

XXXV. NATURE.

Nature seems remote and detached, because the soul surveys her by means of the extremest senses, imposing on herself the notion of difference and remoteness through their predominance, and thereby losing that of her own oneness with it. Yet nature is not separate from me; she is mine alike with my body; and in moments of true life, I feel my identity with her; I breathe, pulsate, feel, think, will, through her members, and know of no duality of being.

---

[12] An allusion to the *Novum Organum* (1620) of Francis Bacon, which urged the inductive method basic to the development of modern science.

[13] The title and theme were likely influenced by Emerson's poem "Each and All," published as "Each in All" in *The Western Messenger* (1839). See Ralph Waldo Emerson, "Each and All," in this volume and n. 22, attached to the text.

[14] God is present but never exhausted in his works. The panentheism expressed in this epigram—that the work of God does not contain him but is instead contained in him—is Platonic in cast (the divine Idea and its copies in creation), but also progressive.

It is in such moods of soul that prophetic visions are beheld, and evangeles published for the joy and hope of mankind.

XXXVI. FLUX.

Solidity is an illusion of the senses. To faith, nothing is solid: the nature of the soul renders such fact impossible. Modern chemistry demonstrates that nine tenths of the human body are fluid, and substances of inferior order in lesser proportion. Matter is ever pervaded and agitated by the omnipresent soul. All things are instinct with spirit.[15]

XXXVII. SEPULTURE AND RESURRECTION.

That which is visible is dead: the apparent is the corpse of the real; and undergoes successive sepultures and resurrections. The soul dies out of organs; the tombs cannot confine her; she eludes the grasp of decay; she builds and unseals the sepulchres. Her bodies are fleeting, historical. Whatsoever she sees when awake is death; when asleep dream.

XXXVIII. TIME.

Organizations are mortal; the seal of death is fixed on them even at birth. The young Future is nurtured by the Past, yet aspires to a nobler life, and revises, in his maturity, the traditions and usages of his day, to be supplanted by the sons and daughters whom he begets and ennobles. Time, like fabled Saturn, now generates, and, ere even their sutures be closed, devours his own offspring.[16] Only the children of the soul are immortal; the births of time are premature and perishable.

XXXIX. EMBRYON.

Man is a rudiment and embryon of God: eternity shall develop in him the divine image.

XL. ORGANIZATION.

Possibly organization is no necessary function or mode of spiritual being. The time may come, in the endless career of the soul, when the facts of incarnation, birth, death, descent into matter and ascension from it, shall comprise no part of her history; when she herself shall survey this human life with emotions akin to those of the naturalist, on examining the relics of extinct races of beings; when mounds, sepulchres, monuments, epitaphs, shall serve but as memoirs of a past state of existence; a reminiscence of one metempsychosis of her life in time.[17]

XLI. SPIRIT AND MATTER.

Divined aright, there is nothing purely organic; all things are vital and inorganic. The microscope is developing this sublime fact. Sense looking at the historic surface beholds what it deems matter, yet is but spirit in fusion, fluent, pervaded by her own immanent vitality and trembling to organize itself. Neither matter nor death are possible: what seem matter and death are sensuous impressions, which, in our sanest moments, the authentic instincts con-

---

[15]This epigram is a particularly good illustration of Alcott's kinetic spirituality.

[16]The Roman agricultural deity Saturn was identified, after Roman contact with Greece, with the last-born of the Greek Titans, Cronos (Time). According to Hesiod *Theogony* (trans. Hugh G. Evelyn-White) 459-60: "These [children] great Cronos swallowed as each came forth from the womb to his mother's knees."

[17]The Platonic doctrine of metempsychosis taught that at death the soul passed into another human or an animal body. See Plato *Phaedo* 80C-82D, 113A, and *Phaedrus* 248C-249C; or, for an account of transmigration with particularly clear Orphic elements, see Plato *Republic* 614B-621B. The language of "descent" into matter and "ascension" from it points as well to Neoplatonism.

tradict. The sensible world is spirit in magnitude, outspread before the senses for their analysis, but whose synthesis is the soul herself, whose prothesis is God.[18] Matter is but the confine of spirit limning her to sense.

XLII. ORDER.

The soul works from center to periphery, veiling her labors from the ken of the senses. Her works are invisible till she has rounded herself in surface, where she completes her organizations.[19] Appearance, though first to sense, is last in the order of generation: she recoils on herself at the acme of sense, revealing herself in reversed order. Historical is the sequel of genetic life.

XLIV. GRAVITATION.

Love and gravity are a twofold action of one life, whose conservative instincts in man and nature preserve inviolate the harmony of the immutable and eternal law of spirit. Man and nature alike tend toward the Godhead. All seeming divergence is overruled by this omnipotent force, whose retributions restore universal order.

XLV. LOVE.

Love designs, thought sketches, action sculptures the works of spirit. Love is divine, conceiving, creating, completing, all things. Love is the Genius of Spirit.

XLVI. LIFE.

Life, in its initial state, is synthetic; then feeling, thought, action are one and indivisible: love is its manifestation. Childhood and woman are samples and instances. But thought disintegrates and breaks this unity of soul: action alone restores it. Action is composition; thought decomposition. Deeds executed in love are graceful, harmonious, entire; enacted from thought merely, they are awkward, dissonant, incomplete: a manufacture, not creations, not works of genius.

XLVII. ACTUAL AND IDEAL.

The actual and ideal are twins of one mother, Reality, who failing to incarnate her conceptions in time, meanwhile contents herself with admiring in each the complement of the other, herself integrant of both. Alway are the divine Gemini intertwined; Pan and Psyche, man and woman, the soul and nature.[20]

---

[18] Alcott most likely takes the language of prothesis and synthesis from Samuel Taylor Coleridge, who used both terms as part of a constructive logic—a kind of metaphysical grammar to eliminate a false antithesis between ideal and real. In this grammar, the first term was the prothesis, the verb substantive (or gerund), which Coleridge conceived as expressing an identity of being and act. This he linked to God, who transcended both thesis (the substantive or noun) and antithesis (the verb)—the second and third terms of his grammar. The fifth term of Coleridge's grammar was the synthesis, the participle that brought together the thesis and antithesis in a union of being and act. (A fourth term, the mesothesis, or infinitive, is not important here.) See Coleridge, *Aids to Reflection,* "Aphorisms on That Which Is Indeed Spiritual Religion," aphorism 2n. In his saying Alcott seems interested in the semantic play of prothesis and synthesis with analysis, which is his own addition. But his understanding of the two former terms is consonant with Coleridge's explanations.

[19] For the significance of circles in articulating Transcendental spirituality, cf. Emerson's essay "Circles" in Ralph Waldo Emerson, *The Collected Works of Ralph Waldo Emerson,* ed. Alfred R. Ferguson et al. (Cambridge: Harvard University Press, Belknap Press, 1971–) 2:177-90.

[20] By Hellenistic times, the Greek mythological brothers Castor and Pollux were known as the Gemini, or Twins. Here, though, Alcott

XLVIII. BEAUTY.

All departures from perfect beauty are degradations of the divine image. God is the one type, which the soul strives to incarnate in all organizations. Varieties are historical: the one form embosoms all forms; all having a common likeness at the base of difference. Human heads are images, more or less perfect, of the soul's or God's head. But the divine features do not fix in flesh; in the coarse and brittle clay. Beauty is fluent; art of highest order represents her always in flux, giving fluency and motion to bodies solid and immovable to sense. The line of beauty symbolizes motion.

XLIX. TRANSFIGURATION.

Never have we beheld a purely human face; as yet, the beast, demon, rather than the man or God, predominate in its expression. The face of the soul is not extant in flesh. Yet she has a face, and virtue and genius shall one day reveal her celestial lineaments: a beauty, a majesty, shall then radiate from her that shall transcend the rapt ideal of love and hope. So have I seen glimpses of this spiritual glory, when, inspired by some thought or sentiment, she was transfigured from the image of the earthly to that of the heavenly, the ignoble melting out of her features, lost in the supersensual life.

L. PROMETHEUS.

Know, O man, that your soul is the Prometheus, who, receiving the divine fires, builds up this majestic statue of clay, and moulds it in the deific image, the pride of gods, the model and analogon of all forms.[21] He chiselled that godlike brow, arched those mystic temples from whose fanes she herself looks forth, formed that miraculous globe above, and planted that sylvan grove below; graved those massive blades yoked in armed powers; carved that heaven-containing bosom, wreathed those puissant thighs, and hewed those stable columns, diffusing over all the grandeur, the grace of his own divine lineaments, and delighting in this cunning work of his hand. Mar not its beauty, spoil not its symmetry, by the deforming lines of lust and sin: dethroning the divinity incarnated therein, and transforming yourself into the satyr and the beast.

LI. REFORM.[22]

The trump of reform is sounding throughout the world for a revolution of all

---

uses the name Gemini to refer to a different set of "twins"—his own Pan and Psyche. Pan, for the Greeks, was a pastoral deity associated with fertility. By contrast, Psyche—who personified the human soul—was a young woman with whom the God Eros (Cupid) fell in love. Although Pan and Psyche were unrelated, Alcott represents them as symbols of the twin aspects of human existence: Pan is the sign of physical nature, Psyche of the immortal soul. Pan is the "actual," Psyche the "ideal."

[21]For Prometheus, see n. 11 to Amos Bronson Alcott, *The Doctrine and Discipline of Human Culture*. One Greek tradition held that Prometheus had given life itself, fashioning "man" as his creation. (See Ovid *Metamorphoses* 1.95-100.) Alcott's metaphor is based on a mythology in which Prometheus is both creator and giver of fire. His allusion to Prometheus's "cunning work" later in the epigram indicates a solid acquaintance with Promethean tales, since Prometheus is depicted as "devious," "clever," "wily," and "crafty." (See, for example, Hesiod *Theogony* 507-616.) The final reference to the satyr—the Greek mythological being who was half human and half animal and noted for its lustfulness—is appropriate in the general context of the extended metaphor.

[22]Here begins the second installment of Alcott's "Orphic Sayings" contributed to *The Dial*. These epigrams appeared in the third issue, published in January 1841.

human affairs. This issue we cannot doubt; yet the cries are not without alarm. Already is the axe laid at the root of that spreading tree, whose trunk is idolatry, whose branches are covetousness, war, and slavery, whose blossom is concupiscence, whose fruit is hate. Planted by Beelzebub, it shall be rooted up. Abaddon is pouring his vial on the earth.[23]

LII. REFORMERS.

Reformers are metallic; they are sharpest steel; they pierce whatsoever of evil or abuse they touch. Their souls are attempered in the fires of heaven; they are nailed in the might of principles, and God backs their purpose. They uproot institutions, erase traditions, revise usages, and renovate all things. They are the noblest of facts. Extant in time, they work for eternity; dwelling with men, they are with God.

LVI. PERSON.

Divinely speaking, God is the only person.[24] The personality of man is partial, derivative; not perfect, not original. He becomes more personal as he partakes more largely of divinity. Holiness embosoms him in the Godhead, and makes him one with Deity.

LVIII. PERSONALITY.

Truth is most potent when she speaks in general and impersonal terms. Then she rebukes everybody, and all confess before her words. She draws her bow, and lets fly her arrows at broad venture into the ages, to pierce all evils and abuses at heart. She wounds persons through principles, on whose phylactery, "thou art the man," is ever written to the eye of all men.[25]

LXI. TEMPTATION.

The man of sublime gifts has his temptation amidst the solitudes to which he is driven by his age as proof of his integrity.[26] Yet nobly he withstands this trial, conquering both Satan and the world by overcoming himself. He bows not down before the idols of time, but is constant to the divine ideal that haunts his heart,—a spirit of serene and perpetual peace.

LXII. LIGHT.

Oblivion of the world is knowledge of heaven,—of sin, holiness,—of time, eternity. The world, sin, time, are interpolations into the authentic scripture of the soul, denoting her lapse from God, innocence, heaven. Of these the child and God are alike ignorant.[27] They have not fallen from their estate of divine intuition, into the dark domain of sense, wherein all is but shad-

---

[23] In the Book of Revelation, Abaddon (Greek Apollyon, or Destroyer) is the angel of the bottomless pit who rules the horde of locusts unleashed by the fifth angel to torture those without the seal of God on their foreheads. See Rev. 9:1-11, esp. 11. In this saying and the next, Alcott's prophetic and apocalyptic voice is uppermost.

[24] Alcott evidently disagrees with his friend Emerson regarding the personality of God. See n. 6 to Ralph Waldo Emerson, Divinity School *Address*.

[25] Again Alcott mixes metaphors. The bow and arrow of a personified Truth suggest a general classical provenance. On the other hand, the phylactery is the small leather box attached to the arm and forehead during prayer and containing the most sacred verses in the Hebrew Bible.

[26] The "man of sublime gifts" is perhaps not the most sublime. (See saying 13.) The two sayings in juxtaposition are a good example of the dialectical and paradoxical nature of Alcott's thought.

[27] Cf. saying 11; and see also n. 27 to Alcott, *Doctrine and Discipline of Human Culture*. Here Alcott's doctrine of the Lapse is tied to his celebration of the child, who has not yet fallen through the weight of the senses.

owy reminiscence of substance and light, of innocence and clarity. Their life is above memory and hope,—a life, not of knowledge, but of sight.

LXIV. SOPHISTRY.[28]

Always are the ages infested with dealers in stolen treasures. Church, state, school, traffic largely in such contraband wares, and would send genius and probity, as of old, Socrates and Jesus, into the markets and thoroughfares, to higgle with publicans and sophists for their own properties. But yet the wit and will of these same vagrants is not only coin, but stock in trade for all the business of the world. Mammon counterfeits the scripture of God, and his partners, the church, the state, the school, share the profit of his peculations on mankind.

LXV. BREAD.

Fools and blind! not bread, but the lack of it is God's high argument. Wouldst enter into life?[29] Beg bread then. In the kingdom of God are love and bread consociated, but in the realm of mammon, bread sojourns with lies, and truth is a starvling. Yet praised be God, he has bread in his exile which mammon knows not of.

LXVI. LABOR.

Labor is sweet; nor is that a stern decree that sends man into the fields to earn his bread in the sweat of his face.[30] Labor is primeval; it replaces man in Eden,—the garden planted by God. It exalts and humanizes the soul. Life in all its functions and relations then breathes of groves and fountains, of simplicity and health. Man discourses sublimely with the divinities over the plough, the spade, the sickle, marrying the soul and the soil by the rites of labor. Sloth is the tempter that beguiles him of innocence, and exiles him from Paradise. Let none esteem himself beloved of the divine Husbandman, unless he earn the wages of peace in his vineyard. Yet now the broad world is full of idlers; the fields are barren; the age is hungry; there is no corn. The harvests are of tares and not of wheat. Gaunt is the age; even as the seedsman winnows the chaff from the wheat, shall the winds of reform blow this vanity away.[31]

LXVIII. DOGMATISM.

The ages dogmatize, and would stifle the freest and boldest thought. Their language is,—our possessions skirt space, and we veto all possible discoveries of time. We are heirs of all wisdom, all excellence; none shall pass our confines; vain is the

---

[28]In ancient Greece the Sophists were traveling teachers who lectured for fees. Plato's *Dialogues* portray them as figures dedicated to the refinements of rhetoric rather than the pursuit of truth, and the pejorative connotations have continued.

[29]Cf. Matt. 19:17. Through much of his life, Alcott practiced what he preached in the advice that follows, as he was often in debt and not able to support his family without the assistance of others.

[30]This hymn to labor may have been influenced by Thomas Carlyle, whose writings—exalting work and the man of action—Alcott had read and admired (although in 1842 the two would meet and quarrel). The epigram, however, is also autobiographical, since Alcott had been farming at Concord to earn a living for himself and his family. His decision to do so had not been purely economic: reformers of the era decried the factory system and the poverty that came after the Panic of 1837; and Alcott, among them, sought a more innocent and ennobling way of life by a return to the soil.

[31]Cf. Matt. 13:24-30, which Alcott has transformed to express his imminent eschatology of reform.

dream of a wilderness of thought to be vanquished by rebellion against us; we inherit the patrimony of God,—all goods in the gift of omnipotence.

LXXIII. SCRIPTURE.

All scripture is the record of life, and is sacred or profane, as the life it records is holy or vile. Every noble life is a revelation from heaven, which the joy and hope of mankind preserve to the world. Nor while the soul endures, shall the book of revelation be sealed.[32] Her scriptures, like herself, are inexhaustible, without beginning or end.

LXXIV. SACRED BOOKS.

The current version of all sacred books is profane. The ignorance and passions of men interpolate themselves into the text, and vitiate both its doctrine and ethics. But this is revised, at successive eras, by prophets, who, holding direct communication with the source of life and truth, translate their eternal propositions from the sacred into the common speech of man, and thus give the word anew to the world.

LXXV. RESURRECTION.

A man must live his life to apprehend it. There have been few living men and hence few lives; most have lived their death. Men have no faith in life. There goes indeed a rumor through the ages concerning it, but the few, who affirm knowledge of the fact, are slain always to verify the popular doubt. Men assert, not the resurrection of the soul from the body, but of the body from the grave, as a revelation of life. Faithless and blind! the body is the grave; let the dead arise from these sepulchres of concupiscence, and know by experience that life is immortal. Only the living know that they live; the dead know only of death.

LXXVI. MIRACLES.

To apprehend a miracle, a man must first have wrought it. He knows only what he has lived, and interprets all facts in the light of his experience. Miracles are spiritual experiences, not feats of legerdemain, not freaks of nature.[33] It is the spiritual sight that discerns whatsoever is painted to sense. Flesh is faithless and blind.

LXXVIII. REVELATION.

Revelation is mediate or immediate; speculative or intuitive. It is addressed to conscience or reason,—to sight or sense. Reason receives the light through mediums and mediators; conscience direct from its source. The light of one is opake; of the other, clear. The prophet, whose eye is coincident with the celestial ray, receives this into his breast, and intensifying there, it kindles on his brow a serene and perpetual day. But the worldling, with face averted from God, reflects divinity through the obscure twilight of his own brain, and remains in the blindness of his own darkness, a deceptive meteor of the night.

LXXX. TEACHER.

The true teacher defends his pupils against his own personal influence. He inspires self-trust. He guides their eyes from himself to the spirit that quickens him. He will have no disciples. A noble artist, he has visions of excellence and revelations of beauty, which he has neither impersonated in character, nor embodied in words. His life and teachings are but studies for yet nobler ideals.

---

[32] A contrary reference, perhaps, to the warning against additions in the Book of Revelation (Rev. 22:18).

[33] Alcott affirms a doctrine of miracles as inner spiritual experience—his statement of the argument that had embroiled Transcendentalists in public controversy with Unitarians.

LXXXI. EXPERIENCE.

A man's idea of God corresponds to his ideal of himself. The nobler he is, the more exalted his God. His own culture and discipline are a revelation of divinity. He apprehends the divine character as he comprehends his own. Humanity is the glass of divinity; experience of the soul is a revelation of God.

LXXXIII. RETRIBUTION.

The laws of the soul and of nature are forecast and preordained in the spirit of God, and are ever executing themselves through conscience in man, and gravity in things. Man's body and the world are organs, through which the retributions of the spiritual universe are justified to reason and sense. Disease and misfortune are memoranda of violations of the divine law, written in the letter of pain and evil.[34]

LXXXIV. WORSHIP.

The ritual of the soul is preordained in her relations to God, man, nature, herself. Life, with its varied duties, is her ordained worship; labor and meditation her sacraments. Whatsoever violates this order is idolatry and sacrilege. A holy spirit, she hallows all times, places, services; and perpetually she consecrates her temples, and ministers at the altars of her divinity. Her censer flames always toward heaven, and the spirit of God descends to kindle her devotions.

LXXXV. BAPTISM.

Except a man be born of water and of spirit, he cannot apprehend eternal life.[35] Sobriety is clarity; sanctity is sight. John baptizes Jesus. Repent, abstain, resolve;—thus purify yourself in this laver of regeneration, and become a denizen of the kingdom of God.

LXXXVI. CARNAGE.

Conceive of slaughter and flesh-eating in Eden.[36]

XCI. GENTLENESS.

I love to regard all souls as babes, yet in their prime and innocency of being, nor would I upbraid rudely a fellow creature, but treat him as tenderly as an infant. I would be gentle alway. Gentleness is the divinest of graces, and all men joy in it. Yet seldom does it appear on earth. Not in the face of man, nor yet often in that of woman (O apostacy,) but in the countenance of childhood it sometimes lingers, even amidst the violence, the dispathy[37] that beset it; there, for a little while, fed by divine fires, the serene flame glows, but soon flickers and dies away, choked by the passions and lusts of sense—its embers smouldering alone in the bosoms of men.

XCII. INDIVIDUALS.

Individuals are sacred: creeds, usages, institutions, as they cherish and reverence the individual. The world, the state, the church, the school, all are felons whensoever they violate the sanctity of the pri-

---

[34]Alcott's explicit reference to disease echoes the health-reform movement of the era, in which his cousin William Alcott was a leader. The epigram also suggests the climate of concern out of which Christian Science and New Thought emerged later in the nineteenth century. For related ideas that provide a metaphysical foundation for mental cure, see Alcott's saying 41.

[35]Cf. John 3:5. Alcott, however, transforms the meaning of the symbol of baptism and the scriptural verse to express his temperance views.

[36]This terse and cryptic epigram expresses Alcott's commitment to vegetarianism.

[37]Alcott here may mean opposite feeling or absence of feeling. For the child, cf. saying 46.

vate heart.[38] God, with his saints and martyrs, holds thrones, polities, hierarchies, amenable to the same, and time pours her vial of just retribution on their heads. A man is divine; mightier, holier, than rulers or powers ordained of time.

XCIV. CHRISTENDOM.

Christendom is infidel. It violates the sanctity of man's conscience. It speaks not from the lively oracles of the soul, but reads instead from the traditions of men. It quotes history, not life. It denounces as heresy and impiety the intuitions of the individual, denies the inspiration of souls, and intrudes human dogmas and usages between conscience and God. It excludes the saints from its bosom, and with these excommunicates, as the archheretic, Jesus of Nazareth also.

XCV. CHRISTIANS.

Christians lean on Jesus, not on the soul. Such was not the doctrine of this noble reformer. He taught man's independence of all men, and a faith and trust in the soul herself. Christianity is the doctrine of self-support. It teaches man to be upright, not supine. Jesus gives his arm to none save those who stand erect, independent of church, state, or the world, in the integrity of self-insight and valor. Cast aside thy crutch, O Christendom, and by faith in the soul, arise and walk. Thy faith alone shall make thee whole.[39]

XCVI. PENTECOST.

The pentecost of the soul draws near.[40] Inspiration, silent long, is unsealing the lips of prophets and bards, and soon shall the vain babblings of men die away, and their ears be given to the words of the Holy Ghost; their tongues cloven with celestial eloquence.

XCIX. ETERNITY.

The soul doth not chronicle her age. Her consciousness opens in the dimness of tradition; she is cradled in mystery, and her infancy invested in fable. Yet a celestial light irradiates this obscurity of birth, and reveals her spiritual lineage. Ancestor of the world, prior to time, elder than her incarnation, neither spaces, times, genealogies, publish her date. Memory is the history, Hope the prophecy of her inborn eternity. Dateless, timeless, she is coeval with God.[41]

C. SILENCE.

Silence is the initiative to wisdom.[42] Wit is silent, and justifies her children by their reverence of the voiceless oracles of the breast. Inspiration is dumb, a listener to the oracles during her nonage; suddenly she speaks, to mock the emptiness of all speech. Silence is the dialect of heaven; the utterance of Gods.

---

[38]Cf. Emerson: "I cannot find language of sufficient energy to convey my sense of the sacredness of private integrity" (Ralph Waldo Emerson, "Lectures on the Times," *The Dial* 3:1 [July 1842]: 12). See also the discussion of self-culture in the introduction to this volume.

[39]Alcott's language reflects such New Testament passages as Luke 17:19 and John 5:8-9.

[40]In the context of these sayings, reference to Pentecost suggests the atmosphere of millennial expectation in which Alcott characteristically lived.

[41]Here Alcott affirms his belief in the preexistence of the soul.

[42]Alcott ends his "Orphic Sayings" by suggesting, in mystical vein, that even sacred conversation must yield to silence. His epigram provides a fitting dialectical conclusion for a collection built on spiritual paradox.

Part III

THEODORE PARKER

INTRODUCTION

"Theodore Parker was our Savonarola, an excellent scholar, in frank and affectionate communication with the best minds of his day, yet the tribune of the people, and the stout Reformer to urge and defend every cause of humanity with and for the humblest of mankind."[1] So wrote Ralph Waldo Emerson some years after Parker's early death as he recalled the beginnings of the Transcendental movement. Emerson's "Savonarola" was a ringing epithet for a man whose combination of eloquence and severity included a willingness to confront established authority in the name of what he thought truth and principle. Scholar, preacher, social reformer, and deeply religious man, Parker brought fire to Transcendental affirmation and spent his mature years demonstrating that the fruit of moral intuition lay for him in a life of action.

Parker was born in 1810 in Lexington, Massachusetts, the youngest of the eleven children of John Parker and Hannah Stearns. Growing up on the farm in Lexington, he received only an irregular education but managed, in 1834, to matriculate at the Harvard Divinity School in preparation for a Unitarian ministry. After graduation, Parker was ordained in 1837 and established at a church in West Roxbury, some twelve miles from Boston. The same year, even before the ordination, he married Lydia Cabot, whom he had courted since 1832 when he taught school in Watertown. Their marriage—troubled for Parker, at least at its beginning—was also saddened by their childlessness.[2] Still, the two compensated in some measure by adopting George Cabot, a child who was a distant cousin to Lydia, and by opening their household to Hannah Stevenson, an older woman who became a combination secretary to Parker and housekeeper-companion to his wife.

Parker read Emerson's *Nature* with keen involvement, and we have already noted his enthusiastic words on hearing the Divinity School Address.[3] But the groundwork for Parker's Transcendentalism had been laid years earlier. By the time he entered the Harvard Divinity School, he had already experienced doubts concerning orthodox Christian teaching, including the validity of Old and New Testament miracles. Even more, from his Watertown days he had pored over French and German thought, and he knew Coleridge's work before he studied at Harvard. Later, at the Divinity School, Parker immersed himself in German biblical scholarship and found the most philosophic help for his thinking

---

[1] Ralph Waldo Emerson, "Historic Notes of Life and Letters in New England," in Ralph Waldo Emerson, *The Complete Works of Ralph Waldo Emerson,* ed. Edward Waldo Emerson, centenary ed. (Boston: Houghton, Mifflin, 1903–1904) 10:344.

[2] For evidence of an unhappy marriage for Theodore Parker, at least initially, see John C. Broderick, "Problems of the Literary Executor: The Case of Theodore Parker," *The Quarterly Journal of the Library of Congress* 23 (1966): 268-70.

[3] See the introduction to Ralph Waldo Emerson, Divinity School *Address,* in this volume.

in the works of Immanuel Kant. He was also intrigued by Neoplatonism and Gnosticism and attracted to the writings of the mystics.[4]

Catalyzed by his encounter with the emerging Transcendental movement, Parker between 1840 and 1842 made three great declarations of faith. The first, the "Levi Blodgett Letter,"[5] was an open letter from the pseudonymous Levi Blodgett to the Unitarian Andrews Norton and his followers who had pursued the miracles question against Emerson and George Ripley. The second, Parker's sermon *A Discourse of the Transient and Permanent in Christianity,* clearly outlined his vision of a religious ideal that went beyond even the most liberal of Unitarian statements. The third, a series of five lectures that Parker delivered in Boston and later (1842) published in revised form as *A Discourse of Matters Pertaining to Religion,* buttressed with Parker's impressive scholarship a logical, but also warmly evangelical, treatment of his religious views.

By the beginning of 1843 the results were clear, and they were painful. The Boston Association of Ministers invited Parker to a "tea" at the home of one of its members for the Unitarian version of a heresy trial. Parker was told that he was neither a Christian nor a Unitarian and was asked to withdraw from the association. He refused on his sense of principle: free inquiry was central to Unitarianism, and there was no doctrinal test for membership in the Boston Association. Without a clear precedent for expulsion, the association officially moved no further. In practice, however, Parker was ostracized, since virtually every minister refused to exchange pulpits with him. By the end of the following year when Parker preached at the First Church a "Thursday lecture" suggesting the possibility of future and greater Christs, the lecture administration was swiftly reordered to preclude any chance that Parker would speak again. The Thursday lectures died in the shuffle, but there was no keeping Parker out of Boston. A group of his friends met as a result of the episode, organized the Twenty-Eighth Congregational Society, and rented the Boston Melodeon building to give substance to their plans. There and later at the Music Hall, Parker presided over the largest congregation in Boston and, it was said, in the United States, preaching the gospel of "absolute religion" and increasingly using his pulpit to protest the evils of slavery.

Not content with preaching, Parker filled his Boston years with lectures on the lyceum circuit and with reform activities, as noted in the introduction. His antislavery work—his greatest cause—was direct and personal, involving the intimidation of slave catchers and confrontations with the law, including in the Anthony Burns case a formal indictment (later dismissed) against Parker himself. In an earlier incident, when Parker aided William and Ellen Crafts, two parishioners who were fugitives from Georgia slavery, he wrote his sermons with a pistol on his desk while he kept Ellen hidden in his house. Upon formalizing

---

[4]John White Chadwick, *Theodore Parker: Preacher and Reformer* (1900; rpt., St. Clair Shores MI: Scholarly Press, 1971) 175. For useful discussions of Parker's intellectual and religious formation, see Henry Steele Commager, *Theodore Parker,* 2d ed. (1947; rpt., Gloucester MA: Peter Smith, 1978) 18-39, 61-71; and Parker's own account, *Theodore Parker's Experience as a Minister,* in Theodore Parker, *The Collected Works of Theodore Parker,* ed. Frances Cobbe (London: Trübner, 1863-1865) 12:264-74.

[5][Theodore Parker], *The Previous Question between Mr. Andrews Norton and His Alumni, Moved and Handled in a Letter to All Those Gentlemen, by Levi Blodgett* (Boston: Weeks, Jordan, 1840).

the Craftses' marriage, he placed a Bible in one of William Crafts's hands and a sword in the other—testimony to Parker's conviction that absolute religion might demand extreme action in support of the higher law.

But such action also demanded extreme energy, and Parker finally paid the price. With consumption in his family history, he contracted the disease and early in 1859, following medical orders, set out for the West Indies and later Europe. He never returned: Parker died and was buried in Florence, Italy, in May 1860.

Even as he was a great preacher and social reformer, Theodore Parker—in a side of his work that his later years sometimes obscured—was also a prodigious scholar. He mastered the principles of some eighteen or twenty languages and used a number in forward-looking biblical studies based on German critical models. The library of eventually twelve thousand volumes at his Boston home overran the fourth floor and crept down the stairs in an imperialism of the printed word that transformed every room except the dining room into a place for books. He read them voraciously and quoted from them easily in sermons and writings, often not identifying the source but assuming, perhaps, that others shared the contents of his well-furnished mind.

Moreover, Parker's writing seemed as voluminous as his reading, with a formidable list of books, pamphlets, and articles published during his lifetime and, after his death, collected works (in editions still not complete) running to fourteen and fifteen volumes.[6] The John White Chadwick bibliography (1900) lists some forty-seven pamphlet sermons and addresses that were published by 1860, beginning in 1840 with the "Levi Blodgett Letter."[7] And the Charles Wendte bibliography in the centenary edition of Parker's works (1907–1911) adds more than 150 items to the Chadwick bibliography. Parker reviewed books for the Unitarian *Christian Examiner* from 1837 to 1858, and from 1840 he contributed articles to *The Dial*. From 1847 to 1850, as chief editor of *The Massachusetts Quarterly Review,* Parker steadily offered pieces to the reading public.

A Discourse of Matters Pertaining to Religion was published in 1842 as Parker's first book. In the next year his translation and amplification of Wilhelm M. L. De Wette's *Critical and Historical Introduction to the Canonical Scriptures of the Old Testament* appeared—a rigorous work of scholarship that surrounded De Wette's study with a veritable encyclopedia of source translations, annotated bibliography, and background material. The same year saw the publication of a volume of collected *Critical and Miscellaneous Writings*. Nearly a decade later, in 1852, came the three-volume collection *Speeches, Addresses, and Occasional Sermons,* to be followed in 1853 by *Sermons of Theism, Atheism and the Popular Theology* and *Ten Sermons of Religion*. Then, in 1855, another collection, *Additional Speeches, Addresses, and Occasional Sermons,* appeared in two volumes including a series of antislavery addresses. In that year, too, Parker published *The Trial of Theodore Parker,* which gave his own account of the proceedings against him in the aftermath of the Anthony Burns incident as well as a "defense" that Parker had never

---

[6]These editions are the Frances Cobbe edition noted above, and Theodore Parker, *The Works of Theodore Parker,* centenary ed. (Boston: American Unitarian Association, 1907-1911). The Cobbe edition contains fourteen volumes, and the centenary edition fifteen. Neither edition contains all of Parker's writings, and both are problematic from an editorial point of view.

[7]The bibliography may be found in Chadwick, *Theodore Parker,* xi-xx.

been able to offer to the court. Finally, later short works included *The Two Christmas Celebrations,* published in 1857, and *Theodore Parker's Experience as a Minister,* published in 1859, an autobiographical account written aboard ship after Parker had left Boston in declining health.

This huge catalog of works is ample testimony that, for Parker, Transcendental intuitions needed to be supported by immersion in a world of detailed scholarship as well as politics and history. He possessed, as Octavius B. Frothingham observed, "acute observation," a "passion for external fact," and a "faith in statistics."[8] In terms of the familiar Coleridgean distinction between the Reason and the Understanding, he gave a far-larger role to the Understanding than either Emerson or Alcott would allow. And yet, as Parker's witness made evident, he was an intensely spiritual man, drawn to the idealism of the Transcendental message and even sentimental in his piety.

In the writings that follow, we trace this complex figure and his many-sided spirituality in excerpts from the unflinching declaration of *The Transient and Permanent in Christianity* and in spirited passages from *A Discourse of Matters Pertaining to Religion.* Finally, in an under-appreciated sermonic classic, we share his reflections in *A Sermon of the Delights of Piety*—delights that the tempestuous Parker never forgot, whatever his involvements in the world of matter and of "man." A Savonarola, perhaps, but in the end Parker possessed a disposition that gave him, in the midst of action, a resonance with the contemplative spirituality of his Transcendental friends.

---

[8]Octavius Brooks Frothingham, *Transcendentalism in New England: A History* (1876; rpt., Gloucester MA: Peter Smith, 1965) 304.

A DISCOURSE OF THE TRANSIENT AND PERMANENT IN CHRISTIANITY

When Theodore Parker published his "Levi Blodgett Letter" in 1840,[1] he was publicly taking sides in a war of words triggered by Emerson's Divinity School *Address*. Andrews Norton had emerged as the most strident of the Unitarian opposition, assailing Emerson and the Transcendentalists in newspaper commentaries and then in his *Discourse on the Latest Form of Infidelity* a year later. In this address Norton's central question was the value of miracles as evidence of the truth and authority of Christianity; and although Emerson chose not to respond, George Ripley entered the fray, precipitating a heated pamphlet debate between himself and Norton.[2]

As Parker read the exchanges between the two, he found himself dissatisfied with Ripley's defense of the Transcendental position and thought that there was more still that could be said. Hence, in the "Levi Blodgett Letter" Parker addressed the "previous question" of how human beings came to have religion in the first place. The answer, for Parker, meant a rejection of both the authority of miracles and the personal (divine) authority of Jesus as evidence for the truth of Christianity. Rather, Christianity was true in that it expressed the intuitive affirmations of the soul with its sense of dependence on God. Seen in this light, Christianity was "absolute religion" and "the perfection of a religion whose germs and first truths [were] innate in the soul."[3]

Thus, Parker's theory of knowledge rested on the internal "evidences" of the spirit, and he was squarely in the Transcendental camp. Then the following year Parker was invited to preach the sermon at the ordination of Charles C. Shackford, a graduate of the Harvard Divinity School (1835) who was assuming pastoral duties at the Hawes Place Church in Boston. Parker delivered his discourse on 19 May 1841 and thereafter, in light of the controversy it raised, had it printed. The first edition was quickly exhausted, so in

---

[1][Theodore Parker], *The Previous Question between Mr. Andrews Norton and His Alumni, Moved and Handled in a Letter to All Those Gentlemen, by Levi Blodgett* (Boston: Weeks, Jordan, 1840).

[2]The relevant pamphlets are Andrews Norton, *A Discourse on the Latest Form of Infidelity* (Cambridge: John Owen, 1839); [George Ripley], *"The Latest Form of Infidelity" Examined: A Letter to Mr. Andrews Norton* (Boston: James Munroe, 1839); Andrews Norton, *Remarks on a Pamphlet Entitled " 'The Latest Form of Infidelity' Examined"* (Cambridge: John Owen, 1839); George Ripley, *Defence of " 'The Latest Form of Infidelity' Examined": A Second Letter to Mr. Andrews Norton* (Boston: James Munroe, 1840); George Ripley, *Defence of " 'The Latest Form of Infidelity' Examined": A Third Letter to Mr. Andrews Norton* (Boston: James Munroe, 1840).

[3][Parker], *Previous Question* ("Levi Blodgett Letter"), in John Edward Dirks, *The Critical Theology of Theodore Parker* (1948; rpt., Westport CT: Greenwood Press, 1970) 150, 152. (Dirks reprints the entire "Levi Blodgett Letter" in an appendix to his study.)

less than a month he came forward with a second. A third edition followed in the same year, and then in 1843 the sermon was republished in *Critical and Miscellaneous Writings.*

A Discourse of the Transient and Permanent in Christianity pursues the themes that appeared in the "Levi Blodgett Letter." Here, however, the emphasis has shifted more clearly from the specific question of miracles to Parker's doctrine of the absolute. Absolute morality and absolute religion, he tells us, are what is permanent in Christianity; doctrines and forms are transient. Christianity is true not because of the authority of its founder or of its holy book (the new German criticism of which the sermon shows he has mastered), but rather because it embodies the absolute. The sanction of Christianity is "the voice of God in your heart," and its end is "to make all men one with God as Christ was one with Him."

It should be evident that Parker in his address articulates a spirituality echoing that of Emerson in the Divinity School *Address*. One could even argue that his categories of the transient and the permanent are not far from Alcott's Platonic delineation, in *The Doctrine and Discipline of Human Culture,* of the Idea and its expression in Jesus (although Parker never took well to Alcott's formulations).[4] Hence, what sets Parker apart from the others is that he makes his case as a Unitarian with every intention of remaining in his ministry. And he makes his case, too, in language in which historical and logical argument as well as scriptural themes and resonances are even more prominent than in the words of Emerson and Alcott. Despite its reasoned and argumentative form, however, Parker's sermon is a document of *religious* as much as theological and critical witness, and what breathes through it is the Transcendental faith that bound him to the others.[5]

---

[4]Parker's biographer Henry Steele Commager wrote that Alcott's "Orphic Sayings" left Parker "mystified" and that he could not "abide" Alcott with his "foggy ways." See Henry Steele Commager, *Theodore Parker,* 2d ed. (1947; rpt., Gloucester MA: Peter Smith, 1978) 44, 284.

[5]The text is excerpted from Theodore Parker, *The Critical and Miscellaneous Writings* (Boston: James Munroe, 1843) 136-69. Neither the Frances Cobbe edition nor the American Unitarian Association edition (see the bibliography) are accurate in their transcription. Punctuation is changed along with capitalization; and, most problematic, in a few places there are minor changes in wording that sometimes alter meaning.

(From) A DISCOURSE OF THE TRANSIENT AND PERMANENT IN CHRISTIANITY

PREACHED AT THE ORDINATION OF MR. CHARLES C. SHACKFORD, IN THE HAWES PLACE CHURCH IN BOSTON, MAY 19, 1841

LUKE xxi, 33. "Heaven and earth shall pass away: but my word shall not pass away."[1]

In this sentence we have a very clear indication that Jesus of Nazareth believed the religion he taught would be eternal, that the substance of it would last forever. Yet there are some, who are affrighted by the faintest rustle which a heretic makes among the dry leaves of theology; they tremble lest Christianity itself should perish without hope. Ever and anon the cry is raised, "The Philistines be upon us, and Christianity is in danger." The least doubt respecting the popular theology, or the existing machinery of the church; the least sign of distrust in the Religion of the Pulpit, or the Religion of the Street, is by some good men supposed to be at enmity with faith in Christ, and capable of shaking Christianity itself. On the other hand, a few bad men and a few pious men, it is said, on both sides of the water, tell us the day of Christianity is past.[2] The latter—it is alleged—would persuade us that, hereafter, Piety must take a new form; the teachings of Jesus are to be passed by; that Religion is to wing her way sublime, above the flight of Christianity, far away, toward heaven, as the fledged eaglet leaves forever the nest which sheltered his callow youth. Let us, therefore, devote a few moments to this subject, and consider what is *Transient* in Christianity, and what is *Permanent* therein. The topic seems not inappropriate to the times in which we live, or the occasion that calls us together. . . .

Looking at the Word of Jesus, at real Christianity, the pure religion he taught, nothing appears more fixed and certain. Its influence widens as light extends; it deepens as the nations grow more wise. But, looking at the history of what men call Christianity, nothing seems more uncertain and perishable. While true religion is

---

[1] The King James (Authorized) Version has "words" where Parker transcribes "word."

[2] The "water" is, of course, the Atlantic Ocean. It is not clear who are the "bad" and who the "pious" who reject Christianity, but generally both groups are deist heirs of the Enlightenment. The "pious" may include some followers of the international Transcendental movement.

always the same thing, in each century and every land, in each man that feels it, the Christianity of the Pulpit, which is the religion taught; the Christianity of the People, which is the religion that is accepted and lived out; has never been the same thing in any two centuries or lands, except only in name. . . .

Let us look at this matter a little more closely. In actual Christianity—that is, in that portion of Christianity which is preached and believed—there seem to have been, ever since the time of its earthly founder, two elements, the one transient, the other permanent. The one is the thought, the folly, the uncertain wisdom, the theological notions, the impiety of man; the other, the eternal truth of God. These two bear perhaps the same relation to each other that the phenomena of outward nature, such as sunshine and cloud, growth, decay, and reproduction, bear to the great law of nature, which underlies and supports them all. As in that case, more attention is commonly paid to the particular phenomena than to the general law; so in this case, more is generally given to the Transient in Christianity than to the Permanent therein.

It must be confessed, though with sorrow, that transient things form a great part of what is commonly taught as Religion. An undue place has often been assigned to forms and doctrines, while too little stress has been laid on the divine life of the soul, love to God, and love to man. Religious forms may be useful and beautiful. They are so, whenever they speak to the soul, and answer a want thereof. In our present state some forms are perhaps necessary. But they are only the accident of Christianity; not its substance. They are the robe, not the angel, who may take another robe, quite as becoming and useful. One sect has many forms; another none. Yet both may be equally Christian, in spite of the redundance or the deficiency. They are a part of the language in which religion speaks, and exist, with few exceptions, wherever man is found. In our calculating nation, in our rationalizing sect, we have retained but two of the rites so numerous in the early Christian church, and even these we have attenuated to the last degree, leaving them little more than a spectre of the ancient form.[3] Another age may continue or forsake both; may revive old forms, or invent new ones to suit the altered circumstances of the times, and yet be Christians quite as good as we, or our fathers of the dark ages. Whether the Apostles designed these rites to be perpetual, seems a question which belongs to scholars and antiquarians; not to us, as Christian men and women. So long as they satisfy or help the pious heart, so long they are good. Looking behind, or around us, we see that the forms and rites of the Christians are quite as fluctuating as those of the heathens; from whom some of them have been, not unwisely, adopted by the earlier church.[4]

---

[3]Parker's "rationalizing sect" is Unitarianism, and the two rites are Baptism and the Lord's Supper. With a diminished notion of sin and a high view of human nature among Unitarians, Baptism had become an initiatory formality. Moreover, with an open communion table in many churches and an increasing discomfort with the Lord's Supper among Unitarian ministers (cf. Emerson's *The Lord's Supper* in this volume), the Holy Communion, too, had grown less important. Still, Unitarians generally accepted the sacraments as ordinances, means of grace through which Christians might come to a new life in Christ.

[4]Similarities between Hellenistic mystery religions and Christian ritual forms had been noticed in the time of the fourth-century church. For a twentieth-century study that illustrates a continuity between Christian forms and Hel-

Again, the doctrines that have been connected with Christianity, and taught in its name, are quite as changeable as the form. This also takes place unavoidably. If observations be made upon Nature,—which must take place so long as man has senses and understanding,—there will be a philosophy of Nature, and philosophical doctrines. These will differ as the observations are just or inaccurate, and as the deductions from observed facts are true or false. Hence there will be different schools of natural philosophy, so long as men have eyes and understandings of different clearness and strength. And if men observe and reflect upon Religion,—which will be done so long as man is a religious and reflective being,—there must also be a philosophy of religion, a theology and theological doctrines. These will differ, as men have felt much or little of religion, as they analyze their sentiments correctly or otherwise, and as they have reasoned right or wrong. Now the true system of Nature which exists in the outward facts, whether discovered or not, is always the same thing, though the philosophy of Nature, which men invent, change every month, and be one thing at London and the opposite at Berlin. Thus there is but one system of Nature as it exists in fact, though many theories of Nature, which exist in our imperfect notions of that system, and by which we may approximate and at length reach it. Now there can be but one Religion which is absolutely true, existing in the facts of human nature, and the ideas of Infinite God. That, whether acknowledged or not, is always the same thing and never changes. So far as a man has any real religion—either the principle or the sentiment thereof—so far he has that, by whatever name he may call it. For, strictly speaking, there is but one kind of religion, as there is but one kind of love, though the manifestations of this religion, in forms, doctrines, and life, be never so diverse. . . .

Now it seems clear, that the notion men form about the origin and nature of the scriptures; respecting the nature and authority of Christ, have nothing to do with Christianity except as its aids or its adversaries; they are not the foundation of its truths. These are theological questions; not religious questions. Their connection with Christianity appears accidental; for if Jesus had taught at Athens, and not at Jerusalem; if he had wrought no miracle, and none but the human nature had ever been ascribed to him; if the Old Testament had forever perished at his birth,—Christianity would still have been the Word of God; it would have lost none of its truths. It would be just as true, just as beautiful, just as lasting, as now it is; though we should have lost so many a blessed word, and the work of Christianity itself would have been, perhaps, a long time retarded.

To judge the future by the past, the former authority of the Old Testament can never return. Its present authority cannot stand. It must be taken for what it is worth. The occasional folly and impiety of its authors must pass for no more than their value;—while the religion, the wisdom, the love, which make fragrant its leaves, will still speak to the best hearts as hitherto, and in accents even more divine, when Reason is allowed her rights. The ancient belief in the infallible inspiration of each sentence of the New Testament is fast changing; very fast. One writer, not a skeptic, but a Christian of unquestioned piety, sweeps off the beginning of Matthew; another, of a different church and equally religious, the end of John. Numerous critics strike off several epistles. The Apocalypse itself is not spared, notwithstanding its concluding

---

lenistic and other pagan rituals, see E. O. James, *Christian Myth and Ritual: A Historical Study* (1933; rpt., Gloucester MA: Peter Smith, 1973).

curse.⁵ Who shall tell us the work of retrenchment is to stop here; that others will not demonstrate, what some pious hearts have long felt, that errors of doctrine and errors of fact may be found in many parts of the record, here and there, from the beginning of Matthew to the end of Acts? We see how opinions have changed ever since the apostles' time; and who shall assure us that they were not sometimes mistaken in historical, as well as doctrinal matters; did not sometimes confound the actual with the imaginary; and that the fancy of these pious writers never stood in the place of their recollection?

But what if this should take place? Is Christianity then to perish out of the heart of the nations, and vanish from the memory of the world, like the religions that were before Abraham? It must be so, if it rest on a foundation which a scoffer may shake, and a score of pious critics shake down. But this is the foundation of a theology, not of Christianity. That does not rest on the decision of Councils. It is not to stand or fall with the infallible inspiration of a few Jewish fishermen, who have writ their names in characters of light all over the world. It does not continue to stand through the forbearance of some critic, who can cut, when he will, the thread on which its life depends. Christianity does not rest on the infallible authority of the New Testament. It depends on this collection of books for the historical statement of its facts. In this we do not require infallible inspiration on the part of the writers, more than in the record of other historical facts. To me it seems as presumptuous, on the one hand, for the believer to claim this evidence for the truth of Christianity, as it is absurd, on the other hand, for the skeptic to demand such evidence to support these historical statements. I cannot see that it depends on the personal authority of Jesus. He was the organ through which the Infinite spoke.⁶ It is

---

⁵Parker's fellow Unitarian Andrews Norton, in his *Evidences of the Genuineness of the Gospels* (1837), had rejected the account of Jesus' birth in the Gospel of Matthew as inauthentic and false. But arguments regarding the canonicity and authenticity of various parts of the New Testament had been forthcoming from German biblical critics since the eighteenth century.

Thus, Johann Gottfried Eichhorn argued in 1794 for a lost Primal Gospel behind the synoptics. According to the first volume of his *Introduction to the New Testament* (1804), the infancy and youth narratives of Matthew and Luke did not come from the Primal Gospel and were added from a later literary source. David Friedrich Strauss (1808–1874), whose *The Life of Jesus, a Critical Treatment* (1835–1836) argued that the Gospels were works of poetic mythmaking that expressed early Christian ideas, especially criticized the Gospel of John. Strauss saw contradictions between the farewell discourses of Jesus in John and the scenario at Gethsemane; and he thought that mythmaking in the Gospel of John was more advanced and self-conscious than in the synoptics. Johann David Michaelis (1717–1791) questioned the inspiration of the epistles of James, Jude, and Hebrews as well as the canonicity of the Book of Revelation (Parker's "Apocalypse"; for its "concluding curse," see Rev. 22: 18-19, and cf. n. 32 to Amos Bronson Alcott, "Orphic Sayings"). Others—including Eichhorn, Friedrich Schleiermacher, and Wilhelm M. L. De Wette—questioned the Pauline authorship of various epistles.

For a discussion of these and related questions concerning the New Testament texts, see Werner Georg Kümmel, *The New Testament: The History of the Investigation of Its Problems,* trans. S. McLean Gilmour and Howard C. Kee (Nashville: Abingdon Press, 1972) 62-143. For a specific account of the New England scene, see Jerry Wayne Brown, *The Rise of Biblical Criticism in America, 1800–1870: The New England Scholars* (Middletown CT: Wesleyan University Press, 1969) esp. 153-70 for a discussion of Parker.

⁶The Christ of Unitarianism was, in the loose

God that was manifested in the flesh by him, on whom rests the truth which Jesus brought to light and made clear and beautiful in his life; and if Christianity be true, it seems useless to look for any other authority to uphold it, as for some one to support Almighty God. So if it could be proved,—as it cannot,—in opposition to the greatest amount of historical evidence ever collected on any similar point, that the gospels were the fabrication of designing and artful men, that Jesus of Nazareth had never lived, still Christianity would stand firm, and fear no evil. None of the doctrines of that religion would fall to the ground; for if true, they stand by themselves. But we should lose,—oh, irreparable loss!—the example of that character, so beautiful, so divine, that no human genius could have conceived it, as none, after all the progress and refinement of eighteen centuries, seems fully to have comprehended its lustrous life. If Christianity were true, we should still think it was so, not because its record was written by infallible pens; nor because it was lived out by an infallible teacher,—but that it is true, like the axioms of geometry, because it is true, and is to be tried by the oracle God places in the breast. If it rest on the personal authority of Jesus alone, then there is no certainty of its truth, if he were ever mistaken in the smallest matter, as some Christians have thought he was, in predicting his second coming.[7]

These doctrines respecting the scriptures have often changed, and are but fleeting. Yet men lay much stress on them. Some cling to these notions as if they were Christianity itself. It is about these and similar points that theological battles are fought from age to age. Men sometimes use worst the choicest treasure which God bestows. This is especially true of the use men make of the Bible. Some men have regarded it as the heathen their idol, or the savage his fetish. They have subordinated Reason, Conscience, and Religion to this. Thus have they lost half the treasure it bears in its bosom. No doubt the time will come when its true character shall be felt. Then it will be seen, that, amid all the contradictions of the Old Testament; its legends so beautiful as fictions, so appalling as facts;[8] amid its predictions that have never been fulfilled; amid the puerile conceptions of

---

sense, Arian—a being more than human but subordinate to God. Through Christ, God's revelation came to humanity, and by the example of his life and death human beings could be inspired to the highest of which they were capable.

[7]The position now known as "consistent eschatology" had already been advanced in the eighteenth century. This view holds that Jesus' understanding of himself and his mission was consistent with the radical hopes of Jewish apocalypticism and that these hopes, proven false, were replaced by doctrinal development in the church. Hermann Samuel Reimarus (1694–1768) was the first modern biblical critic to argue the case for consistent eschatology, and in the *Wolfenbüttel Fragments,* published posthumously from 1774 to 1778, he portrayed Jesus as a deluded apocalypticist whose cry on the cross, "My God, my God, why hast thou forsaken me?" (Matt. 27:46), admitted the failure of his hopes.

Parker knew the *Wolfenbüttel Fragments,* but he was especially drawn to the work of David Friedrich Strauss, who also accepted the thesis of consistent eschatology. Indeed, Strauss's monologues "Transient and Permanent Elements in Christianity" (1838) almost surely provided the title and theme for Parker's sermon; and, although critical, he had reviewed Strauss's *Life of Jesus* in the Unitarian *Christian Examiner* in 1840.

[8]Here Parker is expressing views in accord with those of the "mythical school" in early German biblical scholarship.

God, which sometimes occur, and the cruel denunciations that disfigure both Psalm and Prophecy, there is a reverence for man's nature, a sublime trust in God, and a depth of piety rarely felt in these cold northern hearts of ours. Then the devotion of its authors, the loftiness of their aim, and the majesty of their life, will appear doubly fair, and Prophet and Psalmist will warm our hearts as never before. Their voice will cheer the young and sanctify the gray-headed; will charm us in the toil of life, and sweeten the cup Death gives us, when he comes to shake off this mantle of flesh. Then will it be seen, that the words of Jesus are the music of heaven, sung in an earthly voice, and the echo of these words in John and Paul owe their efficacy to their truth and their depth, and to no accidental matter connected therewith. Then can the Word,—which was in the beginning[9] and now is,—find access to the innermost heart of man, and speak there as now it seldom speaks. Then shall the Bible,—which is a whole library of the deepest and most earnest thoughts and feelings and piety and love, ever recorded in human speech,—be read oftener than ever before, not with Superstition, but with Reason, Conscience, and Faith fully active. Then shall it sustain men bowed down with many sorrows; rebuke sin; encourage virtue; sow the world broad-cast and quick with the seed of love, that man may reap a harvest for life everlasting.

With all the obstacles men have thrown in its path, how much has the Bible done for mankind. No abuse has deprived us of all its blessings. You trace its path across the world from the day of Pentecost to this day. As a river springs up in the heart of a sandy continent, having its father in the skies and its birth-place in distant, unknown mountains; as the stream rolls on, enlarging itself, making in that arid waste a belt of verdure, wherever it turns its way; creating palm groves and fertile plains, where the smoke of the cottager curls up at even-tide, and marble cities send the gleam of their splendor far into the sky;—such has been the course of the Bible on the earth. Despite of idolaters bowing to the dust before it, it has made a deeper mark on the world than the rich and beautiful literature of all the heathen. The first book of the Old Testament tells man he is made in the image of God; the first of the New Testament gives us the motto, Be perfect as your Father in heaven.[10] Higher words were never spoken. How the truths of the Bible have blest us. There is not a boy on all the hills of New England; not a girl born in the filthiest cellar which disgraces a capital in Europe, and cries to God against the barbarism of modern civilization; not a boy nor a girl all Christendom through, but their lot is made better by that great book.

Doubtless the time will come when men shall see Christ also as he is. Well might he still say: "Have I been so long with you, and yet hast thou not known me?"[11] No! we have made him an idol, have bowed the knee before him, saying, "Hail, king of the Jews;" called him "Lord, Lord!" but done not the things which he said.[12] The history of the Christian world might well be summed up in one word of the evangelist—"and there they crucified him,"[13] for there has never been an age when men did not crucify the Son of God afresh. But if error prevail for a time and grow old in the world, truth will triumph at the last, and then we shall see the Son of God

---

[9]Cf. John 1:1.

[10]See Gen. 1:26-27 and Matt. 5:48.
[11]See John 14:9.
[12]Cf. John 19:3 and Luke 6:46.
[13]See Luke 23:33.

as he is. Lifted up he shall draw all nations unto him.¹⁴ Then will men understand the Word of Jesus, which shall not pass away. Then shall we see and love the divine life that he lived. How vast has his influence been. How his spirit wrought in the hearts of his disciples, rude, selfish, bigoted, as at first they were. How it was wrought in the world. His words judge the nations.¹⁵ The wisest son of man has not measured their height. They speak to what is deepest in profound men; what is holiest in good men; what is divinest in religious men. They kindle anew the flame of devotion in hearts long cold. They are Spirit and Life. His truth was not derived from Moses and Solomon; but the light of God shone through him, not colored, not bent aside. His life is the perpetual rebuke of all time since. It condemns ancient civilization; it condemns modern civilization. Wise men we have since had, and good men; but this Galilean youth strode before the world whole thousands of years,—so much of Divinity was in him. His words solve the questions of this present age. In him the Godlike and the Human met and embraced, and a divine Life was born. Measure him by the world's greatest sons;—how poor they are. Try him by the best of men,—how little and low they appear. Exalt him as much as we may, we shall yet, perhaps, come short of the mark. But still was he not our brother; the son of man, as we are; the Son of God, like ourselves?¹⁶ His excellence, was it not human excellence? His wisdom, love, piety,—sweet and celestial as they were,—are they not what we also may attain? In him, as in a mirror, we may see the image of God, and go on from glory to glory, till we are changed into the same image, led by the spirit which enlightens the humble.¹⁷ Viewed in this way, how beautiful is the life of Jesus. Heaven has come down to earth, or rather, earth has become heaven. The Son of God, come of age, has taken possession of his birthright. The brightest revelation is this,—of what is possible for all men, if not now at least hereafter. How pure is his spirit, and how encouraging its words. "Lowly sufferer," he seems to say, "see how I bore the cross. Patient laborer, be strong; see how I toiled for the unthankful and the merciless. Mistaken sinner, see of what thou art capable. Rise up, and be blessed."

But if, as some early Christians began to do, you take a heathen view, and make him a God, the Son of God in a peculiar and exclusive sense—much of the significance of his character is gone. His virtue has no merit; his love no feeling; his cross no burthen; his agony no pain. His death is an illusion; his resurrection but a show.¹⁸ For if he were not a man, but a god, what are all these things; what his words, his life, his

---

¹⁴Cf. John 12:32. Note, too, that the following sentence evokes the scriptural verse with which Parker began the sermon (Luke 21:33).

¹⁵Cf. Isa. 2:4, which Parker echoes with small changes.

¹⁶Parker expresses an exalted view of human nature here. In general, though, as the rest of the passage suggests, he thought more in terms of the "infinite perfectibility" of human nature than of an existing ontological state of perfection-in-divinity. For a discussion (although perhaps overstated) of Parker's views and their departure from Emerson's, see John Edward Dirks, *The Critical Theology of Theodore Parker* (1948; rpt., Westport CT: Greenwood Press, 1970) 26-27; and, for a more general statement, 127-29.

¹⁷Cf. 2 Cor. 3:18.

¹⁸This is probably a reference to Docetic belief. In the early church, the Docetists taught that the manhood of Jesus was not real and that, as God, he could not mingle with the impure material world or experience suffering. But Parker ignores the "both-and" position (both a God and a man) of Christian orthodoxy.

excellence of achievement?—It is all nothing, weighed against the illimitable greatness of Him who created the worlds and fills up all time and space! Then his resignation is no lesson; his life no model; his death no triumph to you or me,—who are not gods, but mortal men, that know not what a day shall bring forth, and walk by faith "dim sounding on our perilous way."[19] Alas, we have despaired of man, and so cut off his brightest hope.

In respect of doctrines as well as forms we see all is transitory. "Every where is instability and insecurity."[20] Opinions have changed most, on points deemed most vital. Could we bring up a Christian teacher of any age,—from the sixth to the fourteenth century, for example, though a teacher of undoubted soundness of faith, whose word filled the churches of Christendom, clergymen would scarce allow him to kneel at their altar, or sit down with them at the Lord's table. His notions of Christianity could not be expressed in our forms; nor could our notions be made intelligible to his ears. The questions of his age, those on which Christianity was thought to depend,—questions which perplexed and divided the subtle doctors,—are no questions to us. The quarrels which then drove wise men mad, now only excite a smile or a tear, as we are disposed to laugh or weep at the frailty of man. We have other straws of our own to quarrel for. Their ancient books of devotion do not speak to us; their theology is a vain word. To look back but a short period, the theological speculations of our fathers during the last two centuries; their "practical divinity;"[21] even the sermons written by genius and piety, are, with rare exceptions, found unreadable; such a change is there in the doctrines.

Now who shall tell us that the change is to stop here? That this sect or that, or even all sects united, have exhausted the river of life, and received it all in their canonized urns, so that we need draw no more out of the eternal well, but get refreshment nearer at hand? Who shall tell us that another age will not smile at our doctrines, disputes, and unchristian quarrels about Christianity, and make wide the mouth at men who walked brave in orthodox raiment, delighting to blacken the names of heretics, and repeat again the old charge "he hath blasphemed"?[22] Who shall tell us they will not weep at the folly of all such as fancied Truth shone only into the contracted nook of their school, or sect, or coterie? Men of other times may look down equally on the heresy-hunters, and men hunted for heresy, and wonder at both. The men of all ages before us, were quite as confident as we, that their opinion was truth; that their notion was Christianity and the whole thereof. The men who lit the fires of persecution, from the first martyr to Christian bigotry down to the last murder of the innocents, had no doubt their opinion was divine. The contest about transubstantiation, and the immaculate purity of

---

[19]Cf. William Wordsworth, *The Excursion*, bk. 3, l. 701, which the quotation resembles. I am indebted to Anthony W. Shipps, librarian for English at the Indiana University Library, for this observation.

[20]Unfortunately, no critical edition of Parker's writings exists, and I am unable to locate the source of the quotation. See also the concluding paragraph, in this volume, in excerpts from Parker's *Discourse of Matters Pertaining to Religion*, where Parker uses the same quotation.

---

[21]That is, practical theology—the branch of the discipline concerned with pastoral and homiletic themes, church polity and administration, and liturgical matters.

[22]Cf. Matt. 9:3.

the Hebrew and Greek texts of the scriptures, was waged with a bitterness unequalled in these days.[23] The Protestant smiles at one, the Catholic at the other, and men of sense wonder at both. It might teach us all a lesson, at least of forbearance. No doubt, an age will come, in which ours shall be reckoned a period of darkness—like the sixth century[24]—when men groped for the wall but stumbled and fell, because they trusted a transient notion, not an eternal truth; an age when temples were full of idols, set up by human folly, an age in which Christian light had scarce begun to shine into men's hearts. But while this change goes on; while one generation of opinions passes away, and another rises up; Christianity itself, that pure Religion, which exists eternal in the constitution of the soul and the mind of God, is always the same. The Word that was before Abraham, in the very beginning, will not change, for that word is Truth. From this Jesus subtracted nothing; to this he added nothing. But he came to reveal it as the secret of God, that cunning men could not understand, but which filled the souls of men meek and lowly of heart. This truth we owe to God; the revelation thereof to Jesus, our elder brother, God's chosen son.

To turn away from the disputes of the Catholics and the Protestants, of the Unitarian and the Trinitarian, of Old School and New School,[25] and come to the plain words of Jesus of Nazareth, Christianity is a simple thing; very simple. It is absolute, pure Morality; absolute, pure Religion; the love of man; the love of God acting without let or hindrance. The only creed it lays down is the great truth which springs up spontaneous in the holy heart—there is a God. Its watchword is, be perfect as your Father in Heaven.[26] The only form it demands is a divine life; doing the best thing, in the best way, from the highest motives; perfect obedience to the great law of God. Its sanction is the voice of God in your heart; the perpetual presence of Him, who made us and the stars over our head; Christ and the Father

---

[23]For transubstantiation, see n. 4 to Ralph Waldo Emerson, *The Lord's Supper*. While it is tempting to suggest Reformation debates, the "contest about transubstantiation" probably means the controversy that arose in the eleventh century in the course of developing the concept. (Note Parker's "the Protestant smiles" in the following sentence.) Berengar of Tours (1000?–1088) argued that bread and wine remained present in the Eucharist and that the words of consecration became an efficacious sign of the body of Christ in heaven. Berengar's theory was opposed by Lanfranc (1005?–1089), who taught what was essentially the doctrine of transubstantiation. In the medieval contest, Lanfranc emerged as the winner. See the discussion in Justo L. Gonzalez, *A History of Christian Thought* (Nashville: Abingdon Press, 1970-1975) 2:148-55.

Controversies regarding the purity of the scriptural texts had erupted in Protestant circles from the time of the Reformation. In the late sixteenth century Protestant scholastics argued strenuously for the integrity of the Hebrew texts, insisting that even the vowel points had been inspired. Later, in the eighteenth century, a storm arose over the *textus receptus,* or "received text," of the New Testament—the Greek text published in 1516 by Desiderius Erasmus (1466?-1536) and not changed after 1533. See Kümmel, *The New Testament,* 40-50.

[24]Part of the so-called Dark Ages after the fall of Rome.

[25]Parker is probably referring to Presbyterians of the Old and New School. Old School Presbyterians were suspicious of Congregational influences on their church and held to doctrinal conservatism. New Schoolers, by contrast, formed the faction less tied to tradition, ecclesiastical structure, and prevailing standards of orthodoxy.

[26]Cf. Matt. 5:48.

abiding within us.[27] All this is very simple; a little child can understand it; very beautiful, the loftiest mind can find nothing so lovely. Try it by Reason, Conscience, and Faith—things highest in man's nature—we see no redundance, we feel no deficiency. Examine the particular duties it enjoins; humility, reverence, sobriety, gentleness, charity, forgiveness, fortitude, resignation, faith, and active love; try the whole extent of Christianity so well summed up in the command, "Thou shalt love the Lord thy God with all thy heart, and with all thy soul, and with all thy mind—thou shalt love thy neighbor as thyself;"[28] and is there anything therein that can perish? No, the very opponents of Christianity have rarely found fault with the teachings of Jesus. The end of Christianity seems to be to make all men one with God as Christ was one with Him; to bring them to such a state of obedience and goodness, that we shall think divine thoughts and feel divine sentiments, and so keep the law of God by living a life of truth and love. Its means are Purity and Prayer; getting strength from God and using it for our fellow men as well as ourselves. It allows perfect freedom. It does not demand all men to *think* alike, but to think uprightly, and get as near as possible at truth; not all men to *live* alike, but to live holy, and get as near as possible to a life perfectly divine. Christ set up no pillars of Hercules, beyond which men must not sail the sea in quest of truth.[29] He says, "I have many things to say unto you, but ye cannot bear them now . . . Greater works than these shall ye do."[30] Christianity lays no rude hand on the sacred peculiarity of individual genius and character. But there is no Christian sect which does not fetter a man. It would make all men think alike, or smother their conviction in silence. Were all men Quakers or Catholics, Unitarians or Baptists, there would be much less diversity of thought, character, and life; less of truth active in the world than now. But Christianity gives us the largest liberty of the sons of God, and were all men Christians after the fashion of Jesus, this variety would be a thousand times greater than now; for Christianity is not a system of doctrines, but rather a method of attaining oneness with God.[31] It demands, therefore, a good life of piety within, of purity without, and gives the promise that whoso does God's will, shall know of God's doctrine.

In an age of corruption, as all ages are, Jesus stood and looked up to God. There was nothing between him and the Father of all; no old word, be it of Moses or Esaias,[32] of a living Rabbi or Sanhedrim of Rabbis; no sin or perverseness of the finite will. As the re-

---

[27]Cf. John 15:4-7, to which Parker adds the Father.

[28]Matt. 22:37, 39.

[29]In the Greek mythological tradition, the tenth of the twelve labors that Hercules, or Heracles, performed to obtain immortality was a symbolic conquest of death by procuring the cattle of Geryon in the faraway western land of Erythia. As a memorial to his journey, Heracles established his Pillars where the Mediterranean Sea opened into the Atlantic Ocean. Thus the Pillars represent the farthest limit of human endeavor, the place beyond which none could venture.

[30]Cf. John 16:12 and 14:12.

[31]For "largest liberty of the sons of God," cf. Rom. 8:21, which Parker may be echoing. Parker's view of oneness with God is not the ecstatic union of much of traditional mysticism. Instead, in an understanding that is ironically closer to Christian orthodoxy, he stresses here a moral union in which the will is active and engaged in the service of God. Note the reference to God's will in the next sentence; and see also Theodore Parker, *A Sermon of the Delights of Piety,* in this volume.

[32]Isaiah.

sult of this virgin purity of soul and perfect obedience, the light of God shone down into the very deeps of his soul, bringing all of the Godhead which flesh can receive.[33] He would have us do the same; worship with nothing between us and God; act, think, feel, live, in perfect obedience to Him; and we never are *Christians* as he was the *Christ*, until we worship, as Jesus did, with no mediator, with nothing between us and the Father of all. He felt that God's word was in him; that he was one with God. He told what he saw—the Truth; he lived what he felt—a life of Love. The truth he brought to light must have been always the same before the eyes of all-seeing God, nineteen centuries before Christ, or nineteen centuries after him. A life supported by the principle and quickened by the sentiment of religion, if true to both, is always the same thing in Nazareth or New England. Now that divine man received these truths from God; was illumined more clearly by "the light that lighteneth every man";[34] combined or involved all the truths of Religion and Morality in his doctrine, and made them manifest in his life. Then his words and example passed into the world, and can no more perish than the stars be wiped out of the sky. The truths he taught; his doctrines respecting man and God; the relation between man and man, and man and God, with the duties that grow out of that relation, are always the same, and can never change till man ceases to be man, and creation vanishes into nothing. No; forms and opinions change and perish; but the Word of God cannot fail.[35] The form Religion takes, the doctrines wherewith she is girded, can never be the same in any two centuries or two men; for since the sum of religious doctrines is both the result and the measure of a man's total growth in wisdom, virtue, and piety, and since men will always differ in these respects, so religious *doctrines* and *forms* will always differ, always be transient, as Christianity goes forth and scatters the seed she bears in her hand.[36] But the *Christianity holy men feel in the heart*—the Christ that is born within us, is always the same thing to each soul that feels it. This differs only in degree and not in kind, from age to age and man to man; there is something in Christianity which no sect from the "Ebionites" to the "latter day saints" ever entirely overlooked.[37] This is that common Christianity, which burns in the hearts of pious men.

Real Christianity gives men new life. It is the growth and perfect action of the Holy Spirit God puts into the sons of men. It makes us outgrow any form, or any system of doctrines we have devised, and approach still closer to the truth. It would lead us to take what help we can find. It would make the Bible our servant, not our master. It would teach us to profit by the wisdom and piety of David and Solomon; but not to sin their sins, nor bow to their idols.[38]

---

[33]Note that Parker emphasizes the moral union of Christ and the Godhead, although—as the passage continues—he does think in terms of an immediate (unmediated) relationship with God. Seen from either of these perspectives, the relationship between Jesus and the Godhead is mystical but not ontological union, and it is a relationship to which human beings may aspire.

[34]Cf. John 1:9.

[35]Cf. Matt. 24:35 and Rom. 9:6, the cadences of which Parker evokes.

[36]Cf. the parable of the sower, Matt. 13:3-23.

[37]The Ebionites were a Jewish-Christian sect of the early Christian Era who taught the exclusive humanity of Jesus and stressed the necessity of adhering to the Mosaic Law. The Church of Jesus Christ of Latter-day Saints is the official name of the Mormon church. At the time of Parker's sermon, the Mormons were considered an extremist sect.

[38]David, although a great and generally pious

It would make us revere the holy words spoken by "godly men of old," but revere still more the word of God spoken through Conscience, Reason, and Faith, as the holiest of all. It would not make Christ the despot of the soul, but the brother of all men. It would not tell us, that even he had exhausted the fulness of God, so that He could create none greater; for with Him "all things are possible,"[39] and neither Old Testament or New Testament ever hints that creation exhausts the creator. Still less would it tell us, the wisdom, the piety, the love, the manly excellence of Jesus, was the result of miraculous agency alone, but, that it was won, like the excellence of humbler men, by faithful obedience to Him who gave his Son such ample heritage. It would point to him as our brother, who went before, like the good shepherd, to charm us with the music of his words, and with the beauty of his life to tempt us up the steeps of mortal toil, within the gate of Heaven. It would have us make the kingdom of God on earth, and enter more fittingly the kingdom on high. It would lead us to form Christ in the heart, on which Paul laid such stress, and work out our salvation by this.[40] For it is not so much by the Christ who lived so blameless and beautiful eighteen centuries ago, that we are saved directly, but by the Christ we form in our hearts and live out in our daily life, that we save ourselves, God working with us, both to will and to do.[41]

Compare the simpleness of Christianity, as Christ sets it forth on the Mount, with what is sometimes taught and accepted in that honored name; and what a difference. One is of God; one is of man. There is something in Christianity which sects have not reached; something that will not be won, we fear, by theological battles, or the quarrels of pious men; still we may rejoice that Christ is preached in any way. The Christianity of sects, of the pulpit, of society, is ephemeral—a transitory fly. It will pass off and be forgot. Some new form will take its place, suited to the aspect of the changing times. Each will represent something of truth; but no one the whole. It seems the whole race of man is needed to do justice to the whole of truth, as "the whole church, to preach the whole gospel."[42] Truth is entrusted for the time to a perishable Ark of human contrivance. Though often shipwrecked, she always comes safe to land, and is not changed by her mishap. That pure ideal Religion which Jesus saw on the mount of his vision,[43] and lived out in the lowly life of a Galilean peasant; which transforms his cross into an emblem of all that is holiest on earth; which makes sacred the ground he trod, and is dearest to the best of men, most true to what is truest in them, cannot pass away. Let men improve never so far in civilization, or soar never so high on the wings of Religion and Love, they can never outgo the flight of truth and Christianity. It will always be above them. It is as if we were to fly towards a Star, which becomes larger

---

king, committed adultery with Bathsheba, the wife of Uriah (2 Sam. 11:2-5), and then saw to it that Uriah was killed by having him placed in the fiercest line of fighting (2 Sam. 11:14-17). Solomon, the son of David by Bathsheba, ruled in a grand manner and married many foreign wives. In his old age, through their influence, he began to worship Gods and Goddesses other than the God of Israel (1 Kings 11:1-8).

[39] Matt. 19:26.

[40] See Gal. 4:19 and Phil. 2:12 (from which Parker omits the "fear and trembling").

[41] Cf. Phil. 2:13.

[42] I am unable to locate the source of the quotation.

[43] The mountain of the transfiguration. See the account in Matt. 17:1-8.

and more bright the nearer we approach, till we enter and are absorbed in its glory.

If we look carelessly on the ages that have gone by, or only on the surfaces of things as they come up before us, there is reason to fear; for we confound the truth of God with the word of man. So at a distance the cloud and the mountain seem the same. When the drift changes with the passing wind, an unpractised eye might fancy the mountain itself was gone. But the mountain stands to catch the clouds, to win the blessing they bear, and send it down to moisten the fainting violet, to form streams which gladden valley and meadow, and sweep on at last to the sea in deep channels, laden with fleets. Thus the forms of the church, the creeds of the sects, the conflicting opinions of teachers, float round the sides of the Christian mount, and swell and toss, and rise and fall, and dart their lightning, and roll their thunder, but they neither make nor mar the mount itself. Its lofty summit far transcends the tumult; knows nothing of the storm which roars below; but burns with rosy light at evening and at morn; gleams in the splendors of the midday sun; sees his light when the long shadows creep over plain and moorland, and all night long has its head in the heavens, and is visited by troops of stars which never set, nor veil their face to ought so pure and high.

Let then the Transient pass, fleet as it will, and may God send us some new manifestation of the Christian faith, that shall stir men's hearts as they were never stirred; some new Word, which shall teach us what we are, and renew us all in the image of God; some better life, that shall fulfil the Hebrew prophecy, and pour out the spirit of God on young men and maidens, and old men and children; which shall realize the Word of Christ, and give us the comforter, who shall reveal all needed things.[44] There are Simeons enough in the cottages and Churches of New England, plain men and pious women, who wait for the Consolation, and would die in gladness, if their expiring breath could stir quicker the wings that bear him on.[45] There are men enough, sick and "bowed down, in no wise able to lift up themselves," who would be healed could they kiss the hand of their Saviour, or touch but the hem of his garment; men who look up and are not fed, because they ask bread from heaven and water from the rock, not traditions or fancies, Jewish or heathen, or new or old; men enough who, with throbbing hearts, pray for the spirit of healing to come upon the waters, which other than angels have long kept in trouble; men enough who have lain long time sick of theology, nothing bettered by many physicians, and are now dead, too dead to bury their dead, who would come out of their graves at the glad tidings.[46] God send us a real religious life, which shall pluck blindness out of the heart, and make us better fathers, mothers, and children; a religious life, that shall go with us where we go, and make every home the house of God, every act acceptable as a prayer. We would work for this, and pray for it, though we wept tears of blood while we prayed.

---

[44]Parker's "Hebrew prophecy" is Joel 2:28. Parker follows Acts 2:16-18 in linking the prophecy of Joel to the Pentecostal outpouring of the Holy Spirit. For Christ's prediction of the Comforter, which Parker echoes, see John 14:26.

[45]A reference to Luke 2:25-32 in which Simeon, who awaited the "consolation of Israel" before his death, recognized the infant Jesus at the time of his presentation in the Temple.

[46]This passage is a veritable collage of scriptural allusions, including Luke 13:11; Mark 5:25-34; Exod. 16:3-15, 17:6; John 5:3-4, 11:1-44; Matt. 8:22.

Such, then, is the Transient, and such the Permanent in Christianity. What is of absolute value never changes; we may cling round it and grow to it forever. No one can say his notions shall stand. But we may all say, the Truth, as it is in Jesus, shall never pass away.[47] Yet there are always some even religious men, who do not see the permanent element, so they rely on the fleeting; and, what is also an evil, condemn others for not doing the same. They mistake a defence of the Truth for an attack upon the Holy of Holies; the removal of a theological error for the destruction of all religion. Already men of the same sect eye one another with suspicion, and lowering brows that indicate a storm, and, like children who have fallen out in their play, call hard names. Now, as always, there is a collision between these two elements. The question puts itself to each man, "Will you cling to what is perishing, or embrace what is eternal?" This question each must answer for himself.

My friends, if you receive the notions about Christianity, which chance to be current in your sect or church, solely because they are current, and thus accept the commandment of men instead of God's truth—there will always be enough to commend you for soundness of judgment, prudence, and good sense; enough to call you Christian for that reason. But if this is all you rely upon, alas for you. The ground will shake under your feet if you attempt to walk uprightly and like men. You will be afraid of every new opinion, lest it shake down your church; you will fear "lest if a fox go up, he will break down your stone wall."[48] The smallest contradiction in the New Testament or Old Testament; the least disagreement between the Law and the Gospel; any mistake of the Apostles, will weaken your faith. It shall be with you "as when a hungry man dreameth, and behold, he eateth; but he awaketh, and his soul is empty."[49]

If, on the other hand, you take the true Word of God, and live out this, nothing shall harm you. Men may mock, but their mouthfuls of wind shall be blown back upon their own face. If the master of the house were called Beelzebub, it matters little what name is given to the household.[50] The name Christian, given in mockery, will last till the world go down. He that loves God and man, and lives in accordance with that love, needs not fear what man can do to him. His Religion comes to him in his hour of sadness, it lays its hand on him when he has fallen among thieves, and raises him up, heals, and comforts him.[51] If he is crucified, he shall rise again. . . .

---

[47]For the truth in Jesus, cf. John 1:17. The rest of the line recalls the scriptural verse that forms the theme of the sermon (Luke 21:33).

[48]This is perhaps a reference to Ezek. 13:4-5 in which, in the King James Version, (foolish) prophets were compared to foxes in the deserts and Israel was chastised for not having "gone up into the gaps, neither made up the hedge for the house of Israel."

[49]See Isa. 29:8.

[50]Cf. Matt. 10:25, which Parker has altered in the service of his point.

[51]Religion, in Parker's metaphor, becomes the good Samaritan. For the parable, see Luke 10:30-37.

A DISCOURSE OF MATTERS PERTAINING TO RELIGION

After his sermon *The Transient and Permanent in Christianity,* Parker felt the sting of ostracism by his ministerial colleagues but also became aware of the interest that his ideas had generated. In this atmosphere, a delegation of prominent citizens invited him to give a course of lectures in Boston. Although at first he declined, Parker later agreed and in the winter of 1841-1842 presented five lectures—entitled "Discourses of Religion"—at the Masonic Temple. Thereafter, in 1842, with amplification and scholarly notes, he had the lectures published as his first book.

The plan of *A Discourse of Matters Pertaining to Religion* reflects its origins in the lecture series. More than 500 pages in its first edition, it is divided into five sections, or books, the first laying the groundwork and the remaining four relating the fundamental scheme to important issues in Christian theology and life. Parker argues for the presence of a religious element in human beings and, in a formulation that reflects the influence of Friedrich Schleiermacher, finds that element in a sense of dependence.[1] The sense of dependence implies, for Parker, the existence of its object; and the intuitive affirmation of God comes by an act of Reason prior to all inductive or deductive arguments. Given these fundamental realities, there are important ramifications for the doctrine of inspiration as well as for an understanding of Jesus, the Bible, and the church. In the four books that remain, Parker takes up these topics one by one, exploring them in light of his exposition of religion in general.

Parker's examination of inspiration below is excerpted from the second book of his work. In a careful and systematic consideration, he has pointed to the analogy between the relation of nature to God and the relation of humans to God. Immanent and active in nature, God is also immanent and active in the human world and so can influence individuals directly. With these ideas as background, Parker analyzes three different theories of inspiration. The first, or rationalistic, view (naturalism), he says, holds that all knowledge comes through the senses and that any notions of God are dependent on the input of the senses with modification through reasoning and reflection. The second, or antiration-

---

[1] Friedrich Schleiermacher built his theological system on a definition of piety (religion) as "the consciousness of being absolutely dependent" and the "feeling of absolute dependence." See Friedrich Schleiermacher, *The Christian Faith,* 2d ed., 4.1-2, 9.1. Parker, in a note to his own text, cites Schleiermacher; but in his usage Parker drops the qualifying adjective "absolute" and speaks of a "sense of dependence." See Theodore Parker, *A Discourse of Matters Pertaining to Religion,* 4th ed. (Boston: Little, Brown, 1856) 17-18; and, for a discussion of possible reasons for Parker's omission, see John Edward Dirks, *The Critical Theology of Theodore Parker* (1948; rpt., Westport CT: Greenwood Press, 1970) 82.

alistic, view (supernaturalism) teaches the same basic doctrine that all knowledge comes through the senses but adds a theory of miracles, viewing divine revelation as a series of interruptions in the natural scheme of things. Parker rejects both naturalism and supernaturalism and proposes instead the third, or natural-religious, view (spiritualism). In this teaching, based on the human sense of dependence, just as there is a supply for physical wants, there is a supply for the spiritual, and God is readily available to the soul.

Parker returns now to the theme of absolute religion that characterized his earlier work in the "Levi Blodgett Letter" and *The Transient and Permanent in Christianity*. In his third book he defines this absolute as the form of religion fitted exactly to the religious and moral constitution of human beings. Using the touchstone of absolute religion, Parker then expounds on issues relating to Jesus, the Bible, and the church. We pass over this material to rejoin him, finally, in excerpts from the conclusion of the work. In a clear application of his spirituality to the American present, Parker turns his discourse to a powerful indictment of slavery, ending where he conceives that all true religion does—in action.

Although, as John White Chadwick remarked, Parker "does not lend himself graciously to condensation or abstraction,"[2] the excerpts presented here are good examples of Parker's rhetoric of spirituality. They demonstrate clearly how he turns a theological exercise into personal affirmation that goes beyond argued rational statement. Without the literary conceits of Bronson Alcott or even the conscious grace of Ralph Waldo Emerson, Parker gives readers the force of his authenticity. These passages reveal the efforts of a man who tried in intellectual terms, as Chadwick wrote, "to communicate to others that which was to him so wonderfully sweet."[3]

---

[2]John White Chadwick, *Theodore Parker: Preacher and Reformer* (1900; rpt., St. Clair Shores MI: Scholarly Press, 1971) 198.

[3]Ibid., 199. The text that follows is from the fourth edition (Boston: Little, Brown, 1856) 201-18, 453-66. This was the final edition published by Parker in his lifetime and represents his mature editorial judgment. The American Unitarian Association edition (vol. 1; see the bibliography) seriously alters capitalization and changes some punctuation. The Cobbe edition (vol. 1; see the bibliography) is better, but in view of its general reputation for carelessness the Little, Brown text seems the wiser choice. Because of limitations of space, Parker's notes to the excerpts have not been included, although in some instances material from the notes has been cited or quoted.

(From) A DISCOURSE OF MATTERS PERTAINING TO RELIGION

CHAPTER VIII
THE NATURAL-RELIGIOUS VIEW, OR SPIRITUALISM

This theory teaches that there is a natural supply for spiritual as well as for corporeal wants; that there is a connection between God and the Soul, as between light and the eye, sound and the ear, food and the palate, truth and the intellect, beauty and the imagination; that as we follow an instinctive tendency, obey the body's law, get a natural supply for its wants, attain health and strength, the body's welfare; as we keep the law of the mind, and get a supply for its wants, attain wisdom and skill, the mind's welfare,—so if, following another instinctive tendency, we keep the law of the moral and religious faculties, we get a supply for their wants, moral and religious truth, obtain peace of conscience and rest for the soul, the highest moral and religious welfare. It teaches that the World is not nearer to our bodies than God to the soul; "for in him we live and move, and have our being."[1] As we have bodily senses to lay hold on Matter and supply bodily wants, through which we obtain, naturally, all needed material things; so we have spiritual faculties to lay hold on God, and supply spiritual wants; through them we obtain all needed spiritual things. As we observe the conditions of the Body, we have Nature on our side; as we observe the Law of the Soul we have God on our side. He imparts truth to all men who observe these conditions; we have direct access to Him, through Reason, Conscience, and the Religious Faculty, just as we have direct access to Nature, through the eye, the ear, or the hand. Through these channels, and by means of a law, certain, regular, and universal as gravitation, God inspires men, makes revelation of truth, for is not truth as much a phenomenon of God, as motion of Matter? Therefore if God be omnipresent and omniactive, this inspiration is no miracle, but a regular mode of God's action on conscious Spirit, as gravitation on unconscious Matter. It is not a rare condescension of God, but a universal uplifting of Man. To obtain a knowledge of duty, a man is not sent away, outside of himself to ancient documents, for the only rule of faith and practice; the Word, is very nigh him, even in his heart, and by this Word he is to try all documents whatever. Inspiration, like God's omnipresence, is not limited to the few writers claimed by the Jews, Christians, or Mahometans,[2] but is coëxtensive with the race. As God fills all Space, so all Spirit; as he influences and constrains unconscious and necessitated

---

[1] Acts 17:28.

[2] Parker here and elsewhere follows accepted Western practice of the period in designating Muslims with their prophet's name. Muslims themselves object because they believe such naming implies that they consider Muhammad divine.

Matter, so he inspires and helps free and conscious Man.

This theory does not make God limited, partial, or capricious. It exalts Man. While it honors the excellence of a religious genius, of a Moses or a Jesus, it does not pronounce their character monstrous, as the supernatural, nor fanatical, as the rationalistic theory; but natural, human, and beautiful, revealing the possibility of mankind. Prayer, whether voluntative or spontaneous, a word or a feeling, felt in gratitude or penitence, or joy, or resignation,—is not a soliloquy of the man, not a physiological function, nor an address to a deceased man; but a sally into the infinite spiritual world, whence we bring back light and truth. There are windows towards God, as towards the World. There is no intercessor, angel, mediator between Man and God; for Man can speak and God hear, each for himself. He requires no advocate to plead for men, who need not pray by attorney. Each man stands close to the omnipresent God; may feel his beautiful presence, and have familiar access to the All-Father; get truth at first hand from its Author. Wisdom, Righteousness, and Love, are the Spirit of God in the Soul of Man; wherever these are, and just in proportion to their power, there is inspiration from God. Thus God is not the author of confusion, but Concord; Faith, and Knowledge, and Revelation, and Reason tell the same tale, and so legitimate and confirm one another.[3]

God's action on Matter and on Man is perhaps the same thing to Him, though it appear differently modified to us. But it is plain from the nature of things, that there can be but one kind of Inspiration, as of Truth, Faith, or Love: it is the direct and intuitive perception of some truth, either of thought or of sentiment. There can be but one mode of Inspiration: it is the action of the Highest within the soul, the divine presence imparting light; this presence as Truth, Justice, Holiness, Love, infusing itself into the soul, giving it new life; the breathing in of the Deity; the in-come of God to the Soul, in the form of Truth through the Reason, of Right through the Conscience, of Love and Faith through the Affections and Religious Element. Is Inspiration confined to theological matters alone? Most surely not. Is Newton less inspired than Simon Peter?[4]

Now if the above views be true, there seems no ground for supposing, without historical proof, there are different kinds or modes of inspiration in different persons, nations, or ages, in Minos[5] or Moses, in Gentiles or Jews, in the first century or the last. If God be infinitely perfect, He does not change; then his modes of action

---

[3] Parker refers readers to the view of inspiration in one of Jonathan Edwards's sermons. The sermon "A Divine and Supernatural Light Immediately Imparted to the Soul by the Spirit of God, Shown to Be Both a Scriptural and Rational Doctrine" is most accessible in Clarence H. Faust and Thomas H. Johnson, eds., *Jonathan Edwards: Representative Selections*, American Century Series, rev. ed. (New York: Hill and Wang, 1962) 102-11.

[4] For Isaac Newton, see n. 13 to Ralph Waldo Emerson, "Self-Reliance." As part of a lengthy note to the passage, Parker observes that "no candid man will doubt that, humanly speaking, it was a more difficult thing to write the Principia than the Decalogue." See Theodore Parker, *A Discourse of Matters Pertaining to Religion*, 4th ed. (Boston: Little, Brown, 1856) 204.

[5] Minos was the legendary king of Crete whose wife, Pasiphae, gave birth by a white bull to the monster Minotaur. Minos was reputed the most kingly of human kings, holding his sceptor from Zeus (Hesiod, Fragment 103) and, in fact, his son. Minos was considered one of the three judges of the underworld.

are perfect and unchangeable. The laws of Mind, like those of Matter, remain immutable and not transcended. As God has left no age nor man destitute, by nature, of Reason, Conscience, Affection, Soul, so he leaves none destitute of inspiration. It is, therefore, the light of all our being; the background of all human faculties; the sole means by which we gain a knowledge of what is not seen and felt; the logical condition of all sensual knowledge; our highway to the world of Spirit. Man cannot, more than Matter, exist without God. Inspiration then, like vision, must be everywhere the same thing in kind; however it differs in degree, from race to race, from man to man. The degree of inspiration must depend on two things: first, on the natural ability, the particular intellectual, moral, and religious endowment, or genius, wherewith each man is furnished by God; and next, on the use each man makes of this endowment. In one word, it depends on the man's Quantity of Being, and his Quantity of Obedience. Now as men differ widely in their natural endowments, and much more widely in the use and development thereof, there must of course be various degrees of inspiration, from the lowest sinner up to the highest saint. All men are not by birth capable of the same degree of inspiration; and by culture, and acquired character, they are still less capable of it. A man of noble intellect, of deep, rich, benevolent affections, is by his endowments capable of more than one less gifted. He that perfectly keeps the soul's law, thus fulfilling the conditions of inspiration, has more than he who keeps it imperfectly; the former must receive all his soul can contain at that stage of his growth. Thus it depends on a man's own will, in great measure, to what extent he will be inspired. The man of humble gifts at first, by faithful obedience may attain a greater degree than one of larger outfit, who neglects his talent. The Apostles of the New Testament, and the true Saints of all countries, are proofs of this. Inspiration, then, is the consequence of a faithful use of our faculties. Each man is its subject; God its source; Truth its only test. But as truth appears in various modes to us, higher and lower, and may be superficially divided, according to our faculties, into truths of the Senses, of the Understanding, of Reason, of Conscience, of the Affections, and the Soul, so the perception of truth in the highest mode, that of Reason, Morals, Philanthropy, Religion, is the highest inspiration. He, then, that has the most of Wisdom, Goodness, Religion, the most of Truth, in the highest modes, is the most inspired.

Now universal infallible inspiration can of course only be the attendant and result of a perfect fulfilment of all the laws of mind, of the moral, affectional, and religious nature; and as each man's faculties are limited, it is not possible to men. A foolish man, as such, cannot be inspired to reveal Wisdom; nor a wicked man to reveal Virtue; nor an impious man to reveal Religion. Unto him that hath more is given. The poet reveals Poetry; the artist Art; the philosopher Science; the saint Religion. The greater, purer, loftier, more complete the character, so is the inspiration; for he that is true to Conscience, faithful to Reason, obedient to Religion, has not only the strength of his own Virtue, Wisdom, and Piety, but the whole strength of Omnipotence on his side; for Goodness, Truth, and Love, as we conceive them, are not one thing in Man, and another in God, but the same thing in each. Thus Man partakes the Divine Nature, as the Platonists, Christians, and Mystics call it. By these means the Soul of All flows into the man; what is private, personal, peculiar, ebbs off before that mighty influx from on high.[6] What is

---

[6]Cf. Ralph Waldo Emerson, "The Over-Soul."

universal, absolute, true, speaks out of his lips, in rude, homely utterance, it may be, or in words that burn and sparkle like the lightning's fiery flash.

This inspiration reveals itself in various forms, modified by the country, character, education, peculiarity of him who receives it, just as water takes the form and the color of the cup into which it flows, and must needs mingle with the impurities it chances to meet. . . . The Spirit inspires Dorcas to make coats and garments for the poor,[7] no less than Paul to preach the Gospel. As that bold man himself has said, "there are diversities of gifts, but the same spirit; diversities of operations, but the same God who worketh all in all."[8] In one man it may appear in the iron hardness of reasoning, which breaks through sophistry, and prejudice, the rubbish and diluvial drift of time. In another it is subdued and softened by the flame of affection; the hard iron of the man is melted and becomes a stream of persuasion, sparkling as it runs.

Inspiration does not destroy the man's freedom; that is left fetterless by obedience. It does not reduce all to one uniform standard, but Habbakuk speaks in his own way, and Hugh de St. Victor in his.[9] The man can obey or not obey; can quench the spirit, or feed it as he will. Thus Jonah flees from his duty; Calchas will not tell the truth till out of danger; Peter dissembles and lies.[10] Each of these men had schemes of his own, which he would carry out, God willing or not willing. But when the sincere man receives the truth of God into his soul, knowing it is God's truth, then it takes such a hold of him as nothing else can do. It makes the weak strong; the timid brave; men of slow tongue become full of power and persuasion. There is a new soul in the man, which takes him as it were by the hair of his head, and sets him down where the idea he wishes for demands. It takes the

---

[7]Dorcas (Tabitha), the woman raised from the dead by Peter in Acts 9:36-41, was described as a woman "full of good works and almsdeeds" (Acts 9:36). When Peter arrived, the widows "stood by him weeping, and shewing the coats and garments which Dorcas made" (Acts 9:39).

[8]See 1 Cor. 12:4 and 6. Parker, whose minor inaccuracies in transcription of the two verses suggest that he is recalling them from memory, also incorrectly identifies the source of the quotation as 1 Cor. 12:8 and following (see Parker, *Discourse of Religion,* 207).

[9]Habakkuk was one of the twelve Minor Prophets whose works appear in the Old Testament. His prophecy, probably written between 605 and 597 B.C., concerns an impending Chaldaean invasion of Judah, but ends with the prediction of the fall of the oppressor and an expression of joy in God. Hugh of St. Victor (1096?–1141), a theologian and mystic, was the most distinguished scholar at the monastery of St. Victor, Paris. Influenced by Platonic and Dionysian thought, he constructed a sacramental and symbolist theology in which all creatures reflect the divine and can lead the soul to contemplation. (For more on this *speculum* [mirror] theology, see n. 16 to Theodore Parker, *A Sermon of the Delights of Piety*.)

[10]Told by the Lord to preach rebuke to Nineveh because of its wickedness, the prophet Jonah went instead to Joppa and got aboard a ship heading for Tarshish, "from the presence of the LORD" (Jon. 1:1-3). Calchas, the priest whose gift of prophecy aided the Greeks in the Trojan War, asked and received from Achilles a promise of protection before he would exercise his powers, since Calchas thought that these powers would anger the king Agamemnon (Homer *Iliad* 1.68-91). (I am indebted to Cynthia King, my former colleague in the Classics Department at Wright State University, for directing me to the first book of *The Iliad*.) Peter, as predicted by Jesus, insisted three times that he did not know Christ and then, when a cock crowed, wept as he recalled Jesus' prophecy (Matt. 26:69-75).

man away from the hall of comfort, the society of his friends; makes him austere and lonely; cruel to himself, if need be; sleepless in his vigilance, unfaltering in his toil; never resting from his work. It takes the rose out of the cheek; turns the man in on himself, and gives him more of truth. Then, in a poetic fancy, the man sees visions; has wondrous revelations; every mountain thunders; God burns in every bush; flames out in the crimson cloud; speaks in the wind; descends with every dove; is All in All.[11] The Soul, deep-wrought in its intense struggle, gives outness to its thought, and on the trees and stars, the fields, the floods, the corn ripe for the sickle, on Men and Women it sees its burden writ. The Spirit within constrains the man. It is like wine that hath no vent. He is full of the God. While he muses the fire burns; his bosom will scarce hold his heart. He must speak or he dies, though the earth quake at his word.[12] Timid flesh may resist, and Moses say, I am of slow speech. What avails that? The Soul says: Go and I will be with thy mouth, to quicken thy tardy tongue.[13] . . . The Priest and the Levite war with the Prophet and do him to death. They brand his name with infamy; cast his unburied bones into the Gehenna of popular shame;[14] John the Baptist must leave his head in a charger;[15] Socrates die the death; Jesus be nailed to his cross; and Justin, John Huss, and Jerome of Prague, and millions of hearts stout as these and as full of God, must mix their last prayers, their admonition, and farewell blessing, with the crackling snap of fagots, the hiss of quivering flesh, the impotent tears of wife and child, and the mad roar of the exulting crowd.[16] Every path where mortal feet now tread secure, has been beaten out of the hard flint

---

[11]See Exod. 19:16, 3:2-4, 24:16-17; Matt. 3:16; 1 Cor. 15:28.

[12]Here Parker (*Discourse of Religion*, 208) refers readers to the famous passage from Lucan's *Civil War* in which Cato, asked by Labienus to consult the oracle of Jupiter Ammon at his temple in Libya concerning the civil war between Pompey and Caesar (49-48 B.C.), responds with deep feeling against the suggestion. Cato says that he received all permitted knowledge from the Creator at birth, and he draws his security not from any oracle but from the certainty of death. See Lucan *Civil War* 9.564-86. But Parker's description of the effect of the Spirit on a man "full of the God" is embellished far beyond the description in Lucan's epic poem—although the sense of a conviction that *must* be spoken is similar.

[13]See Exod. 4:10, 12.

---

[14]Gehenna, near Jerusalem, was from ancient times considered a place of pollution, known for the human sacrifices, especially to Moloch, that took place there. Later Jews regarded it as a site marked by divine retribution for grave sinners such as apostates, and in the New Testament Gehenna became the place of dread and final punishment after the Last Judgment.

[15]That is, a meat platter. See Matt. 14: 6-11.

[16]For the death of Socrates, see Plato *Phaedo* 116A-118; and for the crucifixion of Jesus, any one of the four Gospel accounts (Matt. 27:1-50; Mark 15:1-37; Luke 22:54-23:46; John 18:12-19:28). Justin (100?–165?), a Hellenistic philosopher who embraced Christianity and used his literary gifts in written apologies for the Christian faith, was scourged and beheaded under the Emperor Marcus Aurelius. John Huss (1369?–1415), the Bohemian religious reformer who in many ways anticipated Martin Luther, was excommunicated from the church and later given a safe-conduct for the Council of Constance; but when his trial opened, he was imprisoned and then burned to death. Jerome of Prague (1370?–1416), a second reformer from Bohemia, had studied with Huss and later spread the teachings of the English reformer John Wycliffe (1329?–1384) on the Continent. He repudiated his beliefs at the Council of Constance, but later retracted his words and followed Huss to the stake.

by prophets and holy men, who went before us, with bare and bleeding feet, to smooth the way for our reluctant tread. It is the blood of prophets that softens the Alpine rock. Their bones are scattered in all the high places of mankind. But God lays his burdens on no vulgar men. He never leaves their souls a prey. He paints Elysium[17] on their dungeon wall. In the populous chamber of their heart, the light of Faith shines bright and never dies. For such as are on the side of God there is no cause to fear.

The influence of God in Nature, in its mechanical, vital, or instinctive action, is beautiful. The shapely trees; the leaves that clothe them in loveliness; the corn and the cattle; the dew and the flowers; the bird, the insect, moss and stone, fire and water, and earth and air; the clear blue sky that folds the world in its soft embrace; the light which rides on swift pinions, enchanting all it touches, reposing harmless on an infant's eyelid, after its long passage from the other side of the universe,—all these are noble and beautiful; they admonish while they delight us, these silent counsellors and sovereign aids. But the inspiration of God in man, when faithfully obeyed, is nobler and far more beautiful. It is not the passive elegance of unconscious things which we see resulting from Man's voluntary obedience. That might well charm us in Nature; in Man we look for more. Here the beauty is intellectual, the beauty of Thought which comprehends the world and understands its laws; it is moral, the beauty of Virtue, which overcomes the world and lives by its own laws; it is religious and affectional, the beauty of Holiness and Love, which rises above the world and lives by the law of the Spirit of Life. A single good man, at one with God, makes the morning and evening sun seem little and very low. It is a higher mode of the divine Power that appears in him, self-conscious and self-restrained.

Now this it seems is the only kind of inspiration which is possible. It is coextensive with the faithful use of Man's natural powers. Men may call it miraculous, but nothing is more natural; or they may say, it is entirely human, for it is the result of Man's use of his faculties; but what is more divine than Wisdom, Justice, Benevolence, Piety? Are not these the points in which Man and God conjoin? If He is present and active in spirit—such must be the perfect result of the action. No doubt there is a mystery in it, as in sensation, in all the functions of Man. But what then? As a good man has said: "God worketh with us both to will and to do."[18] Mind, Conscience, the affections, and the Soul mediate between us and God, as the senses between us and matter. Is one more surprising than the other? Is the one to be condemned as spiritual mysticism or Pantheism? Then so is the other as material mysticism or Pantheism. Alas, we know but in part;[19] our knowledge is circumscribed by our ignorance.

Now it is the belief of all primitive nations that God inspires the wise, the good, the holy. Yes, that he works with Man in every noble work. No doubt their poor conceptions of God degraded the doctrine and ascribed to the Deity what came from their disobedience of his law.

The wisest and holiest men have spoken in the name of God. Minos, Moses,

---

[17]The paradise of classical literature.

[18]Cf. Phil. 2:13, which Parker has changed from second to first person.

[19]Cf. 1 Cor. 13:12, "Now I know in part."

Zoroaster, Confucius, Zaleucus, Numa,[20] Mahomet, profess to have received their doctrine straightway from Him. The sacred persons of all nations, from the Druid[21] to the Pope, refer back to his direct inspiration. From this source the Sibylline oracles, the responses at Delphi, the sacred books of all nations, the Vedas and the Bible, alike claim to proceed.[22] Pagans tell us no man was ever great without a divine afflatus falling upon him. Much falsity was mingled with the true doctrine, for that was imperfectly understood, and violence, and folly, and lies were thus ascribed to God. . . . No doubt there have been men of a high degree of inspiration, in all countries; the founders of the various religions of the world. But they have been limited in their gifts, and their use of them. The doctrine they taught had somewhat national, temporal, even personal, in it, and so was not the Absolute Religion.[23] No man is so great as human Nature, nor can one finite being feed forever all his brethren. So their doctrines were limited in extent and duration.

Now this inspiration is limited to no sect, age, or nation. It is wide as the world, and common as God. It is not given to a few men, in the infancy of mankind, to monopolize inspiration and bar God out of the soul. You and I are not born in the dotage and decay of the world. The stars are beautiful as in their prime; "the most ancient Heavens are fresh and strong;"[24] the bird merry as ever at its clear heart. God is still everywhere in nature, at the line, the pole, in a mountain or a moss. Wherever a heart beats with love; where Faith and Reason utter their oracles there also is God, as formerly in the heart of seers and prophets. Neither Gerizim[25] nor Jerusalem, nor the soil that Jesus blessed, so holy as the good man's heart; nothing so full of God. This

---

[20]For Zoroaster, see n. 30 to Ralph Waldo Emerson, Divinity School *Address*. Tradition holds that Zaleucus (fl. 650 B.C.?) of Locris, Italy, was the author of the earliest codification of law among the Greeks. Numa is Numa Pompilius, the legendary Roman king who followed after Romulus and, like Zaleucus, was a lawgiver.

[21]A Druid was a priest in the early Celtic religion of Ireland, Britain, and Gaul, and probably elsewhere—a member of an upper-class cadre in a religion of highly developed ritual with concerns centering on the natural world and its deities.

[22]Parker's "Sibylline oracles" may be the Sibylline books, traditionally ascribed to the inspired prophetess (sibyl) of Apollo who dwelled at the Greek Cumae, and consulted in Rome from the time of the republic during periods of calamity or distress. Or, as likely, Parker may be referring to the Sibylline Oracles, produced between 200 B.C. and A.D. 200 by Jewish writers with Christian additions. These oracles, claiming to be the inspired utterances of Greek sibyls, attained widespread popularity among Christians for their apocalyptic and messianic prophecies. For the oracle at Delphi, see n. 3 to Ralph Waldo Emerson, "The Problem"; and for the Vedas, see n. 25 to Ralph Waldo Emerson, *Nature*.

[23]In Parker's conclusion, excerpted in this volume, he makes it evident that he believes genuine (and not popular) Christianity can be identified with absolute religion. Hence, while Parker is surely radical in his understanding of the Christian message, at least in theory he would still rank Christianity above other religions.

[24]Cf. William Wordsworth, "Ode to Duty" (1804), l. 56.

[25]Gerizim—located in the Samaritan Hills near ancient Shechem—was the biblical mount of blessings (Deut. 11:29, 27:12; Josh. 8:33). In Samaritan tradition Gerizim was the sacred mountain where Abraham was said to have prepared to sacrifice his son Isaac (Gen. 22:1-14, although Gerizim is not named).

inspiration is not given to the learned alone, not to the great and wise, but to every faithful child of God. The world is close to the body; God closer to the soul, not only without but within, for the all-pervading current flows into each. The clear sky bends over each man, little or great; let him uncover his head, there is nothing between him and infinite space. So the ocean of God encircles all men; uncover the soul of its sensuality, selfishness, sin, there is nothing between it and God, who flows into the man, as light into the air. Certain as the open eye drinks in the light, do the pure in heart see God, and he that lives truly feels him as a presence not to be put by.[26]

But this is a doctrine of experience as much as of abstract reasoning. Every man who has ever prayed—prayed with the mind, prayed with the heart greatly and strong, knows the truth of this doctrine, welcomed by pious souls. There are hours, and they come to all men, when the hand of destiny seems heavy upon us; when the thought of time misspent; the pang of affection misplaced or ill-requited; the experience of man's worse nature and the sense of our own degradation, come over us. In the outward and inward trials, we know not which way to turn. The heart faints and is ready to perish. Then in the deep silence of the soul; when the man turns inward to God, light, comfort, peace dawn on him. His troubles—they are but a dew-drop on his sandal. His enmities or jealousies, hopes, fears, honors, disgraces, all the undeserved mishaps of life, are lost to the view; diminished, and then hid in the mists of the valley he has left behind and below him. Resolution comes over him with its vigorous wing; Truth is clear as noon; the soul in faith rushes to its God. The mystery is at an end.

It is no vulgar superstition to say men are inspired in such times. They are the seed-time of life. Then we live whole years through in a few moments, and afterwards, as we journey on in life, cold, and dusty, and travel-worn and faint, we look to that moment as a point of light; the remembrance of it comes over us like the music of our home heard in a distant land. Like Elisha in the fable, we go long years in the strength thereof.[27] It travels with us, a great wakening light; a pillar of fire in the darkness,[28] to guide us through the lonely pilgrimage of life. These hours of Inspiration, like the flower of the aloe-tree, may be rare, but are yet the celestial blossoming of Man; the result of the past, the prophecy of the future. They are not numerous to any man. Happy is he that has ten such in a year, yes, in a lifetime.

Now to many men, who have but once felt this—when Heaven lay about them, in their infancy, before the world was too much with them, and they laid waste their

---

[26]Cf. Emerson's "transparent eyeball" in *Nature*, ch.1; Matt. 5:8. In a note (*Discourse of Religion*, 215), Parker refers readers who may "like to settle questions by *authority*" to "the doctrine of the more spiritual writers of the Old and New Testaments, especially of John and Paul." "It seems to me," he adds, "this was the doctrine of Jesus himself."

[27]Parker may be conflating the biblical account of Elisha with an incident recorded concerning Elijah, his prophetic predecessor. Fleeing from the wrath of Jezebel, Elijah was provided by an angel with food in the wilderness for the forty days and forty nights of his journey (1 Kings 19:1-8). In a later episode, Elisha asked to inherit a double portion of Elijah's spirit (2 Kings 2:9) and thereafter saw Elijah in a whirlwind ascend into heaven. So Elisha took up the mantle of Elijah, and Elijah's spirit rested on him (2 Kings 2:10-15, 2:16-9:3, 13:14-21).

[28]Cf. Exod. 13:21.

powers, getting and spending,[29]—when they look back upon it, across the dreary gulf, where Honor, Virtue, Religion, have made shipwreck and perished with their youth, it seems visionary, a shadow, dream-like, unreal. They count it a phantom of their inexperience; the vision of a child's fancy, raw and unused to the world. Now they are wiser. They cease to believe in inspiration. They can only credit the saying of the priests, that long ago there were inspired men; but none now; that you and I must bow our faces to the dust, groping like the Blind-worm and the Beetle; not turn our eyes to the broad, free Heaven; that we cannot walk by the great central and celestial light which God made to guide all who come into the world, but only by the farthing-candle of tradition, poor and flickering light which we get of the priest, which casts strange and fearful shadows around us as we walk, that "leads to bewilder and dazzles to blind."[30] Alas for us if this be all!

But can it be so? Has Infinity laid aside its Omnipresence, retreating to some little corner of space? No. The grass grows green; the birds chirp as gaily; the sun shines as warm; the moon and the stars walk in their pure beauty, sublime as before; morning and evening have lost none of their loveliness; not a jewel has fallen from the diadem of night. God is still there; ever present in Matter, else it were not; else the serpent of Fate would coil him about the All of things; would crush it in his remorseless grasp, and the hour of ruin strike creation's knell.

Can it be then, as so many tell us, that God, transcending Time and Space, immanent in Matter, has forsaken Man; retreated from the Shekinah[31] in the Holy of Holies, to the court of the Gentiles; that now he will stretch forth no aid, but leave his tottering child to wander on, amid the palpable obscure, eyeless and fatherless, without a path, with no guide but his feeble brother's words and works; groping after God if haply he may find him; and learning, at last, that he is but a God afar off, to be approached only by mediators and attorneys, not face to face as before? Can it be that Thought shall fly through the Heaven, his pinion glittering in the ray of every star, burnished by a million suns, and then come drooping back, with ruffled plume and flagging wing, and eye which once looked undazzled on the sun, now spiritless and cold—come back to tell us God is no Father; that he veils his face and will not look upon his child; his erring child! No more can this be true. Conscience is still God-with-us; a Prayer is deep as ever of old; Reason as true; Religion as blest. Faith still remains the substance of things hoped for, the evidence of things not seen.[32] Love is yet mighty to cast out fear.[33] The Soul still searches the deeps of God; the pure in heart see him.[34] The substance of the Infinite is not yet exhausted, nor the well of Life drunk dry. The Father is near us as ever, else Reason were a traitor, Morality a hollow form, Religion a mockery, and Love a hideous lie. Now, as in the days of Adam, Moses, Jesus, he that is faithful to Reason, Conscience,

---

[29]Cf. William Wordsworth, "Ode: Intimations of Immortality from Recollections of Early Childhood," l. 66; and idem, "The world is too much with us," ll. 1-2, in *Miscellaneous Sonnets*.

[30]I am unable to locate the source of the quotation.

[31]The word *Shekinah* was used by ancient Jews to indicate the presence of God manifest in his dwelling among humankind.

[32]Cf. Heb. 11:1.

[33]Cf. 1 John 4:18.

[34]Cf. 1 Cor. 2:10; Matt. 5:8.

Heart and Soul, will, through them, receive inspiration to guide him through all his pilgrimage.

THE CONCLUSION

I. Of the Popular Theology

THEOLOGY is the science of Religion. It treats of Man, God, and the Relation between Man and God, with the duties which grow out of that relation. It is both queen and mother of all science; the loftiest and most ennobling of all the speculative pursuits of Man. But the popular theology of this day is no science at all, but a system of incoherent notions, woven together by scholastic logic, and resting on baseless assumptions. The pursuit thereof in the ecclesiastical method does not elevate. There is in it somewhat not holy. It is not studied as science, with no concern except for the truth of the conclusion. We wish to find the result as we conceived it to be; as Bishop Butler has said, "People habituate themselves to let things pass through their minds, rather than to think of them. Thus by use they become satisfied merely with seeing what is said, without going any further."[35] Our Theology has two great Idols, the BIBLE and CHRIST; by worshipping these, and not God, only, we lose much of the truth they both offer us. Our theology relies on assumptions, not ultimate facts; so it comes to no certain conclusions; weaves cobwebs, but no cloth.

The popular Theology rests on these main assumptions; the Divinity of the Churches, and the Divinity of the Bible. What is the value of each? It has been found convenient to assume both. Then it has several important aphorisms, which it makes use of as if they were established truths, to be employed as the maxims of geometry, and no more to be called in question. Amongst these are the following: Man under the light of nature is not capable of discovering the moral and religious truth needed for his moral and religious welfare; there must be a personal and miraculous mediator between each man and God; a life of blameless obedience to the law of Man's nature will not render us acceptable to God, and insure our well-being in the next life; we need a superhuman being to bear our sins, through whom alone we are saved; Jesus of Nazareth is that superhuman, and miraculous, and sin-reconciling mediator; the doctrine he taught is Revealed Religion, which differs essentially from Natural Religion; an external and contingent miracle is the only proof of an eternal and necessary truth in Morals or Religion; God formerly transcended the laws of Nature and made a miraculous revelation of some truth; he does not now inspire men as formerly. Each of these aphorisms is a gratuitous assumption, which has never been proved, and of course all the theological deductions made from the aphorisms, or resting on these two main assumptions, are without any real foundation. Theologians have assumed their facts, and then reasoned as if the fact were established, but the conclusion was an inference from a baseless assumption. Thus it accounts for nothing. . . .

II. Of the Popular Christianity

Coming away from the theology of our time, and looking at the public virtue, as revealed in our life, political, commercial, and social, and seeing things as they are, we must come to this conclusion; either Christianity—considered as the Absolute Religion—is false and utterly detestable,

---

[35]Parker has taken the lines, minus a phrase, from Joseph Butler's preface to his second edition (1729) of *Fifteen Sermons Preached at the Rolls Chapel*. See Joseph Butler, *The Works of Joseph Butler, D.C.L.*, ed. W. E. Gladstone (Oxford: Clarendon Press, 1896) 2:2.

or else modern society, in its basis and details, is wrong, very wrong. There is no third conclusion possible. Religion demands a divine life; society one mean and earthly. Religion says—its great practical maxim—We that are strong ought to bear the burdens of the weak; society, we that are strong must make the weak bear our burdens, and do this daily. The strong do not always compel the weak as heretofore, with a sword, nor violently bind them mainly in fetters of iron; they compel with an idea, and chain with manacles unseen, but felt. Men most eminent in defence of the popular theology are loudest in support of American Slavery.[36] . . .

In Absolute Religion we have what is wide as the East and the West; deep and high as the Nadir and Zenith; certain as Truth, and everlasting as God. But in our life we are heathens. He that fears God becomes a prey. To be religious, with us, in speech and action, a man must take his life in his hand, and be a lamb among the wolves.[37] Does our Christianity enter the counting-room; the senate house; the jail? Does it look on ignorance and poverty, seeking to root them out of the land? The religious doctrine of work and wages is a plain thing; he that wins the staple from the maternal earth; who expends strength, skill, taste, on that staple, making it more valuable; who aids men to be healthier, wiser, better, more holy, he does a service to the race; does the world's work. To get commodities won by others' sweat, by violence and the long arm, is Robbery, the ancient Roman way; to get them by cunning and the long head, is Trade, the modern Christian way. What say Reason and Jesus to that? No doubt the Christianity of the Pulpit is a poor thing. Words cannot utter its poverty; it is neither meat nor drink;[38] the text saves the sermon. But the Christianity of daily life, of the street, that is still worse, the whole Bible could not save it. The history of society is summed up in a word: Cain killed Abel;[39] that of real Religion also in a word: Christ died for his brother.

From ancient times we have received two priceless treasures: The Sunday, as a day of rest, social meeting, and religious instruction; and the institution of Preaching, whereby a living man is to speak on the deepest of subjects. But what have we made of them? Our Sabbath, what a weariness is it; what superstition defiles its sunny hours! And Preaching—what has it to do with life? Men graceless and ungifted make it handiwork; a sermon is the Hercules-pillar and *ultima Thule* of dulness.[40] The Popular Religion is unmanly and sneaking. It dares not look Reason in the

---

[36]In the South after 1830 almost the entire clerical establishment supported slavery. Since the Bible seemed to countenance slavery (see, for example, 1 Tim. 6:1), those who held to a strict and literal reading of Scripture as the inspired word of God (the "popular theology") found it relatively easy to argue the proslavery case. Significantly, the reference here to slavery does not appear in Parker's first edition.

[37]Cf. Luke 10:3.

[38]Cf. John 6:55.

[39]See Gen. 4:1-9.

[40]For the Pillars of Hercules, see n. 29 to Theodore Parker, *A Discourse of the Transient and Permanent in Christianity*. Thule, the ancient designation for the northernmost part of Europe, was an island discovered about 310 B.C.—perhaps modern-day Norway, Iceland, or the Shetland Islands. *Ultima Thule,* literally (Latin) "farthest Thule," became a metaphorical expression to suggest a place distant beyond imagining or the most far-reaching goal conceivable. Finally, for Parker's estimate of preaching, cf. Emerson, Divinity School *Address.*

face, but creeps behind tradition and only quotes. It has nothing new and living to say. To hear its talk one would think God was dead, or at best asleep. We have enough of Church-going, a remnant of our fathers' veneration, which might lead to great good; reverence still for the Sabbath, one of the best institutions the stream of time has brought us; we have still admiration for the name of Jesus. A soul so great and pure could not have lived in vain. But to call ourselves Christians after his kind of Religion, while we are keeping slaves and stoning prophets—may God forgive that mockery![41] Are men to serve God by lengthening the creed and shortening the commandments; making long prayers and devouring the weak;[42] by turning Reason out of doors and condemning such as will not believe our Theology, nor accept a priest's falsehood in God's name?

Religion is Life. Is our Life Religion? No man pretends it. No doubt there are good men in all Churches, and out of all Churches; there have been such in the hold of pirate-ships and robbers' dens. I know there are good men and pious women, and I would go leagues long to sit down at their blessed feet and kiss their garments' hem;[43] but what are the mass of us? Disciples of Absolute Religion? Christians after the fashion of Jesus of Nazareth? No! only Christians in tongue.[44] It is an imputed righteousness that we honor;[45] not ours, but borrowed of Tradition; an "historical Christianity" that was, but is no more. A man is a Christian if he goes to meeting in a fashionable place; pays his pew-tax; bows to the parson; believes with his sect; is good as other people. That is our religion; what is lived, what is preached; "like people, like priest," was never more true.[46]

It is not that we need new forms and symbols, or even the rejection of the old. Baptism and the Supper are still beautiful and comforting to many a soul. A spiritual man can put spirit upon these. To many they are still powerful auxiliaries. They commune with God now and then—through bread and wine, as others hold converse with Him forever, through the symbols of Nature, the winds that wake the "soft and soul-like sound" of the pine tree;[47] through the earliest violets of spring and the last leaf of autumn; through calm and storm, and stars and blooming trees and winter's snows and summer's sunshine. A religious man never lacks symbols of its own, elements of communion with God. What we want is the SOUL of Religion, Religion that thinks and works; its SIGN will take care of itself.

With us Religion is a nun; she sits, of week days, behind her black veil, in the meeting-house; her hands on her knees; making her creed more unreadable; damning "infidels" and "carnal Reason;" she only comes out in the streets of a Sunday, when the shops are shut, and temptation out of sight and the din of business is still as a

---

[41] Again, the reference to slavery (and the stoning of prophets) did not appear in Parker's first edition. As early as 1835 brickbats were thrown at a meeting at which the abolitionist minister Samuel J. May (1797–1871) was speaking, and the poet John Greenleaf Whittier (1807–1892), also an ardent abolitionist, was pelleted with stones.

[42] Cf. Mark 12:40.

[43] The metaphor conflates themes from Luke 10:39 and 7:38 and Matt. 9:20.

[44] Cf. 1 Cor. 13:1.

[45] Cf. Rom. 4:22; James 2:23.

[46] See Hos. 4:9.

[47] See the poem by Samuel Taylor Coleridge, "Hymn before Sun-rise, in the Vale of Chamouny," l. 61. I am indebted to Professor John Beer of Peterhouse, Cambridge, for the identification.

baby's sleep. All the week, nobody thinks of that joyless vestal. Meantime strong-handed Cupidity, with his legion of devils, goes up and down the earth, and presses Weakness, Ignorance, and Want into his service; sends Bibles to Africa on the deck of his ship, and Rum and Gunpowder in the hold, knowing that the Church he pays will pray for "the outward bound." He brings home, most Christian Cupidity, images of himself God has carved in ebony; to enslave and so Christianize and bless the sable son of Ethiopia! Verily we are a Christian people; zealous of good-works; drawing nigh unto God—with our lips![48] Lives there a savage tribe our sons have visited, that has not cause to curse and hate the name of Christians, who have plundered, polluted, slain, enslaved their children? Not one the wide world round, from the Mandans to the Malays.[49] If there were but half the Religion in all Christendom, that there is talk of it during a "Revival," in a village; at the baseness, political, commercial, social baseness daily done in the world, such a shout of indignation would go up from the four corners of earth, as should make the ears of Cupidity tingle again, and would hustle the oppressor out of creation.

The Poor, the Ignorant, the Weak, have we always with us, inasmuch as we do good unto them, we serve God; inasmuch as we do it not unto the least of them, we blaspheme God and cumber the ground we tread on.[50] Was there no meaning in that old word, "He that knew his Lord's will and did it not, shall be beaten with many stripes?"[51] They are already laid upon us. Religion meant something with Paul; something with Jesus; what does it mean with us? A divine life from infancy to age; divine all through? Oh, no; a cheaper thing than that; it means talk, creed-making, and creed-believing, and creed-defending. We Christians of the "nineteenth century," have many "inventions to save labor;" among them a process by which "a man is made as good a Christian in five minutes as in fifty years."[52] Behold Christianity made easy! Do men love Religion and its divine life, as Gain and Trade? Is it the great moving principle with us; something loved for itself; something to live by? Oh, no. Nobody pretends it.

No wonder "ministers cannot bear to hear the truth spoken;"[53] five minutes' talk will not weigh down fifty years' work, save in the Church's balance. The Christianity of the Churches stands at the corner of the street, and bellows till all rings again from Cape Sable to the Lake of the Woods,[54] if a single "heretic" lifts up his voice, though never so weak, in the obscurest corner of the earth; but Giant Sin may go through the land with his hideous rout; may ride roughshod over the poor, and burn the standing

---

[48]Cf. Titus 2:14; Matt. 15:8.

[49]The Mandans are a Siouan-speaking American Indian people who were found by the Lewis and Clark Expedition (1804) on the site of modern Mandan, North Dakota. The Malays dwell in the Malayan Peninsula in southeastern Asia and the huge island group, formerly known as the East Indies, adjacent to it.

[50]Cf. Mark 14:7 and Matt. 25:40, which Parker has modified to suit his purposes here.

[51]Cf. Luke 12:47. Parker is probably quoting from memory.

[52]Parker may be caricaturing a revival preacher here.

[53]I am unable to locate the source of the quotation.

[54]Parker is referring to Cape Sable Island, the southernmost place in Nova Scotia. His Lake of the Woods is a large region of land and lake in the pine-forest area of northern Minnesota and on into Manitoba and Ontario.

corn and poison the waters of the nation, and shake the very Church till the steeple rock—and there shall not a dog wag his tongue. When did the Christianity of the churches leave a heresy unscathed; when did it ever denounce a popular sin—the desolation of intemperance, our butchery of the Indians, the soul-destroying traffic in the flesh and blood of men "for whom Christ died?"[55] These things need no comment. They tell their own tale. Where is the infidelity of this age? Read the sectarian newspapers. We have a theological Religion to defend with tracts, sermons, ministers, and scandal. It needs all that to defend it.

No wonder young men, and young women too, of the most spiritual stamp, lose their reverence for the Church, or come into it only for a slumber, irresistible, profound, and strangely similar to death. What concord hath freedom with slavery? Talent goes to the world, not the churches. No wonder Unbelief scoffs in the public print, "beside what that grim wolf, with privy paw, daily devours apace, and nothing said;"[56] there is an unbelief, worse than the public scoffing, though more secret, which needs not be spoken of. No wonder the old cry is raised, "The Church in danger," as its crazy timbers sway to and fro if a strong man treads its floors. But what then? What is true never fails. Religion is permanent in the race; Christianity everlasting as God. These can never perish, through the treachery of their defenders, or the violence of their foes. We look round us, and all seems to change; what was solid last night, is fluid and passed off to-day; the theology of our fathers is unreadable; the doctrines of the middle-age "divines" is deceased like them. Shall our mountain stand? "Everywhere is instability and insecurity."[57] It is only men's heads that swim; not the stars that run round. The Soul of man remains the same; Absolute Religion does not change; God still speaks in Mind and Conscience, Heart and Soul; is still immanent in his children. We need no new forms; the old, Baptism and the Supper, are still beautiful to many a man, and speak blessed words of religious significance. Let them continue for such as need them. We want real Christianity, the absolute Religion, preached with faith and applied to life; Being Good and Doing Good. There is but one real Religion; we need only open our eyes to see that; only live it, in love to God, and love to Man, and we are blest of Him that liveth forever and ever.

---

[55]See Rom. 14:15. I am indebted to Anthony W. Shipps, librarian for English at the Indiana University Library, for this identification. The temperance movement, a lively force during these years, was one to which Parker lent his active support. With the Indian Removal of 1838, forcing some 17,000 Cherokee from their ancestral lands in the Southeast to be resettled (those who lived) in Indian Territory across the Mississippi, the awareness of white American outrages committed against the Indians must have been fresh in Parker's mind.

[56]Cf. John Milton, *Lycidas,* ll. 128-29.

[57]Parker also uses this quotation (source unknown) in *The Transient and Permanent in Christianity.* See the excerpts in this volume.

A SERMON OF THE DELIGHTS OF PIETY

This sermon belongs to the third and most-renowned period of Parker's ministry, when he preached from the Music Hall in Boston. Its text was first delivered there in 1853 and repeated in 1855 at the Yearly Meeting of the Progressive Friends held at Longwood, in Chester County, Pennsylvania. Later the Friends printed the sermon in their proceedings for that year, and it eventually appeared in both the Cobbe and American Unitarian Association editions of Parker's works.

A Sermon of the Delights of Piety is a particularly balanced statement of Parker's mature spirituality and, at first glance, seems a far cry from the harsher formulas and data-laden texts he adopted in his antislavery sermons. Yet closer scrutiny reveals that there is little discrepancy between the militant Parker who carried the banner of social reform and the quieter, more "devout" person who speaks here. Parker had, as Octavius B. Frothingham succinctly put it, a "two-fold power of blasting and of blessing"[1]; and, more important, his radical activism grew organically from his understanding of moral intuition. (Indeed, by this time he had identified the moral law as one of three primary human intuitions, along with God and immortality.) In the present sermon, Parker traces the movement from love and delight in God to love and delight in the material world and then in one's fellow human beings, with the last spilling over into action through moral endeavor. Although he only implies the scheme in these words, in his view sentiment and idea must yield, in human evolutionary progress, to the riper fruit of action.

If there is a social and religious evolutionism in Parker's understanding, there is also a piety that echoes Jonathan Edwards and his delight in the beauty of God.[2] Moreover, there are resonances of the mystical tradition, and it is surely no accident that Parker decided to preach his sermon before an audience of Quakers. The repudiation of mysticism that occurs in the early section—along with a rejection of superstition and fanaticism—is, if carefully read, a rejection of only one form of the mystical impulse, that of the quietistic sort. Such mysticism possesses, as Parker expresses it, "a great idea and a great sentiment" but not "a great will." By contrast, the piety he enjoins involves "the complete Will to serve God" alongside a true idea of him and "the Feeling of perfect Love." This piety expresses the deep *com*munion with God that is basic to much of Western mys-

---

[1]Octavius Brooks Frothingham, *Transcendentalism in New England: A History* (1876; rpt., Gloucester MA: Peter Smith, 1965) 309.

[2]For the best discussion of the beauty of God in the thought of Jonathan Edwards, see Roland A. Delattre, *Beauty and Sensibility in the Thought of Jonathan Edwards: An Essay in Aesthetics and Theological Ethics* (New Haven: Yale University Press, 1968). See also William A. Clebsch, "The Sensible Spirituality of Jonathan Edwards," in *American Religious Thought: A History*, Chicago History of American Religion (Chicago: University of Chicago Press, 1973) 11-56.

ticism, with its suspicion of total unitive consciousness. It is also a piety in which communion overflows into action, much as—to give a strong case—in the piety of the Spirit mystics of the sixteenth-century Radical Reformation, men who were impelled by their sense of the inward Spirit to take up the sword.[3]

Finally, there is a tenderness and even sentimentality in Parker's spirituality here. We meet in it the Father-Mother God who figured in his public prayers at the Music Hall, and we gain an insight into his sense of the divine compassion. It is perhaps only a coincidence in Parker's spiritual teaching, but the male-female deity is a great symbol of the mystical tradition, the compelling sign of the two-in-one. For Parker, at any rate, the Father-Mother provides the divine stamp of approval for a spirituality in which matter and "man" as well as devotion and action play their part.[4]

---

[3]The best general account of the Spirit mystics is Rufus M. Jones, *Spiritual Reformers in the Sixteenth and Seventeenth Centuries* (London: Macmillan, 1914). Thomas Muentzer (1488?–1525) is the classic case of a militant Spirit mystic; see the account of his life in Eric W. Gritsch, *Reformer without a Church* (Philadelphia: Fortress Press, 1967).

[4]For a discussion of the mystical significance of the male-female God (couched with reference to the Mormon tradition), see Catherine L. Albanese, "Mormonism and the Male-Female God: An Exploration in Active Mysticism," *Sunstone* 6:2 (March-April 1981): 54-55. The text that follows is that published in the *Proceedings of the Pennsylvania Yearly Meeting of Progressive Friends* (New York: John F. Trow, Printer, 1855) 41-54. Again, because of problems with both the American Unitarian Association and Cobbe editions (see the bibliography), it seemed wisest to use the edition of the text that appeared during Parker's lifetime—after his (second) delivery of the sermon, to the Progressive Friends. Two obvious typographical errors in this text have been corrected here (see par. 9, ll. 5-6, "Accordingly," and par. 18, l. 23, "their"), but spelling, capitalization, and punctuation remain Parker's own.

A SERMON

OF THE DELIGHTS OF PIETY

Delivered at the Opening Session of the Yearly Meeting of Progressive Friends, held at Longwood (near Kennett Square), Chester County, Pa., on First Day morning, 20th of Fifth month, 1855.

MY FRIENDS:—This morning I ask your attention to SOME THOUGHTS ON THE DELIGHTS OF PIETY.

WE are all connected with the World of Matter, with the World of Man, and with the World of God. In each of these spheres we have duties to do, rights to enjoy, which are consequent on the duties done. Our existence first, and next our welfare, depends on doing the duties and enjoying the rights. Thereof we may do much, and enjoy much, or do little and enjoy no more. The Quantity of our threefold happiness will depend on the amount of duties done, and of the rights enjoyed; but the Quality of the happiness is also largely within our control; and we may derive our habitual delight from any one of these three sources—the material, the human, and the Divine; or we may draw from all of these. We may content ourselves with the lowest quality of human delights, or we may reach up and get the highest and dearest quality thereof.

Religion, in its wide sense, includes man's relation to all three—to the World of Matter, the World of Man, and the World of God; it regulates a man's duties and rights, and consequent enjoyments, in all these three spheres of human consciousness—for Religion, in the large sense of that word, is the service of God with every limb of the body, with every faculty of the spirit, with every power we possess over matter or over man.

But there is a purely subjective and internal part of Religion, which is the heart of the whole of it, and whence its streams of life are sent forth! I mean Piety. At first, Piety includes directly only man's relation to the World of God, and controls and regulates the duties thereof, the rights therein, and the enjoyment therefrom. But the roots of all other human relations, of all the rest of religion, strike down into this, and are not only steadied and supported, but they are nourished thereby. So all of religion, in its concretest form, comes ultimately out of this internal element which I call piety.

By piety, I mean the normal action of the strictly religious faculty—the soul—considered as purely internal and subjective. It is our consciousness of God, our feeling of the world of God, and of all which belongs thereto.

This piety is a feeling which, at first, seems to be simple, and not capable of being analyzed and decomposed into other elements. But when you look at the matter a moment, you see it must be attended by the Idea of God, and, as a condition of complete and perfect piety, that idea must be the *true* idea—of God considered as Infinite Power, Infinite Wisdom, Infinite Justice, Infinite Holiness and Infinite Love—for if you think, as many do, that God is not perfect, but is an ugly devil, it is plain that your feeling towards God, and your internal experience of God, must be exactly the opposite of what it will be if you consider Him as infinitely perfect in power, wisdom, justice, affection, and holiness. In the state of complete and perfect piety, the spirit of man embraces into one unity of consciousness several elements, namely: First, an Idea of God, a conception of Him as Infinite; next, the Feeling of perfect Love for God, of perfect Trust in Him, and of Tranquillity and Rest with God; and, as a third thing, the complete Will to serve God by a way that corresponds to His nature, and to your nature likewise. Then, as a consequent result of these three things, there comes this—a supreme Delight and Rejoicing in God!

It seems to me that these things make up a complete and perfect piety, normal and total. So it includes a great Thought—the idea of Infinite God; a great Feeling—absolute love and trust in God; and a great Will—the resolution to serve Him by the means which He has provided. These things are separated by reflection, and may be analytically examined; for purposes of philosophy and understanding, it is necessary to do this; but for purposes of pure piety and religion it is not necessary; but we conceive of this as one simple thing not decomposable. This composite consciousness we call Piety, and define it commonly by its chief and largest element which enters thereinto, the Love of God—for the feeling of God implies the idea of Him as lovely, and leads unavoidably to the resolution to serve Him by the means that He has provided.

Now, this Piety is distinguished from three abnormal forms of action of the religious faculty.

It is distinguished, first, from Superstition; that is, the action of man's religious faculty combined with the false idea of God, namely: that He is not lovely and beautiful, but fearful and ugly. Accordingly the superstitious man thinks that God must be feared first of all; and the internal worship of God is accordingly, with that man, Fear, and nothing but fear. Then he thinks that outwardly God must be served by some mode of action that is deformed and ugly, and violates the native instincts of man; that He must be served by mutilation, in old times, of the body, and, in our times, of the spirit—now of the intellect, then of the conscience, then of the affections, or of the religious faculty itself. This is a very common idea of God and a very common idea of religion. God is thought to be ugly, and religion of course is ugly! Superstition is Fear before God, and when I speak of piety and its delights, I do not speak of superstition and any delight connected with that.

Then next, Piety is distinguished from Fanaticism. That is the action of the religious faculty attended by the idea that God is not only fearful and ugly, but that he is malignant also, and hates certain men. Accordingly, the notion follows that God is to be served by Cruelty to other men; by depriving them of rights which we value ourselves and do not wish to be deprived of. Fanaticism is Hate before God, as Superstition is Fear before him. Fanaticism is a far greater evil than Superstition, but in our day it is far less common. Examples of Fanaticism you find in the Spanish Catholics, who built the Inquisition, to persecute alike Catholic and Protestant, Mahometan and Jew; in the Protestants, who drove the fathers of New England and Pennsylvania from England and Holland to this the American wilderness; examples of it do you find in the Puritan fathers themselves, who persecuted Quakers and Baptists, and put them to death.[1] Nay, Quakers themselves, though sinning less than other Christians, have yet sometimes been guilty of this offence.[2]

This form of Piety is, thirdly, distinguished from Mysticism. Mysticism is the action of the religious element, attended by the idea that man is nothing, and that God designs to crush him down, not into non-resistance, but into mere passivity; that the religious action is all God asks for, and that is to be purely internal. So, according to the mystic, God is to be served not with all the faculties He has given, but only with this religious faculty, acting to produce emotions of reverence, trust, love, and the rest. Mysticism is sloth before God, as Superstition is Fear, and Fanaticism is Hate before God. It exists still in some of the Churches, which cultivate only emotions of reverence, of trust, of love, and the like, but never let the love of God come out of the heart in the shape of the love of man.

In Superstition and Fanaticism there is not a great Idea, but a mean and false one, not a great Sentiment of Love to God, but a mean one of Fear before Him, and of Hate towards men. But both of these do excite a great Will, and accordingly superstitious men, and still more fanatical men, have always been distinguished for an immensity of will. In Mysticism there may be a great idea and a great sentiment; there cannot be a great will. Complete and perfect Piety unites all three,—the great Thought—of the infinity of God; the great Feeling—of absolute love for Him; and the great Will—the resolution to serve Him.

I have thought it necessary at the outset to make this distinction between true Piety and Superstition, Fanaticism and Mysticism, for two reasons. First, the religious faculties in action are as liable to mistake and error as the hand or the foot, or any faculty that we possess; and we should therefore guard against mistakes which have already been made, and into which ourselves are liable to fall. Then, secondly, I make this distinction and dwell upon it because each of these three things is often set up as Piety itself, and a man is told he can have no real Piety in one Church without Superstition; in another, without Fanaticism; and in a third, without Mysticism.

---

[1] Quaker "Publishers of Truth" arrived in Boston in 1656 and were expelled; thereafter, the General Court of Massachusetts Bay speedily enacted a series of measures against them. But the Friends persisted in returning to Boston in a direct challenge to Massachusetts law, and between 1659 and 1661 four Quakers were hanged. Roger Williams (1603?–1683), the founder of the Baptist church in Rhode Island, was earlier expelled from the Massachusetts Bay Colony; his colleague and supporter in Rhode Island Dr. John Clarke had—with two additional Baptist believers—been fined, flogged, and jailed in Massachusetts Bay.

[2] Parker, in alluding to a Quaker fanaticism that deprived others of their rights, was probably referring to the period from the late seventeenth into the eighteenth century when a middle-class Society of Friends institutionalized the movement in a series of legalistic rules and forms (concerning dress, speech, and discipline), which in practice contradicted the original Quaker doctrine of the inner light. Parker may also have been recalling more recent Friends history in the nineteenth century, when doctrinal disputes over authority resulted in several ecclesiastical splits within Quakerism. For a readily accessible account, see Geoffrey Hubbard, *Quaker by Convincement* (Baltimore: Penguin Books, 1974) 33-58.

Now real Piety is the safeguard of all other forms of happiness; it is the greatest of human joys. Our delight in the world of God far transcends all our delight in the world of matter or in the world of man. If I am sure of God, sure of His infinite power, wisdom, justice, love and holiness, then I am sure of every thing else. I know that He has planned all things wisely, and will finally bring out all things well. Then I have a foundation on which I can build other things, and build securely. Then the universe—the world of matter and the world of man—looks permanent; I can rely on it. But without this certainty of God, I am not sure of any thing, uncertainty hedges me in on every side. Now I doubt, then I fear, next I despair; for if all things depend on chance, as the atheist says—the blind action of blind forces—then there is no security that any thing is planned wisely or will turn out well; and if they depend on an imperfect God, changeable, wilful, capricious, as the popular theology teaches, then there is the same lack of certainty, and I am not sure that God planned wisely or provides well. If they depend on an ugly and malignant God, as so many persons still teach, and some believe,—why, there is no hope; there is fear—yes, despair! In my nature there is a great demand for happiness, for immortality, for heaven. Logically, according to the light of nature, that demand, which comes of my constitution, implies the promise to pay; but if I am not sure of God, then I have only the promise to pay in my nature, but there is no Endorser on the note; there is no Security lodged as collateral for payment, and I cannot trust the promissor. This misfortune is a very deep one, and it is felt also in all the popular Churches that are about us.

Thus my consciousness of God colors all the other facts of consciousness; my world of matter and my world of man take their complexion from my world of God.

This is not theory alone, it is plain fact; you see examples of it every where. My consciousness of God comes into every relation that I have in life—to my business, to my pleasure, to my affection. Go into rigid Calvinistic Churches; look at the faces of men, listen to their prayers, read their hymns, see what passages are selected from the Bible; then go with these men to their homes, and see how their children are brought up in fear, in trembling, and with dread of God,—counting religion as something unnatural,—and see how a mistake in the idea of God comes out and colors all the man's life. Then, to go to the opposite extreme, take the atheistic party which has risen up in our times, read their books, and see them declare that the idea of immortality is the greatest curse left for mankind,—not the common idea, but any idea of immortality,—hear them proclaim that the great function of the philosopher is to re-establish the flesh in its domineering over the spirit of man, and you see how their absence of the idea of God colors their consciousness and penetrates into every relation.[3]

But if I know the Infinite God, then I know that He is perfect Cause and perfect Providence, and that He makes and administers the world of matter from perfect motives, of perfect material, for a perfect purpose, and as a perfect means thereto, and that the perfect motive is love, the desire to bless every thing that he makes; then I am sure that the end is foreseen and provided for, that all the action of the universe, whether right or wrong, of the great universe as a whole, and of you and me, the little atoms which compose it, of each na-

---

[3] For a useful discussion of American atheism and agnosticism in Parker's era, see James Turner, *Without God, Without Creed: The Origins of Unbelief in America* (Baltimore: Johns Hopkins University Press, 1985) 73-167.

tion, community, family, and individual—I am sure that all this has been foreseen and provided for, and so administered by the Infinite God that there shall be no absolute evil befalling the greatest genius or the humblest idiot; that no mote which peoples the sun's beams, that no mortal man, whether he be Judas the betrayer or Jesus the crucified, shall fail of never-ending bliss at last. Discipline there is, and must be, but only as means to the noblest and most joyous end.[4] This I say I am sure of, for it follows logically from the very idea of the Infinite Perfect God. Nay, the religious instinct anticipates induction,[5] and declares this with the spontaneous womanly logic of human nature itself.

Now to any man who thinks, this is a matter of the very utmost importance; to one who does not think, it is of no consequence at all. But if a man thinks, earnest and deep, this conclusion is the most vital. When I am satisfied on this point, then I can enjoy the world of matter and the world of man, and I can apply the human means which are in my power to the human end which I wish to bring to pass. I have then no doubt of the final result, no fear of that; I am concerned about to-day and to-morrow, about my doing my duty and my brother doing his; I am not at all concerned about eternity, and about God doing God's duty.

I confess I wonder that every man who lives does not have this confidence and enjoy it; it seems so natural, and is so instinctive also, and it squares so completely with the very highest science which man attains to; and then as you think about it, why, the infinite perfection of God springs into your eye at once,—so that I wonder that any man who thinks at all does not come to this conclusion, that God is infinitely perfect, perfect Cause and perfect Providence, and made all and superintends all from a perfect motive, for a perfect purpose, and as a perfect means, and will ultimately bless every thing that He has created. And yet, natural as this is, instinctively as we get at it, philosophical as it certainly is, there is no sect of Christians or un-Christians which has laid this down as its great corner stone. There is not, as I have said before, a single sect of men in this whole globe of land which declares, consistently the infinite perfection of God; even the Unitarians, in their "creed" recently promulgated, though they say they believe the absolute perfection of God, yet do not understand what it means, and do not venture to say that no man shall be everlastingly damned; they wish it may be so, they dare not think it surely is so.[6] That of course implies that

---

[4] Here Parker is preaching the Universalist doctrine that all will be saved. American Unitarianism and mature Universalism were virtually identical in belief; however, while Unitarian preachers avoided references to eternal damnation in their sermons, they did not make positive Universalism an important theme. Unitarianism and Universalism eventually did merge in 1961 to form the Unitarian Universalist Association.

[5] That is, inductive reasoning, or reasoning from particular cases to general truths. In traditional fashion, Parker associates such reasoning with maleness and links the "religious instinct" to "womanly logic" (intuition).

[6] In 1853 the Executive Committee of the American Unitarian Association, in a direct reaction to Parker and his radicalism, issued a lengthy "declaration of opinion" that, for all practical purposes, was a creed. Its essence was contained in one of three summary resolutions claiming that the action of the American Unitarian Association rested on divine authority as contained in the Gospel and as established on the miraculous intervention of God to redeem the human race. See *The Twenty-Eighth Re-*

they wish what God is not good enough to wish; and of course implies that they are better in their wishes than God in his wishes, and accordingly, that they are nearer to infinite perfection than God himself. And yet the Unitarians have less of this than any other sect in Christendom. You go into any other Church,—I will except in a large measure the Universalist Church,[7]—and you are frightened with the ghastly image of God which is gibbeted before you in horror.

But, in addition to this sense of permanent security, the Piety I speak of furnishes the highest, the deepest, and the most intimate delight which mortal man knows or can know here on the earth. I am very far from denying the value of other forms of delight, even of those which come wholly from the world of matter. Every sense has its function, and that function is attended with pleasure, with joy. All these natural and normal delights ought to be enjoyed by every man; it is a sullenness toward God not to rejoice and thus appreciate his beautiful world when we can. St. Bernard walked all day, six or seven hundred years ago, by the shores of the Lake of Geneva, with one of the most glorious prospects in the whole world before him—mountain, lake, river, clouds, gardens, every thing to bless the eye—and that monk never saw a thing all day long. He was thinking about the Trinity, and when he reached home some one spoke to him of the beauty he must have seen; and the austere, sour-hearted monk said he had seen nothing. He thought it was a merit, and his chroniclers record it in his praise.[8] It al-

---

port of the American Unitarian Association, with the Addresses at the Anniversary (Boston: American Unitarian Association, 1853); and, for a good discussion, William R. Hutchison, *The Transcendentalist Ministers: Church Reform in the New England Renaissance* (Boston: Beacon Press, 1965) 128-35.

[7]The old saw is that the Universalists thought God was too good to damn mankind and the Unitarians thought man was too good to be damned. The Universalist church owed its denominational beginnings to John Murray (1741–1815) who, in 1779, organized a Universalist congregation in Gloucester, Massachusetts. Others with similar views concerning universal salvation institutionalized their followings in Pennsylvania, New Jersey, New Hampshire, and in the city of Boston. The chief differences between Unitarians and Universalists became those of class status and spiritual style, the Unitarians being paragons of middle- and upper-class urban respectability and the Universalists poorer and simpler rural people.

[8]This story concerning Bernard of Clairvaux (1090–1153), founder of the Cistercian order, famed churchman, mystical theologian, antagonist of heterodoxy, and preacher of the Second Crusade, is contained in early lives of the saint and the popular medieval *Golden Legend* (*Legenda Aurea*) of Jacobus de Voragine, where Parker may have read it. But neither *The Golden Legend* nor the *Vita Prima* and *Vita Secunda* embellish the story of the "lake of Lausanne" as Parker does—or record that Bernard was thinking about the Trinity. Indeed, although Bernard was passionately involved in proceedings against Gilbert de la Porrée (1076–1154) at the Council of Reims (1148) for supposedly heretical views regarding the Trinity, contemplation of the Trinity was hardly the center of Bernardine spirituality. Parker's antipathy to his spiritual style may have suggested this depiction of Bernard the Trinitarian by the radical Unitarian. For the story, see Jacobus de Voragine, *The Golden Legend* (1255?), trans. Granger Ryan and Helmut Ripperger (New York: Longmans, Green, 1941) 472; J. P. Migne, *Patrologia Latina* 185, *Vita Prima* 3.2.4 (col. 306), and *Vita Secunda* 16.45 (col. 496). I am indebted to Bernard McGinn of the University of Chicago for helping me locate the sources of this anecdote and other material concerning Bernard in nn. 11 and 12 below.

ways seemed to me rather impious in the stout-hearted man, a proud fling at God, which Voltaire would have been ashamed of.[9] Mr. Beecher, with more wholesome piety, says in his poetic way, "The sweet-brier is country cousin to the rose."[10] There is a touch of religious recognition in all his love of Nature, which to me seems more truly pious than the proud flights and profound thoughts in the seven hundred and forty-four letters of St. Bernard,[11] and all his sharp and acute, and rather glorious sermons too. To me it always seemed irreverent in that great man that he boasted that he only eat his dinner, but never tasted it, as if his mouth were a mill and no more; it was certainly a fling at the good God, though the Saint meant it otherwise.[12] That great soul which made an ox's crib at Bethlehem holy ground, and the central point of many a pilgrimage, never flouted at God's world in that sort. He saw a lesson in the flight of the raven; in the savorless salt there was a sermon; there is a beatitude in the dry grass of the baking-kettle of a poor woman in the company going up to Jerusalem to hear him preach; and the great eyes which saw God so clearly dwelt with pleasure on the lilies of the valley, and said, "Suffer little children to come unto me and forbid them not."[13]

God made the world of matter exceeding beautiful, and meant it should be rejoiced in by these senses of ours: at these five doors what a world of loveliness comes in and brushes against the sides with its garment, and leaves the sign of God's

---

[9]Voltaire, or François-Marie Arouet (1694–1778), the French deist and philosopher of the Enlightenment, advocated a simple religion of nature with a morality derived from nature's law. He displayed, moreover, a lively interest in the environment as well as in various travels and voyages.

[10]Parker's quotation is a close paraphrase of lines from a sermon by Henry Ward Beecher: "But a wild-brier starts a genial feeling. It is the country cousin of the rose." See Henry Ward Beecher, "A Discourse of Flowers," in *Star Papers; or, Experiences of Art and Nature* (New York: J. C. Derby, 1855) 101. I am indebted to Conrad Wright of the Harvard Divinity School for suggesting the source of the quotation to me. The material that Beecher collected in *Star Papers* had appeared previously in the New York *Independent,* and Parker probably read an edition or account of Beecher's discourse earlier than that of 1855 (unless, of course, he revised the 1855 version of his own sermon to include the Beecher quotation after reading the discourse in *Star Papers*). Henry Ward Beecher (1813–1887) was no doubt the most-celebrated preacher of nineteenth-century America. The son of the well-known Lyman Beecher (1775–1863), he presided from 1847 at the Plymouth Congregational Church in Brooklyn, New York, as a liberal evangelical minister with a gift for popular and romantic style.

[11]How Parker arrived at the number 744 remains a mystery. Bernard was renowned for his epistolary habit, but the Migne edition—a reprinting of the edition of D. Joannis Mabillon, *S. Bernardi Opera Omnia* (1667)—contains 495 letters, including a series judged of doubtful authenticity, and the modern critical edition of Jean Leclercq includes 547 letters. See Migne, *Patrologia Latina* 182, and Bernard of Clairvaux, *Sancti Bernardi Opera,* ed. J. Leclercq (Rome: Editiones Cistercienses, 1957–) vols. 7 and 8.

[12]See Jacobus de Voragine, *Golden Legend,* 468, and Migne, *Patrologia Latina* 185, *Vita Prima* 1.4.20 (col. 238) and 1.7.33 (col. 247). There is probably a historical (and physical) basis for accounts of Bernard's insensitivity to the taste of things, since he is known to have suffered from a serious gastric disorder.

[13]Parker has considerably embellished the Gospel narratives in this passage. Cf. Luke 12:24, perhaps conflated with Matt. 6:26; Matt. 5:13, 6:28; Luke 18:16, 23:28-31.

presence on our doorposts and lintels.[14] Think you God made the world so fair, every flower a sister to a star, and did not mean men's eyes to see, and men's hearts to take a sacrament thereat? Our daily bread is a delight which begins in babyhood, and only ends when the Infinite Mother folds us to her arms and gives us the bread which does not perish in the using.[15] The humblest senses have their pleasure. The fly feeding on a berry crushed by accident on a bush, lets one a good way into the mystery of God's providence. The sights in Nature, the sounds thereof,—they are all means of delight. I am sometimes astonished to see how full of happiness a single day may be made, and that at the very cheapest rate, by the sights which come to the eye, and the sounds to the ear, at no cost but opening and listening. These are sacraments by which man communes with God.[16] It is surely churlish to turn away from the table which He spreads before every man. It is a painful sight and a sad thought to remember how many men there are in this Christian land of ours, and still more in others, who are debarred from this pleasure. We think it a sad thing, and it surely is, that every man should not have a Bible in his house, and power to read it; and great-hearted Christians make large sacrifices to put the words of Esaias, and Amos, and Paul, and Jesus into the hands of every man. But should we not also be ashamed that the greater, diviner Scriptures of God are not in every Christian's understanding, before his eye, and in his consciousness? That also is a reproach.

Then come those higher delights from the use of the senses and the mind better cultivated; from the Beauty of Nature and Art, and Common Life. I cannot now dwell at length on our delight in the world of men, only recall to your memory what every man experiences,—the joy of affection, of love in all its forms, connubial, parental, filial, related, friendly, and all that. It seems to me that ascetic preachers often undervalue this. And I remember to have heard a man, of a good deal of power too, declare that a man's love for his garden, his house, his ox, his horse, his wife, and his children, was all nonsense, and absurdity; nay, "a sin" in the eyes of God, and just as he loved these things the more, he loved God the less; and if he loved Him supremely, he would care for nothing but God! I do not value at a low rate the happiness which comes from the union of the world of matter with the world of man, from our industry, its process and its results. I wish every earnest man knew what satisfaction there is in putting your human nature upon material nature, and making it take your image—now a form of use, then a form of beauty. I do not think we make account enough of this, or set sufficient store by this

---

[14]Cf. Exod. 12:7 and Deut. 11:20.

[15]Cf. John 6:5-13, 31-35. Note that here the theme of God the Mother is introduced. As he develops the idea later in the sermon, Parker joins the theme of the divine Mother to that of the divine Father in a spirituality of tenderness and sentiment that perhaps has mystical overtones, as the introduction (in this volume) to the sermon suggests.

[16]Parker's reflections here and above in the text bring to mind medieval *speculum* (mirror) theology. A classic example is the *Itinerarium Mentis ad Deum* (*The Mind's Road to God*) of Bonaventura (1221-1274), in which the universe is seen as a mirror reflecting God. The sensible world is a ladder for ascent to God; and the soul begins its quest for God by contemplating his traces in nature. There is no evidence here, of course, that Parker had read Bonaventura or other medieval writers who shared his views. For Bonaventura's treatise, see Saint Bonaventura, *The Mind's Road to God,* trans. and ed. George Boas, The Library of Liberal Arts (Indianapolis: Bobbs-Merrill, 1953).

source of delight. To put human nature upon material nature, in the shape of a grand statue or a grand picture—every body thinks that is a great delight; but so it is to put human nature upon material nature in the form of a shoe, or a shirt, or a carriage, or a house, or a stocking, or a loaf of bread, or a nail, a farm, a garden, or a steam engine, or any thing you will; there is the same triumph of mind over matter in the one case as in the other, and when we get a little wiser we shall see what a real joy is in this, and at one end of society there will be no idleness and shirking, and at the other no drudgery and being crushed by excess of toil. God made man to live with matter, and made them both so that there should be good neighborhood between the two, and man should get delight from the contact. God made men so that they might live with each other, and get deeper, dearer, and truer delight from that intimacy. Do not think, I say, that I undervalue either of these forms of well-being. Let a man have all that he can get of both, and communicate in both kinds through this sacrament, with thankfulness of heart.[17] But I must say that I think the delight which comes from the world of God, the joys of Piety as a normal consciousness and experience of God, a great way surpass all these other delights I have just named. Yes, compared with the others, this is what womanhood is compared with girlhood or babyhood. I say this from my own experience; but it is not my experience alone,— every deep-hearted saint who rejoiced in the world of matter and the world of man, and then took fast hold on the world of God, tells us the same thing. What brave words have come to us from Jesus of Nazareth, from Paul of Tarsus, from Thomas à Kempis, and William Law, and Isaac Watts,[18] and that great stout-hearted man whose foot was so deep in the world of matter, whose hands went so largely into the world of men, and whose soul took hold so strongly on the world of God—Martin Luther: what brave words these have left us of their experience in the world of God. Nay, how full of the deepest and richest experience of this kind were the lives of the saints of the Quaker Church! What joy had Fox, and Nayler, and Penn, and Woolman, and Scott,[19] and all those pious

---

[17]That is, communicate through the world of matter and through the world of man, the two species (like bread and wine) of the sacrament of natural well-being.

[18]Thomas à Kempis (1380?–1471), or Thomas Hemerken, the most probable author of *The Imitation of Christ* (see n. 10 to Ralph Waldo Emerson, "The Over-Soul"), was a German Augustinian monk and priest, a gifted devotional writer, and a preacher and spiritual adviser sought by many in his day. William Law (1686–1761) was the English spiritual writer whose *Serious Call to a Devout and Holy Life* (1728), influenced by fourteenth-century German mystical writers, has been hailed as a post-Reformation spiritual classic, second only to John Bunyan's *Pilgrim's Progress*. In his later spiritual development, Law arrived at a conviction similar to the Quaker doctrine of the inner light. Isaac Watts (1674–1748), an English Nonconformist pastor, early retired from an active ministry but continued to devote himself to hymn writing and has been called the founder of English hymnody. Parker may have especially approved the Unitarian tendency of his later years.

[19]George Fox (1624–1691) recorded his religious experience in his well-known *Journal*, published posthumously (1694). Fox preached a mystical doctrine of the Holy Spirit, the inner light to guide a person from within. (See also n. 31 to Ralph Waldo Emerson, *Nature*.) James Nayler (1617?-1660), converted to the Quaker teaching of the inner light, was so compelling a figure that some thought of him as the Christ. Among his many tracts was *How Sin Is*

souls—women and men, who learned to lie low in the hand of God, and rejoice in their consciousness of Him and the visitations of the Eternal Love!

What exquisite delights they are which make up our experience and enjoyment of God! The aspect of beauty, in every form, is always a joy—in the shape and color of a blade of grass, a nut, a fly's wing, a pearl found in a muscle of a New Hampshire brook. What higher delight is there in the beauty of the human form! Beauty is made up of these four things—completeness as a whole, perfection of the parts, fitness of each part for its function, and correspondence with the faculties of man. These four things make up the statics and dynamics of beauty. Now, looked at with the intellectual and æsthetic part of human consciousness, God is absolute beauty. He is the beauty of being, self-existence; the beauty of power, almightiness; of intellect, all-knowingness; of conscience, all-righteousness; of affection, all-lovingness; of the soul, all-holiness; in a word, He is the Absolute, the altogether Beautiful. As men take delight in mere sensuous loveliness of beautiful things, a rose, a lily, a dewdrop, a sunset, a statue or a star, or man's or woman's handsome face, all heedless of their use—so a contemplative man may take rapturous joy in the absolute beauty of God—infinitely attractive to every spiritual faculty of man—having that fourfold loveliness, completeness as a whole, perfection of parts, fitness of function, and adaptation to our human nature.

But this beauty of God is a source of delight to few men; it cannot be relished without a great development of the religious faculty, and also a profound culture of the intellectual and æsthetic faculties; and besides, is somewhat too abstruse and transcendental in its nature for the busy world of men, who want something they can grasp with a thicker and hotter hand. I mention it, and dwell upon it, because it lies so much out of the way of common preaching, and because also it is real and lies within the reach of every man who can cultivate his understanding and his religious faculty. But I pass briefly over this, because to many men it seems as moonshine when compared with the clear daylight of other forms of religious joy.

Then there is this feeling of security and trust in God. I feel God not as a King, power alone, but as a Father; yea, as a Mother, and I know that God loves me with tenderest affection, that He loves every human soul with all of his infinite power, wisdom, justice, love and holiness.[20] Now it is a delight to be beloved by any one; the

---

Strengthened and How It Is Overcome (1657). William Penn (1644–1718), who founded Pennsylvania Colony, was prolific in his written testimony to Quakerism, with nearly 100 pamphlets and books appearing while he was still alive. During a period of imprisonment in the Tower of London, he produced in 1669 the classic of Quaker religious practice *No Cross, No Crown*. John Woolman (1720–1772) was an American Quaker from New Jersey who, while still in his twenties, began an ardent and lifelong campaign against slavery. His *Journal,* published posthumously in 1774, recounts his active work and quietistic spiritual experience from 1756. Parker's "Scott" is most probably Job Scott (1751–1793), a Rhode Island Quaker who, like Woolman, was a quietist and yet actively involved in social-reform effort. His *Journal of the Life, Travels and Gospel Labours of That Faithful Servant and Minister of Christ Job Scott* (1797) offers a personal record of his spiritual life and a commentary on matters of religious concern.

[20]Here Parker develops his theme of God as both Father and Mother, a theme that has been adumbrated earlier in the sermon (see n. 15 above).

affection which a cat, or dog, or horse, or ox feels for a man is a delight to that man; to know that some human being holds you in esteem, in affection, watches for you and watches over you, and takes delight in your well-being—why, what a joy that is! Everybody knows it. I speak not now of the active affection which loves back again, but of the passivity of spirit which only joys in being loved by other men. Yet in receiving such love from mortal man there is often this hindrance—the man often wishes it to be exclusive to him alone; for he thinks his friend has so little affection that he wants it all, and would break other men's pitchers which are let down to the finite, private well of his friend's affection; so there is a strife between the herdsmen of Abraham and of Lot, a quarrel which troubles the well, and breaks the pitchers, and muddies the water itself.[21] But as the affection of the infinite God is boundless, not to be exhausted, as from the very nature of God He must have infinite love, so no man need be jealous of Him and fearful we shall not get our share, because publicans and sinners enter into the joy of their Lord.[22] When the elder brother comes near the house of the Infinite God, he hears the music and dancing, and is not wroth, but falls on his brother's neck and kisses him, and finds himself in the finding of the lost, and lives anew in the living of the dead.[23]

I know the delight of being loved, for I have sunned myself in the affection of father and mother, and brother and sister, and wife and relative, and if anybody knows the beauty and blessedness of friendship, I think that I do, for I have sounded its depths and tasted its joy. But the love that I have received from mortal men, from father, and mother, wife and relative, and friend—it is but little, nay, it is nothing, compared to the still and calm delight which I feel from consciousness of being loved by the Infinite God. My mortal friends love me, perhaps, through their weakness; they are not good enough to love a better man; God loves me for his strength, for his infinity. They are exclusive, perhaps loving others the less from loving me the more; but God includes all, the heathen, the Hebrew, the Mahometan, the Atheist and the Christian; nay, Cain, Iscariot, the kidnapper, are all folded in the arms of the Infinite Mother, who will not suffer absolute evil to come to the least or the worst of these, but so tempers the mechanism of humanity that all shall come to the table of blessedness at last![24] Death itself is no limit. God's love is eternal also, providing retribution for all I do; but pain is medicine. What is not delight is discipline, the avenue to nobler joy.

Feeling a consciousness of this Divine love for me, knowing that it is joined with infinite power, wisdom, justice and holiness, that it is perfect Cause to plan and perfect Providence to administer—why, all the sorrows and sufferings of life, how easily they are borne! I writhe in mortal

---

[21] The account of the strife between the herdsmen of Abraham and those of Lot is recorded in Gen. 13:1-12, but the issue of the use of a well as the reason for the quarrel is present only by implication. Parker may be confusing the incident with that recounted in Gen. 26:17-22, in which strife develops between the herdsmen of Isaac and those of the land of Gerar concerning three wells that were dug. The wells in this episode were the same that had been dug during the lifetime of Isaac's father, Abraham, and then stopped after his death.

[22] Cf. Matt. 9:11 and 25:21 (23), which Parker has conflated.

[23] For the parable of the prodigal son, see Luke 15:11-32. Parker has altered the account to suit his purposes.

[24] Parker again affirms the Universalist teaching of salvation for all.

agony, but my Father's arms are round me—the agony is still. I am not recognized by the world, my little merit is not acknowledged, not appreciated, it is so small; but God recognizes and appreciates it, and smiles down on the little good I do, and it is not lost. Nobody feels for me or with me; but the great God sympathizes with me. I have his infinite power and his infinite love heeding me every moment. I am tormented by the loss of friends—father, mother, wife, child; my dearest of the nearest are gone; but the Infinite Mother folds me to her bosom, and her tenderness wipes the tears from my eyes; I fall asleep in the Infinite Arms, remembering that no harm has happened to those who are taken, and there is a place in store for the one that is left. I know that no evils are absolute and lasting; nay, before the creation of the world, all the errors, the mistakes and the sins which you, or I, or the human race, would commit, were foreseen by the Infinite Father, were provided for long before they came to pass, and shall, all of them, be rounded off at last into a whole of infinite bliss, infinite love towards each child that he has created, towards Cain, towards Iscariot, the kidnapper, and the victims of a world of cruelty and wrong.

I can look on the world's suffering and sorrow, on the wars and slavery, the poverty, drunkenness and crime, the dreadful want which pines in cities, the vice we pile up in jails to perish in malignant rot, the more vicious vice which builds those jails; I can look on all the sad heart-break of mankind, and I know it will be all overruled by the Creator in His machinery of the world so that infinite good shall come at last. Of all the world's suffering and transgression, none came by superhuman chance, and so is a world accident; none by superhuman malignity, and is a world curse. The history of man is the calculated consequence of the faculties God put in man, known beforehand to the Infinite Cause, provided by the Infinite Providence, and made to serve his purpose of eternal love.

Then there comes the rising up of all my spirit in one great act of gratitude, reverence and trust, one great feeling of love to God, and this fills me with unbounded delight. Passive to receive God's love, I am active to return it with love again.[25] I just now spoke of the delight of being loved by mortal men! and then of the intimate joy of conscious love received from God! But as our highest joy is of action, and not merely of receiving, as it is more blessed to give affection than to receive even that, so the joy which a man feels from his conscious love of the Infinite God far surpasses even the delight which he has from being loved by the Father.

My affection for my earthly friends is checked by the limitations of their character; thus far and no farther is the rule:

> "For the fondest, the fairest, the truest that met,
> Man still found the need to forgive and forget."[26]

But as God is infinitely perfect, absolutely loveable, so there is no limit without to my power of loving Him, and my affection grows with the love of God which it feeds upon, and becomes greater, wider, deeper, nicer in its refinement, and brings a greater and greater accession of delight.

Then I have in God the sense of security, of permanent welfare which it brings; this imparts a steadiness to the action of all

---

[25]Here and in what follows Parker returns to the theme of the human activity in relation to God that he associates with true piety (to be distinguished, in his view, from the quietism of mysticism).

[26]I am unable to locate the source of the quotation.

the faculties; it gives energy, vigor, quickness, to the intellect, strengthens the will, sharpens the conscience, widens the heart, blesses with its own beatitude every faculty that I possess. My delight in God increases each special joy in the things of matter or in the persons of men; I love the world the more, because I know it is God's world, even as a dry leaf, given by a lover, is dearer than all pearls from whoso loves us not! I love my proper business better, by fireside and street-side, in market and in shop, because I know that it is the way of serving God, bringing about His divine end by my human means. I love my brothers and sisters, my father and mother, wife and child, far more, because my heart is filled with reverence and love to God.

In the sunshine of life, every human joy is made more joyous by this delight in God. When these fail, when health is gone, when my eye is dim, when my estate slips through my hands, and my good name becomes a dishonor, when death takes the nearest and dearest of my friends, then my consciousness of God comes out, a great light in my darkness, and a very present help in my time of trouble. In wet weather in the spring, every hill abounds with water, the brooks run over in their affluence, and all the hill-sides and plains are green; but, when week after week there is no dew nor rain, and month after month the heavens impart no germinative moisture to the ground, the little streams dry up, the surface springs are choked with heat and dust, then we go to the well, that is bored into the primeval rock, embosomed in the mountain, and drink cool sweet water that never fails.[27]

This delight is for you and me, and every one of us; and when we have this pure abstract enjoyment, which comes of Piety in our soul, then the love of God will run over into morality, into love of men in every form! and, in addition to these dear delights of Piety, we shall have the joys of philanthropy, of justice, of wisdom, and of all human consciousness in its thousand forms!

---

[27] Although Parker is surely not repeating explicit biblical texts here, the passage has scriptural overtones, evoking Exod. 17:6 and John 4:14.

Part IV

HENRY DAVID THOREAU

INTRODUCTION

When Henry Seidel Canby wrote his appreciative biography of Henry David Thoreau close to fifty years ago, he remarked that there were "a half-dozen possible biographies of Thoreau, depending upon the view the biographer takes of his subject."[1] Canby was right; and Thoreau—had he conferred with his biographer—no doubt would have agreed. "Time is but the stream I go a-fishing in," he confided in *Walden,* the book that was later to establish a reputation as his masterpiece.[2] If so, Thoreau had drawn from the water samples of many species, each one for a time engaging his imagination and energy.

Descended from French and Scotch ancestors, David Henry Thoreau (he later reversed the order of his given names) was born at Concord, Massachusetts, in 1817, the third of the four children of John Thoreau and Cynthia Dunbar. After some years of moving with his family he grew up in Concord, supported by the pencil-making business established by his father. By 1833 he matriculated at Harvard, and in 1837 he graduated as an honor student.

Then, when young Thoreau turned to teaching at the Concord School, he found himself in a head-on confrontation with the school committee over his refusal to administer corporal punishment. He resigned. So began a lifelong pattern in which, for stretches of time, Thoreau employed himself in one activity or another—ready to move to something else, but growing in a commitment to writing. For several years (1838-1841) he taught in a private school that he had established, at first alone and later with his brother, John. Then (and likewise in 1847), he lived with the Emerson family, making himself valuable as a general handyman and friend. Again, with Emerson arranging affairs, Thoreau spent six months tutoring the sons of Emerson's brother William on Staten Island, meanwhile cultivating acquaintanceships with New York literary lights and especially Horace Greeley, editor of the *New-York Tribune.*

Unhappy away from home, Thoreau returned to Concord and set to work in the family pencil factory. Earlier he had already initiated a series of improvements in the pencil-manufacturing process, and—with pencils that could compete in quality with German-made ones—he had in large measure been responsible for the growing prosperity of the family business. Now he once more found ways to improve the industrial process and became totally absorbed. When the finer graphite Thoreau's improvements had produced was found ideal for new electrotype printing, the Thoreaus gave up pencil making altogether, and their son helped with the burdens brought by greater success. From 1858, as his father's health failed and he finally died, the younger Thoreau gradually took over the

---

[1] Henry Seidel Canby, *Thoreau* (Boston: Houghton Mifflin, Riverside Press, 1939) xvi.
[2] See, in this volume, Henry David Thoreau, *Walden,* ch.2.

details of the graphite business until his own decline and early death in 1862 (no doubt hastened by the graphite dust that could only have aggravated his tubercular tendency).[3]

But the sometime pencil and graphite maker also practiced professional surveying; lectured in Concord and elsewhere; went on various hiking and boating excursions; and, from 1845 to 1847, spent more than two years living on Emerson's Concord property at Walden Pond. Thoreau's *Week on the Concord and Merrimack Rivers* and, to a large extent, *Walden* were products of these years. Earlier, from 1837, he had begun to keep a journal. As the years passed, Thoreau's journal writing became a consuming activity, and into his later notebooks he poured seemingly endless information concerning the natural species he observed. Intrigued, too, with American Indian life and remains, by 1860 he filled some eleven or twelve notebooks on Indian materials.

Thoreau had one brief romance as a young man (the girl turned him down when he proposed marriage), but he remained a bachelor. At the same time family and domesticity were values for him, and—although he sought and protected his times of solitude—he maintained enduring relationships with family and friends. Known for his blunt speech and acerbic wit, he kept a sensitive spirit and loyal heart. It is against this background that his much-vaunted renunciations of society must be set, for they were never renunciations of a community of kin and friendship but, instead, of the institutional structures that Thoreau believed were oppressive to the individual spirit.

Thus, when he found his name added to tax rolls used to assess support for public worship in Massachusetts, Thoreau bridled—and like others at the time—signed off. As the introduction noted, his well-remembered night in jail climaxed a period (of several years) during which he disdained to pay his poll tax. (The chance for later and similar episodes was avoided by the prepayment of his tax by an aunt or others.) After John Brown and his party raided the United States arsenal at Harpers Ferry, West Virginia, in 1859, the impassioned Thoreau came to Brown's defense publicly. In Brown, he saw principle triumphant over every obstacle, willing to engage in any sacrifice to realize itself. And Thoreau's antislavery, fed by the example of various members of his family and his own compassion for escaped slaves (he was a "conductor" on the Underground Railroad to Canada), was also fed by his outrage at the encroachment of the state on the lives of private individuals.

Transcendentalism had grown naturally for Thoreau. In his childhood his mother had taken the family on long walks to admire nature, and he also loved to roam in the country around Concord alone. As early as 1835, on leave from Harvard College, he had met and talked with Orestes A. Brownson, who later participated in initial meetings of the Transcendental Club. Then, when Emerson's *Nature* appeared, the book became for Thoreau a scripture and guide. Later, through Emerson, Thoreau was introduced to prominent Transcendentalists and under Emerson's sponsorship published his early literary contributions in *The Dial*, even editing the April 1843 number of the journal. In fact, some thought that the younger man was imitating Emerson, and the suspicion grew to be an embarrassment to Thoreau. Gradually, too, he found his own stride as a writer, living out

---

[3]For useful discussions of Thoreau's involvement with his family's business, see Walter Harding, *The Days of Henry Thoreau* (New York: Alfred A. Knopf, 1965) 56-57, 157-59, 261-63, 396-97, 409.

in word and work the Transcendental ethic of self-culture and becoming increasingly radical in his embrace of its teaching. Like Emerson, he spurned the planned communities of his friends at Brook Farm and Fruitlands; and like him, too, he found himself drawn to Eastern literature, pursuing his interest in Oriental spirituality even more than Emerson.

Moreover, as lover of nature and cultivator of the individual spirit, Thoreau learned especially to cherish the particular. In his mature years he became a taxonomist of Transcendental nature, celebrating each species and delighting in catalogs of appearance, quality, and characteristic. His friend Emerson tended to see the forest, while Thoreau, more and more, saw the separate trees. The two grew apart from the late 1840s, and their relationship became strained. But Thoreau still came to Emerson's assistance in practical needs, and Emerson was the one who eulogized Thoreau at his funeral (although the "eulogy," to be sure, was somewhat critical).[4]

Thoreau's literary legacy extends to twenty volumes in the standard Walden edition of 1906, which contains most (but not all) of his works and includes fourteen volumes of journals.[5] His first book, *A Week on the Concord and Merrimack Rivers,* appeared in 1849, as did his famous essay "Civil Disobedience"—under the title "Resistance to Civil Government" in Elizabeth Palmer Peabody's *Aesthetic Papers*. Five years later, in 1854, *Walden* was published. Beyond these major contributions, there were pieces (mostly essays) in various periodicals, including Thoreau's review essay "The Natural History of Massachusetts," which appeared in *The Dial* in 1842, and some poetry, which was also printed in the Transcendental journal.

Later, posthumous publications quickly expanded the list of volumes by Thoreau. The year after his death a collection of essays was published under the title *Excursions,* mostly a series of explorations of his Concord surroundings. Then, (William) Ellery Channing—the man who had been Thoreau's closest friend and companion on his excursions—with Thoreau's sister Sophia and others, edited his travel writings to produce *The Maine Woods* (1864), *Cape Cod* (1865), and *A Yankee in Canada, with Anti-Slavery and Reform Papers* (1866). Meanwhile, Emerson edited a collection of *Letters to Various Persons* that was published in 1865.

Records of the spirit, Thoreau's writings were the records, too, of a man who—like a Transcendental cat—led many lives. Chronicler of the natural world in and near Concord, family member and friend, resister of the state, master of the simple life, ascetic, contemplative, prophet, and sensuous adventurer on untried traveling paths and waterways, Thoreau called himself in his journal "a mystic, a transcendentalist, and a natural philosopher to boot."[6] He was, indeed, all of these; and the lesson that emerges from his

---

[4] For Emerson's eulogy, see Ralph Waldo Emerson, *Thoreau,* in *The Complete Works of Ralph Waldo Emerson,* ed. Edward Waldo Emerson, centenary ed. (Boston: Houghton, Mifflin, 1903–1904) 10:449–85.

[5] Henry David Thoreau, *The Writings of Henry David Thoreau,* Walden ed. (Boston: Houghton Mifflin, 1906). Volumes 7 through 20 of this edition contain Thoreau's journals. A new critical edition of Thoreau's writings is now being published; see the various titles in the series The Writings of Henry D. Thoreau, ed. Walter Harding et al. (Princeton: Princeton University Press, 1971–).

[6] Thoreau, *Journal* (5 March 1853), in *Writings* (Walden ed.) 11:4.

days of absorption in each facet of his world is the significance of the present for creating an eternity of value and worth. Hence, we examine, in the following pages, a series of "presents" lived by this man of many biographies—observing him in youth as he shapes his spirituality in *A Week on the Concord and Merrimack Rivers,* sharing his encounter with the sacred in the wilderness of *The Maine Woods,* and experiencing the biting force of his quarrel with the state for conscience sake in "Civil Disobedience." Finally, in *Walden,* with Thoreau at the height of his powers, we learn anew that the unexamined life is not worth living; and we ponder the message left by this man who marched, in all his life roles, to the beat of a different drummer.[7]

---

[7] See the words of Socrates according to Plato *Apology* 38A, and, in this volume, Thoreau, *Walden,* ch. 18.

A WEEK ON THE CONCORD AND MERRIMACK RIVERS

Late in the summer of 1839 Henry David Thoreau and his older brother, John, traveled down the Concord River and up the Merrimack, hiking to the White Mountains before their return. The two-week trip seemed only a carefree interlude between school terms for the brothers, but subsequent events made the vacation the theme of Henry Thoreau's first book. Because of bad health John had to leave the school in 1841, and Henry, not wanting to continue alone, closed it. Then, in January 1842, John contracted lockjaw from a minor cut, and his death followed soon after. The blow to Henry was profound, and he displayed sympathetic symptoms of lockjaw for several weeks.

It was in this context that Thoreau conceived the idea of writing an account of the trip on the Concord and Merrimack as a memorial to his brother. By the spring of 1845 he went to live at Walden Pond, where he would find the solitude to write. In the work that resulted, Transcendental spirituality reconstituted the bare facts of the journey contained in Thoreau's vacation diary. The two-week excursion was compressed, in effect, into one literary week; and the trip into the White Mountains—with a passing mention of the week that it involved—occupied only a portion of the chapter devoted to Thursday. Moreover, into the travel narrative of each of the days Thoreau wove reflective essays. The book was, as William J. Wolf said, "an exploration by river into the stream of thought."[1] Thoreau's journey was a healing time, and the river—the symbol of his progress—revealed along its banks the foliage of autumn (although it was late summer) because autumn best expressed his grief and its transmutation into Transcendental wisdom.

Throughout the book Thoreau illustrated how much he had read in the spiritual classics of the East. And he showed, too, how extensive was his knowledge of Western classics. He also included numerous samples of his own poetry along with the poetry of others to explore his themes. Such a synthesis from the first proved too challenging for most readers. In order to have his work printed, Thoreau found it necessary to guarantee his Boston publisher James Munroe and Company against loss. On that basis the book appeared in 1849, but by 1853 only 200 of the 1,000 copies printed were sold and seventy-five had been given away. The publisher returned the remainder—more than 700 copies—to the author.

Nonetheless, Thoreau's work must be seen as a classic, the value of which has only begun to be understood. In the selections printed below, we have some of the most sig-

---

[1] William J. Wolf, *Thoreau: Mystic, Prophet, Ecologist* (Philadelphia: United Church Press, Pilgrim Press, 1974) 49. Unfortunately, literary critics have seen the essays as unwieldy digressions. See, for example, Henry Seidel Canby, *Thoreau* (Boston: Houghton Mifflin, Riverside Press, 1939) 271-73; and Walter Harding, *The Days of Henry Thoreau* (New York: Alfred A. Knopf, 1965) 247-48.

nificant of the religious reflections and experiences recounted in Thoreau's *Week*. First, on Sunday, he juxtaposes the Sabbath of nature with the Sabbath of the disapproving churchgoers who observe the brothers on their voyage, and he gives us his critical estimate of Christianity. Then, on Monday, Thoreau discourses at length on the (Indian) *Bhagavad Gita,* and—after an evening that evokes the mystical as he listens to a far-off drummer—on Tuesday he climbs Saddleback, or Greylock, Mountain. Here, Thoreau experiences a sense of the sacred that makes the mountain, as William Wolf wrote, "the mountain of theophany, the symbolical Sinai of Thoreau's Transcendentalism."[2] In a concluding series of vignettes, on Friday Thoreau pleads for a natural life, meditates on spiritual astronomy and discovery, and finally—in the context of the autumnal journey home to Concord—gives his ode to silence. We leave him with his brother fastening their boat to the wild apple tree.[3]

---

[2] Wolf, *Thoreau,* 52.

[3] The text is excerpted from Henry David Thoreau, *The Writings of Henry David Thoreau,* Walden ed. (Boston: Houghton Mifflin, 1906) 1:11-420.

(From) A WEEK ON THE CONCORD AND MERRIMACK RIVERS

CONCORD RIVER

I had often stood on the banks of the Concord, watching the lapse of the current, an emblem of all progress, following the same law with the system, with time, and all that is made; the weeds at the bottom gently bending down the stream, shaken by the watery wind, still planted where their seeds had sunk, but ere long to die and go down likewise; the shining pebbles, not yet anxious to better their condition, the chips and weeds, and occasional logs and stems of trees that floated past, fulfilling their fate, were objects of singular interest to me, and at last I resolved to launch myself on its bosom and float whither it would bear me.

SUNDAY

As we thus dipped our way along between fresh masses of foliage overrun with the grape and smaller flowering vines, the surface was so calm, and both air and water so transparent, that the flight of a kingfisher or robin over the river was as distinctly seen reflected in the water below as in the air above. The birds seemed to flit through submerged groves, alighting on the yielding sprays, and their clear notes to come up from below. We were uncertain whether the water floated the land, or the land held the water in its bosom. It was such a season, in short, as that in which one of our Concord poets sailed on its stream, and sung its quiet glories.

"There is an inward voice, that in the stream
Sends forth its spirit to the listening ear,
And in a calm content it floweth on,
Like wisdom, welcome with its own respect.
Clear in its breast lie all these beauteous thoughts,
It doth receive the green and graceful trees,
And the gray rocks smile in its peaceful arms."[1]

And more he sung, but too serious for our page. For every oak and birch, too, growing on the hilltop, as well as for these elms and willows, we knew that there was a graceful ethereal and ideal tree making down from the roots, and sometimes Nature in high tides brings her mirror to its foot and makes it visible.[2] The stillness was

---

[1] William Ellery Channing (the Younger), "The River," ll.1-7. See William Ellery Channing, *Poems* (1843), reprinted in William Ellery Channing, *The Collected Poems of William Ellery Channing the Younger, 1817-1901*, ed. Walter Harding (Gainesville FL: Scholars' Facsimiles & Reprints, 1967) 81.

[2] In Hindu literature the cosmos forms a huge tree with its roots in the sky and branches growing toward the earth—powerfully suggesting the divine ambience of the tree. See *Rig Veda* 1.24.7; *Katha Upanishad* 6.1; *Bhagavad Gita* 15.1-3. Thoreau may have absorbed a notion of the cosmic tree from Hindu sources. For a comparative discussion of the tree, see Mircea Eliade, *Patterns in Comparative Religion*, trans. Rosemary Sheed (Cleveland: World Publishing, Meridian Books, 1963) 273-78.

intense and almost conscious, as if it were a natural Sabbath, and we fancied that the morning was the evening of a celestial day. The air was so elastic and crystalline that it had the same effect on the landscape that a glass has on a picture, to give to it an ideal remoteness and perfection. The landscape was clothed in a mild and quiet light, in which the woods and fences checkered and partitioned it with new regularity, and rough and uneven fields stretched away with lawn-like smoothness to the horizon, and the clouds, finely distinct and picturesque, seemed a fit drapery to hang over fairyland. The world seemed decked for some holiday or prouder pageantry, with silken streamers flying, and the course of our lives to wind on before us like a green lane into a country maze, at the season when fruit-trees are in blossom. . . .

The sun lodged on the old gray cliffs, and glanced from every pad; the bulrushes and flags seemed to rejoice in the delicious light and air; the meadows were a-drinking at their leisure; the frogs sat meditating, all Sabbath thoughts, summing up their week, with one eye out on the golden sun, and one toe upon a reed, eying the wondrous universe in which they act their part; the fishes swam more staid and soberly, as maidens go to church; shoals of golden and silver minnows rose to the surface to behold the heavens, and then sheered off into more sombre aisles; they swept by as if moved by one mind, continually gliding past each other, and yet preserving the form of their battalion unchanged, as if they were still embraced by the transparent membrane which held the spawn; a young band of brethren and sisters trying their new fins; now they wheeled, now shot ahead, and when we drove them to the shore and cut them off, they dexterously tacked and passed underneath the boat. Over the old wooden bridges no traveler crossed, and neither the river nor the fishes avoided to glide between the abutments. . . .

Just before reaching the Merrimack, the people coming out of church paused to look at us from above, and apparently, so strong is custom, indulged in some heathenish comparisons; but we were the truest observers of this sunny day. According to Hesiod,—

"The seventh is a holy day,
For then Latona brought forth golden-rayed Apollo,"[3]

and by our reckoning this was the seventh day of the week, and not the first. . . .

In my Pantheon, Pan still reigns in his pristine glory, with his ruddy face, his flowing beard, and his shaggy body, his pipe and his crook, his nymph Echo, and his chosen daughter Iambe; for the great god Pan is not dead, as was rumored.[4] No god ever dies. Perhaps of all the gods of New England and

---

[3] Hesiod *Works and Days* 770-71. But Thoreau is quoting out of context, since Hesiod is here discussing the days of the ancient Greek *month*. In fact, in an important work on Thoreau's classicism, Ethel Seybold found "no evidence that Thoreau read his works." See Ethel Seybold, *Thoreau: The Quest and the Classics,* Yale Studies in English, vol. 116 (1951; rpt., Hamden CT: Archon Books, 1969) 71 n. 3.

[4] Thoreau's clever play on words—"Pantheon, Pan"—is achieved only by bringing together separate elements from Roman and Greek religion. The Pantheon is the Roman temple dedicated to all the Gods. For the Greek pastoral deity Pan, see n. 20 to Amos Bronson Alcott, "Orphic Sayings." According to Greek mythology, Pan loved the nymph Echo, and Iambe was their daughter. With her wit and wisdom, Iambe was thought to have invented the iambic verse produced in satiric compositions by the Ionian Greeks.

of ancient Greece, I am most constant at his shrine.

It seems to me that the god that is commonly worshiped in civilized countries is not at all divine, though he bears a divine name, but is the overwhelming authority and respectability of mankind combined. Men reverence one another, not yet God. If I thought that I could speak with discrimination and impartiality of the nations of Christendom, I should praise them, but it tasks me too much. They seem to be the most civil and humane, but I may be mistaken. . . .

There are various, nay, incredible faiths; why should we be alarmed at any of them? What man believes, God believes. Long as I have lived, and many blasphemers as I have heard and seen, I have never yet heard or witnessed any direct and conscious blasphemy or irreverence; but of indirect and habitual, enough. Where is the man who is guilty of direct and personal insolence to Him that made him?

One memorable addition to the old mythology is due to this era,—the Christian fable. With what pains, and tears, and blood these centuries have woven this and added it to the mythology of mankind! The new Prometheus.[5] With what miraculous consent, and patience, and persistency has this mythus been stamped on the memory of the race! It would seem as if it were in the progress of our mythology to dethrone Jehovah, and crown Christ in his stead. . . .

I trust that some may be as near and dear to Buddha, or Christ, or Swedenborg,[6] who are without the pale of their churches. It is necessary not to be Christian to appreciate the beauty and significance of the life of Christ. I know that some will have hard thoughts of me, when they hear their Christ named beside my Buddha, yet I am sure that I am willing they should love their Christ more than my Buddha, for the love is the main thing, and I like him too. . . .

Most people with whom I talk, men and women even of some originality and genius, have their scheme of the universe all cut and dried,—very *dry,* I assure you, to hear, dry enough to burn, dry-rotted and powder-post, methinks,—which they set up between you and them in the shortest intercourse; an ancient and tottering frame with all its boards blown off. They do not walk without their bed.[7] Some, to me, seemingly very unimportant and unsubstantial things and relations are for them everlastingly settled,—as Father, Son, and Holy Ghost, and the like. These are like the everlasting hills to them.[8] But in all my wanderings I never came across the least vestige of authority for these things. They have not left so distinct a trace as the delicate flower of a remote geological period on the coal in my grate. The wisest man preaches no doctrines; he has no scheme; he sees no rafter, not even a cobweb, against the heavens. It is clear sky. If I ever see more clearly at one time than at another, the medium through which I see is

---

[5]The Greek God Prometheus suffered and endured pain because he brought benefit to humankind. Like Christ, he mediated between the divine and human worlds. See n. 11 to Amos Bronson Alcott, *The Doctrine and Discipline of Human Culture,* and n. 21 to Alcott, "Orphic Sayings."

[6]Although many of Emanuel Swedenborg's followers were organized as the Church of the New Jerusalem, still others admired the Swedish seer and mystic through his writings but did not join the church.

[7]Thoreau is perhaps making an ironic play on the words of Jesus in Matt. 9:6.

[8]Cf. Gen. 49:26.

clearer. To see from earth to heaven, and see there standing, still a fixture, that old Jewish scheme! What right have you to hold up this obstacle to my understanding you, to your understanding me! You did not invent it; it was imposed on you. Examine your authority. Even Christ, we fear, had his scheme, his conformity to tradition, which slightly vitiates his teaching. He had not swallowed all formulas. He preached some mere doctrines. As for me, Abraham, Isaac, and Jacob are now only the subtilest imaginable essences, which would not stain the morning sky. Your scheme must be the frame-work of the universe; all other schemes will soon be ruins. The perfect God in his revelations of himself has never got to the length of one such proposition as you, his prophets, state. Have you learned the alphabet of heaven and can count three? Do you know the number of God's family? Can you put mysteries into words? Do you presume to fable of the ineffable? Pray, what geographer are you, that speak of heaven's topography? Whose friend are you, that speak of God's personality? Do you, Miles Howard, think that he has made you his confidant? Tell me of the height of the mountains of the moon, or of the diameter of space, and I may believe you, but of the secret history of the Almighty, and I shall pronounce thee mad. Yet we have a sort of family history of our God,—so have the Tahitians of theirs,[9]— and some old poet's grand imagination is imposed on us as adamantine everlasting truth, and God's own word. Pythagoras says, truly enough, "A true assertion respecting God is an assertion of God;" but we may well doubt if there is any example of this in literature.[10]

The New Testament is an invaluable book, though I confess to having been slightly prejudiced against it in my very early days by the church and the Sabbath-school, so that it seemed, before I read it, to be the yellowest book in the catalogue. Yet I early escaped from their meshes. It was hard to get the commentaries out of one's head and taste its true flavor. I think that Pilgrim's Progress is the best sermon which has been preached from this text; almost all other sermons that I have heard, or heard of, have been but poor imitations of this.[11] It would be a poor story to be prejudiced against the Life of Christ because the book has been edited by Christians. In fact, I love this book rarely, though it is a sort of castle in the air to me, which I am permitted to dream. Having come to it so recently and freshly, it has the greater charm, so that I cannot find any to talk with about it. I never read a novel, they have so little real life and thought in them. The reading which I love best is the scriptures of the several nations, though it happens that I am better acquainted with those of the Hindoos, the Chinese, and the Persians, than of the Hebrews, which I have

---

[9]Thoreau was fascinated by "native" life. See the chapter "Natives to the World," in John Aldrich Christie, *Thoreau as World Traveler* (New York: Columbia University Press, 1965) 211-30. Note also the lines above in Thoreau's text that echo, in rhetorical structure and theme, the Book of Job (cf. Job 38:4-7, 16-20).

[10]For Pythagoras, see n. 26 to Ralph Waldo Emerson, *Nature*. The quotation is from [Jamblichus of Chalcis], *Iamblichus' Life of Pythagoras; or, Pythagoric Life, Accompanied by . . . a Collection of Pythagoric Sentences*, trans. Thomas Taylor (London: Printed by A. J. Valpy, 1818) 196. But the saying is not from Pythagoras. Rather, it is a Pythagorean fragment among Taylor's "Select Sentences" attributed to Sextus the Pythagorean (fl. 300? B.C.).

[11]Cf. Alcott's attraction to *Pilgrim's Progress* as noted in the introduction to part 2, "Amos Bronson Alcott."

come to last.¹² Give me one of these bibles, and you have silenced me for a while. When I recover the use of my tongue, I am wont to worry my neighbors with the new sentences; but commonly they cannot see that there is any wit in them. Such has been my experience with the New Testament. I have not yet got to the crucifixion, I have read it over so many times. I should love dearly to read it aloud to my friends, some of whom are seriously inclined; it is so good, and I am sure that they have never heard it, it fits their case exactly, and we should enjoy it so much together,—but I instinctively despair of getting their ears. They soon show, by signs not to be mistaken, that it is inexpressibly wearisome to them. I do not mean to imply that I am any better than my neighbors; for, alas! I know that I am only as good, though I love better books than they.

It is remarkable that, notwithstanding the universal favor with which the New Testament is outwardly received, and even the bigotry with which it is defended, there is no hospitality shown to, there is no appreciation of, the order of truth with which it deals. I know of no book that has so few readers. There is none so truly strange, and heretical, and unpopular. To Christians, no less than Greeks and Jews, it is foolishness and a stumbling-block.¹³ There are, indeed, severe things in it which no man should read aloud more than once. "Seek first the kingdom of heaven." "Lay not up for yourselves treasures on earth." "If thou wilt be perfect, go and sell that thou hast, and give to the poor, and thou shalt have treasure in heaven." "For what is a man profited, if he shall gain the whole world, and lose his own soul? Or what shall a man give in exchange for his soul?" Think of this, Yankees! "Verily, I say unto you, if ye have faith as a grain of mustard seed, ye shall say unto this mountain, Remove hence to yonder place, and it shall remove; and nothing shall be impossible unto you."¹⁴ Think of repeating these things to a New England audience! thirdly, fourthly, fifteenthly, till there are three barrels of sermons! who, without cant, can read them aloud? Who, without cant, can hear them, and not go out of the meeting-house? They never *were* read, they never *were* heard. Let but one of these sentences be rightly read, from any pulpit in the land, and there would not be left one stone of that meeting-house upon another.¹⁵

---

¹²William Wolf has argued that the remark is tongue-in-cheek and not to be taken literally—unless perhaps Thoreau is referring to the Old Testament or (more likely) to a new appreciation of the entire Bible after being freed from its Christian editors. See William J. Wolf, *Thoreau: Mystic, Prophet, Ecologist* (Philadelphia: United Church Press, Pilgrim Press, 1974) 58. Thoreau's reading of Eastern works dated mainly from the time of his sojourn in the Emerson household, beginning in 1841, where he had access to the books in Emerson's library. Arthur Christy noted that Thoreau's first (published) journal entry on Oriental reading in 1838 displayed "more maturity and wider reading than Emerson's early entries," but he also cited evidence that during his years at Harvard Thoreau withdrew no Eastern books from the college library. See Arthur Christy, *The Orient in American Transcendentalism: A Study of Emerson, Thoreau, and Alcott* (1932; rpt., New York: Octagon Books, 1978) 188. Specific "scriptures . . . of the Hindoos, the Chinese, and the Persians" included the Indian (Thoreau's "Hindoo") *Bhagavad Gita, Laws of Manu,* and *Samkhya Karika;* the Chinese *Analects of Confucius* and other Confucian works, among them the writings of Mencius; and the Persian *Gulistan* of Sa'di.

¹³Cf. 1 Cor. 1:23.

¹⁴See Matt. 6:33 (although Thoreau has supplied "kingdom of heaven" for "kingdom of God"); 6:19; 18:21; 16:26; 17:20.

¹⁵Cf. Matt. 24:2; Mark 13:2; Luke 19:44, 21:6.

Yet the New Testament treats of man and man's so-called spiritual affairs too exclusively, and is too constantly moral and personal, to alone content me, who am not interested solely in man's religious or moral nature, or in man even. I have not the most definite designs on the future. Absolutely speaking, Do unto others as you would that they should do unto you is by no means a golden rule, but the best of current silver.[16] An honest man would have but little occasion for it. It is golden not to have any rule at all in such a case. The book has never been written which is to be accepted without any allowance. Christ was a sublime actor on the stage of the world. He knew what he was thinking of when he said, "Heaven and earth shall pass away, but my words shall not pass away."[17] I draw near to him at such a time.[18] Yet he taught mankind but imperfectly how to live; his thoughts were all directed toward another world. There is another kind of success than his. Even here we have a sort of living to get, and must buffet it somewhat longer. There are various tough problems yet to solve, and we must make shift to live, betwixt spirit and matter, such a human life as we can.[19]

A healthy man, with steady employment, as wood-chopping at fifty cents a cord, and a camp in the woods, will not be a good subject for Christianity. The New Testament may be a choice book to him on some, but not on all or most of his days.

---

[16]For the Golden Rule, cf. Matt. 7:12.

[17]Matt. 24:35.

[18]Cf. Ps. 69:18; James 4:8.

[19]Thoreau's own concern for practical matters—his father's pencil-making business, the needs of the Emerson household, the details of building a hut and planting a crop at Walden Pond—gives evidence that he lived what he preached.

He will rather go a-fishing in his leisure hours. The Apostles, though they were fishers too, were of the solemn race of sea-fishers, and never trolled for pickerel on inland streams. . . .

I was once reproved by a minister who was driving a poor beast to some meeting-house horse-sheds among the hills of New Hampshire, because I was bending my steps to a mountain-top on the Sabbath, instead of a church, when I would have gone farther than he to hear a true word spoken on that or any day. He declared that I was "breaking the Lord's fourth commandment," and proceeded to enumerate, in a sepulchral tone, the disasters which had befallen him whenever he had done any ordinary work on the Sabbath. He really thought that a god was on the watch to trip up those men who followed any secular work on this day, and did not see that it was the evil conscience of the workers that did it. The country is full of this superstition, so that when one enters a village the church, not only really but from association, is the ugliest looking building in it, because it is the one in which human nature stoops the lowest and is most disgraced. Certainly, such temples as these shall ere long cease to deform the landscape. There are few things more disheartening and disgusting than when you are walking the streets of a strange village on the Sabbath, to hear a preacher shouting like a boatswain in a gale of wind, and thus harshly profaning the quiet atmosphere of the day. You fancy him to have taken off his coat, as when men are about to do hot and dirty work.

If I should ask the minister of Middlesex to let me speak in his pulpit on a Sunday, he would object because I do not pray as he does, or because I am not ordained. What under the sun are these things?

Really, there is no infidelity, nowadays, so great as that which prays, and keeps the Sabbath, and rebuilds the churches. The sealer of the South Pacific preaches a truer doctrine. The church is a sort of hospital for men's souls, and as full of quackery as the hospital for their bodies. Those who are taken into it live like pensioners in their Retreat or Sailor's Snug Harbor, where you may see a row of religious cripples sitting outside in sunny weather. Let not the apprehension that he may one day have to occupy a ward therein discourage the cheerful labors of the able-souled man. While he remembers the sick in their extremities, let him not look thither as to his goal. One is sick at heart of this pagoda worship. It is like the beating of gongs in a Hindoo subterranean temple.[20] In dark places and dungeons the preacher's words might perhaps strike root and grow, but not in broad daylight in any part of the world that I know. The sound of the Sabbath bell far away, now breaking on these shores, does not awaken pleasing associations, but melancholy and sombre ones rather. One involuntarily rests on his oar, to humor his unusually meditative mood. It is as the sound of many catechisms and religious books twanging a canting peal round the earth, seeming to issue from some Egyptian temple and echo along the shore of the Nile, right opposite to Pharaoh's palace and Moses in the bulrushes, startling a multitude of storks and alligators basking in the sun.

Everywhere "good men" sound a retreat, and the word has gone forth to fall back on innocence. Fall forward rather on to whatever there is there. Christianity only hopes. It has hung its harp on the willows, and cannot sing a song in a strange land. It has dreamed a sad dream, and does not yet welcome the morning with joy.[21] The mother tells her falsehoods to her child, but, thank Heaven, the child does not grow up in its parent's shadow. . . .

A man's real faith is never contained in his creed, nor is his creed an article of his faith. The last is never adopted. This it is that permits him to smile ever, and to live even as bravely as he does. And yet he clings anxiously to his creed, as to a straw, thinking that that does him good service because his sheet anchor does not drag. . . .

MONDAY[22]

The wisest conservatism is that of the Hindoos. "Immemorial custom is tran-

---

[20]Cave temples—carved out of the living rock—came to India through Buddhism, but later during the reign of the Guptas (320-500?) Hindu cave temples began to appear. According to H. Daniel Smith of Syracuse University, the use of gongs is a regular feature of Bengali worship, but there are no great cave temples in Bengal. Moreover, as Jack Hawley of the University of Washington has suggested, "gongs" evokes the Far East; what one hears, typically, in Hindu temples is *bells*. Hence, Thoreau may have conflated images absorbed from his reading, or gleaned information from an inaccurate travel account, or both. In fact, as Professor Smith has noticed, the reference to gongs should be read as part of an extended metaphor based on 1 Cor. 13:1 that runs through the rest of the paragraph. I am indebted to Professors Hawley and Smith and also to Fred W. Clothey of the University of Pittsburgh.

[21]Cf. Ps. 137:2, 4; Gen. 40:4-5; Ps. 30:5.

[22]Thoreau has been contrasting contemplation and activity, and in this context he has reflected on the claims of the political state and those of conscience. His attention now turns to the conservatism of Hinduism, which he examines with comparative intent.

scendent law," says Menu.²³ That is, it was the custom of the gods before men used it.²⁴ The fault of our New England custom is that it is memorial. What is morality but immemorial custom? Conscience is the chief of conservatives. "Perform the settled functions," says Kreeshna in the Bhagvat-Geeta; "action is preferable to inaction. The journey of thy mortal frame may not succeed from inaction." "A man's own calling, with all its faults, ought not to be forsaken. Every undertaking is involved in its faults as the fire in its smoke." "The man who is acquainted with the whole should not drive those from their works who are slow of comprehension, and less experienced than himself." "Wherefore, O Arjoon, resolve to fight," is the advice of the god to the irresolute soldier who fears to slay his best friends.²⁵ It is a sublime conservatism; as wide as the world, and as unwearied as time; preserving the universe with Asiatic anxiety, in that state in which it appeared to their minds. These philosophers dwell on the inevitability and unchangeableness of laws, on the power of temperament and constitution, the three *goon,* or qualities,²⁶ and the circumstances, or birth and affinity. The end is an immense consolation; eternal absorption in Brahma.²⁷ Their speculations never venture beyond their own table-lands, though they are high and vast as they. Buoyancy, freedom, flexibility, variety, possibility, which also are qualities of the Unnamed, they deal not with. The undeserved reward is to be earned by an everlasting moral drudgery; the incalculable promise of the morrow is, as it were, weighed. And who will say that their conservatism has not been effectual? . . .

Christianity, on the other hand, is humane, practical, and, in a large sense, radical. So many years and ages of the gods those Eastern sages sat contemplating Brahm, uttering in silence the mystic "Om,"²⁸ being absorbed into the essence

---

²³*Laws of Manu* 1.108. Thoreau read the classic Indian code of jurisprudence in the edition titled *Institutes of Hindu Law; or, The Ordinances of Menu, according to the Gloss of Culluca, Comprising the Indian System of Duties Religious and Civil,* trans. William Jones (London: Rivingtons and Cochran, 1825).

²⁴Neither the explicit text nor context of *The Laws of Manu* suggests this reading. Rather, the laws are *divinely prescribed.* But in a deeper sense Thoreau is right, since *Manu* is grounded in the doctrine of correspondence and sees human law as an expression of the divine order of things.

²⁵*Bhagavad Gita* 3.8; 18.48; 3.29; 2.18. The *Bhagavad Gita,* technically a poem within the larger epic *Mahabharata,* recounts the dialogue between the warrior prince Arjuna and his charioteer who is, in fact, Lord Krishna, the manifestation of the God Vishnu. In a struggle over the familial kingdom, Arjuna, one of the Pandavas, is arrayed with his brothers to fight his cousins, the Kauravas, and their army (kin more than "best friends," as Thoreau has it). Arjuna's hesitancy and depression concerning the ensuing battle occasion the classic discourse of Krishna. Thoreau read the *Gita* in English translation in *The Bhagvat-Geeta; or, Dialogues of Kreeshna and Arjoon,* trans. Charles Wilkins (London: Nourse, 1785).

²⁶Thoreau's three *goon* are the three *gunas,* the qualities of *sattva* (purity, goodness), *rajas* (passion, restlessness, action), and *tamas* (darkness, inertia). These qualities—arising in *prakriti* (nature) and stimulated by the Lord's power—interact to bring about the many-faceted world. The *gunas* are considered in *Bhagavad Gita* 14.1-27; 18.7-41; passim.

²⁷Thoreau's "Brahma" is Brahman, the power or essence that permeates the cosmos and the pure consciousness that is the Absolute (see n. 16 to Ralph Waldo Emerson, "Brahma").

²⁸Om, the most sacred sound (or mantra) in the ancient Vedic (sacred Indian) scriptures (see

of the Supreme Being, never going out of themselves, but subsiding farther and deeper within; so infinitely wise, yet infinitely stagnant; until, at last, in that same Asia, but in the western part of it, appeared a youth, wholly unforetold by them,—not being absorbed into Brahm, but bringing Brahm down to earth and to mankind; in whom Brahm had awaked from his long sleep, and exerted himself, and the day began,—a new avatar.[29] The Brahman had never thought to be a brother of mankind as well as a child of God. Christ is the prince of Reformers and Radicals. Many expressions in the New Testament come naturally to the lips of all Protestants, and it furnishes the most pregnant and practical texts. There is no harmless dreaming, no wise speculation in it, but everywhere a substratum of good sense. It never *reflects,* but it *repents.* There is no poetry in it, we may say, nothing regarded in the light of beauty merely, but moral truth is its object. All mortals are convicted by its conscience.

The New Testament is remarkable for its pure morality; the best of the Hindoo Scripture, for its pure intellectuality. The reader is nowhere raised into and sustained in a higher, purer, or *rarer* region of thought than in the Bhagvat-Geeta. Warren Hastings, in his sensible letter recommending the translation of this book to the Chairman of the East India Company, declares the original to be "of a sublimity of conception, reasoning, and diction almost unequaled," and that the writings of the Indian philosophers "will survive when the British dominion in India shall have long ceased to exist, and when the sources which it once yielded of wealth and power are lost to remembrance."[30] It is unquestionably one of the noblest and most sacred scriptures which have come down to us. Books are to be distinguished by the grandeur of their topics even more than by the manner in which they are treated. The Oriental philosophy approaches easily loftier themes than the modern aspires to; and no wonder if it sometimes prattle about them. It only assigns their due rank respectively to Action and Contemplation, or rather does full justice to the latter. Western philosophers have not conceived of the significance of Contemplation in their sense. Speaking of the spiritual discipline to which the Brahmans[31] subjected themselves, and the

---

n. 25 to Emerson, *Nature*), came to symbolize the reality of all sounds and so of the whole universe. Like the Word in the Gospel of John (John 1:1), it was the sound-sign that, because of its intrinsic quality, represented God—here as impersonal Reality.

[29]Thoreau is, of course, referring to Jesus of Nazareth. In Hinduism, an avatar is an incarnation or descent of the God, especially Vishnu. The sleep of "Brahm," in the most well-known version of the myth, is the period during the night of Brahma (4,320,000 years of human time) when the God Vishnu sleeps—an interval when the exhausted world has been destroyed, only to be recreated when Vishnu, as Brahma, awakens and a new day of Brahma begins. For brief allusions, see *Bhagavad Gita* 8.17; 9.7.

[30]Warren Hastings (1732–1818), the first governor-general for British India, sought to promulgate knowledge of the Indian classics in the English-speaking world, promoting the Asiatic Society of Bengal to study Asian culture and eliciting the Charles Wilkins translation of the *Bhagavad Gita,* the first English translation of the poem. The lines that Thoreau quotes are from the dedicatory epistle of 7 October 1784, which Hastings wrote to Nathaniel Smith, chairman of the Court of Directors of the East India Company, to accompany the translation. The letter formed the introduction to the 1785 volume. The material may be found in *Bhagvat-Geeta,* trans. Charles Wilkins, 10, 13.

[31]Here the members of the priestly caste. (See n. 25 to Emerson, *Nature*.)

wonderful power of abstraction to which they attained, instances of which had come under his notice, Hastings says:—

"To those who have never been accustomed to the separation of the mind from the notices of the senses, it may not be easy to conceive by what means such a power is to be attained; since even the most studious men of our hemisphere will find it difficult so to restrain their attention, but that it will wander to some object of present sense or recollection; and even the buzzing of a fly will sometimes have the power to disturb it. But if we are told that there have been men who were successively, for ages past, in the daily habit of abstracted contemplation, begun in the earliest period of youth, and continued in many to the maturity of age, each adding some portion of knowledge to the store accumulated by his predecessors; it is not assuming too much to conclude, that as the mind ever gathers strength, like the body, by exercise, so in such an exercise it may in each have acquired the faculty to which they aspired, and that their collective studies may have led them to the discovery of new tracts and combinations of sentiment, totally different from the doctrines with which the learned of other nations are acquainted; doctrines which, however speculative and subtle, still as they possess the advantage of being derived from a source so free from every adventitious mixture, may be equally founded in truth with the most simple of our own."[32]

"The forsaking of works" was taught by Kreeshna to the most ancient of men, and handed down from age to age, "until at length, in the course of time, the mighty art was lost."[33]

"In wisdom is to be found every work without exception," says Kreeshna.

"Although thou wert the greatest of all offenders, thou shalt be able to cross the gulf of sin with the bark of wisdom."

"There is not anything in this world to be compared with wisdom for purity."[34]

"The action stands at a distance inferior to the application of wisdom."[35]

The wisdom of a Moonee "is confirmed, when, like the tortoise, he can draw in all his members, and restrain them from their wonted purposes."[36]

"Children only, and not the learned, speak of the speculative and the practical

---

[32] The lines are again from Hastings's dedicatory epistle in *Bhagvat-Geeta,* trans. Charles Wilkins, 9. The Hastings epistle speaks of the "discovery of new tracks," not "tracts," and the latter does not appear in uncorrected proofs for the (original) 1849 edition of Thoreau's *Week.* (See Henry David Thoreau, *A Week on the Concord and Merrimack Rivers,* ed. Carl F. Hovde et al., The Writings of Henry D. Thoreau [Princeton: Princeton University Press, 1980] 579, 552.) In the Hastings text, the passage begins with a reference to "this separation of the mind," but Thoreau has changed "this" to "the" to suit his literary needs. Moreover, in this—as in some succeeding quotations from the Wilkins translation—punctuation has been slightly altered. Finally, in the quotations from the *Gita* that follow, there are other minor variants from the Wilkins text.

[33] See *Bhagavad Gita* 4.2. The Wilkins translation titles this chapter ("lecture") of the *Gita* "Of the Forsaking of Works"—hence the first phrase of Thoreau's quotation. Yet Krishna's repeated message in the poem is not the renunciation of action but rather of the fruits that action may bring.

[34] *Bhagavad Gita* 4.33, 36, 38.

[35] Ibid. 2.49. In its context the line signifies "mere" action with, as its motive, the fruit of action.

[36] Ibid. 2.58. A *muni* (Thoreau's and Wilkins's "Moonee") is a Hindu sage and inspired ascetic, known for wisdom, superhuman powers, and participation in the divine nature, and especially understood as vowed to silence.

doctrines as two. They are but one. For both obtain the selfsame end, and the place which is gained by the followers of the one is gained by the followers of the other."

"The man enjoyeth not freedom from action, from the non-commencement of that which he hath to do; nor doth he obtain happiness from a total inactivity. No one ever resteth a moment inactive. Every man is involuntarily urged to act by those principles which are inherent in his nature. The man who restraineth his active faculties, and sitteth down with his mind attentive to the objects of his senses, is called one of an astrayed soul, and the practicer of deceit. So the man is praised, who, having subdued all his passions, performeth with his active faculties all the functions of life, unconcerned about the event."[37]

"Let the motive be in the deed and not in the event. Be not one whose motive for action is the hope of reward. Let not thy life be spent in inaction."

"For the man who doeth that which he hath to do, without affection, obtaineth the Supreme."[38]

"He who may behold as it were inaction in action, and action in inaction, is wise amongst mankind. He is a perfect performer of all duty."[39]

"Wise men call him a *Pandeet*, whose every undertaking is free from the idea of desire, and whose actions are consumed by the fire of wisdom. He abandoneth the desire of a reward of his actions; he is always contented and independent; and although he may be engaged in a work, he as it were doeth nothing."[40]

"He is both a Yogee and a Sannyasee who performeth that which he hath to do independent of the fruit thereof; not he who liveth without the sacrificial fire and without action."[41]

"He who enjoyeth but the Amreeta which is left of his offerings obtaineth the eternal spirit of Brahm, the Supreme."[42]

What, after all, does the practicalness of life amount to? The things immediate to

---

[37]Ibid. 5.4-5; 3.4-7. The "principles which are inherent in . . . nature" are the *gunas* (see n. 26 above). For "event," read "outcome," or "fruit of the action."

[38]*Bhagavad Gita* 2.47; 3.19. For "without affection," understand "without attachment or emotional involvement."

[39]Ibid. 4.18. There is inaction in action because the wise person understands that action does not involve the essence of the self, but only the mind, body, and senses. There is action in inaction because, as a spiritual discipline, such "inaction" is itself an active practice to suppress the tendency toward activity.

[40]Ibid. 4.19-20. The "*Pandeet*" is a pundit—a person wise in spiritual matters, or a sage.

[41]Ibid. 6.1. The "Yogee" of the text is a yogin; that is, one who practices yoga, the spiritual discipline that aims to bring unification of the self and to realize the oneness of the self (*atman*) with Brahman. A "Sannyasee," or *sannyasin,* is a member of one of the upper Hindu castes who, in the last phase of life, retires from the household to live a solitary life in the forest as an ascetic and religious contemplative. The reference to living "without the sacrificial fire" alludes to the relinquishment by the former householder of his ritual responsibility to the Gods to keep the sacrificial fires and to perform sacrifices. Living "without action" means living according to the contemplative spiritual discipline of yoga.

[42]Ibid. 4.31. In Vedic and Hindu myth, *amrita* (the "Amreeta" of Thoreau's text) was the drink of immortality. In this text *amrita* is understood as food (nectar) that is the remains of sacrifice. In its context, the text views the various practices of yoga—renunciations and austerities, regulation of breathing and of food intake—as sacrificial actions that, performed in the proper spirit, will lead to the attainment of Brahman.

be done are very trivial. I could postpone them all to hear this locust sing. The most glorious fact in my experience is not anything that I have done or may hope to do, but a transient thought, or vision, or dream, which I have had. I would give all the wealth of the world, and all the deeds of all the heroes, for one true vision. But how can I communicate with the gods, who am a pencil-maker on the earth, and not be insane?[43]

"I am the same to all mankind," says Kreeshna; "there is not one who is worthy of my love or hatred."[44]

This teaching is not practical in the sense in which the New Testament is. It is not always sound sense in practice. The Brahman never proposes courageously to assault evil, but patiently to starve it out. His active faculties are paralyzed by the idea of caste, of impassable limits of destiny and the tyranny of time. Kreeshna's argument, it must be allowed, is defective. No sufficient reason is given why Arjoon should fight.[45] Arjoon may be convinced, but the reader is not, for his judgment is *not* "formed upon the speculative doctrines of the *Sankhya Sastra.*"[46] "Seek an asylum in wisdom alone;"[47] but what is wisdom to a Western mind? The duty of which he speaks is an arbitrary one. When was it established? The Brahman's virtue consists in doing, not right, but arbitrary things. What is that which a man "hath to do"? What is "action"? What are the "settled functions"? What is "a man's own religion," which is so much better than another's? What is "a man's own particular calling"? What are the duties which are appointed by one's birth? It is a defense of the institution of castes, of what is called the "natural duty" of the Kshetree, or soldier, "to attach himself to the discipline," "not to flee from the field," and the like.[48]

---

[43]For Thoreau's activities as a pencil maker, see the biographical introduction to Thoreau in this volume. An obvious error, "de" for "be," has been corrected in the second sentence of this paragraph.

[44]*Bhagavad Gita* 9.29.

[45]Krishna gives not one but a series of arguments to urge Arjuna to fight: (1) only the body can be killed, and the soul is indestructible (ibid. 2.18-25, 30); (2) death is inevitable for any being that has been born (ibid. 2.27); (3) Arjuna will be dishonored before other men if he does not fight (ibid. 2.34-36); (4) the battle opens the door of heaven for Arjuna, and if he wins he will enjoy earth (ibid. 2.32, 37); and (5) it is Arjuna's duty as a member of the warrior caste to do battle without regard to the result; to refuse to do so would constitute sin (ibid. 2.31, 33, 38).

[46]Ibid. 2.39. The term *sankhya,* or *samkhya* —the name of one of the six orthodox religio-philosophical systems of later Hinduism—is used throughout the epic *Mahabharata,* including the *Bhagavad Gita,* for the religious "way" of knowledge (in the *samkhya* sense of discernment, or discriminating reason). In the *Gita* it is only one path—proposed alongside the way of action (in following one's "natural" caste duty without attachment to the fruits of action) and the way of devotion (in loving attention to Krishna, which in the end is celebrated as the best way to salvation). The content of *samkhya* is dualistic, positing as the two ultimate realities spirit, or *purusha,* and matter (nature), or *prakriti,* and from *prakriti* the three *gunas* (see n. 26 above). In Thoreau's quotation here, *sastra* is a general expression to indicate written *samkhya* teachings; the use of the term rests on Wilkins's mistranslation of the Sanskrit.

[47]*Bhagavad Gita* 2.49.

[48]For "Kshetree," read "Kshatriya," a member of the warrior and ruling caste, second highest of the four major castes of traditional India. Arjuna, in the *Bhagavad Gita,* is a Kshatriya. For the (free) quotations, cf. ibid. 18.43; 4.42. But the "natural" caste duty of the

But they who are unconcerned about the consequences of their actions are not therefore unconcerned about their actions.

Behold the difference between the Oriental and the Occidental. The former has nothing to do in this world; the latter is full of activity. The one looks in the sun till his eyes are put out; the other follows him prone in his westward course. There is such a thing as caste, even in the West; but it is comparatively faint; it is conservatism here. It says, forsake not your calling, outrage no institution, use no violence, rend no bonds; the State is thy parent. Its virtue or manhood is wholly filial. There is a struggle between the Oriental and Occidental in every nation; some who would be forever contemplating the sun, and some who are hastening toward the sunset. The former class says to the latter, When you have reached the sunset, you will be no nearer to the sun. To which the latter replies, But we so prolong the day. The former "walketh but in that night, when all things go to rest in the night of *time*. The contemplative Moonee sleepeth but in the day of *time*, when all things wake."[49]

To conclude these extracts, I can say, in the words of Sanjay, "As, O mighty Prince! I recollect again and again this holy and wonderful dialogue of Kreeshna and Arjoon, I continue more and more to rejoice; and as I recall to my memory the more than miraculous form of Haree, my astonishment is great, and I marvel and rejoice again and again! Wherever Kreeshna the God of devotion may be, wherever Arjoon the mighty bowman may be, there too, without doubt, are fortune, riches, victory, and good conduct. This is my firm belief."[50]

I would say to the readers of Scriptures, if they wish for a good book, read the Bhagvat-Geeta, an episode to the Mahabharat, said to have been written by Kreeshna Dwypayen Veias,—known to have been written by ___, more than four thousand years ago,—it matters not whether three or four, or when,—translated by Charles Wilkins.[51] It deserves to be read with reverence even by Yankees, as a part of the sacred writings of a devout people; and the intelligent Hebrew will rejoice to find in it a moral grandeur and sublimity akin to those of his own Scriptures.

To an American reader, who, by the

Kshatriya does *not* include attachment to the discipline of *samkhya*, or knowledge (*jnana*) yoga.

[49]Ibid. 2.69. Wilkins has translated "walketh" for "wakes" or "waketh." In the verse itself, the subject of the first clause—the one who wakes when all others sleep—is the man of self-control, the one who has withdrawn his senses from their objects. Such a person is fully awakened to Reality; at the same time, this individual—a sage, or man of vision—sees in the everyday world the confused murkiness of nighttime.

[50]Ibid. 18.76-78. Sanjaya ("Sanjay") was the reporter who narrated the discourse that arose between Krishna and Arjuna. Hari (the text's "Haree") is a name that, after the time of the Vedas, was commonly used to refer to Vishnu; Krishna is the manifestation of God, or Vishnu, in the *Gita*.

[51]Thoreau's "Kreeshna Dwypayen Veias" (both the spelling and the information are from the Hastings introduction in *Bhagvat-Geeta*, trans. Charles Wilkins, 5) is Krishna-Dvaipayana, called Vyasa, traditionally hailed as the compiler of the core of the *Mahabharata* (see n. 61 to Emerson, *Nature*). Moreover, the *Gita* is not nearly so old as Thoreau's source (the Hastings introduction) indicates. (Thoreau's immediate disclaimer of interest perhaps hints of uneasiness about the dating.) Rather, in its present form the *Bhagavad Gita* is probably a product of the second century A.D. with early versions dating, perhaps, from the second century B.C.

advantage of his position, can see over that strip of Atlantic coast to Asia and the Pacific, who, as it were, sees the shore slope upward over the Alps to the Himmaleh Mountains,[52] the comparatively recent literature of Europe often appears partial and clannish; and, notwithstanding the limited range of his own sympathies and studies, the European writer who presumes that he is speaking for the world is perceived by him to speak only for that corner of it which he inhabits. . . . In comparison with the philosophers of the East, we may say that modern Europe has yet given birth to none. Beside the vast and cosmogonal philosophy of the Bhagvat-Geeta, even our Shakespeare seems sometimes youthfully green and practical merely. Some of these sublime sentences, as the Chaldæan oracles of Zoroaster,[53] still surviving after a thousand revolutions and translations, alone make us doubt if the poetic form and dress are not transitory, and not essential to the most effective and enduring expression of thought. *Ex oriente lux*[54] may still be the motto of scholars, for the Western world has not yet derived from the East all the light which it is destined to receive thence.

It would be worthy of the age to print together the collected Scriptures or Sacred Writings of the several nations, the Chinese, the Hindoos, the Persians, the Hebrews, and others, as the Scripture of mankind. The New Testament is still, perhaps, too much on the lips and in the hearts of men to be called a Scripture in this sense. Such a juxtaposition and comparison might help to liberalize the faith of men. This is a work which Time will surely edit, reserved to crown the labors of the printing-press. This would be the Bible, or Book of Books, which let the missionaries carry to the uttermost parts of the earth. . . .

We had found a safe harbor for our boat, and as the sun was setting carried up our furniture, and soon arranged our house upon the bank, and while the kettle steamed at the tent door, we chatted of distant friends and of the sights which we were to behold, and wondered which way the towns lay from us. Our cocoa was soon boiled, and supper set upon our chest, and we lengthened out this meal, like old voyageurs, with our talk. Meanwhile we spread the map on the ground, and read in the Gazetteer when the first settlers came here and got a township granted. Then, when supper was done and we had written the journal of our voyage, we wrapped our buffaloes about us and lay down with our heads pillowed on our arms, listening awhile to the distant baying of a dog, or the murmurs of the river, or to the wind, which had not gone to rest. . . .

Far in the night, as we were falling asleep on the bank of the Merrimack, we heard some tyro beating a drum incessantly, in preparation for a country muster, as we learned, and we thought of the line,—

"When the drum beat at dead of night."[55]

---

[52] For the Himalaya ("Himmaleh") Mountains, see n. 14 to Ralph Waldo Emerson, "Self-Reliance."

[53] For Zoroaster, see n. 30 to Ralph Waldo Emerson, Divinity School *Address*. The so-called "Chaldaean Oracles of Zoroaster" were a collection of short fragments attributed dubiously to Zoroaster and gleaned for the most part from the writings of Neoplatonic philosophers. All of the fragments were written in Greek.

[54] Literally, "from the East, light."

[55] The line that the "tyro," or young soldier, evokes is from the Scottish poet Thomas Campbell (1777–1844), "Hohenlinden" (l. 6).

We could have assured him that his beat would be answered, and the forces be mustered. Fear not, thou drummer of the night; we too will be there. And still he drummed on in the silence and the dark. This stray sound from a far-off sphere came to our ears from time to time, far, sweet, and significant, and we listened with such an unprejudiced sense as if for the first time we heard at all. No doubt he was an insignificant drummer enough, but his music afforded us a prime and leisure hour, and we felt that we were in season wholly. These simple sounds related us to the stars. Ay, there was a logic in them so convincing that the combined sense of mankind could never make me doubt their conclusions. I stop my habitual thinking, as if the plow had suddenly run deeper in its furrow through the crust of the world. How can I go on, who have just stepped over such a bottomless skylight in the bog of my life? Suddenly old Time winked at me,—Ah, you know me, you rogue,—and news had come that IT was well. That ancient universe is in such capital health, I think undoubtedly it will never die. Heal yourselves, doctors; by God I live.

> Then idle Time ran gadding by
> And left me with Eternity alone;
> I hear beyond the range of sound,
> I see beyond the verge of sight,—[56]

I see, smell, taste, hear, feel, that everlasting Something to which we are allied, at once our maker, our abode, our destiny, our very Selves; the one historic truth, the most remarkable fact which can become the distinct and uninvited subject of our thought, the actual glory of the universe; the only fact which a human being cannot avoid recognizing, or in some way forget or dispense with.[57]

> It doth expand my privacies
> To all, and leave me single in the crowd.[58]

I have seen how the foundations of the world are laid, and I have not the least doubt that it will stand a good while.[59]

> Now chiefly is my natal hour,
> And only now my prime of life.
> I will not doubt the love untold,
> Which not my worth nor want hath bought,
> Which wooed me young and wooes me old,
> And to this evening hath me brought.[60]

What are ears? what is Time? that this particular series of sounds called a strain of music, an invisible and fairy troop which never brushed the dew from any mead, can be wafted down through the centuries from Homer to me, and he have been conversant

---

[56] The lines may be found, with some small changes, in Thoreau's poem "Inspiration" (ll. 43-44, 29-30), which appeared in the *Commonwealth*, 19 June 1863. See Henry David Thoreau, *The Collected Poems of Henry Thoreau*, ed. Carl Bode (Chicago: Packard, 1943) 231.

[57] In this passage Thoreau translates the message of his poem into the language of prose (cf. Thoreau, "Inspiration," ll. 16, 25-28, 74, in Thoreau, *Collected Poems*, 230, 231, 233); and, as Carl Bode observes regarding the entire poem (ibid., 375), the lines in their expression parallel the Emersonian doctrine of the Oversoul. William Bysshe Stein has argued that the closing pages of "Monday" (which in part are excerpted here) demonstrate Thoreau's practice of the yoga of sound. See William Bysshe Stein, "Thoreau's First Book, A Spoor of Yoga: The Orient in *A Week on the Concord and Merrimack Rivers*," *Emerson Society Quarterly* 41 (1965): 15.

[58] See Thoreau, "Inspiration," ll. 39-40, in Thoreau, *Collected Poems*, 231.

[59] Cf. Job 38:4.

[60] The material, with some changes, again may be found in Thoreau, "Inspiration," ll. 45-46, 69-72, in Thoreau, *Collected Poems*, 231, 232.

with that same aerial and mysterious charm which now so tingles my ears? What a fine communication from age to age, of the fairest and noblest thoughts, the aspirations of ancient men, even such as were never communicated by speech, is music! It is the flower of language, thought colored and curved, fluent and flexible, its crystal fountain tinged with the sun's rays, and its purling ripples reflecting the grass and the clouds. A strain of music reminds me of a passage of the Vedas, and I associate with it the idea of infinite remoteness, as well as of beauty and serenity, for to the senses that is farthest from us which addresses the greatest depth within us.[61] It teaches us again and again to trust the remotest and finest as the divinest instinct, and makes a dream our only real experience. We feel a sad cheer when we hear it, perchance because we that hear are not one with that which is heard.

> Therefore a torrent of sadness deep
> Through the strains of thy triumph is heard to sweep.[62]

The sadness is ours. The Indian poet Calidas says in the Sacontala: "Perhaps the sadness of men on seeing beautiful forms and hearing sweet music arises from some faint remembrance of past joys, and the traces of connections in a former state of existence."[63] As polishing expresses the vein in marble, and grain in wood, so music brings out what of heroic lurks anywhere. The hero is the sole patron of music. That harmony which exists naturally between the hero's moods and the universe, the soldier would fain imitate with drum and trumpet. When we are in health, all sounds fife and drum for us; we hear the notes of music in the air, or catch its echoes dying away when we awake in the dawn. Marching is when the pulse of the hero beats in unison with the pulse of Nature, and he steps to the measure of the universe; then there is true courage and invincible strength. . . .

TUESDAY[64]

LONG before daylight we ranged abroad, hatchet in hand, in search of fuel, and made the yet slumbering and dreaming wood resound with our blows. Then with our fire we burned up a portion of the loitering night, while the kettle sang its homely strain to the morning star. We tramped about the shore, waked all the muskrats, and scared up the bittern and birds that were asleep upon their roosts; we hauled up and upset our boat, and washed it and rinsed out

---

[61] For the importance of sound in Vedic literature, see *Rig Veda* 1.164.45-46. See also n. 28 above.

[62] The lines are Thoreau's and may be found, titled by the first line, in Thoreau, *Collected Poems*, 84.

[63] For the "*Sacontala*" of "Calidas" (trans. Sir William Jones, 1790), read the "*Shakuntala*" of "Kalidasa." Considered the greatest figure in the literature of classical Sanskrit, Kalidasa (fl. 5th cent. ? A.D.) was a dramatist and poet at court during the Gupta period. The *Shakuntala* is his most acclaimed work. The lines themselves may be found in Kalidasa, *Shakuntala*, act 5. See, in twentieth-century translation, Kalidasa, *Translations of Shakuntala and Other Works,* trans. Arthur W. Ryder (1912; rpt., London: J. M. Dent, 1933) 53.

[64] On Sunday and Monday, Thoreau pondered questions regarding religion, but in his reverie as he listened to the drumbeat of the young soldier he began his move to the narration of direct religious experience. In the recollected episode on Saddleback (Greylock) Mountain that he gives us here, the experience of the sacred is at its most intense in the *Week*. For a discussion, see Jonathan Bishop, "The Experience of the Sacred in Thoreau's *Week*," *ELH* 33 (March 1966): 66-91.

the clay, talking aloud as if it were broad day, until at length, by three o'clock, we had completed our preparations and were ready to pursue our voyage as usual; so, shaking the clay from our feet, we pushed into the fog.

Though we were enveloped in mist as usual, we trusted that there was a bright day behind it. . . . I once saw the day break from the top of Saddle-back Mountain in Massachusetts, above the clouds. As we cannot distinguish objects through this dense fog, let me tell this story more at length.

I began in the afternoon to ascend the mountain, whose summit is three thousand six hundred feet above the level of the sea, and was seven or eight miles distant by the path.[65] My route lay up a long and spacious valley called the Bellows, because the winds rush up or down it with violence in storms, sloping up to the very clouds between the principal range and a lower mountain. There were a few farms scattered along at different elevations, each commanding a fine prospect of the mountains to the north, and a stream ran down the middle of the valley, on which, near the head, there was a mill. It seemed a road for the pilgrim to enter upon who would climb to the gates of heaven. Now I crossed a hayfield, and now over the brook on a slight bridge, still gradually ascending all the while with a sort of awe, and filled with indefinite expectations as to what kind of inhabitants and what kind of nature I should come to at last. It now seemed some advantage that the earth was uneven, for one could not imagine a more noble position for a farmhouse than this vale afforded, farther from or nearer to its head, from a glen-like seclusion overlooking the country at a great elevation between these two mountain walls. . . .

I made my way steadily upward in a straight line, through a dense undergrowth of mountain laurel, until the trees began to have a scraggy and infernal look, as if contending with frost goblins, and at length I reached the summit, just as the sun was setting. Several acres here had been cleared, and were covered with rocks and stumps, and there was a rude observatory in the middle which overlooked the woods. I had one fair view of the country before the sun went down. . . .

I was up early and perched upon the top of this [observatory] tower to see the daybreak, for some time reading the names that had been engraved there, before I could distinguish more distant objects. An "untamable fly" buzzed at my elbow with the same nonchalance as on a molasses hogshead at the end of Long Wharf.[66] Even there I must attend to his stale humdrum. But now I come to the pith of this long digression. As the light increased, I discovered around me an ocean of mist, which by chance reached up exactly to the base of the tower, and shut out every vestige of the earth, while I was left floating on this fragment of the wreck of a world, on my carved plank, in cloudland; a situation which required no aid from the imagination to render it impressive. As the light in the east steadily increased, it revealed to me more clearly the new world into which I had risen in the night, the new *terra firma* perchance of my future life.[67] There was not a crevice

---

[65]Thoreau is close. The mountain is not quite 3,500 feet above sea level.

[66]Long Wharf, in Boston, was a merchant's mecca, port of entry for goods from all over the world. The huge cask of molasses would be typical.

[67]Literally, the Latin phrase means "solid land"; Thoreau may be suggesting a more solid grounding.

left through which the trivial places we name Massachusetts or Vermont or New York could be seen, while I still inhaled the clear atmosphere of a July morning,—if it were July there. All around beneath me was spread for a hundred miles on every side, as far as the eye could reach, an undulating country of clouds, answering in the varied swell of its surface to the terrestrial world it veiled. It was such a country as we might see in dreams, with all the delights of paradise. There were immense snowy pastures, apparently smooth shaven and firm, and shady vales between the vaporous mountains; and far in the horizon I could see where some luxurious misty timber jutted into the prairie, and trace the windings of a watercourse, some unimagined Amazon or Orinoko, by the misty trees on its brink. As there was wanting the symbol, so there was not the substance of impurity, no spot nor stain. It was a favor for which to be forever silent to be shown this vision. The earth beneath had become such a flitting thing of lights and shadows as the clouds had been before. It was not merely veiled to me, but it had passed away like the phantom of a shadow, σκιᾶς ὄναρ,[68] and this new platform was gained. As I had climbed above storm and cloud, so by successive days' journeys I might reach the region of eternal day, beyond the tapering shadow of the earth; ay,—

> "Heaven itself shall slide,
> And roll away like melting stars that glide
> Along their oily threads."[69]

But when its own sun began to rise on this pure world, I found myself a dweller in the dazzling halls of Aurora, into which poets have had but a partial glance over the eastern hills, drifting amid the saffron-colored clouds, and playing with the rosy fingers of the Dawn, in the very path of the Sun's chariot, and sprinkled with its dewy dust, enjoying the benignant smile, and near at hand the far-darting glances of the god.[70] The inhabitants of earth behold commonly but the dark and shadowy under side of heaven's pavement; it is only when seen at a favorable angle in the horizon, morning or evening, that some faint streaks of the rich lining of the clouds are revealed. But my muse would fail to convey an impression of the gorgeous tapestry by which I was surrounded, such as men see faintly reflected afar off in the chambers of the east. Here, as on earth, I saw the gracious god

> "Flatter the mountain-tops with sovereign eye,
> . . . .
> Gilding pale streams with heavenly alchemy."

But never here did "Heaven's sun" stain himself.

But, alas, owing, as I think, to some

---

[68] The Greek phrase σκιᾶς ὄναρ is used proverbially for something unreal or fleeting and means, literally, "the dream of a shadow."

[69] Giles Fletcher, *Christs Victorie, and Triumph in Heaven, and Earth, over and after Death* (1610), bk. 1, stanza 38, ll. 4-6. Thoreau follows a modernized spelling and punctuation. I am indebted to the work of Ernest E. Leisy in "Sources of Thoreau's Borrowings in *A Week*," *American Literature* 18:1 (March 1946): 37-44, for assistance in the identification of this quotation and others that follow.

[70] Aurora is the Latin name for the Greek Eos, the Goddess of the dawn, who went before the golden chariot of her brother Helios (the Sun God) each morning in the sky. In classical poetry, favorite epithets for the Goddess of the dawn were "rosy-fingered" and "saffron-robed," both of which Thoreau evokes here. The Sun God later was identified with Apollo, who was called the "far-darter" because of his associations with archery (see n. 12 to Emerson, Divinity School *Address*).

unworthiness in myself, my private sun did stain himself, and

> "Anon permit the basest clouds to ride
> With ugly wrack on his celestial face,"—

and before the god had reached the zenith the heavenly pavement rose and embraced my wavering virtue, or rather I sank down again into that "forlorn world," from which the celestial sun had hid his visage,—

> "How may a worm that crawls along the dust,
> Clamber the azure mountains, thrown so high,
> And fetch from thence thy fair idea just,
> That in those sunny courts doth hidden lie,
> Clothed with such light as blinds the angel's eye?
> How may weak mortal ever hope to file
> His unsmooth tongue, and his deprostrate style?
> Oh, raise thou from his corse thy now entombed exile!"[71]

In the preceding evening I had seen the summits of new and yet higher mountains, the Catskills,[72] by which I might hope to climb to heaven again, and had set my compass for a fair lake in the southwest, which lay in my way, for which I now steered, descending the mountain by my own route, on the side opposite to that by which I had ascended, and soon found myself in the region of cloud and drizzling rain, and the inhabitants affirmed that it had been a cloudy and drizzling day wholly.

---

[71] William Shakespeare, Sonnet 33, ll. 2, 4, 14, 5-6, 7; Fletcher, *Christs Victorie, and Triumph*, bk. 1, stanza 43, ll. 1-8.

[72] The peaks of the New York Catskills are generally about 3,000 feet above sea level, but Slide Mountain and Hunter Mountain reach to well over 4,000 feet.

FRIDAY[73]

Here on the stream of the Concord, where we have all the while been bodily, Nature, who is superior to all styles and ages, is now, with pensive face, composing her poem Autumn, with which no work of man will bear to be compared.

In summer we live out of doors, and have only impulses and feelings, which are all for action, and must wait commonly for the stillness and longer nights of autumn and winter before any thought will subside; we are sensible that behind the rustling leaves, and the stacks of grain, and the bare clusters of the grape, there is the field of a wholly new life, which no man has lived; that even this earth was made for more mysterious and nobler inhabitants than men and women. In the hues of October sunsets, we see the portals to other mansions than those which we occupy, not far off geographically,—

---

[73] "Tuesday," "Wednesday," and "Thursday" have all passed. On "Wednesday," Thoreau left behind the solitude of the Greylock of "Tuesday" for a long reflection on friendship, which is also, for him, a source of revelation. On "Thursday," the brothers struck out from the river for their week-long hike into the White Mountains; but Thoreau did not offer details and instead shared his meditations about, on the one hand, settlers and Indians and, on the other, literary themes. As we rejoin Thoreau on "Friday," the journey is all but complete, and the brothers' boat is heading home to Concord. Thoreau's thoughts have turned to poetry, literary genius, the legacy of the pseudonymous Gaelic poet Ossian, and the signs of autumn along the river. Historical reverie and reflections on science as art have engaged him, until—rowing with neither the wind nor the current for support—he has returned to his literary meditations, thinking of Geoffrey Chaucer and then poetry in general. It is at this point that we rejoin the narrative.

"There is a place beyond that flaming hill,
  From whence the stars their thin appearance shed,
A place beyond all place, where never ill,
  Nor impure thought was ever harbored."[74]

Sometimes a mortal feels in himself Nature,—not his Father but his Mother stirs within him, and he becomes immortal with her immortality.[75] From time to time she claims kindredship with us, and some globule from her veins steals up into our own. . . .

Men nowhere, east or west, live yet a *natural* life, round which the vine clings, and which the elm willingly shadows. Man would desecrate it by his touch, and so the beauty of the world remains veiled to him. He needs not only to be spiritualized, but *naturalized,* on the soil of earth. Who shall conceive what kind of roof the heavens might extend over him, what seasons minister to him, and what employment dignify his life! Only the convalescent raise the veil of nature. An immortality in his life would confer immortality on his abode. The winds should be his breath, the seasons his moods, and he should impart of his serenity to Nature herself. But such as we know him he is ephemeral like the scenery which surrounds him, and does not aspire to an enduring existence.[76] . . .

We need pray for no higher heaven than the pure senses can furnish, a *purely* sensuous life. Our present senses are but the rudiments of what they are destined to become.[77] We are comparatively deaf and dumb and blind, and without smell or taste or feeling. Every generation makes the discovery that its divine vigor has been dissipated, and each sense and faculty misapplied and debauched. The ears were made, not for such trivial uses as men are wont to suppose, but to hear celestial sounds. The eyes were not made for such groveling uses as they are now put to and worn out by, but to behold beauty now invisible. May we not *see* God? Are we to be put off and amused in this life, as it were with a mere allegory? Is not Nature, rightly read, that of which she is commonly taken to be the symbol merely? When the common man looks into the sky, which he has not so much profaned, he thinks it less gross than the earth, and with reverence speaks of "the Heavens," but the seer will in the same sense speak of "the Earths," and his Father who is in them. "Did not he that made that which is *within* make that which is *without* also?" What is it, then, to educate but to develop these divine germs called the senses? for individuals and states to deal magnanimously with the rising generation, leading it not into temptation,—not teach the eye to squint, nor attune the ear to profanity. But where is the instructed teacher? Where are the *normal* schools?[78]

---

[74]Fletcher, *Christs Victorie, and Triumph,* bk. 1, stanza 6, ll. 1-4.

[75]Thoreau's immortal "Mother" is not, as for Theodore Parker (cf. his *Sermon of the Delights of Piety),* the compassionate side of a personal Father-Mother God, but instead the divinity of Nature.

[76]Cf. Thoreau's reflections in these lines to those of Emerson's "Orphic poet" in *Nature,* ch. 8.

[77]The passage that unfolds evokes themes similar to those of Emerson in *Nature,* ch. 8. Yet more than Emerson, Thoreau hails the possibilities of earth and senses, mending the rift between real and ideal worlds in the experience of the ideal through the senses. Thoreau does not cease to be a philosophical idealist in his *Week,* but here he brings the idealism, literally, down to earth.

[78]Note Thoreau's pun on "*normal*

A Hindoo sage said, "As a dancer, having exhibited herself to the spectator, desists from the dance, so does Nature desist, having manifested herself to soul. Nothing, in my opinion, is more gentle than Nature; once aware of having been seen, she does not again expose herself to the gaze of soul."[79]

It is easier to discover another such a new world as Columbus did, than to go within one fold of this which we appear to know so well; the land is lost sight of, the compass varies, and mankind mutiny; and still history accumulates like rubbish before the portals of nature. But there is only necessary a moment's sanity and sound senses, to teach us that there is a nature behind the ordinary, in which we have only some vague preëmption right and western reserve as yet. We live on the outskirts of that region. Carved wood, and floating boughs, and sunset skies are all that we know of it. We are not to be imposed on by the longest spell of weather. Let us not, my friends, be wheedled and cheated into good behavior to earn the salt of our eternal porridge, whoever they are that attempt it. Let us wait a little, and not purchase any clearing here, trusting that richer bottoms will soon be put up. It is but thin soil where we stand; I have felt my roots in a richer ere this. I have seen a bunch of violets in a glass vase, tied loosely with a straw, which reminded me of myself.

I am a parcel of vain strivings tied
   By a chance bond together,
Dangling this way and that, their links
   Were made so loose and wide,
      Methinks,
   For milder weather.

A bunch of violets without their roots,
   And sorrel intermixed,
Encircled by a wisp of straw
   Once coiled about their shoots,
      The law
   By which I'm fixed.

A nosegay which Time clutched from out
   Those fair Elysian fields,[80]
With weeds and broken stems, in haste,
   Doth make the rabble rout
      That waste
   The day he yields.

---

schools"—institutions of higher eduction for the training mostly of elementary-school teachers as well as schools that are up-to-standard and in the context natural, educating according to nature. The quotation, earlier in the passage, seems a dramatic construction to emphasize the message of the seer.

[79] The quotation is from Isvara Krishna *Samkhya Karika* (trans. Henry Thomas Colebrooke) 59, 61. I am indebted to Willard L. Johnson of San Diego State University for pointing to the *Samkhya Karika* as the source of the quotation. Thoreau read the work in the 1837 edition: Iswara Krishna, *The Sankhya Karika; or, Memorial Verses on the Sankhya Philosophy,* trans. Henry Thomas Colebrooke (with *The Bhashya, or Commentary of Gaurapada* [sic], trans. and ed. Horace Hayman Wilson), Oriental Translation Fund of Great Britain and Ireland, Publications 46 (London: A. J. Valpy, 1837). In the lines quoted, the relationship of nature (*prakriti*) to the soul (*purusha*) is seen in classical Indian terms as manifested in the dance of (feminine) nature before the soul, the passive spectator and "enjoyer" of what nature manifests for his liberation. Once known or understood by the soul, nature has accomplished her purpose and leaves his presence. But Thoreau has taken the lines out of context and used them to express his sense of profound opportunity lost when the senses are not rightly educated and employed. For *samkhya* teaching, see n. 46, above.

[80] That is, Elysium, the paradise of classical literature.

And here I bloom for a short hour unseen,
    Drinking my juices up,
  With no root in the land
    To keep my branches green,
        But stand
      In a bare cup.

Some tender buds were left upon my stem
    In mimicry of life,
  But ah! the children will not know,
    Till time has withered them,
        The woe
      With which they're rife.

But now I see I was not plucked for naught,
    And after in life's vase
  Of glass set while I might survive,
    But by a kind hand brought
        Alive
      To a strange place.

That stock thus thinned will soon redeem its hours,
    And by another year,
  Such as God knows, with freer air,
    More fruits and fairer flowers
        Will bear,
      While I droop here.[81]

This world has many rings, like Saturn, and we live now on the outmost of them all.[82] None can say deliberately that he inhabits the same sphere, or is contemporary, with the flower which his hands have plucked, and though his feet may seem to crush it, inconceivable spaces and ages separate them, and perchance there is no danger that he will hurt it. What do the botanists know? Our lives should go between the lichen and the bark. The eye may see for the hand, but not for the mind. We are still being born, and have as yet but a dim vision of sea and land, sun, moon, and stars, and shall not see clearly till after nine days at least. That is a pathetic inquiry among travelers and geographers after the site of ancient Troy.[83] It is not near where they think it is. When a thing is decayed and gone, how indistinct must be the place it occupied!

The anecdotes of modern astronomy affect me in the same way as do those faint revelations of the Real which are vouchsafed to men fom time to time, or rather from eternity to eternity. When I remember the history of that faint light in our firmament which we call Venus, which ancient men regarded, and which most modern men still regard, as a bright spark attached to a hollow sphere revolving about

---

[81]The poem is Thoreau's and appears, titled by its first line, in Thoreau, *Collected Poems,* 81-82. In 1837 Thoreau had tossed the poem, titled in Latin "*Sic Vita*" ("Thus Life"), with a bunch of violets, into the window of Mrs. Lucy Jackson Brown, a woman in her late thirties (Emerson's sister-in-law) whom Thoreau admired. See Walter Harding, *The Days of Henry Thoreau* (New York: Alfred A. Knopf, 1965) 105-107, and Henry Seidel Canby, *Thoreau* (Boston: Houghton Mifflin, Riverside Press, 1939) 72-74. "*Sic Vita*" was later published in *The Dial* in 1841 and finally appeared in Thoreau's *Week*.

[82]Thoreau follows a spiritual geography that locates the spiritually unenlightened at the most peripheral, or outer, circle and, by implication, the sacred in the central, or inmost, place. Significantly, the "map" accords with the mystical and metaphysical tradition of the West. For the similar thoughts of Emerson, see Ralph Waldo Emerson, *The Journals and Miscellaneous Notebooks of Ralph Waldo Emerson,* ed. William H. Gilman et al. (Cambridge: Harvard University Press, Belknap Press, 1960–), 5 (17 June 1836): 177.

[83]It was not until 1871 that Heinrich Schliemann (1822–1890), an amateur archaeologist from Germany, correctly located the site of ancient Troy and began excavations there.

our earth, but which we have discovered to be *another world,* in itself,—how Copernicus, reasoning long and patiently about the matter, predicted confidently concerning it, before yet the telescope had been invented, that if ever men came to see it more clearly than they did then, they would discover that it had phases like our moon, and that within a century after his death the telescope was invented, and that prediction verified, by Galileo,[84]—I am not without hope that we may, even here and now, obtain some accurate information concerning that OTHER WORLD which the instinct of mankind has so long predicted. Indeed, all that we call science, as well as all that we call poetry, is a particle of such information, accurate as far as it goes, though it be but to the confines of the truth. If we can reason so accurately, and with such wonderful confirmation of our reasoning, respecting so-called material objects and events infinitely removed beyond the range of our natural vision, so that the mind hesitates to trust its calculations even when they are confirmed by observation, why may not our speculations penetrate as far into the immaterial starry system, of which the former is but the outward and visible type? Surely, we are provided with senses as well fitted to penetrate the spaces of the real, the substantial, the eternal, as these outward are to penetrate the material universe. Veias, Menu, Zoroaster, Socrates, Christ, Shakespeare, Swedenborg,—these are some of our astronomers. . . .

Thus thoughtfully we were rowing homeward to find some autumnal work to do, and help on the revolution of the seasons. Perhaps Nature would condescend to make use of us even without our knowledge, as when we help to scatter her seeds in our walks, and carry burs and cockles on our clothes from field to field. . . .

As it grew later in the afternoon, and we rowed leisurely up the gentle stream, shut in between fragrant and blooming banks, where we had first pitched our tent, and drew nearer to the fields where our lives had passed, we seemed to detect the hues of our native sky in the southwest horizon. The sun was just setting behind the edge of a wooded hill, so rich a sunset as would never have ended but for some reason unknown to men, and to be marked with brighter colors than ordinary in the scroll of time. Though the shadows of the hills were beginning to steal over the stream, the whole river valley undulated with mild light, purer and more memorable than the noon. For so day bids farewell even to solitary vales uninhabited by man. Two herons (*Ardea herodias*), with their long and slender limbs relieved against the sky, were seen traveling high over our heads,—their lofty and silent flight, as they were wending their way at evening, surely not to alight in any marsh on the earth's surface, but, perchance, on the other side of our atmosphere, a symbol for the ages to study, whether impressed upon the sky or sculptured amid the hieroglyphics of Egypt.[85] Bound to some northern meadow,

---

[84]For Nicholas Copernicus and Galileo Galilei, see n. 13 to Emerson, "Self-Reliance." According to the ancient Ptolemaic theory, the earth—which was stationary—formed the center of the universe, and the heavenly bodies revolved around it. The planets moved in their own (small) circles with their centers revolving about the earth in much larger spheres. With the aid of the telescope, Galileo observed that Venus passed through phases like the moon and argued that therefore it was a dark body that, like the earth, received its light from the sun.

---

[85]The *Ardea herodias* is the great blue heron, about fifty inches long and with a crest on its head. Note Thoreau's reference to the "hiero-

they held on their stately, stationary flight, like the storks in the picture, and disappeared at length behind the clouds. Dense flocks of blackbirds were winging their way along the river's course, as if on a short evening pilgrimage to some shrine of theirs, or to celebrate so fair a sunset.

"Therefore, as doth the pilgrim, whom the night
  Hastes darkly to imprison on his way,
Think on thy home, my soul, and think aright
Of what's yet left thee of life's wasting day:
  Thy sun posts westward, passed is thy morn,
  And twice it is not given thee to be born."[86]

The sun-setting presumed all men at leisure, and in a contemplative mood; but the farmer's boy only whistled the more thoughtfully as he drove his cows home from pasture, and the teamster refrained from cracking his whip, and guided his team with a subdued voice. The last vestiges of daylight at length disappeared, and as we rowed silently along with our backs toward home through the darkness, only a few stars being visible, we had little to say, but sat absorbed in thought, or in silence listened to the monotonous sound of our oars, a sort of rudimental music, suitable for the ear of Night and the acoustics of her dimly lighted halls;

"Pulsae referunt ad sidera valles,"[87]

and the valleys echoed the sound to the stars. . . .

As the truest society approaches always nearer to solitude, so the most excellent speech finally falls into Silence.[88] Silence is audible to all men, at all times, and in all places. She is when we hear inwardly, sound when we hear outwardly. Creation has not displaced her, but is her visible framework and foil. All sounds are her servants, and purveyors, proclaiming not only that their mistress is, but is a rare mistress, and earnestly to be sought after. They are so far akin to Silence that they are but bubbles on her surface, which straightway burst, an evidence of the strength and prolificness of the under-current; a faint utterance of Silence, and then only agreeable to our auditory nerves when they contrast themselves with and relieve the former. In proportion as they do this, and are heighteners and intensifiers of the Silence, they are harmony and purest melody.

Silence is the universal refuge, the sequel to all dull discourses and all foolish acts, a balm to our every chagrin, as welcome after satiety as after disappointment; that background which the painter may not daub, be he master or bungler, and which, however awkward a figure we may have made in the foreground, remains ever our inviolable asylum, where no indignity can assail, no personality disturb us.

The orator puts off his individuality, and is then most eloquent when most silent. He listens while he speaks, and is a

---

glyphics of Egypt,'' and see n. 2 to Emerson, *Nature,* for a brief discussion. The evocative power of the symbol was felt by Thoreau as well as by Emerson. (See, for a second instance, Henry David Thoreau, *Walden,* ch. 17, par. 5, in this volume.)

[86]The lines, with minor changes, are from William Drummond, ''No Trust in Time,'' *Flowers of Sion; or, Spiritual Poems* (1623), ll. 9-14.

[87]Vergil *Eclogues* 6.84. Thoreau immediately repeats the Latin line in translation.

[88]After linking the stars of heaven to spiritual depth and contemplative silence, Thoreau hymns a final tribute to the silence. In the tradition of the mystics, he tells us that sounds and words in the end must yield before the wisdom of the unspoken. The yoga of sound falls away, ultimately, in the yoga of silence.

hearer along with his audience. Who has not hearkened to her infinite din? She is Truth's speaking-trumpet, the sole oracle, the true Delphi and Dodona, which kings and courtiers would do well to consult, nor will they be balked by an ambiguous answer.[89] For through her all revelations have been made, and just in proportion as men have consulted her oracle within, they have obtained a clear insight, and their age has been marked as an enlightened one. But as often as they have gone gadding abroad to a strange Delphi and her mad priestess, their age has been dark and leaden. Such were garrulous and noisy eras, which no longer yield any sound, but the Grecian or silent and melodious era is ever sounding and resounding in the ears of men.

A good book is the plectrum with which our else silent lyres are struck. We not unfrequently refer the interest which belongs to our own unwritten sequel to the written and comparatively lifeless body of the work. Of all books this sequel is the most indispensable part. It should be the author's aim to say once and emphatically, "He said," ἔφη.[90] This is the most the bookmaker can attain to. If he make his volume a mole whereon the waves of Silence may break, it is well.

It were vain for me to endeavor to interpret the Silence. She cannot be done into English. For six thousand years men have translated her with what fidelity belonged to each, and still she is little better than a sealed book.[91] A man may run on confidently for a time, thinking he has her under his thumb, and shall one day exhaust her, but he too must at last be silent, and men remark only how brave a beginning he made; for when he at length dives into her, so vast is the disproportion of the told to the untold that the former will seem but the bubble on the surface where he disappeared. Nevertheless, we will go on, like those Chinese cliff swallows, feathering our nests with the froth which may one day be bread of life to such as dwell by the seashore.[92]

We had made about fifty miles this day with sail and oar, and now, far in the evening, our boat was grating against the bulrushes of its native port, and its keel recognized the Concord mud, where some semblance of its outline was still preserved in the flattened flags which had scarce yet erected themselves since our departure; and we leaped gladly on shore, drawing it up and fastening it to the wild apple tree, whose stem still bore the mark which its chain had worn in the chafing of the spring freshets.

---

[89] For the oracle at Delphi, see n. 3 to Ralph Waldo Emerson, "The Problem." Dodona, located in Epirus, was the oldest of the Greek religious oracles and considered sacred to the God Zeus. Note, finally, the (mystical) paradox Thoreau expresses in the metaphor: silence—like a speaking trumpet, or megaphone, intensifying the sound of a voice for a crowd—intensifies the revelation of truth.

[90] Thoreau has translated the Greek verb *ephe* in the phrase immediately preceding it.

[91] Thoreau assumes that the writing of sacred scriptures was begun six thousand years before his time. But like his contemporaries, he overestimates by modern scholarly standards. The earliest (Sumerian) sacred texts have been dated from probably the middle of the third millennium B.C.

[92] Cliff swallows, or eaves swallows (genus *Petrochelidon*), build mud nests resembling bottles in appearance, in the sides of cliffs or beneath eaves. They are mostly North American, and Thoreau's reference to "Chinese" cliff swallows is a testimony to the breadth of his reading. For a general discussion, see Christie, *Thoreau as World Traveler*.

THE MAINE WOODS

The Maine Woods began with three separate journeys into the wilderness in the state of Maine—in 1846, again in 1853, and finally in 1857. Thoreau explored by boat and by land, absorbing all that he could of Indian life and culture in the area. Repeatedly, he juxtaposed the indigenous past with the American present and future, seemingly compelled by inner necessity to come to terms with the ancient roots of land and people.

The first two trips in Maine resulted in essays that were published during Thoreau's lifetime: "Ktaadn and the Maine Woods," which appeared in five separate installments in John Sartain's *Union Magazine of Literature and Art* in 1848, and "Chesuncook," which appeared in *The Atlantic Monthly* in 1858. In the final weeks before he died, Thoreau was making revisions in a third essay, "The Allegash and East Branch"; and he had already prepared an appendix that covered material, much of it botanical, from all three of the essays. In fact, his friend (William) Ellery Channing recollected that Thoreau's last distinct words before he died were "moose" and "Indians."[1] Thus, when *The Maine Woods* was published in Boston by Ticknor and Fields in 1864, it represented its author's own intentions. Thoreau had selected the title and roughly planned the organization of the work. His editors—his sister Sophia and his friend Channing—were simply executing, as they could, his wishes.

The narrative below is taken from the first of the Maine essays, titled in the book "Ktaadn." It was late during the second summer of his stay at Walden Pond that Thoreau made this, his first expedition to the Maine country. A cousin, George A. Thatcher, had invited Thoreau to accompany him on an inspection of some property located on the Penobscot River's West Branch. Thatcher worked in lumbering, and two of his friends from Bangor, Maine, who also had lumbering interests joined them, as did two boaters, George McCauslin and Thomas Fowler, to guide and carry their hired bateau.

For Thoreau, the journey's center and climax was his solitary hike to the peak of Mount Katahdin, named by the Indians in a word thought to mean "highest land." The mountain was, indeed, the highest place in Maine, soaring nearly 5,300 feet above sea level and surrounded by craggy and forbidding country above the tree line. Euro-Americans had climbed it for the first time only in 1804; and if we follow Thoreau's summary of earlier expeditions, his was the fifth successful attempt to reach the top.[2] But the ascent was not without cost, and Thoreau came away deeply impressed by the wild energies of the moun-

---

[1] See the accounts in William Ellery Channing, *Thoreau: The Poet-Naturalist* (Boston: Roberts, 1873) 319, and Walter Harding, *The Days of Henry Thoreau* (New York: Alfred A. Knopf, 1965) 461-62, 466.

[2] See Henry David Thoreau, *The Writings of Henry David Thoreau*, Walden ed. (Boston: Houghton Mifflin, 1906) 3:4.

tain, his Transcendental confidence in intuitive reason and an organic relationship to nature shaken. In the lonely secret of Katahdin's summit, he experienced the power aspect of the holy that Mircea Eliade has called a "kratophany."[3] If there had been ecstasy on Saddleback Mountain in Thoreau's *Week on the Concord and Merrimack Rivers,* there was a species of terror on this one. Thoreau later articulated the complex emotion of the kratophany in the classical and Miltonic language that forms the basic metaphorical structure of his account, naming the aboriginal powers of the mountain in the vocabulary of the European heritage. He had found paradise on Saddleback, but he lost it in the realm of darker spirits on the summit of Katahdin, and he would never forget the experience.

In the excerpt that follows, we join Thoreau briefly in the privileged hours of the first trip to Maine, when he saw the heights of the mountain. The raw and elemental danger of his contact with Katahdin, as he shows us, left him with questions more than answers and a lasting sense of the ambiguity of the sacred.[4]

---

[3] For the kratophany, or manifestation of the sacred as power, see Mircea Eliade, *Patterns in Comparative Religion,* trans. Rosemary Sheed (Cleveland: World Publishing, Meridian Books, 1963) 14-19.

[4] The text is excerpted from Thoreau, *Writings* (Walden ed.), 3:65-79.

(From) THE MAINE WOODS

KTAADN

At length we reached an elevation sufficiently bare to afford a view of the summit, still distant and blue, almost as if retreating from us. A torrent, which proved to be the same we had crossed, was seen tumbling down in front, literally from out of the clouds. But this glimpse at our whereabouts was soon lost, and we were buried in the woods again. The wood was chiefly yellow birch, spruce, fir, mountain-ash, or round-wood, as the Maine people call it, and moose-wood. It was the worst kind of traveling; sometimes like the densest scrub oak patches with us. The cornel, or bunch-berries, were very abundant, as well as Solomon's-seal and mooseberries. Blueberries were distributed along our whole route: and in one place the bushes were drooping with the weight of the fruit, still as fresh as ever. It was the 7th of September. Such patches afforded a grateful repast, and served to bait the tired party forward. When any lagged behind, the cry of "blueberries" was most effectual to bring them up. Even at this elevation we passed through a moose-yard, formed by a large flat rock, four or five rods square, where they tread down the snow in winter. At length, fearing that if we held the direct course to the summit, we should not find any water near our camping-ground, we gradually swerved to the west, till, at four o'clock, we struck again the torrent which I have mentioned, and here, in view of the summit, the weary party decided to camp that night.

While my companions were seeking a suitable spot for this purpose, I improved the little daylight that was left in climbing the mountain alone. We were in a deep and narrow ravine, sloping up to the clouds, at an angle of nearly forty-five degrees, and hemmed in by walls of rock, which were at first covered with low trees, then with impenetrable thickets of scraggy birches and spruce trees, and with moss, but at last bare of all vegetation but lichens, and almost continually draped in clouds. Following up the course of the torrent which occupied this,—and I mean to lay some emphasis on this word *up*,—pulling myself up by the side of perpendicular falls of twenty or thirty feet, by the roots of firs and birches, and then, perhaps, walking a level rod or two in the thin stream, for it took up the whole road, ascending by huge steps, as it were, a giant's stairway, down which a river flowed, I had soon cleared the trees, and paused on the successive shelves, to look back over the country.[1] The torrent was from fifteen to thirty feet wide, without a tributary, and seemingly not diminishing in breadth as I advanced; but still it came rushing and roaring down, with a copious tide, over and amidst masses of bare rock, from the very clouds, as though a waterspout had just burst over the mountain. Leaving this at last, I began to work my way, scarcely less arduous than Satan's anciently through Chaos, up the

---

[1] Seen in relationship to what follows, Thoreau's "giant's stairway" announces the classical and Miltonic schema that provide the metaphors for interpreting his Katahdin experience.

nearest though not the highest peak.² At first scrambling on all fours over the tops of ancient black spruce trees (*Abies nigra*),³ old as the flood, from two to ten or twelve feet in height, their tops flat and spreading, and their foliage blue, and nipped with cold, as if for centuries they had ceased growing upward against the bleak sky, the solid cold. I walked some good rods erect upon the tops of these trees, which were overgrown with moss and mountain cranberries. It seemed that in the course of time they had filled up the intervals between the huge rocks, and the cold wind had uniformly leveled all over. Here the principle of vegetation was hard put to it. There was apparently a belt of this kind running quite round the mountain, though, perhaps, nowhere so remarkable as here. Once, slumping through, I looked down ten feet, into a dark and cavernous region, and saw the stem of a spruce, on whose top I stood, as on a mass of coarse basket-work, fully nine inches in diameter at the ground. These holes were bears' dens, and the bears were even then at home. This was the sort of garden I made my way *over*,⁴ for an eighth of a mile, at the risk, it is true, of treading on some of the plants, not seeing any path *through* it,—certainly the most treacherous and porous country I ever traveled.

> "Nigh foundered on he fares,
> Treading the crude consistence, half on foot,
> Half flying,"⁵

But nothing could exceed the toughness of the twigs,—not one snapped under my weight, for they had slowly grown. Having slumped, scrambled, rolled, bounced, and walked, by turns, over this scraggy country, I arrived upon a side-hill, or rather side-mountain, where rocks, gray, silent rocks, were the flocks and herds that pastured, chewing a rocky cud at sunset. They looked at me with hard gray eyes, without a bleat or a low.⁶ This brought me to the skirt of a cloud, and bounded my walk that night. But I had already seen that Maine country when I turned about, waving, flowing, rippling, down below.

When I returned to my companions, they had selected a camping-ground on the torrent's edge, and were resting on the ground; one was on the sick list, rolled in a blanket, on a damp shelf of rock. It was a savage and dreary scenery enough, so

---

²Thoreau refers to the "nearest peak" since Katahdin possesses four peaks, the highest being the southern. For Satan's passage through the endless ocean of Chaos, in a misbegotten pilgrimage to seek paradise in the Garden of Eden, cf. John Milton, *Paradise Lost*, bk. 2, ll. 890-1055, and bk. 3, ll. 417-539, in which Satan comes upon the Gate of Heaven (ll. 498-525; cf. the "giant's stairway" of n. 1 above). Milton's vision is built in part on Greek mythology, in which Chaos, the "yawning" or void, is the source from which the primeval Gods arise (cf. Hesiod *Theogony* 116-49).

³The standard botanical name for the black spruce is now *Picea mariana*. Scientific names for the black spruce in use in the nineteenth century included *Abies mariana*, *Picea nigra*, and *Pinus nigra*. *Abies nigra* seems to be a conflation of the first two. In the earlier essay "Ktaadn and the Maine Woods" (1848), Thoreau allowed an identification of the black spruce as *"pinus nigra"* to stand. I am indebted to Walter Tulecke of Antioch College for his assistance in identifying Thoreau's tree.

⁴This may be an ironic allusion to Satan's entry into the Garden of Eden (cf. Milton, *Paradise Lost*, bk. 4, ll. 172-284).

⁵The lines, chronicling Satan's journey to the throne of Chaos, are ibid., bk. 2, ll. 940-42.

⁶Cf. Satan's entry into paradise as a wolf among the flocks, ibid., bk. 4, ll. 183-87, 192; and the reference to the flocks in Eden, ibid., ll. 252-53.

wildly rough, that they looked long to find a level and open space for the tent. We could not well camp higher, for want of fuel; and the trees here seemed so evergreen and sappy, that we almost doubted if they would acknowledge the influence of fire; but fire prevailed at last, and blazed here, too, like a good citizen of the world. Even at this height we met with frequent traces of moose, as well as of bears. As here was no cedar, we made our bed of coarser feathered spruce; but at any rate the feathers were plucked from the live tree. It was, perhaps, even a more grand and desolate place for a night's lodging than the summit would have been, being in the neighborhood of those wild trees, and of the torrent. Some more aërial and finer-spirited winds rushed and roared through the ravine all night, from time to time arousing our fire, and dispersing the embers about. It was as if we lay in the very nest of a young whirlwind. At midnight, one of my bed-fellows, being startled in his dreams by the sudden blazing up to its top of a fir tree, whose green boughs were dried by the heat, sprang up, with a cry, from his bed, thinking the world on fire, and drew the whole camp after him.

In the morning, after whetting our appetite on some raw pork, a wafer of hard-bread, and a dipper of condensed cloud or waterspout, we all together began to make our way up the falls, which I have described; this time choosing the right hand, or highest peak, which was not the one I had approached before. But soon my companions were lost to my sight behind the mountain ridge in my rear, which still seemed ever retreating before me, and I climbed alone over huge rocks, loosely poised, a mile or more, still edging toward the clouds; for though the day was clear elsewhere, the summit was concealed by mist. The mountain seemed a vast aggregation of loose rocks, as if some time it had rained rocks, and they lay as they fell on the mountain sides, nowhere fairly at rest, but leaning on each other, all rocking stones, with cavities between, but scarcely any soil or smoother shelf. They were the raw materials of a planet dropped from an unseen quarry, which the vast chemistry of nature would anon work up, or work down, into the smiling and verdant plains and valleys of earth. This was an undone extremity of the globe; as in lignite we see coal in the process of formation.

At length I entered within the skirts of the cloud which seemed forever drifting over the summit, and yet would never be gone, but was generated out of that pure air as fast as it flowed away; and when, a quarter of a mile farther, I reached the summit of the ridge, which those who have seen in clearer weather say is about five miles long, and contains a thousand acres of table-land, I was deep within the hostile ranks of clouds, and all objects were obscured by them. Now the wind would blow me out a yard of clear sunlight, wherein I stood; then a gray, dawning light was all it could accomplish, the cloud-line ever rising and falling with the wind's intensity. Sometimes it seemed as if the summit would be cleared in a few moments, and smile in sunshine; but what was gained on one side was lost on another. It was like sitting in a chimney and waiting for the smoke to blow away. It was, in fact, a cloud-factory,—these were the cloud-works, and the wind turned them off done from the cool, bare rocks. Occasionally, when the windy columns broke in to me, I caught sight of a dark, damp crag to the right or left; the mist driving ceaselessly between it and me. It reminded me of the creations of the old epic and dramatic poets, of Atlas, Vulcan, the Cyclops, and Prometheus.[7] Such was Caucasus and the

---

[7]Atlas, the Cyclopes, and Prometheus all

rock where Prometheus was bound. Æschylus had no doubt visited such scenery as this.[8] It was vast, Titanic, and such as man never inhabits.[9] Some part of the beholder, even some vital part, seems to escape through the loose grating of his ribs as he ascends. He is more lone than you can imagine. There is less of substantial thought and fair understanding in him than in the plains where men inhabit. His reason is dispersed and shadowy, more thin and subtile, like the air. Vast, Titanic, inhuman Nature has got him at disadvantage, caught him alone, and pilfers him of some of his divine faculty. She does not smile on him as in the plains. She seems to say sternly, Why came ye here before your time. This ground is not prepared for you. Is it not enough that I smile in the valleys? I have never made this soil for thy feet, this air for thy breathing, these rocks for thy neighbors. I cannot pity nor fondle thee here, but forever relentlessly drive thee hence to where I *am* kind. Why seek me where I have not called thee, and then complain because you find me but a stepmother? Shouldst thou freeze or starve, or shudder thy life away, here is no shrine, nor altar, nor any access to my ear.

> "Chaos and ancient Night, I come no spy
> With purpose to explore or to disturb
> The secrets of your realm, but . . .
> .   .   .   .   .   as my way
> Lies through your spacious empire up to
>   light."[10]

---

figure in the *Theogony* of Hesiod (ll. 507-20 and 746-50; 139-46; 521-67 and 613-16). Atlas, the son of the Titan Iapetus and Clymene, the daughter of Ocean, was the brother of Prometheus and the upholder of the sky. For Prometheus, see n. 11 to Amos Bronson Alcott, *The Doctrine and Discipline of Human Culture,* and n. 21 to Amos Bronson Alcott, "Orphic Sayings." Vulcan, or Mulciber, is cited in various places in the *Metamorphoses* of Ovid (2.5, 106; 4.173-89; 9.251, 263; 12.614; 13.289; passim). The Roman counterpart of the Olympian deity Hephaestus, Vulcan was God of fire—at first as a destructive force but later, under Greek influence, as a creative and tempering deity. Finally, the Cyclops is probably Polyphemus—one of a race of lawless one-eyed giants, although in a tradition distinct from that of the Cyclopes who appear in Hesiod's creation myth. In Homer *Odyssey* 9.216-542, Polyphemus devours members of Ulysses' crew but, deceived by the wiles of Ulysses and blinded by him, unwittingly lets the hero and his remaining men escape.

[8]A reference to Aeschylus's tragedy *Prometheus Bound* in which Prometheus, who had angered Zeus by befriending and assisting humankind, was bound in punishment to a rock on the desolate shores of Scythia in the Caucasus. It may be significant that, although reluctantly, Hephaestus (Roman Vulcan) had executed Zeus's orders, riveting Prometheus to the rock (cf. Aeschylus *Prometheus Bound* 12-81).

[9]The Titans were the twelve primordial Gods and Goddesses of ancient Greek religion (Hesiod *Theogony* 132-38, 207-10). Cronos, one of their original number, engaged in the primeval revolt, castrating his father Uranus (Heaven) at the instigation of Ge (Earth) and so destroying his power. But the Titans in turn were conquered by Zeus, the son of Cronos, and forced into Tartarus (Hesiod *Theogony* 154-210, 607-819). Milton refers briefly to the Titans in *Paradise Lost,* bk. 1, ll. 507-21. Here, however, Thoreau uses the adjective "Titanic" to suggest the overwhelming and ruthless power of the landscape.

[10]Milton, *Paradise Lost,* bk. 2, ll. 970-74, with minor, nonsubstantive changes. The words are Satan's at the throne of Chaos. In quoting Milton's Satan in the context of his earlier reference to Aeschylus's Prometheus, Thoreau has caught the spirit of proud defiance that links the two (cf. Moses Hadas, *A History of Greek Literature* [New York: Columbia University Press, 1950] 81). Perhaps, as well, he identifies part

The tops of mountains are among the unfinished parts of the globe, whither it is a slight insult to the gods to climb and pry into their secrets, and try their effect on our humanity. Only daring and insolent men, perchance, go there. Simple races, as savages, do not climb mountains,—their tops are sacred and mysterious tracts never visited by them. Pomola is always angry with those who climb to the summit of Ktaadn.[11]

. . .

I found my companions where I had left them, on the side of the peak, gathering the mountain cranberries,[12] which filled every crevice between the rocks, together with blueberries, which had a spicier flavor the higher up they grew, but were not the less agreeable to our palates. When the country is settled, and roads are made, these cranberries will perhaps become an article of commerce. From this elevation, just on the skirts of the clouds, we could overlook the country, west and south, for a hundred miles. There it was, the State of Maine, which we had seen on the map, but not much like that,—immeasurable forest for the sun to shine on, that eastern *stuff* we hear of in Massachusetts. No clearing, no house. It did not look as if a solitary traveler had cut so much as a walking-stick there. . . .

Setting out on our return to the river, still at an early hour in the day, we decided to follow the course of the torrent, which we supposed to be Murch Brook,[13] as long as it would not lead us too far out of our way. We thus traveled about four miles in the very torrent itself, continually crossing and recrossing it, leaping from rock to rock, and jumping with the stream down falls of seven or eight feet, or sometimes sliding down on our backs in a thin sheet of water. . . . At one place we were startled by seeing, on a little sandy shelf by the side of the stream, the fresh print of a man's foot, and for a moment realized how Robinson Crusoe felt in a similar case;[14] but at last we remembered that we had struck this stream on our way up, though we could not have told where, and one had descended into the ravine for a drink. The cool air above and the continual bathing of our bodies in mountain water, alternate foot, sitz, douche, and plunge baths, made this walk exceedingly refreshing, and we had traveled only a mile or two, after leaving the torrent, before every thread of our clothes was as dry as usual, owing perhaps to a peculiar quality in the atmosphere.

After leaving the torrent, being in doubt about our course, Tom threw down his pack at the foot of the loftiest spruce tree at hand, and shinned up the bare trunk some twenty

---

of his own inner spirit, at least as he began to climb Katahdin. His next sentences, echoing Milton and implicitly characterizing himself, suggest the same.

[11]The Indian deity Pomola is the stormbird, the Thunderer who, according to Penobscot tribal tradition, dwells on the mountain of Katahdin. Thoreau's observation regarding the sacredness of mountaintops for "simple" and "savage" peoples (read American Indian and similar cultures) is a generalization that, when geographical requirements are met, is upheld by the comparative study of religions. But mountains are also sacred in many citied traditions—e.g., those of Japan and ancient Israel.

[12]Lingonberries or cowberries.

[13]Murch Brook, to the south-southwest of Mount Katahdin, ran south and emptied into the West Branch of the Penobscot River.

[14]The account of Robinson Crusoe's discovery of "the Print of a Man's naked Foot on the Shore" may be found in Daniel Defoe, *The Life and Strange Surprizing Adventures of Robinson Crusoe, of York, Mariner (1719)*, ed. J. Donald Crowley (London: Oxford University Press, 1972) 153-54.

feet, and then climbed through the green tower, lost to our sight, until he held the topmost spray in his hand. . . . To Tom we cried, "Where away does the summit bear? where the burnt lands?" The last he could only conjecture; he descried, however, a little meadow and pond, lying probably in our course, which we concluded to steer for. On reaching this secluded meadow, we found fresh tracks of moose on the shore of the pond, and the water was still unsettled as if they had fled before us. A little farther, in a dense thicket, we seemed to be still on their trail. It was a small meadow, of a few acres, on the mountain-side, concealed by the forest, and perhaps never seen by a white man before, where one would think that the moose might browse and bathe, and rest in peace. Pursuing this course, we soon reached the open land, which went sloping down some miles toward the Penobscot.

Perhaps I most fully realized that this was primeval, untamed, and forever untamable *Nature,* or whatever else men call it, while coming down this part of the mountain. We were passing over "Burnt Lands," burnt by lightning, perchance, though they showed no recent marks of fire, hardly so much as a charred stump, but looked rather like a natural pasture for the moose and deer, exceedingly wild and desolate, with occasional strips of timber crossing them, and low poplars springing up, and patches of blueberries here and there. I found myself traversing them familiarly, like some pasture run to waste, or partially reclaimed by man; but when I reflected what man, what brother or sister or kinsman of our race made it and claimed it, I expected the proprietor to rise up and dispute my passage. It is difficult to conceive of a region uninhabited by man. We habitually presume his presence and influence everywhere. And yet we have not seen pure Nature, unless we have seen her thus vast and drear and inhuman, though in the midst of cities. Nature was here something savage and awful, though beautiful. I looked with awe at the ground I trod on, to see what the Powers had made there, the form and fashion and material of their work. This was that Earth of which we have heard, made out of Chaos and Old Night.[15] Here was no man's garden, but the unhandseled globe.[16] It was not lawn, nor pasture, nor mead, nor woodland, nor lea, nor arable, nor waste land. It was the fresh and natural surface of the planet Earth, as it was made forever and ever,—to be the dwelling of man, we say,—so Nature made it, and man may use it if he can. Man was not to be associated with it. It was Matter, vast, terrific,—not his Mother Earth that we have heard of, not for him to tread on, or be buried in,—no, it were being too familiar even to let his bones lie there,—the home, this, of Necessity and Fate.[17] There

---

[15] For the phrase "Chaos and Old Night," cf. Milton, *Paradise Lost,* bk. 1, l. 543; and cf., too, Milton's restatement in which "eldest Night'' and *"Chaos"* are the "Ancestors of Nature" (ibid., bk. 2, ll. 894-95) and Night is enthroned as consort of Chaos (ibid., ll. 959-63). Chaos and Night precede the generation of Earth in Aristophanes *Birds* 694-702, based on an early Greek account.

[16] Again the allusion is surely Miltonic. Unlike Satan, Thoreau has not passed through the Abyss to the Garden of Eden (see n. 2 above) but is still passing through an uninaugurated ("unhandseled") world.

[17] For Necessity and Fate, see n. 1 to Ralph Waldo Emerson, "Fate." See also Hesiod *Theogony* 217-22, 904-906, in which the three Fates are portrayed as avenging and ruthless, the givers of evil (and good) to humanity. Thoreau records here and in the following passage his sense of estrangement from the earth that has become not "Mother" but "Matter." See Robert F. Sayre, *Thoreau and the American Indians* (Princeton: Princeton University Press, 1977) 165-66.

was clearly felt the presence of a force not bound to be kind to man. It was a place for heathenism and superstitious rites,—to be inhabited by men nearer of kin to the rocks and to wild animals than we.[18] We walked over it with a certain awe, stopping, from time to time, to pick the blueberries which grew there, and had a smart and spicy taste. Perchance where *our* wild pines stand, and leaves lie on their forest floor, in Concord, there were once reapers, and husbandmen planted grain; but here not even the surface had been scarred by man, but it was a specimen of what God saw fit to make this world. What is it to be admitted to a museum, to see a myriad of particular things, compared with being shown some star's surface, some hard matter in its home! I stand in awe of my body, this matter to which I am bound has become so strange to me. I fear not spirits, ghosts, of which I am one,—*that* my body might,—but I fear bodies, I tremble to meet them. What is this Titan that has possession of me? Talk of mysteries! Think of our life in nature,—daily to be shown matter, to come in contact with it,—rocks, trees, wind on our cheeks! the *solid* earth! the *actual* world! the *common sense! Contact! Contact! Who* are we? *where* are we? . . .

---

[18]Thoreau stands in the Puritan tradition in linking the wilderness and the Indians (cf. Pomola in the text above) to Satanic forces and the powers of Chaos. See Roderick Nash, *Wilderness and the American Mind,* 3d ed. (New Haven: Yale University Press, 1982) 23-30, 90-92; Peter N. Carroll, *Puritanism and the Wilderness: The Intellectual Significance of the New England Frontier, 1629-1700* (New York: Columbia University Press, 1969) 65-86; and Sayre, *Thoreau and the American Indians, 166.*

CIVIL DISOBEDIENCE

After Thoreau, in July 1846, spent his often-chronicled night in jail for tax refusal, people in Concord continued to question him about the episode. Finally Thoreau, who was active in the local Concord lyceum, gave them a formal answer in two lectures delivered at the lyceum in January and February 1848. It is not clear if the second lecture was a repetition, revision, or second installment of the first, but the material in the lectures had no doubt come together over some years. Thus, as he spoke, Thoreau's thoughts turned on what he called "The Rights & Duties of the Individual in relation to Government."[1] The justification of the night in jail became an opportunity to declare his Transcendental view of the nature of government and law and the meaning of individual freedom and responsibility.

More than a year later Elizabeth Palmer Peabody wrote to Thoreau, asking him to contribute his manuscript of the Concord lectures to the new periodical she was planning to publish. With some protestation, Thoreau—who was in the midst of correcting proofs for his *Week on the Concord and Merrimack Rivers*—agreed to send it. Hence, in May 1849, now titled "Resistance to Civil Government," the essay appeared in the first—and only—issue of *Aesthetic Papers*. At the time it elicited scarcely any response from reviewers, but four years after Thoreau's death, it was reprinted with changes—mostly in punctuation and capitalization—in *A Yankee in Canada, with Anti-Slavery and Reform Papers* (Boston: Ticknor and Fields, 1866). This time the title had been changed (whether by Thoreau before his death is not clear), and the familiar "Civil Disobedience" made its appearance at the head of the essay. Still, though, Thoreau's words did not excite serious interest.

Yet the content of the essay *is* serious. Indeed, Thoreau's text is a prophetic—if sometimes ambiguous—statement of the individual's relationship to the state. As Thoreau demonstrates in his exposition, even spirituality is a political act, with external consequences. Thoreau argues on the basis of conscience that unjust laws should be broken. He finds the proper place for a just man to be prison. And, with his own species of political shrewdness, he notes that if just men were in prison they would clog the workings of the state.

As this last suggests, behind the essay and running through it is a perceived opposition between mechanical and organic spheres. The state, for Thoreau, is a machine beset by the friction of injustice, which can only be tolerated to a point. Unfortunately, the masses

---

[1] Thoreau so titled his work in a letter to Emerson. See Henry David Thoreau to Ralph Waldo Emerson, 23 February 1848, in Henry David Thoreau, *The Correspondence of Henry David Thoreau,* ed. Walter Harding and Carl Bode (Washington Square: New York University Press, 1958) 208. For the lyceum (above in the text), see the introduction to part 1, "Ralph Waldo Emerson."

also perform as machines, lacking the organic power of the principled individual. Thus, nature is the implicit ground on which Thoreau stands as he articulates his theory of the state, and in new form he is voicing his conviction that a human being is called to live a natural life.[2]

There has, of course, been a legacy of Western protest against the absolute claims of the state.[3] But, with the years of neglect falling away, in the twentieth century it is the Thoreauvian statement that has captured the radical imagination. For individuals from Mohandas K. Gandhi in the Indian struggle against Britain, to members of the Danish Resistance in their defiance of the Nazis, and to Martin Luther King, Jr., in the American civil rights movement, Thoreau's "Civil Disobedience" has provided a textbook for non-violent resistance. Whether read as a call for creative anarchy, for passive resistance, for indifference to the state, or for constructive action on its behalf, the excerpts included here help suggest why Thoreau's manifesto continues to live in our time.[4]

---

[2]Sherman Paul wrote summarizing the argument of "Civil Disobedience": "Man's primary allegiance—the unspecified premise of Thoreau's essay—was not to the state but to nature." See Sherman Paul, *The Shores of America: Thoreau's Inward Exploration* (Urbana: University of Illinois Press, 1958) 245; see also 240-41, 243, 246-47.

[3]Classical, Jewish, and Christian sources are part of the legacy. See, for example, Antigone's defiance of the state in order to bury her brother in compliance with divine laws, in Sophocles *Antigone* 74-75, 432-40 (which almost surely influenced Thoreau's statement); and Socrates' words in his trial before the citizens of Athens, in Plato *Apology* 29A-D. Cf., too, the Hebrew prophets who, in the name of their God, pitted themselves against the kings of Israel, as Elijah against Ahab in 1 Kings 17:1-18:46; and the Christian tradition of dissent cited, for example, in Daniel B. Stevick, *Civil Disobedience and the Christian* (New York: Seabury Press, 1969) 39-77.

[4]The text is excerpted from Henry David Thoreau, *The Writings of Henry David Thoreau,* Walden ed. (Boston: Houghton Mifflin, 1906) 4:356-87. Editors of the essay have disagreed about whether the 1849 version in *Aesthetic Papers* or the 1866 edition in *A Yankee in Canada* is the more authoritative. Wendell Glick chose the text from 1849 as the copy-text in the new Princeton edition of Thoreau's writings and gave his reasons in Henry David Thoreau, *Reform Papers,* ed. Wendell Glick, The Writings of Henry D. Thoreau (Princeton: Princeton University Press, 1973) 316-21. On the other hand, Walter Harding used the version first published in 1866 in his *Variorum Civil Disobedience,* explaining his decision in Henry David Thoreau, *The Variorum Civil Disobedience,* ed. Walter Harding (New York: Twayne Publishers, 1967) 27. It is the 1866 edition that, as we have seen, first uses the familiar title "Civil Disobedience" and that reprints Thoreau's essay in the form in which it has become classic. Hence, I have chosen to follow the standard Walden (1906) edition of the essay, which substantively agrees with the text of 1866. Aside from the title there is only one substantive revision of the 1849 text (an addition) in the selections included here. This has been indicated in a note in the appropriate place. It seems likely that Thoreau was responsible for this revision: it was his continuing habit to rework and refine sentences, and the addition is so bold that it is not likely the work of an editor.

(From) CIVIL DISOBEDIENCE

I HEARTILY accept the motto, "That government is best which governs least;" and I should like to see it acted up to more rapidly and systematically.[1] Carried out, it finally amounts to this, which also I believe,—"That government is best which governs not at all;"[2] and when men are prepared for it, that will be the kind of government which they will have. Government is at best but an expedient; but most governments are usually, and all governments are sometimes, inexpedient. The objections which have been brought against a standing army, and they are many and weighty, and deserve to prevail, may also at last be brought against a standing government.[3] . . .

But, to speak practically and as a citizen, unlike those who call themselves no-government men, I ask for, not at once no government, but *at once* a better government.[4] Let every man make known what kind of government would command his respect, and that will be one step toward obtaining it.

After all, the practical reason why, when the power is once in the hands of the people, a majority are permitted, and for a long period continue, to rule is not because they are most likely to be in the right, nor because this seems fairest to the minority, but because they are physically the strongest. But a government in which the majority rule in all cases cannot be based on justice, even as far as men understand it. Can there not be a government in which

---

[1] Although this motto has often been linked to Thomas Jefferson, it came from *The United States Magazine and Democratic Review*, where it appeared on the title page (and cover) as "The best government is that which governs least." The nineteenth-century periodical was concerned with social issues, and several articles by Thoreau were published in its pages. In this and many of the notes that follow, I am indebted to the annotations of Walter Harding in *The Variorum Civil Disobedience* and to the textual notes to the essay by Wendell Glick in *Reform Papers*. See Henry David Thoreau, *The Variorum Civil Disobedience*, ed. Walter Harding (New York: Twayne Publishers, 1967) 59-63, and Henry David Thoreau, *Reform Papers*, ed. Wendell Glick, The Writings of Henry D. Thoreau (Princeton: Princeton University Press, 1973) 322-26.

[2] The quotation marks here are almost surely an editorial device by Thoreau to draw notice to his revised version of the motto.

[3] Traditional republican ideology opposed standing armies. With changing times in the nineteenth century, advocates in a small-but-vocal peace movement by the late 1830s were making known their objections to standing armies and militias. Then, in the context of the Mexican War, objections to armies grew louder and more numerous. See Alice Felt Tyler, *Freedom's Ferment: Phases of American Social History from the Colonial Period to the Outbreak of the Civil War* (1944; rpt., New York: Harper & Row, Harper Torchbooks, 1962) 413-16.

[4] The so-called "no-government men" were anarchists. The leading ones of the mid-nineteenth century were, in fact, Thoreau's fellow citizens in Massachusetts. See Richard Drinnon, "Thoreau's Politics of the Upright Man," in John H. Hicks, ed., *Thoreau in Our Season* (Amherst: University of Massachusetts Press, 1962) 156-57.

majorities do not virtually decide right and wrong, but conscience?—in which majorities decide only those questions to which the rule of expediency is applicable? Must the citizen ever for a moment, or in the least degree, resign his conscience to the legislator? Why has every man a conscience, then? I think that we should be men first, and subjects afterward. It is not desirable to cultivate a respect for the law, so much as for the right. The only obligation which I have a right to assume is to do at any time what I think right. It is truly enough said that a corporation has no conscience;[5] but a corporation of conscientious men is a corporation *with* a conscience. Law never made men a whit more just; and, by means of their respect for it, even the well-disposed are daily made the agents of injustice. A common and natural result of an undue respect for law is, that you may see a file of soldiers, colonel, captain, corporal, privates, powder-monkeys, and all, marching in admirable order over hill and dale to the wars, against their wills, ay, against their common sense and consciences, which makes it very steep marching indeed, and produces a palpitation of the heart. They have no doubt that it is a damnable business in which they are concerned; they are all peaceably inclined. Now, what are they? Men at all? or small movable forts and magazines, at the service of some unscrupulous man in power? Visit the Navy-Yard, and behold a marine, such a man as an American government can make, or such as it can make a man with its black arts,— a mere shadow and reminiscence of humanity, a man laid out alive and standing, and already, as one may say, buried under arms with funeral accompaniments, though it may be,—

"Not a drum was heard, not a funeral note,
    As his corse to the rampart we hurried;
Not a soldier discharged his farewell shot
    O'er the grave where our hero we buried."[6]

The mass of men serve the state thus, not as men mainly, but as machines, with their bodies.[7] They are the standing army, and the militia, jailers, constables, *posse comitatus*,[8] etc. In most cases there is no free exercise whatever of the judgment or of the moral sense; but they put themselves on a level with wood and earth and stones; and wooden men can perhaps be manufactured that will serve the purpose as well. Such command no more respect than men of straw or a lump of dirt. They have the same sort of worth only as horses and dogs. Yet such as these even are commonly esteemed good citizens. Others—as most legislators, politicians, lawyers, ministers, and office-holders—serve the state chiefly with their heads; and, as they rarely

---

[5] Walter Harding, suggesting Thoreau's apparent source, cites the statement of the eminent English jurist Sir Edward Coke (1552-1634) in his case of Sutton's Hospital: "Corporations . . . have no souls." See Thoreau, *Variorum Civil Disobedience*, 59.

[6] The lines form the first stanza of Charles Wolfe, "Burial of Sir John Moore at Corunna" (1816), a poem that was a favorite of Thoreau. The term *marine* (above in the text) refers to a soldier serving the navy.

[7] Thoreau moves from guns and war to the theme of the machine and mechanical that pervades the essay. Cf. these lines to declarations in the opening paragraphs of Henry David Thoreau, *Walden*, ch. 1: "He [the laboring man] has no time to be anything but a machine," and "The mass of men lead lives of quiet desperation."

[8] Literally in Latin, "society is empowered." Note, too, the reference to the "moral sense" in the following sentence. The idea of the moral sense was a basic concept in Scottish commonsense philosophy (see the introduction to this volume).

make any moral distinctions, they are as likely to serve the devil, without *intending* it, as God. A very few—as heroes, patriots, martyrs, reformers in the great sense, and *men*—serve the state with their consciences also, and so necessarily resist it for the most part; and they are commonly treated as enemies by it. A wise man will only be useful as a man, and will not submit to be "clay," and "stop a hole to keep the wind away," but leave that office to his dust at least:[9]—

"I am too high-born to be propertied,
To be a secondary at control,
Or useful serving-man and instrument
To any sovereign state throughout the world."[10]

He who gives himself entirely to his fellow-men appears to them useless and selfish; but he who gives himself partially to them is pronounced a benefactor and philanthropist.

How does it become a man to behave toward this American government to-day? I answer, that he cannot without disgrace be associated with it. I cannot for an instant recognize that political organization as *my* government which is the *slave's* government also.

All men recognize the right of revolution; that is, the right to refuse allegiance to, and to resist, the government, when its tyranny or its inefficiency are great and unendurable. But almost all say that such is not the case now. But such was the case, they think, in the Revolution of '75.[11] If one were to tell me that this was a bad government because it taxed certain foreign commodities brought to its ports, it is most probable that I should not make an ado about it, for I can do without them. All machines have their friction; and possibly this does enough good to counterbalance the evil. At any rate, it is a great evil to make a stir about it. But when the friction comes to have its machine, and oppression and robbery are organized, I say, let us not have such a machine any longer. In other words, when a sixth of the population of a nation which has undertaken to be the refuge of liberty are slaves, and a whole country is unjustly overrun and conquered by a foreign army, and subjected to military law, I think that it is not too soon for honest men to rebel and revolutionize. What makes this duty the more urgent is the fact that the country so overrun is not our own, but ours is the invading army.[12]

---

[9]Cf. William Shakespeare, *Hamlet*, act 5, sc. 1, ll. 236-37.

[10]William Shakespeare, *King John*, act 5, sc. 2, ll. 79-82.

[11]Thoreau dates the American Revolution from the firing of the first shots at Lexington and Concord, 19 April 1775. The sentence that follows alludes indirectly to prerevolutionary measures imposed by the British to collect duties on imported goods.

[12]Note the machine image applied to the government, above in the passage. United States Census figures for 1840 indicate nearly 2,500,000 slaves out of a total population of almost 17,100,000, roughly 14.6 percent, or more than one-seventh of the nation. By the Census of 1850, there were more than 3,200,000 slaves in a population of almost 23,200,000—about 13.8 percent or, now, less than one-seventh of the total population. Hence, Thoreau's estimate of the proportion of the population enslaved is slightly high, perhaps reflecting statistics from an antislavery source. Finally, Thoreau's reference to the country "unjustly overrun and conquered by a foreign army" is an allusion to the United States' invasion of Mexico in 1846 and events thereafter.

Paley, a common authority with many on moral questions, in his chapter on the "Duty of Submission to Civil Government," resolves all civil obligation into expediency; and he proceeds to say that "so long as the interest of the whole society requires it, that is, so long as the established government cannot be resisted or changed without public inconveniency, it is the will of God . . . that the established government be obeyed,—and no longer. This principle being admitted, the justice of every particular case of resistance is reduced to a computation of the quantity of the danger and grievance on the one side, and of the probability and expense of redressing it on the other." Of this, he says, every man shall judge for himself.[13] But Paley appears never to have contemplated those cases to which the rule of expediency does not apply, in which a people, as well as an individual, must do justice, cost what it may. If I have unjustly wrested a plank from a drowning man, I must restore it to him though I drown myself.[14] This, according to Paley, would be inconvenient. But he that would save his life, in such a case, shall lose it.[15] This people must cease to hold slaves, and to make war on Mexico, though it cost them their existence as a people. . . .

All voting is a sort of gaming, like checkers or backgammon, with a slight moral tinge to it, a playing with right and wrong, with moral questions; and betting naturally accompanies it. The character of the voters is not staked. I cast my vote, perchance, as I think right; but I am not vitally concerned that that right should prevail. I am willing to leave it to the majority. Its obligation, therefore, never exceeds that of expediency. Even voting *for the right* is *doing* nothing for it.[16] It is only expressing to men feebly your desire that it should prevail. A wise man will not leave the right to the mercy of chance, nor wish it to prevail through the power of the majority. There is but little virtue in the action of masses of men. When the majority shall at length vote for the abolition of slavery, it will be because they are indifferent to slavery, or because there is but little slavery left to be abolished by their vote. *They* will then be the only slaves. Only *his* vote can hasten the abolition of slavery who asserts his own freedom by his vote.

I hear of a convention to be held at Baltimore, or elsewhere, for the selection of a candidate for the Presidency, made up chiefly of editors, and men who are politicians by profession; but I think, what is it to any independent, intelligent, and respectable man what decision they may

---

[13]The quotation (substantively correct) and final paraphrase are from William Paley, *The Principles of Moral and Political Philosophy,* bk. 6, ch. 3. (The ellipsis in the quotation is Thoreau's.) The work was originally published in 1785, and Paley's complete title for the chapter is "The Duty of Submission to Civil Government Explained." Charles R. Anderson observes that Thoreau's first title for his essay ("Resistance to Civil Government") was likely chosen "to emphasize his opposition to Paley" (Charles R. Anderson, ed., *Thoreau's Vision: The Major Essays* [Englewood Cliffs NJ: Prentice-Hall, Spectrum, 1973] 198). If so, the title of Paley's chapter 4 is equally significant: "Of the Duty of Civil Obedience, as Stated in the Christian Scriptures." Indeed, the sequence of these chapters and the reference to Paley in Thoreau's essay may be an argument that Thoreau himself changed its title to the later "Civil Disobedience."

[14]Cf. Cicero *De officiis* (trans. Walter Miller) 3.23 (89).

[15]Cf. Matt. 16:25.

[16]Thoreau's criticisms of voting were reflected in his actions, for he did not vote.

come to?[17] Shall we not have the advantage of his wisdom and honesty, nevertheless? Can we not count upon some independent votes? Are there not many individuals in the country who do not attend conventions? But no: I find that the respectable man, so called, has immediately drifted from his position, and despairs of his country, when his country has more reason to despair of him. He forthwith adopts one of the candidates thus selected as the only *available* one, thus proving that he is himself *available* for any purposes of the demagogue. His vote is of no more worth than that of any unprincipled foreigner or hireling native, who may have been bought. O for a man who is a *man,* and, as my neighbor says, has a bone in his back which you cannot pass your hand through! Our statistics are at fault: the population has been returned too large. How many *men* are there to a square thousand miles in this country? Hardly one. Does not America offer any inducement for men to settle here? The American has dwindled into an Odd Fellow,—one who may be known by the development of his organ of gregariousness, and a manifest lack of intellect and cheerful self-reliance; whose first and chief concern, on coming into the world, is to see that the almshouses are in good repair; and, before yet he has lawfully donned the virile garb, to collect a fund for the support of the widows and orphans that may be; who, in short, ventures to live only by the aid of the Mutual Insurance company, which has promised to bury him decently.[18]

It is not a man's duty, as a matter of course, to devote himself to the eradication of any, even the most enormous, wrong; he may still properly have other concerns to engage him; but it is his duty, at least, to wash his hands of it, and, if he gives it no thought longer, not to give it practically his support. If I devote myself to other pursuits and contemplations, I must first see, at least, that I do not pursue them sitting upon another man's shoulders. I must get off him first, that he may pursue his contemplations too. See what gross inconsistency is tolerated. I have heard some of my townsmen say, "I should like to have them order me out to help put down an insurrection of the slaves, or to march to Mexico;—see if I would go;" and yet these very men have each, directly by their allegiance, and so indirectly, at least, by their money, furnished a substitute. The soldier is applauded who refuses to serve in an unjust war by those who do not refuse to sustain the unjust government which makes

---

[17] In May 1848 the nominating convention of the Democratic party was held in Baltimore, Maryland. Thoreau's alienation from their deliberations proved to have cause in terms of his concerns. The Democratic platform contained an antiabolitionist plank declaring its judgment that Congress lacked power to control the "domestic institutions" of the states and explicitly warning against abolitionist efforts to "interfere" with slavery. The platform also supported the Mexican War and hailed American soldiers in the conflict who had "crowned" the nation with "imperishable glory." See Donald Bruce Johnson, comp., *National Party Platforms,* rev. ed. (Urbana: University of Illinois Press, 1978) 1:11.

[18] After 1840, with the decline of religious reservations, the life insurance industry grew rapidly. Thoreau's reference to the "organ of gregariousness" for the member of the Odd Fellows (above in the text) evokes the language of phrenology (see n. 150 to Thoreau, *Walden*). His allusion to donning the "virile garb" recalls the *toga virilis,* or toga of manhood, which Roman males began to wear on reaching the age of puberty. Finally, cf. Thoreau's view of philanthropy here to his statement in the concluding paragraphs of *Walden,* ch. 1.

the war; is applauded by those whose own act and authority he disregards and sets at naught; as if the state were penitent to that degree that it hired one to scourge it while it sinned, but not to that degree that it left off sinning for a moment. Thus, under the name of Order and Civil Government, we are all made at last to pay homage to and support our own meanness. After the first blush of sin comes its indifference; and from immoral it becomes, as it were, *unmoral,* and not quite unnecessary to that life which we have made.

The broadest and most prevalent error requires the most disinterested virtue to sustain it. The slight reproach to which the virtue of patriotism is commonly liable, the noble are most likely to incur. Those who, while they disapprove of the character and measures of a government, yield to it their allegiance and support are undoubtedly its most conscientious supporters, and so frequently the most serious obstacles to reform. Some are petitioning the State to dissolve the Union, to disregard the requisitions of the President.[19] Why do they not dissolve it themselves,—the union between themselves and the State,—and refuse to pay their quota into its treasury? Do not they stand in the same relation to the State that the State does to the Union? And have not the same reasons prevented the State from resisting the Union which have prevented them from resisting the State?

How can a man be satisfied to entertain an opinion merely, and enjoy *it?* Is there any enjoyment in it, if his opinion is that he is aggrieved? If you are cheated out of a single dollar by your neighbor, you do not rest satisfied with knowing that you are cheated, or with saying that you are cheated, or even with petitioning him to pay you your due; but you take effectual steps at once to obtain the full amount, and see that you are never cheated again. Action from principle, the perception and the performance of right, changes things and relations; it is essentially revolutionary, and does not consist wholly with anything which was. It not only divides States and churches, it divides families; ay, it divides the *individual,* separating the diabolical in him from the divine.[20]

Unjust laws exist: shall we be content to obey them, or shall we endeavor to amend them, and obey them until we have succeeded, or shall we transgress them at once? Men generally, under such a government as this, think that they ought to wait until they have persuaded the majority to alter them. They think that, if they should resist, the remedy would be worse than the evil. But it is the fault of the government itself that the remedy *is* worse than the evil. *It* makes it worse. Why is it not more apt to anticipate and provide for reform? Why does it not cherish its wise minority? Why does it cry and resist before it is hurt? Why does it not encourage its citizens to be on the alert to point out its faults, and *do* better than it would have them? Why does it always crucify Christ, and excommunicate Copernicus and Luther,[21] and

---

[19] It is not clear what specific incident Thoreau has in mind, but a number of radical abolitionists, including William Lloyd Garrison and Wendell Phillips—and some disunionist politicians—urged the dissolution of state bonds to the union. With state independence they would not be submitting to a government that supported slavery.

[20] Here Thoreau seems to suggest at the same time a doctrine of sin, within a traditional Judeo-Christian dualistic scheme, and an Emersonian affirmation of the Oversoul.

[21] For Copernicus, who actually was not excommunicated (his treatise on the solar system did not appear until he was dying), see n. 13 to Ralph Waldo Emerson, "Self-Reliance." Martin Luther (1483–1546) received the censure of excommunication in 1520 from Pope Leo X.

pronounce Washington and Franklin rebels?

One would think, that a deliberate and practical denial of its authority was the only offense never contemplated by government; else, why has it not assigned its definite, its suitable and proportionate, penalty? If a man who has no property refuses but once to earn nine shillings for the State, he is put in prison for a period unlimited by any law that I know, and determined only by the discretion of those who placed him there; but if he should steal ninety times nine shillings from the State, he is soon permitted to go at large again.

If the injustice is part of the necessary friction of the machine of government, let it go, let it go: perchance it will wear smooth,—certainly the machine will wear out. If the injustice has a spring, or a pulley, or a rope, or a crank, exclusively for itself, then perhaps you may consider whether the remedy will not be worse than the evil; but if it is of such a nature that it requires you to be the agent of injustice to another, then, I say, break the law. Let your life be a counter-friction to stop the machine.[22] What I have to do is to see, at any rate, that I do not lend myself to the wrong which I condemn.

As for adopting the ways which the State has provided for remedying the evil, I know not of such ways. They take too much time, and a man's life will be gone. I have other affairs to attend to. I came into this world, not chiefly to make this a good place to live in, but to live in it, be it good or bad. A man has not everything to do, but something; and because he cannot do *everything*, it is not necessary that he should do *something* wrong. It is not my business to be petitioning the Governor or the Legislature any more than it is theirs to petition me; and if they should not hear my petition, what should I do then? But in this case the State has provided no way: its very Constitution is the evil. This may seem to be harsh and stubborn and unconciliatory; but it is to treat with the utmost kindness and consideration the only spirit that can appreciate or deserves it. So is all change for the better, like birth and death, which convulse the body.

I do not hesitate to say, that those who call themselves Abolitionists should at once effectually withdraw their support, both in person and property, from the government of Massachusetts, and not wait till they constitute a majority of one, before they suffer the right to prevail through them. I think that it is enough if they have God on their side, without waiting for that other one.[23] Moreover, any man more right than his neighbors constitutes a majority of one already.

I meet this American government, or its representative, the State government, directly, and face to face, once a year—no more—in the person of its tax-gatherer; this is the only mode in which a man situated as I am necessarily meets it; and it then says distinctly, Recognize me; and the simplest, the most effectual, and, in the present posture of affairs, the indispensablest mode of treating with it on this head, of expressing your little satisfaction with and love for it, is to deny it then. My civil neighbor, the tax-gatherer, is the very man I have to deal with,[24]—for it is, after all, with men and

---

[22]Note, again, the mechanical imagery that is Thoreau's continuing metaphor for government.

[23]Cf. the saying attributed to Presbyterian founder John Knox (1505–1572): "A man with God is always in the majority."

[24]The tax collector—and jailer—in Concord was Samuel ("Sam") Staples, Thoreau's "civil neighbor" who even offered, according to one

not with parchment that I quarrel,—and he has voluntarily chosen to be an agent of the government. How shall he ever know well what he is and does as an officer of the government, or as a man, until he is obliged to consider whether he shall treat me, his neighbor, for whom he has respect, as a neighbor and well-disposed man, or as a maniac and disturber of the peace, and see if he can get over this obstruction to his neighborliness without a ruder and more impetuous thought or speech corresponding with his action. I know this well, that if one thousand, if one hundred, if ten men whom I could name,—if ten *honest* men only,—ay, if *one* HONEST man, in this State of Massachusetts, *ceasing to hold slaves,* were actually to withdraw from this copartnership, and be locked up in the county jail therefor, it would be the abolition of slavery in America. For it matters not how small the beginning may seem to be: what is once well done is done forever. But we love better to talk about it: that we say is our mission. Reform keeps many scores of newspapers in its service, but not one man.
. . .

Under a government which imprisons any unjustly, the true place for a just man is also a prison. The proper place to-day, the only place which Massachusetts has provided for her freer and less desponding spirits, is in her prisons, to be put out and locked out of the State by her own act, as they have already put themselves out by their principles. It is there that the fugitive slave, and the Mexican prisoner on parole, and the Indian come to plead the wrongs of his race should find them;[25] on that separate, but more free and honorable, ground, where the State places those who are not *with* her, but *against* her,[26]—the only house in a slave State in which a free man can abide with honor. If any think that their influence would be lost there, and their voices no longer afflict the ear of the State, that they would not be as an enemy within its walls, they do not know by how much truth is stronger than error, nor how much more eloquently and effectively he can combat injustice who has experienced a little in his own person. Cast your whole vote, not a strip of paper merely, but your whole influence. A minority is powerless while it conforms to the majority; it is not even a minority then; but it is irresistible when it clogs by its whole weight. If the alternative is to keep all just men in prison, or give up war and slavery, the State will not hesitate which to choose. If a thousand men were not to pay their tax-bills this year, that would not be a violent and bloody measure, as it would be to pay them, and enable the State to commit violence and shed innocent blood. This is, in fact, the definition of a peaceable revolution, if any such is possible. If the tax-gatherer, or any other public officer, asks me, as one has done, "But what shall I do?" my answer is, "If you really wish to do anything, resign your office."[27] When the subject has refused allegiance, and the officer has re-

---

account, to pay Thoreau's tax himself if Thoreau was "hard up." Later Staples frequently worked as an assistant to Thoreau when he was surveying. See Walter Harding, *The Days of Henry Thoreau* (New York: Alfred A. Knopf, 1965) 199, 202-206.

[25] Thoreau shared with Emerson (see the introduction to this volume) a concern regarding the ill-treatment of American Indians. For an extended discussion, see Robert F. Sayre, *Thoreau and the American Indians* (Princeton: Princeton University Press, 1977).

[26] A play, probably, on the saying of Jesus. Cf. Matt. 12:30.

[27] An autobiographical reference to Thoreau's conversation with Samuel Staples that led to the jail incident.

signed his office, then the revolution is accomplished. But even suppose blood should flow. Is there not a sort of blood shed when the conscience is wounded? Through this wound a man's real manhood and immortality flow out, and he bleeds to an everlasting death. I see this blood flowing now.

I have contemplated the imprisonment of the offender, rather than the seizure of his goods,—though both will serve the same purpose,—because they who assert the purest right, and consequently are most dangerous to a corrupt State, commonly have not spent much time in accumulating property. To such the State renders comparatively small service, and a slight tax is wont to appear exorbitant, particularly if they are obliged to earn it by special labor with their hands. If there were one who lived wholly without the use of money, the State itself would hesitate to demand it of him. But the rich man—not to make any invidious comparison—is always sold to the institution which makes him rich. Absolutely speaking, the more money, the less virtue; for money comes between a man and his objects, and obtains them for him; and it was certainly no great virtue to obtain it. It puts to rest many questions which he would otherwise be taxed to answer; while the only new question which it puts is the hard but superfluous one, how to spend it. Thus his moral ground is taken from under his feet. The opportunities of living are diminished in proportion as what are called the "means" are increased. The best thing a man can do for his culture when he is rich is to endeavor to carry out those schemes which he entertained when he was poor. Christ answered the Herodians according to their condition. "Show me the tribute-money," said he;—and one took a penny out of his pocket;—if you use money which has the image of Cæsar on it, and which he has made current and valuable, that is, *if you are men of the State,* and gladly enjoy the advantages of Cæsar's government, then pay him back some of his own when he demands it. "Render therefore to Cæsar that which is Cæsar's, and to God those things which are God's,"[28]—leaving them no wiser than before as to which was which; for they did not wish to know.

When I converse with the freest of my neighbors, I perceive that, whatever they may say about the magnitude and seriousness of the question, and their regard for the public tranquillity, the long and the short of the matter is, that they cannot spare the protection of the existing government, and they dread the consequences to their property and families of disobedience to it. For my own part, I should not like to think that I ever rely on the protection of the State. But, if I deny the authority of the State when it presents its tax-bill, it will soon take and waste all my property, and so harass me and my children without end. This is hard. This makes it impossible for a man to live honestly, and at the same time comfortably, in outward respects. It will not be worth the while to accumulate property; that would be sure to go again. You must hire or squat somewhere, and raise but a small crop, and eat that soon. You must live within yourself, and depend upon yourself always tucked up and ready for a start, and not have many affairs. A man may grow rich in Turkey even, if he will be in all respects a good subject of the Turkish government.[29] Confucius said: "If a state is governed by the principles of reason, poverty and misery are subjects of shame; if a state is not governed by the principles of

---

[28]Cf. Matt. 22:19-21.

[29]The "sick man of Europe" in the nineteenth century, Turkey was enduring a lengthy period of decline at the time Thoreau was writing.

reason, riches and honors are the subjects of shame."[30]... It costs me less in every sense to incur the penalty of disobedience to the State than it would to obey. I should feel as if I were worth less in that case.

Some years ago, the State met me in behalf of the Church, and commanded me to pay a certain sum toward the support of a clergyman whose preaching my father attended, but never I myself. "Pay," it said, "or be locked up in the jail." I declined to pay. But, unfortunately, another man saw fit to pay it. I did not see why the schoolmaster should be taxed to support the priest, and not the priest the schoolmaster; for I was not the State's schoolmaster, but I supported myself by voluntary subscription. I did not see why the lyceum should not present its tax-bill, and have the State to back its demand, as well as the Church. However, at the request of the selectmen, I condescended to make some such statement as this in writing:—"Know all men by these presents, that I, Henry Thoreau, do not wish to be regarded as a member of any incorporated society which I have not joined." This I gave to the town clerk; and he has it.[31] The State, having thus learned that I did not wish to be regarded as a member of that church, has never made a like demand on me since; though it said that it must adhere to its original presumption that time. If I had known how to name them, I should then have signed off in detail from all the societies which I never signed on to; but I did not know where to find a complete list.

I have paid no poll-tax for six years.[32] I was put into a jail once on this account, for one night; and, as I stood considering the walls of solid stone, two or three feet thick, the door of wood and iron, a foot thick, and the iron grating which strained the light,[33] I could not help being struck with the foolishness of that institution which treated me as if I were mere flesh and blood and bones, to be locked up. I wondered that it should have concluded at length that this was the best use it could put me to, and had never thought to avail itself of my services in some way. I saw that, if there was a wall of stone between me and my townsmen, there was a still more difficult one to climb or break through before they could get to be as free as I was. I did not for a moment feel confined, and the walls seemed a great waste of stone and mortar. I felt as if I alone of all my townsmen had paid my tax. They plainly did not know how to treat me, but behaved like persons who are underbred. In every threat and in every compliment there was a blunder; for they thought that my chief desire was to stand the other side of that stone wall. I could not but smile to see how industriously they locked the door on my meditations, which followed them out again without let or hindrance, and *they*

---

[30]*Analects of Confucius* 8.13. Thoreau himself probably translated the sentence, from a French version in Confucius et Mencius, *Les Quatre Livres de philosophie morale et politique de la Chine,* trans. M. G. [Jean Pierre Guillaume] Pauthier (Paris: Charpentier, 1841).

[31]Thoreau's name was as a matter of course added to the tax rolls in support of the religious society that became the First Parish. But in 1840, when he received a tax bill, he was adamant in refusing to pay—hence, his well-known "signing off." The selectmen (above in the text) were members of Concord's official board that served to administer public affairs and to transact public business.

[32]The poll tax was not a voting tax but rather a head tax on every adult male between twenty and seventy years of age.

[33]Concord, along with Cambridge the official seat of Middlesex County, possessed a solid granite jailhouse three stories tall and well fortified.

were really all that was dangerous. As they could not reach me, they had resolved to punish my body; just as boys, if they cannot come at some person against whom they have a spite, will abuse his dog. I saw that the State was half-witted, that it was timid as a lone woman with her silver spoons, and that it did not know its friends from its foes, and I lost all my remaining respect for it, and pitied it.[34]

Thus the State never intentionally confronts a man's sense, intellectual or moral, but only his body, his senses. It is not armed with superior wit or honesty, but with superior physical strength. I was not born to be forced. I will breathe after my own fashion. Let us see who is the strongest. What force has a multitude? They only can force me who obey a higher law than I. They force me to become like themselves.[35] I do not hear of *men* being *forced* to live this way or that by masses of men. What sort of life were that to live? When I meet a government which says to me, "Your money or your life," why should I be in haste to give it my money? It may be in a great strait, and not know what to do: I cannot help that. It must help itself; do as I do. It is not worth the while to snivel about it. I am not responsible for the successful working of the machinery of society. I am not the son of the engineer.[36] I perceive that, when an acorn and a chestnut fall side by side, the one does not remain inert to make way for the other, but both obey their own laws, and spring and grow and flourish as best they can, till one, perchance, overshadows and destroys the other. If a plant cannot live according to its nature, it dies; and so a man. . . .

They who know of no purer sources of truth, who have traced up its stream no higher, stand, and wisely stand, by the Bible and the Constitution, and drink at it there with reverence and humility; but they who behold where it comes trickling into this lake or that pool, gird up their loins once more, and continue their pilgrimage toward its fountain-head.[37]

---

[34] Emerson, who disapproved of Thoreau's action in refusing his tax and going to jail, shared to some extent his friend's estimate of the state as a pitiable object. He called it, in his journal, "a poor good beast who means the best" and "a poor cow who does well by you." "It cannot eat bread as you can," he wrote, "let it have without grudge a little grass for its four stomachs." See Ralph Waldo Emerson, *The Journals and Miscellaneous Notebooks of Ralph Waldo Emerson,* ed. William H. Gilman et al. (Cambridge: Harvard University Press, Belknap Press, 1960–), 9 (July 1846): 446. Alcott, who supported Thoreau's act, recorded in his own journal that Emerson "thought it mean and skulking, and in bad taste. I defended it," he added, "on the grounds of a dignified non-compliance with the injunction of civil powers." See Amos Bronson Alcott, *The Journals of Amos Bronson Alcott,* sel. and ed. Odell Shepard (Boston: Little, Brown, 1938) 183-84 (25 July 1846).

[35] The laws of the state were superseded, for Thoreau, by the transcendent law expressed through conscience, the voice within, or through the exceptional human being who led a life empowered by the higher law. For a different but related development of the idea, see Thoreau, *Walden,* ch. 11. A useful treatment of the doctrine of the higher—or, in another metaphor, fundamental—law and Thoreau's contribution to it may be found in Ralph Henry Gabriel, *The Course of American Democratic Thought,* 2d ed. (New York: Ronald Press, 1956) 14-19, 48-52.

[36] Again Thoreau returns to the metaphor of the machine to express his negative estimate of government in society. Note, too, the contrast with organic life (for the individual) that follows.

[37] Thoreau's language to some extent evokes

No man with a genius for legislation has appeared in America. They are rare in the history of the world. There are orators, politicians, and eloquent men, by the thousand; but the speaker has not yet opened his mouth to speak who is capable of settling the much-vexed questions of the day. We love eloquence for its own sake, and not for any truth which it may utter, or any heroism it may inspire. Our legislators have not yet learned the comparative value of free trade and of freedom, of union, and of rectitude, to a nation. They have no genius or talent for comparatively humble questions of taxation and finance, commerce and manufactures and agriculture. If we were left solely to the wordy wit of legislators in Congress for our guidance, uncorrected by the seasonable experience and the effectual complaints of the people, America would not long retain her rank among the nations. For eighteen hundred years, though perchance I have no right to say it, the New Testament has been written; yet where is the legislator who has wisdom and practical talent enough to avail himself of the light which it sheds on the science of legislation?

The authority of government, even such as I am willing to submit to,—for I will cheerfully obey those who know and can do better than I, and in many things even those who neither know nor can do so well,—is still an impure one: to be strictly just, it must have the sanction and consent of the governed. It can have no pure right over my person and property but what I concede to it. The progress from an absolute to a limited monarchy, from a limited monarchy to a democracy, is a progress toward a true respect for the individual. Even the Chinese philosopher was wise enough to regard the individual as the basis of the empire.[38] Is a democracy, such as we know it, the last improvement possible in government? Is it not possible to take a step further towards recognizing and organizing the rights of man? There will never be a really free and enlightened State until the State comes to recognize the individual as a higher and independent power, from which all its own power and authority are derived, and treats him accordingly. I please myself with imagining a State at last which can afford to be just to all men, and to treat the individual with respect as a neighbor; which even would not think it inconsistent with its own repose if a few were to live aloof from it, not meddling with it, nor embraced by it, who fulfilled all the duties of neighbors and fellow-men. A State which bore this kind of fruit, and suffered it to drop off as fast as it ripened, would prepare the way for a still more perfect and glorious State, which also I have imagined, but not yet anywhere seen.[39]

Emerson's imagery of the Oversoul. See the second paragraph of Ralph Waldo Emerson, "The Over-Soul." For Thoreau's phrase "gird up their loins," cf. Luke 12:35; Eph. 6:14; 1 Pet. 1:13; and Prov. 31:17.

[38]This sentence does not appear in the *Aesthetic Papers* edition of the essay. The line no doubt refers to Confucius (551?–479? B.C.), for whom the good man was the foundation of the good state—although never in a democratic context. See, for example, *Analects of Confucius* 13.6, 13; 15.8-9, 32; passim.

[39]Cf. the closing paragraphs in Thoreau, *Walden,* ch. 18, with references to resurrection and dawn. Thoreau, like Emerson, Alcott, and Parker, awaited a future that fulfilled his millennial hope.

WALDEN

On Independence Day in 1845 Henry David Thoreau moved into a rough cabin he had built on the shores of Walden Pond in Concord. The land on which the cabin stood was owned by his friend Emerson, who allowed Thoreau the use of it in exchange for some practical services. Here Thoreau lived until 6 September 1847, pursuing his writing and also his spiritual concerns. Thoreau was still close to village, family, and friends, though, and the interest of townspeople sparked him to offer two lectures at the Concord lyceum in early 1847. The lectures formed portions of the earliest draft of his book *Walden,* but thwarted by the failure of *A Week on the Concord and Merrimack Rivers,* he continued to revise and expand the text. By the time Ticknor and Fields of Boston published *Walden; or, Life in the Woods* in 1854, Thoreau's manuscript was in its eighth draft.[1]

Now, however, Thoreau's work registered a modest success. Publication was preceded by excerpts in John Sartain's *Union Magazine of Literature and Art* and Horace Greeley's *New-York Tribune.* Reviews were mixed but, on balance and with qualifications, favorable. Ticknor and Fields printed 2,000 copies, and by 1859 the print run was exhausted. Then, in 1862, the publishers agreed to reprint the book, and 280 copies reappeared only a few weeks after Thoreau's death.[2]

Still, it was a quiet start for a complex work that was to be brought again and again into print, not only in English but in numerous other languages as well. As the decades passed, some hailed *Walden* for its superb writing; others have read it as a satiric indictment of nineteenth-century American materialism, and still others as a kind of survivalist manual for the self-reliant. Early critics saw it as a delightful nature book; and others in the twentieth century have seen it as a *Transcendental* nature book, sensitive to the spiritual hieroglyphic of correspondence in the natural world. In similar vein, some have understood it as a classic of spirituality.[3]

---

[1] In his important study in 1957, J. Lyndon Shanley identified seven versions of *Walden* and an eighth fair copy for the printer. See J. Lyndon Shanley, *The Making of* Walden: *With the Text of the First Version* (Chicago: University of Chicago Press, 1957) esp. 18-33.

[2] See the useful accounts of the publication and printing history of *Walden* in Henry David Thoreau, *Walden,* ed. J. Lyndon Shanley, The Writings of Henry D. Thoreau (Princeton: Princeton University Press, 1971) 368-77, esp. 368-69; and Walter Harding, *The Days of Henry Thoreau* (New York: Alfred A. Knopf, 1965) 330-31, 334-41.

[3] For a synopsis of the various interpretations of *Walden* through the years, see Walter Harding, "Five Ways of Looking at *Walden,*" in John H. Hicks, ed., *Thoreau in Our Season* (Amherst: University of Massachusetts Press, 1962) 44-57; and Walter Harding, introduction to Henry David Thoreau, *The Variorum Walden,* ed. Walter Harding (1962; rpt., New York: Washington Square Press, 1967) xx-xxiii. Probably the best study of the Transcendental and spiritual dimensions of *Walden* is contained in Sherman Paul, *The Shores of America: Thoreau's Inward Exploration* (Urbana: University of Illinois Press, 1958) 255-353.

Walden is, in fact, all of these, directed by the deliberate intent with which Thoreau conducted his experiment. For the book poses major religious questions concerning the meaning of life and how it is to be lived. *Walden's* "Brahmanical" passages point eastward, and the sojourn by the pond, with its celebration of the morning sun, may be read as an exercise in yoga, with its goal a spiritual awakening or enlightenment. Or, as Robert F. Sayre has argued, Thoreau's work may be viewed as the record of a vision quest, resembling the pattern found in American Indian religions.[4] Still more, Thoreau's collapse of his stay at the pond into a single great year (analogous to the collapse of time in his *Week*) results in a seasonal evocation of pagan and Christian themes of death and rebirth. And the dying-rising God of *Walden* may be understood as the nameless divinity Thoreau found in nature and in self. In the end, *Walden* is a book about freedom, about the liberation that Thoreau knew, through discipline and ecstasy both, in the years that must have been the high point of his life.

In the pages that follow, we recapture a few selected moments from Thoreau's life at the pond. We listen to his sounds and behind them his deeper silence. Economy, we learn, is ultimately spiritual, and the best getting and spending concern nonmaterial food and drink. Even more, morning is the time to crow. So long as the sun rises, the spring thaws the ice, and the insect gnaws its way out of the wood, there will be rebirth and resurrection.[5]

---

[4]See Robert F. Sayre, *Thoreau and the American Indians* (Princeton: Princeton University Press, 1977) 59-100. For a good account of the yoga of *Walden*, see Frank MacShane, "*Walden* and Yoga," *The New England Quarterly* 37:3 (September 1964): 322-42; see also Arthur Christy, *The Orient in American Transcendentalism: A Study of Emerson, Thoreau, and Alcott* (1932; rpt., New York: Octagon Books, 1978) 199-233.

[5]Sherman Paul wrote that Thoreau's "economy was spiritual: to get and spend one's life." See Paul, *Shores of America,* 308, as well as the extended discussion, ibid., 303-12.

The text of *Walden* is excerpted from Henry David Thoreau, *The Writings of Henry David Thoreau,* Walden ed. (Boston: Houghton Mifflin, 1906) 2:3-367.

(From) WALDEN

I
ECONOMY

When I wrote the following pages, or rather the bulk of them, I lived alone, in the woods, a mile from any neighbor, in a house which I had built myself, on the shore of Walden Pond, in Concord, Massachusetts, and earned my living by the labor of my hands only. I lived there two years and two months. At present I am a sojourner in civilized life again.

I should not obtrude my affairs so much on the notice of my readers if very particular inquiries had not been made by my townsmen concerning my mode of life, which some would call impertinent, though they do not appear to me at all impertinent, but, considering the circumstances, very natural and pertinent. Some have asked what I got to eat; if I did not feel lonesome; if I was not afraid; and the like. Others have been curious to learn what portion of my income I devoted to charitable purposes; and some, who have large families, how many poor children I maintained. I will therefore ask those of my readers who feel no particular interest in me to pardon me if I undertake to answer some of these questions in this book. In most books, the *I*, or first person, is omitted; in this it will be retained; that, in respect to egotism, is the main difference. We commonly do not remember that it is, after all, always the first person that is speaking. I should not talk so much about myself if there were anybody else whom I knew as well. Unfortunately, I am confined to this theme by the narrowness of my experience. Moreover, I, on my side, require of every writer, first or last, a simple and sincere account of his own life, and not merely what he has heard of other men's lives; some such account as he would send to his kindred from a distant land; for if he has lived sincerely, it must have been in a distant land to me. Perhaps these pages are more particularly addressed to poor students. As for the rest of my readers, they will accept such portions as apply to them. I trust that none will stretch the seams in putting on the coat, for it may do good service to him whom it fits.

I would fain say something, not so much concerning the Chinese and Sandwich Islanders[1] as you who read these pages, who are said to live in New England; something about your condition, especially your outward condition or circumstances in this world, in this town, what it is, whether it is necessary that it be as bad as it is, whether it cannot be improved as well as not. I have travelled a good deal in Concord; and everywhere, in shops, and offices, and fields, the inhabitants have appeared to me to be doing penance in a thousand remarkable ways. . . .

I see young men, my townsmen, whose misfortune it is to have inherited farms, houses, barns, cattle, and farming tools; for these are more easily acquired than got rid of. Better if they had been born in the open pasture and suckled by a wolf,[2] that they

---

[1] That is, Hawaiians.

[2] An allusion, perhaps, to the twins Romulus (the legendary founder of Rome) and Remus. According to tradition they were abandoned but suckled by a she-wolf and saved.

might have seen with clearer eyes what field they were called to labor in. Who made them serfs of the soil? Why should they eat their sixty acres, when man is condemned to eat only his peck of dirt?[3] Why should they begin digging their graves as soon as they are born? They have got to live a man's life, pushing all these things before them, and get on as well as they can. How many a poor immortal soul have I met well-nigh crushed and smothered under its load, creeping down the road of life, pushing before it a barn seventy-five feet by forty, its Augean stables never cleansed,[4] and one hundred acres of land, tillage, mowing, pasture, and wood-lot! The portionless, who struggle with no such unnecessary inherited encumbrances, find it labor enough to subdue and cultivate a few cubic feet of flesh.

But men labor under a mistake. The better part of the man is soon plowed into the soil for compost. By a seeming fate, commonly called necessity, they are employed, as it says in an old book, laying up treasures which moth and rust will corrupt and thieves break through and steal.[5] It is a fool's life, as they will find when they get to the end of it, if not before. . . .

Most men, even in this comparatively free country, through mere ignorance and mistake, are so occupied with the factitious cares and superfluously coarse labors of life that its finer fruits cannot be plucked by them. Their fingers, from excessive toil, are too clumsy and tremble too much for that. Actually, the laboring man has not leisure for a true integrity day by day; he cannot afford to sustain the manliest relations to men; his labor would be depreciated in the market. He has no time to be anything but a machine.[6] How can he remember well his ignorance—which his growth requires—who has so often to use his knowledge? . . .

I sometimes wonder that we can be so frivolous, I may almost say, as to attend to the gross but somewhat foreign form of servitude called Negro Slavery, there are so many keen and subtle masters that enslave both North and South. It is hard to have a Southern overseer; it is worse to have a Northern one;[7] but worst of all when you are the slave-driver of yourself. Talk of a divinity in man! Look at the teamster on the highway, wending to market by day or night; does any divinity stir within him?[8] His highest duty to fodder and water his horses! What is his destiny to him compared with the shipping interests? Does not he drive for Squire Make-a-stir?[9] How

---

[3]Walter Harding links Thoreau's language here to the English proverb, "We must eat a peck of dirt before we die," found as early as 1709 in Oswald Dykes's *English Proverbs*. See the note by Harding in Henry David Thoreau, *The Variorum Walden*, ed. Walter Harding (1962; rpt., New York: Washington Square Press, 1967) 257. In this chapter and throughout *Walden*, I am indebted to Harding's annotations in *The Variorum Walden* and also to those of Philip Van Doren Stern in Henry D. Thoreau, *The Annotated* Walden: *Walden; or, Life in the Woods*, ed. Philip Van Doren Stern (New York: Clarkson N. Potter, 1970).

[4]A reference in Greek mythology to the fifth of the twelve labors performed by Heracles (Hercules) to win immortality. Details vary; but in one account Heracles diverted the Alpheus and Peneus rivers from their banks, and their waters flowed through the Augean stables, carrying away the filth.

[5]Cf. Matt. 6:19.

[6]Cf. the excerpts from Henry David Thoreau, "Civil Disobedience," in this volume.

[7]Thoreau is probably alluding to the Northern industrial system as linked to a form of wage slavery and human exploitation.

[8]Cf. Joseph Addison, *Cato*, act 5, sc. 1, l. 7.

[9]The name may have been prompted by

godlike, how immortal, is he? See how he cowers and sneaks, how vaguely all the day he fears, not being immortal nor divine, but the slave and prisoner of his own opinion of himself, a fame won by his own deeds. Public opinion is a weak tyrant compared with our own private opinion. What a man thinks of himself, that it is which determines, or rather indicates, his fate. Self-emancipation even in the West Indian provinces of the fancy and imagination,—what Wilberforce is there to bring that about?[10] Think, also, of the ladies of the land weaving toilet cushions[11] against the last day, not to betray too green an interest in their fates! As if you could kill time without injuring eternity.

The mass of men lead lives of quiet desperation. What is called resignation is confirmed desperation. From the desperate city you go into the desperate country, and have to console yourself with the bravery of minks and muskrats. A stereotyped but unconscious despair is concealed even under what are called the games and amusements of mankind. There is no play in them, for this comes after work. But it is a characteristic of wisdom not to do desperate things.

When we consider what, to use the words of the catechism, is the chief end of man,[12] and what are the true necessaries and means of life, it appears as if men had deliberately chosen the common mode of living because they preferred it to any other. Yet they honestly think there is no choice left. But alert and healthy natures remember that the sun rose clear. It is never too late to give up our prejudices. No way of thinking or doing, however ancient, can be trusted without proof. What everybody echoes or in silence passes by as true to-day may turn out to be falsehood to-morrow, mere smoke of opinion, which some had trusted for a cloud that would sprinkle fertilizing rain on their fields. What old people say you cannot do, you try and find that you can. Old deeds for old people, and new deeds for new. . . .

I think that we may safely trust a good deal more than we do. We may waive just so much care of ourselves as we honestly bestow elsewhere. Nature is as well adapted to our weakness as to our strength. The incessant anxiety and strain of some is a well-nigh incurable form of disease. We are made to exaggerate the importance of what work we do; and yet how much is not done by us! or, what if we had been taken sick? How vigilant we are! determined not to live by faith if we can avoid it; all the day long on the alert, at night we unwillingly say our prayers and commit ourselves to uncertainties. So thoroughly and sincerely are we compelled to live, reverencing our life, and denying the possibility of change. This is the only way, we say; but there are

---

Thoreau's familiarity with John Bunyan's *Pilgrim's Progress* (1678; 1684). Walter Harding notes that it is in the tradition of the classic. See Thoreau, *Variorum Walden,* 257.

[10]William Wilberforce (1759–1833) campaigned for twenty years in Parliament for the abolition of the slave trade in the British Empire, and when this was effected in 1807, he continued to work for the abolition of slavery itself.

[11]Handworked pieces placed in women's dressing rooms. The reference to the last day and the succeeding line suggest that Thoreau may be measuring busywork against a biblical injunction such as Eph. 5:16.

[12]The original source of the allusion (common parlance in Thoreau's time) is "The Shorter Catechism" appended to *The New-England Primer* (first published between 1687 and 1690). See *The New-England Primer,* enl. ed. of 1727, ed. Paul Leicester Ford (1897; rpt., New York: Teachers College, Columbia University, 1962) [38].

as many ways as there can be drawn radii from one centre. All change is a miracle to contemplate; but it is a miracle which is taking place every instant. Confucius said, "To know that we know what we know, and that we do not know what we do not know, that is true knowledge."[13] When one man has reduced a fact of the imagination to be a fact to his understanding, I foresee that all men will at length establish their lives on that basis.

Let us consider for a moment what most of the trouble and anxiety which I have referred to is about, and how much it is necessary that we be troubled, or at least careful. It would be some advantage to live a primitive and frontier life, though in the midst of an outward civilization, if only to learn what are the gross necessaries of life and what methods have been taken to obtain them; or even to look over the old day-books of the merchants, to see what it was that men most commonly bought at the stores, what they stored, that is, what are the grossest groceries.[14] For the improvements of ages have had but little influence on the essential laws of man's existence: as our skeletons, probably, are not to be distinguished from those of our ancestors. . . .

Most of the luxuries, and many of the so-called comforts of life, are not only not indispensable, but positive hindrances to the elevation of mankind. With respect to luxuries and comforts, the wisest have ever lived a more simple and meagre life than the poor. The ancient philosophers, Chinese, Hindoo, Persian, and Greek, were a class than which none has been poorer in outward riches, none so rich in inward. We know not much about them. It is remarkable that *we* know so much of them as we do. The same is true of the more modern reformers and benefactors of their race. None can be an impartial or wise observer of human life but from the vantage ground of what *we* should call voluntary poverty. Of a life of luxury the fruit is luxury, whether in agriculture, or commerce, or literature, or art. There are nowadays professors of philosophy, but not philosophers. Yet it is admirable to profess because it was once admirable to live. To be a philosopher is not merely to have subtle thoughts, nor even to found a school, but so to love wisdom as to live according to its dictates, a life of simplicity, independence, magnanimity, and trust. It is to solve some of the problems of life, not only theoretically, but practically. . . .

If I should attempt to tell how I have desired to spend my life in years past, it would probably surprise those of my readers who are somewhat acquainted with its actual history; it would certainly astonish those who know nothing about it. I will only hint at some of the enterprises which I have cherished.

In any weather, at any hour of the day or night, I have been anxious to improve the nick of time, and notch it on my stick

---

[13]*Analects of Confucius* 2.17. The translation is almost surely by Thoreau himself, from a French version in Confucius et Mencius, *Les Quatre Livres de philosophie morale et politique de la Chine,* trans. M. G. [Jean Pierre Guillaume] Pauthier (Paris: Charpentier, 1841), or in another French edition of Pauthier's work. (See the citation by Wendell Glick in Henry David Thoreau, *Reform Papers,* ed. Wendell Glick, The Writings of Henry D. Thoreau [Princeton: Princeton University Press, 1973] 325; and also, Lyman V. Cady, "Thoreau's Quotations from the Confucian Books in *Walden,*" *American Literature* 33:1 [March 1961]: 21-23.)

[14]Punning was only one device employed by Thoreau in *Walden* to express a humor that was often pointed and insightful.

too;[15] to stand on the meeting of two eternities, the past and future, which is precisely the present moment;[16] to toe that line. You will pardon some obscurities, for there are more secrets in my trade than in most men's, and yet not voluntarily kept, but inseparable from its very nature. I would gladly tell all that I know about it, and never paint "No Admittance" on my gate.

I long ago lost a hound, a bay horse, and a turtle-dove, and am still on their trail.[17] Many are the travellers I have spoken concerning them, describing their tracks and what calls they answered to. I have met one or two who had heard the hound, and the tramp of the horse, and even seen the dove disappear behind a cloud, and they seemed as anxious to recover them as if they had lost them themselves.

To anticipate, not the sunrise and the dawn merely, but, if possible, Nature herself! How many mornings, summer and winter, before yet any neighbor was stirring about his business, have I been about mine! No doubt, many of my townsmen have met me returning from this enterprise, farmers starting for Boston in the twilight, or woodchoppers going to their work. It is true, I never assisted the sun materially in his rising, but, doubt not, it was of the last importance only to be present at it.

So many autumn, ay, and winter days, spent outside the town, trying to hear what was in the wind, to hear and carry it express! I well-nigh sunk all my capital in it, and lost my own breath into the bargain, running in the face of it. If it had concerned either of the political parties, depend upon it, it would have appeared in the Gazette with the earliest intelligence. At other times watching from the observatory of some cliff or tree, to telegraph any new arrival; or waiting at evening on the hill-tops for the sky to fall, that I might catch something, though I never caught much, and that, manna-wise, would dissolve again in the sun.[18]

For a long time I was reporter to a journal, of no very wide circulation, whose editor has never yet seen fit to print the bulk of my contributions, and, as is too common with writers, I got only my labor for

---

[15]This is likely an identification with Robinson Crusoe's way of keeping time. See Daniel Defoe, *The Life and Strange Surprizing Adventures of Robinson Crusoe, of York, Mariner* (1719), ed. J. Donald Crowley (London: Oxford University Press, 1972) 64.

[16]Cf. Thomas Carlyle, *On Heroes, Hero-Worship, and the Heroic in History* (1841), lect. 5: "One Life, a little gleam of Time between two Eternities." The theme of the significance of the present, familiar in the mystical tradition, is a recurring one in *Walden*.

[17]This mysterious line and the sentences that follow have spawned numerous (and often elaborate) interpretations of source and meaning. (See the discussion in Thoreau, *Variorum Walden*, 259-62). In a letter to B. B. Wiley in 1857, Thoreau offered his one extended response to the question of the meaning of hound, horse, and dove: "How shall we account for our pursuits if they are original? We get the language with which to describe our various lives out of a common mint. If others have their losses, which they are busy repairing, so have I *mine*, & their hound & horse may *perhaps* be the symbols of some of them. But also I have lost, or am in danger of losing, a far finer & more etherial treasure, which commonly no loss of which they are conscious will symbolize—this I answer hastily & with some hesitation, according as I now understand my own words" (Henry D. Thoreau to B. B. Wiley, 26 April 1857, in Henry David Thoreau, *The Correspondence of Henry David Thoreau*, ed. Walter Harding and Carl Bode [Washington Square: New York University Press, 1958] 478).

[18]Cf. Exod. 16:11-35.

my pains.[19] However, in this case my pains were their own reward.

For many years I was self-appointed inspector of snow-storms and rain-storms, and did my duty faithfully; surveyor, if not of highways, then of forest paths and all across-lot routes, keeping them open, and ravines bridged and passable at all seasons, where the public heel had testified to their utility.

I have looked after the wild stock of the town, which give a faithful herdsman a good deal of trouble by leaping fences; and I have had an eye to the unfrequented nooks and corners of the farm; though I did not always know whether Jonas or Solomon worked in a particular field to-day; that was none of my business. I have watered the red huckleberry, the sand cherry and the nettle-tree, the red pine and the black ash, the white grape and the yellow violet, which might have withered else in dry seasons.

In short, I went on thus for a long time (I may say it without boasting), faithfully minding my business, till it became more and more evident that my townsmen would not after all admit me into the list of town officers, nor make my place a sinecure with a moderate allowance. My accounts, which I can swear to have kept faithfully, I have, indeed, never got audited, still less accepted, still less paid and settled. However, I have not set my heart on that. . . .

Finding that my fellow-citizens were not likely to offer me any room in the court house, or any curacy or living anywhere else, but I must shift for myself, I turned my face more exclusively than ever to the woods, where I was better known. I determined to go into business at once, and not wait to acquire the usual capital, using such slender means as I had already got. My purpose in going to Walden Pond was not to live cheaply nor to live dearly there, but to transact some private business with the fewest obstacles; to be hindered from accomplishing which for want of a little common sense, a little enterprise and business talent, appeared not so sad as foolish.
. . .

The customs of some savage nations might, perchance, be profitably imitated by us, for they at least go through the semblance of casting their slough annually;[20] they have the idea of the thing, whether they have the reality or not. Would it not be well if we were to celebrate such a "busk," or "feast of first fruits," as Bartram describes to have been the custom of the Mucclasse Indians?[21] "When a town

---

[19]Thoreau may intend here his personal journal, or, perhaps, *The Dial*—surely small in circulation (several hundred subscribers)—which declined to publish a number of his compositions under the editorships of both Margaret Fuller and Emerson.

[20]That is, as the snake sheds its skin. Thoreau's reference to "savage nations" is typical of his time.

[21]Bartram is William Bartram (1739-1823), the naturalist son of the botanist John Bartram. William Bartram recorded his observations during his travels in the southeastern United States, from 1773 to 1777, in the well-known *Travels through North and South Carolina, Georgia, East and West Florida, the Cherokee Country, the Extensive Territory of the Muscogulges, or Creek Confederacy, and the Country of the Chactaws* (Philadelphia: Printed by James & Johnson, 1791). The terms Thoreau quotes here are from Bartram, *Travels*, pt. 4, ch. 3, p. 509. The "busk" is the green corn feast, a major ceremonial among the Southeastern tribes in general, held when the green corn first became fit to eat. The "Mucclasse Indians" were those from the town or tribe of "Mucclasse," or Muklasa, one of the villages in the Creek Confederacy. But the context of Bartram's description suggests that he is engaged in a more general discussion of the busk among all of the (Upper) Creek, or "Muscogulge," Indians.

celebrates the busk," says he, "having previously provided themselves with new clothes, new pots, pans, and other household utensils and furniture, they collect all their worn out clothes and other despicable things, sweep and cleanse their houses, squares, and the whole town, of their filth, which with all the remaining grain and other old provisions they cast together into one common heap, and consume it with fire. After having taken medicine, and fasted for three days, all the fire in the town is extinguished. During this fast they abstain from the gratification of every appetite and passion whatever. A general amnesty is proclaimed; all malefactors may return to their town."

"On the fourth morning, the high priest, by rubbing dry wood together, produces new fire in the public square, from whence every habitation in the town is supplied with the new and pure flame."

They then feast on the new corn and fruits, and dance and sing for three days, "and the four following days they receive visits and rejoice with their friends from neighboring towns who have in like manner purified and prepared themselves."[22]

The Mexicans also practised a similar purification at the end of every fifty-two years, in the belief that it was time for the world to come to an end.[23]

I have scarcely heard of a truer sacrament, that is, as the dictionary defines it, "outward and visible sign of an inward and spiritual grace,"[24] than this, and I have no doubt that they were originally inspired directly from Heaven to do thus, though they have no Biblical record of the revelation. . . .

I confess that I have hitherto indulged very little in philanthropic enterprises.[25] I have made some sacrifices to a sense of duty, and among others have sacrificed this pleasure also. There are those who have used all their arts to persuade me to undertake the support of some poor family in the town; and if I had nothing to do—for the devil finds employment for the idle[26]—I

---

[22]The several paragraphs of quotation are again, with some omissions and other variations, from Bartram, *Travels,* pt. 4, ch. 3, pp. 509-10.

[23]Thoreau is referring to the account of the festival of the Aztecs in William H. Prescott, *History of the Conquest of Mexico with a Preliminary View of the Ancient Mexican Civilization and the Life of the Conqueror, Hernando Cortés* (New York: Harper, 1843) bk. 1, ch. 4. With new-fire rites, the sacrifice of a (human) victim, the cleansing and whitening of houses, the breaking of old vessels and their replacement by new, the festival (as Prescott described it) evidenced major motifs of a purification ritual.

[24]The definition is standard for the period. In his copy of *Walden,* (William) Ellery Channing noted that the definition could be found in the 1822 edition of Walker's dictionary. See Thoreau, *Annotated* Walden, 203; and John Walker, *A Critical Pronouncing Dictionary and Expositor of the English Language* (London: Printed for J. Richardson, 1822) 535.

[25]In the paragraphs that follow, Thoreau takes up the questions of Concord residents concerning his charitable activity, questions to which he has alluded earlier. Thoreau's response echoes the Emersonian proclamation in "Self-Reliance" (see Ralph Waldo Emerson, "Self-Reliance"). It is also not too far from the message, reiterated in the mystical tradition, of the higher duty and activity of contemplation (although, to be sure, Thoreau couches his argument in terms of personal integrity rather than contemplation).

[26]Walter Harding points here to the old English proverb, "The devil finds work for idle hands," transcribed as early as 1670 in John Ray's *Compleat Collection of English Proverbs* (see Thoreau, *Variorum Walden,* 274).

might try my hand at some such pastime as that. However, when I have thought to indulge myself in this respect, and lay their Heaven under an obligation by maintaining certain poor persons in all respects as comfortably as I maintain myself, and have even ventured so far as to make them the offer, they have one and all unhesitatingly preferred to remain poor. While my townsmen and women are devoted in so many ways to the good of their fellows, I trust that one at least may be spared to other and less humane pursuits.[27] You must have a genius for charity as well as for anything else. As for Doing-good, that is one of the professions which are full.[28] Moreover, I have tried it fairly, and, strange as it may seem, am satisfied that it does not agree with my constitution. Probably I should not consciously and deliberately forsake my particular calling to do the good which society demands of me, to save the universe from annihilation; and I believe that a like but infinitely greater steadfastness elsewhere is all that now preserves it. But I would not stand between any man and his genius; and to him who does this work, which I decline, with his whole heart and soul and life, I would say, Persevere, even if the world call it doing evil, as it is most likely they will.

I am far from supposing that my case is a peculiar one; no doubt many of my readers would make a similar defence. At doing something,—I will not engage that my neighbors shall pronounce it good,—I do not hesitate to say that I should be a capital fellow to hire; but what that is, it is for my employer to find out. What *good* I do, in the common sense of that word, must be aside from my main path, and for the most part wholly unintended. . . .

There is no odor so bad as that which arises from goodness tainted. It is human, it is divine, carrion. If I knew for a certainty that a man was coming to my house with the conscious design of doing me good, I should run for my life, as from that dry and parching wind of the African deserts called the simoom, which fills the mouth and nose and ears and eyes with dust till you are suffocated, for fear that I should get some of his good done to me,—some of its virus mingled with my blood.[29] No,—in this case I would rather suffer evil the natural way. A man is not a good *man* to me because he will feed me if I should be starving, or warm me if I should be freezing, or pull me out of a ditch if I should ever fall into one. I can find you a Newfoundland dog that will do as much.[30] Philanthropy is not love for one's fellow-man in the broadest sense. . . .

I would not subtract anything from the

---

[27]Thoreau had, in fact, done much—probably more than his fellow citizens in Concord—to help improve the lot of poor Irish immigrants who labored there. See Frank Buckley, "Thoreau and the Irish," *The New England Quarterly* 13:3 (September 1940): 389-400. Thoreau's revolt seems directed mostly against the self-righteous style of conscious "do-gooders."

[28]Thoreau's use of the expression "Doing-good" may be an allusion either to the *Essays to Do Good* of Cotton Mather (1710) or to the *Dogood Papers* of Benjamin Franklin (1722). For Thoreau's use of *genius* in the passage, cf. n. 3 to Amos Bronson Alcott, *The Doctrine and Discipline of Human Culture.*

[29]For a discussion of Thoreau's reading concerning the African continent, see John Aldrich Christie, *Thoreau as World Traveler* (New York: Columbia University Press, 1965) 162-86, esp. 168-69. *Virus* is not used in the sense of infectious disease—a later concept—but in the older sense of venom or poison.

[30]Cf. Lydia to Julia in Richard B. Sheridan, *The Rivals,* act 1, sc. 2: "Obligation! why a water spaniel would have done as much!"

praise that is due to philanthropy, but merely demand justice for all who by their lives and works are a blessing to mankind. I do not value chiefly a man's uprightness and benevolence, which are, as it were, his stem and leaves. Those plants of whose greenness withered we make herb tea for the sick serve but a humble use, and are most employed by quacks. I want the flower and fruit of a man; that some fragrance be wafted over from him to me, and some ripeness flavor our intercourse. His goodness must not be a partial and transitory act, but a constant superfluity, which costs him nothing and of which he is unconscious. This is a charity that hides a multitude of sins.[31] The philanthropist too often surrounds mankind with the remembrance of his own cast-off griefs as an atmosphere, and calls it sympathy. We should impart our courage, and not our despair, our health and ease, and not our disease, and take care that this does not spread by contagion. From what southern plains comes up the voice of wailing? Under what latitudes reside the heathen to whom we would send light? Who is that intemperate and brutal man whom we would redeem? If anything ail a man, so that he does not perform his functions, if he have a pain in his bowels even,—for that is the seat of sympathy,[32]—he forthwith sets about reforming—the world. . . .

I believe that what so saddens the reformer is not his sympathy with his fellows in distress, but, though he be the holiest son of God, is his private ail. Let this be righted, let the spring come to him, the morning rise over his couch, and he will forsake his generous companions without

apology. My excuse for not lecturing against the use of tobacco is, that I never chewed it, that is a penalty which reformed tobacco-chewers have to pay; though there are things enough I have chewed which I could lecture against. If you should ever be betrayed into any of these philanthropies, do not let your left hand know what your right hand does,[33] for it is not worth knowing. Rescue the drowning and tie your shoe-strings. Take your time, and set about some free labor.

Our manners have been corrupted by communication with the saints.[34] Our hymn-books resound with a melodious cursing of God and enduring Him forever.[35] One would say that even the prophets and redeemers had rather consoled the fears than confirmed the hopes of man. There is nowhere recorded a simple and irrepressible satisfaction with the gift of life, any memorable praise of God. All health and success does me good, however far off and withdrawn it may appear; all disease and failure helps to make me sad and does me evil, however much sympathy it may have with me or I with it. If, then, we would indeed restore mankind by truly Indian, botanic, magnetic, or natural means,[36] let us first be as simple and well as Nature ourselves, dispel the clouds

---

[31]Cf. 1 Pet. 4:8.

[32]That the bowels were the "seat of sympathy" was a time-honored understanding. Cf., for example, Song of Sol. 5:4.

[33]Cf. Matt. 6:3.

[34]Cf. 1 Cor. 15:33.

[35]Thoreau's line inverts the language of the catechism. See n. 12 above.

[36]White Americans showed considerable fascination with American Indian healing. By 1813 *The Indian Doctor's Dispensatory* of Peter Smith prescribed herbal remedies for household use; and American Indian cures were likewise employed in the Thomsonian system of natural herbs from the 1820s. For animal magnetism, or mesmerism, a healing method that had become popular, see n. 73 to Ralph Waldo Emerson, *Nature*.

which hang over our own brows, and take up a little life into our pores. Do not stay to be an overseer of the poor, but endeavor to become one of the worthies of the world.

I read in the Gulistan, or Flower Garden, of Sheik Sadi of Shiraz, that "they asked a wise man, saying: Of the many celebrated trees which the Most High God has created lofty and umbrageous, they call none azad, or free, excepting the cypress, which bears no fruit; what mystery is there in this? He replied: Each has its appropriate produce, and appointed season, during the continuance of which it is fresh and blooming, and during their absence dry and withered; to neither of which states is the cypress exposed, being always flourishing; and of this nature are the azads, or religious independents.—Fix not thy heart on that which is transitory; for the Dijlah, or Tigris, will continue to flow through Bagdad after the race of caliphs is extinct: if thy hand has plenty, be liberal as the date tree; but if it affords nothing to give away, be an azad, or free man, like the cypress."[37]

---

[37]Sa'di *Gulistan* (trans. James Ross, 1823) 8.105. Muslihuddin Sa'di (Saadi or Sadi; fl. 1200?–1290?) was a Persian mystical poet, the most popular of the Persian poets—considered after his death a Sufi saint—and popular as well among the American Transcendentalists. The *Gulistan,* or *Rose Garden* (1258?) is a collection of didactic tales, written in prose but interspersed with verse. The caliph ("race of caliphs") was the religiopolitical head of the Islamic state.

Here in the complete text appear the lines of the English Cavalier poet Thomas Carew taken from his masque *Coelum Brittanicum* (1661), which Thoreau appended in somewhat modernized form and under the titles "Complemental Verses" and "The Pretensions of Poverty." The poem stands distinct from the chapter, printed on a separate page.

II
WHERE I LIVED, AND WHAT I LIVED FOR

I purpose to describe more at length, for convenience putting the experience of two years into one. As I have said, I do not propose to write an ode to dejection, but to brag as lustily as chanticleer in the morning, standing on his roost, if only to wake my neighbors up.[38]

When first I took up my abode in the woods, that is, began to spend my nights as well as days there, which, by accident, was on Independence Day, or the Fourth of July, 1845, my house was not finished for winter, but was merely a defence against the rain, without plastering or chimney, the walls being of rough, weather-stained boards, with wide chinks, which made it cool at night. The upright white hewn studs and freshly planed door and window casings gave it a clean and airy look, especially in the morning, when its timbers were saturated with dew, so that I fancied that by noon some sweet gum would exude from them.[39] To my imagi-

---

[38]In the 1854 edition, this sentence (minus the introductory clause, "As I have said") appeared on the title page of *Walden,* and Thoreau's initial reference is to that sentence. The theme of awakening (Thoreau's version of Transcendental "newness") is here signaled clearly. For a useful discussion of what follows, illuminating its links to Indian thought, see William Bysshe Stein, "The Hindu Matrix of *Walden:* The King's Son," *Comparative Literature* 22:4 (Fall 1970): 303-18. For "ode to dejection," cf. the poem of Samuel Taylor Coleridge, "Dejection: An Ode" (1802).

[39]The sweet gum tree, used for building and cabinetmaking, produces a fragrant balsam. Thoreau is pointing to the treelike character of his house with its timber in a near-natural state. William Bysshe Stein sees throughout this chapter and the previous one, "Economy"—

nation it retained throughout the day more or less of this auroral character, reminding me of a certain house on a mountain which I had visited a year before.[40] This was an airy and unplastered cabin, fit to entertain a travelling god, and where a goddess might trail her garments. The winds which passed over my dwelling were such as sweep over the ridges of mountains, bearing the broken strains, or celestial parts only, of terrestrial music. The morning wind forever blows, the poem of creation is uninterrupted; but few are the ears that hear it. Olympus is but the outside of the earth everywhere.[41]. . .

Every morning was a cheerful invitation to make my life of equal simplicity, and I may say innocence, with Nature herself. I have been as sincere a worshipper of Aurora as the Greeks.[42] I got up early and bathed in the pond; that was a religious exercise, and one of the best things which I did. They say that characters were engraven on the bathing tub of King Tchingthang to this effect: "Renew thyself completely each day; do it again, and again, and forever again."[43] I can understand that. Morning brings back the heroic ages. I was as much affected by the faint hum of a mosquito making its invisible and unimaginable tour through my apartment at earliest dawn, when I was sitting with door and windows open, as I could be by any trumpet that ever sang of fame.[44] It was Homer's requiem; itself an Iliad and Odyssey in the air, singing its own wrath and wanderings.[45] There was something cosmical about it; a standing advertisement, till for-

---

and, indeed, throughout the book—a recurring homology, or correspondence, of "body, house, and cosmos" patterned on Indian religious thought. From this perspective, Thoreau's building and inhabiting his house become forms of ritual action, of yoga. See Stein, "Hindu Matrix," 304-305, passim; and William Bysshe Stein, "The Yoga of Walden: Chapter 1 (Economy)," *Literature East and West* 8:1 & 2 (June 1969): 1-26.

[40]The "certain house on a mountain" was that of a "saw-miller" in the Catskills, as recorded in Thoreau's journal. See Henry David Thoreau, *The Writings of Henry David Thoreau,* Walden ed. (Boston: Houghton Mifflin, 1906), 7 (5 July 1845): 361.

[41]These lines, ending with the reference to Mount Olympus, the traditional home of the Gods in Greek mythology, suggest the eclectic nature of Thoreau's spirituality. Besides Olympus there is the presence of the spirit (the "winds" and "morning wind") echoing the Judeo-Christian tradition. The description of Thoreau's spiritual discipline that follows points to the correspondence between the creation of nature and the creation of the self, a process that William Bysshe Stein links to Hindu *samkhya* teaching (see Stein, "Hindu Matrix," 308-309; and, for *samkhya,* n. 46 to Henry David Thoreau, *A Week on the Concord and Merrimack Rivers*).

---

[42]For Aurora, see n. 70 to Thoreau, *Week.*

[43][Confucian School] *The Great Learning* 2.1. King Tching-thang is T'ang, who according to tradition established the Shang dynasty in about 1500 B.C. The translation is almost surely Thoreau's from the M. G. Pauthier (French) translation (see n. 13 above). Although Thoreau was probably not aware of the fact, the engraving warned the king of the importance of maintaining the purity and uprightness of his character. According to Confucian teaching, it was a predecessor's moral corruption that had led to the collapse of his dynasty. See Cady, "Thoreau's Quotations," 24-25. I am indebted to Cady's work for the identification of "Confucian" quotations in later references as well.

[44]Cf. the English poet Felicia D. Hemans (1793-1835), "The Landing of the Pilgrim Fathers in New England," l. 12.

[45]Cf. Homer *Iliad* 1.1-2; and Homer *Odyssey* 1.1-2.

bidden,[46] of the everlasting vigor and fertility of the world. The morning, which is the most memorable season of the day, is the awakening hour. Then there is least somnolence in us; and for an hour, at least, some part of us awakes which slumbers all the rest of the day and night. Little is to be expected of that day, if it can be called a day, to which we are not awakened by our Genius,[47] but by the mechanical nudgings of some servitor, are not awakened by our own newly acquired force and aspirations from within, accompanied by the undulations of celestial music, instead of factory bells, and a fragrance filling the air—to a higher life than we fell asleep from; and thus the darkness bear its fruit, and prove itself to be good, no less than the light. That man who does not believe that each day contains an earlier, more sacred, and auroral hour than he has yet profaned, has despaired of life, and is pursuing a descending and darkening way. After a partial cessation of his sensuous life, the soul of man, or its organs rather, are reinvigorated each day, and his Genius tries again what noble life it can make. All memorable events, I should say, transpire in morning time and in a morning atmosphere. The Vedas say, "All intelligences awake with the morning."[48] Poetry and art, and the fairest and most memorable of the actions of men, date from such an hour. All poets and heroes, like Memnon, are the children of Aurora, and emit their music at sunrise.[49] To him whose elastic and vigorous thought keeps pace with the sun, the day is a perpetual morning. It matters not what the clocks say or the attitudes and labors of men. Morning is when I am awake and there is a dawn in me. Moral reform is the effort to throw off sleep. Why is it that men give so poor an account of their day if they have not been slumbering? They are not such poor calculators. If they had not been overcome with drowsiness, they would have performed something. The millions are awake enough for physical labor; but only one in a million is awake enough for effective intellectual exertion, only one in a hundred millions to a poetic or divine life. To be awake is to be alive. I have never yet met a man who was quite awake. How could I have looked him in the face?

We must learn to reawaken and keep ourselves awake, not by mechanical aids, but by an infinite expectation of the dawn, which does not forsake us in our soundest sleep. I know of no more encouraging fact than the unquestionable ability of man to elevate his life by a conscious endeavor. It is something to be able to paint a particular picture, or to carve a statue, and so to make a few objects beautiful; but it is far more

---

[46] When an advertisement is to be repeated in succeeding issues of a newspaper, the printer's sign "tf" for "till forbidden" indicates its continuing status.

[47] For "Genius," see n. 3 to Alcott, *Doctrine and Discipline of Human Culture*. Note the contrast in the passage between mechanical, external stimuli and organic, internal Genius.

[48] *Samhita of the Sama-Veda* (trans. J. Stevenson) 2.19.16. The *Sama Veda,* one of the four Vedas, is the sacred text that contains knowledge of chants. The *samhitas* were hymns collected in a separate section (one of four) in each Veda.

[49] According to Greek mythology the mother of Memnon, the king of Ethiopia, was Eos (i.e., Latin Aurora, the Goddess of the dawn), who was able to win immortality for her son from the God Zeus. The Greeks linked the privileged Memnon with the Egyptian Pharaoh Amenhotep III (1411?–1375 B.C.). A huge statue of the pharaoh, still standing at Thebes, emits a sound when the earliest rays of the sun shine on it, and it was said in antiquity that the musical sound was a greeting from Memnon to his mother.

glorious to carve and paint the very atmosphere and medium through which we look, which morally we can do. To affect the quality of the day, that is the highest of arts. Every man is tasked to make his life, even in its details, worthy of the contemplation of his most elevated and critical hour. If we refused, or rather used up, such paltry information as we get, the oracles would distinctly inform us how this might be done.

I went to the woods because I wished to live deliberately, to front only the essential facts of life, and see if I could not learn what it had to teach, and not, when I came to die, discover that I had not lived. I did not wish to live what was not life, living is so dear; nor did I wish to practise resignation, unless it was quite necessary. I wanted to live deep and suck out all the marrow of life, to live so sturdily and Spartan-like[50] as to put to rout all that was not life, to cut a broad swath and shave close, to drive life into a corner, and reduce it to its lowest terms, and, if it proved to be mean, why then to get the whole and genuine meanness of it, and publish its meanness to the world; or if it were sublime, to know it by experience, and be able to give a true account of it in my next excursion.[51] For most men, it appears to me, are in a strange uncertainty about it, whether it is of the devil or of God, and have *somewhat hastily* concluded that it is the chief end of man here to "glorify God and enjoy him forever."[52]

Still we live meanly, like ants; though the fable tells us that we were long ago changed into men; like pygmies we fight with cranes; it is error upon error, and clout upon clout, and our best virtue has for its occasion a superfluous and evitable wretchedness.[53] Our life is frittered away by detail. An honest man has hardly need to count more than his ten fingers, or in extreme cases he may add his ten toes, and lump the rest. Simplicity, simplicity, simplicity! I say, let your affairs be as two or three, and not a hundred or a thousand; instead of a million count half a dozen, and keep your accounts on your thumb-nail. In the midst of this chopping sea of civilized life, such are the clouds and storms and quicksands and thousand-and-one items to be allowed for, that a man has to live, if he would not founder and go to the bottom and not make his port at all, by dead reckoning,[54] and he must be a great calculator indeed who succeeds. Simplify, simplify. Instead of three meals a day, if it be necessary eat but one; instead of a hundred dishes, five; and reduce other things in

---

[50]For the Spartan life-style, see n. 17 to Emerson, "Self-Reliance."

[51]Thoreau's characteristic name for his travel essays was "excursions."

[52]"Shorter Catechism" *New-England Primer* 1 (see n. 12 above). Thoreau, however, adds the adverb *here* to his sentence before quoting.

[53]The "fable" is that of Aeacus. In ancient Greek myth the king of Oenopia, he turned to his father, Zeus, for help when a plague destroyed most of his people. Because of the piety of his son, Zeus changed ants into human beings (called Myrmidons) and the country was repopulated. For pygmies fighting cranes, cf. the advance of the Trojans to fight the Achaeans (Greeks) in Homer *Iliad* 3.1-6. For "clout upon clout," cf. "New England Annoyances," in John Warner Barber, *Historical Collections . . . Relating to the History and Antiquities of Every Town in Massachusetts, with Geographical Descriptions* (Worcester: Dorr, Howland, 1841) 195.

[54]William Bysshe Stein has called attention to the pun here. "Dead reckoning" is a mode of navigating without the guidance of the heavenly bodies, without—in the deeper sense—divine assistance. See Stein, "Hindu Matrix," 314.

proportion. Our life is like a German Confederacy, made up of petty states, with its boundary forever fluctuating, so that even a German cannot tell you how it is bounded at any moment.[55] The nation itself, with all its so-called internal improvements,[56] which, by the way are all external and superficial, is just such an unwieldy and overgrown establishment, cluttered with furniture and tripped up by its own traps, ruined by luxury and heedless expense, by want of calculation and a worthy aim, as the million households in the land; and the only cure for it, as for them, is in a rigid economy, a stern and more than Spartan simplicity of life and elevation of purpose. It lives too fast. Men think that it is essential that the *Nation* have commerce, and export ice, and talk through a telegraph, and ride thirty miles an hour, without a doubt, whether *they* do or not;[57] but whether we should live like baboons or like men, is a little uncertain. If we do not get out sleepers,[58] and forge rails, and devote days and nights to the work, but go to tinkering upon our *lives* to improve *them,* who will build railroads? And if railroads are not built, how shall we get to heaven in season?[59] But if we stay at home and mind our business, who will want railroads? We do not ride on the railroad; it rides upon us.[60] Did you ever think what those sleepers are that underlie the railroad? Each one is a man, an Irishman,[61] or a Yankee man. . . .

Why should we live with such hurry and waste of life? . . . Hardly a man takes a half-hour's nap after dinner, but when he wakes he holds up his head and asks, "What's the news?" as if the rest of mankind had stood his sentinels. Some give directions to be waked every half-hour, doubtless for no other purpose; and then, to pay for it, they tell what they have dreamed. After a night's sleep the news is as indispensable as the breakfast. "Pray tell me anything new that has happened to a man anywhere on this globe,"—and he

---

[55] After the dissolution of the Holy Roman Empire, the German Confederation was only a loose alliance, and boundary problems were endemic. The unification of Germany as an empire was not finally effected until 1871 with Otto von Bismarck.

[56] Thoreau is alluding to political issues of the time regarding public works at the expense of the federal government.

[57] New England did a thriving business exporting ice both at home and abroad. See Thoreau's own description of an ice-harvesting at Walden Pond and his comment on the final destinations of the ice in ch. 16. Samuel F. B. Morse demonstrated the effectiveness of his American telegraph to Congress in 1844. With the introduction of the railroad in the decade from 1830 to 1840, a transportation revolution was effected; an average speed of thirty or thirty-five miles an hour was astonishing to a generation previously accustomed to the stagecoach.

[58] That is, the wooden ties for railroad beds, on which the rails are laid. Notice the pun—the ties *and* the men who work on the railroad "days and nights."

[59] An ironic reference to Nathaniel Hawthorne's satiric short story "The Celestial Railroad" (1843), plotted as a contemporary *Pilgrim's Progress*. Two of the perils encountered therein are a Giant Transcendentalist and a bustling Vanity Fair served by the new railroad line.

[60] Cf. Ralph Waldo Emerson, "Ode: Inscribed to W[illiam] H[enry] Channing" (1846), ll. 50-51, in Emerson, *The Complete Works of Ralph Waldo Emerson,* ed. Edward Waldo Emerson, centenary ed. (Boston: Houghton, Mifflin, 1903-1904) 9:78.

[61] The Irish came pouring into Boston and other East Coast cities from the 1840s, and their labor was exploited in Thoreau's America to build the railroads.

reads it over his coffee and rolls, that a man has had his eyes gouged out this morning on the Wachito River; never dreaming the while that he lives in the dark unfathomed mammoth cave of this world, and has but the rudiment of an eye himself.[62] . . .

What news! how much more important to know what that is which was never old! "Kieou-he-yu (great dignitary of the state of Wei) sent a man to Khoung-tseu to know his news. Khoung-tseu caused the messenger to be seated near him, and questioned him in these terms: What is your master doing? The messenger answered with respect: My master desires to diminish the number of his faults, but he cannot come to the end of them. The messenger being gone, the philosopher remarked: What a worthy messenger! What a worthy messenger!"[63] The preacher, instead of vexing the ears of drowsy farmers on their day of rest at the end of the week,—for Sunday is the fit conclusion of an ill-spent week, and not the fresh and brave beginning of a new one,[64]—with this one other draggle-tail of a sermon, should shout with thundering voice, "Pause! Avast! Why so seeming fast, but deadly slow?"[65]

Shams and delusions are esteemed for soundest truths, while reality is fabulous. If men would steadily observe realities only, and not allow themselves to be deluded, life, to compare it with such things as we know, would be like a fairy tale and the Arabian Nights' Entertainments.[66] If we respected only what is inevitable and has a right to be, music and poetry would resound along the streets. When we are unhurried and wise, we perceive that only great and worthy things have any permanent and absolute existence, that petty fears and petty pleasures are but the shadow of the reality. This is always exhilarating and sublime. By closing the eyes and slumbering, and consenting to be deceived by shows, men establish and confirm their daily life of routine and habit everywhere, which still is built on purely illusory foundations.[67] Children, who play life, discern

---

[62]Thoreau's "Wachito" is the Ouachita River, formerly known as the Washita, which empties into the Red River system in Louisiana. Talk of eye gouging was almost a standard literary device in some regional Southern literature of the period—a metaphor for the wildness the frontier was said to engender. The reference to the "dark unfathomed mammoth cave" is an allusion to Mammoth Cave in southwest central Kentucky, where small, sightless fish live in the water underground. Cf. too, Thomas Gray, "Elegy Written in a Country Churchyard" (1751), st. 14, l. 2.

[63]*Analects of Confucius* 14.26. The translation is almost surely Thoreau's from the French edition of M. G. Pauthier. The Pauthier translation renders the name "Kieou-pe-yu," and the "h" in *Walden* is an error. "Khoung-tseu" is Master K'ung, or Confucius. Arthur Waley doubts that the final, repeated phrase of the saying signifies approval (see *The Analects of Confucius,* trans. Arthur Waley [London: George Allen & Unwin, 1938] 187 n. 4). Waley's own translation reads, "What a messenger, what a messenger!"

[64]The Sabbath, according to the biblical model, is the last—not the first—day of the week (Gen. 2:2-3).

[65]Perhaps, as Walter Harding suggests (*Variorum Walden,* 269), this may be an allusion to the renowned nautical preaching of Father Edward Taylor (1793–1871), the Methodist missionary who presided over Seaman's Chapel in Boston.

[66]The *Arabian Nights,* or *Thousand and One Nights,* the collection of anonymous stories written in Arabic in which Scheherazade tells one tale a night for 1,001 nights in order to prevent her royal husband from murdering her.

[67]The language of "shows" and "illusory foundations" as well as the quotation that follows (see n. 69) suggest the Indian provenance

its true law and relations more clearly than men, who fail to live it worthily, but who think that they are wiser by experience, that is, by failure.[68] I have read in a Hindoo book, that "there was a king's son, who, being expelled in infancy from his native city, was brought up by a forester, and, growing up to maturity in that state, imagined himself to belong to the barbarous race with which he lived. One of his father's ministers having discovered him, revealed to him what he was, and the misconception of his character was removed, and he knew himself to be a prince. So soul," continues the Hindoo philosopher, "from the circumstances in which it is placed, mistakes its own character, until the truth is revealed to it by some holy teacher, and then it knows itself to be *Brahme.*"[69] I perceive

that we inhabitants of New England live this mean life that we do because our vision does not penetrate the surface of things. We think that that *is* which *appears* to be. If a man should walk through this town and see only the reality, where, think you, would the "Mill-dam" go to?[70] If he should give us an account of the realities he beheld there, we should not recognize the place in his description. Look at a meeting-house, or a court-house, or a jail, or a shop, or a dwelling-house, and say what that thing really is before a true gaze, and they would all go to pieces in your account of them. Men esteem truth remote, in the outskirts of the system, behind the farthest star, before Adam and after the last man.[71] In eternity there is indeed something true and sublime. But all these times and places and occasions are now and here. God himself culminates in the present moment, and will never be more divine in the lapse of all the ages. And we are enabled to apprehend at all what is sublime and noble only by the perpetual instilling and drenching of the reality that surrounds us.

---

of Thoreau's thinking here. (For a related example, see his quotation from the *Samkhya Karika* in Thoreau, *Week;* and see n. 79 to the text.) Indian religious thought from about the sixth century B.C. dwelled on the problem of *samsara,* the fleeting passage of life, which could give no lasting security. For a specifically Christian formulation of the problem of transience, cf. Theodore Parker, *A Discourse of the Transient and Permanent in Christianity.*

[68]For the superior discernment of children, cf. Alcott, *Doctrine and Discipline of Human Culture;* and see n. 27 to the text.

[69]The quotation is attributed by Horace Hayman Wilson to Vijnana Bhikshu (Vijnanabhikshu)—a sixteenth-century commentator on the (fourteenth-century?) *Samkhya-pravacana-Sutra,* itself a commentary on the *Samkhya Karika.* Wilson's quotation may be found in Isvara Krishna *Samkhya Karika* (trans. Henry Thomas Colebrooke, with *The Bhasya or Commentary of Gaudapada,* trans. and ed. Horace Hayman Wilson) 72 (Comment). For the 1837 edition of the *Samkhya Karika* from which Thoreau took the quotation, see n. 79 to Thoreau, *Week.* For "*Brahme,*" read "Brah-

man"; and see n. 16 to Ralph Waldo Emerson, "Brahma," for its mystical import. Finally, cf. Thoreau's use of the story of the forester who is in reality a king's son to Emerson's use of the theme from the induction to William Shakespeare's *Taming of the Shrew* in which, as a joke, an awakened sot is told he is a (noble) lord. See Emerson, "Self-Reliance," and also n. 24 to the text.

[70]The "Mill-dam" was the shopping district of Concord, and "meeting-house," "court-house," and "jail"—mentioned later in the passage by Thoreau—were all located there. Note, too, Thoreau's continuing distinction, based on Indian thought, between appearance and reality.

[71]For Thoreau's spiritual geography, see n. 82 to Thoreau, *Week.* For the significance of the present (below in the passage), cf. n. 16 above.

The universe constantly and obediently answers to our conceptions; whether we travel fast or slow, the track is laid for us. Let us spend our lives in conceiving then. The poet or the artist never yet had so fair and noble a design but some of his posterity at least could accomplish it.

Let us spend one day as deliberately as Nature, and not be thrown off the track by every nutshell and mosquito's wing that falls on the rails. Let us rise early and fast, or break fast, gently and without perturbation; let company come and let company go, let the bells ring and the children cry,— determined to make a day of it. Why should we knock under and go with the stream? Let us not be upset and overwhelmed in that terrible rapid and whirlpool called a dinner, situated in the meridian shallows. Weather this danger and you are safe, for the rest of the way is down hill. With unrelaxed nerves, with morning vigor, sail by it, looking another way, tied to the mast like Ulysses.[72] If the engine whistles, let it whistle till it is hoarse for its pains. If the bell rings, why should we run? We will consider what kind of music they are like. Let us settle ourselves, and work and wedge our feet downward through the mud and slush of opinion, and prejudice, and tradition, and delusion, and appearance, that alluvion which covers the globe, through Paris and London, through New York and Boston and Concord, through Church and State, through poetry and philosophy and religion, till we come to a hard bottom and rocks in place, which we can call *reality,* and say, This is, and no mistake; and then begin, having a *point d'appui,* below freshet and frost and fire, a place where you might found a wall or a state, or set a lamp-post safely, or perhaps a gauge, not a Nilometer, but a Realometer, that future ages might know how deep a freshet of shams and appearances had gathered from time to time.[73] If you stand right fronting and face to face to a fact, you will see the sun glimmer on both its surfaces, as if it were a cimeter, and feel its sweet edge dividing you through the heart and marrow, and so you will happily conclude your mortal career. Be it life or death, we crave only reality. If we are really dying, let us hear the rattle in our throats and feel cold in the extremities; if we are alive, let us go about our business.

Time is but the stream I go a-fishing in.[74] I drink at it; but while I drink I see the sandy bottom and detect how shallow it is. Its thin current slides away, but eternity remains. I would drink deeper; fish in the sky, whose bottom is pebbly with stars. I cannot count one. I know not the first letter of the alphabet. I have always been regretting that I was not as wise as the day I was born. The intellect is a cleaver; it discerns and rifts its way into the secret of things. I do not wish to be any more busy with my hands than is necessary. My head is hands and feet. I feel all my best faculties concentrated in it. My instinct tells me that my head is an organ for burrowing, as some creatures use their snout and fore paws, and with it I would mine and burrow my way

---

[72]Ulysses had himself tied to the mast of his ship in order that he might hear the seductive songs of the Sirens and yet not sail to them, which would bring certain death to himself and his crew. See Homer *Odyssey* 12.154-200.

[73]For "*point d'appui,*" read "point of support," or "fulcrum." The ancient Nilometer was a well constructed on the bank of the Nile River, both at Memphis and on the island of Elephantine, with marks to measure the rise of the water. See Strabo *Geography* 17.1.48, and Diodorus of Sicily 1.36.11.

[74]Once again, in this passage, the fleeting quality of temporal life (the Indian *samsara*) and the innate wisdom of the young are suggested.

through these hills. I think that the richest vein is somewhere hereabouts; so by the divining-rod[75] and thin rising vapors I judge; and here I will begin to mine.

IV
SOUNDS[76]

I did not read books the first summer; I hoed beans. Nay, I often did better than this. There were times when I could not afford to sacrifice the bloom of the present moment to any work, whether of the head or hands. I love a broad margin to my life. Sometimes, in a summer morning, having taken my accustomed bath,[77] I sat in my sunny doorway from sunrise till noon, rapt in a revery, amidst the pines and hickories and sumachs, in undisturbed solitude and stillness, while the birds sang around or flitted noiseless through the house, until by the sun falling in at my west window, or the noise of some traveller's wagon on the distant highway, I was reminded of the lapse of time. I grew in those seasons like corn in the night, and they were far better than any work of the hands would have been. They were not time subtracted from my life, but so much over and above my usual allowance. I realized what the Orientals mean by contemplation and the forsaking of works.[78] For the most part, I minded not how the hours went. The day advanced as if to light some work of mine; it was morning, and lo, now it is evening, and nothing memorable is accomplished. Instead of singing like the birds, I silently smiled at my incessant good fortune. As the sparrow had its trill, sitting on the hickory before my door, so had I my chuckle or suppressed warble which he might hear out of my nest.[79] My days were not days of the week, bearing the stamp of any heathen deity, nor were they minced into hours and fretted by the ticking of a clock;[80] for I lived like the Puri Indians, of whom it is said that "for yesterday, to-day, and to-morrow they have only one word, and they express the variety of meaning by pointing backward for yesterday, forward for to-morrow, and

---

[75] A divining rod is a forked instrument used to detect the presence of water or minerals when, users attest, the rod dips markedly downward over the elements sought.

[76] In the previous chapter Thoreau has discussed reading as a serious activity worthy of consecrated hours. Now he leaves his books for another form of consecrated action. Critics have cited these lines as the record of mystical experience (see, for example, Thoreau, *Variorum Walden,* xxii), and a close reading suggests at least a deep meditative state. Thoreau's morning yoga is surely akin to his experience of the "yoga of sound" as he heard the distant tyro beating a drum (see "Monday" in Thoreau, *Week,* and nn. 41 and 57 to the text; for a useful discussion of the yoga of *Walden,* see also Frank MacShane, "*Walden* and Yoga," *The New England Quarterly* 37:3 [September 1964]: 322-42).

[77] The bath was intended as a spiritual as well as physical cleansing.

[78] Cf. Thoreau's quotations from the *Bhagavad Gita* and his reflections on them in "Monday" of his *Week.* But the "forsaking of works" is not the forsaking of action in the sense of spiritual awareness. There is a subtle irony in Thoreau's language in the passage.

[79] This may be an oblique reference to a meditation mantra, in Indian religious practice a sound repeated, not for its intellectual content, but for its power to center the mind and to make real the truth expressed in the sound. (Cf. n. 28 to Thoreau, *Week.*)

[80] Roman names for the days of the week, based on the names of planetary deities, were inherited by Western Europeans. In the English language the Latin names were retained in translation, or the names of Germanic deities were substituted. With the introduction of the factory system in New England, the organic time of the farmer began to give way before the "clock time" of the factories.

overhead for the passing day."[81] This was sheer idleness to my fellow-townsmen, no doubt; but if the birds and flowers had tried me by their standard, I should not have been found wanting. A man must find his occasions in himself, it is true. The natural day is very calm, and will hardly reprove his indolence. . . .

V
SOLITUDE

Sometimes, when I compare myself with other men, it seems as if I were more favored by the gods than they, beyond any deserts that I am conscious of; as if I had a warrant and surety at their hands which my fellows have not, and were especially guided and guarded. I do not flatter myself, but if it be possible they flatter me. I have never felt lonesome, or in the least oppressed by a sense of solitude, but once, and that was a few weeks after I came to the woods, when, for an hour, I doubted if the near neighborhood of man was not essential to a serene and healthy life. To be alone was something unpleasant. But I was at the same time conscious of a slight insanity in my mood, and seemed to foresee my recovery. In the midst of a gentle rain while these thoughts prevailed, I was suddenly sensible of such sweet and beneficent society in Nature, in the very pattering of the drops, and in every sound and sight around my house, an infinite and unaccountable friendliness all at once like an atmosphere sustaining me, as made the fancied advantages of human neighborhood insignificant, and I have never thought of them since. Every little pine needle expanded and swelled with sympathy and befriended me. I was so distinctly made aware of the presence of something kindred to me, even in scenes which we are accustomed to call wild and dreary, and also that the nearest of blood to me and humanest was not a person nor a villager, that I thought no place could ever be strange to me again.—

> "Mourning untimely consumes the sad;
> Few are their days in the land of the living,
> Beautiful daughter of Toscar."[82]

Some of my pleasantest hours were during the long rain-storms in the spring or fall, which confined me to the house for the afternoon as well as the forenoon, soothed by their ceaseless roar and pelting; when an early twilight ushered in a long evening in which many thoughts had time to take root and unfold themselves. . . . Men frequently say to me, "I should think you would feel lonesome down there, and want to be nearer to folks, rainy and snowy days and nights especially." I am tempted to reply to such,—This whole earth which we inhabit is but a point in space. How far apart, think you, dwell the two most distant inhabitants of yonder star, the breadth

---

[81]Except for a small difference in Thoreau's transcription, the quoted material on the Puri of eastern Brazil may be found in Ida Pfeiffer, *A Lady's Voyage round the World: A Selected Translation from the German of Ida Pfeiffer*, trans. Mrs. Percy [Jane] Sinnett (New York: Harper, 1852) 36.

[82]The lines, from Ossian's poem "Croma," may be found in the blank-verse translation of Patrick MacGregor. See Ossian [James Macpherson], *The Genuine Remains of Ossian*, trans. Patrick MacGregor (London: Smith, Elder, 1841) 193. The publication of the poems of "Ossian" was a great literary imposture in the eighteenth century. Subsequent investigation showed that the third-century "remains" of Ossian were a mixture of traditional Gaelic poetry and much original poetry by the Scotsman James Macpherson. Notwithstanding this denunciation, Patrick MacGregor's translation appeared in the nineteenth century; and Thoreau—though aware of the controversy—like many others was drawn to Ossian.

of whose disk cannot be appreciated by our instruments? Why should I feel lonely? is not our planet in the Milky Way? This which you put seems to me not to be the most important question. What sort of space is that which separates a man from his fellows and makes him solitary? I have found that no exertion of the legs can bring two minds much nearer to one another. What do we want most to dwell near to? Not to many men surely, the depot, the post-office, the bar-room, the meeting-house, the school-house, the grocery, Beacon Hill, or the Five Points, where men most congregate,[83] but to the perennial source of our life, whence in all our experience we have found that to issue, as the willow stands near the water and sends out its roots in that direction. This will vary with different natures, but this is the place where a wise man will dig his cellar. . . .

Any prospect of awakening or coming to life to a dead man makes indifferent all times and places. The place where that may occur is always the same, and indescribably pleasant to all our senses. For the most part we allow only outlying and transient circumstances to make our occasions. They are, in fact, the cause of our distraction. Nearest to all things is that power which fashions their being.[84] *Next* to us the grandest laws are continually being executed. *Next* to us is not the workman whom we have hired, with whom we love so well to talk, but the workman whose work we are.

"How vast and profound is the influence of the subtle powers of Heaven and of Earth!"

"We seek to perceive them, and we do not see them; we seek to hear them, and we do not hear them; identified with the substance of things, they cannot be separated from them."

"They cause that in all the universe men purify and sanctify their hearts, and clothe themselves in their holiday garments to offer sacrifices and oblations to their ancestors. It is an ocean of subtle intelligences. They are everywhere, above us, on our left, on our right; they environ us on all sides."[85]

We are the subjects of an experiment which is not a little interesting to me. Can we not do without the society of our gossips a little while under these circumstances,—have our own thoughts to cheer us? Confucius says truly, "Virtue does not remain as an abandoned orphan; it must of necessity have neighbors."[86]

With thinking we may be beside ourselves in a sane sense. By a conscious effort of the mind we can stand aloof from actions and their consequences; and all things, good and bad, go by us like a tor-

---

[83] Beacon Hill, in Boston, is the site of the State House and a hub of sophisticated Boston society. Five Points, in New York—in Thoreau's day to the north of the City Hall but now no longer existing—had acquired an opposite reputation as a dilapidated and criminal section of the city.

[84] Again, an instance of Thoreau's spiritual geography of periphery and center (see n. 82 to Thoreau, *Week*).

[85] [Tzu Sse] *The Doctrine of the Mean* 16.1-3. The work contains the teaching of the Confucian school. The translation of the three sayings is almost surely Thoreau's from the French version by M. G. Pauthier. Lyman Cady has noted that the *Walden* translation's "subtle powers" were *kwei-shen,* spirits both demonic and benevolent, set in the context of ancestor worship. See Cady, "Thoreau's Quotations," 26-27.

[86] *Analects of Confucius* 4.25. The Confucian aphorism is directed toward a social and political agenda, but Thoreau is able to use the saying to suit his purposes.

rent.[87] We are not wholly involved in Nature. I may be either the drift-wood in the stream, or Indra in the sky looking down on it. I *may* be affected by a theatrical exhibition; on the other hand, I *may not* be affected by an actual event which appears to concern me much more. I only know myself as a human entity; the scene, so to speak, of thoughts and affections; and am sensible of a certain doubleness by which I can stand as remote from myself as from another. However intense my experience, I am conscious of the presence and criticism of a part of me, which, as it were, is not a part of me, but spectator, sharing no experience, but taking note of it; and that is no more I than it is you. When the play, it may be the tragedy, of life is over, the spectator goes his way. It was a kind of fiction, a work of the imagination only, so far as he was concerned. This doubleness may easily make us poor neighbors and friends sometimes.

I find it wholesome to be alone the greater part of the time. To be in company, even with the best, is soon wearisome and dissipating.[88] I love to be alone. I never found the companion that was so companionable as solitude. We are for the most part more lonely when we go abroad among men than when we stay in our chambers. A man thinking or working is always alone, let him be where he will. Solitude is not measured by the miles of space that intervene between a man and his fellows. . . .

VII
THE BEAN-FIELD[89]

This is the result of my experience in raising beans. Plant the common small white bush bean[90] about the first of June, in rows three feet by eighteen inches apart, being careful to select fresh round and unmixed seed. First look out for worms, and supply vacancies by planting anew. Then look out for woodchucks, if it is an exposed place, for they will nibble off the earliest tender leaves almost clean as they go; and again, when the young tendrils make their appearance, they have notice of it, and will shear them off with both buds and young pods, sitting erect like a squirrel. But above all harvest as early as possible, if you would escape frosts and have a fair and salable crop; you may save much loss by this means.

This further experience also I gained. I said to myself, I will not plant beans and corn with so much industry another summer, but such seeds, if the seed is not lost, as sincerity, truth, simplicity, faith, innocence, and the like, and see if they will not grow in this soil, even with less toil and manurance, and sustain me, for surely it

---

[87]In the passage that follows, Thoreau describes a doubleness that in his case seems largely natural but, as the sentence indicates, may also be deliberately elicited. Thus, such a doubleness may be the product of a conscious meditation technique. The reference to Indra (Indian God of thunder and war, and greatest of Gods in the *Rig Veda*), the "theatrical exhibition," and the "spectator" suggest an Indian provenance. The technique itself is unexceptional in certain forms of Hindu meditative teaching. Cf. Thoreau's quotation from the *Samkhya Karika* in "Friday" of his *Week;* and see n. 79 to the text. And for Indra, cf. Emerson's reference to the "strong gods" in his poem "Brahma"; and see n. 19 to the text.

[88]Cf. the theme of this passage to Seneca [the Younger] *Epistles* 7.1. Cf., too, Thomas à Kempis *The Imitation of Christ* 1.20. (For Thomas à Kempis, see n. 18 to Theodore Parker, *A Sermon of the Delights of Piety.*)

[89]After his chapter "Visitors," Thoreau devotes most of the present chapter to an account of his work growing beans.

[90]That is, the navy bean.

has not been exhausted for these crops.[91] Alas! I said this to myself; but now another summer is gone, and another, and another, and I am obliged to say to you, Reader, that the seeds which I planted, if indeed they *were* the seeds of those virtues, were wormeaten or had lost their vitality, and so did not come up. Commonly men will only be brave as their fathers were brave, or timid. This generation is very sure to plant corn and beans each new year precisely as the Indians did centuries ago and taught the first settlers to do,[92] as if there were a fate in it. I saw an old man the other day, to my astonishment, making the holes with a hoe for the seventieth time at least, and not for himself to lie down in! But why should not the New Englander try new adventures, and not lay so much stress on his grain, his potato and grass crop, and his orchards,—raise other crops than these? Why concern ourselves so much about our beans for seed, and not be concerned at all about a new generation of men? We should really be fed and cheered if when we met a man we were sure to see that some of the qualities which I have named, which we all prize more than those other productions, but which are for the most part broadcast and floating in the air, had taken root and grown in him. Here comes such a subtile and ineffable quality, for instance, as truth or justice, though the slightest amount or new variety of it, along the road. Our ambassadors should be instructed to send home such seeds as these, and Congress help to distribute them over all the land.[93] We should never stand upon ceremony with sincerity. We should never cheat and insult and banish one another by our meanness, if there were present the kernel of worth and friendliness. We should not meet thus in haste. Most men I do not meet at all, for they seem not to have time; they are busy about their beans. We would not deal with a man thus plodding ever, leaning on a hoe or a spade as a staff between his work, not as a mushroom, but partially risen out of the earth, something more than erect, like swallows alighted and walking on the ground:—

"And as he spake, his wings would now and then
Spread, as he meant to fly, then close again,—"[94]

so that we should suspect that we might be conversing with an angel. Bread may not always nourish us; but it always does us good, it even takes stiffness out of our joints, and makes us supple and buoyant, when we knew not what ailed us, to recognize any generosity in man or Nature, to share any unmixed and heroic joy.

Ancient poetry and mythology suggest, at least, that husbandry was once a

---

[91] In keeping with the law of correspondence, Thoreau finds analogies between cultivating a crop and cultivating virtue. In fact, he did not plant his beans the second season at Walden Pond. Moreover, he did not eat any of his bean crop of the first year but exchanged it for rice (see Thoreau, *Writings*, 2:179).

[92] In the manuscript of William Bradford's *History of Plymouth Plantation* (1650?), the (Pawtuxet) Indian Squanto was said to have taught the Pilgrims to plant corn. See Alexander Young, ed., *Chronicles of the Pilgrim Fathers of the Colony of Plymouth from 1602 to 1625* (Boston: Charles C. Little and James Brown, 1841) 230-31. (The complete version of Bradford's *History* did not appear until 1856.)

[93] At the time, members of the United States Congress supplied seeds without charge to constituents who asked for them.

[94] Words of the shepherd Evangelus describing the apparition of an angel announcing the Virgin Birth, in Francis Quarles, *The Shepheards Oracles* (1646), eclogue 5, ll. 130-31.

sacred art;[95] but it is pursued with irreverent haste and heedlessness by us, our object being to have large farms and large crops merely. We have no festival, nor procession, nor ceremony, not excepting our cattle-shows and so-called Thanksgivings,[96] by which the farmer expresses a sense of the sacredness of his calling, or is reminded of its sacred origin. It is the premium and the feast which tempt him. He sacrifices not to Ceres and the Terrestrial Jove, but to the infernal Plutus rather.[97] By avarice and selfishness, and a grovelling habit, from which none of us is free, of regarding the soil as property, or the means of acquiring property chiefly, the landscape is deformed, husbandry is degraded with us, and the farmer leads the meanest of lives. He knows Nature but as a robber. Cato says that the profits of agriculture are particularly pious or just (*maximeque pius quaestus*),[98] and according to Varro the old Romans "called the same earth Mother and Ceres, and thought that they who cultivated it led a pious and useful life, and that they alone were left of the race of King Saturn."[99]

We are wont to forget that the sun looks on our cultivated fields and on the prairies and forests without distinction. They all reflect and absorb his rays alike, and the former make but a small part of the glorious picture which he beholds in his daily course. In his view the earth is all equally cultivated like a garden. Therefore we should receive the benefit of his light and heat with a corresponding trust and magnanimity. What though I value the seed of these beans, and harvest that in the fall of the year? This broad field which I have looked at so long looks not to me as the principal cultivator, but away from me to influences more genial to it, which water and make it green. These beans have results which are not harvested by me. Do they not grow for woodchucks partly? The ear of wheat (in Latin *spica,* obsoletely

---

[95]By mid-August 1851, Amos Bronson Alcott had lent Thoreau his copy of the *Rei Rusticae* ("*Things Rustic*"), a volume containing the works of the ancient Roman writers on husbandry—Cato, Varro, Columella, and Palladius. See the discussion in Ethel Seybold, *Thoreau: The Quest and the Classics,* Yale Studies in English, vol. 116 (1951; rpt., Hamden CT: Archon Books, 1969) 70-71.

[96]Walter Harding notes that Concord was the site of an annual cattle show or county fair. See Thoreau, *Variorum Walden,* 293. In this period there was no annual national Thanksgiving observance. Thanksgiving festivals were sporadic and local events.

[97]Ceres, the Roman equivalent of the Greek Demeter, was the Goddess of grain. Thoreau calls Jupiter or Jove—the Roman counterpart of the Greek Zeus—"Terrestrial Jove," probably to stress his agrarian connections. Because thunder and rain—atmospheric phenomena with agricultural import—were associated with Jupiter, and also perhaps because of his amorous exploits that demonstrated his fertility, a religious logic could bring him down to earth. Cf. Varro *Rerum Rusticarum* (*On Agriculture*) 1.1.5. Finally, Plutus, although often confused with the Roman Pluto, was a separate Greek deity (note Thoreau's conflation of Roman and Greek names), God of agricultural prosperity and then of wealth and riches in a more general sense. Here Plutus is probably "infernal" because Thoreau perceives riches as corrupting.

[98]Cato *De Agri Cultura* (*On Agriculture*) 1.4. The Latin *quaestus,* which Thoreau has translated "profits," signifies in its context "profession" or "trade."

[99]Varro *Rerum Rusticarum* (*On Agriculture*) 3.1.5. The translation is Thoreau's. For Saturn—the "Sower"—see n. 16 to Amos Bronson Alcott, "Orphic Sayings." Associated in Roman culture with the seed and the harvest, Saturn was the father, among other deities, of Jupiter and Ceres.

speca, from *spe,* hope) should not be the only hope of the husbandman; its kernel or grain (*granum,* from *gerendo,* bearing) is not all that it bears.[100] How, then, can our harvest fail? Shall I not rejoice also at the abundance of the weeds whose seeds are the granary of the birds? It matters little comparatively whether the fields fill the farmer's barns. The true husbandman will cease from anxiety, as the squirrels manifest no concern whether the woods will bear chestnuts this year or not,[101] and finish his labor with every day, relinquishing all claim to the produce of his fields, and sacrificing in his mind not only his first but his last fruits also.

IX
THE PONDS[102]

A lake is the landscape's most beautiful and expressive feature. It is earth's eye; looking into which the beholder measures the depth of his own nature. The fluviatile trees next the shore are the slender eyelashes which fringe it, and the wooded hills and cliffs around are its overhanging brows. . . .

It is a soothing employment, on one of those fine days in the fall when all the warmth of the sun is fully appreciated, to sit on a stump on such a height as this,[103] overlooking the pond, and study the dimpling circles which are incessantly inscribed on its otherwise invisible surface amid the reflected skies and trees. Over this great expanse there is no disturbance but it is thus at once gently smoothed away and assuaged, as, when a vase of water is jarred, the trembling circles seek the shore and all is smooth again. Not a fish can leap or an insect fall on the pond but it is thus reported in circling dimples, in lines of beauty, as it were the constant welling up of its fountain, the gentle pulsing of its life, the heaving of its breast. The thrills of joy and thrills of pain are undistinguishable. How peaceful the phenomena of the lake! Again the works of man shine as in the spring. Ay, every leaf and twig and stone and cobweb sparkles now at mid-afternoon as when covered with dew in a spring morning. Every motion of an oar or an insect produces a flash of light; and if an oar falls, how sweet the echo!

In such a day, in September or October, Walden is a perfect forest mirror, set round with stones as precious to my eye as if fewer or rarer. Nothing so fair, so pure, and at the same time so large, as a lake, perchance, lies on the surface of the earth. Sky water. It needs no fence. Nations come and go without defiling it. It is a mirror which no stone can crack, whose quicksilver will never wear off, whose gilding Na-

---

[100]Cf. Varro *Rerum Rusticarum* 1.48.2-3. Thoreau delighted in philological reflection (see also ch. 17) and—following the law of correspondence—like Emerson (cf. *Nature,* ch. 4) pursued an organic and intrinsic connection between words and the things they signified. For a helpful discussion in the context of earlier New England theology, see Philip F. Gura, *The Wisdom of Words: Language, Theology, and Literature in the New England Renaissance* (Middletown CT: Wesleyan University Press, 1981) 107-44.

[101]Cf. Matt. 6:25-26.

[102]In the previous chapter, "The Village," Thoreau has given a general account of his trips into town each day or two and briefly recounted the incident of his night in jail. The present chapter is a reflection on Walden Pond and other ponds in the area, and the first excerpted paragraph is a particularly strong statement of the doctrine of correspondence. If the eye provides entry to the spirit, a lake—"earth's eye"—is a mirror of the self, with even the "fluviatile trees"—intimately related to the water—a part of the correspondence.

---

[103]A hilltop.

ture continually repairs; no storms, no dust, can dim its surface ever fresh;—a mirror in which all impurity presented to it sinks, swept and dusted by the sun's hazy brush,—this the light dust-cloth,—which retains no breath that is breathed on it, but sends its own to float as clouds high above its surface, and be reflected in its bosom still.

A field of water betrays the spirit that is in the air. It is continually receiving new life and motion from above. It is intermediate in its nature between land and sky. On land only the grass and trees wave, but the water itself is rippled by the wind. I see where the breeze dashes across it by the streaks or flakes of light. It is remarkable that we can look down on its surface. We shall, perhaps, look down thus on the surface of air at length, and mark where a still subtler spirit sweeps over it.[104] . . .

Of all the characters I have known, perhaps Walden wears best, and best preserves its purity. Many men have been likened to it, but few deserve that honor. Though the woodchoppers have laid bare first this shore and then that, and the Irish have built their sties by it, and the railroad has infringed on its border, and the ice-men have skimmed it once, it is itself unchanged, the same water which my youthful eyes fell on;[105] all the change is in me.

It has not acquired one permanent wrinkle after all its ripples. It is perennially young, and I may stand and see a swallow dip apparently to pick an insect from its surface as of yore. It struck me again to-night, as if I had not seen it almost daily for more than twenty years,—Why, here is Walden, the same woodland lake that I discovered so many years ago; where a forest was cut down last winter another is springing up by its shore as lustily as ever; the same thought is welling up to its surface that was then; it is the same liquid joy and happiness to itself and its Maker, ay, and it *may* be to me. It is the work of a brave man surely, in whom there was no guile![106] He rounded this water with his hand, deepened and clarified it in his thought, and in his will bequeathed it to Concord. I see by its face that it is visited by the same reflection; and I can almost say, Walden, is it you?

> It is no dream of mine,
> To ornament a line;
> I cannot come nearer to God and Heaven
> Than I live to Walden even.
> I am its stony shore,
> And the breeze that passes o'er;
> In the hollow of my hand
> Are its water and its sand,
> And its deepest resort
> Lies high in my thought.[107]

The cars[108] never pause to look at it; yet

---

[104]Again in keeping with the teaching of correspondence, contemplating the "natural fact" of water and wind leads Thoreau to ponder the "spiritual fact" of an existence beyond the present. (For "natural facts" and "spiritual facts," see Emerson, *Nature*, ch. 4.)

[105]Emerson had purchased his land on Walden Pond, on which Thoreau's cabin stood, to save it from the woodcutters. For Irish immigrants, see n. 61 above. The railroad, which ran by one end of Walden Pond, graphically illustrated the less-than-wilderness character of Thoreau's retreat. For the "ice-men," see Thoreau's description in ch. 16; and see also n. 57 above.

[106]Cf. the words of Jesus regarding Nathanael in John 1:47.

[107]The poem, with its mystical identification with the pond, is Thoreau's and appears, titled by its first line, in Henry David Thoreau, *Collected Poems of Henry Thoreau,* ed. Carl Bode (Chicago: Packard, 1943) 26. (See also Bode's note to the poem on 341.)

[108]Railroad cars.

I fancy that the engineers and firemen and brakemen, and those passengers who have a season ticket and see it often, are better men for the sight. The engineer does not forget at night, or his nature does not, that he has beheld this vision of serenity and purity once at least during the day. Though seen but once, it helps to wash out State Street[109] and the engine's soot. One proposes that it be called "God's Drop."[110] . . .

Since the wood-cutters, and the railroad, and I myself have profaned Walden, perhaps the most attractive, if not the most beautiful, of all our lakes, the gem of the woods, is White Pond;—a poor name from its commonness, whether derived from the remarkable purity of its waters or the color of its sands.[111] . . .

White Pond and Walden are great crystals on the surface of the earth, Lakes of Light. If they were permanently congealed, and small enough to be clutched, they would, perchance, be carried off by slaves, like precious stones, to adorn the heads of emperors; but being liquid, and ample, and secured to us and our successors forever, we disregard them, and run after the diamond of Kohinoor.[112] They are too pure to have a market value; they contain no muck. How much more beautiful than our lives, how much more transparent than our characters, are they! We never learned meanness of them. How much fairer than the pool before the farmer's door, in which his ducks swim! Hither the clean wild ducks come. Nature has no human inhabitant who appreciates her. The birds with their plumage and their notes are in harmony with the flowers, but what youth or maiden conspires with the wild luxuriant beauty of Nature? She flourishes most alone, far from the towns where they reside. Talk of heaven! ye disgrace earth.[113]

XI
HIGHER LAWS[114]

As I came home through the woods with my string of fish, trailing my pole, it being now quite dark, I caught a glimpse of a woodchuck stealing across my path, and felt a strange thrill of savage delight, and was strongly tempted to seize and devour him raw; not that I was hungry then, except for that wildness which he repre-

---

[109]The heart of the financial sector in Boston.

[110]Emerson in his journal called the much-smaller Goose Pond, less than a quarter of a mile to the northeast of Walden Pond, "the Drop or God's Pond." See Ralph Waldo Emerson, *The Journals and Miscellaneous Notebooks of Ralph Waldo Emerson,* ed. William H. Gilman et al. (Cambridge: Harvard University Press, Belknap Press, 1960–), 7 (9 April 1840): 491.

[111]White Pond, considerably smaller than Walden, is more than two miles to the southwest and across the Sudbury River.

[112]The Koh-i-noor diamond, which came to light in India in 1739, was more than 186 carats in weight and was subsequently recut to more than 106 carats and included among the crown jewels of Britain.

[113]A clear and striking statement of Thoreau's religious naturalism, which pervades *Walden*. Cf. also his aspiration for a "*purely sensuous life,*" in "Friday" of his *Week*.

[114]In the previous chapter, "Baker Farm," Thoreau went fishing after an unsuccessful attempt to "convert" an Irishman in whose hut he had taken shelter from a storm. Now, in "Higher Laws," he expands on themes suggested in that chapter. Thoreau's esteem for purity, seen in his earlier chapter on Walden and other ponds, will become even more apparent.

sented.[115] Once or twice, however, while I lived at the pond, I found myself ranging the woods, like a half-starved hound, with a strange abandonment, seeking some kind of venison which I might devour, and no morsel could have been too savage for me. The wildest scenes had become unaccountably familiar. I found in myself, and still find, an instinct toward a higher, or, as it is named, spiritual life, as do most men, and another toward a primitive rank and savage one, and I reverence them both. I love the wild not less than the good.[116] The wildness and adventure that are in fishing still recommended it to me. I like sometimes to take rank hold on life and spend my day more as the animals do. Perhaps I have owed to this employment and to hunting, when quite young, my closest acquaintance with Nature. They early introduce us to and detain us in scenery with which otherwise, at that age, we should have little acquaintance. Fishermen, hunters, woodchoppers, and others, spending their lives in the fields and woods, in a peculiar sense a part of Nature themselves, are often in a more favorable mood for observing her, in the intervals of their pursuits, than philosophers or poets even, who approach her with expectation. She is not afraid to exhibit herself to them.[117] . . .

Moreover, when at the pond, I wished sometimes to add fish to my fare for variety. I have actually fished from the same kind of necessity that the first fishers did. Whatever humanity I might conjure up against it was all factitious, and concerned my philosophy more than my feelings. I speak of fishing only now, for I had long felt differently about fowling, and sold my gun before I went to the woods. Not that I am less humane than others, but I did not perceive that my feelings were much affected. I did not pity the fishes nor the worms. This was habit. As for fowling, during the last years that I carried a gun my excuse was that I was studying ornithology, and sought only new or rare birds. But I confess that I am now inclined to think that there is a finer way of studying ornithology than this. It requires so much closer attention to the habits of the birds, that, if for that reason only, I have been willing to omit the gun. Yet notwithstanding the objection on the score of humanity, I am compelled to doubt if equally valuable sports are ever substituted for these; and when some of my friends have asked me anxiously about their boys, whether they should let them hunt, I have answered, yes,—remembering that it was one of the best parts of my education,—*make* them hunters, though sportsmen only at first, if possible, mighty hunters at last, so that they shall not find game large enough for them in this or any vegetable wilderness,— hunters as well as fishers of men.[118] . . .

---

[115]This well-known confession by Thoreau of his identification with wilderness forces introduces a searching discussion of the disciplined life and sets the tone for what follows: Thoreau's pursuit of asceticism must be read in the context of his quest for the ecstasy embodied in wildness and the liberty of spirit it obliquely proclaims.

[116]Cf. Rom. 7:22-23.

[117]Again Thoreau evokes the theme—familiar in Indian *samkhya* teaching—of nature exhibiting herself before the spectator soul. Cf. his quotation from the *Samkhya Karika* in "Friday" of his *Week;* and see n. 79 to the text.

Cf., too, Thoreau's reflections on "doubleness" in ch. 5. The *samkhya* view, in which nature both imprisons the soul and arouses it to seek its liberation, almost surely forms part of the background for the present chapter.

[118]Cf. Matt. 4:19. John B. Pickard argues that the "main metaphor" of this chapter is "an elaborate expansion of Christ's demand that His Apostles be fishers of men, catching the spiri-

Such is oftenest the young man's introduction to the forest, and the most original part of himself. He goes thither at first as a hunter and fisher, until at last, if he has the seeds of a better life in him, he distinguishes his proper objects, as a poet or naturalist it may be, and leaves the gun and fish-pole behind. The mass of men are still and always young in this respect.[119] In some countries a hunting person is no uncommon sight. Such a one might make a good shepherd's dog, but is far from being the Good Shepherd.[120] I have been surprised to consider that the only obvious employment, except wood-chopping, ice-cutting, or the like business, which ever to my knowledge detained at Walden Pond for a whole half-day any of my fellow-citizens, whether fathers or children of the town, with just one exception, was fishing. Commonly they did not think that they were lucky, or well paid for their time, unless they got a long string of fish, though they had the opportunity of seeing the pond all the while. They might go there a thousand times before the sediment of fishing would sink to the bottom and leave their purpose pure; but no doubt such a clarifying process would be going on all the while.[121] The Governor and his Council faintly remember the pond, for they went a-fishing there when they were boys; but now they are too old and dignified to go a-fishing, and so they know it no more forever. Yet even they expect to go to heaven at last. If the legislature regards it, it is chiefly to regulate the number of hooks to be used there; but they know nothing about the hook of hooks with which to angle for the pond itself, impaling the legislature for a bait.[122] Thus, even in civilized communities, the embryo man passes through the hunter stage of development.

I have found repeatedly, of late years, that I cannot fish without falling a little in self-respect. I have tried it again and again. I have skill at it, and, like many of my fellows, a certain instinct for it, which revives from time to time, but always when I have done I feel that it would have been better if I had not fished. I think that I do not mistake. It is a faint intimation, yet so are the first streaks of morning. There is unquestionably this instinct in me which belongs to the lower orders of creation; yet with every year I am less a fisherman, though without more humanity or even wisdom; at present I am no fisherman at all.[123] But I see that if I were to live in a wilderness I should again be tempted to become a fisher and hunter in earnest. Beside, there is something essentially un-

---

tual rather than the physical.'' See John B. Pickard, ''The Religion of 'Higher Laws,' '' in Richard Ruland, ed., *Twentieth Century Interpretations of* Walden: *A Collection of Critical Essays* (Englewood Cliffs NJ: Prentice-Hall, 1968) 89. But the Gospel command of Jesus has been transformed in Thoreau's construction. Here fishing is an inner quest for the self or spirit rather than a missionary venture directed toward others (see n. 122 below; and cf. also the introductory paragraphs of ch. 18).

[119]In Thoreau's evolutionary version of the teaching of correspondence, ''lower'' laws may light the path to higher ones. See also the comment by John B. Pickard linking this chapter to the theme of rebirth and renewal (Pickard, ''Religion of 'Higher Laws,' '' 87).

[120]Cf. John 10:1-16. For ice cutting (below in the text), see Thoreau's description of an ice harvest in ch. 16; and see also n. 57 above.

[121]Thoreau introduces the theme of purification, a leading motif of this chapter.

[122]Thoreau's concern here is an ascetic and metaphysical fishing, a way of life that in pursuit of purity aims at final clarity and union of self and nature.

[123]Thoreau refers to the time when he is writing—later than his sojourn at Walden Pond.

clean about this diet and all flesh, and I began to see where housework commences, and whence the endeavor, which costs so much, to wear a tidy and respectable appearance each day, to keep the house sweet and free from all ill odors and sights. Having been my own butcher and scullion and cook, as well as the gentleman for whom the dishes were served up, I can speak from an unusually complete experience. The practical objection to animal food in my case was its uncleanness; and besides, when I had caught and cleaned and cooked and eaten my fish, they seemed not to have fed me essentially. It was insignificant and unnecessary, and cost more than it came to. A little bread or a few potatoes would have done as well, with less trouble and filth. Like many of my contemporaries, I had rarely for many years used animal food, or tea, or coffee, etc.; not so much because of any ill effects which I had traced to them, as because they were not agreeable to my imagination.[124] The repugnance to animal food is not the effect of experience, but is an instinct. It appeared more beautiful to live low and fare hard in many respects; and though I never did so, I went far enough to please my imagination. I believe that every man who has ever been earnest to preserve his higher or poetic faculties in the best condition has been particularly inclined to abstain from animal food, and from much food of any kind. . . .

It is hard to provide and cook so simple and clean a diet as will not offend the imagination; but this, I think, is to be fed when we feed the body; they should both sit down at the same table. Yet perhaps this may be done. The fruits eaten temperately need not make us ashamed of our appetites, nor interrupt the worthiest pursuits. But put an extra condiment into your dish, and it will poison you. It is not worth the while to live by rich cookery. Most men would feel shame if caught preparing with their own hands precisely such a dinner, whether of animal or vegetable food, as is every day prepared for them by others. Yet till this is otherwise we are not civilized, and, if gentlemen and ladies, are not true men and women. This certainly suggests what change is to be made. It may be vain to ask why the imagination will not be reconciled to flesh and fat. I am satisfied that it is not. Is it not a reproach that man is a carnivorous animal? True, he can and does live, in a great measure, by preying on other animals; but this is a miserable way,—as any one who will go to snaring rabbits, or slaughtering lambs, may learn,—and he will be regarded as a benefactor of his race who shall teach man to confine himself to a more innocent and wholesome diet. Whatever my own practice may be, I have no doubt that it is a part of the destiny of the human race, in its gradual improvement, to leave off eating animals, as surely as the savage tribes have left off eating each other when they came in contact with the more civilized.[125]

---

[124]The practice of vegetarianism and abstinence from stimulants had a small but devoted following in Thoreau's America. See, for example, the description of Bronson Alcott's Fruitlands in the introduction to this volume; and for a discussion in the context of the mid-nineteenth-century health-reform movement, see John B. Blake, "Health Reform," in Edwin S. Gaustad, ed., *The Rise of Adventism: Religion and Society in Mid-Nineteenth-Century America* (New York: Harper & Row, 1974) 30-49. Thoreau himself was often (but not always) vegetarian; however, when he used meat and animal products, he used them sparingly. He also practiced, as he indicates, an abstinence from stimulants.

[125]Thoreau, like his contemporaries, distinguishes sharply between "savage" and "civilized" peoples in a way of thinking inherited from the Enlightenment and elaborated by romanticism.

If one listens to the faintest but constant suggestions of his genius,[126] which are certainly true, he sees not to what extremes, or even insanity, it may lead him; and yet that way, as he grows more resolute and faithful, his road lies. The faintest assured objection which one healthy man feels will at length prevail over the arguments and customs of mankind. No man ever followed his genius till it misled him. Though the result were bodily weakness, yet perhaps no one can say that the consequences were to be regretted, for these were a life in conformity to higher principles. If the day and the night are such that you greet them with joy, and life emits a fragrance like flowers and sweet-scented herbs, is more elastic, more starry, more immortal,—that is your success. All nature is your congratulation, and you have cause momentarily to bless yourself. The greatest gains and values are farthest from being appreciated. We easily come to doubt if they exist. We soon forget them. They are the highest reality. Perhaps the facts most astounding and most real are never communicated by man to man. The true harvest of my daily life is somewhat as intangible and indescribable as the tints of morning or evening. It is a little star-dust caught, a segment of the rainbow which I have clutched.

Yet, for my part, I was never unusually squeamish; I could sometimes eat a fried rat with a good relish, if it were necessary. I am glad to have drunk water so long, for the same reason that I prefer the natural sky to an opium-eater's heaven.[127] I would fain keep sober always; and there are infinite degrees of drunkenness. I believe that water is the only drink for a wise man; wine is not so noble a liquor; and think of dashing the hopes of a morning with a cup of warm coffee, or of an evening with a dish of tea! Ah, how low I fall when I am tempted by them! Even music may be intoxicating. Such apparently slight causes destroyed Greece and Rome, and will destroy England and America.[128] Of all ebriosity, who does not prefer to be intoxicated by the air he breathes? I have found it to be the most serious objection to coarse labors long continued, that they compelled me to eat and drink coarsely also. But to tell the truth, I find myself at present somewhat less particular in these respects. I carry less religion to the table, ask no blessing; not because I am wiser than I was, but, I am obliged to confess, because, however much it is to be regretted, with years I have grown more coarse and indifferent. Perhaps these questions are entertained only in youth, as most believe of poetry. My practice is "nowhere," my opinion is here. Nevertheless I am far from regarding myself as one of those privileged ones to whom the Ved refers when it says, that "he who has true faith in the Omnipresent Supreme

---

[126] For "genius," see n. 3 to Alcott, *Doctrine and Discipline of Human Culture*. In Emersonian terms, "genius" is here the "self" of self-reliance, the individual witness to and manifestation of the Oversoul.

[127] Walter Harding notes that use of opium was "comparatively prevalent in Thoreau's day." See Thoreau, *Variorum Walden*, 301. The specific reference is a likely allusion to the book by Thomas De Quincey, *Confessions of an English Opium-Eater* (1822).

[128] An allusion to the popularly held view that Greece and Rome crumbled from within through moral decline and corruption. For the Transcendentalists and many other nineteenth-century Americans, nature was associated with innocence and purity, a powerful elixir against the decay of the Old World. It followed that, for some, living naturally—as close to nature as possible—was a matter of serious moral concern.

Being may eat all that exists," that is, is not bound to inquire what is his food, or who prepares it; and even in their case it is to be observed, as a Hindoo commentator has remarked, that the Vedant limits this privilege to "the time of distress."[129]

Who has not sometimes derived an inexpressible satisfaction from his food in which appetite had no share? I have been thrilled to think that I owed a mental perception to the commonly gross sense of taste, that I have been inspired through the palate, that some berries which I had eaten on a hillside had fed my genius. "The soul not being mistress of herself," says Thseng-tseu, "one looks, and one does not see; one listens, and one does not hear; one eats, and one does not know the savor of food."[130] He who distinguishes the true savor of his food can never be a glutton; he who does not cannot be otherwise. A puritan may go to his brown-bread crust with as gross an appetite as ever an alderman to his turtle. Not that food which entereth into the mouth defileth a man, but the appetite with which it is eaten.[131] It is neither the quality nor the quantity, but the devotion to sensual savors; when that which is eaten is not a viand to sustain our animal, or inspire our spiritual life, but food for the worms that possess us. If the hunter has a taste for mud-turtles, muskrats, and other such savage tidbits, the fine lady indulges a taste for jelly made of a calf's foot, or for sardines from over the sea, and they are even. He goes to the mill-pond, she to her preserve-pot. The wonder is how they, how you and I, can live this slimy, beastly life, eating and drinking.

Our whole life is startlingly moral. There is never an instant's truce between virtue and vice. Goodness is the only investment that never fails. In the music of the harp which trembles round the world it is the insisting on this which thrills us.[132]

---

[129] The material from both "Ved" (Veda) and "commentator" may be found in Rajah Rammohun Roy, trans., *Translation of Several Principal Books, Passages, and Texts of the Veds, and of Some Controversial Works on Brahmunical Theology*, 2d ed. (London: Parbury, Allen, 1832) 21. Roy's text itself is a free and highly interpretive condensation of Badarayana *Vedanta Sutras* 3.4.28. But the ultimate source of the (misrepresented) Vedic quotation is the *Chandogya Upanishad* 5.2.1. The "Hindoo commentator" is Roy (1772?–1833), who in 1828 founded the monotheistic Hindu reformist society called the Brahmo Samaj—hence the rendering "Supreme Being." The "Vedant" of Roy and Thoreau is the *Vedanta Sutras* (or *Brahma Sutras*), of which Roy had published his interpretive abridgment and translation in 1816. It is this work that Thoreau read, included in Roy's *Translation of the Veds*. For a modern reprint of Roy's 1832 text, see William Bysshe Stein, ed., *Two Brahman Sources of Emerson and Thoreau* (Gainesville FL: Scholars' Facsimiles & Reprints, 1967).

[130] [Confucian School] *The Great Learning* 7.2. The translation is almost surely Thoreau's from the French text by M. G. Pauthier. Thoreau suggests the reason for a purification of the senses in his use of the quotation, which in its Chinese context involves consideration of "rectification" of the mind. For Thoreau, through discipline mind and senses will be unified, and the senses will *attend* to the world in a presence to it that brings awareness of the spirit.

[131] Cf. Mark 7:15, which Thoreau has recast to suit his literary needs.

[132] This sentence and the remainder of the paragraph are built on Thoreau's private pun on the harp. On the one hand, it is the familiar musical instrument on which one may "touch a string or move a stop." On the other, it is the "telegraph harp," the music of the wind, or "zephyr," running through the telegraph wires like the ancient classical "music of the spheres." The telegraph harp is the sign in sound of universal law. For a discussion, see Seybold, *Thoreau*, 71-73.

The harp is the travelling patterer for the Universe's Insurance Company, recommending its laws, and our little goodness is all the assessment that we pay. Though the youth at last grows indifferent, the laws of the universe are not indifferent, but are forever on the side of the most sensitive. Listen to every zephyr for some reproof, for it is surely there, and he is unfortunate who does not hear it. We cannot touch a string or move a stop but the charming moral transfixes us. Many an irksome noise, go a long way off, is heard as music, a proud, sweet satire on the meanness of our lives.

We are conscious of an animal in us, which awakens in proportion as our higher nature slumbers. It is reptile and sensual, and perhaps cannot be wholly expelled; like the worms which, even in life and health, occupy our bodies.[133] Possibly we may withdraw from it, but never change its nature. I fear that it may enjoy a certain health of its own; that we may be well, yet not pure. The other day I picked up the lower jaw of a hog, with white and sound teeth and tusks,[134] which suggested that there was an animal health and vigor distinct from the spiritual. This creature succeeded by other means than temperance and purity. "That in which men differ from brute beasts," says Mencius, "is a thing very inconsiderable; the common herd lose it very soon; superior men preserve it carefully."[135] Who knows what sort of life would result if we had attained to purity? If I knew so wise a man as could teach me purity I would go to seek him forthwith. "A command over our passions, and over the external senses of the body, and good acts, are declared by the Ved to be indispensable in the mind's approximation to God."[136] Yet the spirit can for the time pervade and control every member and function of the body, and transmute what in form is the grossest sensuality into purity and devotion. The generative energy, which, when we are loose, dissipates and makes us unclean, when we are continent invigorates and inspires us. Chastity is the flowering of man; and what are called Genius, Heroism, Holiness, and the like, are but various fruits which succeed it. Man flows at once to God when the channel of purity is open. By turns our purity inspires and our impurity casts us down. He is blessed who is assured that the animal is dying out in him day by day, and the divine being established. Perhaps there is none but has cause for shame on account of the inferior and brutish nature to which he is allied. I fear that we are such gods or demigods only as fauns and satyrs,[137] the

---

[133] A reference to the animalcular theory, the early form of what became in the later nineteenth century bacteriological theory and science. The "reptile" (above in the text and repeated in the following paragraph) may have been suggested by the short story of Nathaniel Hawthorne, "Egotism; or, the Bosom Serpent," in *Mosses from an Old Manse* (1846). See Frank Davidson, "Thoreau's Contributions to Hawthorne's *Mosses*," *The New England Quarterly* 20:4 (December 1947): 538.

[134] Thoreau records such an incident in his journal in June 1850. See Thoreau, *Writings*, 8:36. For a reflection on health similar to Thoreau's following observation, see the final paragraph, in this volume, of ch. 17.

[135] Mencius *Works,* bk. 4, pt. 2, 19.1. The translation is almost surely Thoreau's from the French text by M. G. Pauthier. The writings of Mencius (371?–288? B.C.) form one of the so-called four books that were held to contain the essence of Confucian thought.

[136] See Roy, *Translation of the Veds,* 19. The quotation is from Roy's condensed version of Badarayana *Vedanta Sutras* (3.4.27; see n. 129 above).

[137] Fauns, in Roman religion counterparts to

divine allied to beasts, the creatures of appetite, and that, to some extent, our very life is our disgrace. . . .

All sensuality is one, though it takes many forms; all purity is one. It is the same whether a man eat, or drink, or cohabit, or sleep sensually. They are but one appetite, and we only need to see a person do any one of these things to know how great a sensualist he is. The impure can neither stand nor sit with purity. When the reptile is attacked at one mouth of his burrow, he shows himself at another. If you would be chaste, you must be temperate. What is chastity? How shall a man know if he is chaste? He shall not know it. We have heard of this virtue, but we know not what it is. We speak conformably to the rumor which we have heard. From exertion come wisdom and purity; from sloth ignorance and sensuality. In the student sensuality is a sluggish habit of mind. An unclean person is universally a slothful one, one who sits by a stove, whom the sun shines on prostrate, who resposes without being fatigued. If you would avoid uncleanness, and all the sins, work earnestly, though it be at cleaning a stable. Nature is hard to be overcome, but she must be overcome. What avails it that you are Christian, if you are not purer than the heathen, if you deny yourself no more, if you are not more religious? I know of many systems of religion esteemed heathenish whose precepts fill the reader with shame, and provoke him to new endeavors, though it be to the performance of rites merely.

I hesitate to say these things, but it is not because of the subject,—I care not how obscene my *words* are,—but because I cannot speak of them without betraying my impurity. We discourse freely without shame of one form of sensuality, and are silent about another. We are so degraded that we cannot speak simply of the necessary functions of human nature. In earlier ages, in some countries, every function was reverently spoken of and regulated by law. Nothing was too trivial for the Hindoo lawgiver, however offensive it may be to modern taste. He teaches how to eat, drink, cohabit, void excrement and urine, and the like, elevating what is mean, and does not falsely excuse himself by calling these things trifles.[138]

Every man is the builder of a temple, called his body, to the god he worships,[139] after a style purely his own, nor can he get off by hammering marble instead. We are all sculptors and painters, and our material is our own flesh and blood and bones. Any nobleness begins at once to refine a man's features, any meanness or sensuality to imbrute them.

John Farmer sat at his door one September evening, after a hard day's work, his mind still running on his labor more or less.[140] Having bathed, he sat down to re-

---

Greek satyrs, were rural Gods, in form part human/part goat and associated with the productivity of earth and animals. For satyrs, see n. 21 to Alcott, "Orphic Sayings." Here the lustfulness of fauns and satyrs is especially implied.

[138]Thoreau is most likely thinking of Manu (or, as he writes, "Menu") and *The Laws of Manu*. For the edition of *The Laws of Manu* that he read, see n. 23 to Thoreau, *Week*. For rules concerning lawful and forbidden food, see *Laws of Manu* 5.1-56; for laws and duties regarding cohabitation, see ibid. 9.40-87; and for rules for voiding excrement and urine, see ibid. 5.134-38. I am indebted to Paul Courtright of the University of North Carolina at Greensboro for his helpful comments on this question.

[139]Cf. 1 Cor. 3:16.

[140]Walter Harding observes that Farmer was a common family name in the Concord of this period, but suggests its use here as a "type name" rather than a specific reference. See Thoreau, *Variorum Walden*, 302.

create his intellectual man. It was a rather cool evening, and some of his neighbors were apprehending a frost. He had not attended to the train of his thoughts long when he heard some one playing on a flute,[141] and that sound harmonized with his mood. Still he thought of his work; but the burden of his thought was, that though this kept running in his head, and he found himself planning and contriving it against his will, yet it concerned him very little. It was no more than the scurf of his skin, which was constantly shuffled off. But the notes of the flute came home to his ears out of a different sphere from that he worked in, and suggested work for certain faculties which slumbered in him. They gently did away with the street, and the village, and the state in which he lived. A voice said to him,—Why do you stay here and live this mean moiling life, when a glorious existence is possible for you? Those same stars twinkle over other fields than these.— But how to come out of this condition and actually migrate thither? All that he could think of was to practise some new austerity, to let his mind descend into his body and redeem it, and treat himself with ever increasing respect.[142]

XVI
THE POND IN WINTER[143]

AFTER a still winter night I awoke with the impression that some question had been put to me, which I had been endeavoring in vain to answer in my sleep, as what— how—when—where? But there was dawning Nature, in whom all creatures live, looking in at my broad windows with serene and satisfied face, and no question on *her* lips. I awoke to an answered question, to Nature and daylight. The snow lying deep on the earth dotted with young pines, and the very slope of the hill on which my house is placed, seemed to say, Forward! Nature puts no question and answers none which we mortals ask. She has long ago taken her resolution. "O Prince, our eyes contemplate with admiration and transmit to the soul the wonderful and varied spectacle of this universe. The night veils without doubt a part of this glorious creation; but day comes to reveal to us this great work, which extends from earth even into the plains of the ether."[144]

---

[141]This was almost surely Thoreau, who loved the flute and played his instrument at Walden Pond.

[142]Thoreau's language is ambiguous here, but in the context of his overall treatment of the theme of purification—for awakened and intensified perception of sense and spirit—he is disparaging John Farmer's efforts.

[143]In chs. 12 through 15, Thoreau has described animal life and offered his well-known account of the battle of the ants in "Brute Neighbors"; with fall in the air has told of building chimney and fireplace, plastering and shingling his house, and bringing in firewood in time for colder weather in "House-Warming"; has recounted memories of former dwellers at the pond and described his few present winter visitors—among them, though unnamed, Channing, Alcott, and Emerson—in "Former Inhabitants; and Winter Visitors"; and has supplied an anecdotal catalog of winter animals and their activities in "Winter Animals."

[144]In a somewhat garbled reference, Philip Van Doren Stern gives the source of this quotation as the *Harivansa,* or *Harivamsa* (see Thoreau, *Annotated* Walden, 405). Certainly, the linguistic flag "O Prince" suggests the *Harivamsa,* and vocabulary and theme are also consistent with it; but I have been unable to locate the quotation. The *Harivamsa* itself is a long addendum to the epic poem *Mahabharata* (within which the *Bhagavad Gita* is also found). Thoreau read the *Harivamsa* in French translation in M. A[lexandre] Langlois, *Harivansa; ou, Histoire de la famille de Hari, ouvrage for-*

Then to my morning work. First I take an axe and pail and go in search of water, if that be not a dream. After a cold and snowy night it needed a divining-rod to find it. Every winter the liquid and trembling surface of the pond, which was so sensitive to every breath, and reflected ever light and shadow, becomes solid to the depth of a foot or a foot and a half, so that it will support the heaviest teams, and perchance the snow covers it to an equal depth, and it is not to be distinguished from any level field. Like the marmots in the surrounding hills, it closes its eyelids and becomes dormant for three months or more. Standing on the snow-covered plain, as if in a pasture amid the hills, I cut my way first through a foot of snow, and then a foot of ice, and open a window under my feet, where, kneeling to drink, I look down into the quiet parlor of the fishes, pervaded by a softened light as through a window of ground glass, with its bright sanded floor the same as in summer; there a perennial waveless serenity reigns as in the amber twilight sky, corresponding to the cool and even temperament of the inhabitants. Heaven is under our feet as well as over our heads. . . .

As I was desirous to recover the long lost bottom of Walden Pond, I surveyed it carefully, before the ice broke up, early in '46, with compass and chain and sounding line. There have been many stories told about the bottom, or rather no bottom, of this pond, which certainly had no foundation for themselves. It is remarkable how long men will believe in the bottomlessness of a pond without taking the trouble to sound it. . . . But I can assure my readers that Walden has a reasonably tight bottom at a not unreasonable, though at an unusual, depth. I fathomed it easily with a cod-line and a stone weighing about a pound and a half, and could tell accurately when the stone left the bottom, by having to pull so much harder before the water got underneath to help me. The greatest depth was exactly one hundred and two feet; to which may be added the five feet which it has risen since, making one hundred and seven.[145] This is a remarkable depth for so small an area; yet not an inch of it can be spared by the imagination. What if all ponds were shallow? Would it not react on the minds of men? I am thankful that this pond was made deep and pure for a symbol.[146] While men believe in the infinite some ponds will be thought to be bottomless. . . .

When I had mapped the pond by the scale of ten rods to an inch,[147] and put down the soundings, more than a hundred in all, I observed this remarkable coincidence. Having noticed that the number indicating the greatest depth was apparently in the

---

mant un appendice du Mahabharata, Oriental Translation Fund [Publications] 36 (Paris: Oriental Translation Fund of Great Britain and Ireland, 1834–1835). Moreover, Thoreau used the Langlois edition to make his own English translation from the *Harivamsa,* finally published many years after his death as Henry David Thoreau, *The Transmigration of the Seven Brahmans: A Translation from the* Harivamsa *of Langlois,* ed. Arthur Christy (New York: William Edwin Rudge, 1931).

[145] Twentieth-century soundings of Walden Pond, using modern instruments, have shown that Thoreau was extraordinarily accurate in his measurement—just two-tenths of a meter off according to one study. See Thoreau, *Variorum Walden,* 312; and Thoreau, *Annotated Walden,* 408.

[146] Cf. Ralph Waldo Emerson, *Nature,* ch. 4: "Particular natural facts are symbols of particular spiritual facts."

[147] Thoreau included his map of the pond in the first (1854) edition of *Walden.*

centre of the map, I laid a rule on the map lengthwise, and then breadthwise, and found, to my surprise, that the line of greatest length intersected the line of greatest breadth *exactly* at the point of greatest depth, notwithstanding that the middle is so nearly level, the outline of the pond far from regular, and the extreme length and breadth were got by measuring into the coves; and I said to myself, Who knows but this hint would conduct to the deepest part of the ocean as well as of a pond or puddle? Is not this the rule also for the height of mountains, regarded as the opposite of valleys? We know that a hill is not highest at its narrowest part. . . .

What I have observed of the pond is no less true in ethics.[148] It is the law of average. Such a rule of the two diameters not only guides us toward the sun in the system and the heart in man, but draw lines through the length and breadth of the aggregate of a man's particular daily behaviors and waves of life into his coves and inlets, and where they intersect will be the height or depth of his character. Perhaps we need only to know how his shores trend and his adjacent country or circumstances, to infer his depth and concealed bottom. If he is surrounded by mountainous circumstances, an Achillean shore,[149] whose peaks overshadow and are reflected in his bosom, they suggest a corresponding depth in him. But a low and smooth shore proves him shallow on that side. In our bodies, a bold projecting brow falls off to and indicates a corresponding depth of thought.[150] Also there is a bar across the entrance of our every cove, or particular inclination; each is our harbor for a season, in which we are detained and partially land-locked. These inclinations are not whimsical usually, but their form, size, and direction are determined by the promontories of the shore, the ancient axes of elevation. When this bar is gradually increased by storms, tides, or currents, or there is a subsidence of the waters, so that it reaches to the surface, that which was at first but an inclination in the shore in which a thought was harbored becomes an individual lake, cut off from the ocean, wherein the thought secures its own conditions,—changes, perhaps, from salt to fresh, becomes a sweet sea, dead sea, or a marsh. At the advent of each individual into this life, may we not suppose that such a bar has risen to the surface somewhere? It is true, we are such poor navigators that our thoughts, for the most part, stand off and on upon a harborless coast, are conversant only with the bights of the bays of poesy, or steer for the public ports of entry, and go into the dry docks of science, where they merely refit for this world, and no natural currents concur to individualize them. . . .

In the winter of '46-7 there came a hundred men of Hyperborean extraction swoop down on to our pond one morning, with many carloads of ungainly-looking farming tools,—sleds, plows, drill-barrows, turf-knives, spades, saws, rakes, and each man was armed with a double-pointed pike-staff, such as is not described in the

---

[148]Thoreau's "scientific" reasoning by analogy now leads him to an extended reflection on ethics, cast within the framework of correspondence that pervades this chapter.

[149]That is, a rocky, mountainous shore, as in the Greek terrain of Achilles, the hero of Homer's *Iliad*.

[150]An observation in keeping with nineteenth-century phrenology, which argued for a correspondence between the shape of the bony structure of the skull and personal character. Cf. n. 18 to Thoreau, "Civil Disobedience."

New-England Farmer or the Cultivator.[151]

. . .

To speak literally, a hundred Irishmen, with Yankee overseers, came from Cambridge every day to get out the ice.[152] They divided it into cakes by methods too well known to require description, and these, being sledded to the shore, were rapidly hauled off on to an ice platform, and raised by grappling irons and block and tackle, worked by horses, on to a stack, as surely as so many barrels of flour, and there placed evenly side by side, and row upon row, as if they formed the solid base of an obelisk designed to pierce the clouds. They told me that in a good day they could get out a thousand tons, which was the yield of about one acre. . . .

Thus it appears that the sweltering inhabitants of Charleston and New Orleans, of Madras and Bombay and Calcutta, drink at my well.[153] In the morning I bathe my intellect in the stupendous and cosmogonal philosophy of the Bhagvat-Geeta, since whose composition years of the gods have elapsed, and in comparison with which our modern world and its literature seem puny and trivial; and I doubt if that philosophy is not to be referred to a previous state of existence, so remote is its sublimity from our conceptions.[154] I lay down the book and go to my well for water, and lo! there I meet the servant of the Bramin, priest of Brahma and Vishnu and Indra, who still sits in his temple on the Ganges reading the Vedas, or dwells at the root of a tree with his crust and water jug.[155]

---

[151]In Greek mythology, the Hyperboreans, dwellers in a far northern land, lived in bliss and enjoyed an unending springtime in their country. In fact, Thoreau is referring to Irish workers, as he indicates below in the text. The Boston-based *New England Farmer* was a journal devoted, obviously, to agriculture. The identity of the "Cultivator" is less clear: both a *New England Cultivator* and a *Boston Cultivator* were, according to Walter Harding, also published in Boston (see Thoreau, *Variorum Walden*, 313).

[152]Thoreau is describing an ice harvest (see n. 57 above). Frederic Tudor, the so-called ice king, was harvesting at Walden Pond because of his trade war with Nathaniel Jarvis Wyeth, his erstwhile partner who had monopolized the regular sources of ice (see Thoreau, *Variorum Walden*, 312).

[153]Charleston, South Carolina, and New Orleans, Louisiana, were port cities for the Southern market in the United States. Madras, Bombay, and Calcutta are Indian port cities.

[154]For the *Bhagavad Gita*, see n. 25 to Thoreau, *Week*. Note, however, that a "cosmogonal philosophy" theorizes concerning the origins of the universe or world, a theme not particularly central to the *Bhagavad Gita*. The reference to "years of the gods" is an allusion to Indian temporal and cosmic speculation in which 360 human years equaled one year of the Gods. The reference to a "previous state of existence" recalls the classic Indian religious teaching of rebirth and transmigration.

[155]For the Brahmin caste, see n. 25 to Emerson, *Nature*. For Brahma, see n. 16 to Emerson, "Brahma." In the *Rig Veda*, Vishnu was only a minor sun deity, but later, merging his identity with that of two other Gods, he attained cosmic importance as the preserver of the world and became known for his numerous "descents," or *avataras*. For Indra, see n. 87 above. Thoreau's linkage of the three Gods signals an ahistorical understanding. Indra figures prominently in earlier Indian religion but then loses most of his importance. The ascendancy of Brahma and Vishnu belongs to a later period. The reference to the Ganges is more accurate though, since it is the most sacred river of India. Finally, the entire passage is gently ironic and, in fact, a subtle but elaborate pun on water (physical and spiritual). And Walter Harding notes that ice was not the only export from Walden Pond to the Hindus, since later Thoreau's writings would be exported as well (Thoreau, *Variorum Walden*, 313).

I meet his servant come to draw water for his master, and our buckets as it were grate together in the same well. The pure Walden water is mingled with the sacred water of the Ganges. With favoring winds it is wafted past the site of the fabulous islands of Atlantis and the Hesperides, makes the periplus of Hanno, and, floating by Ternate and Tidore and the mouth of the Persian Gulf, melts in the tropic gales of the Indian seas, and is landed in ports of which Alexander only heard the names.[156]

XVII
SPRING

At length the sun's rays have attained the right angle, and warm winds blow up mist and rain and melt the snowbanks, and the sun dispersing the mist smiles on a checkered landscape of russet and white smoking with incense, through which the traveller picks his way from islet to islet, cheered by the music of a thousand tinkling rills and rivulets whose veins are filled with the blood of winter which they are bearing off.[157]

Few phenomena gave me more delight than to observe the forms which thawing sand and clay assume in flowing down the sides of a deep cut on the railroad through which I passed on my way to the village, a phenomenon not very common on so large a scale, though the number of freshly exposed banks of the right material must have been greatly multiplied since railroads were invented. The material was sand of every degree of fineness and of various rich colors, commonly mixed with a little clay. When the frost comes out in the spring, and even in a thawing day in the winter, the sand begins to flow down the slopes like lava, sometimes bursting out through the snow and overflowing it where no sand was to be seen before. Innumerable little streams overlap and interlace one with another, exhibiting a sort of hybrid product, which obeys half way the law of currents, and half way that of vegetation. As it flows it takes the forms of sappy leaves or vines, making heaps of pulpy sprays a foot or more in depth, and resembling, as you look down on them, the laciniated, lobed, and imbricated thalluses of some lichens;[158] or you are reminded of coral, of leopards' paws or birds' feet, of brains or lungs or bowels, and excrements of all kinds. It is a

---

[156]Thoreau supplies here a list of fabled and exotic places. Atlantis, the huge island of Platonic myth (see, for example, Plato *Timaeus* 24D-25D), was located near the Straits of Gibraltar. The land of the Hesperides—daughters of Night in Greek mythology—lay at the farthest western edge of earth. Hanno (fl. 480? B.C.), a navigator from Carthage in northern Africa, likely explored the West African coast as far south as what is now Sierra Leone. Ternate and Tidore, volcanic islands in present-day eastern Indonesia in the Molucca Sea, were part of the Spice Islands (the Moluccas). The Persian Gulf, of course, lies to the southwest of Iran, separating it from present-day Saudi Arabia. Alexander the Great, or Alexander III of Macedon (356–323 B.C.), secured Greece and the Balkan Peninsula, entered Egypt without resistance, and conquered much of Asia, subduing Asia Minor, Syria, Palestine, the Persian Empire, and northwestern India to the far side of the Indus River. For a full discussion of Thoreau's extensive travels of the mind and spirit, see Christie, *Thoreau as World Traveler*.

[157]Thoreau has written of the ice breaking up on the ponds. Now he turns to a description of other signs of spring.

[158]Thoreau is using botanical terms. A *thallus* is an undifferentiated plant lacking roots, stem, and leaves. That it is laciniated means that its lobes are extremely irregular and probably pointed, and that it is imbricated means that, at the same time, the lobes overlap one another like rooftop shingles.

truly *grotesque* vegetation, whose forms and color we see imitated in bronze, a sort of architectural foliage more ancient and typical than acanthus, chiccory, ivy, vine, or any vegetable leaves;[159] destined perhaps, under some circumstances, to become a puzzle to future geologists. The whole cut impressed me as if it were a cave with its stalactites laid open to the light. The various shades of the sand are singularly rich and agreeable, embracing the different iron colors, brown, gray, yellowish, and reddish. When the flowing mass reaches the drain at the foot of the bank it spreads out flatter into *strands,* the separate streams losing their semi-cylindrical form and gradually becoming more flat and broad, running together as they are more moist, till they form an almost flat *sand,* still variously and beautifully shaded, but in which you can trace the original forms of vegetation; till at length, in the water itself, they are converted into *banks,* like those formed off the mouths of rivers, and the forms of vegetation are lost in the ripple-marks on the bottom.

The whole bank, which is from twenty to forty feet high, is sometimes overlaid with a mass of this kind of foliage, or sandy rupture, for a quarter of a mile on one or both sides, the produce of one spring day. What makes this sand foliage remarkable is its springing into existence thus suddenly. When I see on the one side the inert bank,—for the sun acts on one side first,—and on the other this luxuriant foliage, the creation of an hour, I am affected as if in a peculiar sense I stood in the laboratory of the Artist who made the world and me,—had come to where he was still at work, sporting on this bank, and with excess of energy strewing his fresh designs about.[160] I feel as if I were nearer to the vitals of the globe, for this sandy overflow is something such a foliaceous mass as the vitals of the animal body. You find thus in the very sands an anticipation of the vegetable leaf. No wonder that the earth expresses itself outwardly in leaves, it so labors with the idea inwardly.[161] The atoms have already learned this law, and are pregnant by it. The overhanging leaf sees here its prototype. *Internally,* whether in the globe or animal body, it is a moist thick *lobe,* a word especially applicable to the liver and lungs and the *leaves* of fat (λείβω, *labor, lapsus,* to flow or slip downward, a lapsing; λοβός, *globus,* lobe, globe; also lap, flap, and many other words,) *externally,* a dry thin *leaf,* even as the *f* and *v* are a pressed and dried *b.*[162] The radicals of *lobe* are *lb,*

---

[159]Representatives of acanthus, chicory, ivy, and vine leaves have all been used for ornamentation in various traditional architectural contexts.

[160]The entire passage preceding and following this affirmation celebrates the emergence of life from a kind of primal chaos, oozing, "excremental," and caught in the act of achieving form. Thus Thoreau's awareness of the unfolding of life in nature leads him to religious ecstasy. In fact, Leo Marx has called Thoreau's movement toward the time of nature in the passage "the movement that redeems machine power" (cf. the railroad bank on which the natural drama is taking place). See Leo Marx, *The Machine in the Garden: Technology and the Pastoral Ideal in America* (New York: Oxford University Press, 1964) 261.

[161]Cf. Thoreau's use of the English verb *labor* here with his linguistic exegesis of the Latin verb (also *labor*) below in the text (see also n. 162 below). Thoreau is punning as he describes the movement into form, and he expresses throughout the passage an understanding of all the world in terms of leaves. Note, too, the pun on *labor* in the context of the following sentence with its "pregnant" atoms.

[162]Cf. this passage to Thoreau's philological

the soft mass of the *b* (single-lobed, or B, double-lobed), with the liquid *l* behind it pressing it forward. In globe, *glb,* the guttural *g* adds to the meaning the capacity of the throat. The feathers and wings of birds are still drier and thinner leaves. Thus, also, you pass from the lumpish grub in the earth to the airy and fluttering butterfly. The very globe continually transcends and translates itself, and becomes winged in its orbit. Even ice begins with delicate crystal leaves, as if it had flowed into moulds which the fronds of water-plants have impressed on the watery mirror. The whole tree itself is but one leaf, and rivers are still vaster leaves whose pulp is intervening earth, and towns and cities are the ova of insects in their axils.

When the sun withdraws the sand ceases to flow, but in the morning the streams will start once more and branch and branch again into a myriad of others. You here see perchance how blood-vessels are formed. If you look closely you observe that first there pushes forward from the thawing mass a stream of softened sand with a drop-like point, like the ball of the finger, feeling its way slowly and blindly downward, until at last with more heat and moisture, as the sun gets higher, the most fluid portion, in its effort to obey the law to which the most inert also yields, separates from the latter and forms for itself a meandering channel or artery within that, in which is seen a little silvery stream glancing like lightning from one stage of pulpy leaves or branches to another, and ever and anon swallowed up in the sand. It is wonderful how rapidly yet perfectly the sand organizes itself as it flows, using the best material its mass affords to form the sharp edges of its channel. Such are the sources of rivers. In the silicious matter which the water deposits is perhaps the bony system, and in the still finer soil and organic matter the fleshy fibre or cellular tissue. What is man but a mass of thawing clay?[163] The ball of the human finger is but a drop congealed. The fingers and toes flow to their extent from the thawing mass of the body. Who knows what the human body would expand and flow out to under a more genial heaven? Is not the hand a spreading *palm* leaf with its lobes and veins? The ear may be regarded, fancifully, as a lichen, *umbilicaria,* on the side of the head, with its lobe or drop.[164] The lip—*labium,* from

---

reflection, based on Varro, in the final paragraph of ch. 7. The best discussion of the linguistic vision of the present passage will be found in Gura, *Wisdom of Words,* 131-37. Thoreau has, in effect, translated the Greek and Latin words he employs. The Greek verb λοβός (*lobos*) means "to pour," "let flow," or "flow." The Latin verb *labor* means "to glide," "slip down or away," or "fall"; its past participle (passive in form but active in meaning) is *lapsus,* "having glided" or "slipped down" or "away," or "fallen." The Greek noun λείβω (*leibo*) designates the lobe of the ear or the liver or a pool. The Latin noun *globus* identifies a globe or ball. Phonetically, "f" and "v" are spoken from the front of the mouth (hence "pressed and dried," close to the air), while "b" is sounded farther back, in the "liquid" interior. Finally, note Thoreau's movement, in his philological exposition here and below in the text, from the liquid (womblike) interior to the dry exterior: language reflects life, and words are, as Emerson said, "signs of natural facts" (see Emerson, *Nature,* ch. 4). Thoreau's painstaking analysis is a proclamation of correspondence.

[163]Cf. Job 12:9.

[164]*Umbilicaria* is the botanical name for a small genus of lichens that in appearance resemble leaves as well as navels. Notice, too, the presence of the embryonic lobe (of the leaf) in the earlobe. Thoreau nuances his text, suggesting at once the leaf and its coming to birth in the shape of the ear.

labor (?)—laps or lapses from the sides of the cavernous mouth.[165] The nose is a manifest congealed drop or stalactite. The chin is a still larger drop, the confluent dripping of the face. The cheeks are a slide from the brows into the valley of the face, opposed and diffused by the cheek bones. Each rounded lobe of the vegetable leaf, too, is a thick and now loitering drop, larger or smaller; the lobes are the fingers of the leaf; and as many lobes as it has, in so many directions it tends to flow, and more heat or other genial influences would have caused it to flow yet farther.

Thus it seemed that this one hillside illustrated the principle of all the operations of Nature. The Maker of this earth but patented a leaf. What Champollion will decipher this hieroglyphic for us, that we may turn over a new leaf at last?[166] This phenomenon is more exhilarating to me than the luxuriance and fertility of vineyards. True, it is somewhat excrementitious in its character, and there is no end to the heaps of liver, lights, and bowels, as if the globe were turned wrong side outward; but this suggests at least that Nature has some bowels, and there again is mother of humanity.[167] This is the frost coming out of the ground; this is Spring. It precedes the green and flowery spring, as mythology precedes regular poetry.[168] I know of nothing more purgative of winter fumes and indigestions. It convinces me that Earth is still in her swaddling-clothes, and stretches forth baby fingers on every side. Fresh curls spring from the baldest brow. There is nothing inorganic. . . .

The first sparrow of spring! The year beginning with younger hope than ever! The faint silvery warblings heard over the partially bare and moist fields from the bluebird, the song sparrow, and the redwing, as if the last flakes of winter tinkled as they fell! What at such a time are histories, chronologies, traditions, and all written revelations? The brooks sing carols and glees to the spring. The marsh hawk, sailing low over the meadow, is already seeking the first slimy life that awakes. The sinking sound of melting snow is heard in all dells, and the ice dissolves apace in the ponds. The grass flames up on the hillsides like a spring fire,—"et primitus oritur herba imbribus primoribus evocata,"[169]—as if the earth sent forth an inward heat to greet the returning sun; not yellow but green is the color of its flame;— the symbol of perpetual youth, the grass-

---

[165]*Labium* is the Latin equivalent for "lip." But Thoreau's etymological derivation of *labium* from "labor" is forced and, as he recognizes, questionable.

[166]Thoreau has already deciphered a radical correspondence between leaf and world. For Jean-François Champollion and the symbol of Egyptian hieroglyphics, see n. 2 to Emerson, *Nature*. For a useful discussion of the reading that influenced Thoreau's hieroglyphic interest, see John T. Irwin, *American Hieroglyphics: The Symbol of the Egyptian Hieroglyphics in the American Renaissance* (New Haven: Yale University Press, 1980) 15-18. Irwin also sees in Thoreau's "leaf" a subtle evocation of the cosmic tree as "an image of language as mediating link between the human and the divine" (ibid., 32). For the cosmic tree, see also n. 2 to Thoreau, *Week*. Notice, finally, Thoreau's pun on turning over a new leaf.

[167]For Thoreau's pun on bowels, cf. n. 32 above.

[168]Mythopoetic theories abounded in the nineteenth-century romantic movement, and Thoreau here reflects the general romantic interest in the connection between myth and poetry and, also, in origins.

[169]Varro *Rerum Rusticarum* (*On Agriculture*) 2.2.14: "And the grass which is called forth by the early rains is just growing" (trans. William Davis Hooper and rev. Harrison Boyd Ash).

blade, like a long green ribbon, streams from the sod into the summer, checked indeed by the frost, but anon pushing on again, lifting its spear of last year's hay with the fresh life below. It grows as steadily as the rill oozes out of the ground. It is almost identical with that, for in the growing days of June, when the rills are dry, the grass-blades are their channels, and from year to year the herds drink at this perennial green stream, and the mower draws from it betimes their winter supply. So our human life but dies down to its root, and still puts forth its green blade to eternity.

Walden is melting apace. There is a canal two rods wide along the northerly and westerly sides, and wider still at the east end. A great field of ice has cracked off from the main body. I hear a song sparrow singing from the bushes on the shore,—*olit, olit, olit,—chip, chip, chip, che char,—che wiss, wiss, wiss.* He too is helping to crack it. How handsome the great sweeping curves in the edge of the ice, answering somewhat to those of the shore, but more regular! It is unusually hard, owing to the recent severe but transient cold, and all watered or waved like a palace floor. But the wind slides eastward over its opaque surface in vain, till it reaches the living surface beyond. It is glorious to behold this ribbon of water sparkling in the sun, the bare face of the pond full of glee and youth, as if it spoke the joy of the fishes within it, and of the sands on its shore,—a silvery sheen as from the scales of a leuciscus,[170] as it were all one active fish. Such is the contrast between winter and spring. Walden was dead and is alive again.[171] . . .

As every season seems best to us in its turn, so the coming in of spring is like the creation of Cosmos out of Chaos and the realization of the Golden Age.[172] . . .

A single gentle rain makes the grass many shades greener. So our prospects brighten on the influx of better thoughts. We should be blessed if we lived in the present always, and took advantage of every accident that befell us, like the grass which confesses the influence of the slightest dew that falls on it; and did not spend our time in atoning for the neglect of past opportunities, which we call doing our duty. We loiter in winter while it is already spring. In a pleasant spring morning all men's sins are forgiven. Such a day is a truce to vice. While such a sun holds out to burn, the vilest sinner may return.[173] Through our own recovered innocence we discern the innocence of our neighbors. You may have known your neighbor yesterday for a thief, a drunkard, or a sensualist, and merely pitied or despised him, and despaired of the world; but the sun shines bright and warm this first spring

---

[170]Generic name for various species of freshwater fish in the Cyprinidae (minnow) family, thought in Thoreau's day to include such varieties as daces, roaches, and shiners.

[171]Cf. Luke 15:24.

[172]The earliest literary source for the myths of the creation of the cosmos from Chaos and of the Golden Age is the ancient Greek poet Hesiod (fl. 8th cent.? B.C.). See, respectively, Hesiod *Theogony* 116-36, and Hesiod *Works and Days* 110-20. Thoreau's source, however, is not Hesiod but the Latin poet Ovid (43 B.C.-A.D. 18). For Ovid, Chaos was a crude elemental mass in strife and disorder, from which God and nature brought an ordered cosmos into being. The Golden Age, preceding the ages of silver, bronze, and iron, was a time of peace, plenty, and unending spring. See Ovid *Metamorphoses* 1.5-112.

[173]Cf. Isaac Watts *Hymns and Spiritual Songs* (1707) 1.88.3-4. For Watts, see n. 18 to Parker, *Sermon of the Delights of Piety*. Notice, too, Thoreau's celebration of the present as the important time—a recurring theme.

morning, recreating the world, and you meet him at some serene work, and see how his exhausted and debauched veins expand with still joy and bless the new day, feel the spring influence with the innocence of infancy, and all his faults are forgotten. There is not only an atmosphere of good will about him, but even a savor of holiness groping for expression, blindly and ineffectually perhaps, like a new-born instinct, and for a short hour the south hillside echoes to no vulgar jest. You see some innocent fair shoots preparing to burst from his gnarled rind and try another year's life, tender and fresh as the youngest plant. Even he has entered into the joy of his Lord.[174] Why the jailer does not leave open his prison doors,—why the judge does not dismiss his case,—why the preacher does not dismiss his congregation! It is because they do not obey the hint which God gives them, nor accept the pardon which he freely offers to all.

"A return to goodness produced each day in the tranquil and beneficent breath of the morning, causes that in respect to the love of virtue and the hatred of vice, one approaches a little the primitive nature of man, as the sprouts of the forest which has been felled. In like manner the evil which one does in the interval of a day prevents the germs of virtues which began to spring up again from developing themselves and destroys them.

"After the germs of virtue have thus been prevented many times from developing themselves, then the beneficent breath of evening does not suffice to preserve them. As soon as the breath of evening does not suffice longer to preserve

---

[174]Cf. Matt. 25:21. But the servant was canny and worldly wise to have doubled the talents; Thoreau's passage is a romantic hymn to the innocence of new birth and infancy.

them, then the nature of man does not differ much from that of the brute. Men seeing the nature of this man like that of the brute, think that he has never possessed the innate faculty of reason. Are those the true and natural sentiments of man?"[175]

"The Golden Age was first created, which without any avenger
Spontaneously without law cherished fidelity and rectitude.
Punishment and fear were not; nor were threatening words read
On suspended brass; nor did the suppliant crowd fear
The words of their judge; but were safe without an avenger.
Not yet the pine felled on its mountains had descended
To the liquid waves that it might see a foreign world,
And mortals knew no shores but their own.
. . . .
There was eternal spring, and placid zephyrs with warm
Blasts soothed the flowers born without seed."[176]

On the 29th of April, as I was fishing from the bank of the river near the Nine-Acre-Corner bridge,[177] standing on the quaking grass and willow roots, where the

---

[175]Mencius *Works,* bk. 6, pt. 1, 8.2. The translation is almost surely Thoreau's from the French text by M. G. Pauthier. For Mencius's writings, see n. 135 above. The Pauthier-Thoreau version is generally more romantic than the later James Legge translation (1895). In fact, the reference to morning especially must have attracted Thoreau to the passage, continuing his theme of new birth in the spring.

[176]Ovid *Metamorphoses* 1.89-96, 107-108. The translation is Thoreau's.

[177]Lee's Bridge across the Sudbury River, southeast of Nine-Acre Corner, itself in the south, southeastern part of the village of Concord. The date was 29 April 1846.

muskrats lurk, I heard a singular rattling sound, somewhat like that of the sticks which boys play with their fingers,[178] when, looking up, I observed a very slight and graceful hawk, like a nighthawk, alternately soaring like a ripple and tumbling a rod or two over and over, showing the under side of its wings, which gleamed like a satin ribbon in the sun, or like the pearly inside of a shell.[179] This sight reminded me of falconry and what nobleness and poetry are associated with that sport. The merlin[180] it seemed to me it might be called: but I care not for its name. It was the most ethereal flight I had ever witnessed. It did not simply flutter like a butterfly, nor soar like the larger hawks, but it sported with proud reliance in the fields of air; mounting again and again with its strange chuckle, it repeated its free and beautiful fall, turning over and over like a kite, and then recovering from its lofty tumbling, as if it had never set its foot on *terra firma*. It appeared to have no companion in the universe,—sporting there alone,—and to need none but the morning and the ether with which it played. It was not lonely, but made all the earth lonely beneath it. Where was the parent which hatched it, its kindred, and its father in the heavens? The tenant of the air, it seemed related to the earth but by an egg hatched some time in the crevice of a crag;—or was its native nest made in the angle of a cloud, woven of the rainbow's trimmings and the sunset sky, and lined with some soft midsummer haze caught up from earth? Its eyry now some cliffy cloud.

Beside this I got a rare mess of golden and silver and bright cupreous fishes, which looked like a string of jewels. Ah! I have penetrated to those meadows on the morning of many a first spring day, jumping from hummock to hummock, from willow root to willow root, when the wild river valley and the woods were bathed in so pure and bright a light as would have waked the dead, if they had been slumbering in their graves, as some suppose. There needs no stronger proof of immortality. All things must live in such a light. O Death, where was thy sting? O Grave, where was thy victory, then?[181]

Our village life would stagnate if it were not for the unexplored forests and meadows which surround it. We need the tonic of wildness,—to wade sometimes in marshes where the bittern and the meadow-hen lurk, and hear the booming of the snipe; to smell the whispering sedge where only some wilder and more solitary fowl builds her nest, and the mink crawls with its belly close to the ground.[182] At the same time that we are earnest to explore and learn all things, we require that all things be mysterious and unexplorable, that land and sea be infinitely wild, unsurveyed and unfathomed by us because unfathomable. We can never have enough of nature. We must be refreshed by the sight of inexhaustible

---

[178] A children's game in which pieces of wood or bone were used to make rhythmical clacking or clapping sounds.

[179] Edwin Way Teale observed that the bird was "undoubtedly a male marsh hawk" (see Thoreau, *Variorum Walden,* 316). The nighthawk is a completely different species, a relative of the whippoorwill and not truly a hawk. But it is known for its twilight dives from the sky to secure insects as it is flying.

[180] A small falcon.

[181] Cf. 1 Cor. 15:55. For "proofs of immortality," cf. Acts 1:3. Thoreau weaves the specifically Christian theme of resurrection into his affirmation of new birth.

[182] Cf. Thoreau's affirmation of wildness in this passage to the introductory paragraph in ch. 11. Note, too, that Thoreau's naturalism encompasses both benign and sterner aspects of nature. He finds meaning in life and in death and, notably, in death by violence.

vigor, vast and titanic features,[183] the sea-coast with its wrecks, the wilderness with its living and its decaying trees, the thunder-cloud, and the rain which lasts three weeks and produces freshets. We need to witness our own limits transgressed, and some life pasturing freely where we never wander. We are cheered when we observe the vulture feeding on the carrion which disgusts and disheartens us, and deriving health and strength from the repast. There was a dead horse in the hollow by the path to my house, which compelled me sometimes to go out of my way, especially in the night when the air was heavy, but the assurance it gave me of the strong appetite and inviolable health of Nature was my compensation for this.[184] I love to see that Nature is so rife with life that myriads can be afforded to be sacrificed and suffered to prey on one another; that tender organizations can be so serenely squashed out of existence like pulp,—tadpoles which herons gobble up, and tortoises and toads run over in the road; and that sometimes it has rained flesh and blood! With the liability to accident, we must see how little account is to be made of it. The impression made on a wise man is that of universal innocence. Poison is not poisonous after all, nor are any wounds fatal. Compassion is a very untenable ground. It must be expeditious. Its pleadings will not bear to be stereotyped. . . .

XVIII
CONCLUSION

If you would learn to speak all tongues and conform to the customs of all nations, if you would travel farther than all travellers, be naturalized in all climes, and cause the Sphinx to dash her head against a stone, even obey the precept of the old philosopher, and Explore thyself.[185] Herein are demanded the eye and the nerve. Only the defeated and deserters go to the wars, cowards that run away and enlist. Start now on that farthest western way, which does not pause at the Mississippi or the Pacific, nor conduct toward a worn-out China or Japan,[186] but leads on direct, a tangent to this sphere, summer and winter, day and night, sun down, moon down, and at last earth down too.

It is said that Mirabeau took to highway robbery "to ascertain what degree of resolution was necessary in order to place one's self in formal opposition to the most

---

[183]Thoreau's language here evokes his experience on Katahdin in *The Maine Woods*. (For "titanic," see n. 9 to Henry David Thoreau, *The Maine Woods*.) Note that the "innocence" of nature (below in the text) is neither sentimental nor uncritically romantic.

[184]Cf. the examples in this and the previous sentence to Thoreau's discovery—as recorded in ch. 11—of the lower jaw of a long-dead hog. The power and importance of nature, for Thoreau, lie in its transcendence of stereotyped human categories (cf. the end of the paragraph in the present chapter), even when they are "higher."

[185]Thoreau has opened the chapter with a veritable catalog of his geographical knowledge (see Christie, *Thoreau as World Traveler*, for further discussion of the theme)—all in the service of the inner geography to which he points (cf. n. 82 to Thoreau, *Week*). For the Sphinx, see n. 29 to Emerson, *Nature*. Cf., too, the rhetorical flavor of Thoreau's description of the Sphinx's suicide to Ps. 91:12. And for the "old philosopher" and his dictum "Explore thyself" ("know thyself"), cf. Socrates in Plato *Apology* 38A.

[186]The reference to the "farthest western way" should be read in the context of the western migration of the period. Thoreau calls China and Japan "worn-out" no doubt because, in keeping with contemporary theories of the stages or cycles of civilization, he viewed these civilizations as grown too old.

sacred laws of society." He declared that "a soldier who fights in the ranks does not require half so much courage as a foot-pad,"—"that honor and religion have never stood in the way of a well-considered and a firm resolve."[187] This was manly, as the world goes; and yet it was idle, if not desperate. A saner man would have found himself often enough "in formal opposition" to what are deemed "the most sacred laws of society," through obedience to yet more sacred laws, and so have tested his resolution without going out of his way. It is not for a man to put himself in such an attitude to society, but to maintain himself in whatever attitude he find himself through obedience to the laws of his being, which will never be one of opposition to a just government, if he should chance to meet with such.[188]

I left the woods for as good a reason as I went there.[189] Perhaps it seemed to me that I had several more lives to live, and could not spare any more time for that one. It is remarkable how easily and insensibly we fall into a particular route, and make a beaten track for ourselves. I had not lived there a week before my feet wore a path from my door to the pond-side; and though it is five or six years since I trod it, it is still quite distinct. It is true, I fear that others may have fallen into it, and so helped to keep it open. The surface of the earth is soft and impressible by the feet of men; and so with the paths which the mind travels. How worn and dusty, then, must be the highways of the world, how deep the ruts of tradition and conformity! I did not wish to take a cabin passage, but rather to go before the mast and on the deck of the world, for there I could best see the moonlight amid the mountains. I do not wish to go below now.[190]

I learned this, at least, by my experiment; that if one advances confidently in the direction of his dreams, and endeavors to live the life which he has imagined, he will meet with a success unexpected in common hours. He will put some things behind, will pass an invisible boundary; new, universal, and more liberal laws will begin to establish themselves around and within him; or the old laws be expanded, and interpreted in his favor in a more liberal sense, and he will live with the license

---

[187]Honoré Gabriel Riquetti, comte de Mirabeau (1749–1791), despite years of dissolute living, was known for his French revolutionary and political activities. Thoreau's quotations come from the unsigned "Mirabeau: An Anecdote of His Private Life," *Harper's New Monthly Magazine* 1:5 (October 1850): 651, although Thoreau has altered the third quotation to suit his semantic needs. For "foot-pad" (see the second quotation), read "highwayman." The hyphen does not occur in the *Harper's* article, which was taken from (an unspecified number of) *Chamber's Edinburgh Journal.*

[188]Cf. Thoreau's observations here to the theme of his essay "Civil Disobedience."

[189]The practical reason for Thoreau's departure was his agreement, while Emerson traveled abroad, to remain with his family and to look after the household.

[190]Thoreau's "before the mast" is no doubt an allusion to *Two Years before the Mast* (1840), the classic narrative by Richard Henry Dana, Jr., Thoreau's former classmate at Harvard. The reference to moonlight may be Thoreau's remembrance of a Hudson-River boat trip in which he and (William) Ellery Channing stayed all night in the ship's bow because of the moonlight. According to Walter Harding, Channing made this connection to the text (see Thoreau, *Variorum Walden,* 318). Finally, note the contrast between going "before the mast" (the place for active sailors) and going "below" (the place for passengers, whose destiny is in the hands of others).

of a higher order of beings. In proportion as he simplifies his life, the laws of the universe will appear less complex, and solitude will not be solitude, nor poverty poverty, nor weakness weakness. If you have built castles in the air, your work need not be lost; that is where they should be. Now put the foundations under them.

It is a ridiculous demand which England and America make, that you shall speak so that they can understand you. Neither men nor toadstools grow so. As if that were important, and there were not enough to understand you without them. As if Nature could support but one order of understandings, could not sustain birds as well as quadrupeds, flying as well as creeping things, and *hīsh* and *whoa,* which Bright can understand, were the best English.[191] As if there were safety in stupidity alone. I fear chiefly lest my expression may not be *extra-vagant* enough, may not wander far enough beyond the narrow limits of my daily experience, so as to be adequate to the truth of which I have been convinced.[192] *Extra vagance!* it depends on how you are yarded. The migrating buffalo, which seeks new pastures in another latitude, is not extravagant like the cow which kicks over the pail, leaps the cowyard fence, and runs after her calf, in milking time. I desire to speak somewhere *without* bounds; like a man in a waking moment, to men in their waking moments; for I am convinced that I cannot exaggerate enough even to lay the foundation of a true expression. . . .

Why should we be in such desperate haste to succeed and in such desperate enterprises? If a man does not keep pace with his companions, perhaps it is because he hears a different drummer. Let him step to the music which he hears, however measured or far away.[193] It is not important that he should mature as soon as an apple tree or an oak. Shall he turn his spring into summer?[194] If the condition of things which we were made for is not yet, what were any reality which we can substitute? We will not be shipwrecked on a vain reality. Shall we with pains erect a heaven of blue glass over ourselves, though when it is done we shall be sure to gaze still at the true ethereal heaven far above, as if the former were not?

There was an artist in the city of Kouroo who was disposed to strive after per-

---

[191] In the original (1854) edition, "*hīsh*" and "*whoa*" appear as "*hush*" and "*who*"—terms, respectively, for urging an ox to go and getting it to stop. (Bright was a common choice as the name for an ox at this time.) Francis H. Allen, who edited the Walden (and Manuscript) edition of Thoreau's writings in 1906 for Houghton Mifflin, changed the terms and later regretted the decision (see Thoreau, *Variorum Walden,* 318).

[192] Thoreau again pursues etymology in the service of his point, stressing the Latin roots of the English word *extravagant,* from *vagari,* "to wander about," and *extra,* "beyond" or "outside of." (Cf. his reflections on the thawing sand on the railroad bank in ch. 17, and on the ear of wheat and grain in ch. 7.) In the terms suggested by Thoreau's argument, the law of correspondence demands extravagant language to awaken people to lead extravagant lives—the only kind that, for Thoreau, are spiritually significant.

[193] Cf. Thoreau's "yoga of sound" in "Monday" of his *Week,* in which Thoreau, while falling asleep, hears and reflects on the drumbeat of the young soldier in the distance. See, too, the lengthy comment by Philip Van Doren Stern on the history of Thoreau's idea in this sentence, in Thoreau, *Annotated* Walden, 442-44.

[194] Cf. Thoreau, "Civil Disobedience": "If a plant cannot live according to its nature, it dies; and so a man."

fection.¹⁹⁵ One day it came into his mind to make a staff. Having considered that in an imperfect work time is an ingredient, but into a perfect work time does not enter, he said to himself, It shall be perfect in all respects, though I should do nothing else in my life. He proceeded instantly to the forest for wood, being resolved that it should not be made of unsuitable material; and as he searched for and rejected stick after stick, his friends gradually deserted him, for they grew old in their works and died, but he grew not older by a moment. His singleness of purpose and resolution, and his elevated piety, endowed him, without his knowledge, with perennial youth. As he made no compromise with Time, Time kept out of his way, and only sighed at a distance because he could not overcome him. Before he had found a stock in all respects suitable the city of Kouroo was a hoary ruin, and he sat on one of its mounds to peel the stick. Before he had given it the proper shape the dynasty of the Candahars was at an end,¹⁹⁶ and with the point of the stick he wrote the name of the last of that race in the sand, and then resumed his work. By the time he had smoothed and polished the staff Kalpa was no longer the pole-star; and ere he had put on the ferule and the head adorned with precious stones, Brahma had awoke and slumbered many times.¹⁹⁷ But why do I stay to mention these things? When the finishing stroke was put to his work, it suddenly expanded before the eyes of the astonished artist into the fairest of all the creations of Brahma. He had made a new system in making a staff, a world with full and fair proportions; in

---

¹⁹⁵Thoreau's "Kouroo" was probably Kurukshetra (cf. *Laws of Manu* 7.193), in the region of Delhi, in northern India. In the *Bhagavad Gita,* Kuru is the eponymous ancestor of the Kauravas whom Arjuna is arrayed to fight (see n. 25 to Thoreau, *Week*). The Charles Wilkins translation, which Thoreau used (1785; see ibid.), speaks of the assembling of the opposing parties at "*Kooroo-kshetra*" (*Bhagavad Gita* 1.1). So far as I have been able to determine, no scholar has located an Indian (or other) source for the parable that follows in the passage; moreover, because of its content and intrinsic character, it has been assumed as virtually certain that the story was created by Thoreau.

¹⁹⁶The reference is obscure, adding strength to conclusions that the entire story is Thoreau's. At least according to standard accounts, there was no dynasty of the Candahars (or Kandahars) in Indian history. Gandhara was the ancient name for the site of modern Kandahar (or Qandahar), in Afghanistan, and its people figure in the epic *Mahabharata*. One Gandharan princess was the wife of Ajamidha, an ancestor of the Kurus, and another, the renowned Gandhari, was the wife of the blind King Dhrtarashtra, father of the Kauravas (Kurus) in the *Bhagavad Gita*. Hence, the "dynasty of the Candahars" may be Thoreau's designation for the reign of the Kuru royal lineage in the *Bhagavad Gita* and the larger *Mahabharata*. Additionally, Thoreau may have conflated the name with recollections of the Candravamsha—the lunar dynasty, or race of kings claiming descent from the moon. Both opposing parties in the *Gita* were understood as so descended.

¹⁹⁷For a Kalpa, or "day of Brahma," see n. 29 to Thoreau, *Week*. Although Indian literature does not make Kalpa the polestar, Indians were aware that over a lengthy course of time a different star would become the polestar. Thus, the reference points especially strongly to the passage of millions of years and the end of a cosmic era. As Walter Harding suggests, Thoreau may have gleaned material about both the Kalpas and the polestar (conflating them in his mind?) from H. T. Colebrooke's *Miscellaneous Essays* (see H[enry] T[homas] Colebrooke, *Miscellaneous Essays* [London: W. H. Allen, 1837] 2:288, 364). Finally, for Brahma, see n. 16 to Emerson, "Brahma."

which, though the old cities and dynasties had passed away, fairer and more glorious ones had taken their places. And now he saw by the heap of shavings still fresh at his feet, that, for him and his work, the former lapse of time had been an illusion, and that no more time had elapsed than is required for a single scintillation from the brain of Brahma to fall on and inflame the tinder of a mortal brain. The material was pure, and his art was pure; how could the result be other than wonderful?[198]

No face which we can give to a matter will stead us so well at last as the truth. This alone wears well. For the most part, we are not where we are, but in a false position. Through an infirmity of our natures, we suppose a case, and put ourselves into it, and hence are in two cases at the same time, and it is doubly difficult to get out. In sane moments we regard only the facts, the case that is. Say what you have to say, not what you ought. Any truth is better than make-believe. Tom Hyde, the tinker, standing on the gallows, was asked if he had anything to say. "Tell the tailors," said he, "to remember to make a knot in their thread before they take the first stitch."[199] His companion's prayer is forgotten.

However mean your life is, meet it and live it; do not shun it and call it hard names. It is not so bad as you are. It looks poorest when you are richest. The fault-finder will find faults even in paradise. Love your life, poor as it is. You may perhaps have some pleasant, thrilling, glorious hours, even in a poor-house. The setting sun is reflected from the windows of the alms-house as brightly as from the rich man's abode; the snow melts before its door as early in the spring. I do not see but a quiet mind may live as contentedly there, and have as cheering thoughts, as in a palace. The town's poor seem to me often to live the most independent lives of any. Maybe they are simply great enough to receive without misgiving. Most think that they are above being supported by the town; but it oftener happens that they are not above supporting themselves by dishonest means, which should be more disreputable. Cultivate poverty like a garden herb, like sage. Do not trouble yourself much to get new things, whether clothes or friends. Turn the old; return to them. Things do not change; we change. Sell your clothes and keep your thoughts. God will see that you do not want society. If I were confined to a corner of a garret all my days, like a spider, the world would be just as large to me while I had my thoughts about me. The philosopher said: "From an army of three divisions one can take away its general, and put it in disorder; from the man the most abject and vulgar one cannot take away his thought."[200] Do not seek so anxiously to be developed, to subject yourself to many influences to be played on; it is all dissipation. Humility like darkness reveals the heavenly lights. The shadows of poverty and meanness

---

[198] The sentence suggests that, for Thoreau, speaking of artistic perfection is another way of speaking of purity. In fact, the parable as a whole throws light on Thoreau's expression of his quest for purity in ch. 11. In the end, aesthetics becomes ethics, but ethics as embodied in human interactions with nature and through art.

[199] Tom Hyde has never been positively identified so far as can be determined; but Walter Harding suggests the possibility (based on a line in a journal entry by Thoreau) that Hyde may appear in the "folklore or fact" of eastern Massachusetts (see Thoreau, *Variorum Walden*, 319).

[200] *Analects of Confucius* 9.25. The translation is probably Thoreau's from the French text by M. G. Pauthier although, curiously, Lyman Cady is silent regarding the quotation (Cady, "Thoreau's Quotations," 20-32).

gather around us, "and lo! creation widens to our view."²⁰¹ We are often reminded that if there were bestowed on us the wealth of Crœsus,²⁰² our aims must still be the same, and our means essentially the same. Moreover, if you are restricted in your range by poverty, if you cannot buy books and newspapers, for instance, you are but confined to the most significant and vital experiences; you are compelled to deal with the material which yields the most sugar and the most starch. It is life near the bone where it is sweetest.²⁰³ You are defended from being a trifler. No man loses ever on a lower level by magnanimity on a higher. Superfluous wealth can buy superfluities only. Money is not required to buy one necessary of the soul.

I live in the angle of a leaden wall, into whose composition was poured a little alloy of bell-metal. Often, in the repose of my mid-day, there reaches my ears a confused *tintinnabulum* from without. It is the noise of my contemporaries. My neighbors tell me of their adventures with famous gentlemen and ladies, what notabilities they met at the dinner-table; but I am no more interested in such things than in the contents of the Daily Times. . . . I delight to come to my bearings,—not walk in procession with pomp and parade, in a conspicuous place, but to walk even with the Builder of the universe, if I may,—not to live in this restless, nervous, bustling, trivial Nineteenth Century, but stand or sit thoughtfully while it goes by. What are men celebrating? They are all on a committee of arrangements, and hourly expect a speech from somebody. God is only the president of the day, and Webster is his orator.²⁰⁴ I love to weigh, to settle, to gravitate toward that which most strongly and rightfully attracts me;—not hang by the beam of the scale and try to weigh less,—not suppose a case, but take the case that is; to travel the only path I can, and that on which no power can resist me. It affords me no satisfaction to commence to spring an arch before I have got a solid foundation. Let us not play at kittlybenders.²⁰⁵ There is a solid bottom everywhere. We read that the traveller asked the boy if the swamp before him had a hard bottom. The boy replied that it had. But presently the traveller's horse sank in up to the girths, and he observed to the boy, "I thought you said that this bog had a hard bottom." "So it has," answered the latter, "but you have not got half way to it yet."²⁰⁶ So it is with the bogs and quicksands of society; but he is an old boy that knows it. Only what is thought, said, or done at a certain rare coincidence is good. I would not be one of those who will foolishly drive a nail into mere lath and plastering; such a deed would keep me awake nights. Give me a ham-

---

²⁰¹Cf. the English author and cleric Joseph Blanco White (1775-1841), "To Night," l. 8.

²⁰²Crœsus (d. 547? B.C.), king of ancient Lydia in Asia Minor, has been remembered most of all for the enormity of his wealth.

²⁰³Cf. the old English proverb, "The nearer the bone, The sweeter the flesh," which has been traced in slightly different form to a line in the ballad by T. Emley, *Maid That Would Mary* (ca. 1557–1558). See James Payne Collier, ed., "Old Ballads from Early Printed Copies," *Percy Society* 1 (1840): 21.

²⁰⁴A reference to Daniel Webster (1782–1852), famed political orator, constitutional lawyer, United States senator from Massachusetts (1827–1841; 1845–1850), and secretary of state (1841–1843; 1850–1852).

²⁰⁵Kittlybenders is a game in which players engage in runs or slides over thin ice, bending but not breaking it.

²⁰⁶The humorous anecdote was carried, according to Walter Harding (Thoreau, *Variorum Walden,* 320), in Concord's *Yeoman's Gazette* for 22 November 1828.

mer, and let me feel for the furrowing. Do not depend on the putty. Drive a nail home and clinch it so faithfully that you can wake up in the night and think of your work with satisfaction,—a work at which you would not be ashamed to invoke the Muse.[207] So will help you God, and so only. Every nail driven should be as another rivet in the machine of the universe, you carrying on the work.

Rather than love, than money, than fame, give me truth. I sat at a table where were rich food and wine in abundance, and obsequious attendance, but sincerity and truth were not; and I went away hungry from the inhospitable board. The hospitality was as cold as the ices. I thought that there was no need of ice to freeze them. They talked to me of the age of the wine and the fame of the vintage; but I thought of an older, a newer, and purer wine, of a more glorious vintage, which they had not got, and could not buy. The style, the house and grounds and "entertainment" pass for nothing with me. I called on the king, but he made me wait in his hall, and conducted like a man incapacitated for hospitality. There was a man in my neighborhood who lived in a hollow tree. His manners were truly regal. I should have done better had I called on him.[208]

How long shall we sit in our porticoes practising idle and musty virtues, which any work would make impertinent? As if one were to begin the day with long-suffering, and hire a man to hoe his potatoes; and in the afternoon go forth to practise Christian meekness and charity with goodness aforethought! Consider the China pride and stagnant self-complacency of mankind.[209] This generation inclines a little to congratulate itself on being the last of an illustrious line; and in Boston and London and Paris and Rome, thinking of its long descent, it speaks of its progress in art and science and literature with satisfaction. There are the Records of the Philosophical Societies, and the public Eulogies of *Great Men!* It is the good Adam contemplating his own virtue. "Yes, we have done great deeds, and sung divine songs, which shall never die,"[210]—that is, as long as *we* can remember them. The learned societies and great men of Assyria,—where

---

[207]Invoking the aid of the Muses—the mythological Greek sisters who were patron deities of the arts—was a time-honored practice for literary artists. Hence, Thoreau is saying that even a practical and mechanical task, if accomplished with awareness and a zeal for perfection, can be a work of art and, by implication, of religion. Note, too, that unlike other instances (cf. ch. 1, above, and Thoreau, "Civil Disobedience," passim) the machine is understood positively in the text below.

[208]The paragraph seems to be another of Thoreau's parabolic narratives, likely based, at least partially, on snatches of reconstructed au-

tobiography. The reference to wine echoes, in spirit, Christian Scripture (cf. Matt. 9:17 and Acts 2:13). Emerson also once wrote of a "divine man" living near him in a hollow tree, but the reference—attributed by Emerson to "Osman," his name for the ideal man—is obscure (see Ralph Waldo Emerson, quoted, for 1841, in Edward Waldo Emerson, *Emerson in Concord: A Memoir Written for the "Social Circle" in Concord, Massachusetts* [Boston: Houghton, Mifflin, 1889] 210).

[209]For this stereotypical view of China, cf. n. 187 above. "Pride," here, should be understood in the sense of smug and static self-satisfaction.

[210]Rather than a quotation, this seems to be a dramatic casting for effect, especially echoing the Psalms in construction. Thus, Thoreau puts into the mouths of his contemporaries a blasphemy: the exaltation of their historical (and, in the language of the twentieth century, ego-based) personalities as divine.

are they?[211] What youthful philosophers and experimentalists we are! There is not one of my readers who has yet lived a whole human life.[212] These may be but the spring months in the life of the race. If we have had the seven-years' itch, we have not seen the seventeen-year locust yet in Concord.[213] We are acquainted with a mere pellicle of the globe on which we live.[214] Most have not delved six feet beneath the surface, nor leaped as many above it. We know not where we are. Beside, we are sound asleep nearly half our time. Yet we esteem ourselves wise, and have an established order on the surface. Truly, we are deep thinkers, we are ambitious spirits! As I stand over the insect crawling amid the pine needles on the forest floor, and endeavoring to conceal itself from my sight, and ask myself why it will cherish those humble thoughts, and hide its head from me who might, perhaps, be its benefactor, and impart to its race some cheering information, I am reminded of the greater Benefactor and Intelligence that stands over me the human insect.

There is an incessant influx of novelty into the world, and yet we tolerate incredible dulness. I need only suggest what kind of sermons are still listened to in the most enlightened countries. There are such words as joy and sorrow, but they are only the burden of a psalm, sung with a nasal twang, while we believe in the ordinary and mean. We think that we can change our clothes only. It is said that the British Empire is very large and respectable, and that the United States are a first-rate power.[215] We do not believe that a tide rises and falls behind every man which can float the British Empire like a chip, if he should ever harbor it in his mind. Who knows what sort of seventeen-year locust will next come out of the ground? The government of the world I live in was not framed, like that of Britain, in after-dinner conversations over the wine.

The life in us is like the water in the river. It may rise this year higher than man has ever known it, and flood the parched uplands; even this may be the eventful year,

---

[211] Thoreau uses Assyria—the west Asian empire that enjoyed an age of glory and of learning in the seventh century B.C.—as an example of a great but ephemeral civilization.

[212] Note the pun on "whole human life"—witty but, in its second sense, a statement of spiritual deficiency.

[213] With "seven-years' itch" Thoreau seems to suggest a general bored and restless state—but short and superficial compared to the life of the seventeen-year locust. This cicada lives for seventeen years but remains underground in a preadult state for almost that entire period. When it finally emerges, the seventeen-year locust matures quickly and survives only a few weeks after reaching adulthood. In the context of the story of the bug encased in the table, in the final paragraph of the text, the locust seems to point to the later symbol of resurrection—a sign of spiritual maturity still to be awaited and sought.

[214] Thoreau is ending his chapter as he began it—with a spiritual geography in which the surface of the globe is only the periphery, and true significance lies elsewhere.

[215] At its height in the late nineteenth and early twentieth centuries, the British Empire encompassed roughly one-quarter of the world's population and territory, with colonies on every continent. When Thoreau was writing, it was still growing; and even without the huge African acquisitions later in the century and the Middle Eastern and African territories added through victory in World War I, it was indeed "very large and respectable." Meanwhile, the United States, which recently (1846-1848) had warred against Mexico with imperialistic aims, had extended its domain to the Pacific Ocean.

which will drown out all our muskrats.[216] It was not always dry land where we dwell. I see far inland the banks which the stream anciently washed, before science began to record its freshets. Every one has heard the story which has gone the rounds of New England, of a strong and beautiful bug which came out of the dry leaf of an old table of apple-tree wood, which had stood in a farmer's kitchen for sixty years, first in Connecticut, and afterward in Massachusetts,—from an egg deposited in the living tree many years earlier still, as appeared by counting the annual layers beyond it; which was heard gnawing out for several weeks, hatched perchance by the heat of an urn.[217] Who does not feel his faith in a resurrection and immortality strengthened by hearing of this? Who knows what beautiful and winged life, whose egg has been buried for ages under many concentric layers of woodenness in the dead dry life of society, deposited at first in the alburnum of the green and living tree, which has been gradually converted into the semblance of its well-seasoned tomb,—heard perchance gnawing out now for years by the astonished family of man, as they sat round the festive board,—may unexpectedly come forth from amidst society's most trivial and handselled furniture, to enjoy its perfect summer life at last!

I do not say that John or Jonathan will realize all this;[218] but such is the character of that morrow which mere lapse of time can never make to dawn. The light which puts out our eyes is darkness to us. Only that day dawns to which we are awake. There is more day to dawn. The sun is but a morning star.[219]

---

[216]This passage, with its river metaphor for "the life in us," evokes Emerson's characterization of human thought as it arises in the Oversoul. Cf. Ralph Waldo Emerson, "The Over-Soul," par. 2. Note, however, the graphic quality of the Thoreau approximation. The muskrat constructs either a burrow (on a bank near water) or a hut (in marshy land) for habitation. In both cases, the muskrat provides an underwater entrance for the higher, above-water structure. But if an area should flood, the muskrat accordingly risks drowning. Here, at any rate, the muskrats seem to symbolize the unwanted—perhaps moral flaws or problems.

[217]Thoreau most likely based his narrative on an account in John Warner Barber, *Massachusetts Historical Collections . . . Relating to the History and Antiquities of Every Town in Massachusetts, with Geographical Descriptions* (Worcester: Dorr, Howland, 1839) 108-109, with which, according to Walter Harding (Thoreau, *Variorum Walden,* 320), he was familiar. There are, however, differences in some details. For the publication history of the anecdote of the insect—used, eventually, by Herman Melville for his short story "The Apple-Tree Table, or Original Spiritual Manifestations" (1856)—see Douglas Sackman, "The Original of Melville's Apple-Tree Table," *American Literature* 11:4 (January 1940): 448-51.

[218]The names *John* and *Jonathan* are probably used here to indicate, respectively, the typical British and American citizen.

[219]Thoreau ends in a resounding statement of his theme of awakening, with a millennial optimism that is characteristic (cf. n. 39 to Thoreau, "Civil Disobedience"). Walter Harding (Thoreau, *Variorum Walden,* 321) notes the similarity of Thoreau's conclusion to the statement in Emerson's essay "Politics" (1844): "We think our civilization near its meridian, but we are yet only at the cock-crowing and the morning star." (See Emerson, *Complete Works,* 3:216-17.)

BIBLIOGRAPHY

The literature concerning American Transcendentalism—especially general studies and studies of Ralph Waldo Emerson and Henry David Thoreau—is vast and many-sided. In the selected bibliography that follows, I have kept the intentions of this volume uppermost and have directed attention, where possible, to materials and interpretations that stress religious themes.

Where I have thought it necessary, I have made brief annotations regarding the materials. In some cases, a book appears in the listing more than once because it is relevant in two distinct categories. Finally, for reason of availability I have generally given complete facts of publication for more recent reprints of older works rather than for the original printings. Given the importance of Transcendentalism to the literary and cultural history of the United States, the range of such reprints is wide and convenient.

I. Transcendentalism and Its General Background

A. Primary Sources

The Dial: A Magazine for Literature, Philosophy, and Religion. 4 vols. July 1840–April 1844. Reprint. New York: Russell & Russell, 1961.

Hochfield, George, ed. *Selected Writings of the American Transcendentalists.* New York: Signet Classics, 1966.

Miller, Perry, ed. *The American Transcendentalists: Their Prose and Poetry.* Garden City NY: Doubleday, Anchor Books, 1957.

_____. *The Transcendentalists: An Anthology.* 1950. Reprint. Cambridge: Harvard University Press, 1971.

B. Anthologies of Criticism

Barbour, Brian M., ed. *American Transcendentalism: An Anthology of Criticism.* Notre Dame IN: University of Notre Dame Press, 1973.

Simon, Myron, and Thornton H. Parsons, eds. *Transcendentalism and Its Legacy.* Ann Arbor: University of Michigan Press, 1966.

Whicher, George F., and Gail Kennedy, eds. *The Transcendentalist Revolt.* Rev. ed. Lexington MA: Heath, 1968.

C. Other Secondary Sources

Albanese, Catherine L. *Corresponding Motion: Transcendental Religion and the New America*. Philadelphia: Temple University Press, 1977.

Boller, Paul F., Jr. *American Transcendentalism, 1830–1860: An Intellectual Inquiry*. New York: G. P. Putnam's Sons, 1974.

Brooks, Van Wyck. *The Flowering of New England*. New York: Dutton, 1936.

Buell, Lawrence. *Literary Transcendentalism: Style and Vision in the American Renaissance*. Ithaca NY: Cornell University Press, 1973.

Christy, Arthur E. *The Orient in American Transcendentalism: A Study of Emerson, Thoreau, and Alcott*. 1932. Reprint. New York: Octagon Books, 1978.

Cooke, George Willis. *An Historical and Biographical Introduction to Accompany* The Dial. 1902. 2 vols. Reprint. New York: Russell & Russell, 1961.

Frothingham, Octavius Brooks. *Transcendentalism in New England: A History*. 1876. Reprint. Gloucester MA: Peter Smith, 1965.

Goddard, Harold C. *Studies in New England Transcendentalism*. 1908. Reprint. New York: Humanities Press, 1969.

Gohdes, Clarence L. F. *The Periodicals of American Transcendentalism*. 1931. Reprint. New York: AMS Press, 1970.

Gura, Philip F. *The Wisdom of Words: Language, Theology, and Literature in the New England Renaissance*. Middletown CT: Wesleyan University Press, 1981.

Hutchison, William R. *The Transcendentalist Ministers: Church Reform in the New England Renaissance*. 1959. Reprint. Boston: Beacon Press, 1965.

Kaplan, Nathaniel, and Thomas Katsaros. *The Origins of American Transcendentalism in Philosophy and Mysticism*. New Haven: College & University Press, 1975.

Kern, Alexander. "The Rise of Transcendentalism, 1815–1860." In *Transitions in American Literary History*, edited by Harry Hayden Clark. 1954. Reprint. New York: Octagon Books, 1967.

Matthiessen, F. O. *American Renaissance: Art and Experience in the Age of Emerson and Whitman*. 1941. Reprint. London: Oxford University Press, 1979.

Miller, Perry. *Nature's Nation*. Cambridge: Harvard University Press, 1967.

Mumford, Lewis. *The Golden Day*. 1926. Reprint. New York: Dover Publications, 1968.

Parrington, Vernon L. "The Transcendental Mind." In *Main Currents in American Thought*. Vol. 2. 1927. Reprint (3 vols. in 1). New York: Harcourt, Brace and World, 1958.

Rose, Anne C. *Transcendentalism as a Social Movement, 1830–1850*. New Haven: Yale University Press, 1981.

Schneider, Herbert W. "The Transcendental Temper." In *A History of American Philosophy*. 2d ed. New York: Columbia University Press, 1963.

Smithline, Arnold. *Natural Religion in American Literature*. New Haven: College and University Press, 1966.

Stoehr, Taylor. *Nay-Saying in Concord: Emerson, Alcott, and Thoreau*. Hamden CT: Archon Books, 1979.

Swift, Lindsay. *Brook Farm: Its Members, Scholars, and Visitors*. 1900. Reprint. Gloucester MA: Peter Smith, n.d.

Wright, Conrad. *The Beginnings of Unitarianism in America*. 1955. Reprint. Hamden CT: Archon Books, 1976.

II. Ralph Waldo Emerson (1803–1882)

A. Primary Sources

Emerson, Ralph Waldo. *The Complete Works of Ralph Waldo Emerson*. Edited by Edward Waldo Emerson. Centenary ed. 12 vols. Boston: Houghton, Mifflin, 1903–1904. Reprint. New York: AMS Press, 1968. (The standard edition of Emerson's writings.)

─────────. *The Collected Works of Ralph Waldo Emerson*. Edited by Alfred R. Ferguson et al. 3 vols. to date. Cambridge: Harvard University Press, Belknap Press, 1971–. (This is the new critical edition being published with the endorsement of the Center for Editions of American Authors of the Modern Language Association of America.)

─────────. *The Early Lectures of Ralph Waldo Emerson*. Edited by Stephen E. Whicher et al. 3 vols. Cambridge: Harvard University Press, Belknap Press, 1966–1972.

─────────. *The Journals of Ralph Waldo Emerson*. Edited by Edward Waldo Emerson and Waldo Emerson Forbes. 10 vols. Boston: Houghton Mifflin, 1909–1914. (The standard edition until recently.)

─────────. *The Journals and Miscellaneous Notebooks of Ralph Waldo Emerson*. Edited by William H. Gilman et al. 16 vols. to date. Cambridge: Harvard University Press, Belknap Press, 1960–. (New critical edition.)

─────────. *The Letters of Ralph Waldo Emerson*. Edited by Ralph L. Rusk. 6 vols. 1939. Reprint. New York: Columbia University Press, 1966.

─────────, and Thomas Carlyle. *The Correspondence of Emerson and Carlyle*. Edited by Joseph Slater. New York: Columbia University Press, 1964.

B. Classic Biography

Rusk, Ralph L. *The Life of Ralph Waldo Emerson*. 1949. Reprint. New York: Columbia University Press, 1967.

C. Other Secondary Sources

Allen, Gay Wilson. *Waldo Emerson: A Biography*. New York: Viking Press, 1981.

Bishop, Jonathan. *Emerson on the Soul*. Cambridge: Harvard University Press, 1964.

Cabot, James E. *A Memoir of Ralph Waldo Emerson*. 2 vols. 1887. Reprint. Folcroft PA: Folcroft Library Editions, 1973.

Carpenter, Frederick Ives. *Emerson and Asia*. 1930. Reprint. Studies in Comparative Literature, no. 35. New York: Haskell, 1969.

─────────. *Emerson Handbook*. 1953. Reprint. New York: Hendricks House, 1967.

Clebsch, William A. "The Hospitable Universe of Ralph Waldo Emerson." In *American Religious Thought: A History*. Chicago History of American Religion. Chicago: University of Chicago Press, 1973.

Duncan, Jeffrey L. *The Power and Form of Emerson's Thought*. Charlottesville: University Press of Virginia, 1973.

Gray, Henry D. *Emerson: A Statement of New England Transcendentalism as Expressed in the Philosophy of Its Chief Exponent*. 1917. Reprint. New York: Frederick Ungar Publishing, 1965.

Hoeltje, Hubert H. *Sheltering Tree: A Story of the Friendship of Ralph Waldo Emerson and Amos Bronson Alcott*. 1943. Reprint. Port Washington NY: Kennikat Press, 1965.

Hughes, Gertrude Reif. *Emerson's Demanding Optimism*. Baton Rouge: Louisiana State University Press, 1984.

McAleer, John. *Ralph Waldo Emerson: Days of Encounter*. Boston: Little, Brown, 1984.

Miller, Perry. "From Edwards to Emerson." In *Errand into the Wilderness*. 1956. Reprint. New York: Harper & Row, Harper Torchbooks, 1964.

Paul, Sherman. *Emerson's Angle of Vision: Man and Nature in American Experience*. 1952. Reprint. Cambridge: Harvard University Press, 1969.

Porte, Joel. *Emerson and Thoreau: Transcendentalists in Conflict*. Middletown CT: Wesleyan University Press, 1966.

_____. *Representative Man: Ralph Waldo Emerson in His Time*. New York: Oxford University Press, 1979.

Robinson, David. *Apostle of Culture: Emerson as Preacher and Lecturer*. Philadelphia: University of Pennsylvania Press, 1982.

Wagenknecht, Edward. *Ralph Waldo Emerson: Portrait of a Balanced Soul*. New York: Oxford University Press, 1974.

Whicher, Stephen E. *Freedom and Fate: An Inner Life of Ralph Waldo Emerson*. 2d ed. Philadelphia: University of Pennsylvania Press, 1971.

Wright, Conrad. "Emerson, Barzillai Frost, and the Divinity School Address." In *The Liberal Christians: Essays on American Unitarian History*. Boston: Beacon Press, 1970.

III. Amos Bronson Alcott (1799–1888)

A. Primary Sources

No full edition of Amos Bronson Alcott's writings exists. Separate editions of his most important works include the following:

Alcott, Amos Bronson. *Concord Days*. 1872. Reprint. Ann Arbor MI: University Microfilms, 1972. (This and subsequent University Microfilms editions are printed books, facsimile photocopies of original editions.)

_____. *The Doctrine and Discipline of Human Culture*. 1836. Reprint. Ann Arbor MI: University Microfilms, 1978. (*Doctrine and Discipline* is the introductory essay that appears in *Record of Conversations on the Gospels* below.)

_____. *Essays on Education (1830–1862) by Amos Bronson Alcott*. Edited by Walter Harding. Gainesville FL: Scholars' Facsimiles & Reprints, 1960.

_____. *New Connecticut: An Autobiographical Poem*. Edited by F. B. Sanborn. 1887. Reprint. Philadelphia: A. Saifer, 1970.

_____. *Observations on the Principles and Methods of Infant Instruction*. Boston: Carter and Hendee, 1830.

_____. *Orphic Sayings*. Introduced by William Peirce Randal. Mt. Vernon NY: Golden Eagle Press, 1939. (100 Orphic sayings from *The Dial*.)

_____. *Ralph Waldo Emerson: An Estimate of His Character and Genius, in Prose and Verse*. 1882. Reprint. Ann Arbor MI: University Microfilms, 1978.

_____. *Record of Conversations on the Gospels* (*Conversations with Children on the Gospels*). 2 vols. 1836–1837. Reprint. New York: Arno Press, 1972.

_____. *Sonnets and Canzonets*. 1882. Reprint. Philadelphia: A. Saifer, 1969.

_____. *Table-Talk*. 1877. Reprint. Ann Arbor MI: University Microfilms, 1978.

_____. *Tablets*. 1868. Reprint. Ann Arbor MI: University Microfilms, 1978.

_____. *The Journals of Bronson Alcott*. Selected and edited by Odell Shepard. 1938. Reprint. 2 vols. Port Washington NY: Kennikat Press, 1966.

_____. *The Letters of A. Bronson Alcott*. Edited by Richard L. Herrnstadt. Ames: Iowa State University Press, 1969.

B. Classic Biography

Shepard, Odell. *Pedlar's Progress: The Life of Bronson Alcott*. 1937. Reprint. New York: Greenwood Press, 1968.

C. Other Secondary Sources

Bedell, Madelon. *The Alcotts: Biography of a Family*. New York: Clarkson N. Potter, 1980.

Dahlstrand, Frederick C. *Amos Bronson Alcott: An Intellectual Biography*. Rutherford NJ: Fairleigh Dickinson University Press, 1982.

Hoeltje, Hubert H. *Sheltering Tree: A Story of the Friendship of Ralph Waldo Emerson and Amos Bronson Alcott*. 1943. Reprint. Port Washington NY: Kennikat Press, 1965.

McCuskey, Dorothy. *Bronson Alcott, Teacher*. 1940. Reprint. New York: Arno Press, 1969.

Peabody, Elizabeth Palmer. *Record of a School, Exemplifying the General Principles of Spiritual Character*. 1835. Reprint. New York: Arno Press, 1969. (This is an account of proceedings in Alcott's classroom at the Temple School by his assistant, who also recorded the "conversations" in *Record of Conversations on the Gospels*.)

Sanborn, Franklin B. *Bronson Alcott at Alcott House, England, and Fruitlands, New England, 1842–1844*. 1908. Reprint. Folcroft PA: Folcroft Library Editions, 1974.

_____, and William T. Harris. *A. Bronson Alcott: His Life and Philosophy*. 2 vols. 1893. Reprint. New York: Biblo and Tannen, 1965.

Sears, Clara Endicott. *Bronson Alcott's Fruitlands*. 1915. Reprint. Philadelphia: Porcupine Press, 1975.

IV. Theodore Parker (1810–1860)

A. Primary Sources

The standard—though neither complete nor accurate—editions of Theodore Parker's writings are the following:

Parker, Theodore. *The Collected Works of Theodore Parker.* Edited by Frances Cobbe. 14 vols. London: Trübner, 1863–1865.

―――――. *The Works of Theodore Parker.* Centenary ed. 15 vols. Boston: American Unitarian Association, 1907–1911.

The three selections by Parker contained in this volume may be found respectively in the works listed below:

Parker, Theodore. *The Critical and Miscellaneous Writings.* Boston: James Munroe, 1843.

―――――. *A Discourse of Matters Pertaining to Religion.* 4th ed. Boston: Little, Brown, 1856.

―――――. "A Sermon of the Delights of Piety." In *Proceedings of the Pennsylvania Yearly Meeting of Progressive Friends, 1855.* New York: John F. Trow, Printer, 1855.

In addition, some materials are contained in the following works:

Collins, Robert E., ed. *Theodore Parker: American Transcendentalist. A Critical Essay and a Collection of His Writings.* Metuchen NJ: Scarecrow Press, 1973.

Commager, Henry Steele, ed. *Theodore Parker: An Anthology.* Boston: Beacon Press, 1960.

Dirks, John E. *The Critical Theology of Theodore Parker.* 1948. Reprint. Westport CT: Greenwood Press, 1970. (Contains the complete text of the "Levi Blodgett Letter.")

Weiss, John. *The Life and Correspondence of Theodore Parker.* 2 vols. 1863. Reprint of 1864 ed. New York: Arno Press, 1969.

B. Classic Biography

Commager, Henry Steele. *Theodore Parker.* 2d ed. 1960. Reprint. Gloucester MA: Peter Smith, 1978.

C. Other Secondary Sources

Brown, Jerry Wayne. "The Enemy Within: Theodore Parker as a Biblical Critic." In *The Rise of Biblical Criticism in America, 1800–1870: The New England Scholars.* Middletown CT: Wesleyan University Press, 1969.

Chadwick, John White. *Theodore Parker: Preacher and Reformer.* 1900. Reprint. St. Clair Shores MI: Scholarly Press, 1971.

Dirks, John E. *The Critical Theology of Theodore Parker.* 1948. Reprint. Westport CT: Greenwood Press, 1970.

Fellman, Michael. "Theodore Parker and the Abolitionist Role in the 1850s." *Journal of American History* 61 (December 1974): 666-84.

Frothingham, Octavius Brooks. *Theodore Parker: A Biography.* Boston: J. R. Osgood, 1874.

Newbrough, George F. "Reason and Understanding in the Works of Theodore Parker." *The South Atlantic Quarterly* 47 (January 1948): 64-75.

Nichols, Charles H. "Theodore Parker and the Transcendental Rhetoric: The Liberal Tradition and America's Debate on the Eve of Secession, 1832–1861." *Jahrbuch für Amerikastudien* 13 (1968): 69-83.

Smith, H. Shelton. "Was Theodore Parker a Transcendentalist?" *The New England Quarterly* 23 (September 1950): 351-64.

Weiss, John. *The Life and Correspondence of Theodore Parker*. 2 vols. 1863. Reprint of 1864 ed. New York: Arno Press, 1969. (While this work contains primary material, it is also the earliest "life" of Parker.)

V. Henry David Thoreau (1817–1862)

A. Primary Sources

Thoreau, Henry David. *The Writings of Henry David Thoreau*. Walden ed. 20 vols. Boston: Houghton Mifflin, 1906. Reprint. New York: AMS Press, 1968. (The traditional standard edition of Thoreau's writings.)

——. The Writings of Henry D. Thoreau. Edited by Walter Harding et al. 7 vols. to date. Princeton: Princeton University Press, 1971–. (This is a series of individual titles that together constitute the new critical edition, published with the endorsement of the Center for Editions of American Authors of the Modern Language Association of America.)

——. *Collected Poems of Henry Thoreau*. Edited by Carl Bode. 1943. Reprint. Baltimore: Johns Hopkins University Press, 1964.

——. *The Correspondence of Henry David Thoreau*. Edited by Walter Harding and Carl Bode. 1958. Reprint. Westport CT: Greenwood Press, 1974.

Miller, Perry, ed. *Consciousness in Concord: The Text of Thoreau's Hitherto "Lost Journal" (1840–1841), Together with Notes and a Commentary*. Boston: Houghton Mifflin, 1958.

B. Classic Biography

Harding, Walter. *The Days of Henry Thoreau*. New York: Alfred A. Knopf, 1965. (Enl. ed., New York: Dover, 1982.)

C. Other Secondary Sources

Anderson, Charles R. *The Magic Circle of Walden*. New York: Holt, Rinehart & Winston, 1968.

Bishop, Jonathan. "The Experience of the Sacred in Thoreau's *Week*." *ELH* 33:1 (March 1966): 66-91.

Blair, John G., and Augustus Trowbridge. "Thoreau on Katahdin." *American Quarterly* 12:4 (Winter 1960): 508-17.

Canby, Henry Seidel. *Thoreau*. 1939. Reprint. Gloucester MA: Peter Smith, 1965.

Christie, John Aldrich. *Thoreau as World Traveler*. New York: Columbia University Press, 1965.

Cook, Reginald L. "Nature Mysticism." In *Passage to Walden*. 2d ed. New York: Russell & Russell, 1966.

Friesen, Victor Carl. *The Spirit of the Huckleberry: Sensuousness in Henry Thoreau*. Edmonton, Canada: University of Alberta Press, 1984.

Garber, Frederick. *Thoreau's Redemptive Imagination*. New York: New York University Press, 1977.

Harding, Walter, and Michael Meyer. *The New Thoreau Handbook*. New York: New York University Press, 1980.

Hicks, John H., ed. *Thoreau in Our Season*. Amherst: University of Massachusetts Press, 1962.

Krutch, Joseph Wood. *Henry David Thoreau*. 1948. Reprint. Westport CT: Greenwood Press, 1973.

MacShane, Frank. "*Walden* and Yoga." *The New England Quarterly* 37:3 (September 1964): 322-42.

Oliver, Egbert S. "Thoreau and the Puritan Tradition." *The Emerson Society Quarterly* 44 (1966): 79-86.

Paul, Sherman. *The Shores of America: Thoreau's Inward Exploration*. 1958. Reprint. Urbana: University of Illinois Press, 1972.

Porte, Joel. *Emerson and Thoreau: Transcendentalists in Conflict*. Middletown CT: Wesleyan University Press, 1966.

Ruland, Richard, ed. *Twentieth Century Interpretations of Walden: A Collection of Critical Essays*. Englewood Cliffs NJ: Prentice-Hall, 1968. (Especially essays by Reginald L. Cook, "Ancient Rites at Walden," and John B. Pickard, "The Religion of 'Higher Laws.' ")

Stein, William Bysshe. "The Hindu Matrix of *Walden*: The King's Son." *Comparative Literature* 22:4 (Fall 1970): 303-18.

??????. "Thoreau's First Book, A Spoor of Yoga: The Orient in *A Week on the Concord and Merrimack Rivers*." *The Emerson Society Quarterly* 41 (1965): 3-25.

??????. "Thoreau's *Walden* and the *Bhagavad Gita*." *Topic* 3 (1963): 38-55.

??????. "Thoreau's *A Week* and *Om* Cosmography." *American Transcendental Quarterly* 11 (1971): 15-37.

??????. "The Yoga of *Walden*: Chapter 1 ('Economy')." *Literature East and West* 8:1 & 2 (June 1969): 1-26.

Wolf, William J. *Thoreau: Mystic, Prophet, Ecologist*. Philadelphia: United Church Press, Pilgrim Press, 1974. (Contains a useful bibliography—including articles and shorter pieces—on Thoreau's religion.)

In addition, the editorial material in the following editions of Thoreau's "Civil Disobedience" and *Walden* may prove useful:

Thoreau, Henry D. *The Annotated* Walden: Walden; or, Life in the Woods. Edited by Philip Van Doren Stern. New York: Clarkson N. Potter, 1970. (Also contains an annotated edition of "Civil Disobedience.")

??????. *The Variorum Civil Disobedience*. Edited by Walter Harding. New York: Twayne Publishers, 1967.

??????. *The Variorum Walden*. Edited by Walter Harding. New York: Twayne Publishers, 1962.

Index

Abaddon, 174
Abolitionism. *See* Slavery
Abraham, 209, 229
Aeolus, 49
Aesthetic Papers, 12, 237, 275-76, 288
Aids to Reflection (Coleridge), 7, 59, 67, 152, 158, 168, 172
Alcott, Abigail May, 16, 18, 149
Alcott, Amos Bronson, 1, 13, 25, 151-52, 169, 173, 175, 177, 202, 288
  biographical sketch, 147-49
  and Coleridge, 158, 167-68, 172, 184
  and correspondence, idea of, 23, 162, 171
  and *The Dial,* 11-12, 164-65
  and Emerson, 32, 72
  and Fruitlands, 14, 16, 149, 161
  on genius, 157-58, 302
  on Jesus, 152, 154, 156, 163, 186
  on Lapse, doctrine of, 7, 72, 167, 174
  on miracles, 176
  and mysticism, 24, 26, 72, 163, 165-67, 178
  and nature, 24, 162, 165
  and Neoplatonism, 7, 26, 46, 72, 149, 152, 159, 161, 164, 167, 171
  "Orphic Sayings," 12, 27, 73, 151, 164-66
  and Plato, 153, 159-61, 164, 171, 186
  and Quakerism, 147
  and slavery, 18
  and the Temple School, 10, 19, 151
  and Thoreau, 287, 312
  and Unitarianism, 5, 176
Alcott, Louisa May, 149
Alcott, William, 177
Alcott House, 19, 148
Alexander the Great, 53, 328
Alfred the Great, 115
Allston, Washington, 107
American Indians, 17, 215-16, 236, 266, 274, 284, 290, 296-97, 299, 312
American Journal of Education, 151

American Unitarian Association, 4
Amrita, 251
Analects of Confucius, 245, 286, 294, 305
Anaxagoras, 125
Andes Mountains, 112, 129
Animal magnetism, 74, 299
Anthony, Saint, 114
Antigone (Sophocles), 66, 276
Apollo, 82, 128, 258
Arabian Nights, 305
Ararat, Mount, 129
Ariel, 66
Arrian (Flavius Arrianus), 95
Asceticism, 161, 165, 316, 318
Assyria, 51, 341
Atlantic Monthly, 132, 135, 266
Atlantis, 328
Atlas, 271
Augustine, Saint, 129
Aurora, 258, 302
Aztecs, 297

Bacon, Francis, 58, 170
Bacon, Roger, 57
Bancroft, George, 6
Baptism, 188
Baptists, 39, 221
Bartram, William, 296
Beecher, Henry Ward, 225
Bentham, Jeremy, 122
Berengar of Tours, 195
Bering, Vitus Jonassen, 125
Berkeley, George, 68
Bernard of Clairvaux, Saint, 224-25
Berserker, 140
Bhagavad Gita, 8, 132, 240, 245, 248-53, 308, 324, 327, 337-38
Biographia Literaria (Coleridge), 158
Bismarck, Otto von, 304
Blavatsky, Helena, 68

Boehme, Jacob, 7-8, 98, 152
Bonaventura, Saint, 226
Boston, 1-2, 4, 8-9, 14, 16, 19, 25, 31, 34, 147-48, 151, 182, 201, 221, 224, 257, 266, 304, 310, 316
Boston Association of Ministers, 182
Boston Cultivator, 327
Boston Daily Advertiser, 18, 164
Boston Infant School Society, 147
Boston Latin School, 31
Boston Quarterly Review, 12, 19, 149, 164
Boston Transcript, 164
Brahma, 132, 248-49, 306, 327
Brahman, 8, 132, 248, 251, 306
Brisbane, Albert, 15
Brook Farm, 8-9, 14-15, 17, 19, 126, 237
Brown, John, 236
Brown, Lucy Jackson, 262
Brown, Thomas, 5
Brownson, Orestes A., 2, 7, 10, 12, 16, 19, 24, 164, 236
Buddhism, 247
Buell, Lawrence, 24-25
Buffon, Georges-Louis Leclerc, comte de, 55
Bunyan, John, 147, 227, 244, 293
Burns, Anthony, 18, 182-83

Cabot, James Elliot, 17, 33, 81, 127
Cabot, Lydia, 181
Caesar, Julius, 114, 207
Calchas, 206
Calvinism, 4-5, 11, 36
Campbell, Thomas, 254
Canby, Henry Seidel, 235
Caratach, 121
Carew, Thomas, 300
Carlyle, Thomas, 6, 32, 141, 175, 295
Catholicism, 36, 99, 103
Cato, 207
Celibacy, 149
Ceres, 313-14
Chadwick, John White, 25
"Chaldaean Oracles of Zoroaster," 121, 254
Champollion, Jean-François, 46-47, 331
Channing, William Ellery (the Elder), 41-42
Channing, (William) Ellery, 2, 12-13, 32, 237, 266, 297
Channing, William Henry (the Younger), 2, 10, 12, 16-17, 19, 304
Chaos, 269, 271, 273-74, 332
Chardon Street Convention, 19
Charles II (king of England), 103
Chaucer, Geoffrey, 259
Cheshire Pestalozzian School, 147
Christian Examiner, 10, 183, 191
Christian Philosopher, The (Mather), 2
Christian Register and Boston Observer, 11

Christian Science, 45, 177
Christian Union, 16
Christianity
 Alcott and, 159
 Emerson and, 41, 43, 58, 80
 and miracles, 43, 181, 185
 and mysticism, 58
 "Orphic Sayings" and, 164
 Parker and, 181, 185-86, 193, 196, 209
 Thoreau and, 240, 290, 334
 and Transcendentalism, 3-4, 6, 9-10, 17, 21-22, 26-28
Christianity as a Purely Internal Principle (Francis), 10
Christie, John Aldrich, 23
Christina (queen of Sweden), 103
Chrysostom, Saint John, 129
Church of England, 36
Church of the Disciples, 16
Church of the New Jerusalem, 45, 99, 243. *See also* Swedenborg, Emanuel; Swedenborgianism
"Civil Disobedience" (Thoreau), 13, 237-38, 275-76, 280
Civil War (Lucan), 207
Clarke, James Freeman, 2, 10-12, 16
Clarke, Dr. John, 221
Clarkson, Thomas, 114
Coke, Sir Edward, 278
Coleridge, Samuel Taylor, 6-7, 32, 45, 53, 59, 62, 65-67, 81, 91, 101, 152, 158, 167-68, 172, 181, 184
Come-outer Convention, 19
Commager, Henry Steele, 15, 18, 186
Concord, Massachusetts, 17, 32, 76, 84, 135, 148, 175, 235-37, 275, 283, 286, 289, 297-98, 306, 313, 323
Concord School, 235
Concord School of Philosophy, 148
Conduct of Life, The (Emerson), 33, 141
Confucianism, 8, 245, 286, 288, 294, 301, 305, 310, 321-22, 339
Consistent eschatology, 191
Consubstantiation, 36
Convention of Non-Resistants, 19
Convention of the Friends of Universal Reform, 19
Conway, Moncure, 17
Copernicus, Nicholas, 112, 262, 282
Correspondence, idea of, 21-26
 Alcott and, 162
 Emerson and, 22- 23, 45, 54, 90, 94, 101, 134, 138, 162
 Thoreau and, 311, 314-15, 318, 330-31
Council of Reims, 224
Cousin, Victor, 7
Crafts, Ellen, 182-83
Crafts, William, 182-83

Critical and Historical Introduction to the Canonical Scriptures of the Old Testament (De Wette), 183
Croesus, 339
Cromwell, Oliver, 103
Cronos, 171
Crowe, Charles, 15
Cudworth, Ralph, 36, 46
Cyclopes, 271

Daedalus, 130
Dana, Richard Henry, Jr., 336
David (king of Israel), 197-98
De Wette, Wilhelm M. L., 183, 190
Delphi, 128, 264
Democratic party, 19, 281
Denderah, 85
Dial, 1-2, 11-12, 32, 57, 127-28, 130, 139, 149, 164-66, 173, 183, 236-37, 262, 296
    second *Dial* (1860), 12
Diogenes, 125
Discourse of Matters Pertaining to Religion, A (Parker), 182-84, 194, 201
Discourse of the Transient and Permanent in Christianity, A (Parker), 13, 182, 184, 185-86, 201-202, 216
Discourse on the Latest Form of Infidelity, A (Norton), 185
Divinity School Address (Emerson), 33, 76, 101, 104, 128, 181, 185-86
Dix, Dorothea, 18
Docetists, 193
Doctrine and Discipline of Human Culture, The (Alcott), 149-52, 165, 167, 186
Dodona, 264
Dorcas, 206
Druids, 209
Dunkers, 39
Dwight, John Sullivan, 12

Eastern thought: and Transcendentalism, 8, 27, 237, 239, 245, 306-307
Ebionites, 197
Echo, 242
Eclecticism, 7, 108
Eddy, Mary Baker, 45
Edwards, Jonathan, 2-3, 204, 217
Eichhorn, Johann Gottfried, 190
Elijah, 210
Elisha, 210
Emerson, Charles Chauncy, 31, 63
Emerson, Edith, 32
Emerson, Edward Bliss, 31, 63
Emerson, Edward Waldo, 32, 34
Emerson, Ellen, 32-33, 127
Emerson, Ralph Waldo, 1-2, 9, 13, 25, 38-42, 50, 67-69, 73, 82, 84-85, 95-96, 112-14, 118, 121, 123-24, 127-31, 141, 148, 157, 164-67, 172, 174, 181, 186, 202, 260, 263, 284, 288, 306, 341
    biographical sketch, 31-33
    and Brook Farm, 14-15, 126, 237
    and correspondence, idea of, 22-24, 45, 54, 90, 94, 101, 134, 138, 162, 314
    and the *Dial*, 11-12, 127, 139, 296
    and Eastern thought, 8, 132, 237
    and Gnosticism, 97, 106, 109, 115
    on Jesus, 76, 79, 81, 101, 138-39
    on miracles, 81-82, 101, 116, 134, 185
    and the moral sentiment, 76-77, 79
    and mysticism, 31, 48, 58, 68, 72, 76, 80, 93, 96, 98, 100, 106, 112, 132-33, 135
    on nature, 23-24, 26-27, 45-46, 101, 120, 127, 134, 138, 162
    and Neoplatonism, 45-48, 68, 72, 76-77, 79-80, 87, 91, 93, 97-98, 108, 139
    and the Oversoul, 48, 76, 80, 87, 91, 93, 97, 100, 114-15, 128, 135, 137, 141, 255, 282, 287, 319, 342
    and the Reason and the Understanding, 59, 65, 81, 99, 184
    and self-culture, 13, 15, 17, 91, 106, 178
    and social reform, 17-18
    and Swedenborgianism, 7, 11, 34, 45, 47, 54, 91, 97, 99, 122
    and Thoreau, 235-37, 245-46, 287, 289, 315-16
    and Unitarianism, 5, 13, 34, 41, 43, 45, 76, 81, 93, 101, 116, 134, 185
    and the *Western Messenger*, 11, 127, 133-34
    and women's rights, 17
Emerson, Waldo, 32, 135, 138
Emerson, William, 34, 235
Enlightenment, 4, 10, 89, 187, 225, 319
Epaminondas, 83
Erasmus, Desiderius, 195
Essay Concerning Human Understanding, An (Locke), 4
Euler, Leonhard, 67
Europe, 6, 8, 19, 183, 285
    Emerson's trip to, 31-32
Everett, Edward, 6
Evil, 109, 158
    good and, 5, 79, 106, 273

"Fate" (Emerson), 33, 141
Faust (Goethe), 143
Fichte, Johann G., 6
Fletcher, John, 121
Follen, Charles T. C., 6
Foot washing, 39
Fourier, Charles, 12, 15, 122
Fourierists, 14-15, 17, 19
Fourth Lateran Council, 36
Fox, George, 34, 58, 227-28

Francis, Convers, 2, 10-11
Franklin, Sir John, 125
French Revolution, 89
Frost, Barzillai, 76, 84
Frothingham, Octavius B., 3, 12, 20, 24, 184, 217
Fruitlands, 9, 14, 16, 149, 161, 237, 319
Fuller, Margaret, 2, 11-13, 15, 19, 24-25, 32, 149, 164, 296
Furness, William H., 2, 10, 13, 81

Galilei, Galileo, 112, 262-63
Gandhi, Mohandas, 276
Garrison, William Lloyd, 17-18, 282
Gehenna, 207
Genius, 153-54, 158, 302, 319
Gerizim, 209
German Brethren, 39
Glas, John, 39
Gnosticism, 68, 91, 97, 106, 109, 115, 182
God, 159, 206, 213, 248, 332
   Alcott on, 162-63, 167, 170, 172, 174
   Berkeley on, 68
   Coleridge on, 172
   Emerson on, 41, 76, 80, 91, 101, 112, 127, 129, 135, 138-39, 174
   as Father-Mother, 218, 226, 229, 260
   of Israel, 198, 211, 276
   and nature, 2-3, 24, 101, 162, 201, 226, 290
   Parker on, 185-86, 191, 193, 196-97, 201-202, 217-18, 226, 229-30, 260
   Plato on, 139, 170
   pre-Socratic conception of, 61
   Puritans and, 2-4
   and self-culture, 14
   Thoreau on, 283, 290
   Unitarianism and, 5, 191, 224
   Universalists and, 224
Goddard, Harold, 3, 24
Goethe, Johann Wolfgang von, 62, 143
Gohdes, Clarence, 12
Gospels, 4, 9, 148, 224, 317. *See also* New Testament
Grace, 2-3, 34, 139, 188
Great Awakening, 4
Greek mythology, 49, 51, 58, 61, 73, 82, 109, 128, 130, 142, 157, 160, 165, 169, 171-73, 188-89, 196, 204, 206, 209, 213, 242-43, 258, 264, 269, 271, 273, 276, 292, 301-303, 307, 313, 322, 326, 328, 332, 340-41
Greeley, Horace, 19, 235, 289
Groton Convention, 19
Gustavus Adolphus (king of Sweden), 115

Habakkuk, 206
Hannibal, 114
Hanno, 328
Harbinger, 8

Harivamsa, 324-25
Harris, William Torrey, 148
Harvard University, 1-2, 4-6, 31, 76, 181, 185, 235-36, 245
Haskins, Ruth, 31
Hastings, Warren, 249-50
Hawes Place Church, 185
Hawthorne, Nathaniel, 15, 304, 322
Hedge, Frederic Henry, 2, 6
Hegel, G. W. F., 154
Herbal medicine, 9, 299
Herbert, George, 49, 72, 101, 139
Hercules, 196, 213, 292
Hesiod, 242, 332
Hesperides, 328
Hieroglyphics, 46-47, 54, 263, 331
Himalayas, 112, 254
Hinduism, 27, 57, 132, 241, 247, 249-52, 301, 311, 321. *See also Bhagavad Gita; Mahabharata; Samkhya Karika; Vedas*
Hoadley, Benjamin, 36
Hoar, Ebenezer Rockwood, 18
Holy Spirit, 3, 228
Homeopathy, 9
Howe, Samuel Gridley, 18
Hudson, Henry, 125
Hugh of St. Victor, 206
Huss, John, 99, 207
Hutchinson, Anne, 3
Hutton, James, 122
Hydropathy, 9

Iambe, 242
Idealism, 1, 3, 6-7, 10, 45, 61, 68, 77, 93, 153, 156, 158-59, 170, 186
Imitation of Christ, The (à Kempis), 96, 227
Independent (New York), 225
Indians. *See* American Indians
Indra, 132, 311, 327
Innocent III (pope), 35
Intuition, 6-7, 10, 24, 76, 97, 115, 185, 201, 217, 267
Isaac, 209, 229
Isaiah, 160

Jackson, Andrew, 8
Jackson, Lydia, 32, 135
Jacobi, Friedrich H., 6
James I (king of England), 103
Jefferson, Thomas, 277
Jehovah, 132
Jerome of Prague, 207
Jesus, 7, 10, 197, 206
   Alcott on, 152, 154, 156, 163
   Emerson on, 76, 79, 81, 101, 138-39
   and the Eucharist, nature of, 36, 195
   and German biblical criticism, 190

Parker on, 185-86, 188, 191, 193, 197, 199-202, 210
Thoreau on, 243, 249, 284, 317
and Transcendentalism, 9, 79, 101
and the Trinity, 41
Unitarianism and, 4-5, 9, 188, 190-91
Joel, 199
John the Baptist, 163
Jonah, 206
Jouffroy, Théodore, 7
Judaism, 36, 38, 174, 191, 207, 209, 211
Justin, 207

Kalidasa, 256
Kant, Immanuel, 6-7, 45, 81, 101, 182
Katahdin, Mount, 23-24, 266-69, 272, 334
Kempis, Thomas à, 96, 227
Kern, Alexander, 2, 7, 10
Kinetic spirituality, 23-24, 171
King, Martin Luther, Jr., 276
King's Chapel, 4
Knox, John, 283
Kratophany, 267
Krishna, 248, 250, 252, 253
Ktaadn. *See* Katahdin, Mount

"Laboring Classes, The" (Brownson), 19
Lane, Charles, 16, 148-49
Lanfranc, 195
Lapse, doctrine of, 7, 72, 167, 174
Last Judgment, 41, 207
Latter-day Saints, 197
Laud, William, 36
Lavoisier, Antoine, 121-22
Law, William, 227
Laws of Manu, 8, 245, 247-48, 323
Leibniz, Gottfried Wilhelm, Baron von, 58
Leonidas, 52
Leopold, Alexander, 73
Lethe, 109, 169
"Levi Blodgett Letter" (Parker), 182, 185-86, 202
Life of Jesus, a Critical Treatment, The (Strauss), 190- 91
Linnaeus, Carolus, 55
Locke, John, 4-6, 10, 101
Lord's Supper, 31, 34, 36, 188
Lovejoy, Elijah P., 17
Luther, Martin, 207, 282
Lutheranism, 36, 99

Mackintosh, James, 101
Macpherson, James, 309
Mahabharata, 68, 248, 252-53, 324, 338
Maine Woods, The (Thoreau), 23, 237-38, 266
Manichaeans, 68
Mann, Horace, 18
Manu, 248, 323. See also *Laws of Manu*

Marsh, James, 6-7, 81
Martineau, James, 10
Massachusetts Quarterly Review, 12, 183
Masséna, André, 89
Mather, Cotton, 2, 298
May, Samuel J., 18, 214
Mazzini, Giuseppe, 19
Memnon, 302
Mencius, 245, 322, 333
Mesmer, Franz Anton, 74
Mesmerism, 74, 299
Metempsychosis, 171
Methodism, 87
Mexican War, 18, 277, 279, 281, 342
Michaelis, Johann David, 190
Miller, Perry, 2, 4, 6
Milton, John, 52, 114, 267-69, 271-73
Minos, 204
Mirabeau, Honoré Gabriel Riquetti, Comte de, 335-36
Miracles, 4, 10, 43, 45, 81-82, 101, 116, 134, 176, 181-82, 185, 202
Molinos, Miguel de, 99
Monadnock, Mount, 132
Moravians, 99
Mormons. *See* Latter-day Saints
Morse, Samuel F. B., 304
Muhammad, 203
Murray, John, 224
Music Hall (Boston), 182, 217
Muslims, 203
Musquetaquid, 135
Mysticism
  Alcott and, 24, 26, 72, 163, 165-67, 178
  and correspondence, idea of, 21-22, 24
  Emerson and, 31, 48, 58, 68, 72, 76, 80, 93, 96, 98, 100, 106, 112, 132-33, 135
  Parker and, 182, 196-97, 217-18, 228, 230
  and Puritanism, 2-3
  and self-culture, 13-14, 106
  Thoreau and, 264, 308
  and Unitarianism, 6

Napoleon, 89, 133
Native Americans. *See* American Indians
Nature
  Alcott and, 24, 162, 165
  Emerson and, 23-24, 26-27, 45- 46, 101, 120, 127, 134, 138, 162
  God in, 2, 22
  Thoreau and, 24, 27, 69, 260, 267, 276, 289-90, 316-18, 329, 334-35
  and Transcendentalism, 9-11, 21-22, 24, 26, 320
  Voltaire on, 225
Nature (Emerson), 10, 13, 32-33, 45-47, 81, 91, 101, 124, 135, 165, 181, 236
Nayler, James, 228

Nebuchadnezzar, 72
Neoplatonism, 254
    Alcott and, 7, 26, 46, 72, 149, 152, 159, 161, 164, 167, 171
    Emerson and, 45-48, 68, 72, 76-77, 79-80, 87, 91, 93, 97-98, 108, 139
    Parker and, 182
    and Transcendentalism, 7- 8
New England Anti-Slavery Society, 18
New England Cultivator, 327
New England Farmer, 327
New Testament, 148, 152, 163, 195, 207, 210. *See also* Gospels
New Thought, 45, 177
New Views of Christianity, Society, and the Church (Brownson), 10
New-York Tribune, 19, 235, 289
Newton, Sir Isaac, 112, 204
Norton, Andrews, 182, 185, 190
Norton, Charles Eliot, 129
Novum Organum (Bacon), 58, 170
Numa, 209

Oberlin, Jean Fréderic, 88
Observations on the Growth of the Mind (Reed), 7
Odysseus, 49. *See also* Ulysses
Oedipus, 130, 141
Oegger, Guillaume, 58
Olcott, Henry S., 68
Olympus, Mount, 301
Oneidans, 14
Opium, 320
Orphic Mysteries, 73, 165
"Orphic Sayings" (Alcott), 12, 27, 73, 149-51, 164-66, 173, 178, 186
Osiris, 82
Ossian, 259, 309
Ossoli, Angelo, 19
Oversoul, 6, 48, 76, 80, 87, 91, 93, 97, 100, 114-15, 128, 135, 137, 141, 255, 282, 287, 319, 342
"Over-Soul, The" (Emerson), 33, 76, 91, 106
Ovid, 332
Owenites, 14

Paley, William, 101, 280
Palmyra, 123
Pan, 173, 242
Paphos, 51
Parker, Theodore, 2, 13, 24, 203-204, 206, 215, 225-26, 229, 288
    and antislavery, 9, 18, 182-83, 202, 213-14, 217
    biographical sketch, 181-84
    and Brook Farm, 15
    and Christianity, 26-27, 181, 185-86, 191, 195-97, 199-202, 209-10, 224, 306
    Emerson on, 181
    on Emerson's Divinity School *Address,* 76, 185-86
    on God, 24, 185-86, 196-97, 201-202, 204, 207, 217-18, 225-26, 229- 31
    on human nature, 193
    and mysticism, 182, 196-97, 217-18, 228, 230
    and Quakerism, 217-18, 221
    and social reform, 19, 216- 17
    and Unitarianism, 16, 182, 185-86, 188, 223, 227
Parmenides, 132
Parrington, Vernon L., 4
Parry, Sir William Edward, 125
Passover, 38
Paul, Saint, 41, 98, 210
Peabody, Elizabeth Palmer, 2, 12, 25, 58, 81, 148-49, 237, 275
Peace Society of Massachusetts, 18
Peale, Norman Vincent, 45
Penn, William, 228
Pentecost, 124, 128, 178, 199
Pestalozzi, Johann Heinrich, 19, 147, 152
Phidias, 123, 128
Phillips, Wendell, 18, 282
Phocion, 53, 125
Phrenology, 281, 326
Pietism, 6, 39, 99
Pilgrim's Progress (Bunyan), 147, 227, 244, 293
Pindar, 53
Pitt, William, 113
Plato, 3, 7, 45, 54, 61, 98, 139, 142, 152, 156, 160, 175, 238
Platonism, 3, 7, 45, 54, 61, 82, 152-53, 159, 161-62, 164, 170- 71, 186, 206
Plotinus, 46, 57, 68, 79, 98, 105, 139, 152, 159
Plutarch, 125
Pollio, Marcus Vitruvius, 62
Pomola, 272
Pope, Alexander, 36, 101
Preliminary Anti-Slavery Society, 18
Presbyterianism, 195
Present, 12
Proclus, 152
Progressive Friends, 217
Prometheus, 157, 173, 243, 271
Prospero, 66
Protestantism, 3-4, 195. *See also* individual denominations
Proteus, 61
Psyche, 173
Puritanism, 2-4, 6, 22, 24, 31, 36, 93, 274
Pythagoras, 57, 112, 244

Quakerism, 3, 6, 25, 34, 147, 217, 221, 227-28
Quietists, 99

Radical, 12
Rappites, 14

Rationale of Religious Inquiry (Martineau), 10
Rationalism, 4-5, 10
Reason and the Understanding, The, 45, 59, 65, 81, 99, 168, 184
Record of Conversations on the Gospels (Alcott), 10, 19, 148-49, 151, 153
Reed, Sampson, 7
Reid, Thomas, 5, 101
Reimarus, Hermann Samuel, 191
Reincarnation, 137
Religious Union of Associationists, 16-17
Remarks on the Four Gospels (Furness), 10
Rerum Rusticarum, 312-14, 331
Ripley, George, 2, 7, 10-15, 19, 81, 182, 185
Roman mythology, 139, 153-54, 171, 207, 209, 258, 271, 291, 302, 308, 313-14, 322, 332
Romanticism, 7-8, 10, 319
Rosetta stone, 46
Russell, William, 52, 151-52
Rye House Plot, 52

Saddleback (Greylock) Mountain, 240, 256, 259, 267
Sa'di, Muslihuddin, 245, 300
Samkhya Karika, 245, 261, 306, 311, 317
Sanborn, Franklin B., 148
Sandeman, Robert, 39
Sandemanians, 39
Sartain, John, 266, 289
Satan, 269, 271, 273
Saturn, 171
Savonarola, 181, 184
Scanderbeg (George Castriota), 115
Scheherazade, 305
Schleiermacher, Friedrich, 6, 190, 201
Schliemann, Heinrich, 262
Scipio Africanus Major, 114
Scott, Job, 228
Scottish common sense philosophy, 5-6, 10, 76, 91, 97, 101, 278
Second Church (Boston), 31, 34, 45, 128-29
Self-culture, 13-14, 17, 24, 26, 91, 106, 152, 165, 178, 237
"Self-Reliance" (Emerson), 33, 76, 91, 106, 133, 167
Sermon of the Delights of Piety, A (Parker), 184, 217
Shackford, Charles C., 185
Shakers, 14, 73-74
Shakespeare, William, 66, 114-15, 306
Shakuntala (Kalidasa), 256
Shekinah, 211
Shepard, Odell, 151, 162, 165, 167
Sibylline Oracles, 209
Simeon, 199
Sin, 158, 161, 188, 282
Slavery, 17-18, 110, 182, 202, 213-14, 217, 228, 236, 279, 281- 82, 293

Society for Christian Union and Progress, 16
Society for the Abolition of Slavery, 17
Socrates, 61, 98, 125, 156, 162, 238, 276, 335
Solomon (king of Israel), 123, 198
Sophists, 175
Sophocles, 66, 276
Soul, 3, 10, 24, 45-47, 57, 61, 68, 73, 76, 80, 87, 91, 95, 119, 152, 159, 162, 165, 167, 169, 171, 178, 185, 202, 206, 226, 261
Specimens of Foreign Standard Literature (Ripley), 13
Sphinx, 58, 130-31, 141, 335
Spiller, Robert E., 46, 51-52, 62, 73, 86
Spinoza, Baruch, 101
Spirit, 3, 21-22, 25, 33-34, 45, 91, 124, 127, 134, 141, 152, 237, 290
Spirit mystics, 218
Staël, Madame Germaine de, 62
Staples, Samuel, 283-84
Stevenson, Hannah, 181
Stewart, Dugald, 5, 101
Stoicism, 87, 95, 120
Strauss, David Friedrich, 190-91
Sulayman the Magnificent, 103
Swedenborg, Emanuel, 7-8, 11, 34, 45, 57, 91, 97, 166, 243
Swedenborgianism, 8, 15, 45, 47, 54, 58, 99, 122, 166

Taylor, Father Edward, 305
Taylor, Jeremy, 129
Taylor, Thomas, 7
Temple School, 10, 19, 148-49, 151
Terminus, 139
Thebes, 122
Theosophy, 68
Thermopylae, 52
Thor, 119
Thoreau, Henry David, 2, 13, 240, 243, 249, 259, 262-63, 265-66, 273-74, 277-78, 280-82, 292, 295, 298, 303-304, 319, 321, 328-29, 333, 336, 341-43
and antislavery, 18, 236, 279, 281-82
biographical sketch, 235-38
on charity, 281, 297-98
and civil disobedience, 18, 275-76, 283-84, 286-87
and Confucianism, 286, 288, 294, 301, 305, 310, 321-22, 333, 339
and correspondence, idea of, 23-24, 311, 314-15, 318, 326, 330-31, 337
and the *Dial,* 12, 236-37, 262, 296
Eastern thought, influence of, 8, 27, 237, 239, 245, 290, 300
and Emerson, 32, 69, 235-37, 246, 260, 289
Greek and Roman mythology, use of, 242-43, 258, 271, 302, 313, 332, 340-41

Hindu and Indian literature, use of, 241, 247-48, 250-53, 261, 301-302, 305-306, 308, 317, 321-24, 327, 337-38
and Indians, 284, 290, 297, 299
and individualism, 15, 18, 27
and the Mexican War, 18, 279, 281
at Mount Katahdin, 266-69, 272
and mysticism, 264, 308
and nature, 24, 27, 69, 260, 267, 276, 289-90, 316-18, 329, 334-35
at Saddleback (Greylock) Mountain, 256-57, 267
and self-culture, 237
and vegetarianism, 319
at Walden Pond, 15, 24, 236, 239, 246, 289, 315, 324-25
and yoga, 255, 264, 290, 301, 308, 337
Thoreau, John, 235, 239
Thoreau, Sophia, 237, 266
Thousand and One Nights. See *Arabian Nights*
Ticknor, George, 6
Ticknor and Fields, 266, 275, 289
Tillich, Paul, 27
Tom Hyde, 339
Tragedie of Bonduca, The (Fletcher), 121
Transcendental Club, 2, 6, 10, 25, 32, 148, 236
Transcendental spirituality, 20-27, 151, 239
Transcendentalism, 1-4, 6, 8-9, 11, 16, 20, 25-27, 32, 127, 150, 164, 236
Transcendentalists, 1-14, 16-21, 23-28, 43, 76, 81, 101, 134, 147, 152, 167, 176, 320
Transient and Permanent in Christianity, The (Parker). See *A Discourse of the Transient and Permanent in Christianity*
Transubstantiation, 36, 195
Trinity, 4-6, 41, 224
Troy, 262
Tucker, Ellen, 31, 123
Turgot, Anne Robert Jacques, 67
Twenty-Eighth Congregational Society, 16, 182
Two Years before the Mast (Dana), 336

Ulysses, 271, 307. *See also* Odysseus
Underground Railroad, 236
Understanding, The. *See* Reason and the Understanding, The
Union Magazine of Literature and Art, 266, 289
Unitarian Christianity (W. E. Channing), 41-42
Unitarianism, 1, 4-6, 9-10, 13, 16, 34, 41, 43, 76, 81, 93, 101, 116, 134, 176, 182, 185-86, 188, 191, 223-24

United States Magazine and Democratic Review, The, 277
Universal Unity, 17
Universalism, 223-24, 229

Van Buren, Martin, 17
Vane, Sir Henry, 52
Vedas, 8, 57, 68, 132, 241, 248, 253, 256, 302, 311, 320-21, 327
Vegetarianism, 9, 165, 177, 319
Very, Jones, 2, 11, 13, 24
Vigilance Committee, 18
Vishnu, 248-49, 253, 327
Vishnu Purana, 132
Voltaire, 225
Vyasa (Viasa), 68, 253

Wake, William, 36
Walden (Thoreau), 13, 235-36, 238, 289-90, 300, 308
Walden Pond, 24, 236, 239, 246, 289, 304, 312, 314-16, 318, 324- 25, 327-28
Warburton, William, 36
Ware, Reverend Henry, 4
Watts, Isaac, 227
Webster, Daniel, 340
Week on the Concord and Merrimack Rivers, A (Thoreau), 13, 23, 236-40, 267, 275, 289-90, 308
Wesley, John, 87
Western Messenger, 10-11, 127, 133-34, 170
Whittier, John Greenleaf, 214
Wilberforce, William, 114, 293
Williams, Roger, 221
Winkelried, Arnold von, 52
Woden, 119
Woman in the Nineteenth Century (Fuller), 12, 19
Women's rights, 15, 17, 19
Woolman, John, 228
Wordsworth, William, 6, 32, 162
Wright, Henry, 148

Xenophanes, 61

Yankee in Canada, with Anti-Slavery and Reform Papers, A (Thoreau), 237, 275-76
Yoga, 8, 251, 264, 290, 301, 308, 337

Zaleucus, 209
Zeno of Citium, 87, 95
Zeus, 142, 157, 204, 264, 271, 302-303, 313
Zinzendorf, Nikolaus von, 99
Zoroastrianism, 87, 121, 209, 254